ALSO BY NEIL SCHAEFFER

The Art of Laughter

The Marquis de Sade

The *Marquis de* *Sade*

A LIFE

NEIL SCHAEFFER

ALFRED A. KNOPF   *New York*   1999

THIS IS A BORZOI BOOK
PUBLISHED BY ALFRED A. KNOPF, INC.

Copyright © 1999 by Troglydyte, Inc.

www.randomhouse.com

Knopf, Borzoi Books, and the colophon are
registered trademarks of Random House, Inc.

Library of Congress Cataloging-in-Publication Data
Schaeffer, Neil, [date]
The Marquis de Sade : a life / Neil Schaeffer.
p.   cm.
Includes bibliographical references and index.
ISBN 0-679-40407-4
1. Sade, marquis de, 1740–1814—Biography. 2. Authors, French—
18th century—Biography. I. Title.
PQ2063.S3S33   1999
843'.6—dc21
[B]   98-12640
CIP

Manufactured in the United States of America

First Edition

FOR

Susan

As if a man were author of himself
And knew no other kin.

Coriolanus 5.3.36–37

CONTENTS

20   The Bastille   326

21   Sodom   336

22   The Revolution   367

23   "Amidst Madmen and Epileptics"   390

24   "Free at Last"   395

25   Citizen Sade   403

26   The Guillotine Beneath Our Windows   438

27   On My Knees, Dying of Hunger   452

28   Charenton   474

     Notes   *517*

     Bibliography   *549*

     Index   *553*

ACKNOWLEDGMENTS

MY GRATITUDE is extended to those who have cared about Sade and my work. In particular, I thank the devoted and indefatigable Sade scholar, Alice M. Laborde, Professor Emerita of French Literature at the University of California at Irvine, who has recently published her masterly and indispensable edition of Sade's correspondence. Above all, her example, but also her kindness and her hospitality, and that of her husband and companion in research, Pierre, have given me the strength to push on when it sometimes seemed that I was imprisoned in my own sort of Bastille. She was extremely generous with her time and wisdom, especially when it came to deciphering photocopies of Sade's letters. I have also received help and encouragement from Virginia Barber, who first suggested that I write a biography; Olwyn Hughes, who read this book in manuscript as well as several versions of the letters I translated; Dr. Stephen Rittenberg; Professor Barbara Gerber; Yannick Marchand; Peter Mayle, who guided me around Provence; Thibault de Sade; Vicky and Steve Weissman; Jane Maude; and Abner Stein, a wonderful friend and counselor. I am grateful to Sonny Mehta, for his faith in me and this book, and I am particularly grateful to my editor, George Andreou, for his unfailing good judgment, his intelligence, and his humor. But nothing could have been accomplished without the love of my wife, to whom this work is dedicated as an emblem of my deepest gratitude.

A NOTE ON TRANSLATION

ALL TRANSLATIONS of Sade are my own. I have also translated all other French texts, except on the rare occasion when one is both available and more convenient in English, and in those cases I have indicated the translator in the endnote and the bibliography. Most of Sade's writing has not been translated, and this lack is particularly felt in the matter of his correspondence, of which only a tiny fragment is available in English. My practice in translation has been to strike a compromise in modernizing Sade's orthography and punctuation, so that the translation retains some flavor of his style and of eighteenth-century conventions without sacrificing readability.

The Marquis de Sade

Son and Heir

*T*HE SMALL, picturesque village of La Coste rises steeply through very narrow cobbled streets and cubist stone houses attached to the face of one of the hills in the Lubéron range of Provence. On the brow stand the jagged stone walls of the ruin that once had been the Marquis de Sade's château of La Coste. Inside, the floors and ceilings have long since fallen, although there are hints—a bit of fancy molding here, a touch of antique and faded paint there—to suggest the life that once animated these rooms. Now the inside is a hollow, open to the pale, intense heat of the Provençal sky. Even as ruins, the thick stone walls are magnificent. Together, these walls and the hollow they protect are a perfect emblem of the castle's former owner.

It is inevitable that one comes to picture Sade behind walls. He lived to be seventy-four, but he spent almost twenty-nine years of his adulthood in various prisons and at the insane asylum at Charenton. What caused the series of imprisonment-release-imprisonment that constituted most of Sade's adult life? What crimes are hidden behind the prison walls, behind the asylum walls, behind the grotesque mask of evil that most people imagine when they try to picture the Marquis de Sade? Behind the ruined walls of La Coste, behind the cruel mask Sade is made to wear in everyone's imagination, there is a mystery, a hollowness, that this book will aim to explore.

When Sade was thirty-eight years old, he himself opened a window that sheds light into the darkness within. During the night of February 16, 1779, asleep in his prison cell in the fortress of Vincennes, he had a vivid dream. He had fallen asleep reading late into the night, as was his habit. All winter, the thick stone walls had kept in the damp and the cold, and because his cell had no chimney, he could make no fire. For two years, he had endured imprisonment in this royal fortress, but not for crimes committed. Rather, he was being held at the pleasure of the King, under a lettre de cachet granted to his mother-in-law, Mme de Montreuil. Thus, at thirty-eight years of age, Sade spent his days sitting in his cell, feeling sorry for himself, wondering what he had done to deserve his fate, and writing angry letters about his predicament to his patient wife, Renée-Pélagie de Montreuil. His sole consolation, he wrote to her, came from reading the recently published life of Petrarch, written by Sade's uncle, Jacques-François-Paul-Aldonze de Sade (the Abbé de Sade). Sade had been sent at the age of four and a half to his uncle's château at Saumane, near La Coste, where he remained until the age of ten, when he left for school in Paris.

On this wintry night in a cold prison, Sade took to bed his uncle's acclaimed life of Petrarch. He then fell asleep over the book and dreamed of the mysterious Laure, the woman whom Petrarch celebrated as the inspiration of his life and poetry. In his book, *Mémoires pour la vie de François Pétrarque,* Sade's uncle made a plausible case for identifying Petrarch's Laure as an ancient member of the noble house of Sade: Laure de Noves, wife of Hugues de Sade. Sade described his dream in a letter to his wife the next day:

It was around midnight. I had just fallen asleep, his *Mémoires* in my hand. Suddenly, she appeared to me. . . . I saw her! The horror of the grave had not at all altered the radiance of her charms, and her eyes still flashed as brilliantly as when Petrarch celebrated them. A black veil enveloped her completely, and her beautiful blond hair loosely floated above. It seemed as if Love, in order to keep her still beautiful, sought to soften all the lugubrious array in which she presented herself to my gaze. "Why suffer in the world?" she asked me. "Come and be reunited with me. No more pain, no more sorrows, no more distress, in the endless space where I abide. Have the courage to follow me there." At these words, I prostrated myself at her feet, I said to her: "Oh my Mother! . . ." But sobs choked my voice. She extended a hand to me, which I covered with my tears. She shed them as well. "It gave me pleasure," she added, "when I lived in this world that you detest, to turn my eyes toward the future. I multiplied my descendants as far as you, *and I did not imagine you so miserable.*" Then, overcome by my despair and my affection, I flung my arms around her neck to hold her back or to follow her, and to bathe her in my tears, but the phantom disappeared. All that remained was my sorrow.

> *O voi che travagliate, ecco il cammino*
> *Venite a me se'l passo altri non serra.*

[O you who suffer, come, this is the way,
Come to me, if you can see your way free.]

Pétr., son. LIX.[1]

At first, it may be startling to realize that this poignant vision, so sad and piteous, was the product of the mind that wrote *Les Cent Vingt Journées de Sodome*, "the most impure tale," Sade himself boasted, "that has ever been written since the world began."[2] It may be surprising to realize that, behind Sade's mask of perverse sexuality and obdurate violence (a myth that he himself helped cultivate), there existed an emotionally needy, tender sensibility that revealed itself in his dream. Tears came to Sade (if only in this dream) as easily as they poured from Jean-Jacques Rousseau, that man of exquisite feeling. In the dream, Sade's humiliations and sufferings had suffused him in a flush of self-pity, as warm as a blush, as passionate as the tears that choke his voice. In this dream—even at the age of thirty-eight—Sade yearned for the embrace of a mother. "Oh my Mother!" he cried out to Laure, prostrate at her feet, as if he were one of the tortured victims of his own fictional erotic fantasies. But when, in his dream, he reached to grasp her, she disappeared and abandoned him to his lonely suffering. If Sade's conscious fantasies turned to erotic violence, especially directed against women, we may ask where and why those underground rivers of rage and sexuality met. Where was the first abandonment, disappointment, even betrayal that lurks behind the beautiful, compassionate Laure of the dream?

The dream's insistence that Laure's beauty was in no way affected by "the horror of the grave," that "the radiance of her charms" was as bright as ever, and that "her eyes still flashed as brilliantly as when Petrarch celebrated them," gives the beginnings of an answer. Oddly, Sade's dream, which denies reality—Laure was dead and decayed—makes Laure's true state all the more evident. Like Faustus' Helen, Sade's Laure is a gaudy ghost imperfectly hidden behind an illusion of glowing beauty. Despite her sparkling eyes and seductive hair, she is an exhalation of the grave. "Oh my Mother!" Sade had cried when he saw her. In life, Sade's mother, like Laure, was impossible to grasp. Remote, embittered, disillusioned with her husband, grieving over the death of her first child, and for the third one, who died soon after its birth, when Sade was just six years old, Sade's mother might as well have lived, like Laure, in some "endless space" where he could not reach her. Indeed, she was to die in the Carmelite convent on the rue d'Enfer in Paris, to which she had retreated perhaps as early as 1747, when her son was seven years old.[3] There is a profound loneliness at the bottom of what may be called the sweet Sade—a loneliness that he could find no way to fill except with rage.

If the sweet side of Sade is focused on some idealized mother figure like Laure, the rest of his dream implies a competition with men of authority, Christ foremost among them. Laure's injunction, "Why suffer in this world? . . . Come and be reunited with me," parodies the excerpt in the sonnet by Petrarch that Sade quotes, in which it is Christ who says, "O you who suffer . . . / Come to me. . . ." Sade would make a painful career for himself by challenging the laws of man and God. Moreover, sacrilege and incest always held an erotic allure for Sade, and these themes are also evident in his dream about his married relative Laure de Noves. In Sade's dream, Laure is the apex of a love triangle. The second position is taken up by her husband. The third position is occupied by a variety of interlopers: Petrarch, Sade's uncle, the Abbé de Sade, and, of course, Sade himself. It is no accident that two books play such an important role in the dream: Petrarch's sonnets and the Abbé's biography of Petrarch that Sade was reading with great admiration as he fell asleep. Laure is complexly attractive, not only as a sexual and familial figure, but also as a muse. In his dream, then, Sade sought to steal the inspirational figure not only of Petrarch, but of his uncle, the Abbé de Sade. Like Prince Hamlet, Sade was enamored of his uncle's beloved. By theft, by incest, by his own rapt will, Sade would make Laure his own muse. His drive to write, precisely like his feverish and often perverse sexuality, was bound together with a powerful need to compete with or attack whatever was forbidden, limited, sanctified.

The Abbé de Sade had a genetic and climatic theory to explain *his* own feverish sexuality. "The passions," he wrote, "take the shape of the head where they are formed." Our sexual nature is a genetic endowment and is therefore "beyond our control." Climate, moreover, can affect the strength of one's original sexual energy. For example, the Abbé wrote, "The sun incites the blood of a man from Provence."[4] Perhaps the Abbé was right. Perhaps the heat of Provence fired the blood.

Under the brilliant sun of Provence, everything is hot. The stones of the earth give off the odors of spice. The valleys are lush and green, and the terraced fields climb the lower slopes to the fortified towns that guard them, towns like Bonnieux, Céreste, Ménerbes, La Coste. From a distance, these villages perched near the tops of the mountains look like the bastions they are, heating up and glowing in the heat. They are reached by roads, once paths, that switch back and forth on their way up to the fortified gate. Inside the walls, spiraling up from the central square with its well or fountain, narrow stone stairways seem gouged between the stone houses. On a bluff above the town of La Coste stood the ancestral home of the Sade family.

On this strategic site, overlooking what had once been crucial Roman roads, stood a fort—in Latin, *castrum*—which may have provided the name "La Coste." During the Middle Ages, La Coste became the possession of the Sade family, who made their fortune in the cloth trade. Possibly one of the most notable was Hugues de Sade, mentioned earlier, who, in 1325, more than four hundred years before Sade's birth, married Laure de Noves. Over the centuries, each heir prospered in his turn, and the château grew in size and changed as architectural styles changed. In Provence, the Sades continued to hold important military and ecclesiastical positions. Sade's father, Jean-Baptiste de Sade (born 1702), was first a captain of dragoons, and later performed ambassadorial missions to Russia, to England, and finally to the Elector of Cologne, where he took up his post six months after his first and only son, Donatien-Alphonse-François, was born on June 2, 1740. At the time of Sade's birth, his mother, Marie-Éléonore de Maillé, who was related to the Prince de Condé, was serving as a lady-in-waiting to the Princesse de Condé. The Sades were especially fortunate, therefore, to have an apartment in the Condé Palace in Paris. Sade's first years would be spent in a scene of magnificence and royal luxury almost unmatched in all of Europe.

On June 2, 1740, Sade was born in the large apartment occupied by his mother in the Condé Palace. The next day, he was brought for baptism to the Church of Saint-Sulpice. His mother and father were not present. Sade was taken by their proxies, an officer in his father's regiment and the wife of another officer. These two, or the servants who carried the infant to church, managed to garble his Christian names. Instead of Donatien-Aldonse-Louis, he was baptized Donatien-Alphonse-François. If Sade resented this muddling of his name, he never commented on it. Throughout his long life, he would use several variants of both his intended and actual Christian names. After the Revolution, for example, he prudently suppressed his noble title and styled himself simply as Citizen Louis Sade. The variety of the names he used on official documents may have saved his life following the Revolution, when, in 1793 and 1794, he spent ten frightful months in several Paris prisons. In the end, his nature was no more fixed than his name. As the times changed, so did he. He appeared to be malleable, a creature of shifting surfaces. But it would be his destiny to become—to turn himself into—a being of myth, a force in the consciousness of humanity, known by only one name: "Sade."

The infant Sade would spend his early years in the splendor of a great palace. Until around the age of four, he was often in the care of nurses. His father was away in Germany. His mother had duties to perform for her patron, the Princesse de Condé, who, four years before Sade saw the light of day, had given birth to an heir, Louis-Joseph de Bourbon. Like many a noble house, the Palace de Condé was often swept by intrigues. Sade's parents had to practice prudence. The year before Sade was born, Minister of Foreign Affairs d'Argenson noted in his *Journal* that the Prince de Condé was very angry with Sade's father because he had not informed him of the Princesse's infidelity, a fact that Mme de Sade, as the companion of the Princesse, would likely have known.⁵ Then, in fairly quick succession, two events occurred that would make Sade's mother's position far more precarious. On January 27, 1740, the Prince de Condé died; a year and a half later, on June 14, 1741, his wife died. This left the young Prince de Condé an orphan, and Mme de Sade without a patron. During this time, the young Prince was supervised by his uncle, the Comte de Charolais, a notorious libertine and a homicidally brutal man. His actions were vastly more horrifying and extreme than any the Marquis de Sade would ever commit in his lifetime. Mme de Sade could provide an essential maternal presence for the orphaned Prince in the Palace de Condé, and her new son, four years junior to the Prince, could become his playmate. Her powerful patrons were dead, and she believed that it would be useful later if her son cemented a strong relationship with the young Prince.

Perhaps Mme de Sade too strongly revealed her hopes for her son. Her first child, a daughter, Caroline-Laure, had been born in 1737, and died at the age of two. Her son, born a year after that tragedy, must have seemed heaven-sent. He would make up for her loss. With her influential social connections, he might do very well. Mme de Sade's husband was away; she must have been pleased with her management of affairs in the wake of the mortal crises that beset the palace. Her scheme to attach her only child to what she believed would turn out to be the glorious career of the young Prince de Condé deserved, she thought, to succeed. It was *her* blood relationship to the Condé family that had brought this branch of the Sade family, as important as they may have been in Provence, to Paris, where they had a free apartment in the palace, and where her husband had prospects for posts of distinction. In the end, perhaps it would not matter if her husband could not manage to stay out of debt, or if he would have to be recalled from the Court of Cologne, questions of mismanagement and scandal tainting his ambassadorial mission there.⁶ At least her son would have his chance.

But, as with so many instances of good fortune that came to Sade throughout his long life, he found a way to turn this into a savage misfortune that almost destroyed him. Abruptly, around the age of four, he was sent from the palace to be raised in Provence, first by his grandmother, and then by his uncle, the Abbé de Sade. Some forty years later, imprisoned in the Bastille, Sade would write a novel, *Aline et Valcour,* that contains an account of his expulsion from what must have been the paradise of the Palace de Condé:

> Allied, through my mother, to the most important people in the
> kingdom; related, through my father, to the most distinguished people
> of the province of Languedoc; born in Paris in the lap of luxury and
> plenty, I believed, as soon as I was able to reason, that nature and for-

tune had conspired to inundate me with their bounties; I believed it because they were foolish enough to tell me so, and this absurd presumption made me arrogant, tyrannical, and fierce; it seemed that everyone was supposed to give in to me, that the whole universe was supposed to flatter my whims, and that all I needed to do was think them to have them satisfied; I will recount for you but one event of my childhood in order to convince you of the dangerous principles that were, with such negligence, permitted to take root in me.

I was born and raised in the palace of the renowned Prince to whom my mother had the honor to be related and who was nearly my own age; they hastened to join me to him, so that, being known to him from my childhood, I would later on be able to obtain his support at every stage of my life; but my pride, at that time, which had as yet heard nothing about this scheme, one day taking offense during our childish games at his arguing with me about something, and something, moreover, to which, for undoubtedly very considerable reasons, he believed himself entitled by his rank, I took revenge for his opposition by repeated blows, and not the slightest respect stopped me, and only force and violence succeeded in separating me from my rival.

This occurred around the time when my father was sent to conduct the negotiations; my mother joined him there, and I was sent to my grandmother's in Languedoc, whose extreme coddling fostered in me all the faults that I have just admitted.[7]

Sade's account focuses on the pride, obstinacy, and combativeness that seek satisfaction heedless of the consequences. In fact, he makes a point of insisting that, at the age of four or so, he was unaware of the consequences of his outburst. At that time, he "had as yet heard nothing" about his mother's "scheme" to profit from his relationship to the Prince. Even if his mother's scheme had been made known to him before he took offense at the Prince's prerogatives, would he, at four, have suppressed his impulse to drub the older boy with such fury that he had to be pulled from him by the palace staff? Would he have behaved better? Sade's pride, his hypersensitivity to insults (real or imagined), his tendency to overreact are at the center of this memory. Self-pride would have been sorely tried in any boy whose family lived by sufferance in another boy's house. Sade tells us that he was a proud, tyrannical, and autocratic child because he had been spoiled, and this spoiling continued when he was sent down to his grandmother's house in Avignon. Perhaps his life would have turned out differently had his father not been absent during those early years in Paris.

In a sense, his mother also must have been absent. Though there is almost no information about how she treated her newborn son, we do know that she was not always present during his infancy. She accompanied her husband on at least one of his ambassadorial missions to Cologne.[8] Certainly, evidence still extant makes it possible to draw a few conclusions about her emotional state and her relationship with her son when he was a young child. The auto-biographical passage under consideration stressed the mother's social standing as superior to the father's. Moreover, it was the mother who conceived the socially ambitious scheme that the son ruined by punching the Prince. The son, to be sure, was a creature of pride, a sin nourished by the indulgence of everyone around him except the Prince. Sade's mother may have spoiled her son, but did she love him? If pride and higher social status were the mother's goals, her son, it would seem, wanted something more. Is it too much to con-jecture that what he wanted was love? Sade's mother appears not to have been a demonstrative or an emotionally generous woman. There is not a single let-ter extant between her and her son. On one occasion, she did write angrily to the lieutenant general of police to complain about libels that were being pub-lished against her son. However, it is clear from her letter that her main inter-est was to protect her own family's name, which "has no stain of dishonor" on it.[9] If during Sade's infancy his mother was too much occupied with other matters, if she was emotionally distant, the consequences can be seen in his attempts throughout his life to acquire and idealize mother figures who seemed able to protect him. Unfortunately, he almost always chose badly. Women like his mother-in-law turned against him, abandoned him, and punished him. Even the dream Laure, deceptively beautiful and nurturing ("Come and be reunited with me"), is also a macabre, grotesque demon, tempting him to suicide. Throughout his life, Sade would find women who re-created the role of the bizarre, two-faced mother who enticed him with promises of love, then used him, and finally betrayed or abandoned him.

When Sade was expelled from the Palace de Condé, he was deprived not only of his mother, but of a brilliant future in society. In the gloom of the Bastille, as Sade described the scene of the fistfight, he could ponder the enor-mity of the opportunity he had wasted. His onetime playmate, the Prince de Condé, had gone on to a distinguished military career. In 1761, when the Prince was asked to help obtain a commission for Sade, the Prince flatly refused. After the Revolution, the Prince led an army of émigrés against the revolutionaries, and returned to Paris with the Restoration of King Louis XVIII, who bestowed high position and honors upon him. Sade's wagon had once been hitched to a princely coach. He not only unhitched it, he broke its wheels so that it could not be used again.

The fistfight scene, as Sade narrated it, is almost dreamlike in character. It seems to float, without strong anchorage in the real world. In Sade's account, no bitterness toward the Prince is evident, nor is there any anger at his own cursed luck. The fight seems to have no consequences. Of course, Sade ends the scene by reporting that, as a result of this contretemps, he was sent down to his grandmother, but he mentions this primarily so that he can conclude the narrative on a note of irony: his punishment put him into the hands of an equally indulgent woman and only served to confirm the very faults that needed correction.

Sade also imposed an ironical trajectory on the plot of this scene and employed other literary devices in order to create a kind of ironically distanced superciliousness from his own experience. He felt that he was above his own life, or, to put it another way, he was withdrawn deep inside himself. During his lifetime, he would learn to be *in* places yet not to be *of* them; to be in the army but not to become a comrade; to be in a Jesuit school but not to be a Christian; to be the president of one of the most revolutionary sections of the Paris Commune (it spawned Robespierre) yet to remain a monarchist; to be locked up as a madman in Charenton but to become one of its principal ornaments and a friend of the director. If, in many ways, he was a chameleon, if he could fit into the most bizarrely opposite of social groupings and movements in eighteenth-century France, he could do so because he was never *of* any of them—never belonged to any of them. What was most furious, tyrannical, and proud in Sade would stay inside him, remain part of his inaccessible inner world, and his most important battles would be fought not in the Palace de Condé, or in the law courts, or in prison, or in the streets of Paris, but in the depths of his own mind.

Sade's grandiosity and ferocity had prevented him from getting along with the Prince de Condé. These qualities would rule throughout his life, for he would acquire no true friends. He would become an angry loner. Indeed, as a child, he must have been often alone. Lacking reactions to his behavior, or mirroring, from people he loved, he failed to develop a reliable or realistic sense of himself, or an understanding of how one person could truly relate to another. His surprising and violent outburst against the Prince (brought about by a turn of events that Sade could never remember) must have startled Sade as much as the Prince. In his later life, he would constantly misjudge people and events. He was always surprised when people grew angry with him for the things he said, or wrote, or did. He had little sense of his relation to, or his impact upon, the world he occupied. It is not too much to say that his primary relationship was with himself. Lonely, introverted, secretly proud, potentially violent, he would have been a difficult boy for any parent to raise.

Obviously, he had little capacity to deal with frustration. He knew what he wanted; he had an inflated sense of entitlement; and he had no ability to marshal internal controls or limits. His fight with the Prince is an early example of what would become a repeating cycle: he would commit transgressions, and these would immediately lead to terrible punishments. Anyone but Sade could have foreseen the consequences of his actions. At some level, we might say, he *did* foresee the coming punishment, and because he did, the punishment itself must be considered the ultimate goal of his behavior. Through his repeated transgressions, he tried to manipulate the outside world into imposing some semblance of order and control upon his unruly internal life. And if he became an object of discipline, this meant that he was not alone in an indifferent world.

Events of his early life may have led Sade to believe that *he* could suffer no ill consequences of his actions. In the summer of 1744, when he was four years old, he accompanied his father to Provence for a festive occasion in Avignon. There, on August 16, 1744, possibly at the house of Sade's grandmother, the village elders of Saumane, one of Sade's father's estates, sent a delegation "to offer their respects to Monseigneur the Marquis de Sade, son of Monseigneur the Comte, lord of this estate upon his joyous arrival in Avignon and to wish him a long and happy life as his heir and successor."[10] The elders of Saumane prostrated themselves before the small boy who would someday become their lord. Though this extraordinary event may seem somewhat comical to us, it was performed in 1744 with all the seriousness that the elders described in their minutes. In not a great many years, the Revolution would overthrow all distinctions between people, who—king, nobleman, or commoner—would all bear the general title of Citizen, and these very villagers or their sons and daughters would become enemies of the Marquis. After the Revolution, Sade's château at La Coste would be thoroughly pillaged and destroyed. But in 1744, the rituals of submission were still endowed with much of their ancient significance.

If the feudal ritual at Avignon swelled young Sade's pride, what happened next certainly deflated it. His father left him there to be raised by his grandmother. When the Comte de Sade returned to the Palace de Condé, he did not stay very long with his wife. At the beginning of the new year, 1745, he left once more for Cologne. He never got there. In February 1745, he was arrested in Zinzic. Apparently he had lost the confidence of both the Elector of Cologne and the French King. There were questions of malfeasance during his previous trip. In any case, neither government was in a hurry to free him from prison, where he stayed until October or November of 1745, when he returned to the Palace de Condé. On August 13, 1746, Mme de Sade gave birth to an apparently premature infant, a girl, Marie-Françoise, who died five days later.[11] The Comte's return may also have put an end to his marriage. After he took up residency at the Palace de Condé in December 1746, he tried for another royal posting, but was never again granted one. In a word, his career was ruined. He knew it, and his wife knew it too. Her disappointment in him, in his infidelities and his failings, finally prompted her to live apart, in the Carmelite convent on the rue d'Enfer in Paris.

As for young Sade, he was not faring better at his grandmother's house in Avignon. She was not able to handle this difficult boy. He remained, as he said, "arrogant, tyrannical, and fierce." Sade's character could not have been formed, as he claimed, by her "extreme coddling." Any grandmother would delight in coddling a grandson who, not yet five, must already have displayed strong signs of that prodigious charm that made him attractive to a great many women throughout his life. And Sade always responded well to coddling. His witty friend and housekeeper, Mlle de Rousset, wrote on April 30, 1779, that she knew how to handle him and how to make him as "docile" as she could wish: "When one rubs you the wrong way, you are like an escaped lion. By going with the nap, you become the most lovable sheep."[12] Sade's uncle, the Abbé, who would soon be entrusted with raising the boy, also reached this conclusion about Sade's temperament. "It would be dangerous," he wrote on June 1, 1765, "to rub him the wrong way."[13] Unquestionably, Sade must have been a very difficult charge for his old grandmother. His character was not formed because she had "coddled" him too much. It would never be possible to coddle Sade too much. He had already developed the seeds of the paranoia that would later discover obstacles to his will in even the most innocuous events or turns of phrase. It was his boyish rage, his "arrogant, tyrannical, and fierce" nature, that Grandmother d'Astouaud could not control.[14] The experiment in entrusting young Sade to his grandmother could not have lasted long. At the beginning of 1745, when Sade was four and a half, he was sent to the Abbé de Sade, his father's brother, to be educated and raised under his masculine authority at the château of Saumane, situated almost twenty miles from Avignon and about fifteen from La Coste.

The fortified château of Saumane was young Sade's home for the next five years. Unlike La Coste, this ancestral estate of the Sade family escaped destruction during the Revolution. Today it looms darkly over the valley much as it did when young Sade was driven there from Avignon. Saumane was a very long way from Paris. And if Avignon was no Paris, even less like Avignon was the château of Saumane. The road from Avignon to Saumane points due east, passing through L'Isle-sur-la-Sorgue, and then, just before Fontaine-de-Vaucluse, the site of Petrarch's retreat, the road turns north and climbs sharply to Saumane. First to be seen are the small village and the church chopped into the brow of the mountain. Then, just above, there is the château. That structure is, in fact, a confused hybrid. It consists of a walled fortress and a large stone house, typical of the region. The house is set within the walls and stands on top of the fortress. Seen from almost any point of view, and in almost any light, it is not a pretty place. Though it is medieval in its origins, there is nothing romantic in its design or appearance. In the wintry gloom, the massive stone walls slope upward without architectural embellishment. The monotony of these dull gray walls is relieved only by firing loops for bows or muskets, and larger loops for cannon. This is a practical, military structure of sheer walls, difficult to scale, and forbidding to the eye. It is surrounded by a deep fosse. Entrance was once gained only by a portcullis. The Abbé himself pronounced Saumane cold and forbidding. He preferred to spend time reading, writing, and otherwise enjoying himself at the estate's farmhouse, called La Vignerme.

For a boy of six, however, the château's complex architecture offered innumerable spaces in which he and his imagination could wander. There were spiraling stone staircases, passageways (some of them secret), and cellars (some of them really caves, hewn out of the natural rock of the mountain). Up above, on the high ramparts, the stones hot in summer, in winter cold from the blustery wind and occasional snow, the view is extensive and thrilling. There are picturesque terraced farms on the hillside across the valley. In the far distance are large mountains. On the ramparts is a shaft (an oubliette) covered by a raised semicircular iron grating. A spiral stone staircase leads down to the guards' quarters and to a cell for prisoners, barrel-vaulted, with a small barred window at one end and a massive wooden door (without a window) at the other. The darkness, the dampness, even in the height of summer, and the weight of solid stone blocks are oppressive. It is a relief as well as a pleasant change to enter the château itself. In one of its magnificent rooms, the center of the vaulted ceiling bears the Sade family coat of arms. Carved in stone worn by time, an awesome eagle with extended wings soars at the center of an eight-pointed star. The guards' room, which was also used as a confessional, has a vaulted ceiling with a peculiar and fascinating acoustical feature. Pressing an ear to the stone groin in one corner of this room allows one to hear perfectly what is said, or even whispered, by a person across the room. In times of plague, it is said, priests were thus able to hear confessions at a safe distance. At the center of the vaulted stone dome is the date: 1595. A magnificent staircase leads to an impressive Renaissance chapel. Near the chapel is a wooden bookcase on hinges. It pulls away like a door to reveal a secret passage whose walls are provided with frequent peepholes and listening places. At the very base of the château, carved out of the natural rock of the mountain, is the most secret room, the treasury. This room is reached by descending a narrow spiral staircase and opening a heavy door. On this level, there are other, equally mysterious rooms, as well as a vast barrel-vaulted stable for the military horses, partly carved out of the natural rock. Velvet lines the lower walls to protect the horses' flanks. Young Sade's intense curiosity and his pride in his heritage would have prompted him to discover every room, every passageway, every peephole.

The three distinct elements of the boy's new home—château, fort, and subterranean caves—became the model for the great and terrible fortresses of his libertine fiction: most notably, the château of Silling in *Les Cent Vingt Journées de Sodome.* The events of these novels frequently take place in an impregnable fortress, sometimes totally isolated from the outside world by its strategic placement on a mountain peak. Inside, there is always an elegant, luxurious dwelling that provides all the comforts and refinements of culture and civilization. Finally, at the deepest level, subterranean cellars become the setting for the most exquisitely horrible depravities—horrors so shocking as to be almost beyond human imagination. This complex of specialized spaces became the diagram—the pure form—of Sade's conception of the structure of society and man's place in it—a very architecture of the brain. Sade's is an embattled view of life. The individual cannot fully exist except by first protecting himself behind defensive walls. Once safe from the power of others and their ideas, he cannot know himself fully except by probing into the darkness at the depth of his nature, as if descending into the very bowels of the earth. Culture, civilization, the individual himself stand like the château—with its beautiful chapel, its lovely painted walls and ceilings, its gilded moldings—between heaven and hell. The lightness of the château's design, its comfort, its significance, like the attributes of civilization itself, have meaning only as a perhaps momentary and unique illumination between the absolute but blinding brilliance of the Provençal sun and the absolute and blinding darkness of the caves below.

When young Sade arrived at Saumane, the Abbé, his father's youngest brother, was forty years old. The Abbé had been educated (as Sade would be in a few years) at the prestigious Jesuit school in Paris, the Collège Louis-le-Grand, where he and Voltaire became friends. The Abbé lived for a long period in Paris, enjoying its literary society and the pleasures of women (he had been the lover of Mme de La Popelinière). In 1733, when the Abbé had been named grand vicar of Toulouse, his friend Voltaire wrote this charming note of congratulation on November 25:

They say that you are going to be a priest and a grand vicar. That's more than a few sacraments at the same time in one family. And that's the reason why you tell me that you are going to renounce love.

> Have you now, then, got it in your brain,
> As soon as you will have the name,
> The dull dignity, of grand vicar,
> That you will all at once refrain
> From Love, and the art of giving pleasure?
> Be as much a priest as you maintain,
> You'll go on loving just the same;
> Were you a bishop or the Holy Father,
> You would love and please again:
> There you see your true career.
> You will love and please and gain
> Forever, equal degrees of fame
> At Church and in the groves of pleasure.[15]

Voltaire certainly knew his friend. The Abbé de Sade was, as his nephew would be, a man of considerable charm and intelligence. He continued to receive appointments in the church. In 1744, he was named Abbé of a rather depleted monastery at Ébreuil, where he spent some of his time when he was away from Saumane. Possibly he brought young Sade there with him. He also continued to visit Paris for the stimulation of friendship, literary society, and the occasional debauch. In 1762, he was arrested in a Paris bordello in the room of a prostitute, La Léonore.[16] Nevertheless, he was valued as a man of judgment in family matters: he helped manage his brother's ruinous affairs in Provence, and his advice was always sought and considered. And, of course, he was celebrated as Petrarch's biographer. From everything that we know of him, he appears to have been a complex and talented man who managed to enjoy his life on his own terms.

There is some debate about how much—if at all—young Sade was influenced by exposure to the sexual life of his uncle.[17] Much of this controversy hinges on a letter Sade wrote in the summer of 1765 to his aunt the Abbesse of Saint-Benoît de Cavaillon, in which he defended himself against charges of sexual misconduct by claiming that the Abbé (who had made these charges against him) was even worse: "Priest though he be, he always keeps a few whores at his place. . . . What is his château but a seraglio? No, even better, it is a b[ordello]."[18] Sade's mean tone and his attempt to shift blame away from himself provide insight into what it must have been like for the Abbé to raise this impulsive, mentally aggressive, shifty boy. The slightest criticism of him, especially when he was in the wrong, immediately provoked him to concoct prevarications, rationalizations, and, if need be, insults against his critic. Sade remembered every word anyone ever said (in prison he would reread his wife's correspondence countless times, memorizing the letters, making marginal notes), and could quote his accuser to show that, whatever he himself had done wrong, it was someone else—his accuser—who had told him to do it. It would be not merely infuriating to try correcting or arguing with Sade, but also a dangerous and dirty business. If someone wanted to tar Sade, Sade would pick up the tar pot, turn, and dump it upon his accuser. Sade had the paranoid's acute sensitivity to attacks, even when none were intended. He was always on the watch for evidence and arguments that would be of use in a counterattack. At times, he counterattacked without provocation. And his defensive strikes were always made at the highest pitch of aggression. He gave back many times worse than he got.

Sade would have to apologize for his attack on his uncle's sexual promiscuity. To be sure, the Abbé was a man of the world. He was no celibate, and young Sade, living at Saumane for nearly six years, must have seen some evidence of his uncle's sexual life. But what Sade saw is undoubtedly less important than the extreme conjectures he made concerning its implications. From everything we know from the Abbé's letters to various correspondents, he was a highly intelligent, conscientious, thoughtful man. It would be a mistake to imply that he was somehow responsible for Sade's later perversity: mental disorders like Sade's begin in early childhood and go very deep indeed. Despite the excessiveness of Sade's attack upon his uncle, he would continue to retain strong attachments to him and to other members of his uncle's household throughout his life.

Conscientious as the Abbé was in taking on the responsibility of raising his difficult nephew, he was not foolish enough to undertake the task alone. He immediately brought into his household two persons who would have a lasting and continuing impact on Sade's life: Mme de Saint-Germain, who would act as a kind of mother figure for the boy, and Jacques-François Amblet, his tutor. The Abbé Amblet had been recommended to Sade's father. Thirty-one years old when he arrived at Saumane in January of 1747,[19] he impressed Sade's uncle as a man of "intelligence and gentleness."[20] Over the years, Amblet developed an unqualified affection for, and loyalty to, his student. After three years at Saumane, he accompanied Sade when the boy went to Paris to attend the Collège Louis-le-Grand. Even when Amblet's formal duties as tutor ended, he continued to be of use to his protégé. When Sade was imprisoned in Vincennes, Amblet was given the task of picking up Sade's young children from school each day. As Sade's wife informed her husband (on January 26, 1782), the children "will not leave with anyone but" Amblet.[21] Gentle Amblet never lost his temper. Ever kind, ever useful—if he had been like an easy father to Sade, now he was an easy grandfather to Sade's children. He, too, knew that Sade could be placated, but not opposed. "Such is my character," Sade wrote after two years in prison at Vincennes, "which has never changed even from childhood—Amblet, who raised me, can attest to it—and which certainly will not change any more."[22] No doubt Amblet had seen many of young Sade's frequent rages, but Amblet's mildness of character helped protect him from Sade's customary violence against authority. Gentle, comforting, bookish, never rubbing Sade the wrong way, always knowing his place in the aristocratic household, Amblet did not rise high enough on the landscape of Sade's imagination to draw forth his thunderbolts.

About Mme de Saint-Germain, a significant figure in Sade's childhood and later life, not much is known. Some biographers believe that her husband was the military hero in the Seven Years' War, Claude-Louis, Comte de Saint-Germain, who, in 1775, became secretary of war. Both the Abbé and Sade's father, during earlier excursions into Parisian society, appear to have known the two of them.[23] In Sade's own "Récit de la campagne de 1758" ("Account of the Campaign of 1758"), which deals with his participation in the Seven Years' War, he mentioned M. de Saint-Germain several times.[24] Throughout his life, Sade said that his thoughts always included Mme de Saint-Germain. On February 3, 1784, he wrote to his wife from Vincennes to say that "after you," Mme de Saint-Germain is "the only woman in the world" he loves and to whom he owes "as much as any son could the respect due a mother." He added, "Not a single day has passed since I came here that I have not thought of her."[25] In fact, Sade so frequently referred to Mme de Saint-Germain as his mother that his wife adopted the same style, calling her *"your mama."*[26] Mme de Saint-Germain herself had earlier established this familiar style in her own letters; in one of them, she referred to Sade as "my child." The intimacy that formed among the members of this small alternative family was such that Mme de Saint-Germain, in this same letter, addressed the Abbé as "my dear Papa."[27] It is important to remember that, as lonely and alienated a life as Sade would make for himself, he nevertheless retained the love of a few individuals from his boyhood years.

Sade's own parents were not a presence during his years at Saumane. The family of sorts that endeavored to raise the boy at Saumane were not likely to rub him the wrong way. Sade could be delightful, inquisitive, and charming. These traits were evident throughout his life, even in very difficult circumstances. Under the gentle instruction of Amblet, and benefiting from the kindness and affection of Mme de Saint-Germain and the tolerance and love of his uncle, Sade spent a relatively happy boyhood at Saumane. The Abbé's considerable library was a wonderful resource for Sade, who throughout his life loved to read. He read everything, from travelers' tales of faraway lands to the ancient classics of Greece and Rome, from treatises on the natural sciences to books on morality. In the library at Saumane, a world full of new and arcane facts, of competing authorities and values, was opened up to him. If it was not always convenient or satisfying to argue with Amblet, Sade could wage private wars of mental chess with the authors of books, and with the ideas these authors expressed. The world of books would always be Sade's best home. Such a spacious domain could be set up even in the most dismal of prisons. Much later in life, Sade would grieve for his personal library of six hundred volumes, destroyed in the sacking of the Bastille.

As fortunate as young Sade was in his provisional parents at Saumane, they were not, after all, his true parents. They could not be treated with the full range of emotions a boy can feel and express toward his actual parents. In the world of books, Sade would find not only antagonists, but also substitute parents. In a sense, Sade, although surrounded with surrogate parents, lived the emotional life of an orphan searching for his true father and mother. Evidence of this search may be found in Sade's excited account of reading the sermons of Père Massillon in the dungeon of Vincennes:

> They raise me up, they enchant me, they ravish me. . . . He is no pedant bristling with sophisms that aim to convince only by terrorizing the mind. It is at the heart that he directs his maxims; it is the heart that he seeks to seduce and it is the heart that he always enthralls. With each word, one finds a loving father who desires his children's happiness; each phrase is what a friend would say to his friend at the edge of a precipice. What purity of soul! what morality![28]

At times, Sade must have felt himself "at the edge of a precipice," and must have wished to be coaxed from the edge by a "loving father." Sade was a combustible mixture of sentiment and rage, of exalted idealism and profound cynicism. To understand him, it is necessary to keep his high ideals in mind. In one sense, these lofty ideals were formed as a consequence of his search for a father—that is, for an ideal authority worthy of absolute admiration. And when that search inevitably failed, Sade's ideals also became a justification for his anger. Anger that is not inspired by commensurate ideals is merely primal rage. At Saumane, young Sade was beginning to learn how to express and refine his anger through discourse, as well as how to argue. This process would continue under the powerful guidance of the Jesuits at the Collège Louis-le-Grand in Paris.

In the fall of 1750, when Sade was ten years old, he took leave of his uncle and boarded the coach for Paris with Amblet. The journey was long and fatiguing: Avignon, Montpellier, Lyons, and on to the north. Outside the coach windows, the towns and cities of southern and central France passed by, often cloaked in darkness. The travelers arose before dawn, put up long after dark in strange and uncomfortable posting inns, until finally the steeples of Paris, like the masts of a great fleet at anchor, rose above the horizon. The journey was more than long. It was a progress from one world, one climate, one language, to another. In Provence, young Sade had come to love the brilliance of its heat and light, the rough grandeur of its mountains, the beauty of its terraced farms, its odd mixture of desert and verdant fields, tropical foods and strong, natural aromas. He had begun to learn that strange dialect, Provençal. In prison, he would ask his wife for packages of Provençal foods and consume them greedily. When he left Provence, he was leaving his homeland, the land of his ancestors. But he knew he was also going to the noblest city in the world to receive a nobleman's education.

The Jesuit school Louis-le-Grand was on the Left Bank, on the rue Saint-Jacques. It was a privileged institution, attracting sons of the highest rank of the nobility. Because of the Jesuits' charitable policy, the school also admitted numbers of poor scholars. Descartes had praised this admissions policy at another Jesuit school, La Flèche, where "there are a number of young men from all parts of France." Descartes praised the egalitarianism of the Jesuits and their "treating the highest and the least of them in essentially the same way."[29] The accommodations for live-in students, or *pensionnaires*, could range from rude dormitory rooms for twelve to fifteen poor students, to elegant apartments for rich nobles who often came with several servants. Indeed, at end of term, the press of the nobility's carriages arriving to pick up their scholars in the rue Saint-Jacques was so dense it created a traffic jam.[30] Young Sade, however, was not to be a participant in such festive scenes, for he was an external, not a live-in, student. This was an economy measure. His father could barely pay the tuition at Louis-le-Grand. Despite the equality that reigned among the resident students, external students, who lived with parents or relatives or, even worse, in rooming houses, were treated differently, almost as outcasts. At the time of Sade's attendance, the school had around five hundred resident and twenty-five hundred external students.[31] Père Rochemonteix notes that resident scholars "were never supposed to speak with or have any relation with the *externes*, from whom they were completely separated, even in class."[32] This segregation, as well as Sade's own withdrawn nature, may account for the fact that he developed no close or lasting relationships with any of his classmates. He never wrote to any of them later, and his correspondence never so much as mentions a single one of them, or any of his instructors.

Little is known about Sade's four years at school. It appears likely that he lived in Amblet's apartment, on the rue des Fossés-Monsieur-le-Prince. Had Sade been a resident student, there would have been no need for Amblet's presence. Sade probably did not live with his mother. Indeed, by then she may well have taken up residence in the Carmelite convent on the rue d'Enfer, in the parish of Saint-Jacques, from which she was never to emerge. Sade's living with Amblet must have buffered the shock that most boys feel on going away to school. However, because he was an outsider, Sade did not have to learn how to live with other boys his age, nor did he have to face the inevitable ragging of older boys. It is worth noting that, when he came to serve in the cavalry during the Seven Years' War, he disdained making friends with his peers and refused to ingratiate himself with his superior officers. In fact, Sade's isolation and mistrust of others began early and continued throughout school and on into the cavalry. At school, it would seem, Sade hid out among that vast majority of nonresident students. Not once in four years does his name appear on the annual lists of prizewinners.[33] This is an extraordinary nonachievement for a boy with Sade's intellect, his analytic and argumentative skills, his love of literature and writing.

At school, Sade must have suppressed not only his talents but also his impulsive rage. Serious infringements of the rules, of course, could be punished with caning. This task was customarily performed not by the priests, but by a layman called the *correcteur*.[34] It may be tempting to speculate on whether Sade's having been whipped at school, and his having observed other boys whipped, had any impact on his later use of flagellation for erotic purposes.[35] It may also be tempting to associate Sade's interest in flagellation with the now famous acknowledgment made by Jean-Jacques Rousseau in his *Confessions.* Rousseau attributed his lifelong and unfulfilled wish to be spanked by a woman to his having been spanked at age eight by Mlle Lambercier.[36] As for Sade's sexual identity, we have to admit that we know nothing of it at Louis-le-Grand. It would be wrong to ascribe Sade's sexual nature to experiences or thoughts he had at school. In fact, his general masochism and his sexual nature had begun to develop in his early childhood. Later, they would converge with explosive effect.

The comparison with Rousseau, however, is instructive on many levels. In the first place, when Rousseau was spanked by Mlle Lambercier, the sexual pleasure he said he derived from this spanking created a shameful desire to have the spanking repeated, but he said that he "never had the courage" to ask for such treatment from any woman.[37] This unspoken yearning was to interfere with all of his later relations with women. Rousseau the boy felt ashamed of his aggressive nature and sought to eliminate aggression from his own mind and from all men and their societies. His ideal, one might say, was a soft world, celebrating man's benevolent and social tendencies. Of course, Rousseau ended by attacking just about everyone and every nation, but he made such attacks, he would have argued, only to make the world a better, a finer place. Sade, on the other hand, came to feel entirely unembarrassed by his aggressive and sexual feelings and by their perversity. The writer of *Les Cent Vingt Journées de Sodome* was hardly squeamish about man's sadistic and masochistic tendencies. Sade was clearly unafraid of the idea that man is driven by his materialistic and sexual instincts. Of course, both Sade and Rousseau ended up attacking the world and being humiliated by it, but they wrote from opposing emotional and mental realms: Sade from the cave and Rousseau from a cloud. They looked at the same things from opposite poles; both are necessary for understanding where we are.

In order to estimate the possible influence of whipping on Sade's character, it must first be acknowledged that no one knows how often, or if at all, young Sade was caned at school. As a day student, he would certainly have had fewer occasions to commit infractions. Moreover, his later behavior in the military shows that his natural tendency was to avoid alliances with his fellows and to stay out of the way of his superiors. Long before Sade got to Louis-le-Grand, his sexual nature as well as his introversion and masochism had been essentially established. The lasting influence of Louis-le-Grand is not so much sexual as intellectual: it consolidated and refined a mentality already obsessed with moral absolutism. He arrived at school with a religious sense that had been fostered in him by Amblet. He also came with a very sensitive nose for injustice, especially (if the fistfight with the Prince was any indication) when he felt himself to be its victim. A sense of right and wrong was, after all, precisely what the Jesuit fathers were trying to instill; their pupils were trained to analyze questions of right and wrong at a highly sophisticated level. It is, in fact, profitable to view Sade's later mentality and his creative work as a satire or parody of the idealistic world-view promulgated by the priests at Louis-le-Grand. Throughout his life, Sade regarded authority figures with a sharp, cynical eye. And because he wanted to find a true hero, a true father, he subjected every conceivable candidate to such a withering and destructive analysis that no one passed (perhaps with the exception of Père Massillon, mentioned above). In this way, he was like Lovelace, the satanic libertine of Samuel Richardson's novel *Clarissa*. Lovelace sought to find a woman worthy of his love. However, when he found a perfect candidate, the sublime Clarissa, he subjected her virtue to a test no one could possibly pass, and thus destroyed the very thing that he sought. The way Lovelace studied women, Sade studied priests—to ferret out their weaknesses, their hypocrisy, their self-deceptions. The wish to *become* someone is a form of emulation or imitation. To become someone in order to prove that person unworthy is parody. Sade played both roles. He sought a father to model himself on, but whenever a candidate presented himself, Sade's satire and cynicism destroyed him. This struggle took place primarily in Sade's mind, not out in the open. He may have had an occasional run-in with the Jesuit fathers, but it is unlikely that he attacked them head-on any more than he attacked or toadied up to his military commanders. Young Sade was much more likely to have waged his wars in his own mind, just as he would later wage them on paper. The constant surveillance and questioning to which the Jesuit fathers customarily subjected their students became a model for the behavior of many of Sade's libertines in their relations with the young objects of their debauchery. A score of Jesuit teachers would provide a schoolboy who possessed Sade's talent for caricature with ample material for many of his later fictional portraits.

Sade's relationship with his own father at this time does not appear to have been very close. The few letters surviving from the Comte de Sade are all concerned with his own debts, his overspent income, his need for funds to keep up appearances, which among other things meant gambling at Court or at the wealthy houses where he occasionally stayed, and his schemes to sell either Saumane or another property to raise tuition for his son, or to buy yet another property at Mazan.[38] In a letter dating from 1752, the Comte informed his brother the Abbé that he was staying at Fontainebleau as a guest of "Mademoiselle," Mlle de Charolais, his former mistress. The society at Court, he said, was never so fine, and he boasted that he had won 16 louis at cards. He also reported the news at Court: the marriage of the Prince de Condé had been delayed. This, by the way, was the same individual, now sixteen, with whom young Sade had come to blows. The marriage of the Prince on May 3, 1752, must have set off some bitter thoughts of lost chances in the mind of Sade's mother. The Comte went on to tell his brother, "I think Madame de Sade is in Paris. M. Amblet will have informed you about how she is doing."[39] The Comte did not know where his wife was; he mentioned his son only as a financial burden. In a letter to the Abbé the following year, he speculated about "advantageously" marrying off his son, then thirteen.[40] While young Sade was at school in Paris with Amblet, his father remained a remote figure, flitting about the brilliant candles of the Court, nearly consumed by his own rising debts and financial speculation, resentful of his son's tuition costs.

The only relief from young Sade's rigorous schoolwork was his summer vacations at the château de Longeville in Champagne, the residence of his father's old friend the Comtesse de Raimond. When Sade was thirteen, and on school vacation with her, Mme de Raimond wrote to his father about how frightened she had been when the boy rode a horse. Amblet, she said, was annoyed that she might infect young Sade with her own fears, but the boy, she insisted, had too much bravery for that to happen. She also reported that young Sade had fallen in love with her friend Mme de Vernouillet. Mme de Raimond said that she had to laugh watching the boy's tongue-tied, naïve struggles with the tender passion, for he treated Mme de Vernouillet more as his mama than his beloved. But the woman he *would* call Mama for the rest of his life, Mme de Saint-Germain, was also a guest there. At one point, Mme de Saint-Germain wrote an impassioned letter to the Comte de Sade, pleading with him to let his son stay on with her and Amblet at the château de Longeville rather than return to college.[41]

Does it appear strange that Sade, in his youth as well as in later life, attracted women who unabashedly wished to mother him and to protect him? Even today, a great many of the important scholars and writers on Sade, and especially those who wish to understand or purify his reputation, are women: Simone de Beauvoir, Angela Carter, Margaret Crosland, Alice Laborde, Annie Le Brun, Francine du Plessix Gray. What is Sade's appeal? It may well be the appeal of the orphan, of a withdrawn but passionate soul that cries out for mothering.

Boys who need mothering, however, eventually grow up, if not quite all the way. Large changes were in store for Sade. His fourth year at school would be his last. He was now fourteen, and ready, or so his father thought, for the next stage in his development. He was enrolled in the training academy for the Chevaux-légers, the King's Light Cavalry, an elite corps that admitted sons from only the best families. Accordingly, in May 1754, a month before Sade's fourteenth birthday, the court genealogist, M. de Clairambault, was asked to draw up a document from evidence supplied by the Abbé certifying the Sade family's ancient nobility. "Their genealogy goes back more than 400 years," M. de Clairambault determined, and Sade "has all the qualifications required to be admitted" into the Chevaux-légers.[42] Sade was then fourteen, but some of his fellow cadets may well have been younger.[43] Of course, Sade would be leaving what after four years had become the familiar world of the Jesuit school. He was leaving Amblet's gentle supervision. He was leaving the spiritual discipline of the Jesuit fathers. His new world would be concerned more with outer things: parades, horsemanship, swordplay, physical discipline. This was as it should have been, what a young man of his age and rank was supposed to do. After all, M. de Clairambault's certificate had noted his family's distinguished military service. Young Sade was right on schedule.

There were several military schools on the Left Bank of the Seine. The King often presided over reviews of the candidates training for his Chevaux-légers. These "military tournaments," a contemporary noted, "attract a great assembly of people of consequence of both sexes. . . . The eagerness of these young men to win the prizes that are awarded to the victors makes these festivals gallant and regular."[44] The physical discipline and the training in Sade's military academy were rigorous, but military life may have been a pleasant change from the intense mental pressure of a Jesuit school. Sade had enjoyed outdoor life at Saumane. He had even frightened Mme de Raimond with his bravery on horseback. Throughout his later years, whether seeing action during the Seven Years' War, or in prison, or during the horrors of the Revolution, he often displayed considerable physical courage. For a while, he must have enjoyed the prospect of joining the Chevaux-légers, with their noble blood, their code of honor and service to king and country. These were ideals to which a brave young cavalier could aspire. Moreover, he could wear their handsome uniform with pride: "Scarlet uniform, edged throughout with gold braid, with frogs; lining, cuffs, collar, jacket, and breeches of white silk; pockets cut crosswise; buttons and buttonholes of silver; epaulet in gold on the right shoulder; white belt braided with gold, hat edged with gold, with a white plume and cockade, heavy boots."[45] Even when he was fully grown, Sade, at around five feet six inches, was of middling height. At age fourteen, on horseback and wearing his scarlet uniform and plumed cockade, he must have felt ten feet tall. Moreover, the Chevaux-légers were garrisoned in Versailles, a brilliant setting for a young officer. Following his course of training, Sade was commissioned a second lieutenant in the King's Foot Guard on December 14, 1755. There would not be much time to enjoy his new uniform in peace.

When Sade turned sixteen, on June 2, 1756, the Seven Years' War had already begun. He experienced his baptism of fire on June 27–28 beneath the walls of Port-Mahon, which Maréchal de Richelieu successfully took by a bloody assault. Sade's bravery was even mentioned in the *Gazette:* "The Marquis de Briqueville and M. de Sade vigorously attacked the *redoute de la Reine* and, after a very fierce and murderous battle, they succeeded in seizing it by assault and by means of scaling ladders, and they held it, when the besieged enemy exploded four mines."[46] An autobiographical passage in his novel *Aline et Valcour* gives the following account of his going off to war:

War began, and I dare boast that I fought well. That native impetuosity of my character, that soul of fire that nature granted me at birth, served only to augment with additional power and energy that fierce quality generally called courage, and that is looked upon, no doubt erroneously, as the sole qualification for our profession.[47]

At the *redoute de la Reine*, the fort sent down a withering fire of musket and cannon as the soldiers approached with flimsy ladders. Even when they scaled the walls and stood on the battlements, the ground below suddenly belched flame and rubble as the retreating enemy set off the mines they had buried. Yet, even though there was death above ground and below, something in Sade burned stronger than courage. "Soul of fire"—Sade's image perfectly describes the crucible within him in which his rage reduced everything to a fiery residue.

On January 14, 1757, Sade was commissioned *cornette*, the officer in charge of the colors, in the regiment of *carabiniers* commanded by his father's friend the Marquis de Poyanne, the Comte de Provence. The following year, Sade took part in the unsuccessful French campaign along the Rhine. From May to December 1758, he wrote a detailed, almost day-by-day account of the confusing maneuvers of this campaign. Sade's style is neither literary nor interesting. The account is as banal, as boring as the daily realities of ordinary warfare. It is concerned with positioning and repositioning troops, making and breaking camp, skirmishing, gaining or losing small advantages, the same towns lost or retaken. In July, for example, the French forces found themselves with the advantage of the high ground overlooking the enemy encampment at Bedburg. Sade wrote in his journal:

> We found them arrayed for battle on the plain below these heights on this side of the river Erft. The high ground made our position very advantageous. The enemy took careful note of it. . . . At midnight, all of their campfires were seen to go out. It was discovered on the 15th, at three o'clock in the morning, that their army had decamped at ten o'clock at night and had crossed back over the Erft. M. de Comtades immediately sent a considerable detachment commanded by M. d'Armentières, but he was not in time. We captured a piece of siege artillery, several deserting soldiers and sutlers.[48]

If an army were to be surprised or caught on low ground, the results could be devastating. On June 22, skirmishing focused around the town of Krefeld, which had just been retaken by a small French force. "The enemy," Sade wrote, were "still at Hüls" and were caught off guard:

They decamped on the same day and, by a forced march, they arrived on the 23rd to attack our camp. The army was surprised to some extent. It had enough time, however, to prepare for battle. The enemy cannonaded us rather fiercely from all sides. . . . Night was coming on; the Comte de Clermont thought it prudent to retreat, which was done in the best order. The enemy took possession of the battlefield, spent the night there, and left the next morning to make camp before Krefeld. We retreated below Cologne.[49]

The campaign of 1758 went much as did the entire war—against France. Sade must have acquitted himself well enough. On April 21, 1759, he was promoted to the rank of captain in the Burgundian Cavalry, a position bought in the usual way, through his father's influence and money. By the time the preliminary peace treaty was signed at Fontainebleau in November 1762, Sade, at age twenty-two, had served in six campaigns.

Sade's adolescence had been spent in barracks, in encampments, and on the field of battle. War, it is sometimes said, makes a man of you. Did it make a man of Sade? In modern times, the immense psychological impact of warfare has come to be understood and expected. Shell shock, battle fatigue, flashbacks, traumatic psychosis, survivor guilt are all well known, even familiar. Sade's account of the 1758 campaign, from which the above two excerpts are a very brief but absolutely representative sample, is written without any emotional coloring whatsoever. How different this style is from his memorable concreteness and vividness of detail in *Les Cent Vingt Journées de Sodome* or in his letters from prison! In them, every molecule of matter is imagined, felt, and given its full weight. Sade's emotional detachment in describing his part in the Seven Years' War may be attributed to the desire of a young officer to write like an old general. This role-playing is a sign of his insecurity, his wish to be like his senior officers, perhaps like his mentor, the Marquis de Poyanne, who had given him a book on military tactics.[50] Certainly, Sade did not write about war as he did because he could not face the crude or low side of life or of war. Rather, his tendency was to view events from an extreme vantage point: the zenith or the nadir; too high or too low. In this case, he chose the overview, idealizing and rationalizing warfare into high strategy, identifying with the godlike vision of the generals, the world of the fathers who know or who ought to know what is right.

If one side of Sade identified with the generals who fought the war on paper, the other side was still an adolescent, attempting to deal with being on his own for the first time. Like any young fellow, he had to make friends, watch his money, avoid the pitfalls of youth, find girls. Camp life, even near a battlefield, was often boring. "At the dinner tables of the officers," the English poet Arthur Young wrote, "you hear only obscene and ridiculous chattering."[51] During the Seven Years' War, another observer noted that "the general quarters are full of valets, party girls, and sutlers. The general officers are occupied only with their pleasures, with high living, with their quarters."[52] Sade, of course, had his own valet, Teissier.[53] He liked girls. He gambled with what funds remained from his small allowance. In the army, gambling was just as much a social necessity as it was at Court. The following is a letter from M. de Castéra[54] to the Comte de Sade, providing news of Sade's trip back to camp after a leave in Paris:

> The dear boy is in fine shape. He is pleasant, agreeable, amusing. . . . The journey put some weight on him and some color in his cheeks, which the pleasures of Paris had somewhat paled; we are taking care of that. Teissier[55] is a treasure whom I exhort him to value highly. Our two horses are giving us some trouble: his is off his feed, and is lame (somewhat); he claims it's out of spite, since, when he gets a chance to run off, he skips like a goat. Mine has received a wound near the withers, but I hope that we will manage well enough. He [Sade] captures and abandons hearts at every stop. His little heart or, rather, *body* is wildly excitable: let the German girls look out! I will do my best to prevent him from committing follies. He has given me his word not to gamble more than a louis a day in the army. But this is a secret that I am not disclosing to you.[56]

Several details are worth noting in this characterization of Sade. M. de Castéra, Sade's traveling companion, appeared to like him. Yet, even though they were about the same age, he felt bound to assume a fatherly authority over Sade, extracting from him a promise to limit his gambling. M. de Castéra also observed a small instance of Sade's characteristic paranoia: Sade somehow came to believe that his horse was persecuting him with a feigned injury. Finally, it is interesting to see Sade's early success at charming women. His power, M. de Castéra observed with a touch of envy, emanated not so much from his "heart"—although, as we shall see later, Sade could be lavishly sentimental. Here, it is attributed, rather, to a physical sensuality, a wild excitability that must have appeared to women as a great urgency in him. M. de Castéra quite accurately caught his companion's character with a few strokes of the pen—his effect on women, and on men too. Although M. de Castéra was perhaps only a year older than Sade, he had become involved in playing a dual and duplicitous role. He was Sade's friend, and he was also an authority figure, undertaking to keep the "dear boy" out of trouble. Sade himself never mentioned M. de Castéra in any of his letters. If there had been any possibility of a real friendship between them, M. de Castéra's betrayal of his confidences to his father must have destroyed whatever trust Sade felt in him.

The Comte de Sade had M. de Castéra's letter copied, doubtless to be sent to his brother the Abbé, to show him what a wastrel his son had become. The Comte attached an angry comment, "You see how that rascal has a louis a day to lose!," adding, "Yet he made me a promise not to bet a sol."[57] It was his father's opinion that Sade would need, if not to reform, at least to apologize for his sins.

This apology seemed to have come in the letter Sade wrote to his former tutor, the Abbé Amblet, following his tiring escapades in Paris, possibly in the spring of 1759. Because the dating of this letter is conjectural, it may be either the first or the second letter we have from Sade's pen. Although it is written to Amblet, who was at that time living with Sade's father, it was clearly meant for the father's eyes:

> The number of sins I have committed during my stay at Paris, my dear Abbé, the manner in which I have behaved toward the kindest father in the world, make him repent of having brought me into it. But may the remorse for having displeased him and the fear of forever losing his friendship sufficiently punish me! All that remains now of those pleasures I once thought real is the most bitter sorrow of having disturbed the kindest of all fathers and the best of all friends. Each morning I arose to seek out pleasure; this thought made me forget everything else. I considered myself happy as soon as I found it, but this so-called happiness faded as soon as my desires, and left me only with regrets. By night, I was in despair; I knew that I had done wrong, but I did not see it except at night, and the next day my reawakening desires drove me once more to pleasure. I completely forgot the thoughts of the night before. Someone suggested a party, I agreed to it, and I thought I was happy, but I saw that I was only committing foolishness and that I was not truly enjoying myself.[58] Quite alone with myself now, the more I think about my conduct, the stranger it seems to me. I see that my father had good reason when he told me that almost everything I did was illusory. Ah! if I had always done only what gave me real pleasure, I would have spared myself a lot of suffering, and I would have much less offended my father. Did I really think that the girls I saw could procure true pleasure for me? Alas! does one ever truly enjoy a happiness that one buys, and love without

tenderness, can it ever be truly sweet? My pride now suffers to think that I was loved only because I was, perhaps, less niggardly in paying than someone else.

I have just now received a letter from my father. He advises me to offer him a general confession. I am going to do it, but I assure you that it will be sincere. I no longer wish to deceive such a gentle father, and one who would still wish to forgive me if I admit my faults to him.

Adieu, my dear Abbé, let me hear from you, I beg of you, even though I will only be able to receive your letters much later, because, being unable to stop anywhere along the way, I will not be able to get your letters until I return to camp. So do not be surprised, my dear Abbé, if you do not hear from me until I turn up.[59]

This is a slippery letter. Sade had just received a very angry and probably threatening letter from "the kindest father in the world"—a father who had also told him that he would never amount to anything because his head was always in the clouds, his thoughts were mere illusions. His father had demanded a "general confession," which Sade promised Amblet he would write. No such letter exists, and it probably was never written. This, then, was the only confession Sade's father was to get, and it was a confession once removed, conveyed through the conduit of Amblet, more beneficent and forgiving than Sade's father, who was, to use Sade's words, "displeased" and "offended."

How afraid of his father was Sade? When he wrote this unctuous confession, how sincere was he? How much, if at all, did his heart tremble before the paternal wrath? The head of a noble household in eighteenth-century France was indeed a formidable figure. Sade's distant cousin the famous revolutionary hero Mirabeau would be imprisoned for sexual misconduct and disobedience under a lettre de cachet obtained by his own father. At the age of nineteen, Sade was dependent upon his father's money and upon his influence for the advancement of his army career. If the Comte de Sade was angry, he would have to be placated. It is not hard to imagine what the Comte de Sade thought of the letter his son sent, not to *him*, but to Amblet—a letter, moreover, that was a deft mixture of flattery and cheek, sincerity and charm. When the Comte de Sade had this letter copied and sent to his brother the Abbé de Sade, he noted, "I am extremely displeased."[60]

The letter is richly, tensely ironical, perhaps the first hint of the writer Sade was to become. His statements are at once true and false. He *was* driven toward whores and party girls. Many soldiers on leave in Paris were. Sade felt remorse the morning after. Who had not? Sade preferred true love to lust; he was a romantic. Who wasn't? The girls had provided pleasure—value for money. Admittedly, this was not the highest form of pleasure, sex combined with tenderness. But if the pleasure of lust was not as exalted as the pleasure of love, it was still pleasure. Sade's renunciation of lust sounded both as true and as false as his other statements. When he said that he was driven by an endless circle of lust and remorse, a cycle that he could not control, he seemed to be telling the truth. But when he promised to stop, he did not seem to be telling the truth. Similarly, he created a pretty picture of an idealized father, but he sounded ironical when he related the picture to his real father and when he promised to write a full confession. In fact, he ended his letter to Amblet with prevarications: Sade claimed that he could not be easily reached, he was in the army after all, letters could miscarry (i.e., his father should not bother to write any more angry letters), and one should not expect to hear from him again until he returned on leave to Paris a year later. The message is a mixture of surface and subterranean meanings. On the surface, there is the creation of an idealized father, the celebration of pure love, the exaggerated suffering and remorse for sexual profligacy. Beneath the surface, there is the implication that fathers, even God, can be duped by flattery and false contrition, that sexual pleasure, even though it does not measure up to true love, is still sexual pleasure, and that repentance in the morning occurs only after one has had a very wild time the night before. The truth is that Sade believed in both the surface and the underbelly of the ironical statement: he was a sinner who believed in sin, but argued that it did not exist; he was, in a sense, almost a fatherless child who invented an even more powerful father than his own in order to cringe before the preposterous idol he himself created; he was both a romantic and a materialist. Charm, confidence, and mastery are evident in this letter, but also desperation, fear, and remorse. Sade was a creature of contradictions, of opposites. What these opposites suggest, what this early and sophisticated use of irony suggests, is that there was no sure center in Sade's personality.

There is another interesting letter that has some claim to be considered as Sade's first extant letter,[61] also an ironic apology. Sade was writing to the officials of the captured town of Clèves, where he was quartered:

Messieurs,

Upon hearing the wonderful news that we just received that Mgr le Duc de Broglie had completely beaten your Hanoverian and Hessian troops, as a good patriot and one keenly interested in the success of my nation, last Sunday, the 22nd of this month, I shot off some fireworks in celebration of that wonderful news, but unfortunately a rocket fell

on the house of M. Streil. It did not cause, Messieurs, any harm or
damage; I am sending you the certificate of the owner of the house. If
circumstances, Messieurs, keep me here some time longer, as I foresee
that occasions for celebration could become more frequent, I will
choose, Messieurs, a field more distant from the town and beyond the
reach of all danger, in which to shoot off my fireworks.[62]

This letter is at once an apology and an insult. It is pleasant to think of Sade,
an officer in the French army, playing with fireworks and almost burning
down a captured town. Impetuosity, boyish enthusiasm, even a certain childishness were to remain features of his personality. In this case, no damage was
done. Perhaps the letter did not need to be written, but simply provided Sade
an opportunity to display his ability at mock apology.

The best evidence of Sade's mentality around this time appears in a letter
to his father dated August 12, 1760, when Sade was twenty years old and writing from an encampment at Obertistein. The beginning of this letter deals
with the details of that summer's campaign. Then Sade discusses the possibility of visiting his father in Provence on his winter leave. He continues:

> You ask me about my way of life, my daily occupations. I am going
> to describe them in detail for you with complete frankness. I am
> accused of liking my sleep; it is true that I am somewhat guilty of this
> fault: I go to bed early and arise late. I very frequently ride out to
> inspect the enemies' position and our own. After three days in a camp,
> I am as familiar with the least ravine as is M. le Maréchal [de Broglie].
> For good or bad, I draw my own conclusions; I speak them, and I am
> praised or blamed according to how little or no common sense they
> contain. Occasionally, I pay visits, but only to M. de Poyanne, or to
> my old comrades from the *carabiniers* or from the Régiment du Roi. I
> do not much stand on ceremony; I do not care for it. Except for M. de
> Poyanne, throughout the campaign, I have not set foot in general
> headquarters. I am quite aware that I am not acting for the best; it is
> necessary to pay court in order to get ahead: but I do not like to do it.
> I am in pain when I hear someone flatter another with a thousand
> things that he often does not believe. He is a tougher man than I who
> plays such a stupid role. To be polite, honest, proud but without arro-
> gance, obliging but without insipidity, to generally suit oneself in
> small ways so long as we do not cause harm, either to ourselves or to
> anyone else; to live well, to amuse oneself without bringing either ruin
> or trouble down upon oneself; having few friends, or perhaps none,

because there simply is no one truly sincere or who would not sacrifice you twenty thousand times over, if the most slender selfish motive on his part were involved; with the equality of character that lets you get along well with everyone, but without ever surrendering yourself to anyone, because no sooner do you do that than you have cause to regret it; to speak most highly of, to offer the greatest praise of those who, often without cause, have spoken very meanly about you without your even suspecting it (because nearly always it is the very people who have the most attractive surface and who seem the most eager for your friendship who deceive you the most). There you have my virtues, there you have those to which I aspire. If I were able to flatter myself that I have a friend, I believe I do have one in the regiment; yet I am not entirely sure of him. He is M——, the son of M. de ————, and he is even, as I believe, somewhat connected to me through our Simiane relatives. He is a boy of considerable merit, extremely pleasant, writing some very lovely poetry, a very fine writer, industrious and knowledgeable in his craft. I am genuinely his friend. I have reason to think him mine. In any case, who can one trust? It is the same with friends as with women: experience often makes one see that the merchandise is false. There you have my entire confession; I open my heart to you not as to a father whom one fears generally without loving, but as to one's most sincere friend, to the most gentle friend I believe I have in the world. Cease to have any reason to pretend to hate me, grant me your love so as never to take it away from me, and trust that I will in no way neglect anything in order to try to deserve it.

. . .

Let me hear from you as soon as possible, I beg of you; you would not imagine the pleasure your letters give me when I get them. But do not write just a few words, as you usually do.[63]

If this letter was meant to be the "general confession" that Sade's father had asked him to make a year earlier, the Comte de Sade must have been baffled by it. "There you have my entire confession," his son claimed. But the only defect he admitted to, "somewhat," was oversleeping: "I am accused of liking my sleep." His admission that his career may have suffered because he would not pay court to his superior officers at camp may be evidence of self-blame: "I am quite aware that I am not acting for the best." If he has a weakness, it is that he cannot act the part of a toady: "He is a tougher man than I who plays such a stupid role." This is, indeed, a peculiar style of confession and self-criticism. Sade had confessed that he was virtuous to a fault! He could not get ahead in the army because he was no hypocrite, no flatterer, no liar. This letter was probably a defensive response to his father's complaints about his lack of progress: he begged his father to stop looking for reasons "to hate me"; he was doing the best he could do, in view of his high moral code. It is natural to want the praise of one's father, and of one's superior officers. But Sade required this praise to have an absolute value. If it were acquired by his dancing attendance at the general's table in the officer's mess, or by means of his social skills and flattery, then Sade did not want it.

On the one hand, Sade idealized fathers, superior officers, and the idea of authority. In an ideal world, Sade believed, his superior virtues would be recognized. On the other hand, he angrily satirized fathers, superior officers, and authority figures for their failures to live up to the ideals they had a duty to uphold. Generals can be flattered. Outrageous! Fathers can become infuriated with their sons for no good reason. Unjust! Virtue, like Sade's, can go unrewarded. Again, unjust! Most people come to accept some compromises to their youthful idealism. Most come to locate themselves somewhere in the middle ground that we call reality. They make some kind of peace between the way they know the world ought to be and the way that it is. This, Sade said, he would not do. Indeed, he *could not* do it. The anger against the "fathers" and against the generals would be repeated again and again throughout Sade's life; it would become anger against priests, against judges, against high government officials, against God. Sade would, throughout his life, blame all his difficulties on others (as he had done when still a child). In one sense, Sade's exquisite sensitivity to the difference between the way things and people *ought* to be and the way they *were* would predispose him, in view of his literary abilities, to a career as a satirist. In fact, a satirist is exactly what he became. This letter and the previous one to Amblet display a sophisticated competence in that genre. It sometimes happens that extreme satirists (like Jonathan Swift) who seem to attack the whole of reality are thought to be insane, and this was a danger lying in wait for Sade. His inability to accept reality, his obsessive identification with a perfect world peopled by a perfect species, his rage at any deviations from the ideal, his paranoid tendency to blame others for his own inadequacies—all of these traits indicate a seriously disturbed psyche. But he had not crossed, and would not cross, the border of reality to enter the country of full psychosis. At times—especially in his fiction—he would come close to psychosis, but he was never insane. For one thing, he always felt the pain of his predicament. He yearned for the love and approval of a father whose life and temperament would never permit him to become the idealized figure Sade had constructed in his absence. Sade begged for his father's love; he begged him to "cease" creating pretexts to hate him; he begged for a letter from him: "But do not write just a few words, as you usually do." It is painful to feel on the verge of an ideal world. It is painful to try to import pure, ideal things into this corrupt, fallen world. It is painful—impossible—to extract love from a totem, an idol. Sade felt the pain and pathos of his predicament, yet he could not give up his need for a perfect world or for a perfect father.

Sade did not have any better success in dealing with his comrades, his peers. If he would not or could not enter into the rivalrous fray of junior officers competing for the attention of the commanding officers, neither could he make friends among these equals, whom he describes as backbiting rogues. Sade's embattled loneliness is painfully evident. His only consolation was his pride in his moral superiority: he would not stoop to their tactics. He mistrusted everyone. Those who seemed the most attractive and friendly—they were the ones "who deceive you the most." Sade condensed his suspicions into a harsh maxim: "It is the same with friends as with women: experience often makes one see that the merchandise is false." Sade's character was now fully formed. He was at twenty what he would be for the rest of his life—an angry loner, a sharp and cynical observer of life and human nature.

If Sade's paranoia excluded his superiors and his equals (and possibly all women) from his trust, that left only his inferiors as potential friends; indeed, Sade would become intimately and sexually involved with some of his valets. Later, we will see a particularly charming and wildly humorous exchange of letters between Sade and one of his valets, whom he called "La Jeunesse." In the army, Sade was able to trust only one young fellow, a relative actually, "a boy of considerable merit, extremely pleasant, writing some very lovely poetry." Wit, some literary ability, and general tractability were attractions to Sade in an inferior. He could sometimes tolerate a young man; he could act the authority figure to the poetical chap in his regiment. At such times, it was as if Sade were making a demonstration, showing the Powers That Be the sort of father, the sort of commanding officer, the sort of God he would like above him. But what Sade usually displayed to these Powers was angry disappointment and satirical fury. He taunted authority with its failures, relentlessly goaded authority into action, even if, as the events of his life demonstrate over and over, authority's actions took the form of reprisals aimed at himself.

CHAPTER 2

Love and Marriage

I N SEPTEMBER or October of 1762, shortly before France signed
the preliminaries of the peace treaty bringing an end to the Seven
Years' War, the Comte de Sade wrote jointly to his brother the
Abbé and his sister Mme de Villeneuve about his son's imminent
demobilization (which took place a few months later, in February 1763). The
Comte de Sade was so "displeased" with his son that he threatened to enter a
monastery "so as not to welcome my son into my house."[1] Of his son, he
added: "I knew it was necessary to get him married early."[2] Now, with the
son's return imminent, Sade's father saw marriage as the only solution to his
son's problems.

The Comte de Sade had begun negotiations for a favorable union as early
as the summer of 1759.[3] He rejected a few early prospects, and during the
spring of 1761, his hopes were first raised and then dashed by the family
of Mlle de Bassompierre.[4] He apparently kept a list of eligible heiresses and
was well informed about their families' finances.[5] In the end, the Comte de
Sade found his son a bride whom Sade never saw until just before the wedding day, Renée-Pélagie de Montreuil. The marriage would have disastrous
consequences.

It may be wondered what kind of father forces his only son into a very
early marriage merely to get rid of him. The Comte de Sade was not a man to
be trifled with. But at the time of the marriage negotiations, neither was he
entirely in his right mind. In 1762, he was sixty years old. He had been long
separated from his wife. His career as a diplomat had ended fifteen years earlier, when his son was still a small boy. He had tried for another position, but
he did not appear to have been trusted by anyone who had the ear of the
King. Instead of simply going down to La Coste and managing his estates, he
remained in Paris, enjoying Court society and evidently living far beyond his
means. His pretensions and improvidence were the only explanation for his
dreadful financial condition in 1763, the year of his son's marriage. According
to the marriage contract, the Comte de Sade each year earned 10,000 livres

from his position as lieutenant general of Bresse, Bugey, Valromey, and Gex, as well as 18,000 to 20,000 livres from his own estates of La Coste, Saumane, Mazan, and the Mas de Cabanes in Provence.[6] This would have been a princely income in Provence. But it was far from enough for a man trying to play the part of a courtier in Paris, Versailles, and Fontainebleau. On the eve of his son's wedding, he was deeply in debt and could not even fulfill the modest financial obligations he had undertaken for the wedding.

The following excerpt of a letter that the Comte de Sade wrote to his aged mother in the summer of 1762, while she was on her deathbed, gives a vivid impression of his unstable mental state:

> I intend to retire into some corner of the world only to contemplate my end and to live alone forgotten by everyone. I will soon bid you an eternal farewell and I will beg forgiveness for all the suffering and pain I have given you. I hope that my son does not give you any more of them. *You may dispose of all my effects that I left down there. I want none of it. I no longer need anything.*
>
> There is a revolution in Russia. The Tsar is in prison. His son is emperor and his wife is regent.
>
> The two bits of trimming that I have sent are for the young girl Aldonse [a servant in his mother's household].
>
> There is a man who claims to have received a letter from God which commanded him to kill his wife and children. He obeyed, he has been put in prison and condemned as insane to the madhouse.[7]

The Comte de Sade's mother would die in a matter of weeks, on September 16. Yet her son is utterly preoccupied with his own problems. Moreover, the stream of peculiar associations from one sentence to the next reveals a disordered and depressed state of mind. He is angry with his son, and then immediately shifts to a discussion of how the Tsar of Russia has been deposed by his wife and son. Finally, there is the bizarre account of a maniac who kills his wife and children. If this letter displays no understanding of or consideration for his mother's plight, it certainly does open a frightful window into the Comte's fear of his own impotence and old age, as well as into his jealousy of and rage against his own son.

For all the Comte de Sade's animosity, Sade always spoke of his father with the highest respect and, despite annoying but ineffectual attempts at rebellion, deferred to him in everything. Sade's idealizing tendency had already been evident in the perfect models he constructed for his superior officers in the army; he did the same for his father. When the real generals, when his real father failed to live up to Sade's ideal conceptions of them (as, indeed, how could they not?), Sade tended to withdraw into an angry depression. But his first wish was to live in a world where he could be directed and controlled by an ideal authority. His paranoid speculations (which will become more evident as time goes on), his sense that he was the object of secret messages and conspiracies against him by powerful forces, are actually a feature of his deeper desire to be controlled by such forces. His submission to his father's marriage scheme was really a submission to the ideal of the powerful father he had fabricated in his own mind. This ideal continued to exist and to operate in Sade long after most boys, through actual experience of their fathers and fatherly types, are obliged to revise their ideals downward. In the end, Sade succumbed to an ideal of his own devising.

Since this period in Sade's life concerns his father's schemes to marry him off, it is well to consider what is known of Sade's affairs of the heart. To be sure, Sade had visited prostitutes in Paris while on leave from the army, and he had left broken hearts in the towns he had passed through. He also gave an account of how he learned German during one of his encampments at Clèves. Having heard "that, in order to learn a language well, it was necessary to sleep regularly and continually with a woman of that country," Sade took the advice: "I rigged myself out with a nice fat baroness who was three or four times my age, and who taught me rather pleasantly. At the end of six months, I spoke German like Cicero!"[8]

Sade's next serious affair also involved an older woman—ten years his senior. It was the summer of 1762, when he was twenty-two years old and garrisoned either at Hesdin, south of Calais, or nearby in Abbeville. In the autumn, the Comte de Sade informed the Abbé of the details of this affair. "Everybody" at Hesdin, he said, "was gossiping about my son's romance." The woman in question, he heard, though "amiable," was ten years older than his son.[9] Forty-five years later, in 1807, near the end of his life, Sade, writing in his *Journal* at the Charenton insane asylum, would recall this summer as a time when he was performing in plays at Hesdin, a summer of love and play-acting that came to a sudden end with the death of his grandmother.[10] There is a tender and romantic quality to Sade's affections, a boyish, hyperbolical idealism in his passions. He wrote a rather intemperate and passionate ultimatum to his father, stating that he was "absolutely determined" to marry the Hesdin woman: "I ask your forgiveness if I am resolved to marry only where my heart leads me. It may deceive me, but its error will be so sweet that I will always prefer it to the most perfect happiness. What most encourages me is the kindness that you had in promising me that you would never compel my feelings."[11] Just as the Comte de Sade was throwing up his hands in disgust, the Duc de Cossé-Brissac, a colonel in Sade's regiment at Hesdin, wrote to say that he had succeeded in talking Sade out of his infatuation. "Your son," he wrote, "has a very tender heart, or at least he easily persuades himself that he is in love and that the same feeling is returned."12

Sade's father had no patience for his son's romantic airs. The Comte preferred to blacken his son's reputation in his letters to his sister and brother back in Provence. For example, in February 1763, he told his brother that he had had a conversation with the major of his son's regiment. According to the Comte, "everything" the major "had to say about him is frightful."13 In another letter to his brother during the same month, he said that he was eager "to be rid of that little fellow, who has not one good quality and who has all the bad ones."14

While the Comte de Sade was trying to mine for gold, his son was bleating away about true love, about following no dictate but that of his heart. He was also having a very good time in Paris. On February 2, the Comte complained to the Abbé: "My son never misses a ball or a play. It is infuriating."15 Sade did enjoy the playhouses. He liked to go backstage and contrive introductions to the actresses. Perhaps he should have seen his father more often. If Sade avoided visiting him, it may have been because these visits always led, if not to arguments, then at least to conflicts which Sade knew he was bound to lose.

In Paris, Sade had also come across Laure de Lauris, a year younger than he was and of a noble Provençal family. Sade met with her on many occasions, notably in her bedroom. His excitable heart was once again smitten. The two lovers talked of marriage even as his father was opening negotiations with one of the uncles of Renée-Pélagie de Montreuil, who, the Comte wrote to his brother, "came to see me yesterday to discuss the marriage of his niece and to indicate its advantages." The Comte then gave the Abbé an account, no doubt provided by Renée's uncle, of the wealth of her father and the various inheritances that would eventually come to her from her aunts and uncles.16 The marriage plan moved forward, but not altogether smoothly. Renée's mother, the formidable Mme de Montreuil, was apparently told by someone that Sade "owed a lot of money and that he was wild." But to the surprise and delight of the Comte, she had replied, "What young man does not commit some follies?" In view of her conciliatory attitude, the Comte predicted success. A more serious difficulty was that the prospective groom knew nothing about this impending marriage. He believed he was in love with and engaged to Laure de Lauris. Also troubling his father was the venereal disease that Sade had contracted. The Comte grumbled that Sade would not see a doctor and was not taking care of it, which could ruin the marriage: "He does not have the time. I asked him to come and dine with me with the *intendant* [of the Veterans' Hospital, Renée's uncle] in order to discuss it, but he did not come and said that he had forgotten."[17] Sade's method of dealing with his father was passive: he avoided him.

Sade had less luck with Laure's father. One morning at the end of March, Sade paid his customary visit to his beloved's bedroom, but the Marquis de Lauris was lying in wait, hiding near the front door. This was a scene from a comedy. Sade placed his foot on the stair, listening. Stealthily, he ascended to Laure's room, as he had always done before, "three times a week," with no one there to stop him.[18] But this morning, scarcely had the lovers time to exchange greetings than the Marquis de Lauris burst into the room. It is not difficult to imagine the cries of surprise, the voice of paternal outrage, the feeble attempts at explanation. Sade insisted that Laure was innocent, that she had never submitted to his passion. But the Marquis de Lauris would not be placated. What he wanted, what he demanded, was that Sade marry his daughter the very next day.

Sade immediately left Paris for Avignon, where he intended to cure his illness and to prepare for his marriage to Laure. The Comte de Sade, in a letter to his brother, described his son's hasty departure from Paris as ignominious: "Day and night, he was afraid of being pursued by the Laurises, whom he thought he constantly saw at his heels."[19] Certainly, Sade had discussed with his father the Marquis de Lauris's demand. Sade wrote a joint letter to Laure and to her father explaining that the "motives of my trip" were not "to elude or to flee from a marriage that I had always desired, and that I assure you I still desire very avidly." Sade claimed that, as soon as his father learned of the matter, "he immediately gave his consent."[20] The passion of Sade's letter to Laure and her father suggests that he really believed that his trip to Avignon, Laure's birthplace, could result in a marriage. Either he misunderstood his own father's reaction, or else he was deliberately misled. Immediately after Sade left, his father wrote to the Abbé gloating that, just as this affair with Laure was coming to an end, the negotiations with the Montreuils were "miraculously" moving forward with renewed force.[21]

In Avignon, it soon became clear to Sade that Laure herself had rejected him. On April 6, 1763, he wrote her a very long, disjointed, passionate, emotionally desperate, and vindictive letter:

> Liar! ingrate! what has become of those promises to love me all your life? who is forcing you to this faithlessness? who is forcing you to break the vows that were to unite us forever? Have you taken my departure for flight? Did you think that I could live and yet fly from you?

Laure had apparently informed Sade that she preferred Paris to Avignon. Sade, calling her a "monster," told her she could stay there. Then, suspecting a human rather than a geographical rival, he hurled this curse at her: "May the deceptions of the scoundrel who will take my place in your heart one day become as odious in your eyes as your faithlessness has become in mine!" Sade slipped into a suicidal reverie reminiscent of his dream of that other Laure, Petrarch's: "Forgive the words of a miserable wretch who is out of his mind, for whom, following the loss of his beloved, death is the only answer. Alas! I am getting closer to it, to that moment which will free me from the life that I detest; my only desires now are for that day to come." Sade portrays Laure de Lauris here just as he would later portray Petrarch's Laure in his dream: she is a two-faced mother figure, the beloved mother with whom he wants to merge, and the indifferent, grotesque, poisonous mother sowing death and causing him to desire it. In this last connection, Sade now accuses Laure of infecting him with a venereal disease, and threatens to tell her new lover about this and more:

> Take care of your health; I am trying to restore mine. But whatever the state of your health, nothing could prevent me from giving you the most passionate proof of my love. . . . The little matter concerning the c[anker] ought to make you a bit more obliging to me. I tell you that I will not hide it from my rival, and this will not be the only secret that I will impart to him.

Following this bit of blackmail, Sade said that he was looking forward to his father's death, when Sade himself would become the Comte de Sade, and thus an even more eligible bachelor:

> Love me forever, my dear friend, and let us bide our time. . . . My father is asking for me again; do not think that it is for a marriage. I am absolutely determined to do nothing of the sort, and never would I want to do it. . . . Love me forever; be true to me, if you do not want to see me dead of a broken heart. Adieu, my sweet child, I adore you and love you a thousand times more than my life.[22]

This is a frenzied, disjointed, mad letter, sounding very much like the letters Sade would sometimes send his wife from prison. It also is kin to a few similar letters that Sade would write to actresses and mistresses who, he felt, had betrayed him. This letter is a kind of compendium of Sade's various and contradictory moods and writing styles, ranging from the abject, suicidal suffering of the romantic lover to the homicidal rage of the lover scorned ("Liar!

ingrate! . . . monster!"); from reasonable discussion of their dilemma to bitter, jealous fantasies about a rival; from tender expressions of undying love to salacious innuendoes and vile suggestions of blackmail. The lack of transition from one mood or argumentative style to the next suggests simultaneity. All of these moods and styles operate equally and at the same time in the writer's mind. It is, if not a cacophony, then a polyphonic aria of many voices, shrieking, crying, moaning, crooning. The letter is also marked by exaggerations and outright lies: for example, "my father, tears in his eyes, only asks as a favor" that the marriage take place in Avignon. All undermine the credibility of the writer and ensure that the letter could have had no good practical effect. No woman receiving a letter like that could possibly think, "Yes, I have been wrong. I will wait for him." Like so many letters Sade would later write, this one, it might be said, was written not by a man to a woman but, rather, by Sade to himself, or to the God in himself, the God of simultaneity, of paradox, of omniscience, who, seeing all, knowing all, could understand Sade, sympathize with him, and perhaps do him justice.

On April 16, 1763, the Comte de Sade wrote to his brother to say that it was now "very important" to see that his son leave Provence for Paris. Typically, however, he also urged economy: "Manage it, I beg you, with the least possible expense." He also warned the Abbé not to entrust their late mother's silver plate to Sade: "He would sell it along the way. Nothing is sacred to him."[23] By the 19th, the Comte de Sade wrote to his sister the Abbesse de Saint-Laurent that matters were moving forward. The Montreuils, he announced, had loaned him the 10,000 livres that he had promised to give to his son for the marriage. Of the Montreuils, he said:

> These are the best people and the most honest people in the world and everybody says that my son is extremely lucky to marry into that family. But I very much pity them for making such a bad acquisition, capable of committing all sorts of follies. He wrote to me yesterday that he was more than ever in love [with Mlle de Lauris], that it was certainly not Mlle de L[auris] who had made him sick. He forgets that he told me that he had not been with anybody else. Fortunately, she does not want him.

The Comte went on to describe the dinner he had had at the Montreuils', noting, however, that his wife "did not want to go" and said she was sick.[24] This was the first time he had seen his future daughter-in-law. It would appear that Renée had been described as no beauty. At the wedding, a month later, one of Sade's relatives characterized her as "not pretty."[25] At this point in the negotiations, as the Comte explained to his sister, had she been quite hideous he would have found something good to say: "I did not find the girl ugly. She is rather handsome, her bosom very pretty, her arms and hands very white, and nothing at all disagreeable, a charming personality. Her mother is extremely pleasant, amusing and witty."[26] For 10,000 livres, the Comte de Sade had reason to be pleased.

On May 1, 1763, the marriage contract of Donatien-Alphonse-François de Sade and Renée-Pélagie Cordier de Montreuil was approved and signed by Louis XV, the Queen, and other members of the royal family at Versailles, a signal honor rendered slightly strange by the absence of the prospective groom. He was still in Provence. Perhaps he was hoping that Laure would somehow appear. At any rate, he was having a good time at the village fête of La Coste. A much bleaker April day sixteen years later, when Sade was in prison in Vincennes, a letter from his friend Mlle de Rousset recalled her own participation in this day of rural gaiety, when she had been a young woman of nineteen. Her brother also had a role in the festivities:

> He composed that little pastoral at the request of Madame your aunt in eight days. At the same time, he coached that entire procession which was in front of you near Saint-Hilaire. Big Gardiol made him miserable by his clumsiness, and I, who was young, I laughed at the grace of some and at the awkwardness of others. I made the decorations for all of the men, and the ribbons for all the shepherdesses and the sheep. . . . Fifteen years! Yes, that was in 1763. Time flows very quickly. . . . What sufferings have we not experienced?[27]

Yes, that must have been a wonderful and comical procession of town officials, musicians, peasants, children, all in costume, all decorated, including the sheep!

On May 2, the Comte de Sade wrote his brother to hurry his son along. He also reminded the Abbé that, since Sade's illness was known to everyone, and especially to the Montreuils through their connections in Avignon, it would be necessary to speak of the venereal disease as a "bout of fever, since that is what I call it here." He also wanted his son, if possible, to bring along three dozen artichokes (very rare in Paris after the recent frosts) and a tuna pâté, all of which would make a very nice (and inexpensive) present to the Montreuils for the wedding.[28] The Comte de Sade had reason to be nervous. The ceremony, scheduled for May 17, was only two weeks away. Sade kept his father on tenterhooks about his arrival until the very last moment. This passive stubbornness was the only type of attack the son would allow himself against his father.

The details of the marriage settlement and of the Comte de Sade's financial difficulties are worth examining briefly. Even a cursory look provides a clearer picture of the situation than Sade himself appeared to have, either because he lacked the strength to question his father or because his father was an able and habitual dissembler. The marriage contract stipulated Renée's dowry and the financial responsibilities of both families. In brief, the Montreuils undertook to give the couple 10,000 livres upon their marriage, to provide Renée with an income of 1,500 livres a year (in addition to an income of 6,000 livres a year from her paternal grandmother), to offer the couple room and board for five years with two servants, and to give them 10,000 livres afterward for setting up their own household. But these incomes represented only a fraction of the almost 300,000 livres due the couple upon the deaths of various members of the Montreuil family.[29] The Montreuils were wealthy and belonged to what was then called the *noblesse de robe*, what today might be called the wealthy executive class. Renée's father, Claude-René de Montreuil, had once been the *président* or presiding judge of the Cour des Aides in Paris, and he still bore that honorary title. His wife was known as "La Présidente." Their influence, like that of their class, was real and growing. Of course, they were extremely eager to ally themselves with the true nobility that a family like Sade's had long represented. For this purpose, the Montreuils—or, rather, Mme de Montreuil, La Présidente, who was the dominant force in her family—were willing to overlook Sade's evident faults and the financial manipulations of his father in order to cement the alliance.

According to the marriage contract, the Comte de Sade's income from his estates of La Coste, Mazan, and Saumane in Provence, and of the Mas de Cabanes in Arles, amounted to 18,000 to 20,000 livres a year, in addition to the 10,000 livres a year from his post as lieutenant general. Though the Comte agreed to give the estates to his son, he reserved the income for himself until his death. Even stranger is the way the Comte de Sade signed over to his son the income from his post as lieutenant general. He had made this transfer retroactive to March 4, 1760. His son and his in-laws therefore expected in a short time to obtain four years of back income from this post: 40,000 livres. They did not get a sou. The Comte had already drawn this income or borrowed against it. Now he claimed that he had used up all the money to pay his son's allowance and expenses during the four years in question. The Comte's assertion that he had, in effect, already given his son this income, and his failure to provide an accounting of the payments, would produce a serious argument in the months following the wedding. Finally, the marriage contract also indicated that the Comte would give his son 10,000 livres. His letter to his sister of April 19, 1763, made it clear that this was the sum he had already borrowed from the Montreuils, and which he promised to repay upon the sale of his house in Glatigny, near Versailles.[30] After the marriage, the Comte de Sade would have no property, but neither would he have any debts. Even such debts as he had incurred in 1757 by, in effect, mortgaging the sale price of his post as lieutenant general, the so-called *brevet de retenue*, thereby borrowing 20,000 livres from Mme de Vigean—even debts such as these became the liability of his son.[31]

It must not have seemed so to Sade, but his marriage was built on unstable financial ground. Contractually, the Montreuils had promised great wealth; it would someday come to Sade upon the death of various relatives, but that was far in the future. On his own side, Sade would not get the money from his father that he expected, and would instead be saddled with his father's considerable debts. Perhaps he should have read the marriage contract with more care.

On May 15, Sade and Renée met at the Montreuils' Paris residence on the rue Neuve-du-Luxembourg to sign the marriage contract. There is no record of a previous meeting of the bride and groom. Indeed, Sade must have only just arrived in Paris from Avignon. He must have brought the artichokes and the pâté. There would be no further nonsense about his following the dictates of his heart; this was a marriage desired by both families. The next day, May 16, Mme de Montreuil took time to write to the Abbé de Sade, who would not attend the ceremony on the following day: "No one could be more deeply touched than I am, Monsieur, by all the expressions of satisfaction that you have generously offered over the alliance that we have the honor to contract with you. I am deeply flattered and delighted in every way. Your nephew could not be more kind and more desirable as a son-in-law because of the judgment, the sweetness of disposition, and the fine education that your cares appear to have inculcated in him."[32] For the Montreuils, this marriage was a dream come true, a confirmation of their wealth, their talents, their improving status in society. For the Comte de Sade, it would mean a clean financial slate. On June 2, he wrote his brother that from now on he could live on his income. "I no longer owe anything," he boasted.[33] At the same time, he was free of a son he did not like or understand.

The marriage was performed on May 17, 1763, after which the couple immediately took up residence in the Montreuils' elegant Paris mansion. The contract stipulated that the Comte de Sade must "emancipate" his son and set him "beyond his paternal authority."[34] At twenty-three, Sade was in fact a few years younger than the conventional age of independence. Despite the new legal status that his father had just conferred upon him, Sade was still quite immature. Far from being "free," he would begin to realize that he had been saddled with his father's debts. And he would discover that he had merely exchanged the oppressive authority of his father for what would prove to be the even more odious authority of his mother-in-law.

Some details of the early days of the marriage come from Sade's father, who took lodgings near his son and daughter-in-law on the rue Basse-du-Rempart. His opinion of his son remained unchanged: he "will never amount to anything. Whatever he does is quite indifferent to me now, but I put a good face on it. . . . All he has is wind in his head and an insatiable appetite for pleasure." The Comte added that his son and new daughter "expressed a desire to go to see the review of the Royal Household." Perhaps they were put up to it by Mme de Montreuil, whose primary goal was to advance in society. The Comte noted that Mme de Montreuil "visits me every day." In any case, the Comte accompanied the newlyweds on this outing and also "gave them a dinner at Marly, at the house of the head steward of the late Mademoiselle [the Comte's old friend the Duchesse du Maine]." The Comte was pleased by his reception there. He was less than pleased by his son's behavior: "No sooner was he there than he conceived the desire not to be there."[35] A month or so later, the Comte complained about his son's fecklessness, in this case his failure to take advantage of the Comte's social connections: "Alas! I arrived here [at Fontainebleau] in order to obtain permission for him [Sade] to ride in the carriages and go hunting with the King. He was supposed to arrive here, but then he did not come, even though I obtained everything. That is his business. I have made up my mind and I will no longer trouble myself over anything."[36]

Nine days after the marriage ceremony, Mme de Montreuil was confident, as she wrote to the Abbé de Sade, that her daughter's "sweetness of character, her attachment to her husband, and her desire to please him" would earn her his lasting love and respect.[37] Sade also wrote to the Abbé about his bride: "I do not know how to praise her enough. I am equally delighted with my father-in-law and my mother-in-law. They look after my interests with an incredible eagerness. I had but faintly glimpsed all the advantages of my new life. All that I can tell you about it is that I am enchanted with it."[38] The Comte conceded that his son "is getting along very well with his wife."[39] On June 9, he wrote to the Abbesse de Saint-Laurent that he had been going to all of the dinner parties that the Montreuil relatives gave in honor of the couple. He also said that on this day he had accompanied Sade and Renée to Versailles, where she was presented at Court by Mlle de Sens.[40] The Comte, however, had earlier noted that in Paris the couple went to the theater every day, costing "at least a louis a day."[41] Clearly, Sade was hoping to introduce Renée to his own passions.

At this time, it is natural to raise the question of how Sade's sexual predilections operated in the context of his marriage. It had been his custom to divide his sex life between good girls and whores. This would remain an important division throughout his life. He generally requested a whipping from the whores, and then asked to whip them. He often asked to sodomize them. Anal intercourse held a particular fascination for him, and he celebrated it in his libertine novels. It is not clear whether he had by this time engaged in passive and active homosexual intercourse, but he certainly did later with his valets. Unlike his father, who had been frequently reported and once arrested for soliciting male prostitutes in the Tuileries Gardens,[42] Sade does not appear to have had an interest in, or to have been willing to run the risk of, such encounters. The myth that has grown around the name "Sade" calls up the image of a beast worse than Gilles de Rais, the murderer of children, or of Jack the Ripper, the Victorian butcher of women. Sade's sex life was not what most people would call normal, but neither was it nearly as abnormal as most people think. Indeed, libertinism in eighteenth-century France was both an accepted and familiar mentality and a type of behavior tolerated (often celebrated) among a significant minority of the privileged class. Sade was, in a sense, living up to a model already well established. His sexual life would find a modern equivalent among a great many film and rock stars. Their public expect and vicariously enjoy their escapades. There is always an actual or an imagined privileged sexual class, and individuals who think they belong to such a class usually can get away with a great deal if they are careful and lucky. Sade was neither.

It has been suggested that Sade introduced his wife to sodomy early in their marriage.[43] Maurice Lever states that on their wedding night Sade could scarcely restrain himself from requiring of his wife the same acts of sodomy that he demanded of whores and that he later depicted in his novels: "There is no question," Lever asserts, "but that Mme de Sade offered herself up without resistance to her husband's requirements," and that anal intercourse was their customary practice.[44] Certainly it was in their repertoire, and he would later tease her about it in his letters to her from prison. But it is doubtful that she acceded to it on their wedding night. The marriage, moreover, required children, and the couple felt the pressure to provide them. Only four months after the wedding, Mme de Montreuil wrote to the Abbé about her happiness with Sade and Renée, but added, "There is but one large disturbance in their household: this is not to be yet able to assure you and me of the title of *grand* [i.e., great-uncle and grandmother]. I desire it, but I await it without impatience. Neither of them comes from infertile stock."[45] Years later, Sade wrote a very short tale (or a long joke), "L'Époux complaisant" ("The Obliging Husband"), about a nobleman, notorious for his devotion to sodomy, who marries a very young and naïve girl. Her mother, considering the groom's tastes, warns her daughter on the eve of the marriage: "I have but one piece of advice for you, my daughter, beware of the first proposition that your husband will make to you, and tell him forcefully: 'No, Monsieur, that is not the way a decent woman does it, *in any other way that you please, but that way, absolutely not. . . .*'" On their marriage night, the husband decides to show consideration for his wife and offers, at least for this first time, to fulfill his marital responsibilities in the approved manner. His bride, however, remembering well her mother's warning, demurs:

> "What do you take me for, Monsieur," she told him, "did you think that I would submit to such things? *In any other way that you please, but that way, absolutely not.*"
>
> . . .
>
> "Very well, Madame, your wish shall be indulged," the Prince said, while taking possession of his cherished sanctum, "I would indeed be sorry if it were said that I had ever sought to displease you."[46]

The joke delightfully turns both on the subversion of maternal authority and on a naïve girl's demand for an aberrant sexual life. It suggests that Sade himself was not as fortunate as the Prince. Sade must have liked this story, because he retold it almost exactly in another short tale, "Soit fait ainsi qu'il est requis" ("Do It the Right Way").[47]

By everyone's account, Renée was gentle and sweet rather than pretty. Her mother hoped that her good heart and willingness to please her husband would make up for her lack of beauty. Sade, however, would describe her as a prude. On their trip to Versailles on June 9, when Renée was presented at Court, the Comte described her for the Abbesse de Saint-Laurent: "The little daughter-in-law is very sweet. I observe nothing ungenerous about her, but my son gives a very bad opinion of her heart to two or three friends who are kept informed."[48] It is unknown who these friends were. Sade had no friends. Perhaps they were invented by the Comte. It is possible that early in his marriage Sade wrote to the Abbé about his disappointment in his wife. Two years later, according to the Abbé, he complained that, though he respected Renée, he found her "too cold and too devout."[49]

A few months after that, in September 1765, he again wrote to his uncle and described in even greater detail his feelings toward his wife and the circumstances of his marriage: "Yes, I would doubtless be much happier if I loved my wife, but am I the master of this particular passion? I have accomplished a miracle, my dear uncle, in vanquishing the repugnance that she inspired in me from the first moment I saw her. But I have never been the master of my feelings. Who knew better than you how I came to be married?" Even so, Sade attempted to hide his repugnance: "I very nearly fooled myself," he claimed, "and the obligation to be false, in numbing the true feelings of my heart, allowed me for a time to find my duty less burdensome." This deception was not easy for a man who liked to think of himself as an idealist in love. He continued his argument: "Weary of being constrained for so long a time and for two years of having said I love you without thinking it, I tried to think it in order to obtain some pleasure in saying it." Gradually, he said, he became somewhat inured to acting the hypocrite in love: "That is where I am now, a frightful situation, doubtless, but less cruel than before. Ah! believe me, my dear uncle, I am more to be pitied than to be blamed."[50] Here was the version of Sade that he liked to promote. He detested hypocrisy. He saw himself as an idealist, a man of feeling, of exquisite sensibility. He was a martyr to his marriage, a martyr to social conventions, on whose altar he had sacrificed the deepest passion of his life, the romantic quest for the one perfect love.

Sade's highly romantic view of love was at odds with conventional eighteenth-century notions of arranged marriages and may appear even more at odds with the now familiar libertine manifesto derived from his own practice with whores, expressed in such novels as *Les Cent Vingt Journées de Sodome*, *Juliette*, and *La Philosophie dans le boudoir*. However, he used the idea of determinism to explain both romantic love ("Am I the master of this particular passion?") and also sexual tastes and perversions. In *Les Cent Vingt Journées*, Sade explains that sexual deviations "depend on our constitution, on our organs, on the manner in which they are affected, and we are no more in control of changing our tastes in this regard than we are of changing the shape of our bodies."[51] There are numerous restatements of this principle of sexual determinism in Sade's letters. Writing to his wife from prison in Vincennes, he argued that he should not be punished for "weaknesses of temperament over which one has no control and which have never done harm to anyone."[52] In a similar way, he discussed a fetish for soiled linen. Of sexual deviations, he wrote to his wife, "However baroque they may be, I always hold them worthy of respect, both because one is not master of them and because, properly understood, the most peculiar and the most bizarre of them always hark back to a principle of refinement."[53] In Sade's deterministic and materialistic model of sexuality, each individual is provided with a certain quantum of daily sexual energy that is in turn routed through predetermined, constitutional paths, and there is nothing anyone can do to change his sexual nature.

Thus, on both the romantic and the materialistic sides, Sade soars or plummets toward a radical view of the extremes of human nature. There is never any middle ground, any in-between. Sade's search for absolutes, both high and low, is immature. Every adult compromises. Reality is an average of most people's compromises. Reality brackets a very large space. As big as it is, Sade sought its limits and went beyond. He wanted things pure, absolute. Oddly enough, then, Sade was idealistic about both love and lust.

In June 1763, a month after his marriage, Sade secretly rented several apartments and *petites maisons* in Paris and its suburbs.[54] A private pleasure palace in the country was not uncommon among the nobility, and Sade, having dutifully married and now having the credit derived from his rich marriage, thought that he too deserved a break. He had every reason to think, as he would later say, that his libertine lifestyle was conventional. Indeed, someone of his rank, with sufficient money and a modicum of discretion, could safely live on both sides of the street. But Sade had little money of his own and even less discretion. In October 1763, within five months of his marriage, the *petite maison* that he rented on the rue Mouffetard would figure in his first arrest and his first, brief imprisonment in the royal fortress of Vincennes.

Sade and his wife planned on spending the summer with the Montreuils at their château, Échauffour, in Normandy. But this otherwise happy period was clouded by the growing understanding of the Comte de Sade's financial chicanery with regard to the marriage contract. A mere week after the marriage was celebrated, Mme de Montreuil realized that something was wrong. On May 26, 1763, she wrote to the Abbé that she saw "clouds forming."[55] Sade was beginning to try to obtain the income of 10,000 livres a year, retroactive from 1760, from the post of lieutenant general that his father turned over to him as part of the marriage contract. This turned out to be a post in name only. Sade and his father had a "discussion" about it early in June; on June 9, the Comte complained to the Abbesse de Saint-Laurent: "I am very sorry for not getting my son to sign a receipt for everything I spent on him."[56]

On September 14, 1763, Mme de Montreuil wrote again to the Abbé from her country home in Normandy, Sade and Renée having arrived around the middle of August. Sade and his father had been constantly wrangling by letter. The Comte, Mme de Montreuil told the Abbé, had been complaining "loudly" about his son to members of the Montreuil family and to his own family, calling him "ungrateful and unnatural."[57] On September 21, the Comte also wrote to the Abbé, complaining that his son now refused to pay the Comte's considerable debts to Mme de Vigean (20,000 livres) and to Teissier. He concluded with unjustifiable bitterness: "So that is how I am repaid for everything I have done for him."[58] On October 20, when Sade had left Normandy for Paris, Mme de Montreuil wrote once again to the Abbé. This is a long and patient, rather than angry letter, detailing all of the maneuvers by which the Comte had sought to avoid acknowledging that he had broken his word. Mme de Montreuil brought to light a few new facts. For example, there was a previously unmentioned debt of 8,000 livres that the Comte owed to someone named Bourg and that his son was now also expected to settle.[59] Moreover, the tailor from whom the Comte had ordered the wedding clothes (cost: 1,600 livres) had not been paid, and the Comte, "with a peremptory tone," simply forwarded the bill to his son for payment. For the first time, Mme de Montreuil revealed that she had sent the Comte the money for the wedding clothes even before the wedding. When her husband had written to the Comte to remind him of these facts, the Comte "replied to M. de Montreuil that he was going to let his son be sued by this tailor and that the court would decide who would have to pay."[60] Mme de Montreuil contented herself with saying that it would be painful for her to see her son-in-law "sued for 1,600 livres that he does not owe." The impossibility of making sense out of the Comte's explanations and prevarications, combined with his effrontery and his dismissive tone, finally wore down the Montreuils. Mme de Montreuil told the Abbé that she could easily destroy the Comte's reasoning in the above letter, but "since to reply to it would require imitating his style, I have deemed it proper to do nothing about it. That is not my style."[61] The correspondence about money matters came to an end. All too soon, Mme de Montreuil would have other things to worry about. A week after this letter was written, her son-in-law was under arrest in Paris.

If Mme de Montreuil, as strong, as powerful, as stubborn as she was, could be defeated by the Comte de Sade, what hope was there for his son? After the initial arguments about money in June, Sade tended to avoid his father. The Comte thought that his son was afraid of him. That was the burden of an anecdote the Comte related to his sister the Abbesse de Saint-Laurent:

Upon arriving in Paris [from Fontainebleau], I intended to sleep, as was my custom, at M. de Montreuil's. My lackey was sent ahead to prepare my bed. The porter told him that he had orders not to allow me to sleep there. I gathered from this that M. le M[arquis—i.e., his son] was in Paris, because this order could not have come from the owners. Alas! I was not put out by it. I slept in the chambermaid's bed.

But he was afraid to meet up with me. The next day, I received a letter from his father-in-law, who informed me that he had left to trot after his little family.[62]

Was it petty, vindictive pride that inspired Sade to have the porter of the Montreuils' house rebuff his father at the door? Was Sade really afraid of his angry father? Did Sade watch the scene from above, the damask curtain slightly parted? To be sure, his father knew where the order came from, knew that his son was there. And the son knew that his father knew.

The next day, when Sade withdrew to Échauffour in Normandy, nothing had been settled, and nothing would be settled. As Mme de Montreuil wrote to the Abbé on September 14, 1763, "The facts that fully justify" Sade, "necessarily condemn" his father.[63] This dilemma produced an emotional and moral paralysis in Sade. According to Mme de Montreuil, who the Comte said was utterly smitten by his son's charm ("She's crazy about him"),[64] this withdrawal was interpreted as an appropriate "respectful silence," which, she said, he had maintained for the past "six weeks"—that is, from the beginning of August.[65] Respectful silence? Or emotional withdrawal, paralysis, and depression? Ever since the Comte's return to Paris, he had been going around to the Montreuil relatives telling them the most dreadful things about his son, and they reported what he said to Sade. Mme de Montreuil wrote to all of her relatives to correct the bad impression given by the Comte, but Sade, she told the Abbé, "was not able to bring himself to write to his father. His feelings were too hurt for that. What could one write in such a situation? I did not think to insist on it too much."[66]

Thus, it becomes clear that Mme de Montreuil was responsible for Sade's earlier attempts to assert his rights. She was able, for a time, to coax Sade into a confrontation with his father, but his heart was not in it. In fact, he had never really tried to win a battle with his father, favoring indirection rather than confrontation when dealing with him. His relationship with his father had never known overt conflict. Conflict with the Comte was, in Sade's mind, linguistic and symbolic, conducted by means of ironical language and ironical or symbolic acts. Mme de Montreuil, on the other hand, was, if anything, the embodiment of pragmatism. She had earnestly tried to win, and to get what rightfully belonged to her son-in-law and to her daughter. She was willing to take the Comte to court, where his chicanery and irrational arguments could easily be demolished. But Sade, whom she thought of as "lovable," "sensitive," and "gentle,"[67] was not up to such a conflict. Mme de Montreuil had wanted an alliance with a noble family, and that was what she had gotten, and what she still had. She surveyed the terrain for the battle, assessed the personnel on both sides, evaluated the stakes, what could be won (money) and lost (a connection to the Comte and his influence at Court), and she simply made a pragmatic decision to let things lie.

For Sade, however, there could be no such détente. If he could not fight with his father in the real world, he would nevertheless find ways to express his anger, ways, alas, that were perhaps only symbolic but still utterly self-destructive.

CHAPTER 3

Scandalous Debauch

*I*N THE eighteenth century, Parisians abandoned Paris in August, as they do to this day. The month that Sade spent with the Montreuils in Normandy was idyllic. In a climate of relaxation and family living, Mme de Montreuil was pleased to get to know her son-in-law better. For his part, Sade could employ the charm he knew elicited the sympathy and kindness of women. The relationship that developed between Sade and his mother-in-law was intimate and teasing. This is how she described him in her letter to the Abbé on October 20, 1763:

> Oh, the rascal! That is what I call him, my little son-in-law. Sometimes I also take the liberty of scolding him: we quarrel, we make up at once. It never gets really serious or goes on very long. Trust is not won in a day. . . . Flighty though he may be, marriage is giving him some mental ballast. If I am not much mistaken, you would notice this improvement if you saw him. As for your niece, whatever desire she has to please you and obey you, she will never scold him. She will love him as much as you would want. The reason is obvious: so far, he has been charming, he loves her deeply, could not treat her better.[1]

This is the first indication that Mme de Montreuil's mind was not entirely given over to calculating for advantage. She felt free to take liberties with Sade, tease him, scold him, even if her daughter would not. And she took pleasure in witnessing the salubrious effects that country living had upon him. In a letter to the Abbé, she writes:

> The tranquillity, inevitable in the country, does a lot of good for his health. He is putting on weight rather nicely. I do not know if it [country life] satisfies his mind as much as his appetites; they are strong; they both need nourishment. Happily, there are always two excellent solutions for that: reading and sleep. You certainly are aware of his taste for both.

{ 54 }

In the sa.1e letter, she makes a point of telling the Abbé that Sade and M. de Montreuil have gone off on an outing to a nearby abbey to visit and talk with its wise and virtuous custodian. There were other pleasures: "A bit of deer hunting in a lovely forest, some horses, especially a cabriolet, are diverting and make the time pass. *Each age has its toys,* and that is very true and very well said."2 Pretty scenery, outings with the formal and dull father-in-law, family dinners with the surprisingly sprightly mother-in-law, evenings of reading books, and nights with his devoted but plain and prudish wife—not exactly Sade's idea of a good time.

Sade, who had neglected to go hunting with the King, suddenly conceived the necessity of going to Paris and then of paying his court at Fontainebleau, where he hoped to solicit a post from the Duc de Choiseul. He also intended to go to the Parlement de Dijon to be invested in his post as lieutenant general. In reporting Sade's plan to the Abbé, Mme de Montreuil had only one anxiety: "On his arrival, he is supposed to go to see his father. I do not know how he will be received. I have a terrible dread about this meeting because of the boy's excitability and the father's harshness."3 Sade bade his wife and mother-in-law adieu on Saturday, October 15, 1763. Perhaps he was "supposed" to see his father only because Mme de Montreuil thought it would be a good thing to do: she may still have retained some hope that the Comte would pay up. But Sade did not go to Fontainebleau, nor would he get to Dijon. And there is no evidence that he saw his father. It is doubtful that he even intended to see him. In fact, he went almost directly to jail.

On his coach ride from Normandy, from one posthouse to the next, as towns and villages ticked by, Sade was thinking only of Paris and his *petite maison* on the rue Mouffetard. He stopped briefly at his apartment in his father-in-law's mansion on the fashionable rue Neuve-du-Luxembourg. On Tuesday, October 18, he sought out a procurer named Mme Du Rameau, who lived above a café on the rue Montmartre, and he hired an occasional prostitute, Jeanne Testard, to accompany him to his *petite maison* for the night. The events of that night prompted Testard the next morning to go straight to the police and to swear a complaint against her client. This document, though long, deserves to be read in full, because it provides the first and the clearest information about Sade's sexuality and his state of mind at this time:

On Wednesday, October 19, 1763, at 6 o'clock in the evening, in our office and before us, Hubert Mutel, lawyer to the Parlement, King's Counselor, Commissioner to the Châtelet de Paris, appeared Jeanne Testard, a girl 20 and a half years old, a fan maker, though also sometimes a party girl, residing on the rue Montmartre near the rue de

Cléry, parish of Saint-Eustache, accompanied by M. Jean-Baptiste Zullot, officer of M. Louis Marais, Inspector of Police, who, after swearing to tell the truth, testified that around three weeks ago she became acquainted with a woman named Du Rameau, a procurer then living in a furnished room on the rue Faubourg-Saint-Honoré and for the past two weeks on the rue Montmartre, at the Café de Montmartre; that yesterday at 8 o'clock in the evening, the above-mentioned Du Rameau had sent for the witness, who came to her room at once, and the above-mentioned Du Rameau proposed a plea-sure party that would earn her two louis d'or at 24 livres; which the witness having agreed to, she [Du Rameau] turned her over to an indi-vidual unknown to the witness, around 22 years old, around 5 feet 7 inches tall,[4] with light-brown hair done up in a net, with a pale com-plexion somewhat marked by smallpox, dressed in a blue overcoat with a red collar and red trim and silver buttons, which individual conducted the witness into a hired coach that was waiting at the door and in which was the servant of the above-mentioned individual, which servant she later learned is called La Grange, and she was driven to the end of Faubourg Saint-Marceau, near the rue Mouffetard, to a *petite maison* with a carriage door painted yellow with iron spikes over it; that, having arrived, he showed her up to a room on the first floor, and after having sent his servant, who had followed him, down to the ground floor, he locked and bolted the door of the above-mentioned room; and, being alone with the witness, the first thing he did was ask her if she was religious, and if she believed in God, in Jesus Christ, and in the Virgin; to which she replied that she did believe in them, and that she observed as best she could the Christian Religion in which she was raised. To which the individual replied with horrible insults and blasphemies, saying that there was no God, that he had proved it, that he had masturbated directly into a chalice that he made use of in that way for two hours in a chapel, saying that J[esus] C[hrist] was a F[uck-ing] B[astard] and the Virgin was a B[itch]. He added that he once had sexual union with a girl with whom he had taken communion, that he had made off with the two communion wafers, had shoved them into that girl's sexual parts, and had sexual congress with her, all the while saying: *If you are God, avenge yourself;* that he then proposed to the witness to go into a room adjoining the said room, warning her that she was going to see something quite unusual; that, having informed him that she was pregnant and that she was afraid to see any-thing capable of frightening her, he replied that these things would not frighten her, and at the same time, he made her go into the adjoining room, and shut himself in there with her; that, upon entering, she was shocked to see four switches and five types of whips, of which three were of cord, one of brass wire, and one of iron wire, which were hanging on the wall, and three ivory statues of Christ on the cross, two engravings of Christ, one engraving of Calvary and another of the Virgin, all decorating the walls, along with a great number of drawings and engravings picturing naked figures in poses of the greatest imaginable indecency; that, having made her examine these various objects, he told her that she had to flog him with the iron-wire whip after having it heated red-hot in the fire, and that afterward he would lash her with whichever of the other whips she preferred; that she by no means consented to these proposals, although he had very urgently pressed her to do so; that, following this, he took down two of the ivory statues of Christ, one of which he trampled underfoot, and upon the other masturbated himself; and, remarking the evident shock and horror shown by the witness, he told her that she had to trample on the crucifix, pointing out to her two pistols on a table and putting his hand upon his sword, ready to draw it from its scabbard, and threatening to run her through; the witness, out of fear for her life, suffered the misfortune of being forced to trample on the crucifix, while at the same time he forced her to utter these wicked words, *B[astard], I don't give a f[uck] about you;* that he had even wanted to make the witness take an enema and discharge on the Christ, which did not occur because of her refusal to do it; that, during the night the witness spent with him without food or sleep, he made her look at and he read to her several poems full of blasphemies and totally contrary to religion, which he told her had been given to him by one of his friends, as much a libertine as himself, and who thought and behaved in the same fashion; that the above-mentioned individual offered to know the witness in a manner contrary to nature, and he pushed the sacrilege to the extreme of forcing the witness to promise him that she would come to him next Sunday at seven o'clock in the morning at the above-mentioned *petite maison* in order to go together to the parish church of Saint-Médard to take communion there and then to make off with the two communion wafers, of which he proposed to burn one and to employ the other in order to perform the same sacrileges and profanations that he said were committed with the girl he mentioned earlier; that at nine o'clock this morning she left the above-mentioned house when the above-mentioned Du Rameau had come to get her; that, before leaving and before the arrival of the above-mentioned Du Rameau, he obliged the witness to give her oath never to reveal any of the things that occurred between them and that he had confided in her, and he made her sign her name to a blank sheet of paper; that, upon leaving the above-mentioned house, she went to the office of the Lieutenant General of Police with the intention of giving him an account of all these facts; that, finding him not in, she sought out M. Marais, in whose absence she spoke with M. Zullot, his assistant, who, after having received orders from the Lieutenant General of Police, brought her before us for the purpose, as she has done, of making the present Statement which she asked us to draw up for her in the interest of justice and to be signed with the above-mentioned M. Zullot in our report.[5]

This deposition was the first of several during the next decade that would be sworn out by prostitutes against Sade. The second case involved a beggar woman or prostitute, Rose Keller, who in April 1768 complained that Sade had tied her down, whipped her, and stabbed her buttocks. The final case occurred at the end of June 1772, when several Marseilles prostitutes hired by Sade complained that he had made them ill by feeding them bonbons laced with the aphrodisiac Spanish fly. The complaint also alleged that he had whipped some of them, as well as obliged them to whip him, and that he engaged in sodomy with two of them and also with his servant Latour.

These accounts of Sade's sexual practices with whores deserve close examination. But first let us make clear that his frequent forays into the sexual demimonde must be understood in terms of the division he felt between idealistic, romantic love and materialistic, sexual lust. Each experience had its own protocols and scenarios, and Sade was certainly capable of both. Something of Sade's superheated passion has already been seen in his love for Laure de Lauris and in his impassioned ultimatum to his father about the girl from Hesdin he wanted to marry. Such romantic ardor can be irresistible, as it was to famous actresses like Colet and Beauvoisin, whose favors he succeeded in obtaining without the monthly support payments and lavish gifts—beyond his means, anyway—which were customarily required. When Sade offered his heart, he was utterly focused on the object of his love, painfully inflamed with lovesickness.

But Sade's pursuit of the other sort of experience was equally exaggerated. It finds a literary correlative in his novel *Les Cent Vingt Journées de Sodome*, a veritable *catalogue raisonné* of six hundred perversions arranged in ascending order of complexity and brutality—literally a crescendo. Each perversion stores a particular quantum of sexual energy, and the novel organizes them as scrupulously as a periodic table arranges the elements. This is the Hobbesian, materialistic version of human love and human nature. In this polarization of love and lust there was, as in all of Sade's thinking, no in-between, no middle ground.

On the night of October 18, just arrived from Normandy and staying at his in-laws' mansion on the rue Neuve-du-Luxembourg, Sade sent out his servant (the so-called La Grange) to hire a coach, and together they drove to a decidedly less fashionable part of town, where Sade sought out a procurer, Du Rameau, above the Café de Monmartre. He knew what he was doing. Perhaps he had used her services before. A month later, on November 16, the Comte reported the bare details of the incident to his brother the Abbé: ". . . rented *petite maison,* furnished on credit, where he went to perform a scandalous debauch coldly and calmly, utterly alone, dreadful blasphemy, about which the girls felt obliged to swear out their deposition."[6] Even if the Comte was mistaken in thinking there was more than one girl, it is interesting that he is offended as much by his son's choice of venue as by the behavior itself. The Comte seems to sniff at the vulgarity of a rented pleasure palace, furnished on credit. It was one thing to be a social libertine, able to afford a real *petite maison* in the country and to give parties for one's friends with the best girls and actresses hired for the occasion. Such events could also be arranged at a few of the more reputable Paris bordellos, such as Brissault's, where a police informer noted, for example, that on January 1, 1762, "Baron de Wangen had given a supper" for his friends "with the girls Dubois and Villette. This supper passed very gallantly."[7] Or one could do as Casanova had done in 1750, when he went with a friend to the Hôtel du Roule, one of the most famous establishments in Paris:

> The woman who kept it had furnished the place with great elegance, and she always had twelve or fourteen well-chosen nymphs, with all the conveniences that could be desired. Good cooking, good beds, cleanliness, solitary and beautiful groves. Her cook was an artist, and her wine-cellar excellent. Her name was Madame Paris; probably an assumed name, but it was good enough for the purpose. Protected by the police, she was far enough from Paris to be certain that those who visited her liberally appointed establishment were above the middle class. Everything was strictly regulated in her house and every pleasure was taxed at a reasonable tariff. The prices were six francs for a breakfast with a nymph, twelve for dinner, and twice that sum to spend a whole night.[8]

In Sade's time, the most notable establishment of this respectable sort was that of Marguerite Stock, alias "La Gourdan."⁹ But Sade was without friends, not sociable, and after a rather different kind of experience.

For one thing, what Sade seemed to want of Jeanne Testard, even more than sex, was a captive audience. Indeed, the entire episode can be seen mostly as a rhetorical rather than a sexual event, as a series of persuasive arguments, each with its own style and persona. "The first thing he did was ask her if she was religious, and if she believed in God, in Jesus Christ, and in the Virgin." A kind of catechism! Do you believe in God, my child? You do? Following this, out pours a flood of blasphemies. Jeanne Testard may have believed in God "as best she could," and thus was prepared to let Sade use her body, but not her soul for 2 louis d'or. First there were curses, and then the argument that God did not exist. Next, Sade told Testard that he once took a whore to church for communion. This sounds like the beginning of a joke, and in a sense it was.

Thus far, Sade had not even touched Jeanne Testard. Although he later masturbated on a statue of Christ, and although he proposed to sodomize her (which she refused, as she had also refused the offer to whip him or to be whipped), there was no sexual union. Sade was all talk. There were obscene poems to be read, stories like the two above to be told, sacrilegious and atheistic taunts to be hurled. This was not so much a night of sex as a kind of libertine salon for two, rooted in literature, argument, philosophy, and satire. Here Sade displayed his mastery of several forms of discourse before a hapless, puzzled, and shocked Jeanne Testard. What must she have thought! Strange as this literary evening was, we may see it in some ways as a model for the novels Sade would write in prison and afterward. These consistently follow a plan of alternating sex scenes with passages philosophizing upon them. For instance, in *Justine, ou les malheurs de la vertu* (which is Sade's parody of one of his favorite author's works, *Pamela, or Virtue Rewarded*, by Samuel Richardson), the naïve, religious, and virtuous heroine preserves her faith despite suffering a series of rapes and perversions, each of which is followed by a philosophical discourse in which her attacker attempts to convince her that morality and religion are mere prejudices, and that what has just happened to her is in accord with Nature and is, in fact, for the best. Sade's literary recitations before Jeanne Testard suggest that there is already a text running in his mind, an anthology comprising bits of stories, obscene verses, satirical gibes against God and religion, arguments in favor of masturbation, of sodomy, of flagellation. In twelve frenzied hours with Testard, without sleep or food, Sade managed to get through samples of each genre. Little wonder Testard was so annoyed when she was finally able to leave, at nine the following morning.

The Testard deposition is also of interest because of what it suggests about Sade's obsession—absolutely evident and fantastically elaborated in his novels—for creating a privileged space, a sanctum for perverse sexuality, like the château of Silling in *Les Cent Vingt Journées de Sodome*, a forbidding and utterly isolated Gothic castle perched on an inaccessible promontory. As in the château, the rooms in Sade's house on the rue Mouffetard each had a particular ambience and purpose. The two where he entertained Jeanne Testard had previously been set aside and decorated to suit his specific taste in sacrilege and flagellation. The first had a door ominously fitted with both a lock and a deadbolt. Here, Sade played the role of the kindly priest to Testard's novice: Tell me, my child, do you believe in God? Then came the sacrilegious libertine, spouting curses. For Testard, being locked and bolted in with a man like that was frightening enough. When it came time to move into the next room, Sade warned her mysteriously about its contents, inciting her anxiety. This was a fearful space, farther away from the bolted door, with safety and civilization on its other side.

The movement, the progress into the depth, has a powerful and rich meaning in the fictional world of Silling. For the libertines, the retreat from civilization frees the mind: the libertine says, "I am alone now, here I am at the world's end."[10] This isolated utopia is ruled by Hobbesian materialism, by the goddess Nature, a force more powerful and more primitive than religion, civilization, the social contract. Here, Sade can imagine the bottom line on the tally sheet of human nature, can narrate, as he says, "the history of the human heart."[11] However, in real life—in a rented furnished house on an unfashionable street, the two rooms with their odd paraphernalia of whips, ivory Christs, and an enema—the whole scene appears tawdry and silly, like the theme rooms in short-stay motels. For prostitutes familiar with a whole range of odd tastes and fetishes and perversions, often the difficult part was not to laugh.

Sade's collection of whips decorating the walls of the inner room should not have upset a prostitute. Flagellation was so frequently requested that bordellos had their own collections of whips. In eighteenth-century France, flagellation was thought to be a cure for impotence. Inspector Louis Marais, who, as head of the vice squad, was responsible for the surveillance of bordellos, said, "Many men are devoted to this extreme, and there is not a bawdy house today that does not have switches ready to perform the ceremony on impotent old lechers."[12] During his tenure, Marais had compiled an enormous fund of information about the operation of bawdy houses, their clients, and their tastes. For example, of the Chevalier de Judde, commander of the Order of Malta, Marais noted that he preferred to bring "his own switches."[13] The philosopher Helvétius, who had become devoted to flagellation in Paris whorehouses, required the same services at home, after he married, in order to make love to his wife.[14] Rousseau, the tenderhearted, idealistic hero of the enlightenment, in his *Confessions* reveals that his "strange taste" for flagellation, a taste that he never had the courage to reveal or to satisfy directly,[15] had its source in a whipping he received during childhood: "Who could have supposed that this childish punishment, received at the age of eight at the hands of a woman of thirty, would determine my tastes and desires, my passions, my very self for the rest of my life?"[16] Sade, the opposite of Rousseau in just about everything, was not so squeamish. Nor would have been the vast majority of the prostitutes frequented by Sade. Thus, when he invited Jeanne Testard to witness "something quite unusual" in the next room, her display of fright might have been just part of the act whores put on to satisfy their clients' fantasies.

Although flagellation was not unusual, sodomy was, and that is what Sade next requested of Testard, to know her "in a manner contrary to nature." It is possible that Testard complied with Sade's desire, but told the police she had refused. Sodomy was, after all, a capital offense. But it is also possible that she really did refuse, just as she had refused to whip him with the red-hot whip, to be whipped herself, or to take an enema. Perhaps her procuress, Du Rameau, had not prepared her for what would be expected of her. Except for threatening her if she refused to trample on the crucifix, Sade was remarkably tolerant of her rejections. Almost the only satisfactions he must have enjoyed were psychological, the pleasure of seeming to shock and frighten an apparently naïve young woman with his verbal audacity. Given the kind of brutalities that whores frequently met with, it is slightly surprising that Testard and her procuress felt it necessary to report Sade to the police.

In many ways, Sade appeared even more naïve than Testard. He was so intent on proving that God did not exist ("he had proved it," he boasted) that he was almost entirely oblivious to the very bad impression he was making on Testard. On this occasion, as on so many others, Sade was too self-absorbed to be aware of the impact of his behavior on those around him. Moreover, he appears to have been a very poor judge of character. He seemed to have thought that Testard would indeed return the following Sunday to fulfill her "promise" to go to church with him in order to get the two communion wafers, etc. He seemed to have faith in the "oath" he made her swear "never to reveal any of the things that occurred between them and that he had confided in her." If there is no God, what did he make her swear on? His book of dirty poetry?

When the procuress Du Rameau came to collect Jeanne Testard at nine o'clock on the morning of October 19, the two of them went directly to the office of Lieutenant General of Police Antoine de Sartine. Sartine held a post roughly comparable to attorney general of the United States. During his long reign, from 1759 to 1774, Sartine's major accomplishment was to perfect the art of police surveillance, turning, for example, the vice squad headed by Inspector Marais into a powerful tool for spying and information gathering. Much of Sade's mental life was a running argument (either acted out or writ-ten down) against God or Authority. *"If you are God, avenge yourself,"* he had shouted. When God did not immediately strike him down with a lightning bolt, Sade achieved an easy, rhetorical victory. But the world was changing. What Sade could not immediately perceive was that his real opponent was not the Biblical God of vengeance, but a quite modern and efficient combina-tion of the secret police and arbitrary imprisonment. It was not God who would punish Sade, but a precursor of the Gulag.

It is still unclear exactly why Jeanne Testard turned Sade in. Even if she were truly scandalized, going to the police would require her to admit that she was a prostitute, and prostitution was against the law. And why did Du Rameau not only tolerate this revelation, but accompany her and allow her-self to be implicated? There is something strange in all this. Procurers bought police protection with the information they provided Inspector Marais. His reports make the nature of this collusion perfectly clear. If Jeanne Testard was new to the trade, Du Rameau was not. One of them, in any case, knew exactly where to go. In Marais's absence, Jeanne Testard finally told her story to his officer, M. Zullot, "who, after having received orders from the Lieu-tenant General of Police," brought her before Commissioner Hubert Mutel to make her deposition at six o'clock in the evening. By the time it was over, she must have been one tired young woman. She had not slept the night before, and now had spent the entire day walking her way through the police bureaucracy. She and Du Rameau must have felt that the trouble was worth their time, that their client was worth reporting. Note that M. Zullot had not presumed, in the absence of his superior, Marais, to authorize the taking of a deposition. It is also suggestive that Testard, Du Rameau, and M. Zullot—that is, everyone involved—immediately understood that this was a matter of great importance, requiring the direct and personal intervention of the high-est judicial and police authority in the land, whose power was exceeded only by that of the King—namely, Lieutenant General of Police Sartine.

Even though Sade was not named in the deposition, and even though Tes-tard perhaps got the name of Sade's servant "La Grange" incorrectly, the police were able to identify Sade and arrest him on October 29, ten days after Testard's deposition. The description of the house on the rue Mouffe-tard, with its yellow carriage door and iron spikes, would have helped the police find the place and the man who rented it. Testard's description of the man and her detailed account of his tastes would also have helped Inspector Marais poll his informants in the sex trade. Marais's superior, Sartine, normally reported to the minister of the King's household, M. de Saint-Florentin. The latter informed the King at Fontainebleau and recommended action, which resulted in the following arrest order to M. Guyonnet, commander of the royal prison of Vincennes, signed by both the King and M. de Saint-Florentin: "Monsieur Guyonnet, I write this letter to authorize you to receive into custody in the donjon of my château of Vincennes the Marquis de Sade and to hold him there until further orders from me."[17]

East of Paris, on the northern edge of the Bois de Vincennes, stands the imposing château of Vincennes, looking much as it did in Sade's day, a great stone pile with four massive towers behind moated stone walls. It is a charmed prospect—viewed, that is, from the outside, sitting at a café, perhaps, under the trees of the Avenue de Paris, beside the gourmet take-out shops and fancy boutiques of the town of Vincennes. The donjon rises above the other buildings of the walled compound that features two classically elegant pavilions, once residences for the King and Queen, as well as the beautiful Sainte-Chapelle completed in the sixteenth century. From medieval times, the *bois* had been a royal hunting ground, and over the centuries it had been built up, first with a royal hunting lodge and then with the dominating donjon, completed in 1370. In the *Très Riches Heures du duc de Berry*, a winter hunting scene is depicted: in the foreground, dogs have brought down a wild boar, their jaws deep into its flesh, blood on the ground. Above the bleak December trees, in the distance and against a cold blue wintry sky, rise the towers of Vincennes, a white confection as delicate as spun sugar.

If the donjon had once been the principal residence of one of the most elegant courts of Europe, by the time Sade saw it, on the night of his arrest, it had long since been supplanted by Versailles and Fontainebleau, and was now the site of a military college and a pottery factory. Even with its walls crumbling, it was an imposing sight, and certainly chilling for anyone to be locked inside. Sade's detention in Vincennes was clearly intended to frighten him into good behavior. A new prisoner would cross a drawbridge lowered over a deep moat, pass into the compound of the donjon, surrounded by sheer, high walls. Above him soared masses of stone: the four towers of the donjon. There are heavy oak doors reinforced with iron and double-locked, and more locked doors up the spiral stone staircase, seemingly carved out of solid rock. The cells have heavy doors. More noise. The ceilings are high and vaulted, but the windows are slots intended for defense. It is clear that this fortress, designed to keep invaders out, would be equally efficient at keeping prisoners in. Sade would have recalled the military features of the fortified château of Saumane, where he had played as a boy. But this was no game. On the day of his arrest and imprisonment, October 29, Sade immediately wrote to Lieutenant General of Police Sartine, pleading that the scandal be limited, because otherwise his relations would cut off his income and he would never be able to return to the cavalry.[18] He beseeched Sartine to forward a letter to his mother-in-law: "This is a favor that I presume to beg of you on my knees, with tears in my eyes. Do me the kindness of reconciling me with a person who is so dear to me and whom I offended so grievously."[19] A few days later, on November 2, 1763, Sade again wrote to Sartine, asking him please to forward his letter to Mme de Montreuil, or at least "to inform my wife of my unhappy fate. Nothing could equal the anxiety that she must be suffering, not hearing anything about me."[20] Sade had left Échauffour on October 15 in order, among other things, to visit the Court of Fontainebleau to further his career. Ironically, he did get to go to Fontainebleau, but as the prisoner of Inspector Marais, and with the purpose of hearing the verdict of the King, through the minister of the King's household, M. de Saint-Florentin.

In trying to send his own letter to Mme de Montreuil, Sade had hoped to put his own light on the calamity. But if Sartine were to write to her, Sade begged him "not to inform my family of the real reason for my detention, I would be utterly ruined in their eyes." Sade appeared willing to have Sartine focus on the book found at his *petite maison,* the one from which he read obscene poems to Testard. It may have been a banned book, or else a manuscript he had collected or written himself. Sade offered Sartine the following in extenuation:

I dare to offer you, Monsieur, a further observation: the date of the regrettable book was only from the month of June, I was married on May 17, and I can assure you that I set foot in the above-mentioned house only in the month of June. After that, I spent three months in the country; a week after I returned, I was arrested. However brief had been the period of my transgressions, I am nonetheless guilty of them; they had occurred long enough to offend the Supreme Being whose just anger I now feel; I almost repent having made these remarks to you: should I be concerned with exonerating myself when I ought to be occupied only with repentance?

Sade, who taunted God so brazenly during his night of debauchery with Testard, now begged Sartine to let him see a priest:

> As utterly miserable as I find myself here, Monsieur, I do not at all complain about my lot; I deserved God's punishment, and I am getting it; to cry over my errors, to abhor my mistakes is my only occupation. Alas! God could have annihilated me without giving me the time to become conscious of them and to acknowledge them. . . . Give me the means of doing it, I beg of you, Monsieur, by allowing me to see a priest. Through his good counsel and my sincere repentance, I hope soon to be able to approach the divine sacraments whose total neglect had become the real cause of my ruin.[21]

In these theatrically abject, contrite letters, Sade involves Sartine in an imagined scene similar to his encounter with Testard. Now it was Sade's turn to be frightened and to grovel—this time before Sartine.

It was not intended that Sade remain long at Vincennes, where he was imprisoned at the King's expense. M. de Saint-Florentin informed Sartine that it was the King's expectation that Sade's family would soon have him transferred to another establishment at their expense.[22] This would have been a fort, Sade's father wrote to the Abbé on November 16:

> I ran to Fontainebleau. I begged for mercy. He was sent back to Normandy to his father-in-law's château, by which means nothing leaked out. They said that he was quite simply returned there. It cost me ten louis for my trip to Fontainebleau and other expenses with which I would have lived for two months. Every three months it is necessary I have some horrifying shocks. Thursday and Friday I kept to my bed with fever. Alas, why has my illness returned? My sufferings are the punishment for my crimes. I kiss the hand that strikes me, and I submit.[23]

Mme de Montreuil would take credit for her son-in-law's eventual release. As she explained to the Abbé, Sade was indebted to his wife and to her family for "the hushing up of a matter that could have ruined him forever and caused him to spend years in a fort."[24] Sade was probably indebted both to his father and to his in-laws. On November 13, the King ordered his release after two weeks of imprisonment in Vincennes, on the condition that he reside with the Montreuils at Échauffour under the surveillance of Inspector Marais. Freedom meant a humiliating journey back to Normandy, without any of the prizes he had proposed to win in Paris and Fontainebleau. Now his name was tainted with scandal, his future virtually ruined. With a dossier on file in Paris and Marais dogging his every step, Sade ought to have realized that any subsequent indiscretions would not go unnoticed.

Back at Échauffour, Sade somehow managed to make his peace with his mother-in-law. Renée accepted the return of her wayward husband with stoicism, as Mme de Montreuil explained to the Abbé at the beginning of January 1764: "You can imagine what must have been her suffering. She has behaved like a virtuous wife." Yes, injured, but loyal. Mme de Montreuil professed now to be "pleased" with Sade's conduct, but, of course, "only future experience can reassure me."[25] Later, on July 17, 1764, after further infuriatingly indiscreet affairs by Sade, Mme de Montreuil would write to the Abbé that she was no longer so easily taken in by Sade's apologies, when, "in an injured tone, he will complain about his fate, about the violence of his passions that sweep him along, about his remorse for having given pain to those who love him."[26] There is an innocence about Sade's confessions, an almost improbable candor and openness of feeling. It is virtually impossible to confess one's adulteries with good result to one's mother-in-law, yet that is exactly what Sade did. She knew all about his affairs, discussed them with him. The question that always tantalizes one in the presence of a charmer is asked by Mme de Montreuil: "Is he sincere, or dissembling?"[27] Nevertheless, there is an obvious intimacy in Sade's relationship with his mother-in-law; it encompasses a whole range of confession, contrition, and promises. It must have been flattering to be the focus of such boyish romantic openness and passion. Such charm.

The winter of 1763–64, following Sade's release from Vincennes, was a penitential season for him at Échauffour. He was under a kind of house arrest, with Inspector Marais responsible for watching him and making sure he did not leave. Inside the château there were letters to write—one to the Abbé, his uncle, whose response happily indicated that he was willing to forget Sade's faults. At the beginning of January 1764, he wrote the Abbé: "I flatter myself that you are indeed willing to accept the certainty that I will never again put myself in a position to commit similar ones."[28] Sade thanked his uncle,[29] as did Mme de Montreuil in a letter this same month,[30] for the Abbé's New Year's gift, a barrel of olive oil from Provence. Both families, the Montreuils and the Sades, were happy to celebrate the news of the January publication of the first of three volumes of the Abbé's *Mémoires pour la vie de François Pétrarque*. Sade's father had been sent copies to present at Versailles. Mme de Montreuil wrote the author that she eagerly looked forward to "many pleasant evenings" reading it when she got her copy.[31] Yes, this was the tranquil life that only a few months earlier, before the Testard affair, Mme de Montreuil had imagined would be so conducive to cementing the newlyweds' relationship and establishing Sade's physical and mental health.

One very promising thing did come of those eight weeks Sade had spent at Échauffour before the Testard affair and may account for his mother-in-law's readiness to forgive. Mme de Montreuil's desire to assume the title of grandmother was well on its way to satisfaction. Sometime in October, just before Sade had rushed off to Paris, Renée had become pregnant. Sade, whose own relation to the idea of fatherhood was problematic, was about to become a father himself. There was one difficulty, a residue of the Testard business, that threatened to have implications for Renée's pregnancy. The King had confined Sade to Échauffour, but Mme de Montreuil had no intention of letting her daughter, whom she called "delicate," give birth so "far from any assistance."[32] On April 3, 1764, M. de Saint-Florentin informed M. de Montreuil that Sade could spend three months in Paris, "where you deem that his presence is necessary."[33] By April 17, Sade and the Montreuils were guests at the château d'Évry, Renée's uncle's house outside Paris. There, Sade realized a special pleasure in inaugurating a private theater, directing and performing in several plays, using family members and friends of the Montreuils and the d'Évrys for his cast. He also added some occasional verse of his own composition to the plays he put on. For example, to Regnard's *Le Retour imprévu,* Sade added the following verses concerning the reconciliation of a father and son:

> Let us pardon everything for this child,
> Since love is his excuse;
> But let him be in future prudent
> And he our pardon not abuse.[34]

Sade enjoyed projecting the image of renewal and harmony. At the conclusion to *L'Avocat Patelin* by Brueys and Palaprat, Sade wrote the verses below to be sung by the character he played, Valère, to Henriette, played by Renée. Following the Testard scandal, Renée was touched to hear her husband say,

> So never let us lose our hope.
> Once, our happiness seemed remote;
> Now my heart is filled with joy,
> A promise of my constancy.
> No mystery to be understood:
> It's but one step from bad to good.

Renée replied in verses concluding with the following couplet:

> I now have nothing more to dread:
> So let us fly from bad to good.[35]

Charming. But for Sade, the reverse course remained a tempting option: it was but one step from good to bad. His good luck and good behavior would hold out for only a few more months.

CHAPTER 4

In the Flames of Passion

OMETIME IN July 1764, Renée gave birth to a child that would live only a few hours. Sade described his loss to the Abbé: "Heaven was not pleased to allow me long to enjoy the happiness of being a father, my dear uncle."[1] In the middle of the very same month, Sade began his impassioned pursuit of Mlle Colet, an actress of the Comédie-Italienne. For the next few years, actresses would be his constant preoccupation.

During the spring of 1764, the King had granted Sade leave from exile at Échauffour to visit Dijon for his installation as lieutenant general of the provinces of Bresse, Bugey, Valromey, and Gex. It was for this very purpose that Sade had intended to go to Dijon the previous October, when he found himself sidetracked by the Testard affair. At the installation on June 26, Sade addressed the Parlement de Bourgogne: "It gives me great satisfaction, Messieurs, to appear before you today, the happiest day of my life. . . . To be worthy of you, this is my only ambition; that one day you will judge me as such, this is my highest wish."[2] Sade's message to the body before which he would represent the King's interests was deferential, modest, emotional. He was twenty-four years old. And as always, he stood in some awe of figures of authority, even as he himself was becoming one. His only declared wish was to be found worthy.

On September 11, the King rescinded his order exiling Sade to Échauffour. Once more, he was living with his wife and the Montreuils in Paris on the rue Neuve-du-Luxembourg. He attended balls, saw all the plays, haunted the backstage, sought introductions to actresses, whom he pursued in person and with passionate letters. He also became a frequent patron of some of the better bordellos and procurers. A good deal of the information about Sade's activities during these years comes from the extant surveillance reports that Inspector Marais filed daily with Sartine, the lieutenant general of police. Marais's reports read like a combination of Krafft-Ebing's *Psychopathia Sexualis* and a high-society gossip column. It was generally understood that the summaries of the reports Sartine prepared for the King were not intended merely for his royal edification. Sade himself was aware that Sartine fashioned them as "*lascivious accounts* that could add some titillation to the private suppers at the Parc-aux-Cerfs."3 Sade had already been caught in the vice police's complex web following the Testard deposition in 1763. After that, Marais, the chief of the vice squad, had been assigned to conduct him into exile at Échauffour and to keep him under surveillance. But even with this experience fresh in his mind, Sade was far from cautious as, over the next few years, he resumed a feverish pursuit of actresses and patronized well-known bawdy houses and procurers—the very sort of people who were known to be Marais's primary informants.

This notable recklessness goes to the heart of Sade's self-image and personality. Partly it was a matter of his sense of invulnerability that seems to have issued from his confidence in the protection conferred by his noble rank. In his class, libertinage was fairly commonplace, perhaps even expected. He deemed whores to be so far beneath him that he could not imagine that their complaints could have any serious consequences for him. Marais may have been the chief of the vice squad, but to Sade he must have appeared an insignificant functionary. When the King allowed him to return to Paris, Sade must have thought—innocently, almost naïvely—that the King had properly set Sartine and Marais straight. There was also a timely intellectual aspect to Sade's elitism. Although his sacrilegious and perverse sexuality had caused a bit of a fuss, he regarded himself as an Enlightenment philosopher challenging the narrow conventionality of religious and sexual taboos. Adapting the materialistic philosophy of Thomas Hobbes and Julien Offroy de La Mettrie, he would argue that, since his sexual tastes were inherent in the constitution given him by nature, fulfilling them could not be an unnatural act. Thus he rationalized his libertinage in terms he believed anyone could understand and accept. But if misguided elitism contributed to Sade's difficulties at this time, one must look as well at a more complex aspect of his personality: his impulse toward self-victimization, the pronounced masochism of his relations with Testard, his desire to be whipped and humiliated, the ease with which he submitted to his father and other authorities, the perverse pleasure he took in apologizing and in expressing remorse. These are all indications of a person courting degradation and disaster, if unconsciously. And we shall have occasion to witness the effects of this impulse throughout his life.

On July 15, 1764, Sade wangled an introduction to the actress Mlle Colet following a play at the Comédie-Italienne. He also managed to accompany her home from the theater. The next day, he sent her the following letter, suggesting that he had long suffered a silent passion for her:

It is difficult to see you and not love you, and still more difficult to love you without telling you. Even so, I kept quiet for a long time, but I can be silent no longer. I am madly in love with you, and I can conceive of no higher happiness for me in the whole world than to spend my life with you and to share my fortune with you.

Deign to give me a word of response, I beg you. If I am fortunate enough for you neither to disdain nor to reject the hopes of the most sincere of men, grant me a meeting where we can come to an agreement; but I warn you that I intend this for life, and there is no point that I would not agree to.

Please burn my letter, or at least show it to no one. If you must disappoint me, do not exult over my misfortune and do not make a public display of it.

Although I was introduced to you, you may not recall my name. I was he upon whom you bestowed the pleasure of conducting you home from the theater on Monday.

My footman will bring me the answer that I beg you to give.

My happiness is in your hands; I cannot live without you.[4]

Mlle Colet was nineteen. Ever since her debut at the Comédie-Italienne at the age of fifteen, she had been the kept mistress of several wealthy gentlemen and noblemen, receiving from them gifts of expensive jewelry or else a monthly stipend. As one of the more enterprising actress-courtesans in Paris, she had inevitably come under the surveillance of Inspector Marais.

Mlle Colet's response to Sade's valet, who carried his letter and waited at her door for her reply, was decidedly unfavorable. She must have chosen to take offense at Sade's offer to share his fortune with her, because Sade immediately wrote her another letter, manically apologizing for the presumed insult:

Ye gods! if only I could fall instantly at your feet, Mademoiselle, to atone for the insult of which you accuse me! Me, capable of insulting you! Ah, I would rather die a thousand deaths! . . . The reputation for virtue and courtesy that you enjoy is, more than anything, I assure you, what determined me to offer you my heart, knowing you only from this excellent reputation that the public accords you and that you so well deserve. . . . Did you really believe that I offered my fortune to buy your kindness? Delicate and sensitive as you are, how you would have had reason to hate me if I had sought to obtain your favor in that way![5]

As in many of Sade's letters, there is a mischievous mixture of histrionic passion in the style of courtly love (his tears, his sighs, death would be preferable to offending her) and deflating irony (her reputation for virtue! her delicacy and sensitivity!). In all likelihood, Colet would have missed the allusions to her reputation for venality. There was a charm in this intriguing amalgam of passionate idealism and smirky sexual taunting. Rather than dismiss him outright, she decided to string him along.

Sade's interest in Mlle Colet did not escape the watchful eye of Inspector Marais, who first mentioned Sade in his regular reports to Sartine in December of 1764. He summarized Sade's previous activities, his imprisonment at Vincennes, his exile at Échauffour, and added that, "in order to occupy his leisure," Sade

> is pleased to give 25 louis a month to Mlle Colet, an actress at the [Théâtre des] Italiens, who is living with the Marquis de Lignerai, who is obliging enough to take a back seat when she finds a good prospect. He is not unaware of her intrigue with M. de Sade, but the latter is beginning to realize that he is being deceived by this girl, and this week he went to work off his passion at Mme Brissault's, of whom he persistently inquired whether she knew me. She told him that she did not. I very strongly advised this woman, without explaining any further, not to furnish him with any girls to go with him to *petites maisons.*[6]

Mme Brissault, called "La Présidente" by her clients, was one of the most successful procurers of the day. It is quite telling that Sade questioned her as to whether she knew a police inspector named Marais. It reveals that he now knew perfectly well what Marais's functions were, and was aware, on some level, that his indiscretions would be self-destructive. For his part, Marais considered that it might be safe to allow Sade to patronize prostitutes at a regulated establishment like Mme Brissault's. Mindful of the Testard affair and of what Sade was capable of in the privacy of his *petite maison*, Marais warned Mme Brissault not to allow him to take any girls away with him.

Marais's next report, on December 21, continued the account of Sade's affair with Colet, noting that Sade felt close enough to Mme Brissault to seek her motherly advice. Of course, one recalls the even deeper relationship Sade had with his mother-in-law, La Présidente de Montreuil. His quest for mothering extended even to the proprietress of one of Paris's famous bordellos. Sade confided to Mme Brissault his jealousy of Colet's other, wealthier lovers, as well as his "apprehensions" that this affair might cause a scandal.[7]

Marais's report for December 28 indicates Sade's displeasure at having to share Colet with anyone. He had very strong views concerning the fidelity of his lovers, and would one day write that the "thought that someone in my arms is perhaps involved with another has always disgusted me, and never in my life have I taken back a woman whom I suspected of having played me false."[8] Concerning Sade's jealousy, Marais observed that he was particularly inflamed by an enormous jewelry chest sent to Colet on Christmas Day. Colet's mother was so concerned about Sade's reaction to the expensive gift that she lied to him about its origin, telling him that it had come from the Duc de Richelieu. Marais believed that the mother "employed this ruse in order to contain, by reason of the respect owed to a rival of such importance, the Comte de Sade's jealousy."[9]

Seven months later, in a letter to the Abbé, Mme de Montreuil took credit for using Sade's jealousy to manipulate him into breaking off the affair with Colet.[10] Mme de Montreuil was not only clever; she was also shameless. She herself had gone to retrieve her son-in-law at Colet's house.[11] While her coach waited in the street, Mme de Montreuil stood in the doorway of one of Paris's notorious actress-courtesans, refusing to leave without her son-in-law! The episode makes clear that Mme de Montreuil had effectively become Sade's parent. His father having completely withdrawn from any involvement with him, she vigorously assumed the management of his crises and of his finances. And from the first, Sade was willing to confide in her. To some extent, he had no choice, since it was to her that apologies were owed after various crises. It must also be allowed that his passionate nature somehow opened up to her.

Confidante though she was, Mme de Montreuil appears not to have relied on Sade alone for information concerning his activities. She knew more than he told her. And she knew before he told her. How, for example, did she know about Colet—where she lived, enough about Colet's other clients so as to convince Sade that he was being two-timed? It seems likely that Sade's mother-in-law had some understanding with Inspector Marais, the best source of information about actresses and prostitutes in all of France. This cooperation may have begun with Mme de Montreuil and Marais's first meeting, when he escorted Sade into exile at Échauffour. It was part of Marais's responsibility to protect the reputation of noble families. He may also have been willing to render personal services at a price. Mme de Montreuil possessed the nerve required to bribe a policeman, just as she would later suborn many of Sade's business agents and lawyers. If Sade believed that Mme de Montreuil would be content with his version of the facts concerning his scandalous adventures, it was one of many miscalculations he would make about his mother-in-law. She was not the sort of person to be bamboozled.

Sade's brief fling with Colet was over by the beginning of the new year. He asked her for his letters back, to which request she evidently responded by hurling insults at his footman. In a final letter to her he began aphoristically, "A woman's vengeance is always contemptible," and went on to complain about her infidelity and about her humiliating refusal to return his letters. He added that he had learned "never to entertain such a cruel passion" as love, and he looked forward never to seeing her again.[12] In fact, Colet died a year later, at the age of twenty-one.

Despite Sade's resolution never to love again, the following month, February 1765, saw him make another leap into epistolary passion. He had just been smitten by the otherwise unidentified Mlle C—— at a ball. In his letter to her of February 20, 1765, he lamented the cruel irony that she had once been offered as his prospective wife.[13] Sade's letter is a bittersweet fantasy about how things might have been. The following is an excerpt:

What delightful days I would have spent with you! Ceaselessly occupied with pleasing you, what enchantment I would have discovered in making your commands my desires! Days, when now an unfortunate marriage, based solely on greed, produces only thorns, would have instead perpetually offered me the roses of springtime. How I would have savored them, these precious days that I now detest. Cherished by the fingers of happiness, they would have flown by all too quickly for me. The longest years would not have been long enough to honor my sweet love. At my wife's feet I would have always worshipped my mistress, and the chains of duty, intertwined with love, would have offered my enraptured heart some blush of happiness. Vain illusion! delusive dream! you came to beguile my passions only to plunge them into the horror that now overwhelms them; you offer me happiness only the better to make me feel my loss.[14]

It is hard to imagine what any woman would have made of this letter, and it is unknown what Mlle C—— thought. In a sense, it is like a literary exercise, an elegy on lost chances. Like some of Sade's other love letters, it reveals a suicidal theme: if he could not have her, he wrote, "how sweet death would seem to me!" And although he had met her only by chance at a ball, the letter evinces an absurd sexual jealousy. He threatened to commit suicide the moment he heard that she had taken another: "I will not survive the happiness of a rival." Like all of Sade's impassioned acts (including his fiction), this letter was not merely occasional, but part of a larger ongoing discourse, part of his life's hidden narrative. Whatever the real attractions of Mlle C——, in

Sade's view she stands as a symbol of that perfect, ideal Love to which he felt entitled, but which was taken from him by his father, who arranged his marriage to Renée. However, even though Sade describes his wife as a "thorn," as opposed to the "rose" that is Mlle C——, the opposition cannot be sustained. By the end of the letter, Mlle C—— becomes, by reason of her unresponsiveness to his needs, a woman of "savage heart."[15] Sade's delirious dream of the perfect love and the perfect woman is doomed. Women would always betray him. Love is finally so exalted, so transcendent, as to be beyond his reach.

Lust was easier to satisfy. On February 8, 1765, Marais reported that Mlle Beaupré slept with Sade twice for 6 louis.[16] On April 26, Marais listed him as third among the lovers of Beauvoisin, paying her 20 louis a month.[17] About twenty-one years old at this time, Beauvoisin was described by a contemporary as a "courtesan with a pretty face, . . . but without a figure, short and stout," for which reason "she had been obliged to leave the Opéra, where she had been a dancer."[18] As early as February, Sade was preparing to spend the summer with her at his château of La Coste. The excuse offered his mother-in-law was that he wanted to familiarize himself with the business affairs of his estates. Mme de Montreuil did not quite believe him, but she hoped that his uncle the Abbé could straighten him out: "Your nephew is getting ready to leave soon for Avignon and tells me he has business to conduct there. Is his presence there really necessary? I am unaware of it; but certainly he will always gain much from being near you; so I am not opposed to it at all."[19] In her letter of May 20, she informed the Abbé that Sade had left on the 9th, and she wondered why she had not yet heard of his arrival in Provence. She again expressed the hope that the Abbé could have a good influence on him:

> He very much needs your advice to settle the flightiness of his mind. He trusts you. That head of his wants to be managed, because, its first impulses always being violent, they are to be dreaded. But his mind is susceptible to reason upon reflection. All he needs is the time to make himself listen, as long as no passion overwhelms him.[20]

But Sade was once again in the throes of passion.

On June 1, 1765,[21] the Abbé de Sade wrote to Mme de Montreuil in response to her anxieties about her son-in-law's whereabouts. The Abbé too must have been wondering where his nephew was, because he had received a letter from him indicating he would arrive at Avignon between May 15 and May 20. In fact, Sade had left for Avignon on May 9. The Abbé, therefore, left his home at Saumane on the 15th, and waited in Avignon until Sade finally turned up on the 21st. The reason for the delay, the Abbé informed Mme de Montreuil, was that Sade had taken some extra days of pleasure along the road with Beauvoisin:

> He had spent four days at Melun with the individual with whom he is now besotted [Beauvoisin]. So that is who delayed his arrival. He assured me he had opened his heart to you on this weakness and even written to you from Lyons about his interlude at Melun. I would like to know if that is true, because that trust in you would give me pleasure and would give me some hope for the future.

If Sade sat at a table at an inn in Lyons (with Beauvoisin beside him?), writing to his mother-in-law about his latest uncontrollable passion, it would not be the first time he shared such information with her, thus further drawing her into his sexual life. The rest of the Abbé's letter went into some detail about how he understood his nephew's personality and behavior. The Abbé's views, for a time, had considerable influence on the way his frequent correspondent Mme de Montreuil tried to manage her difficult son-in-law. After all, the Abbé had been almost a father to young Sade. The Abbé wrote:

> Only you and I, Madame, have a bit of influence over him, but what can we do? Not much just now; he must sow his oats; he is now in the flames of passion, and you are right to say that his is a mind that wants to be controlled; but it would be dangerous, as his father has done, to rub him the wrong way; that would drive him to the most extreme indiscretions. It is only through gentleness, indulgence, reasoning that you can hope to reclaim him. You have begun the process, Madame, one can do no better. He has a great deal of trust and respect for you; sooner or later, you will accomplish what you wish.
>
> The current fancy worries me but little; less than a month's dalliance in these parts, and he will think of her no more; but that will be only to replace her with a new one. There's the rub, and I very much fear that he will be like that until he is past his youth. I talked to him a good deal about his wife, as you can well imagine; he appreciates all of her virtues, he spoke of her with the highest praise; he feels friendship for her and a good deal of respect: he would be in despair to displease her, but he finds her too cold and too devout for him, and there you see what makes him seek out amusement elsewhere. When he has passed through the age of heated passions, he will recognize the value of the wife you have bestowed upon him; but he must get past this age,

which will last much longer than we would wish. May God grant that he does not give too much pain to you and to me! If we act together, we will be able to parry the blows. He told me that his wife remained ignorant of his follies and that he would be in despair if she found out; that is something, anyway.

The Abbé proposed to visit Sade at La Coste the following week, after which, he promised Mme de Montreuil, "I will have the honor to give you an account of what I will discover."[22] The Abbé would get an eyeful.

When Sade arrived at La Coste with Beauvoisin, the villagers had prepared a welcoming celebration for their lord and lady. They gathered at the château and sang a simple Provençal song:

> O happy tidings
> they just announced
> *derida*
> our Marquis has married
> a lovely maid
> *couci couça*
> And here she is![23]

Sade did not explain that Beauvoisin was not Mme de Sade. Perhaps he did not want to break the mood of the occasion. He may also have had a puckish desire to see how his actress friend played out the role of a marquise. In any case, many did believe that Beauvoisin was Mme de Sade.

By the time of his uncle's arrival, Sade was already living the high life. He put on balls, entertainments, and especially plays for the local gentry. He had so much enjoyed directing and performing in plays the year before, at the château d'Évry, that he had outfitted a room at La Coste to be used as a theater, and for the following year was planning a considerably more ambitious construction for the same purpose. All of this cost money. By the end of the summer, Sade was almost 5,000 livres in debt.

Mme de Montreuil was beginning to lose patience. She wrote to the Abbé on July 17, foreseeing the trouble Sade would bring when he returned to Paris in the fall:

He will come back exhausted in every way, giving me all sorts of worries and torments, using every trick that he knows in order to extract some money to pay 5,000 livres of debts, whose bill he has sent to his wife, and then beginning all over again with new expenses. He can be certain that, as much as I am ready to hide his follies from his wife or to excuse them so as not to put a boundless distance between them, to the same extent would I have the firm resolve to make her aware of them and to convince her of her wretched fate when that proves necessary in order to divert her from far greater suffering in perpetuating her error; and I am soon going to be pushed to it if he does not stop me by a sincere change, which he is not capable of.[24]

Sade had frequently expressed his concern that his wife remain shielded from his indiscretions. Mme de Montreuil had cooperated in this conspiracy, persuaded that her son-in-law's immaturity and his obsessive need to sow his wild oats would pass in time. Moreover, like so many women, she appears to have been charmed by Sade, by his disarming candor, his extremely passionate nature, perpetually gripped by emotions—not only sexual ones, but also tenderness, lovesickness, remorse. This range of passion was doubtless beyond the bounds of Mme de Montreuil's middle-class proprieties. Perhaps inevitably, she found herself induced to come onto the stage of his psychodrama and play a role that must have held some attractions and aroused her curiosity. But in protecting her daughter from Sade's affairs, she had allowed herself to become an active participant in them. She knew of all his complaints about her daughter's sexual shortcomings. It was because Mme de Montreuil had such a strong interest in preserving at least the appearance of an alliance with the noble class that she waited so patiently for her son-in-law to reform. For his part, Sade felt that he had at last found someone who understood and accepted him as he was. Eventually, Mme de Montreuil would lose patience, breaking the spell of this mutual seduction. And when her essentially pragmatic mind had finally decided to write Sade off as a bad bargain, he would experience a profound betrayal.

That summer, Mme de Montreuil worried not only about the rising cost of Sade's adventure, but also about the public scandal he was causing at La Coste by passing Beauvoisin off as his wife:

However justified I may be from past experience in expecting anything on the part of M. de Sade, I would not have thought him capable of this excess of indecency in his idiotic love affairs. . . . Secret infidelities are an error with regard to his wife and to me, but this public misconduct, in front of his whole province, offensive to his neighbors, will cause him irreparable harm if it becomes known here [in Paris], and how will it not be known? . . . And then, in an injured tone, he will complain about his fate, about the violence of his passions that sweep him along, about his remorse for having given pain to those who love him.[25]

Mme de Montreuil had already begun to consider stronger measures against Sade and Beauvoisin: "For that I could easily get whatever I might require from the minister, but that would cause a scandal and be dangerous for him." In the meantime, she urged the Abbé never to let Sade "out of your sight, because one succeeds with him only by not leaving him alone for a second." The Abbé had always advised gentle measures, suggesting that harsh treatment was counterproductive. But now Mme de Montreuil was trying to goad him into acting against his own nature and better judgment: "Pay him another visit to see what is going on there, if he is still as much taken with her. Thunder, speak firmly; out of respect for you, he will be obliged at least to put on an appearance of decency there." Her strategy sought to make the lovers feel "uncomfortable" in their nest. Then "they will grow tired of each other," and "the nymph will decide all the more quickly to depart." During this affair, Mme de Montreuil and her son-in-law had written several letters (now lost) back and forth to each other. In one, Mme de Montreuil informed the Abbé, Sade wrote that "he has already begun to be disgusted with" Beauvoisin. Mme de Montreuil urged the Abbé to exploit any "storm clouds" or any "quarrels that may occur." If the Abbé should succeed in bringing the affair to an end, she warned him not to "let him follow after her. Keep him by you for a long time without letting him stray. Keep him busy." Mme de Montreuil concluded the letter by wondering why her son-in-law did not leave off pursuing these expensive, high-class mistresses. In fact, she "would prefer" him to have a country mistress down in Provence: "They are always less dangerous than kept mistresses."[26]

But the Abbé did not or could not bring the affair to an end. After the Abbé's visit at La Coste, Sade avoided him, and when the Abbé wrote to Sade, Sade replied intemperately. The Abbé had been goaded into writing strong letters, not only to his nephew, but also to some of his relations, notably his sister the Abbesse of Saint-Benoît de Cavaillon. When she in turn criticized Sade, Sade countered with an extremely sarcastic letter in which he accused the Abbé of running a bordello at Saumane (see page 518, n. 17). Sade's dream summer down in Provence was ending in bitterness on all sides.

Sade tried to repair some of the damage. Apparently upset by the Abbé's "harsh reproaches," he wrote to his uncle to say that his conscience was clear: "I do not regard my honor or my integrity compromised . . . and I reproach myself for no villainy whatsoever." If the Abbé felt offended, Sade offered him this charming reassurance:

Of the wrong against you, my dear uncle, never believe me capable of it, the women I see may foul my mind, but never my heart. What is certain is that I always find in probing my heart to its depths, the feelings of gratitude and of friendship that it owes you, however much its master wishes to surrender it to a woman, she never will extinguish those feelings in it, they are written there by your kindnesses, there they will be inscribed forever.[27]

Later, Sade would also apologize to his uncle for nastily alluding to the château of Saumane as a bordello.

Around the middle of August 1765, Sade shut up his château at La Coste and sneaked into Paris with Beauvoisin. Mme de Montreuil and Sade's wife were, as usual, still at Échauffour. But Sade's entrance into Paris did not go unnoticed or unreported to Mme de Montreuil, as she informed the Abbé on August 26:

I know that his valet arrived at my house in Paris on the 20th with his trunks. He said that his master had sent them before, that he would arrive in a few days. I am quite confident that he is already there, and that he is staying at la Demoiselle's [Beauvoisin]. . . . If I were in Paris, I would go myself to take him away at the very door of that girl, just as I did with another one [Colet] a year ago.[28]

On September 8, Mme de Montreuil informed the Abbé that Sade was still in Paris, "living more at Mlle B[eauvoisin]'s house than at mine." She also wrote to her son-in-law, threatening not to help him pay off his debts unless he came at once to Échauffour.[29]

Mme de Montreuil's information was correct. Sade had returned with Beauvoisin on August 20. The next day, the two of them appeared before the royal notary, M. Pontelier, and signed a contract by which Beauvoisin paid Sade 10,000 livres against an annuity of 500 livres he would pay her for life. To raise the cash, Beauvoisin had sold some of her jewelry the day before. There is no indication that Sade ever paid her the annual income he promised.[30] It remains a mystery why Beauvoisin gave money to one of her lovers—a surprising reversal of the usual procedure. Perhaps she was speculating that she would live longer than the twenty years it would take to earn back her initial investment. Fictitious loans were a frequent means by which mistresses guaranteed their incomes against the possible claims of their dissipated clients' families.[31] In Sade's case, however, it appears that Beauvoisin did pay him the 10,000 livres.

Toward the middle of September, Sade began to see that it would be prudent to improve his relationship with his mother-in-law, whose threatening letters had begun to sound quite earnest. On September 8, Mme de Montreuil had informed the Abbé that she was fed up with her son-in-law's prevarications: "I was not pleased with his tone, and I replied with some harshness."[32] Sade decided that it would be a good idea to spend some time with her and his wife. He arrived at Échauffour on September 15, late in the night. They saw him, as Mme de Montreuil said in a brief note to the Abbé the following morning, "only for a moment," and because Renée was present, "he spoke only of indifferent matters."[33] In a letter to the Abbé, Mme de Montreuil reported that his mood was "gay enough." Privately, he told his mother-in-law that his romance with Beauvoisin was cooling, but Mme de Montreuil told the Abbé that Sade "still loves her."[34] This was Renée's first meeting with her husband in four months; he had parted from her to go to La Coste on May 9. Sade was again living under one roof with two women whom he was obliged to treat very differently: his devout and virtuous wife, whose good opinion of him he wished to preserve, and his mother-in-law, to whom he revealed his worst nature and whose understanding and sympathy he valued. If one is tempted to conclude that he must have been aware that he was living a lie with one of them, one might as easily say that he was living a lie with both of them, or, to put it another way, he was living the truth with both of them. Such was the flexibility of his deeply divided nature.

As chance would have it, Sade's conciliatory stay was shorter than expected. Early in November, he was informed of a crisis in Beauvoisin's health and immediately set out to join her in Paris, telling his wife (there was no need to lie to Mme de Montreuil) that he had to visit a friend in Provence. Beauvoisin had been pregnant since the previous March, but was unclear which of her many lovers at that time was the father. To Mme de Montreuil, Sade appeared distraught, "completely upset." She tried to stop him from going, without success. She could console herself that this trip at least produced no scandal. It remains unclear whether Beauvoisin suffered a miscarriage or gave birth to a healthy baby. Mme de Montreuil's comment to the Abbé drips with hostility: "In her condition, I do not imagine she was much of a source of pleasure." Of her son-in-law, she added, "It is unfortunate that he does not love the one he ought to love."[35]

As had been planned, Mme de Montreuil and her daughter arrived in Paris on November 14. Ten days later, Sade rented yet another secret trysting place, this one an apartment at Versailles.[36] But it would not be for Beauvoisin. Inspector Marais's report for December 13, 1765, listed her as fully back in action. She returned to the theater "like a new star": "Her lying-in made her more beautiful, and the young M. de Saint-Contest immediately surrendered to her charms, and in deference to him, she has cast off M. de Louvois and M. de la Boulaye."[37] There is no mention of Sade. Their relationship appears to have cooled before a break at the beginning of the new year. On January 3, 1766, Marais reported, "M. le Comte de Sade has ceased all commerce with Mlle de Beauvoisin."[38] Perhaps written around this time is an undated letter Sade wrote to Beauvoisin and preserved, along with his other letters to his actress-lovers, in his manuscript anthology, *Oeuvres diverses,* containing his early works, 1758 to 1769:

> So you are now unmasked, you monster! . . . Go, and you return me to my senses; for the rest of my life, I will despise you, you and your sort. . . . Adieu, seize your new conquest, and may you detach yourself from him using the same base arts that you employed with me. . . . So be happy, I will not trouble your success; enjoy it, if you can, despite the depths of despair into which you plunge me.[39]

Sade's affairs all began in the superheated language of high romance, and they all ended in the equally superheated language of despair and disillusionment. He felt both these extremes with equal sensitivity.

Sade immediately found consolation. Marais noted in his report of January 3, 1766, that Sade met "Mlle Dorville, a strapping and pleasant girl, recently escaped from Mme Hecquet's seraglio," whom he paid 10 louis a month to be her second lover, behind the Chevalier Elchin—i.e., Lord Elgin—who paid 4 louis a visit.[40] It is possible to imagine that a passionate letter of introduction Sade wrote to "Mlle D——, of the Opéra," and which he also preserved in his *Oeuvres diverses,* was written to Mlle Dorville. Sade's first line is very like the one he used in his letter to Colet: "It is difficult to see you and not love you." To Mlle D——, Sade wrote: "To see you and to love you, Mademoiselle, is the work of a moment." Sade told both women that he had been smitten at the theater. In this case, he said, he persuaded a mutual acquaintance, M. Bourneville, an officer in the guards, to speak to her for him. That "unhappy day" at the theater, Sade claimed,

> will mark the season of my misfortune if you do not take pity on my extreme love, which now nothing can surmount. . . . Permit me to come to visit you today, even for a moment, at whatever time you wish, or tomorrow, you set the time. I assure you, I will be absolutely discreet. I will always follow your orders: I will be your slave. Ah! 'tis

the hands of love will plait my chains. May I have the honor of wearing them![41]

The two preceding letters, the angry one to Beauvoisin and the plaintive one
to Mlle D——, may have been written in the same month. In any case, they
perfectly exemplify the two opposite poles of the same passionate mind.

On January 18, 1766, Sade was involved in a sort of contretemps that is
common in a large city. At the beginning of the month, he had rented a stable
in Paris.[42] He was now keeping a private coach. On the 18th, while he was
driving across the Place des Victoires with his servant, his cabriolet was
blocked by a hired coach driven by one Paul Lefèvre, who had stopped to discharge a passenger. A dispute ensued. The Marquis, in a fury, stepped down
from his carriage, brandishing his sword, then struck the offending horses
with the flat of the blade. He had no control over himself or his weapon. The
point entered the belly of one of the horses. Sade was obliged to pay the
coachman 24 livres (half of what he paid Jeanne Testard) for the treatment of
the horse and for damages.[43] The injury Sade inflicted on the horse, probably
unintentionally, was slight. Nevertheless, the incident reveals a rage that
always burned just beneath the surface, a rage that could easily explode when
met by the small and inevitable provocations of everyday life.

At the beginning of 1766, when Sade was rejected by Beauvoisin and he
had his traffic altercation, he had been involved in attempting to authenticate
the antiquity of his noble lineage to the satisfaction of the royal genealogist,
M. de Baujon. In the spring, Sade wrote to the Abbé about this matter in a
letter that helps us understand his activities during the coming summer in
Provence. The "very difficult" M. de Baujon was now demanding the original
genealogical documents, not copies. Sade therefore proposed to come to visit
his uncle at his Abbaye d'Ébreuil, whereupon he and his uncle would then go
to Avignon by the beginning of June in order to collect the necessary documents.[44] Sade's visit to Provence in June 1766 did not in the least resemble the
sexual fandango of the previous summer with Beauvoisin.[45] This brief trip
was all business, and he carried the papers back to Paris himself at the end of
June. It is very likely that, while he was in Provence, he spent a few weeks at
La Coste, supervising the renovations that he had commissioned the previous
summer, including a new complex of rooms for his wife and a new theater,
capable of seating sixty guests, to replace the makeshift room he had previously used. A private theater was a status symbol of the time, and it suited
Sade's own taste and pretensions. Judging from actual bills from the workmen
involved in the renovation, Sade's improvements cost between 3,000 and
4,000 livres.[46] If Mme de Montreuil did not complain, perhaps it was because

these expenditures produced tangible, relatively unobjectionable results. But to her dismay, his spending on courtesans and actresses resumed quickly with his return to Paris. In the fall of 1766, Sade's name reappeared in Inspector Marais's weekly reports. On September 26, Marais recorded the breakup two weeks earlier of Sade and a young dancer from the Opéra, Mlle Le Roy.[47] On November 4, Sade paid 200 livres for four and half months' rent on a *petite maison* at Arcueil, just outside Paris.[48] His noisy parties with whores at this house in a respectable and quiet village would annoy his neighbors, and one unfortunate incident would bring him once more to the attention of the police.

As the new year of 1767 began, the health of Sade's father, which had been in decline for several years, took a sudden turn for the worse. He died on January 24 at the age of sixty-five, leaving his estate in "disastrous financial condition,"[49] with perhaps 85,000 livres of debts.[50] On the day his father died, Sade wrote of his grief to the Abbé: "I know not what words to use, or how to describe my sorrow, it is inexpressible, my dear uncle."[51] Accompanied by his father-in-law, Sade attended the burial two days later. His passionate nature and reverence for the idea his father represented produced a grief that touched Mme de Montreuil's heart. "The manner in which his son felt this loss and was affected by it," she wrote to the Abbé, "totally reconciles me to him. Be a father to him, Monsieur, he cannot find a better one than you."[52] Mme de Montreuil well understood that at twenty-six her son-in-law still needed a paternal figure.

In the same letter, Mme de Montreuil recorded an interesting conversation she had had with her son-in-law the month before. She had been trying to induce Sade to reform by telling him that his uncle the Abbé was angry with him. (She had also tried, apparently with some success, to get the Abbé to renounce his characteristic tolerance and patience, and to act more decisively with his nephew.) One day, Sade informed her that he had received letters from his uncle demonstrating that the Abbé was not angry with him at all. Sade accused Mme de Montreuil of trying to poison his uncle's mind against him. Mme de Montreuil described this conversation with her son-in-law:

> "My uncle is not as angry as you led me to believe," he [Sade] told me, "here's a letter from him in which he calls me his dear nephew, so you can see very plainly that we are not at odds."—I don't believe any of it, let's have a look. He shows me. Indeed, I do glimpse: "My dear nephew." But he never allowed me to read any further. Two weeks ago he told me: "I got a letter from my uncle. You must have told him

some rather bizarre things, devoid of any common sense, because I don't understand anything of all that my uncle writes me about it." I wrote nothing but the plain truth. Our conversation was interrupted, and that is where it stays. I have not wanted to ask to see the letters, since I was already reprimanded about it.[53]

Mme de Montreuil's account reveals the seductive, coy, teasing relationship Sade had established with his mother-in-law. In the drawing room of the Montreuil mansion in Paris, Sade enters with a letter from his uncle and piques Mme de Montreuil's curiosity. She is a very curious woman, and she has reason to be. Sade tells her that she is wrong, that his uncle is not as angry as she says. As proof, he folds the letter to reveal only the salutation, "My dear nephew," and teases her by refusing to show the rest. For once, Sade knows a secret about her, her constant meddling, her constant letter-writing, her constant need to know everything, to control everything. Two weeks later, he repeats the performance with another letter from the Abbé, and accuses Mme de Montreuil of telling the Abbé lies. She would like to know what the letters say, but cannot swallow her pride to ask. Perhaps the Abbé will write back and tell her. . . . For a moment, this powerful woman—the moral and practical head of her household (her husband is almost never mentioned)—for an instant, she seems happy to behave almost helplessly, almost girlishly, as she pouts over her son-in-law's reprimand. Such was the relationship possible with a Mother. A Father was quite another matter.

On January 23, 1767, the day before Sade's father died, Inspector Marais noted in his weekly reports that Sade was back with Beauvoisin, the "monster" who had jilted him a year before. This information came from the Chevalier de Jeaucourt, Beauvoisin's primary lover, who told Marais that she was seeing many other men, including Sade, with whom she had appeared in public.[54] By April 19, when Mme de Montreuil wrote to the Abbé, she was not only aware of Sade's renewed affair with Beauvoisin, but knew exactly when it had begun, leading one to believe that she did have some access to Marais or to his reports. Mme de Montreuil wrote: "La B[eauvoisin] has totally resumed her domination over him, and since the death of his father, she has employed it. When it comes to her, he is totally blind." In the same letter, she informed the Abbé that her daughter was now nearly five and a half months pregnant.[55] Mme de Montreuil hoped that the birth of a child would cement the marriage, but she had her doubts: "The father does not seem so eager for it. He is occupied with rather more interesting objects." Mme de Montreuil informed the Abbé that Sade intended to leave for Provence on the following day: "I confess that this pleases me greatly, for it will provide at least a period of calm. What a pity! he has everything necessary to be happy by making those he lives with happy. If he would only be reasonable and well behaved, and not betray himself with worthless creatures."[56]

During the summer of 1767, Sade spent some time with his uncle at Saumane, then went on to La Coste, where renovations were almost complete. On July 1, Mme de Montreuil wrote to the Abbé that by mid-month her daughter would enter her ninth month of pregnancy: "She is very big and her child very active. He will take after his father." Mme de Montreuil noted that she had not heard from the Abbé in a long time and wondered if Sade was hiding something, or was otherwise up to his old tricks. She acknowledged that Sade was sending Renée letters regularly enough, but she wondered whether they were sincerely written. Her daughter told her only that Sade said he was in good health but "suffering a good deal from the heat."[57] Despite the heat, Sade, now head of the family and lord of his estates, had asked the council of La Coste to arrange both a mass for his dead father and the traditional ceremony acknowledging the new lord. This feudal ritual took place on August 9, when the officials and council members of the community appeared before Sade, who was seated in an armchair. The elders bared their heads, knelt before him, and pledged their loyalty.[58] It was but twelve years before the Revolution, when the whole feudal order of the Ancien Régime would be swept away. But on this hot summer day, Sade insisted on his prerogatives, and he received the homage of his subjects.

Sade's other activities during this summer remain unclear. Among his biographers, only Laborde believes he returned to Paris in time to see his first son and heir, Louis-Marie, born on August 27, 1767.[59] At the very beginning of the marriage, Mme de Montreuil had yearned for the title of grandmother. In the course of time, because of Sade's imprisonment and his wife's distraction, the task of rearing this child, as well as the two others born later, would fall to her. For now, she and her daughter were thrilled with the new and healthy baby boy. If they had hoped that fatherhood would change Sade, they would soon find that his indiscretions were growing more dangerous.

CHAPTER 5

The Arcueil Affair

AFTER THE Testard affair in 1763, Sade had come to know Inspector Marais personally. Nevertheless, knowing Marais and the nature of his work did not stop Sade from continuing and even escalating activities that must necessarily become known to Marais, then to Lieutenant General of Police Sartine, and ultimately to the King. A perversely intimate relationship was to develop between the noble libertine who challenged all authority, and the hired gumshoe of the state. Sade taunted not only God, but also this little minion of authority. Some part of him wanted Marais as a witness to his attacks on decency.

Marais's report of October 16, 1767, predicted worse things to come:

> One will soon be hearing about M. le Comte de Sade's horrors; he is making every possible effort to induce Mlle Rivière of the Opéra to live with him and has offered her twenty-five louis a month on condition that, on the days she would not be at the theater, she would come to see him at his *petite maison* at Arcueil. This young lady refused him, because she was being kept by M. Hocquart de Coubron, but M. de Sade continues to pursue her, and, in waiting to wear her down, this week he tried as well as he could to persuade La Brissault to supply him with girls to go and sup with him at his *petite maison*. This woman constantly refused him, knowing more or less what he is capable of, but he will apply to others who are less scrupulous or do not know him, though they certainly will hear of him before long.[1]

Marais understood that there was a kind of sliding scale to Sade's sexual objects: if he could not get a famous actress, then he would go to the most reputable bordello, that of Mme Brissault. If he was barred there, he would send his valet to obtain common whores. In the end, Sade himself would go out and personally solicit beggars and streetwalkers, and the *petite maison* that he was renting at Arcueil would soon become the focus of national and even international attention.

Sade had begun paying rent on the house in November 1766.[2] M. Jean-François Vallée, the *procureur fiscal* for the town, informed the police about the new tenant's activities. "He has caused a great deal of scandal," Vallée claimed, "ever since he arrived." Vallée charged that, "day and night," Sade brought "persons of both sexes there for the purpose of debauchery, that, furthermore, he is known as a very violent man, having insulted and struck several persons."[3] Vallée also reported that in February 1768 Sade entertained at Arcueil four prostitutes who had been hired by his valet in Faubourg Saint-Antoine. The prostitutes, according to Vallée, were whipped and given dinner for a fee of slightly less than a louis apiece.[4] Another neighbor, Mme Pontier, "heard that Sade often brought girls or women to his house, but never heard that he had mistreated them."[5] Vallée also claimed that Sade had a dispute with a coachman over the fare for carrying some prostitutes to the house in Arcueil.[6] Sade's angry sexual fantasies could no longer be contained within the walls of the most discreet and fashionable bordellos. He was now on the verge of becoming a scandalous public figure. It was not so much what went on in his house at Arcueil that brought Sade to grief. Rather, it was his apparently uncontrollable disregard for authority and public opinion. Sade was courting disaster. On Easter Sunday, April 3, 1768, it befell him with a vengeance. By the end of that fatal day, Rose Keller would charge him with physical and sexual abuse.[7]

On the most sacred day in the Christian calendar, Sade had planned a special séance at Arcueil. He was up and about early. He instructed his valet, Jacques-André Langlois, to procure a few prostitutes and to bring them to his *petite maison*. When Sade reached Arcueil, just past noon, two would be waiting for him in the kitchen. Despite this prospect, Sade went to the Place des Victoires at nine in the morning and struck a pose, leaning against the railing beneath the statue of Louis XIV. Perhaps his own difficulties in obtaining girls from La Brissault had made him doubt whether his valet would be successful. He may have wished to exercise his own skill at procuring a possibly naïve victim (Rose Keller, the woman he was about to meet, would claim she was merely a beggar, whereas Sade said that she was a streetwalker). At her deposition on April 21 for the criminal division of the High Court, known as La Tournelle, Keller would claim that she had just emerged from mass at Les Petits Pères. "Do you believe in God?" was the first thing Sade had asked Jeanne Testard. Observing Rose Keller emerging from church might have piqued Sade's interest.[8] She said that at 9 a.m. she was standing at the Place des Victoires, begging. One man had just given her a sol when another, Sade, beckoned to her. He was wearing a gray frock-coat and had a hunting knife at his belt. In one hand he carried a cane; in the other, an almost white fur muff.

Keller approached the stranger. She was thirty-six years old and the widow of Charles Valentin, an apprentice pastry cook. Her work had been spinning cotton, but for the past month she had been unemployed and was begging. Born in Strasbourg, she spoke French poorly and with a heavy German accent—so poorly, in fact, that one village woman of Arcueil to whom she later talked was not able to understand her entirely.[9] For the past month, Keller had been renting a room at the shop of a tailor whose name she did not know. For her two depositions she gave two different addresses. She may have been misunderstood; she may have been confused; she may not have had any fixed residence. When she approached Sade, she said, he asked her to come with him to clean his room. Sade claimed that he asked her to come with him without specifying any purpose. She testified that she believed his request was for some purpose other than cleaning his room and had objected that she was not what he imagined. He replied, she said, that he only wanted her as a servant and that he would give her wages and food. In her second deposition, Keller mentioned the wages as 1 écu—that is, 3 livres, or a sixteenth of what Sade had paid Jeanne Testard. Keller agreed to Sade's proposal and accompanied him to a house near the Nouvelle Halle, where he took her to a room furnished with armchairs and a yellow chaise longue. Was this yet another secret apartment that Sade kept for libertine purposes? Here, she said, Sade asked her to accompany him to his country house, and she replied that she was indifferent as to where she earned her bread. He left her alone in the room for an hour while he ran some errands.

On his return, Sade put Keller in a carriage, sat down beside her, closed the blinds, and fell silent. Later on, she said, he asked her if she knew where she was. She replied that she could not possibly know, since she could not see anything. Sade fell silent once more and drifted off to sleep. The journey to suburban Arcueil took perhaps two hours, and they arrived at around twelve-thirty in the afternoon. When they reached Sade's rented house, he led Keller to a green side door and asked her to wait while he went around to the front door to let her in. He then conducted her across a small garden to a bedroom with two canopy beds overlooking a larger garden. There he bade her wait, and he double-locked the door. Sade's precautions of closing the coach blinds during the journey and then locking her in the room suggest that he was aware that Keller was not a prostitute of the same sort as the two hired by his valet who were waiting below in the kitchen. Sade, occupied below, did not return to Keller for an hour.

When he did return, he simply said to Keller, "M'love, come downstairs."

They crossed the same garden and entered a small room. Sade told her to get undressed. When she asked him why, he said it was to have a good time. She protested. He replied that, if she did not take off her clothes, he would kill her and bury her in the garden. He left her for a time, during which she stripped to her chemise. When he returned, he had taken off his clothes and donned an old sleeveless vest. He also had wound a white handkerchief around his head. He must have looked like a workman or a butcher. This was his whipping costume. When he saw her still in her chemise, he told her that this garment would have to go as well. She said that she would rather die. He pulled it off over her head, then led her naked into an adjoining room whose windows were darkened by closed drapes. It is worth recalling that Sade had conducted an initial interview with Jeanne Testard in one room and then induced her to enter a second, more dangerous room where he had his whips and obscene pictures. There are stations of the cross, as it were, in the ritual unfolding of Sade's sexual fantasies. This is seen most clearly in his libertine novels, where there are specialized spaces devoted to particular activities. The movement is always into the depths, deeper into the interior: "M' love, come downstairs."

The day after her ordeal, Keller told a woman[10] that the room in which she had undressed contained many bunches of switches, and these had alarmed her. Psychological torture by the inducement of progressively greater fear was also a feature of Sade's night with Jeanne Testard. In the center of the innermost room at the Arcueil house was a daybed covered with a red-and-white calico print. He made Keller lie facedown on this bed and tied down her hands and legs. Then he took a fistful of switches and caned her. Keller claimed that he had made several incisions in her buttocks with a small knife. In her second deposition, she also said that he had struck and bruised her back with a stick.

One should pause here to note Sade's denial, in his own deposition, of some of the major points of Rose Keller's complaint. He said that in the room near the Nouvelle Halle he made it clear to her that he wanted her for *"une partie de libertinage."* He denied threatening her with death. He said she undressed voluntarily. He denied tying her down. He admitted he whipped her with a *"martinet de cordes à nœuds"*—a whip with knotted thongs. He denied using birch rods, or a knife, or any stick. He denied that she had cried out or had made any protest. Later, he discussed the affair with Inspector Marais, who reported that Sade "strongly and steadfastly maintained only to have whipped the girl." Sade insisted "that it never occurred to him to scar her, that he cannot imagine what could have caused this creature to make such a charge, and that he is fully persuaded that, if the High Court orders verification by expert surgeons, they will find no trace of any scar."[11] Indeed, none was found. On the very night of this incident, the authorities at Arcueil had sent for the local surgeon, Pierre-Paul Le Comte, to examine Keller. He made a cursory examination that night and a complete one the following day, by order of the court at Arcueil. He found no knife cuts or incisions whatsoever, and no bruises to suggest a beating with a stick. He also found no rope marks on her wrists or feet that suggested Keller had been tightly bound and under duress. He did find small round marks, and perhaps a dozen shallow flaps of skin, or excoriations, consistent with a whipping. Either Keller was truly new to such proceedings and imagined that the sensation of being whipped was like that of being cut with a knife, or else she was embellishing the details to make her case more sensational. The knife incisions were the most notorious details of the case, and almost every newspaper and gossip sheet of the time reported this and even magnified the affair into a kind of vivisectionist bloodbath. It is reasonable to accept the disinterested conclusions of the surgeon. Undoubtedly, a whipping had occurred. Prostitutes understood the role they were expected to play. There was a certain amount of pain suffered, and a good deal of feigning on both sides. What is interesting is how completely Sade had misjudged Keller, just as he had earlier misjudged Jeanne Testard: both women went straight to the police. It was not that Sade was a poor judge of character. On the contrary, he was a charmer, adept at sizing up people, manipulating them, knowing just how far he could go. Two factors may account for his miscalculation on this and other occasions. First, when sexual frenzy was upon him, he lost touch with reality. And, second, a major purpose of his sexual misconduct was to challenge authority and to see how far he could go. His interest was in finding the edge; it is small wonder that he frequently toppled over it.

To return to the little room beside the garden: Rose Keller claimed that Sade renewed the whipping seven or eight times (Sade said three or four). After each whipping, Keller claimed that Sade had dripped hot wax on her wounds, specifying white wax, and also a red wax that has a much higher melting point.[12] Sade denied that he had tortured Keller with melted wax. Rather, he claimed that after each episode of whipping he had applied dabs of a wax-based salve to heal the wounds. The surgeon Le Comte testified that he found no burn marks on Keller and no traces of red wax, though he did find some drops of white wax. Within ten days, on April 13, the Marquise du Deffand reported to Horace Walpole in England that Sade, "far from disavowing or blushing at his crime, claimed that he had performed a highly commendable act, and had provided a great service to the public by discovering a salve that instantly healed wounds."[13] There is no evidence that Sade said any such thing, but every aspect of the scandal at Arcueil was immediately exaggerated and sensationalized to satisfy the intense public interest in this case.

Rose Keller claimed that she had responded to the whippings with cries of protest. Sade testified that she made no sound, and if she had, they would have been heard by the other people then in the house. He claimed that, on the second or third whipping, she said she was beginning to feel unwell, and he continued for only one more repetition. Keller said he produced a knife and threatened to kill her and bury her in the garden if she did not cease her outcry. She then begged him not to kill her, because she had not yet gone to Easter mass and taken communion, to which Sade had replied that he would confess her himself, and even tried to make her confess to him. The day after this incident, Keller told a woman that she had asked Sade if he intended to make her suffer death as Christ had suffered, and Sade had replied that to do so would only increase his pleasure. This detail caused almost as much of a sensation as the claim about knife incisions. Sacrilege had been the overriding feature of Sade's night with Jeanne Testard—his cursing God, his trampling on the crucifix, his misuse of the communion wafer, etc. Perhaps Sade *had* joked with Keller about confessing her himself. This may seem rather tame stuff today, but only a few years earlier, on July 1, 1766, the Chevalier de la Barre, aged twenty, had been decapitated in Paris for sacrilegious acts.[14] Sade's whipping of Keller and his offer to confess her appeared to parody the crucifixion. Mme de Saint-Germain wrote to the Abbé on April 18: "The public outcry against him is raised beyond all expression. Judge it for yourself: it is presumed that he enacted that silly flagellation as a mockery of the Passion. All of that is too ridiculous to be believed."[15] But we know what Sade was capable of. Easter Sunday would have given an extra piquancy to his debauch, as would sexualizing the suffering of Christ by inflicting a parody of his crucifixion upon a prostitute. With Rose Keller, as with Jeanne Testard, no mutual sexual act had occurred. When he was with Testard, Sade had masturbated on the crucifix. Keller was lying facedown on the daybed, listening to Sade's banter about the confessional, when he suddenly burst into loud and frightful cries. He had been masturbating, and the sacrilegious banter had finally provoked his orgasm.

Sade untied Keller, took her back to the adjoining room, and brought her a basin of water and a towel to wash herself. After wiping, she found the towel bloody. He then brought a vial of a liquid that she was instructed to apply to the wounds, which caused her to suffer burning pains. Now fully clothed, she was brought some bread, a cold dish of boiled beef, and a carafe of wine. After eating, Keller was conducted upstairs to the first room, where Sade told her that he would let her leave in the evening. She told him that she hoped she could leave early, because she did not want to have to sleep on the road back to Paris. He reassured her, she said, replying that he had no wish to inconvenience her. Sade's and Keller's testimonies agree on these facts. Sade added that she in no way appeared disturbed or upset. He then locked her in the room, one story up from the large garden. If he grossly misread her state of mind at this point, he also made another costly mistake: he left the food tray and cutlery behind.

After a time, Keller thought of escape. She hooked the door from the inside, and then used the knife to pry open one of the shutters. With some large pins, she fastened together the covers from the two beds in the room, then tied them to an oak crossbar in the window. By this means, she was able to slide down to the garden. When she reached the far wall of the garden, she clambered over it with the aid of a trellis, but she scraped and bruised her left wrist when she fell on the other side. Then she scrambled across a field and stumbled to the main street of the village of Arcueil. At this point, she heard Sade's valet Langlois in pursuit, calling out to her to return, for his master wished to speak with her. She refused. Langlois held up a purse and told her he wished to pay her. Again she refused, and continued her flight into the center of the town. Distraught, her hand painful and bleeding, her clothes disheveled and torn, she came upon a village matron, Marguerite Sixdeniers, to whom she tearfully told her tale of horror. Two other women came up, Mmes Bajou and Pontier. They found Rose Keller's story and condition serious enough to take her at once to see M. Vallée, the *procureur fiscal,* who directed them to the château of Arcueil to see the registrar to the court, Charles Lambert. They arrived at the château at around six in the evening. At the same time, Sade was leaving his *petite maison* to return to his wife and in-laws at their house on the rue Neuve-du-Luxembourg in Paris. As Mme de Saint-Germain so well expressed it in her letter of April 18, this Easter Sunday would be "a day forever cursed for the House of Sade."[16]

At the château of Arcueil, Mme Lambert welcomed Rose Keller and her excited escort of townswomen. As Keller recounted the day's events, Mme Lambert became so upset that she was forced to retire. If Keller had difficulty expressing herself in her new language, she nevertheless could see the effect of her words. By 8 p.m., M. Gersant de la Bernardière, an officer of the constabulary of Bourg-la-Reine, had arrived to take down Keller's first deposition. He ordered the surgeon Le Comte to examine her. Finally, Keller was given refuge and a place to sleep in a neighboring cow barn.

On the following day, April 4, Charles-René Coignet, judge at Arcueil, heard Keller's complaint and opened an investigation that continued on April 6 with the depositions of witnesses. On April 5, Mme Lambert saw fit to relocate Keller and make her a guest at the château. Mme Lambert had regained sufficient composure to hear Keller's story through to its conclusion. By April 7, news of the scandal and the legal proceeding had already reached Mme de Montreuil. Amblet and Claude-Antoine Sohier, attorney and court prosecutor, were summoned to an early-morning conference on the rue Neuve-du-Luxembourg. Then they were immediately dispatched to Arcueil to see if Rose Keller was willing to settle the matter. Later that day, when Amblet and Sohier arrived at the château of Arcueil, they found Keller in bed, complaining that her sufferings prevented her from earning a living. She offered to withdraw her complaint for 3,000 livres—an extraordinary sum (she had been willing to work the day for 1 écu, or 3 livres). Sohier protested; Keller stood her ground. Sohier made a counteroffer of 1,800 livres; Keller split the difference and demanded 2,400 livres. The two negotiators returned to Paris to consult with Mme de Montreuil, who sent them straight back with orders to settle at all costs. On their return, they found Keller sitting up in her room and chatting with an audience of women. Sohier could not resist telling her rather sarcastically, "It's pretty clear that you are not as ill as you claimed." Even so, they paid her the 2,400 livres, plus 168 more that she demanded for bandages and medicines, and she signed a document withdrawing her complaint.[17] It was over, or so it seemed. Sade had once again been saved by Mme de Montreuil. But whereas Mme de Montreuil had succeeded in dealing with the Testard affair and the consequences of his escapades with actresses, this time she could not keep the truth from her daughter.

In a long letter of self-justification, Sade's "Grande Lettre," written to his wife from prison at Vincennes on February 20, 1781, he referred to the Keller affair as that "adventure at Arcueil." He characteristically minimized his responsibility for his fate, portraying himself in this case as the victim of Keller, an "untruthful and scheming woman" who was out "to get some money."[18] Keller turned out to have been nobody's fool. Sade, caught up in the dreamscape of his sexual frenzy, had seriously misjudged her character and her reactions to him. He had, moreover, once again relied too heavily on his rank for protection. He would also blame the judges and the legal system, for, although Mme de Montreuil had bought off Keller, the Paris courts would soon take up the case. In a short story entitled "Le Président mystifié" ("The Judge Confounded"), Sade satirized judges who are "more deeply moved to compassion for the whipped backside of a streetwalker than for the people whom they claim they protect."[19] Sade professed little sympathy for whores. In his eyes, as long as they were paid, they could have no complaint. In his novel *Aline et Valcour,* he praised a judge for telling a prostitute who appeared before him to lodge a complaint about a client: "Change your occupation, . . . or if this one suits you, put up with its thorns."[20] This subject of whores' backsides was a frequent, often humorous topic of Sade's letters to his wife. In July 1783, he wrote from prison: "One can be guilty of every abuse and of every imaginable wickedness, so long as one maintains respect for the backsides of whores: that is the main thing, and the reason is perfectly simple: the whores pay [i.e., protection], and we do not. When I get out of here, I must also try to obtain some police protection: like a whore, I too have an ass, and I would be quite happy to have it respected."[21]

Rage, self-pity, bewilderment. Sade never really understood what he had done wrong. There are many causes for this detachment from reality. Pride in his class, his sense of his own honor as a noble, as an officer in the army, and as the head of an important family—these were roles he felt he fulfilled with the greatest virtue. He represented the blindness of the Ancien Régime, standing on their privileges only two decades away from the guillotine. He also felt a strong sense of personal entitlement. His self-absorption, his narcissism, his lack of sympathy for others could easily come to the fore and at times overwhelm him, propelling him into an egotistical frenzy.

Although Sade was philosophically an idealist about many things, including love, there were many other matters, including sex, about which he was a materialist. He saw sex as a natural function no different (he would say) from moving his bowels, and just as necessary. If he felt a desire (inspired by his own nature, and ultimately therefore by Mother Nature) to hire a prostitute to whip her backside, what business was it of the state or the church to interfere with this contract? Sade liked to see himself as the victim of authority, and he felt compelled to challenge all authority as arbitrary and narrow. He liked to think of himself as a philosopher engaged in a debate on individual freedom and the limitations imposed by religion and government. However, if Sade meant his acts as a symbolic defiance of abstract authority, it was real-world, actual authority (embodied in the police and in judges) that would punish him, and quite severely. This invariably came as a complete surprise to Sade. He simply could not comprehend what was happening to him, how he had got where he was. Rage, self-pity, bewilderment—these were the legacy of that "adventure at Arcueil."

Sade never thanked his mother-in-law for buying off Rose Keller. On the contrary, he frequently expressed his resentment over her tactics. In his "Grande Lettre," mentioned above, he complained that Mme de Montreuil "had stupidly paid" Keller the money she wanted. But that had not silenced Keller, who, according to Sade, spread rumors about his "experiments" and about "corpses" buried in his garden. "This idea," Sade bitterly complained, "too well served the rage of my enemies for them not to use it as a sauce to spice anything that might happen to me."[22] Moreover, the precedent of paying Keller, Sade felt, later on prompted another woman to try the same ploy: "She knew about the one hundred louis [the equivalent of 2,400 livres] paid at Arcueil."[23] Sade had wanted to fight Keller's charges in court and be proved innocent. Mme de Montreuil's paying Keller to drop the charges, he felt, stained his reputation. As shall be seen, it is doubtful he could have won in court. Forces more powerful than he could successfully fight were quickly lining up against him.

Although Keller had signed the papers withdrawing her charges on April 7, news of the affair spread rapidly and was exaggerated with each telling. On April 8, the King moved to imprison Sade at the château of Saumur on the Loire River, about 190 miles from Paris. The King's action pre-empted judicial sanctions, and may have been recommended by the Montreuils for that purpose. Nevertheless, further legal action would be taken by the criminal division of the High Court in Paris, which opened its investigation into the "horrible crime that occurred at Arcueil" in which a woman was "tied to a table" and suffered "several incisions made on her body."[24] Among the five presiding judges of this court was Louis-Paul Pinon, who had a country house at Arcueil and may therefore have taken a personal interest in punishing the man who had been ruining the neighborhood. In any event, the court acted very quickly to depose witnesses, to make a search of Sade's *petite maison*, and to order his arrest and appearance. Mme de Saint-Germain blamed the court's interference on "a malicious minister" whose machinations were designed to take the case out of the King's hands and "to return the matter to the jurisdiction" of the criminal court.[25] Since Sade was already under royal arrest and could not appear, the court and the King were thrown into a conflict that the court could not win.

On April 9, Sade's former tutor, Abbé Amblet, was prudently sent to the *petite maison* at Arcueil to secure any valuables there, but also, no doubt, to remove any incriminating evidence. When the court investigators arrived on April 20, Sade's gardener let them in, and they found the rooms that Keller occupied just as she had described them. But they found nothing else: no whips, no obscene pictures, no collection of ivory crosses. The investigators carefully searched the entire house, basement, and grounds, looking into everything, under mattresses, into every cupboard. When they found a secretary and a cellar door locked, they called in a locksmith. At each closet, each location, the same phrase is repeated throughout their report, *"rien trouvé."*[26]

Amblet provided another service to his former pupil: he was permitted to be Sade's escort on the journey to Saumur. En route, on April 12, Sade wrote to his uncle, the Abbé: "An unfortunate affair has just got me arrested and transported to the château of Saumur. . . . If the story becomes public scandal in the country, you can maintain its falsity and say that I am with my regiment. . . . Write to me, I beg of you, my dear uncle, do not abandon me."[27] There is the familiar tone of bewilderment and self-pity, and an urgent scheme to control damage by managing public opinion in Provence. On the way to Saumur, Amblet wrote to Mme de Saint-Germain asking her "not to abandon" her "child." On April 18, Mme de Saint-Germain wrote to the Abbé about her own bewilderment:

> How to begin? how to present the details of all the horrors that are charged against this unfortunate person who, if one believes him, is guilty merely of foolish indiscretion, and who has already suffered more than enough? . . . I have defended him and I continue to defend him as much as I can, but how can I answer those who have seen the reports and the depositions of the witnesses, who have observed that woman escape over a wall, despite her wounds. . . . If that is true, he is crazy. But that is not true.

For her part, Mme de Saint-Germain believed that Sade "is now the victim of a malicious public."[28]

After a few weeks at Saumur, Sade was transferred by order of the King to the fortress of Pierre-Encize, near Lyons, where he would be guarded much more closely than in the relative freedom he enjoyed at Saumur. When Inspector Marais arrived at the château of Saumur to collect his prisoner, he found Sade eating "at the commandant's table." The commandant, M. du Petit-Thouars, embarrassed by this discovery of his leniency to a prisoner, "begged" Marais "as a favor on my return not to mention this at all, because it could harm him." According to Marais, Sade "seemed very surprised to see me," and was worried about the meaning of the transfer. Marais explained that the transfer was really in Sade's interest: if the King appeared to punish Sade severely enough, the court would relent. But there would be two problems that would haunt Sade then as today: Sade's own nature, and the public's fascination with the myth that was already growing about him in 1768. Marais referred to these two factors in the final paragraph of his report to M. de Saint-Florentin, minister of the King's household: "Everyone in the province knows his history. At Saumur, at Lyons, at Moulins, and at Dijon, it is the talk of the town, and if I have been able to judge properly from M. de Sade's conversation, he seems repentant about it only on account of the detention that it makes him suffer today, because at heart he is still the same."[29]

The public interest in the Arcueil affair threatened to ruin the attempt to quash the scandal by keeping Sade in prison under royal authority. The Tournelle court continued its proceedings. On April 19, it ordered Sade to appear. The next day, the bailiff searched the Montreuil mansion on the rue Neuve-du-Luxembourg for Sade. Sade, of course, was not there and could not appear at court: he was in prison. Newspaper accounts and gossip sheets popularized the affair and its consequences, a story too good to leave alone or unembellished. The *Courrier du Bas-Rhin* for April 20 called Sade another Bluebeard and reported that many young girls were seen to enter his house, never to leave again. A gossip sheet in Leyden published the often repeated charges that Sade had been experimenting with a magic salve and that there were bodies buried in his garden at Arcueil.[30] Reports like these prompted Sade's mother to write to Lieutenant General of Police Sartine to demand legal action against their publishers, the only extant letter by her.[31] Writing to Sartine from her convent on May 24, she adopted an angry and peremptory tone toward this extremely powerful minister. She complained that he had done nothing to stop "the blackest calumnies that are openly published against my son." In particular, she protested that the *Gazette de Hollande* had just printed an account of the Arcueil affair "in the blackest shades possible." She continued:

> To dishonor someone throughout the whole world, what a disgrace! The scoundrels who have committed such a horror deserve to be locked up for the rest of their lives, and one does not dishonor someone so closely related to me with impunity. At least let them make true accusations; to embellish to the point they have done is something criminal. My race has no stain of dishonor to reproach itself for, and one must know how to respect a family that is worthy of respect in every way. But to dare speak in that way about mine! Villains and wretches like those deserve to be hanged![32]

She acknowledged that her son would stand or fall in court on the merits of the case, but complained about leaks of the court depositions, which propagated false charges even before the case was formally heard. Her argument was forceful. She implicated Sartine himself for allowing these slanders to be published. At age fifty-six, she sounded strong, concerned about herself, angry about her honor, and quite alone.

By June 1, Sade, still in prison, missed another appearance at court. However, on June 3, royal commands were issued for Inspector Marais to bring Sade to Paris so that the prisoner could present to the court a royal *lettre d'abolition*, effectively annulling a legal procedure that had become an embarrassment to the nobility and to the King. Thus, Sade was returned to Paris and imprisoned at the Conciergerie. On June 10, he made his deposition for the Tournelle court, which ceded authority in this matter to the superior court of the Grand Chamber, which alone could receive Royal Letters of Abolition. As was the custom, Sade appeared with bared head and upon his knees. The chief judge, Charles-Augustin de Maupeou, accepted the King's letter and pronounced the symbolic penalty of 100 livres to pay for bread for the other prisoners of the Conciergerie. Following this ceremony, Marais conducted Sade back to the château of Pierre-Encize, where he was to remain in prison at the King's pleasure. On June 13, Mme de Montreuil wrote of the good news to the Abbé, and appeared to take credit for the result by saying that she had spent the past two days "making visits of thanks." Even though her influence could not have extended higher than her own class, Mme de Montreuil was beginning to sound like the head of the Sade family, a role she would find increasingly congenial. In the end, however, the King and his advisers had acted in their own interests to put an end to an embarrassment to the nobility. They would have agreed with Mme de Montreuil's conclusion to her letter: "A dishonorable business, and one that cannot be condoned, could not have ended better."[33]

Throughout this ordeal, the reaction of Sade's wife remains unknown. Mme de Montreuil's letters to the Abbé gave only one detail about her daughter. In her letter of April 26, she mentioned Renée literally as an afterthought, a postscript: "I have not at all mentioned Mme de Sade. It is easy to imagine her suffering."[34] Renée's husband and her mother had conspired to deceive her, to protect her from knowledge of Sade's previous scandals. Now that she was forced to face the truth, she began to display the courage and loyalty that were to be harshly tested during the years ahead. Immediately after her husband had been returned to Pierre-Encize in June, Renée swallowed her pride and wrote to the minister of the King's household to ask for special privileges for her husband. On July 29, the minister wrote to M. de Bory, commandant of Pierre-Encize, granting permission for Renée to visit her husband "only two or three times during the period that this lady will stay at Lyons."[35] Renée did not appear to have her mother's support for the journey she was about to make to Lyons. In fact, she had to sell her diamonds to pay for the trip.[36]

Sade's mood improved. He began to employ his charm upon Commandant de Bory. Marais had criticized Commandant du Petit-Thouars for allowing Sade to take excessive liberties at Saumur. Earlier, in 1763, Sade had written abject letters to the commandant of Vincennes, M. Guyonnet, and also to Lieutenant General of Police Sartine. Over the years, Sade would have occasion to write many letters to a variety of prison heads and high police officials. A collection of these letters would make a book, a kind of genre of wheedling, special pleading, extenuation, rationalization, self-pity, self-destructive fits of rage, hollow threats, manipulation, fulsome flattery, operatic remorse—the whole gamut of Sade's complex and conflicted feelings and stances toward authority. Sade was to spend almost twenty-nine years behind one sort of bars or another. In a sense, if all the commandants of Sade's various prisons could be rolled into one, he would represent one of the most stable and significant figures in Sade's life, a sort of father figure, at times susceptible to being manipulated and charmed by Sade's cleverness, at other times the stern, punitive arm of God's vengeance on earth. Even when these authority figures behaved in a perfectly professional or neutral way toward Sade, he nevertheless projected one or the other of these two images of authority upon them, and responded to the self-created fictions by adopting the corresponding stance. He could be either charming in an almost boyish, seductive manner, or the tragic hero of a psychodrama, the doomed challenger to authority, ready to face, indeed almost eager, to suffer the inevitable punishment.

Sade's success in charming Commandant du Petit-Thouars had certainly come to the attention of the minister of the King's household, Saint-Florentin, through Marais's report. The same sort of thing may have happened to Commandant de Bory. On August 24, Saint-Florentin wrote him a firm letter, reminding him of his responsibilities and complaining about "the excessive liberty which I am informed you allow your prisoners to enjoy."[37] Although Saint-Florentin gave Renée permission for only a few visits to her husband, she stayed longer at Lyons than had been expected, and the number of her visits increased without further authorization from Paris. Sade could be very charming, and his young, sweet wife must also have had an impact upon the already tender heart of M. de Bory, who broke the rules in order to allow some of the visits to be conducted in complete privacy. Sometime around the end of September, during one of the private visits, Renée became pregnant with the child that would be born on June 27, 1769, Sade's second son, Donatien-Claude-Armand.

The scandal surrounding Sade was dissipating. On November 4, 1768, Saint-Florentin responded to a letter from Sade's mother of the previous day requesting the King to free her son and allow him to go into exile on one of his estates. The speed of the minister's reply and his asking, on behalf of the King, exactly which of Sade's estates was intended, suggested that a favorable response was imminent. On November 5, Saint-Florentin issued new orders to the commandant: Renée could visit as often as she liked. On November 16,

Saint-Florentin conveyed the King's order to set Sade free on condition that he immediately leave Lyons and proceed directly to exile on his estate of La Coste.[38]

Sade made his way down to La Coste to fulfill the King's order. His wife, however, returned to Paris. On January 11, 1769, Sade's father-in-law, M. de Montreuil, wrote to the Abbé to inform him that Renée "has decided to lie in in Paris rather than in Provence."[39] In the same month, Sade, now at La Coste, wrote to invite the Abbé to a ball and a play on February 10 in his new theater, to be performed, he boasted, "by the best actors from the Marseilles troupe."[40] It would appear that Sade had already violated the royal order of exile by traveling down to Marseilles. As impresario, Sade desired a respectable as well as a large audience. Mme de Montreuil would later make fun of Sade for spending so much money to build a fashionable theater in his château and then inviting "the whole province," filling the seats with a very unfashionable audience of farmers and middle-class village officials.[41] Sade was sensitive to this problem from the beginning. He asked his uncle to bring along his houseguest, the Marquis de Rochechouart: "That would produce a marvelous effect—and would raise my credit in the country, rather necessary following all that has happened." Sade also asked his uncle: "Try to get a few girls from L'Isle or Mazan to come along that day. They will find a supper and a ball, and even some beds, if they wish."[42] Sade was twenty-eight years old, but he was almost adolescent in his enthusiasm for his new theater, for new toys, for new provocations.

On April 12 of this same year, an inventory of the contents of Sade's château described the new theater. There were decorations for three stage sets, all of them interesting: first, a public square; second, a salon; and, third, a prison.[43] Sade had taken Jeanne Testard from the street to an interview room in his house, and finally to his locked inner sanctum. He brought Keller from the Place des Victoires to his fancy paneled bedroom at Arcueil, and finally to the dark and locked room below. Taken together, the sets he chose for his theater have an uncanny resemblance to the architecture of his imagination and to the course of his own life.

Although Sade may have appeared carefree and debonair in his retreat at La Coste, someone in Paris was then making up her mind to become his most implacable foe. Ever since Sade's release and his return to La Coste, Mme de Montreuil had been corresponding with him in an effort to get an accurate account of his wrecked finances. It was her view that all of his debts should be consolidated and paid off by means of a loan at the lower interest rate then available. But Sade prevaricated. In January 1769, he had sent her phony accounts, written up, according to Mme de Montreuil, "by his secretary (an apprentice actor, they say, who, for this reason, has a strong need to please him)."[44] This opinion and the following information come from an extremely long and detailed letter of March 2, 1769, in which Mme de Montreuil gave the Abbé her analysis of Sade's financial situation and what should be done about it. She evidently had some source of information about what was going on at La Coste other than the Abbé, who had not written to her for some time. Perhaps she had already suborned François-Elzéar Fage, one of Sade's lawyers. According to Mme de Montreuil's own calculations, at the time of the Arcueil affair Sade had "foolishly" spent around 16,000 livres "on his *petites maisons*, on his mistresses, on his maintenance, debts that he carefully kept hidden from me, always saying that he owed nothing, that he paid for everything in cash." She found Sade's debts considerable. Moreover, she noted that during the previous year Renée had sent 1,200 livres of her own money to Sade's mother, "who could not and would not wait longer, herself hounded by creditors." Sade's neglect of his mother's semiannual pension prompted Mme de Montreuil to complain, "Every six months it is the same old song." Mme de Montreuil asked the Abbé, "Is this the time to give parties and to waste money on foolish things, at the expense of legitimate debts?" At La Coste, Sade either did not answer her letters, or else replied with "banter" and "irrationalities." Mme de Montreuil claimed that, following Sade's marriage five years earlier, he had wasted 66,000 livres "for his pleasures over and above his income." From what we know about Sade's expenditures on prostitutes and actresses, this figure appears highly improbable.[45] Nevertheless, Mme de Montreuil had changed her mind about her son-in-law, and having done so, she would never change back. She told the Abbé that Sade's continuing and increasing wrongdoing has "forced me to discontinue my correspondence with him." In the end, she told the Abbé, "I abandon him to you, Monsieur. . . . As for me, I give up."[46]

Mme de Montreuil was also disappointed in the Abbé. He had not proved to be as effective or even as concerned as she had wished. He, too, did not answer her letters. Even her own daughter had begun to be rebellious. When Mme de Montreuil was disputing with Sade over the consolidation loan, Renée had gone on her own and "without informing me about it" to consult with a lawyer.[47] Renée had clearly grown as an independent person. Indeed, her mother's treatment of Sade was forcing Renée to become more independent. Mme de Montreuil's anger at Sade, her forceful handling of Rose Keller, her attempts to control Sade and his finances, her rage against his failures to do what she wanted—all of this anger took possession of a great deal of emotional territory within the family and left Renée little space in which to stake out her own anger against her husband. She could have allowed herself to remain swallowed up by her powerful mother. However, if she was to become a person in her own right, there was no place left to go but toward her husband. Renée must also have become aware of the momentous change that was taking place in her mother's attitude toward Sade, a change that made Mme de Montreuil consider some very harsh measures. In the above-mentioned letter to the Abbé, Mme de Montreuil wrote that it would have been better "that he remain for a long time in a secure fort perfectly quiet, out of the reach of temptations or at least beyond the possibility of succumbing to them, and even further reason for urging his wife to separate from him."[48] Mme de Montreuil's talk about breaking the marriage would help to drive her daughter further toward her husband. Renée was beginning to display some of the grit and independence that she would need for the hard years ahead.

On March 4, 1769, only two days after Mme de Montreuil's very long letter to the Abbé concerning Sade's finances, she wrote him a much shorter but even more biting one.[49] She had learned that the Abbé himself had attended one of Sade's plays at La Coste, and she expressed her annoyance thus:

> I hear that he has given a fête, a ball, a play, and all that goes with it, and what actresses! It was doubtless acceptable in itself, since I was assured that you graced it with your approbation and your presence, and this made it quite forgivable in my eyes, considering the person who gave it; but leniency does not have the same effect on every temperament, it can lead him to commit a very grave mistake and to have more serious consequences than he imagines.

Even though Mme de Montreuil tried (unsuccessfully) to soften her contempt and anger at the Abbé's "leniency," she could not resist a harsher comment: "I confess that I would not have been as indulgent as you. I would rather have set fire to the room if I had no other means of preventing it." In conclusion, she said that, even though she had not forced her daughter to stay in Paris, she was nevertheless happy that Renée was not in Provence: "I would be in a continual state of agony to think of her locked up in an isolated château with that sort of mentality."[50]

Sade would soon be reunited with Renée—not at La Coste, but in Paris. Sade's mother had petitioned the King to lift her son's exile to La Coste so that he could return to Paris, ostensibly for medical attention. Sade did suffer from painful hemorrhoids. Mme de Montreuil, however, did not quite credit the report of her son-in-law's illness. Surely there were doctors in Provence—at Avignon or Montpellier, for example—who could treat Sade's problem. She did not favor his return to Paris, where he might succumb once again to the temptations of the demimonde and exert even greater influence over her now rebellious daughter. It galled Mme de Montreuil to realize that the matter had been taken out of her hands. A year after the Arcueil affair, the scandal had died down sufficiently to permit the King to allow Sade's return. On April 2, Saint-Florentin wrote back to Sade's mother giving the King's permission.[51] Mme de Montreuil, however, in a letter to the Abbé on April 17, claimed that the minister's letter had been sent to *her*.[52] Mme de Montreuil had the politician's knack of taking credit for things that she, in fact, opposed.

On April 24, Sade left La Coste for Paris in high spirits. Earlier, he had sent Mme de Montreuil an authorization for 10,000 livres—only "half of what is needed," she informed the Abbé, "but it is always like that," with Sade.[53] As Sade entered the Montreuil mansion on the rue Neuve-du-Luxembourg, he knew he would have to win back his mother-in-law's confidence. This, he believed, would not be difficult, not with a new child on the way. On June 28, 1769, the day after his birth, Donatien-Claude-Armand was baptized in the presence of his godparents, M. de Montreuil and Sade's mother. Sade was also present at the ceremony, but, because of the scandal still tainting his name, there were no noble guests in attendance, as at the baptism of his first son. In a letter to the Abbé on June 29, Mme de Montreuil informed him of the birth and grudgingly admitted that Sade was "performing the functions of a good husband." She wondered, however, if she was again being bamboozled: "Only time will tell if this is a tactic or true affection and dedication."[54] In her next letter to the Abbé, on August 22, Mme de Montreuil once again commented on her son-in-law's charm: "He easily enough writes what one wants to hear." The question was, could he be believed? Following Sade's brief medical leave, he was obliged to return to La Coste. Mme de Montreuil, however, prevented her daughter from accompanying him, having no desire "to expose her to new scandals." She asked the Abbé to try to make Sade see reason, and accept this separation, "because whatever he says, it will not turn out otherwise. One could accomplish by force what it would be much wiser for him to let happen by mutual agreement. And his wife will not have any say in the matter. He must not presume that he can make us tremble with his I WANT."[55] Sade's noble, autocratic manner once had made the Montreuils tremble. Things were different now. They would not get any better.

In the fall of 1769, Sade made a trip to the Low Countries, visiting such cities as Brussels, Rotterdam, Amsterdam, and Utrecht. He recorded his impressions of the trip in seven journal-letters written from various cities from September 25 to October 23. His account of his first stop, Brussels, is typical of the others he would write. He described the town, its notable buildings, its museums, its theater, its mercantile and social life, the exact cost of its best inn. In this first letter, Sade told his imaginary correspondent, "I thought it indispensable to go into all the details."[56] The Dutch people, Sade reported, keep their houses in immaculate condition: "You always find door-mats at the entrances ready for you to wipe your feet, and if you should unfor-tunately enter without this ceremony, they fly into a rage against you." Sade, it would seem, had made this mistake himself. If, as he would say, the life of any narrative is in the details, one can read his accounts of this visit to Hol-land without ever guessing the identity of its famous author, or the purpose of his trip, or even whether he was having a good time. To be sure, he saw Charlemagne's sword at Brussels, visited the tapestry factory there and the natural history room in Prince Charles's palace with its extensive exhibit of fish, praised the beauty of a tree-lined walk from The Hague to the village of Scheveling on the sea, admired the tulip displays of Leyden and Haarlem, was impressed by the windmills near Amsterdam and the dike system between Amsterdam and Utrecht. Sade's style is pedestrian, the commentary trite. There is only one clue that he is the author: he always notes whether each city had a theater. Antwerp, he observed, did not. He reported that the men of this city "have no other pleasure than to go and smoke and drink beer at the cabaret." This provoked Sade into one of the few emotional displays of these letters: "Judge from that, Madame, what a delightful life their wives must lead here!" At Amsterdam, Sade found life "rather somber," the men "phlegmatic," "cold," concerned only with business, and their wives "usually rather ugly and generally sullen." If Sade had tried to impart some of his warmth to these women, his journal records neither the attempt nor his success. Perhaps he was depressed by recent events. Perhaps he was awed by this first attempt to write in a serious genre: a gentleman's travelogue. Much more interesting were the love letters he earlier wrote to Laure de Lauris and Colet—letters that he carefully preserved in the family archives. But the best of his writing—including the best of his letters and novels—would be written in the crucible of prison.

Presumably, Sade returned to Paris following his trip to the Low Coun-tries, but there are no letters or other indications of what his life was like dur-ing the winter of 1769–70. He must have been behaving himself: Inspector Marais recorded no new indiscretions. The spring of 1770 would see a con-certed effort on the part of Mme de Montreuil to get Sade a commission in the army. She had hoped to accomplish this the previous year, to get "permis-sion [for him] to join his regiment on the first of June." As she had written to the Abbé on March 2, 1769, this would be "crucial to his honor, to his reha-bilitation of his public image."[57] Now, in March 1770, Mme de Montreuil tried again to advance her son-in-law's career by petitioning the King to permit Sade to reappear at Court. However, on March 24, Saint-Florentin replied that he did not think it wise to make such a request at this time, because the unfavorable impressions of Sade "are still too fresh to be forgotten." Saint-Florentin said that he would not forward the request, for its certain refusal "would do him [Sade] considerably more harm in his regiment."[58]

On July 1, 1770, Sade was not yet able to join his regiment of Burgundian Cavalry in garrison at Fontenay-le-Comte, near the Atlantic Ocean, in Poitou. When he finally showed up on August 1, he was provoked into an altercation with his superior officer, Major de Malherbe, presiding in the absence of the Comte de Saignes, lieutenant colonel of the regiment. Perhaps Major de Malherbe had been offended by Sade's tarnished reputation. In any case, he prevented Sade from taking up his post. When Sade argued with him, he was put under arrest. Mme de Montreuil wrote at once to the wife of Marc-Antoine-René de Voyer, the Marquis de Paulmy d'Argenson, who supervised Sade's regiment. Mme de Montreuil glossed over her son-in-law's affair at Arcueil as "a troublesome adventure" due to "a lively imagination" and "bad company." According to her, malicious gossip "turned a youthful folly into a serious matter." She even falsely claimed that Sade had received the King's permission to reappear at Court.[59] Despite Mme de Montreuil's attempt, Sade was forced to leave his post. After his departure, it is unclear where he went or what he did for the next six months.[60] On March 13, 1771, Sade was clearly in Paris, and petitioning the secretary of war for a promotion to *mestre de camp* in the cavalry. This honorary title of colonel without pay was conferred by the King. When Sade broke a long silence on March 19 to write to the Abbé about his promotion, he seemed full of boyish enthusiasm about his "exciting news": "The King has just appointed me colonel on my leaving the cavalry, so here I am, as it were, with a foot in the stirrup and certain to make my way." Sade's optimism, however, was extremely short-lived. He vaguely alluded to his mounting financial crisis in his letter to the Abbé: "I must tell you of my eagerness to get rid of my Mas de Cabanes."[61] Far from having put his foot in the stirrup, Sade was obliged by this promotion to give up his place in the Burgundian Cavalry. In effect, he had been promoted up and out, had gone as high as he would get. Moreover, he would hold this title of *mestre de camp* for only a few months. In June, his need for cash to pay his debts would force him to sell his new title for 10,000 livres.

By April 1771, Sade's wife was in her ninth month of pregnancy. On April 17, she gave birth in Paris to Madeleine-Laure, her third child, conceived the previous July, just before Sade went off to join his regiment. That had been a happier time. Renée had some hope for her husband's career and thought she could stand by him, even against her mother's advice. Now, for the first time during a pregnancy, Renée's mother was not beside her. Mme de Montreuil was in the country, at Vallery, with Sade's two boys. She wrote the Abbé from there about the birth on April 27, noting that "indispensable business kept her in the country." She said she was sorry, but added, "Such is her destiny and mine. One must submit to it as to everything that does not depend on us." Mme de Montreuil hoped that her new granddaughter would inherit her own "patience": "I consider this the most requisite virtue for women."62 While she waited for her son-in-law to learn good middle-class values, like prudence and thrift, Mme de Montreuil's patience had been sorely tried.

Even as his third child was coming into the world, Sade was scrambling desperately for money. On April 24, his lawyer Fage wrote to Ripert, his agent at Mazan, about how Sade "constantly informs me of his need for money." There were also continuing construction costs on his estate.63 In May, Sade wrote to Fage of his plans to come to La Coste the following autumn, where he expected to live "with the greatest economy."64 For this purpose, he asked Fage to make sure that his garden was well planted, so that he could enjoy its produce. In the same letter, Sade listed his current debts as 26,000 livres, for which 13,400 livres were absolutely necessary immediately.65 During the same month, Sade wrote to Fage another clear but desperate account of his situation and his needs. He needed the 13,400 livres without fail because an unnamed creditor refused any extension beyond July 1. Sade added, rather piteously, that if he did not get the money, "I am ruined in the eyes of my wife."66 Though Mme de Montreuil had a very comprehensive idea of her son-in-law's financial situation, this knowledge was kept from Renée by both her husband and her mother. It is not clear who Sade's implacable creditor was. Perhaps it was one of his father's creditors, Mme Vigean or Teissier. As late as March 27, 1779, when Sade was imprisoned in Vincennes, his friend Mlle de Rousset wrote to say that Teissier, who had not yet been paid, "has been babbling scandal for an infinite time, and has made the strongest threats."67 When the mysterious loan fell due on July 1, 1771, Sade did not have the money to pay it, nor had Fage been able to arrange a loan against Sade's future income and the proposed sale of the Mas de Cabanes.

Sade's relationship to money and debts is similar to his attitude toward sex. He courted financial as well as sexual disaster. A more prudent man might have managed both spheres of his existence with less risk. But there is something callow, blithe, innocent, boyish in the way, time and again, he pulled his house down upon his own head. For Sade, money, like sex, brought him into a power struggle with others. It provided him with a way of figuring and measuring his own strength and worth in relation to them. Oddly enough, one of Sade's private words for some sort of sex play with his wife was "measuring." Imprisoned in Vincennes, he wrote to his wife in May 1779 to say that he looked forward to her first visit. Their separation, he said, had made him grow "devilishly wild at going so long without *measuring*."[68] Sade used both money and sex to measure his own worth. Both were means by which he challenged limitations, taboos, and figures of authority. It should not be surprising that Sade, who at the age of thirty-one had already twice been imprisoned for sexual indiscretions, was now about to be thrown into a debtor's prison.

Sex and money equally involved Sade in high dramas of intrigue and conspiracy. He and his mother-in-law conspired to keep Renée ignorant of both his financial and his sexual delinquencies. Moreover, just as Sade had pleaded with Lieutenant General of Police Sartine not to tell Renée the true reason for his arrest over the Testard affair, so did he now plead with his own lawyer Fage not to allow Renée to learn of his financial crisis, or else "I'm ruined in the eyes of my wife." Sade did not seem to be aware of or inhibited by the humiliating spectacle he was making of himself before his own employee. In the throes of the frenzied crises that Sade himself created, nothing mattered. He cringed and whined before Fage, tearfully prostrated himself before Sartine, produced a slew of abject apologies for Mme de Montreuil. If he whipped the naked buttocks of Rose Keller as a parody of the Easter Passion, he ended up bareheaded and literally on his knees before the High Court in Paris while a crowd of curious citizens watched and gossiped about his life of sin. Supremacy or humiliation—these were states of excitation that had equal attraction for Sade.

In his libertine sex life and in his management or mismanagement of his finances, Sade allowed to develop—or, rather, himself created—a climate of extreme tension and high drama. If, on three or four occasions, he was caught in his own web of sexual misconduct, we can only assume that there were a great many other events that could have ended equally disastrously. Similarly, his financial condition was never stable, and he never took the steps necessary to make it so. In both spheres of life, Sade enjoyed the thrill, the risk, the challenge of skating on thin ice. The wonder is that he did not fall through it more often. Interestingly, Sade's letters about love and sex and his letters about money are interchangeable in their display of highly dramatic attitudinizing. First he wooed at the feet of actress-courtesans; then, after a time, feeling betrayed, he excoriated them as monsters. During the financial crisis of the summer and fall of 1771, Fage too fell under Sade's whip. Writing to Fage at the beginning of September, Sade complained:

> In God's name, my dear Monsieur Fage, have some regard for my horrible situation, nothing has arrived and I see the time passing. Why are you, then, delaying sending me the 12,000 francs, since you have found them. . . . In the name of all that you hold most dear, hurry. The situation is extremely critical, it is frightful.[69]

Here is the conclusion of another letter to Fage, without date, but clearly from the same time: "In God's name, do not lose a minute, Monsieur, and send me the 12,000 francs at once. You would not believe to what difficulty and to what despair you will reduce me if you waste a minute. Hurry, hurry, I implore you."[70] From a period nearer the end of Sade's life, a time after the Revolution, here are a few excerpts from his letters to Gaspard-François-Xavier Gaufridy, who became his lawyer in 1774:

> Adieu, dear lawyer. In the name of God, some money, some money, some money.[71]

> This is what I am asking you for, *it's money*, this is what I want, *it's money*, this is what I need, *it's money*.[72]

> It is on my knees that I am begging you to permit not a second's delay. . . .[73]

> Adieu, I repeat, gentle and barbarous friend; remember that I am indeed starving to death, remember that you are to some degree the cause of the frightful misfortune in which I find myself. . . .[74]

> Today is Sunday. In going to mass, have you at least asked pardon of God for *tearing me apart*, for *flaying me*, for *torturing me* as you have done for the past three years?[75]

When Sade needed money, he could be quite shameless. The following letter was probably written in the fall of 1771 to an Abbé d'Armand, begging for a loan of 15 louis, of which 5 were needed at once:

> If, in the meantime, it were possible for you to send me five by the bearer, I would be in a situation to await the ten others, and by extri-

cating me from the greatest difficulty, you would do me the greatest service that one can do. Two hours after you are pleased to send me the sum of five louis that I request of you, you will receive my note from me for the said sum payable without fail on the first of January.[76]

It comes as a shock that Sade was now reduced to begging for 3 louis more than he had paid for a night with Jeanne Testard in 1763.

The financial crisis during the summer of 1771 that had spawned so many feverish letters to and from Fage finally ended badly for Sade. He defaulted on the loan payment due on July 1. Sometime during the summer, Sade's unknown creditor had him arrested and imprisoned in Fort-l'Évêque, from which he gained his release on September 1 or 2 after paying 3,000 livres and promising the remainder by October 15. These details were communicated in a letter to Fage on September 9 by Sade's secretary Albaret.[77] Mme de Montreuil may have had a hand in Sade's arrest. Albaret would soon be employed by her, and future events would also prove Fage to be under her influence. Both Albaret and Fage (among 139 other people) were prominent in a list Sade compiled in March 1785 in a letter to his wife: "LIST OF *LA PRÉSIDENTE'S* ALLIES AND OF THOSE PEOPLE WHO HAVE GIVEN HER AID IN ALL THIS, WHETHER BY COUNSEL OR BY ACTIONS OR REVELATIONS CONCERNING ME."[78] When Sade got out of Fort-l'Évêque and learned that Albaret had told Fage that the date for the next promissory note was October 15, Sade exploded and fired him on the spot. Sade described the problem Albaret had created in a letter to Fage soon after the event:

It is with incredible astonishment, Monsieur, that I have learned today that, instead of continuing to press you, my secretary M. Albaret had informed you that I no longer required the money until the middle of October. This fellow made that up out of whole cloth, Monsieur, and he is totally deceived. It is on the first of October, and not the fifteenth, that I need it. This stupid blunder in which I suspect some malice has earned him his discharge, which I have just given him.[79]

Sade, of course, did have enemies, but he was also paranoid and kept lists (as just noted) of real and imagined plots and insults. His state of frenzy can be seen in the following letter to Fage toward the end of September, perilously close to the October deadline for his promissory note: "You are reducing me to absolute despair. And you push me to the point that if, on

September 25, I do not have this money, there will not be any other alternative for me but to blow my brains out."[80] Somehow, it is not clear exactly how, the money was found and sent in time. Perhaps only Mme de Montreuil had a true understanding of Sade's complicated financial situation. For Sade, ignorance or denial was not only bliss: it provided the climate of danger that also prompted him periodically to experience shame, rage, and gratitude.

CHAPTER 6

Fatal Passion

*I*N THE fall of 1771, Sade packed up his family in Paris and began the journey down to La Coste. He brought his children along: his two sons—Louis-Marie, four years old; and Donatien-Claude-Armand, two—as well as his five-month-old daughter, Madeleine-Laure. Their governess, Mlle Langevin, was also in attendance. This would be Renée's first trip to La Coste. Now she would see the new apartment that Sade had prepared for her, as well as the other improvements he had made to the house and grounds. She would also see the new theater that had so much angered her mother. Finally, the seigneur's family would be at home in the château overlooking the village of La Coste and the attractive patchwork of terraced fields. After so much scandal and heartbreak, Renée had reason to hope that her marriage would take root there, as everything else did in that fertile ground.

Unfortunately, this season of happiness would bring forth fruit that would prove bitter, even poisonous. Shortly after the Sades set up house at La Coste, Renée's younger sister, Anne-Prospère de Launay, arrived for a visit. Many mysteries still cloak this important and intriguing person in Sade's life. The winter and spring of 1771–72 would emerge as a paradigm of the various facets of Sade's emotional, mental, artistic, and sexual life. For the first time in his marriage, he was living on his own with his wife and children. He was out from under the watchful eye of his mother-in-law. Here, on his estates in Provence, Sade was the head of his family and the lord of a considerable number of dependents, servants, civil officials, farmers, and others at La Coste, Mazan, and Saumane. He was also about to savor the product of his efforts of the past few years—the inauguration of a drama festival in the theaters he had constructed or refurbished in his houses at La Coste and Mazan. For this purpose, at the end of February, he went down to Marseilles to hire, for 800 livres plus expenses, an acting couple, M. Bourdais and his wife, who would perform in the plays he was to direct from Easter 1772 until the following November.[1] The memory of his debts and of debtors' prison was banished from his mind. This would be a season of delights, of dreams finally come true.

When Anne-Prospère de Launay arrived at La Coste, she was a month or two away from her twentieth birthday.[2] Renée was thirty and Sade thirty-one. Anne-Prospère had been living a secluded existence in a convent[3] as a *chanoi-nesse*, a resident who had not and probably would not take vows. She was waiting until her family could make a suitable match for her. In May 1763, when Sade married Renée, Anne-Prospère was present at the ceremony. At that time, however, she was not quite eleven and a half years old. A year later, Anne-Prospère, along with other members of her family, acted in plays that Sade put on at the château d'Évry. Afterward, if Sade saw his sister-in-law from time to time in Paris or at the Montreuil country estate at Échauffour, there is no record of their meeting, and no clue to the nature of their relationship before she arrived at La Coste in the fall of 1771.

This was to be a winter of balls, and visits, and plays, and horseback rides or long walks to nearby villages. The Sades had finally come to La Coste, and the Marquis, for one, intended to enjoy himself. Sade had a voracious sweet tooth. A confectioner, Légier, kept an account of the sweets he carried up to the château for the ten months beginning December 1771. This list included almonds and almond paste, white and brown sugar, sugared almonds, candied and jellied quince and kumquats, various cakes, spices, soaps.[4] The bills of another tradesman, a shoemaker named Silvestre from the nearby town of Ménerbes, show that Sade bought a pair of boots for himself, slippers for his wife and Anne-Prospère, and shoes for his sons, his sister-in-law, and his servants Latour, André, and Lefèvre. Renée and Anne-Prospère both chose a rose-colored silk fabric for their footwear.[5] Sade's major expenses, however, went to establishing his two theaters at La Coste and Mazan.

Sade's first production, an original composition, was scheduled for Monday, January 20, 1772, at La Coste. He was having trouble attracting a well-born or even a gentle audience for his performances. On January 15, Sade wrote a personal invitation to M. Girard of Lourmarin, a village about eight miles from La Coste. M. Girard, it seemed, had not responded to an earlier invitation, and now Sade tried to flatter this complete stranger into attending his play. "I very much desire your opinion," he wrote, and added, "Spectators and critics as enlightened as you, Monsieur, are precious."[6] But if Sade could not get the audience he wanted, he would have to deal with the audience he got.

The regular repertory season opened on Sunday, May 3, and performances alternated weekly between Sade's theaters at La Coste and Mazan. At a cost of 70 livres for each performance, Sade had to hire someone to provide refreshments, candles for lighting, stagehands, a hairdresser, and two police officers "to prevent riots."7 When Mme de Montreuil learned about Sade's plays, she was infuriated over their expense and offended by the class of people her son-in-law was entertaining. In a letter to the Abbé on May 29, she complained about Sade's debts and about these new "extravagances." She conceded that there was no harm in putting on plays "within one's own society of equals" (she was recalling the salon theater at her relative's château d'Évry). But it was a consummate folly, she went on, to lower oneself and make a spectacle of oneself before the entire province: "If such a thing has always been his ruling passion, not to say his madness, he is master of his own person and of his actions up to a point, but he ought not, and he definitely will not, contrive to further compromise his wife and his sister-in-law." She vowed to refuse help to Sade in settling his debts: "I am tired of being his dupe; one makes sacrifices for decent and reasonable things, but not to perpetuate extravagances." Then Mme de Montreuil drifted off into a vengeful reverie: "When he has wasted everything, he will send me back his wife and children, to whom he scarcely pays any attention, and whom I will certainly welcome. Then he can go and suffer his fate . . . where misfortune and misery beckon, a fate which will not suit him!"8

If Mme de Montreuil indulged in fantasies of vengeance against Sade, he was often thinking of her as well. One of the main characters of his first extant play, *Le Philosophe soi-disant* (*The Self-Styled Philosopher*), is the pleasure-loving and sexually aggressive La Présidente de Pouval. When Sade invited M. Girard to a comedy of his own composition to be performed at La Coste on January 20, 1772, this was probably the play. The cast of characters includes a pair of young lovers (the coquettish Clarice and her admiring Cléon), and the redoubtable widow La Présidente, who finally wins and dominates the rationalist philosopher Ariste. This performance, put on well before Sade started the regular season on May 3, when he added some professional actors from Marseilles to the troupe, must have relied for its casting on the occupants of La Coste. In all likelihood, Sade played the philosopher, Renée the widow, and Anne-Prospère the frisky coquette. The rationalist and pleasure-phobic philosopher is a man whose rule of life is "to despise softness, to fly from luxury, to do good, to hate evil." Like Sade himself, Ariste professes himself to be without any prejudices or affectations of mind or manners: "I have no prejudices at all, I depend upon no one, I see but few people, I love no one, and I say whatever I think."9 La Présidente also professes herself to be a philosopher of sorts:

ARISTE: You, Madame! and of what school? Stoic, Epicurean?
LA PRÉSIDENTE: Oh! my word, the name makes no difference.
    I have ten thousand écus of income, and I spend them very

pleasantly. I have good wine from Champagne that I drink with my friends. I am in good health. I do what I please, and I live and let live. That's my creed.

ARISTE: That's all very well said, and exactly what Epicurus taught.

LA PRÉSIDENTE: Oh! I can assure you that no one has taught me; all of that comes straight from me. For the past twenty years I have read nothing but my wine list and the menu for my supper!

ARISTE: On this basis, you ought to be the happiest woman in the world!

LA PRÉSIDENTE: Happy, me! I am in need of a husband after my own taste. My Président was an imbecile. He was good only in court; he understood the law, but that's all. I want a man who understands how to love me, who occupies himself with me alone. . . .

ARISTE (more tenderly): You will find a thousand of them, Madame, and . . .

LA PRÉSIDENTE: . . . I know that I am not pretty, but ten thousand écus of income as a wedding present are worth more than the attractions of a Clarice; and although love be rare in this age, one ought to get it for ten thousand écus![10]

In her pragmatism, her realism, her resolve, Sade's portrait of La Présidente bears more than a passing resemblance to the character of his mother-in-law, La Présidente de Montreuil. La Présidente de Pouval and Sade's mother-in-law both derived their titles from their husbands' role as judges. La Présidente de Pouval called her husband a legal dullard who left her unsatisfied and was good for nothing else in life. Mme de Montreuil hardly ever mentioned her husband in any of her letters. Sade almost never mentioned him, and when he did it was almost always with contempt.

In the above scene, Sade gave the victory to La Présidente over Ariste. "Excellent, Madame, excellent!" Sade has Ariste exclaim to La Présidente. "Do you realize that there are few minds like yours? What courage, what strength!"[11] Later in the play, Sade would tip the scales the other way, putting some of his own strong views into the mouth of the philosophical Ariste. In response to La Présidente's admission that she is not pretty, Ariste replies: "So what! Madame, do you not know that ugliness and beauty exist only in the mind? Nothing is beautiful, nothing is ugly in itself. As many men, as many tastes."[12] Sade's most favored rhetorical gambit for challenging rules and authority in general was to search travel literature (a genre which in the eighteenth century was a primitive form of today's comparative ethnography) in order to find remote laws, customs, and mores that were not only different from, but in direct opposition to, those of France and those of the Ten Commandments. Sade would come to wield the weapon of cultural relativism with indiscriminate violence, seeking to ridicule all rules as codifications of localized prejudice; his goal was to shatter the very idea of authority: "As many men, as many tastes." In *Le Philosophe soi-disant*, La Présidente de Pouval teases Ariste to apply his philosophy to a list of her own physical faults, beginning with her plumpness. This is his answer: "Ah! Madame, plumpness, which is an excess with us, is a beauty in Asia." To her complaint about her long nose, he tells her to examine the busts of antiquity:

LA PRÉSIDENTE: At least they do not have this wide mouth and these thick lips.

ARISTE: Thick lips, Madame, are the main attraction of African beauties; they are like two cushions where sweet and voluptuous pleasures lie. As to a rather wide mouth, I know of nothing that gives more openness and gaiety to the face.

LA PRÉSIDENTE: That is true, as long as the teeth are good, but unfortunately . . .

ARISTE: Go to Siam: good-looking teeth are for the lower class, and it is considered a disgrace to have them. Everything that is called beauty depends upon the caprices of human tastes, and the only real beauty is whatever charms us.[13]

The action of this entertaining little comedy is to make a mockery of the philosophical Ariste's rationality, as well as his pride in his virtue. In the end, succumbing to La Présidente's income and her supposed charms, Ariste declares his love for her, only to be humiliated. Even though the play makes fun of both Ariste and La Présidente, some of their characteristics survive the ridicule: La Présidente's pragmatic materialism and Ariste's polemical demolition of conventional cultural values. These are distinguishing aspects of Sade's own mentality. It is interesting that he divided the two strains of his own personality and way of thinking equally between the two antagonists of his play. The weakness of his own core personality required an antagonist to give energy and meaning to his thoughts and feelings.

The final scene is chillingly reminiscent of Sade's penchant for winning symbolic but Pyrrhic victories. After succumbing to La Présidente, Ariste embraces her while she slips a rose-colored ribbon around his neck and parades him in humiliation about the stage. This detail reminds one of the color-coded ribbons worn by the young sex slaves of *Les Cent Vingt Journées de Sodome.* As Ariste begs for mercy from "this state of debasement," from this "humiliation," La Présidente retorts in "triumph": "I want you to consider it an honor to be mine and to bear my chains."[14] Thus, in this very early work by Sade, several tendencies of his mind are evident that would obtain full expression later: his propensity to sexualize power struggles and to find as much satisfaction in humiliation as in victory; his tendency to explode fragments of his soul onto the stage and to arrange these parts of himself, these characters, into argumentative stances, as in La Présidente's pragmatic materialism and Ariste's aggressive idealism. His own weakened core personality disposed Sade to the idea of acting, the idea of trying on and casting off many provisional roles, and he was equally attracted to the idea of directing, of assuming absolute authority over these provisional fragments of himself. His theatrical festival at La Coste and Mazan during the winter and spring of 1772 promised the fulfillment of his deepest wishes.

Sade's pleasures would prove to be expensive. In addition to M. Bourdais and his wife, Sade also hired an orchestra conductor and a troupe of ten other actors and actresses headed by M. Dutilleul and his wife.[15] Sade planned to put on performances from May 3 to October 22, 1772, beginning at La Coste and repeating each play anywhere from four to ten days later at Mazan. He chose safe, bankable works by Voltaire, Diderot, Destouches, Gresset, Saurin, Regnard, Rochon de Chabannes, and others. He may have intended to put on a play of his own, *Le Mariage du siècle,* of which only a plot summary and a few sketchy scenes remain. To this summary, Sade attached two possible casts of characters: one, a wish list of professional actors, including the famous Molé (François-René Molet) of the Comédie-Française; and the other including M. Bourdais of the 1772 company, with Anne-Prospère as the heroine married to Sade himself. He cast Renée in a lesser role.[16] If Sade's casting choices in this play are any indication of his practice in the others, he and the two women in his household were very busy learning and rehearsing their parts. Sade had his hands full keeping his Thespian household in order. Sade's uncle the Abbé wrote Fage about Sade's problems:

I am of your opinion concerning my nephew's passion for plays, which, as you see, is pushed to the extreme, and which would have soon ruined him if it lasted. I have thus far said nothing to him about that, because I recognize the futility of my arguments. But I see with pleasure that the trouble of reconciling the actors with each other and the trouble of their perpetual scheming and dissension, the difficulty of finding money to defray these expenses, the obstacles that constantly come up to stand in the way of satisfying this passion, begin to damp on it, and I am only awaiting an opportune moment to strike the death blow. It would have already been done if his wife were willing to act in concert with me and if she were less kindly disposed toward her husband's capricious fancies.[17]

The Abbé here seemed unusually put off by his nephew's behavior. It was certainly strange for him to offer his personal criticisms about the Sades to their employee Fage. Perhaps the Abbé was jealous of all the fun Sade was having. Perhaps he had noticed the attraction that was developing between Sade and Anne-Prospère, an attraction that would quickly grow into a love affair. This forbidden, incestuous relationship would blight the lives of both lovers when Mme de Montreuil found out about it.

The Abbé himself appears to have been powerfully smitten by Anne-Prospère's charms. There is a fragment of a letter from Anne-Prospère to him. Although the letter is undated, it clearly refers to their relationship and to a period after Anne-Prospère returned to her parents' house in Paris; there she was kept safely out of scandal's way by her mother. Anne-Prospère sounded chastened and unhappy. "You know as well as I," she wrote the Abbé, "that our relatives are often not our best friends." She continued, expressing her envy of the Abbé's "solitude" at Saumane: "Paris bores me; society is tiresome. My only happy moments are those I spend in my apartment, where I retire as often as possible, and where solitary study provides the only diversion from the suffering of my life." After the scandal of her trip to Provence, Anne-Prospère sounded depressed, hopeless, and disillusioned. She also appeared hungry for some "diversion." In her despair, she teased the Abbé about the compliments he had made to her in his letters. "Is it just gallantry?" she asked him. Or "Can I believe you?"[18] When they first met, in the winter of 1771–72, she had been twenty years old and the Abbé sixty-six. He must have replied to her letter questioning his gallantry with more passion than she could cope with. He had to apologize for the warmth of his expression of love. Apparently, she had written to the Abbé to beg, as a favor "upon which my reputation, my honor, and, perhaps, my very life depend," that he renounce his love of her and "replace it with a more tranquil sentiment." "I am fully determined to do whatever you want," the Abbé replied; "the question is whether I can. You want a man of Provence to love like a man of the Auvergne. That is not possible." Here, the Abbé, like Sade, insisted that there was a climatic determinism to the nature of the sex drive. "The movements of the heart," the Abbé explained, depend "on the circulation of the blood, which is beyond our control. The sun incites the blood of a man from Provence; the snow congeals the blood of a man from the Auvergne." The Abbé told Anne-Prospère that he could not change the way he felt: "My feelings for you will remain where they are in my heart, because it is not in my power to weaken them or to make them conform to your view." But he promised not to disturb her peace of mind; he promised to "don an Auvergnian mask over my Provençal friendship." He described what he meant by that:

> I would like to spend my life with you: but I will not see you at all. I burn to go to Clermont: but I will not go. If I heeded the promptings of my heart, I would write to you every day, and my letters would be full of love and warmth: but to please you, my letters, few and far between, will try to coolly imitate the style of the Auvergne. I trust I can flatter myself that, shielded by this mask, your reputation and your life will be protected.
>
> If you should need anything else from me that is in my power, you have only to ask. But if you want me to keep the promise that I am making, take care not to cross the limits that you yourself have drawn. "Ah, my dear uncle, how I love you! ever since I met you, you have never left my mind!" My niece, is that the style of friendship in the Auvergne? I am warning you that I look upon that declaration as an incursion into my province. If you continue in that way, I will no longer be responsible for myself: I will gather up all my warmth, I will melt all your snow, and so loose a torrent that will overwhelm you.
>
> Do you not find it amusing, my dear niece, that I find your letters too passionate and that I am complaining of the immoderation of your love?[19]

The Abbé's letter, explaining away his passion as a consequence of the sunny climate of Provence, sounds very much like Sade's explanation of his own uncontrollable sexual temperament.

When Anne-Prospère de Launay joined the Sades at La Coste in the fall of 1771, her brother-in-law soon won her heart. The beginning of Sade's affair with Anne-Prospère was described by Renée in a *requête*, or petition, that she dictated in 1774 to her lawyer Gaufridy for the Châtelet, the court, in Paris:

> She [Renée] was with the Marquis de Sade, her husband, on his estate of La Coste in Provence; she was joined there by Mlle de Launay, her sister, under the pretext of keeping her company and of enjoying the more tranquil atmosphere there; sharing in her devotion to her

husband and her love for her children, for a long time she enjoyed there that peace that nothing should have disturbed, and the attentions of her husband did not permit her to suspect that a fatal passion would have soon become the source of a series of misfortunes and calamities.[20]

Renée's phrase "fatal passion" perfectly describes and condenses a whole constellation of attitudes in her husband that inevitably, even obsessively, propelled him toward whatever was challenging, extreme, passionate, and forbidden. In defense of her husband, Renée described with some bitterness her sister, Anne-Prospère's arrival upon this scene of domestic bliss. What was Renée trying to imply by describing her sister's visit as made "under the pretext of keeping her company and of enjoying the more tranquil atmosphere" at La Coste? Her sister's visit, she suggested, was not innocent from the beginning; there was some ulterior and previous motive for it. Had Renée reason to suspect her husband and her sister?

On December 1, 1771, Anne-Prospère had been given the task of making an inventory of Sade's linen. At the bottom of the page, Renée had written these cryptic words: *"evil plan frightful frightful."*[21] Perhaps these words refer to her husband's affair with her sister, but it must be noted that they could have been written well after December 1. In her *requête*, Renée testified that she did not suspect this "fatal passion" until after June 1772. Eventually, Renée would know everything about her husband's sexual tastes, come to tolerate his escapades, and help cover them up. Really, she had no choice. If she had not broken with Sade over the Keller affair—something her mother seemed to want at that time and during the financial crisis that followed—then she would have to stick with him now. Possibly, Renée had a row with her mother over going down to La Coste with Sade and their children. After all, Mme de Montreuil had already written to the Abbé, "I would be in a continual state of agony to think of her locked up in an isolated château with that sort of mentality."[22] Yet that is exactly where she allowed Renée to go, and her favorite daughter, Anne-Prospère, soon followed.

This inconsistency in Mme de Montreuil's behavior has prompted one biographer, Jean-Jacques Pauvert, to speculate that the "only conclusion possible" was that Mme de Montreuil and Renée were aware of an earlier intrigue between Sade and Anne-Prospère that had begun sometime between November 1769 and November 1771, and that Mme de Montreuil allowed the three of them to leave for La Coste, where the scandal could be better contained.[23] However, Mme de Montreuil's letter to the Abbé of May 29, 1772, already extensively quoted above (see page 115), reveals her thinking. She was giving her son-in-law room in which to fail, fully expecting that he would ruin himself financially. True, her newly independent-minded daughter Renée would suffer in the process, but she too deserved a lesson, and soon she would come crawling back with her children. Mme de Montreuil's letter betrayed no anxiety about the moral situation of her unmarried daughter, Anne-Prospère. She was concerned only about social disgrace. Her two daughters were being "compromised" in Sade's theatrical productions when he had them appear onstage before the riffraff of the province. It is absurd to imagine that Mme de Montreuil would have tolerated an affair between Sade and Anne-Prospère at La Coste or anywhere else. Her experience of Sade's previous adventures led her to believe that he was attracted to actress-courtesans and common prostitutes. She did not imagine that Anne-Prospère, a *chanoinesse*, was at risk, or that her son-in-law would seduce a member of his own family. In the years to come, her rage against him and her unrelenting determination to have him imprisoned for life are evidence of her shock and her desire for vengeance because of his affair with her younger daughter.

The very things that Mme de Montreuil expected would protect Anne-Prospère—her religious education and her relation to Sade—were especially attractive to him. Sacrilege was an important element in his sex acts with both Jeanne Testard and Rose Keller. Incest was an obsessive feature of his libertine novels. Of countless examples, consider the following description of two perversions in *Les Cent Vingt Journées de Sodome:* "In order to combine incest, adultery, sodomy, and sacrilege, he embuggers his married daughter with a Host";[24] "A devotee of incest, a great lover of sodomy, in order to combine this crime with those of incest, murder, rape, sacrilege, and adultery, has himself embuggered by his son with a Host, rapes his married daughter, and kills his niece."[25] For Sade, perverse sex acts constitute a kind of polemical argument designed to initiate a dialogue with some higher authority. Seducing Mme de Montreuil's favorite daughter can be seen as a perverse way of continuing his subliminal dialogue with his mother-in-law and of enlarging the scope of his ambiguous relationship with her.

Sade could not and would not deny his passions. Indeed, he celebrated them, since they were given to him by Nature. In a poem titled "La Vérité," Sade wrote, "Nothing is sacred," and added,

> Of all things, great and small, Whore Nature is mother,
> And all of us are ever cherished at her breast,
> Monsters and scoundrels as much as the good and just.[26]

In his notes to this poem, he elaborated his argument: "Let us give ourselves indiscriminately to everything our passions suggest, and we will always be happy. . . . Conscience is not the voice of Nature; do not be fooled by it, for it is only the voice of prejudice."[27] In celebrating the primacy of Nature, Sade made a romantic leap back to an era previous to the civilizing and socializing structures of law and religion; previous, in the life of the individual, to the development of conscience. In this primitive place, all man's impulses can be fully felt and freely indulged. This is what Nature's logic intended, according to Sade. Previous to the incest taboo, for example, and the limitations of law and religion, there was such a thing as the "natural" man. "After all, there is no need to prohibit something that no one desires to do, and a thing that is forbidden with the greatest emphasis must be a thing that is desired." This is not Sade, but Freud in *Totem and Taboo*.[28] Like Freud, Sade had a feel for man's nature and for the predicament of a life lived somewhere between the spheres of animals and angels. Again, the center held no attraction for Sade. When he moved to occupy the low ground, his assault was hypothetical: Let us see how low we can get and what arguments we can make to hold on to this tenuous position. Sade occupied rhetorical territory not to colonize and defend it, but to see how it felt and what would happen when he got there. His excursions into the lower depths of human nature were almost experimental, almost hypothetical, almost humorous.

Anne-Prospère certainly knew of Sade's scandalous reputation. Yet she was charmed by him. It was clear to her that her sister loved him despite the troubles he got into. There he was at La Coste, a nobleman on his own land, lordly, witty, amusing, intelligent, curious, charming. And he was particularly interested in her. A month earlier, she had been in her convent. Now she was rehearsing leading-lady parts with Sade the actor, with Sade the director, for a theatrical festival that would be the talk of the district. Sade would later use play-acting as a device for seduction in *L'Union des arts, ou les ruses de l'amour*, a play in which the Comte de Vercueil disguises himself as an actor-director-author in order to woo the lovely Émilie against her father's wishes. Since Émilie will take part in the play, Verceuil says that he will have "a perfect opportunity to speak easily to the dear object of my heart. During the rehearsals, I will describe my love to her, I will express it to her during the performances."[29] His acting advice to Émilie is ironic and self-serving: "During the passionate scenes, always keep before your eyes the person who loves you most in the world."[30] Events at La Coste were to duplicate events in this play. In Sade's theaters at Mazan and La Coste, Anne-Prospère was introduced to a troupe of professional actors and actresses, a class of people whose mores and freedoms were entirely new to her. Suddenly, she was the center of attention.

In February, Sade wrote a note to Ripert, his agent at Mazan, to prepare the house for a visit: "We will arrive at supper, my sister-in-law, myself, a chambermaid, and a valet."[31] While accompanying Sade back and forth between his two houses, his two theaters, Anne-Prospère fell in love with her leading man and director. In a short time, this affair would destroy them both.

CHAPTER 7

Marseilles

*T*HE IDYLLIC spring of 1772 was about to explode under two pressures that Sade could not seem to control: money and perverse sex. In June, both needs would propel him from La Coste to Marseilles. Unlike his other escapades, this would be a trip from which he would never recover.

By the middle of June, Sade's theatrical festival at La Coste and Mazan was well into its second month of operation. His plan was to put on plays through October, and three had already been performed. As Mme de Montreuil had hoped and the Abbé had predicted, Sade was in need of money. In her letter to the Abbé on May 29 (see page 115), she told the Abbé that Sade had asked her to help him settle his debts, 60,000 livres, all due on July 1. The death of Renée's paternal grandmother six months earlier would provide a considerable inheritance for Sade and his wife. But Mme de Montreuil claimed that the money was still unavailable. She would not send it without guarantees, and without knowing exactly on what it would be spent.[1] It was in this same letter that Mme de Montreuil expressed her wish to see Sade ruin himself so that she could reclaim her daughter and grandchildren.

On Saturday, June 20, Sade wrote an angry letter to Fage, his lawyer at Apt, who was having trouble finding the money needed to pay bills and to fulfill Sade's orders: "When I send you an order, I find it very strange that you send it back without any answer and without performing what I ask of you. . . . If it is a question of a bad mood on your part, Monsieur, and if the details of my business are troublesome to you, have the goodness to let me know and do not employ such an unseemly device for informing me of it."[2]

A day or two later, Sade again wrote angrily to Fage, announcing that he was leaving for Marseilles "to get my money there."[3] On June 20, Sade was ten days away from bankruptcy. Moreover, the expenses of his acting troupe had to be paid. Some of the actors were lodged at L'Isle-sur-la Sorgue, and on his way back from Marseilles, Sade would stop there to pay bills of some 250 livres.[4] The actors performed last on Monday, June 22, at La Coste. Sade had almost a week before the next performance, on Monday, June 29, at Mazan, and he intended to combine pleasure with business on his trip to Marseilles.

On the morning of Tuesday, June 23, Sade bade farewell to Renée and Anne-Prospère and took the road to Marseilles, accompanied by his valet, Latour. When they arrived that evening, they put up at the Hôtel des Treize-Cantons. "The view of Marseilles, in the approach, is not striking," wrote the English poet Arthur Young when he stopped there in 1789. However, he added, "the population, if we may judge from the throng in the streets, is very great."[5] Sade, in his novel *La Marquise de Gange*, wrote of Marseilles that there was "no more interesting tableau than that various multitude of individuals from all nations whom commerce roused into the greatest activity." The port was also a scene of pleasure, and Sade observed that there were "numerous concerts at various sites on this magnificent quay, this crowd of the idle curious or of people at their business mingling, thronging together, especially for pleasure, the wild gaiety of this lively and vigorous people." All of this, Sade said, made "the port of Marseilles one of the most striking spectacles in the whole world."[6] The city boasted theaters and, naturally, a red-light district. All of these attractions, especially the last two, would occupy Sade for the next few days.[7]

Sade may have been involved in business on his first full day in Marseilles, but by Thursday, he was ready for amusement. Latour well understood his role as procurer of girls for his master. He knew Sade's tastes, and he knew his way around the red-light district. However, Latour's search on Thursday met with no success. He first tried Jeanne Nicou, age nineteen, a prostitute living on the rue Saint-Ferréol-le-Vieux. When she refused to come to Sade's hotel room, he himself went to see her, and proposed, as she would testify, "to know her from behind." She declined. The next night, Friday, Sade was back, saying that he would like to bring her some anise candies. On this occasion, her friend Catherine Charles, age twenty-three, was present and observed that Sade "asked for several girls to be brought to him, which was refused, and before leaving, he said that tomorrow [Saturday] he wanted to bring them some anise in order to make them fart and to receive the farts in his mouth." Saturday, the day of the orgy, Latour was back, both before and after the orgy, and attempted to arrange a date for Sade with Nicou, but again without success.

On the first day that Latour tried his luck with Jeanne Nicou, he also accosted Marianne Laverne, age eighteen, telling her that "his master had come to this city for the purpose of amusing himself with girls and that he preferred them very young." Latour explained that his master could not visit Laverne that very night because "he was having supper with some actors," but would come the next night, Friday, at eleven o'clock. It is worth noting that on Saturday, between the orgy in the morning and a tryst with another prostitute late at night, Sade treated another actor, Sébastien des Rosières, to supper. Actors, sex, and money—these were the ruling themes of Sade's visit to Marseilles, as they had been for the past eight months at La Coste and Mazan. In fact, it was from Marseilles that Sade had hired his troupe of actors. The suppers Thursday and Saturday provided opportunities to catch up on theater gossip and to boast about the success of his drama festival.

Friday night, although Sade had an appointment at eleven with Laverne, he had earlier visited Nicou to discuss his anise candies. There appeared to be, if not desperation, a certain urgency in Sade's and Latour's efforts to arrange a party. There was not much time left, because Sade would have to leave on Sunday to be at Mazan for Monday's performance. Sade's failure with Nicou was only compounded when, at eleven, Latour called on Laverne and found that she had broken the date and was off on a sailing party. Latour then made a date with a woman living in the same establishment as Laverne, one Marianne (also called Mariannette) Laugier, age twenty. Latour told her that his master would come to see her the following morning, Saturday, "but he wanted to have several girls." Laugier managed the arrangements for the next morning with efficiency. Three of the four prostitutes lived in the same establishment: Laugier, the above-mentioned Laverne, and another, Rose (also called Rosette) Coste, twenty. At eight o'clock on Saturday morning, Latour appeared at Laugier's room to convey his master's objection to visiting her there, "because her house was too much in view." Instead, he proposed that they all meet two hours later at the apartment of another prostitute, Marie (also called Mariette) Borelly, age twenty-three. Her rooms were on the third floor of a house on the rue d'Aubagne.

At ten in the morning, the four prostitutes were waiting as Sade and his valet climbed the stairs and entered the apartment. Latour, a tall man, his face marked by smallpox, was jauntily decked out in a blue-and-yellow-striped sailor's costume, the same one he had worn since his arrival. Had Sade himself chosen this nautical costume for their seaside frolic? Next to his lanky and somewhat comical valet, the much shorter Sade sported a plumed hat, a gray frock-coat with blue lining, and marigold-colored silk pants and vest. An épée hung at his side, a hunting knife at his belt. In his hand was a cane with a gold knob. When he removed his hat, the whores noted that he was rather handsome, full-faced, and blond. The first thing he did was extract a handful of coins from his pocket and ask the girls to guess the amount. They may have thought that the winner would be rewarded with this fistful of change—a game one plays with children, like giving them candy. But just as there was to be an unwelcome surprise in the anise candies Sade would offer them, so now the reward for this guessing game was only the honor of going first. Marianne Laverne won, and the three others were sent into the next room.

When Sade was alone with Laverne and his valet, he locked the door, a simple act in and of itself, but perhaps threatening to the woman with him. He had her lie on the bed with Latour while he whipped her with one hand and masturbated Latour with the other. This ambidextrous, acrobatic simultaneity became a feature of Sade's hyperbolically complicated and truly impossible sex tableaux in his erotic fiction. Next, Sade took from his pocket a gray leather pouch, from this removed a crystal box edged with gold, and offered Marianne Laverne some candy. Eat a lot, he told her; the candies would make her pass wind. She ate seven or eight of them. Have some more, he told her, but she refused. He proposed that either he or "Monsieur le Marquis," as he called Latour, know her from behind, for which he offered a surcharge of 1 louis. This she refused to permit. He then produced a whip that he had brought with him, which had at the tips of its lashes pins stained with blood. He asked her to whip his backside with it. After three strokes, however, her courage failed her. He wanted her to whip him harder, but she refused to continue. He therefore asked her to send out for a broom of brambles. The errand was quickly run by Borelly's servant, Jeanne-Françoise Lemaire, age forty-two. Laverne then gave Sade many strokes with this broom, even as he asked her to do it harder. When Sade was done with Laverne, she retired to the kitchen, complaining of stomach pains. Borelly's servant gave her a glass of water. Later, while each of the other prostitutes took her turn in the room, Laverne felt worse and sent Borelly's servant down to bring back a cup of coffee.

Next in the room was Marie Borelly. Sade had her undress and position herself at the foot of the bed, where he gave her some blows with the broom before asking her to give him a considerable number of blows with it. When this process was completed, he inscribed with his knife on the mantel of the fireplace the number of strokes he had received. Four days later, when the police searched the premises, they found the following numbers carved in the mantel in the following order:

215

179

225

240

If these numbers represent the actual number of strokes Sade received that day, the total came to 859. After being beaten with the broom, and after manually arousing both Borelly and Latour, Sade mounted Borelly from behind on the bed and apparently sodomized her while Latour did the same to him. Borelly added the detail that for this act Sade moistened his fingers and brought them to his backside, and Latour likewise moistened his fingers and brought them to the same spot. Afterward she went into the next room with the others. It was fortunate for her that Sade did not offer her any of the candies.

It was now Rose Coste's turn. Sade had her lie on the bed with Latour, who aroused her while Sade with one hand beat her with the broom, and with the other aroused Latour. Sade offered her a louis to be sodomized by Latour, but she refused. Coste was not offered any of the candies.

Finally, Marianne Laugier's turn came. Sade first aroused her, and then told her that he wanted to whip her, for he still had twenty-five strokes to give. However, when Laugier noticed the bloody pins at the tips of the lashes, she wanted to leave. Sade asked the first of the four prostitutes, Marianne Laverne, to join them. Then he locked Laugier and Laverne in with him and Latour and put the key in his pocket. He offered them both the box of candies: Laverne, who had already been made ill, refused, and Laugier took only a few, but immediately spit them out. Then Sade, whom Latour at this time called "Lafleur," flogged both of them with the broom. Afterward, Sade brought his nose to Laverne's backside. She had been the only one who had eaten any of the candies, and he now asked her whether they had not yet produced the intended effect. Evidently not. He asked Laugier to masturbate Latour, which she refused to do. He had Laverne lie facedown on the bed and made the reluctant Laugier stand by the bed and watch as he whipped Laverne and aroused Latour. Then, as he lay on Laverne's back and presumably sodomized her, he had Latour sodomize him. This act so filled Laugier with horror, she testified, that she could no longer keep to her post as voyeur. Unable to leave through the locked door, she retreated to the window. Her emotions, she said, overwhelmed her, and she burst into tears.

It was over. Sade paid each woman 6 livres, an eighth of what he had paid Jeanne Testard nine years earlier. Before he left, Sade asked them to accompany him later that night on an excursion out to sea, but they refused. As Sade and Latour descended the stairs, they met Borelly's maid on the way up, carrying the cup of coffee for Marianne Laverne. The maid noticed that Latour spoke to his master, telling him to give her something, whereupon Sade opened his purse and gave her a tip. A spectator might have thought that on this occasion the valet had taken some liberty in presuming to instruct his master.

The morning debauch concluded, the day was still young, and Sade looked forward to new pleasures before he would have to leave the next day. Toward evening, he sent Latour out to ask Marianne Laugier once again if she would accompany Sade on a boat trip that night, but she continued to refuse. By nine o'clock, the indefatigable Latour appeared once more at the room of the prostitute Jeanne Nicou, who had rejected all previous advances on Thursday and Friday. Her answer remained the same. However, on the same street, Latour approached another prostitute, Marguerite Coste, age twenty-five, and made arrangements for his master to visit her. Latour left his handkerchief with her as a guarantee of his return and hurried back to Sade's hotel. Sade, meanwhile, was being fitted for clothes by a tailor in his room. At around nine in the evening, he was visited by the actor Sébastien des Rosières, who begged Sade to deliver a letter on his journey home. Sade dismissed the tailor and was having supper with des Rosières when Latour entered and told his master of his successful mission.

Later that night, in Marguerite Coste's room, Sade again drew out his crystal box of candies. She ate a few. When he encouraged her to eat more, she declined. He said he gave them to all the girls, and he pressed her—she would later say that he forced her—to eat all of them. After a time, he asked her if she felt anything happening in her stomach. Then he proposed enjoying her from behind and in several other ways even more offensive to her. In her deposition, she said she had refused these overtures. It is unlikely that she, or the other prostitutes who claimed they had declined, would have incriminated themselves to the police by admitting to sodomy. In a later deposition, Coste denied that Sade had ever proposed sodomy, admitting that she was "poorly informed on this subject."[8] However, she added that Sade "put his tongue to her anus and asked her to fart into his mouth." After he took his pleasure of her in the normal manner, he put 6 livres on the table and left.

This long day was now truly over, and in a very real sense, although he did not yet realize it, so was his life as a free man. If some readers are inclined to say that Sade *ought* to have been behind bars because of the scenes just described, let them consider the fact that flagellation and, to a lesser degree, sodomy were typical of the commerce between prostitutes and their clients in the eighteenth century. The English artist William Hogarth included a whip hanging on the wall above the prostitute's bed in his series illustrating *The Harlot's Progress*. The jurist and sexologist Richard von Krafft-Ebing, among others, noted that flagellation can be a stimulant to erection: "This effect of flagellation is used by weakened debauchees to help their diminished power;

and this perversity—not perversion—is very common."9 So inconsequential was flagellation that it did not form any part of the subsequent criminal indictment against Sade. During the final scene at Borelly's apartment, Sade told Marianne Laugier that he had twenty-five strokes of the broom still to give. He had apparently begun the morning's debauch with a definite number in mind, a magical, ritualistic number, perhaps. If the numbers marked on the mantel are to be believed, Sade received incredibly more than he gave. Since the numbers of strokes he received are not rounded off, they had a significance different from the predetermined number of strokes to be given, representing the actual number of strokes Sade received sufficient to produce the desired erection. Years later, in prison, he would refer to his difficulty in achieving orgasm while masturbating. He wrote to his wife to ask her to consult a physician about his condition. At the age of thirty-two, his reliance upon flagellation in Borelly's apartment suggests some congenital or psychic obstruction to normal sexuality. Sade's dependence upon whipping dates back at least to the Testard affair in 1763. The numbers on the mantel also suggest Sade's unusual degree of curiosity about his own sexuality. In prison he would keep a detailed log of the frequency and quality of his masturbations and emissions.10 In addition to a powerful but problematic sex drive, there seems to have been in Sade an almost scientific objectivity.

On that day in Borelly's apartment, Sade was neither sadistic nor masochistic, in the strict sense of these terms. His goal was neither to inflict nor to receive pain. To be sure, he had frightened two of the prostitutes with the needle-tipped whip that he brought with him, but it was used only perfunctorily and only upon himself. None of the prostitutes complained about being flogged with the broom, nor did any of them remark that the extraordinary number of strokes Sade received caused him either pain or injury—no welts, no blood. The whipping he received appeared necessary to provoke the psychic and physical stimulation sufficient to produce a number of erections. One cannot be certain about the number of his orgasms, or, indeed, whether any occurred. When he had masturbated while whipping Rose Keller, his orgasm was accompanied by loud and frightful cries. The Marseilles prostitutes reported no such phenomenon.

In view of the natural interest in Sade's sexuality raised by reviewing his morning's activity in Borelly's apartment, the reader may wish to examine the relevant details of the "Vanille et Manille" letter that Sade wrote to Renée from Vincennes after seven years of imprisonment. Sade had been using vanilla as a kind of aphrodisiac to promote orgasms. His code word "manille" refers to masturbation, supported by the intromission of dildos in his anus. That is probably what he meant when he wrote, "One good long hour in the morning comprises *five manilles*, artfully calibrated from 6 to 9." In prison, Sade described the dildos he used as measuring from six to nine inches in circumference. He added that "in the evening" he spent "a good half-hour" for three more manilles "in smaller proportions." He regarded this masturbatory activity as "nothing to raise an outcry over." "It causes no inconvenience," he said, and added, "In fact, it does good." Some parts of the letter remain difficult to decipher. However, it is clear that orgasm and ejaculation were problematical and often painful events. He told his wife that he must have "a constitutional defect," and he wished to consult a doctor about it. To illustrate his difficulty better, he used the image of a kind of sexual "arrow" ready to fly from a "bow" that is "taut and well drawn." "I want it to shoot," he said, "but the arrow will not fly." The frustration drove him crazy, gave him "the vapors," an eighteenth-century medical term referring to a state of "nerves" or hypochondria. If this energy was relieved after being too long bottled up, the result was a frightfully painful orgasm, a "seizure" that was "virtually an epileptic fit," involving "convulsions, spasms, as well as cries of pain." It is clear that Sade believed that sexual energy built up in a kind of pressurized hydraulic system that required regular purging for the sake of good mental and physical health. The cause of his seizures, he said, was "*the extreme thickness of the fluid*—as if one wished to force cream through the very narrow neck of a bottle." He believed that, when regular purging did not occur, the pressurized seminal fluid would become thickened, back up, and cause physiological and psychological damage. In attempting to explain his dilemma to his wife, perhaps the most revealing image he chose was the following: "Picture a gun charged with a ball, and such a ball whose nature is to grow larger in proportion to its stay in the gun; if you shoot the gun after a few days, the explosion will be mild; if you allow the ball to grow larger, in being discharged it will burst the gun."[11] Whether sexual energy is an arrow that can never be released from a drawn bow, or whether it is an ever-thickening fluid unable to escape a pressurized hydraulic system, or whether it is an expanding bullet in a gun, sexual energy for Sade is dangerous, explosive, deadly. It is interesting that he looked for his imagery and the source of his sexual problem inside himself. His sexual dilemma is tragic: he is full of poison that must be purged; but it is very difficult to accomplish, requiring special measures, even drugs; if he fails, he will explode. Sade's letter is a remarkably open inquiry into his own sexual nature, which he himself acknowledged was not normal.

The letter confirms that Sade's interest in some of the central features of the Marseilles affair continued throughout his life. The counting of the broom strokes bears a relationship to the pacing and the technique of his masturbations mentioned in the letter. Obsessive masturbation in solitary confinement, although unhealthy, is not uncommon. Sade defended his practice because of the unavailability of a sex partner in prison, and he developed it on the basis of his understanding of his own mental and physical constitution. The numbering of experiences, or sensations, and the establishment of a "regime" suggests that Sade constructed a scientific model derived from his own experimentation.

This letter is also important for understanding the Marseilles affair because of Sade's admission that he used vanilla as an aphrodisiac drug to stimulate regular masturbation. His interest in drugs dated back at least to the Marseilles affair in 1772, and most probably began earlier. The use of cantharides, the so-called Spanish fly, was fairly common in libertine circles. The Duc de Richelieu employed the drug in candies so often that such bonbons came to be known as *pastilles de Richelieu*. In small doses, the drug acts as a sexual stimulant by irritating the urethral canal. In larger doses, it can seriously irritate other internal organs, even causing death. Sade later denied he had drugged the women. On October 26, 1781, he wrote to his wife from Vincennes, "I swear on all that I hold most sacred that there was not anything the least bit harmful in the anise candies of the girls at Marseilles."[12] The police did recover samples of the candy that Borelly's servant swept up from the floor of the room and then threw out the window into the street. Chemical analysis of these candies and of a sample of the vomit of one of the prostitutes revealed nothing unusual. Of course, the chemist was looking for evidence of arsenic poisoning, the original diagnosis of the physician who attended the women. Sade claimed that the women could very likely have fallen ill from tainted food at the supper they had together,[13] and that the prostitute he saw at night, Marguerite Coste, could have been sickened by the "peculiar remedies" of a street doctor who had been called to her bedside.[14] On the other hand, only those prostitutes who ate the candy, Marianne Laverne in the morning and Marguerite Coste at night, fell ill, and their symptoms were consistent with an overdose of cantharides. Sade did not need to drug prostitutes to have sex with him. Indeed, women of better reputation found him attractive and interesting enough on his own. After all, he had just recently succeeded in making his sister-in-law his mistress. It is likely that he was interested in Spanish fly just as he was interested in almost everything that had to do with sex: his primary motivation was curiosity. If he misjudged the dosage he administered, like his earlier misjudgments of the effect he had on Jeanne Testard and Rose Keller, this mistake would prove costly.

Sade also appears to have believed that the drug, or else the anise that flavored it, was a carminative. If the aphrodisiac in his candies excited a person sexually against his or her will, Sade believed that it would also excite a person to pass wind involuntarily. A similar motif was present in his request that Jeanne Testard take an enema. There are countless examples in Sade's libertine writing of individuals perversely savoring the unsavory, sexualizing just about everything and anything—everything, that is, except normal sexual intercourse. For example, on the twenty-fifth day of *Les Cent Vingt Journées de Sodome*, the four libertines receive in their mouths hundreds of farts produced by means of a drug in the food of their sex slaves.[15] There is also an account of a man who required a whore to drink a large quantity of "anise water" and "a large glass of a balsamic liquor," both intended to provoke the passing of wind.[16] This libertine then tells the whore to let fly while he "hermetically glues" his mouth to her anus and swallows every fart "in ecstasy."[17]

There is something inherently humorous in the perversions, something inherently incongruous in the pervert's preference for his particular fetish or his particular sexual object over the normal goals of sexuality. The Marseilles affair reveals something infantile and silly in Sade, his nose buried in Marianne Laverne's buttocks, waiting to savor the perfume of her drug-induced farts. What he awaited was a fart he could swallow; this event is a parody of inspiration, the Divine Afflatus, a secret message from the interior, from the unknown. It is perhaps too early to discuss Sade's philosophy of the sexual perversions; this discussion will be more appropriate with regard to *Les Cent Vingt Journées de Sodome*, written in the Bastille, when Sade had the time to organize his thoughts on the subject. Still, it is worthwhile here to situate the Marseilles affair within the framework of hyperbolic parody that existed in his previous two scandalous affairs. With Jeanne Testard, there was sacrilege, the attack on God's existence, the sexualizing and misuse of God's body in the Eucharist wafer, the preference for sodomy. With the flagellation of Rose Keller on Easter Sunday, there was sacrilege, and a parody and sexualizing of Christ's Passion. And here, in the Marseilles affair, in addition to the religious crime of sodomy (which, whether heterosexual or homosexual, is a parody of procreative intercourse), there is a parody of the Annunciation through the reading of what goes on in a woman's belly by the reports from below and behind. Sade's childish curiosity and fear of what went on inside a woman's belly remained very active during his mature years.

Sade's fear of women is most evident in his belief that his mother-in-law, Mme de Montreuil, was filled with venom. This is a typical passage, from a letter he wrote to his wife on May 21, 1781, from Vincennes: "Like the snake, it seems she wants to spit out all her venom before dying. Come, then, let her at least make haste, the abominable reptile, even were we to be poisoned with all the stinking bile that might still remain in her filthy guts."[18] A few months later, Sade complained that Renée's letters were being "poisoned with your mother's bile,"[19] just as his children's letters to him were "completely poisoned by the black, bilious venom of my vile torturer," Mme de Montreuil.[20] Sade was not speaking metaphorically; he actually believed that he was being poisoned in prison. In various letters to his wife, he accused the commandant of Vincennes, Charles-Joseph de Rougemont, of trying to poison him with drugs.[21] Even after Sade was transferred to the Bastille, he continued to believe that drugs were put in his food. He attributed his very serious and chronic eye inflammation to the treatment prescribed by the prison oculist: powder of cantharides.[22] It is clear, then, that Sade believed that some people, particularly his mother-in-law, can harbor, like snakes, secret reservoirs of poison within their bodies.

It is reasonable to presume that Sade felt that his own insides were dangerous and poisonous, as witnessed by his hydraulic theory of sexual energy and semen, and the need to purge them regularly (even obsessively) in order to avoid dangerous consequences. A psychiatrist would say that Sade's fears about poison were projections of his own poisonous wishes directed at the rectums, bowels, and stomachs of the Marseilles prostitutes. He drugged the candy in order to give the prostitutes severe stomach cramps, from which he hoped to receive literally some inspiration about what goes on inside a woman. Sade's actions at Marseilles represent, or act out, a very young child's curiosity about, and vengeance against, woman's role as child-bearer and child-nurturer. Preferring a woman's rectum to her vagina and womb denies her first role; imagining her and her food to be full of poison and corruption, as evidenced by her farts, denies her second role.

Sade's bisexuality—the mutual understanding evident between him and Latour, indicating that this was not the first time they had behaved in this way—was also a feature of his infantile, anal organization. One might view Sade's behavior as a retreat or regression from genital sexuality, which is the goal of the Oedipal stage of development. Anal intercourse is a more primitive, infantile explanation for where babies come from. It denies the procreative function of a woman's genitals and womb; by ignoring the true state of her genitalia, it avoids facing the horrifying possibility that she may have suffered castration, the Oedipal punishment; and it also denies the difference in the sexes, by presuming that, since both the boy and his mother have anuses, the boy can, as readily as his mother, be loved by his father. The wish to interfere or else take part in the coupling of his parents obtains dramatic representation in Sade's placing himself between Marianne Laverne, whom he was sodomizing, and Latour, who was sodomizing him. The interchangeability of the sexes is mirrored in the interchangeability of identity and class: Laverne testified that Sade called his valet "Monsieur le Marquis" and his valet called Sade "Lafleur." Sade, as the feminine "flower," was being embuggered by the Marquis. This arrangement was similar to the one Sade proposed to perform with Jeanne Testard in 1763: he would put the communion wafer, the body of Christ, up her vagina, where it would be followed by his own penis, which would then presumably embugger Christ. This anal-sadistic fantasy is a parody of the holy family and is a kind of unimmaculate conception. The Virgin Mary becomes a whore, her son fucks her, and he is himself fucked by Sade. *"Avenge yourself,"* Sade had shouted on a similar occasion, inviting God to descend and assume the vengeful, aggressive position at Sade's rear, the position occupied for the moment by Latour. Sade's position in the middle is both aggressive and passive. He mediates powerful forces, but does not become one himself. He is a kind of parenthesis between the mother and the father, identifying with both, communicating between both, commenting on and ridiculing both, but becoming neither. Sade's infantile sexual organization left a similar parenthesis or gap in his character, a void that was never to be overcome, because it could not be filled by a strong sense of his own self. Perhaps more than anyone else before or since, Sade would be driven to know the extremes of human nature at the edges of the gap that was the weakness of his central character.

In addition to his notorious libertine fictions, Sade would write his less famous idealistic novels and plays. If the world was full of poisonous individuals, including himself, it was necessary to imagine someone who was absolutely pure, someone who was free from the corruption of life. It was necessary to imagine the perfect mother. His dream of Petrarch's Laure was, in part, such a vision. Another can be seen in the following passage, written some thirty years after the Marseilles affair, when Sade was incarcerated in the insane asylum at Charenton. He intended the following paragraph for inclusion in a letter to his mistress's young son, Charles Quesnet:

> I often told you, a mother is a friend that Nature gives us but once and whom nothing in the world can compensate us when we have had the misfortune to lose her. We never again find anything that takes her place: the poisonous characteristics of mankind, their knavery, their calumnies, their wickedness, infect us without restraint. We fly to the bosom of a friend, of a wife; but, oh my dear Quesnet, what a difference! We never again experience those unselfish attentions of a mother, that precious love that never wavers in the slightest: in short, oh my dear friend, nevermore to feel such hands![23]

One might dismiss this panegyric as avuncular sentimentality, but two extremes were always in Sade's mind, equally real and valid: the poisonous and the pure.

As an extremist, Sade made a shambles of life. When he left Marseilles to return home on Sunday morning, June 28, 1772, Marianne Laverne and Marguerite Coste, the two prostitutes who had eaten the candies, were ill. Suffering from stomach cramps and vomiting dark bile, Coste required a doctor. Her landlady informed the police. By Tuesday, June 30, an investigation had begun. Marie Borelly's apartment was searched; all four prostitutes were interviewed, as well as others, including the prostitute Jeanne Nicou and the actor des Rosières. As the week progressed, Coste remained ill; Laverne's condition was similar but much less serious. The investigation and the criminal indictment for sodomy and poisoning proceeded very quickly under the direction of the King's prosecutor at Marseilles, M. de Mende, who signed the arrest order on July 4, exactly one week after the orgy in Borelly's apartment. One week later, on the morning of Saturday, July 11, the bailiff for the village of Apt and several police officers arrived at La Coste to arrest Sade and Latour. Sade had received early notice of the brewing scandal and the criminal proceedings going on at Marseilles. When the police arrived at the château, they found his lawyer Fage waiting for them. Fage told them that Sade and Latour had left a week earlier and he did not know where they had gone. The police searched all the rooms and questioned the servants and the neighbors. No one knew anything. In Sade's absence, the bailiff fulfilled his orders by officially seizing all of Sade's property and money.

Sade's continuing failure to appear at court to answer the charges of poisoning and sodomy helped to speed the criminal proceedings against him. Meanwhile, the public at Marseilles and also at Paris were eager to receive details, however exaggerated or false, about the scandal. Bachaumont's *Mémoires secrets* for July 25, 1772, contains the following entry:

It is reported from Marseilles that M. le Comte de Sade, who caused such a scandal in 1768 [the Keller affair], for the deranged atrocities he perpetrated against a girl under the pretext of testing some ointment, has recently provided a spectacle in this city at first rather amusing, but dreadful in its consequences. He had given a ball to which he invited a great many people, and for the dessert he slipped in some chocolate candies so delicious that a great many people devoured them. There was more than enough, so no one went without; but he had them made with Spanish fly. The effect of this medication is well known: it is such that whoever ate them, inflamed by lewd desires, gave themselves over to all the extremes to which the most passionate lust could carry them. The ball degenerated into one of those licentious orgies renowned among the Romans: the most virtuous women were not able to resist the sexual fury that agitated them. It was in this way that M. de Sade seduced his sister-in-law, with whom he has run off, in order to avoid the punishment that he deserves. Several people are dead from the excesses which they indulged in their depraved profligacy, and others remain seriously ill.[24]

This sample stands for many others and indicates the passion for sexual gossip then, as now. It shows that the Keller affair at Arcueil was not forgotten. The Marseilles scandal also aroused interest at Court, the site of the most intense gossip. M. de Saint-Florentin, who, as minister of the King's household, had signed the order to arrest Sade over the Testard affair in 1763, and who had since been named Duc de La Vrillière, wrote from Compiègne on July 15 to the *intendant* of Provence asking why he had not been informed about such a serious matter that was on everyone's lips.[25]

The heat of public opinion worked against Sade. He may also, unwittingly, have made a political enemy of Chancellor Maupeou, who for the past two years had been successfully waging a legal war to gain control of the traditional justice system represented by Sade's father-in-law, the Président de Montreuil. Possibly Maupeou intended to use Sade's scandal to humiliate M. de Montreuil, the honorary presiding judge of the Cour des Aides in Paris. Sade had made himself a symbol of the excesses of the noble class. Maupeou, moreover, was one of the judges involved in the legal process concerning the Rose Keller affair at Arcueil, a process from which Sade had somehow wriggled free. Writing from Vincennes in 1781, Sade would list Maupeou as one of his worst enemies.[26] Chancellor Maupeou may have pushed forward the precipitous and ultimately faulty legal proceedings against Sade at Marseilles—"faulty" because the verdict against Sade would be overturned on appeal in 1778. There was, for example, no evidence of poisoning; the two prostitutes who had become ill withdrew their complaint in the middle of the proceedings; and there was no proper legal foundation for the charge of sodomy. But because of the enmity of Maupeou, and in the feverish climate of opinion during the summer of 1772, Sade was an easy target, almost a willing one.

When Sade and Latour failed to surrender themselves at Marseilles on September 2, the Parlement ruled them in contempt, found them guilty of poisoning and sodomy, and sentenced them to be consigned over to the executioner, conducted to the cathedral, and obliged to "perform honorable penance . . . in their shirts, on their knees, with heads and feet bare, a rope around their necks, each holding in his hands a lit yellow wax candle of one-pound weight." Having begged "forgiveness of God, of the King, and of the Court," the prisoners would be brought to a scaffold erected at the Place Saint-Louis, where Sade would be beheaded and Latour "hanged and strangulated to death, following which the body of the said Lord de Sade and that of the said Latour will be burned and their ashes thrown to the wind."[27] On September 11, this sentence was confirmed by the court of Aix; the next day, it was carried out there by proxy in the absence of Sade and Latour—that is, by means of effigies of the two condemned men, which were burned at the Place des Prêcheurs. This symbolic, bloodless ceremony would have a very practical significance for the absent Sade. The sentence of death by default meant that, unless he surrendered himself to the court within five years, he could afterward be considered legally dead. In the meantime, he had lost his civil rights and had been effectively deprived of his income, his estates, and his position as head of his family. A few months later, on December 18, a family council of elder relatives was held at Avignon. Renée was then entrusted with the administration of her children's education and of their property, and also of her husband's affairs. In a legal sense, the escapade at Marseilles had killed Sade.

Following the Keller affair, Sade had displayed a kind of hapless insouciance. Once again, after the Marseilles affair, he was incapable of facing the crisis he created. He spent part of July in hiding, following the police search of his house on July 11. The full burden of managing this crisis fell on Renée, who had been forced by recent circumstances to become far more effective. Amidst the scandal and the shambles left by her fleeing husband, Renée also had to deal with her discovery at this time of his affair with her sister. Nevertheless, as Renée stated in her *requête*, she "flew to Marseilles with this very sister." At Marseilles, however, she saw that the authorities were prosecuting the case against her husband with "the most excessive haste."[28] Back at La Coste, Renée worked on a plan to quash the legal proceedings, just as she had seen her mother succeed in buying off Rose Keller during the Arcueil affair. By August, Renée's agent in Marseilles, the lawyer M. de Carmis, had managed to persuade Marguerite Coste and Marianne Laverne to withdraw their complaints.[29] Even so, the legal process against Sade continued without abatement. Renée's maneuvers appeared promising, but they required money. On August 1, Fage noted, "The news from Marseilles could not be better. The business looks as good as one could wish," then added, "But money is needed, money! without which nothing can be done."[30] On August 10, Renée wrote to Ripert about her urgent need. A postscript was added to her letter, probably by the Abbé, authorizing Ripert to pay her: "Pay it, since M. de Sade wishes it, and send her her money."[31] By the third week in August, Renée's father arrived at La Coste from Paris. On August 25, he advanced her 3,000 livres.[32] The presence and financial support of M. de Montreuil prompted Fage on September 11 to tell Ripert to try to calm Sade's creditors: "More than ever, efforts are being made to put everything in order. M. de Montreuil has left by coach for Paris for this purpose."[33]

Renée's father's visit to La Coste produced an anecdote that Sade related to his friend Mlle de Rousset nearly ten years after the event. It concerns M. de Montreuil's flirtation or fling with Sade's promiscuous servant woman, Gothon:

> Gothon had, it is claimed, the loveliest . . . The devil take it! what is to be done now? The dictionary has no synonym for this word, and decency prevents me from spelling out all its letters, were there but two. . . . All right, then, yes! in truth, Mademoiselle, it was the loveliest a[ss] that fled down the mountains of Switzerland for more than a century. . . . That was her reputation. M. le Président de Montreuil . . . could not refuse a moment of his free time for the sweet contemplation of that renowned star. This was what established that remarkable reputation that the unfortunate Gothon enjoyed for the rest of her life. And the magistrate whom I named— all the more so since he was a connoisseur in this particular feature, whose taste he had perfected upon the sublime beauties of the capital—was perfectly suited to make a rational evaluation of such an item.[34]

Perhaps it was M. de Montreuil's meditation on Gothon that detained him at La Coste for two weeks and delayed his arrival at Aix until September 7, where the Parlement of Aix quickly ratified the Marseilles court's death sentence against Sade and Latour, which was performed in absentia at Aix on September 12 on the Place des Prêcheurs. M. de Montreuil, it would appear, was ineffective and had no great desire to be otherwise. His journey down from Paris had taken two weeks. Reaching La Coste on August 22, he still could easily have been in Marseilles before the rendering of the verdict there on September 7, the very day he left La Coste for Aix. Evidently the Montreuils—that is, Mme de Montreuil—had decided to allow the criminal proceedings to run their course. The courts and public opinion were against Sade. Mme de Montreuil had concluded that her son-in-law was a failure and that the best she could do was to minimize the damage he could do and to gain as much control as she could over his finances while protecting her daughter's dowry. M. de Montreuil spent more time with Sade's relatives in Provence than with the jurists at Aix. Mme de Montreuil wanted to solidify her relations with Sade's relatives before attempting, a few months later, to place her daughter in control of Sade's finances.

During the summer months of 1772, while Renée was trying to scrape up money for the lawyers who were dealing with the Marseilles prostitutes, Sade was probably in hiding somewhere in Provence. As yet, his affair with Anne-Prospère was known to no one but Renée; it would be discovered only after September, when Sade and Anne-Prospère fled to Italy.[35] If, on his trip to Provence, M. de Montreuil had discovered that Sade had run off with Anne-Prospère, he would not have encouraged Sade's lawyer Fage to believe that the Montreuils would settle their son-in-law's debts. Indeed, when Mme de Montreuil did find out, she made Sade pay with his freedom. Thus, it would appear that Sade's trip to Italy with Anne-Prospère was very brief—perhaps no more than three weeks in September, for she was back at La Coste by October 2. Sade then took up residency in Chambéry, in Savoy, part of the Kingdom of Sardinia, where, according to official records, he arrived on October 27 with his valets Latour and Carteron and an unknown woman who was variously reported as being his wife or his sister-in-law. Whoever this mystery woman was, she was not Anne-Prospère, who by that time was with Renée at the château d'Évry. Brief as Sade's Italian trip with his sister-in-law was, as far as Mme de Montreuil was concerned, he had crossed a line. When, according to Renée's *requête*, Sade imprudently revealed his hiding place to his mother-in-law,[36] Mme de Montreuil successfully petitioned the Duc d'Aiguillon, the French minister of foreign affairs, who on November 17 asked the King of Sardinia's ambassador to Paris, Comte Ferrero de la Marmora, to arrange for the arrest and imprisonment of Sade. This courtesy was granted the French government, and Sade and Latour were arrested on December 8 in a rented house on the outskirts of Chambéry. The next day, Sade was conducted to the mountain fortress of Miolans, about twelve miles to the east, where he would remain for five months.

Why had Sade, who risked arrest for a capital conviction in Marseilles, and who had seduced Mme de Montreuil's favorite daughter, written to ask for her help "against the injustice that was pursuing him"? Was it stupidity? Why had he given Mme de Montreuil his address? Renée said that he was "deluding himself." His delusion, his wish, was to put himself into the competent hands, and to throw himself on the mercy of the Good Mother. He had done something like this before, on at least one stunning occasion.

His fistfight with the Prince de Condé had perhaps been in part a call for attention, but his mother had reacted by sending him away. When Sade seduced Mme de Montreuil's favorite daughter and then revealed his hiding place, he forced his mother-in-law to do the same thing. This was the first time, but it would not be the last, that she sent him to prison.

The evidence for Sade's elopement with his sister-in-law to Italy comes from the correspondence of various Sardinian officials involved in the arrest and imprisonment of Sade. For example, Comte Ferrero de la Marmora reported that "Sade must be a rather bad sort," adding, "I am told that he is in love with his sister-in-law."[37] The Comte could have been "told" this only by the Duc d'Aiguillon, who got it from Mme de Montreuil. Following Sade's arrest at Chambéry, Comte Sallier de la Tour, governor of the Duchy of Savoy, interrogated Albaret, one of Sade's servants, from whom he learned about Sade's "abduction of Mademoiselle de Launay, his sister-in-law, whom he took to Venice and into a part of Italy under the name of his wife, and with the privileges due to that title." The Comte concluded that in Sade they were dealing with "a hardened mind, without religion, without morality, and prepared to go to any extreme."[38] As late as July 1773, the Comte's official correspondence continued to refer to Mme de Montreuil's "very pressing interest" that any papers or letters "not be made public, since," according to Mme de Montreuil, "mention is made of her younger daughter, who had been seduced by the Comte de Sade, her brother-in-law."[39] Mme de Montreuil had been assiduous in acquiring any papers, presumably love letters to and from Anne-Prospère, that Sade might have possessed at the time of his arrest. In particular, Mme de Montreuil demanded "a small box or wooden casket, thought to be red in color, with leather decoration, which also contains some papers."[40] So successful were her efforts that there remains not one letter between Sade and Anne-Prospère that can cast light on the details of their relationship.

In a few short months, Sade, who was supposed to be on his best behavior after the Keller affair, had managed to poison some prostitutes and to seduce his wife's sister. Now he had not just the police and the law courts ranged against him, but an even more implacable force, Mme de Montreuil. Why couldn't he behave? Or, at least, why couldn't he be more careful? To be sure, Sade had countless arguments to justify his sexual tastes and practices. He was made differently from most men. His difficult orgasms and peculiar tastes were constitutional or genetic endowments, and he argued that they could not be changed. Moreover, since they were inspired in him by nature, how could they be unnatural? Besides, he would not change them even if he could: it was an issue of personal pride and also of philosophy. But whenever he practiced his philosophy, he was thrown in prison. Certainly his practices were designed to flout the rules he held in such contempt, the rules to which he felt so superior. When he seduced his sister-in-law, when he frightened Jeanne Testard with sacrilegious talk, when he bullied Rose Keller, when he made the Marseilles prostitutes sick, why didn't he know that he would get into trouble?

It was not simply that Sade lacked a strong connection to reality (although that appears to be true). Part of him sensed that his actions would cause trouble. He designed them to be provocative. If orgasms were problematical for him, so was living. He needed extra excitement to feel that he was alive, both sexually and emotionally. He could not live and function moderately. And so he forced his feelings to an extreme pitch, and the world responded by hitting back very hard. Both the crime and the punishment were equally necessary and meaningful to him, for he had no internal controls. A clue to his character can be found in the way he described the sexualized rifle: it was difficult to make it fire (and that was painful), and then there was a dreadful and painful explosion when it finally did go off. In Sade's metaphor, as in his life, there was no happy medium. His life was always lived in dilemma. Lacking a strong sense of his own self, and lacking the ability to live and find pleasure in the middle range, he forced himself to the extremes of life and thereby provoked the world into forcibly applying limits to his behavior. Lacking internal controls, Sade needed the world to supply some balance, and so he provoked total strangers and family members alike into forcing a state of equilibrium on him. But balance was not a condition that he found natural, and when it was forced upon him from outside, he could not live with it long. In the Bastille, at nearly forty years of age, he wrote, "I have noticed from long experience that it made no difference whether one behaved well or badly, and that it was only those who cause a racket, make a fuss, who get anything."[41] It had begun with his striking the Prince: when he could not get attention for being good or express his rage against his parents, he duly found a lesser target. But even at middle age, he was still trying to determine how to get what he wanted, and he could not think of a better way than the one that had got him into trouble over and over throughout his life. His way was to cause trouble and to provoke punishment. His way made him feel alive and brought him into some relationship (however punishing) with figures of authority whose attention he still required.

Over the years, Sade's provocations had grown more and more extreme. More and more they reflected the confusion at the core of his being and of his sexuality. If the Marseilles affair revealed an almost childlike quest to find out what goes on inside the belly of a woman, Sade's seduction of his sister-in-law would soon reveal what goes on inside the head of a very angry mother-in-law. In every practical sense, his affair with Anne-Prospère was the worst miscalculation he ever made. In another sense, that affair would finally get him what he had been looking for. It goes without saying that he would not be pleased.

CHAPTER 8

In Prison at Miolans

WHEN SADE arrived at Chambéry on October 27, 1772, he immediately set about finding lodgings at an inn, the Pomme d'Or, for himself, using one of his other titles, the "Comte de Mazan," his two valets (Carteron and Latour), and a mystery woman, sometimes identified as his wife, at other times as his sister-in-law, Anne-Prospère. Once settled, he also developed a friendship with a fellow lodger and countryman, M. de Vaulx, who would provide him invaluable and even risky assistance. After a week or so, Sade's female companion departed; at the beginning of November, he rented a country house on the outskirts of Chambéry.

As with his other scandals, Sade thought that, if he could lie low for a time, the Marseilles troubles would be forgotten. He even believed that he could write to Mme de Montreuil for help. A sincere display of contrition and she would fix everything, forgive and forget, just as she had done in the past. He did not know that she was already making arrangements for his arrest.

In his rented house, Sade lived discreetly and quietly. For one thing, he was ill. A doctor had been summoned. When Mme de Montreuil heard about this illness, she was sufficiently concerned to make a particular inquiry in a letter to the Sardinian ambassador to Paris, the Comte de la Marmora. She wanted to know exactly why her son-in-law had been visited by a doctor named Thonin on November 20. "It is a matter of considerable interest to his family," she wrote to the ambassador, "to know for certain where this matter stands."[1] Mme de Montreuil, it would seem, was concerned about a venereal disease—one that might have infected her daughter Anne-Prospère.

By November 28, a month after Sade had arrived in Chambéry, Mme de Montreuil's negotiations for his arrest had been satisfactorily concluded. All that remained was for her to send a trustworthy person to Chambéry to identify Sade.[2] In the meantime, on December 5, orders were issued to arrest the "Comte de Mazan" at once, so as to prevent his escape while they were waiting for a proper identification.[3] On the night of December 8, around nine o'clock, the Comte de la Chavanne, an officer in the army, arrived at Sade's house with two adjutants and a troop of soldiers. Before approaching the door, he took the precaution of having the house surrounded. According to the Comte, Sade appeared "as much astonished as distressed" when placed under arrest. He was in a state of shock. Without a quarrel, he "immediately gave over his weapons, consisting of a pair of pistols and his épée." Except for his valet Latour, Sade was quite alone in the house; there was no female companion. Having left his and Anne-Prospère's baggage at Nice, he had few comforts or possessions, "since but one portemanteau contained all of them." Following Mme de Montreuil's precise instructions, the Comte de la Chavanne searched the house, but found no letters or papers of any consequence. These indignities concluded, he thought it wise to keep Sade guarded in his room by the two adjutants.[4]

The next morning, at seven o'clock, Sade was put into a coach rented by the Comte for the journey to the fortress prison of Miolans, about fifteen miles east of Chambéry. The Comte took the precaution of placing one of his adjutants in the coach and guarding it with four men on horseback. If Sade entertained any hope of escape, the journey to Miolans must have been chilling. This virtually inaccessible medieval castle stood on a rocky outcropping overlooking the Vallée de l'Isère. In the distance, on clear days, there were panoramic views of snow-capped peaks from Mont Blanc to Mont Aiguille. But in bad weather, the clouds descended below the fortress, and Sade could feel as much a prisoner of nature as of man.

The commandant of the fortress of Miolans, Louis de Launay, welcomed Sade upon his arrival and had him sign an oath of obedience. De Launay advised his superior, the Comte de la Tour, that a guard would lock Sade's room each night and sleep outside his door. The cells in the tower of the donjon had been given ironical names. The lowest one, dampened and chilled by the water of the fosse, was called Enfer (The Inferno). Above was Purgatoire, and higher still was Trésor. At the next level up was the apartment for Commandant de Launay. Above him were two cells, Petite Espérance and Grande Espérance. The top floor was called Paradis. Sade was led into the cell called Grande Espérance—Great Expectation.

How a man adapts to imprisonment says a good deal about him. When Sade entered Miolans at the end of 1772, he was thirty-two years old. As it turned out, he would live to seventy-four, a very long time, spending almost twenty-nine years of it in prison. From 1777 until his death in 1814, he lived almost twenty-eight of the thirty-seven years behind bars. Sade's relations with prison guards and officials—and, at a higher level, with the King and with the state—would become as meaningful and important as his personal relationships with his wife, his children, his mother-in-law. Miolans is the first imprisonment of Sade about which there exists a good deal of information, in the form of correspondence of prison officials and letters and petitions written by Sade himself, by his wife, and by his mother-in-law. The record of this experience provides the first glimpse into the dark cells that would become Sade's world for most of the rest of his life.

On December 10, the day after his incarceration, Sade wrote from his cell the first of many letters to the Comte de la Tour, the governor of the Duchy of Savoy at Chambéry. He began with an absurd apology for not having dropped by immediately to introduce himself when he arrived: "The principal purpose of my letter is to ask you to accept my excuses for my negligence in having paid you my respects." Then he thanked the Comte for his many "kindnesses": "my gratitude for them is inexpressible." More flattery: "I am aware of all the honor Your Excellency has at Court, I am equally aware of his honest and sensitive soul, whose highest pleasure is kindness toward the unfortunate." Having thus buttered up the governor, Sade asked for some favors. He wanted his servant Carteron to be able to visit him freely in prison and "to perform on the outside the small errands that are necessary each day." Sade also requested "the free transmission of my letters"—that is, the lifting of the censorship of his correspondence. The most astonishing mixture of flattery and audacity is seen in a request to be set free on his own recognizance in the town of Chambéry. If this favor were granted, Sade promised, "on my word of honor, and I am not accustomed to break this oath, not to leave the town of Chambéry." Is not the word of honor of an officer and a gentleman sufficient among equals? Sade took care to sign the letter with his military rank: "Mestre de Camp de Cavalerie."[5] The tone here is the same one Sade adopted when he wrote to Sartine after his first arrest, over the Testard affair: he is fawning, abject, manipulative. By whatever means, a prisoner seeks every favor, every advantage, no matter how trifling. If one favor is granted, the next, perhaps a bigger one, may come more easily. And who knows which privilege will lead to freedom or to a means of escape?

Sade set to work in his new surroundings. There were letters to be written, protests, petitions. He had to win over the governor and to cow the commandant. He had to curry favor with the prison staff. And for that, he needed money. He had to devise some safe means of communication, so that he could buy help from outside, and that required money as well. He also had to obtain information about Mme de Montreuil's intentions. For this, he was impatiently awaiting the return from Paris of his servant Carteron, whom he had sent off to his mother-in-law and his wife with letters full of complaint.

When Carteron finally returned to Chambéry on December 16, he was interrogated by the Comte de la Tour before being given permission to visit Sade
in a supervised meeting. According to Carteron, the Montreuils "were doing
their best to arrange some accommodation over the unfortunate affair" at
Marseilles,[6] but the news from Paris did nothing to cheer up the prisoner.
Immediately, Sade sent Carteron on another mission, this time to Nice, to
collect the baggage he had left there. For one thing, Sade had few clothes (all
he had, according to the Comte de la Tour's memorandum, was "one rather
shabby surtout,"[7] and it would be a cold winter on the edge of the Alps. For
another, the red box of papers that so much aroused Mme de Montreuil's
interest might prove useful.

Sade's haggling for small advantages continued—especially on the issues
of uncensored mail and of Latour's freedom to run errands in town. In a letter
to the Comte de la Tour on December 28, Sade asked him to tell Commandant de Launay that Latour was not to be constrained. Characterizing de
Launay's treatment of him as "despotism," Sade also complained that the
commandant refused to forward one of Sade's letters to the Comte, and that
de Launay "has persisted in this refusal with a tone and in a manner which my
birth and my military rank scarcely permit me to submit to." By contrast,
Sade professed himself to be "constantly overwhelmed by new kindnesses
from Your Excellency," the Comte. Bad father, good father. And, of course,
after this flattery, Sade would ask a favor of the Comte: he wanted a "certificate" testifying to his good behavior while he had resided at Chambéry.[8] Even
though the Comte reported that Sade did behave like "a man of honor and in
an irreproachable manner," he had to decline writing such a certificate,
because he did not know what Sade "would try to do with it."[9] Sade pretended not to be aware of the rebuff. On December 31, he would remind the
Comte of this never-granted favor, adding fulsome expressions of gratitude:
"Your Excellency is asked to accept all my thanks for the certificate that he did
me the honor to promise me, I beg him not to forget it." The rest of Sade's letter contained further complaints about Commandant de Launay: how he did
not follow the rules, and how he imposed new, even more restrictive orders.[10]

Sade's attempts to inveigle preferential treatment for himself were not
working. Things were in fact getting worse. The new restrictions he complained about were explained by the commandant in a letter to the Comte on
the first day of the new year: "I have had to reclose the door to the donjon, no
longer permitting him to take his exercise in the Bas-Fort,[11] just as I informed
Your Excellency, which deeply upset him, along with two letters that he
received from his mother-in-law and from his wife, laden with reproaches."[12]
The news from home was not good either. In Sade's letter to the Comte on

December 31, there is a puzzling sentence asking the Comte to inform his superiors "that I am thirty-two years old, that I have been married for ten, that I have full possession of my estates, that until this moment I have always promptly paid for whatever I have bought, and that I have no wish to put myself under any conservator."[13] The letters from his wife and mother-in-law that had so infuriated him must have imparted the news that this month the family council had given Renée control over his property and of their children's education. Some of his rage over the matter may have been redirected onto Commandant de Launay, who, Sade thought, was changing the rules of the prison to spite him.

When de Launay denied Sade the use of the Bas-Fort, Sade's reaction was so strong that the commandant was obliged to regard "this gentleman" as "extremely dangerous."[14] A few days later, Sade fell ill, as a consequence, the commandant believed, of his "enormous rage" and his "extreme suffering."[15] On January 13, 1773, Sade had a furious confrontation with de Launay, who described the "scene" in a letter to the Comte de la Tour. The commandant reported that, just as he began to speak with Sade, the prisoner let fly a barrage of "the most atrocious invectives." The commandant, recognizing that his presence would only create "a much greater scene," wisely retired. He offered the following explanation of Sade's antipathy to him:

> The principal reason . . . is that, after having tried to persuade me that in France one was able to pay to rescind lettres de cachet, and thus leave prison, and that I was the sole person who was capable of rendering him this service, but having received from me a strong negative, he presumed to win me over more effectively by having delivered from Chambéry some gifts, wine, coffee, and chocolate, which he had delivered to my kitchen, and which I immediately sent back to him, telling him that I receive presents from no one.[16]

Sade tried to bluff this provincial officer about French law, and to offer him money to buy back the lettre de cachet. Then came the parcel of sweets. Finally, a flood of invectives. Sade's method with the commandant was to run sweet, then sour: first blandishments, then a screaming fit.

Whereas his unpredictable behavior kept the commandant off balance, Sade was uniformly sweet-tempered with the Comte de la Tour, to whom he offered this version of the episode with de Launay:

> Monsieur,
>   Deeply moved by all your kindnesses, I cannot stop expressing all

my gratitude for them, except perhaps to wish that Monsieur de Launay would try to put them into execution; but it is impossible to make
him understand, Monsieur, that he must fulfill the minister's orders,
just as Your Excellency informed him to do, yet he continues, and
therefore contrary to these very orders of the minister, to keep me
closely locked up here. I urgently ask you to restore order here; we
have just had another violent crisis with this commandant, of which
Monsieur Ansart,[17] a witness, could give an account to Your Excellency. I am not accustomed to be spoken to with words like F[ucker]
and B[ugger], and M. de Launay's very indecent way of expressing
himself forced me to answer him somewhat sharply. I ask you, in all
kindness, Monsieur, to put me under the orders of M. le Major,[18] a
man replete with correctness and courtesy; I dare warn you, Monsieur,
that this is the means to avoid any untoward scenes in the future.
If there are some expenses involved in the change, I am prepared to
pay them; but obtain it, I conjure you, and be certain, Monsieur, that
there will always be a real danger in putting a man of honor and of
some education under the orders of M. de Launay.

I am, with respect for Your Excellency, your very humble and very
obedient servant.

The Marquis de Sade.[19]

Sade's explanation of his argument with de Launay is absurd, as is his offer to
pay to be supervised by someone other than the commandant. It was, however, supported by a letter of complaint he managed to have his wife write to
de Launay. "Not only have you not executed the order for leniency that you
received concerning [my husband]," she wrote, "but you are lacking in
respect and in the attentions that are required of you and that are due him."
She concluded by repeating Sade's hollow threat, "I am immediately removing him from under your orders," and she added a threat of her own: "My
family and I are going to give an account of your actions to your ambassador."[20] It would have greatly pleased Sade to see how much bureaucratic ink
was spilled by the Sardinian prison and diplomatic officials over Renée's
letter.[21]

If Sade tried to play the commandant and the Comte de la Tour off each
other, they consciously played a similar game with him, a timeless tactic of
prison officials and policemen: good cop, bad cop. According to Commandant de Launay, it was best to try to keep Sade in a state of dependency and
uncertainty, somewhere "between fear and gratitude."[22] In Paris, Ambassador
Ferrero de la Marmora agreed: "Only by the mixture of kindness and

severity," privileges and punishments, would Sade be brought "to submit" to the prison's regulations.[23] The ambassador assured the Comte that, "without the slightest difficulty and without risk of receiving any reproaches" from the family (that is, from Mme de Montreuil), Commandant de Launay could "withdraw privileges and considerations" from Sade that the commandant "deemed to be harmful, and of which he [Sade] rendered himself unworthy by his caprices and by his petulance."[24]

In this game of jailer and prisoner, it might at first appear that the latter has no power, no advantages whatsoever. But in practice, there is always some negotiation between the two for the prisoner's good behavior. And Sade did have a special advantage over the felons and sociopathic madmen then incarcerated at Miolans. Unlike them, he was a prisoner of state, incarcerated at the pleasure of the King of Sardinia as a courtesy to the French Court. Mme de Montreuil's petition to Sardinian officials and their own correspondence make it clear that Sade was to be accorded special treatment, that he was to be given, as Ambassador de la Marmora put it, "all the considerations due his rank," provided "they are consistent with his security." The family, he added, would like "to soften the lot of this unfortunate gentleman who was deprived of liberty only for his own good."[25] Aware of the special consideration he was to be accorded, Sade used it as a wedge to widen his privileges and his freedom to operate within the prison.

Sade used his own version of the carrot-and-stick approach with the prison officials. On January 13, he savagely berated de Launay over the withdrawal of his exercise privileges in the Bas-Fort. Four days later, he treated him to lunch. But on that very same day, Sade also wrote to the Comte de la Tour to complain that "M. de Launay, more deaf, more blind, and more mute than the Israelites ever were, wishes neither to understand nor to execute the said orders, despite all the explanations of them that he has received from you."[26] A week later, Sade again treated the commandant to lunch.[27] This time, Commandant de Launay, with evident relief, informed the Comte de la Tour that "the Marquis de Sade has become much calmer than during the previous period."[28] Here was the same effortless alternation between imperious unruliness and charm that Sade had practiced since childhood.

Sade's punitive rages and complaints provided a smokescreen for a more important purpose. It had become clear to him that the only way he would get out of this fortress prison would be to escape from it. Mme de Montreuil had proved obdurate, and Sade had no personal influence with the King of Sardinia—or, for that matter, with the King of France. His personal-expense records at Miolans from December 24, 1772, to January 27, 1773, give some indication of his tactics to subvert prison rules and to engineer an escape.

Sade was charged during this period for eight meals (dinner or supper), provided to "a messenger from Chambéry." This messenger, one Joseph Violon,
was later punished with three months in prison and then banishment for his
part in Sade's escape, and for smuggling letters in and out of Miolans. During
the same period and for the following few months, until mid-March, Sade
provided many more meals to Lieutenant Duclos of the garrison of Miolans,
who was also punished in the aftermath of Sade's escape. During the period of
March 7–16, Sade daily supped with Duclos.[29] This pattern of bribery and
fraternization came to the notice of Commandant de Launay and the Comte
de la Tour over what might be called the affair of the watch.

On February 13, 1773, Sade sent a messenger (no doubt Violon) with a letter for the Comte de la Tour in Chambéry, asking for 12 louis d'or from the
money that was presumably being held for Sade. He said he wanted to purchase a watch. The Comte naturally became suspicious about how Sade could
have gained access to a private messenger. He also suspected that the watch
purchase was only a "pretext" for obtaining some ready cash, especially since
the Comte knew that Sade already had a watch when he was arrested. The
messenger admitted upon interrogation that Sade's letter had been conveyed
to him by Lieutenant Duclos, which led the Comte to conclude that "Duclos
is selling his services" and that he might help Sade to escape. The Comte
ordered Commandant de Launay to say nothing about this discovery, but to
observe closely both Sade and Duclos.[30]

Imagine the Comte's surprise when he found out that his letter had never
reached Commandant de Launay. On February 15, Sade wrote the Comte the
following explanation about how the Comte's letter had ended up in Sade's
hands:

> Monsieur,
>   This morning someone came to my room with a letter from Your
> Excellency, presenting it as your response to one that I had the honor
> to write to you the day before yesterday [asking for money to buy the
> watch]. My first impulse had been to read it with alacrity. Imagine my
> astonishment and my despair when I realized that the packet con-
> tained only one letter for me and the other for M. de Launay. I am not
> able to express to Your Excellency how desperate I had been in my
> eagerness to open this letter, without even noticing the address. I am
> not sending it to M. de Launay, feeling quite certain that he would
> accuse me perhaps of motives very far from my way of thinking, and I
> would prefer to return it to Your Excellency, who, treating me with
> more justice, would better understand my actions and would see in

them merely an inadvertent mistake. I have the honor to give my word of honor to Your Excellency that, recognizing from the first line that the letter was not for me, I read no further and I instantly put it back into the packet and sealed it in order to have it sent to you by the first courier, begging you to excuse me and to be fully persuaded that I had done absolutely nothing wrong in this accident, of which I stand ready to give even more complete explanations to Your Excellency if you require. As to the request that I had the honor to make to you, it was based only on the information that came to me that Your Excellency had funds for me. A thousand pardons for having believed it, and my eagerness for that watch is not so great that I cannot wait for it. The one I have belongs to my wife: as they wrote me from Paris that she was going to come, I regarded it as a duty to return it to her at once, and an indulgence to replace it. However, I will postpone this slender indulgence until some money arrives, and I would be in despair to abuse the kind offers that Your Excellency generously gave me in this circumstance. I beg him to please save them for more pressing occasions, and to accept the profound respect with which I have the honor to be Your Excellency's very humble and very obedient servant.[31]

Sade was quite adept at apologizing. Indeed, a part of him felt that he had done nothing wrong.

Although he was quick to implicate "someone," possibly Duclos, for the theft of the letter, Sade would admit years later that he himself had plucked it, unopened, off de Launay's desk.[32] What child would believe that Sade had not read it straight through to the end? He gives himself away in his explanation that the watch really belonged to his wife, a claim that makes sense only in response to the suspicion the Comte expresses well into his letter to de Launay. Of course Sade had read it all, including the proposed tactics for thwarting his escape. Now each side knew what the other was up to, although neither would admit it.

The affair of the watch and the stolen letter prompted a burst of investigative activity by Commandant de Launay, who informed the Comte de la Tour on February 19 that, though he could not discover the name of the messenger, he had learned from his interrogation of Duclos that a letter from Sade had been secretly conveyed to a French gentleman lodging at the Pomme d'Or in Chambéry.[33] Although his identity was not yet known, he would turn out to be the mysterious M. de Vaulx, whom Sade had befriended when he too was a lodger there. But the discovery that "most concerns me," the commandant added, "is that M. Duclos has developed a relationship" with Sade, and "that

the two of them dine together every night."[34] On February 26, the commandant informed the Comte that, during further interrogation, Duclos categori-
cally denied transmitting letters for Sade. But the commandant concluded
that "a very close relationship" existed between Sade and Duclos, and that
there was no point in censoring Sade's mail, since he was able to send and
receive letters secretly anyway.[35]

Sade, in fact, had better information than the prison officials. On February 15, when he wrote that unctuous letter to the Comte de la Tour, he already
knew that his wife was coming to Miolans to visit him. The first news that
the Comte had of this prospect came several days after February 26, when
Ambassador Ferrero de la Marmora, having learned of the trip from Mme de
Montreuil, tried to warn him about it. A few days later, the ambassador again
wrote from Paris, this time to report a conversation he had had with the Duc
d'Aiguillon, the French minister of foreign affairs, who was obviously receiving his information from Mme de Montreuil. The Duc dismissed Renée as "a
woman misinformed and exploited by the influence that her husband, whom
she still loves, unfortunately wields over her mind." If she should turn up in
Savoy, he added, it would be "essential" to "prevent her from seeing him" and
to oblige her politely to return to France.[36]

Renée's not-so-secret trip to Savoy to help her husband escape, or at least
to see him and supply him with money, had been planned through their clandestine correspondence. She would write in care of M. de Vaulx at the
Pomme d'Or in Chambéry; young Violon would carry the mail to Duclos at
Miolans, who would give it to Sade. Violon would have a bite to eat at the
prison canteen before he took the return packet of letters back to the Pomme
d'Or. Renée's trip to Savoy was one of the most curious episodes in Sade's life,
and certainly in the life of his wife. For one thing, although her trip began as a
secret, as soon as she prepared to leave her mother's house in Paris, Mme de
Montreuil became suspicious and alerted the Duc d'Aiguillon. Escorting
Renée on her journey was a servant, Albaret, one of those persons whom Sade
had obsessively singled out over the years for special denunciation.[37] When
Albaret went to work for Mme de Montreuil, he brought with him a very
good understanding of his former master's behavior and way of thinking.

When Renée and Albaret reached Lyons, instead of proceeding south to
La Coste, as she had told her mother she would, she had her coach take the
road east to Chambéry; it arrived at six in the evening on March 6, 1773. Her
comical disguise in male clothing and her other tactics might have fit well
into an Italian opera, but they were to fool no one in Chambéry. Renée and
Albaret stopped for the night at an inn, probably the Pomme d'Or, where, no
doubt, she met with the mysterious facilitator of her secret correspondence,

M. de Vaulx. Renée and Albaret registered as two Frenchmen, the brothers Dumont. It is difficult to imagine Mme de Sade, the mother of three, sporting a frock-coat and britches. The Comte de la Tour himself said that he "would never have suspected that this could possibly be Mme la Marquise de Sade dressed as a man."[38] However, since he had been warned to watch out for her, when the brothers Dumont departed at noon the next day, the Comte, beginning to suspect, questioned the postilion, who said they had stopped at Montmélian because of some illness. That very evening, Albaret was dispatched by Renée from Montmélian to the fortress of Miolans with a letter from her for Commandant de Launay.

Renée's letter was as transparent a lie as her disguise. First, although it was delivered by Albaret on March 7 from Montmélian in Savoy, only nine miles from Miolans, Renée predated it "March 5" and affected to have sent it from Barraux, France, fourteen miles southwest of Miolans. In it, she claimed to have fallen ill with a severe cold on her journey to Provence, and although she had hoped to be able to stop off at Miolans to see her husband, this was no longer possible. Nevertheless, she was worried about her husband's health, and she begged the commandant to allow the bearer of her letter a private interview with her husband, even if only for fifteen minutes. This the commandant refused to do, for it was against his orders. Early the next morning, Monday, March 8, the commandant sent a letter by courier to inform the Comte de la Tour at Chambéry that his suspicions were correct. Renée's disguise and her maneuvers had been exploded, although she did not yet know this.

When Albaret returned from his fruitless visit with the commandant, Renée immediately sent off an angry letter to the Department of Internal Affairs at Turin. She continued to claim that she was on the outskirts of Savoy, on her way to Provence. She said that she was in "despair" over the refusal of visiting privileges, and she threatened to go to see the King of Sardinia to plead her case personally: "He is just. He is great. . . . I would be heard by him." Renée went on to make a very narrow legal argument. She conceded that one king may ask to have one of his subjects arrested by another king. This royal deference she acknowledged was conventional. However, she argued that such a royal prisoner ought merely to be detained, not closely imprisoned: "If your Master owes to mine the detention of my husband, this deference cannot go so far as to prevent him from seeing the friends he has at Chambéry."[39] The elegance of her argument and her style, so different from her usual letters, suggests that, when she stopped at the Pomme d'Or in Chambéry, M. de Vaulx had a letter of instructions from her husband waiting for her there.

On the same day, Renée sent Albaret from Montmélian to Chambéry to deliver a deceptive letter to the Comte de la Tour which she pretended was written at Barraux on March 5, although she actually wrote it at Montmélian on March 8. She claimed that she was ill at Barraux and that it was now "impossible" for her to fulfill her intention of visiting her husband. "I am very anxious for news of him," she told the Comte. "This circumstance and my illness oblige me to ask one of my friends to come to present his respects to you and to ask your permission to see M. de Sade even for a moment in order to discuss his affairs with him."[40] This visit could be the linchpin of Sade's escape plan. Of course, when the Comte de la Tour met with "M. Dumont," or Albaret, and read this letter, he was fully aware of Renée's deception, and he played his role well, asserting that the prisoner was in perfect health, which Mme de Sade could verify by sending a letter. The Comte offered to facilitate its delivery and to obtain a speedy response from Sade.

The next day, Tuesday, March 9, Renée, still dressed in men's clothes at Montmélian, again sent Albaret to the Comte to renew the request for permission to visit the prisoner. He was again refused. He then produced an unsealed letter from Renée to her husband, which the Comte read and, finding nothing amiss, sent on to the fort. As he was leaving, Albaret asked the Comte to arrange for a team of horses at Montmélian for Friday, March 12, when they would return to Lyons.

Albaret's third visit to the Comte at Chambéry occurred on March 10 or 11.[41] This time, the Comte felt that Albaret was trying to play on his sympathy: Mme de Sade, Albaret said, remained far too ill to leave, as planned, on Friday, March 12. Departure had to be postponed until Sunday, March 14, when, in fact, she did leave Montmélian for La Coste. The Comte, somehow managing not to laugh, told Albaret to transmit his regrets over Mme de Sade's poor state of health and to suggest to her that she really ought to get out of that miserable inn where she was lodging.

By this time, it was all too clear that Renée had no hope whatsoever of seeing her husband. But if that was her only goal, why had she adopted the masculine disguise and pretended to be at Barraux in France when she was really in Savoy? As we shall see, it is possible to imagine a plausible escape plan based on the facts that are known, for an escape attempt must have been the only reason for Renée's deceptions.[42]

Except for Lieutenant Duclos, whom Sade had a particular reason to bribe for his help in smuggling letters in and out of the prison, Sade's most frequent companion at dinner and supper was François de Songy, Baron de l'Allée, incarcerated almost a year before Sade, on February 22, 1772, for attempted murder, and considered "a very dangerous man when drinking, disturbs the peace, threatens murder."[43] He would turn out to be Sade's partner and fellow fugitive when the escape was finally accomplished. Over food and wine, their conversation would have come around to one of the Baron's more astonishing exploits. A little more than two years earlier, on the night of December 4, 1770, the Baron masterminded and managed the escape of one of his friends from a prison in Bonneville. He and four friends had paid a visit to the prisoner at eight o'clock, and when it was time to leave, the Baron had the prisoner put on the clothes and wig of one of the visitors. Thus disguised, the prisoner was able to walk out.[44]

Commandant de Launay had learned that Sade "was expecting to leave on the 7th" of March. In fact, Sade had packed his bags, the commandant informed the Comte de la Tour.[45] Did Sade believe that his wife had come bringing orders for his release?[46] Being in secret communication with Renée, he knew that he had no hope at all for a release through his wife's efforts. Perhaps his packed bags had some role in his escape plan. In any case, on the day in question, the brothers Dumont arrived at Montmélian, and one of them (Albaret) went on to Miolans. "One hour before nightfall," the commandant reported, Dumont appeared, "a rather well-dressed man," bearing Mme de Sade's letter from Barraux, and asking for a private interview with the prisoner.[47] Had the private interview been granted, Sade would have attempted the escape plan the Baron de l'Allée had used at Bonneville and put on M. Dumont's fine clothes. With darkness falling to assist his disguise, he would have slipped away while Dumont created a diversion by fulminating over his packed bags and his wife's failure to get him a release.

Renée remained at Montmélian for a week, until March 14. When the escape plan miscarried because of Albaret's inability to obtain a private interview, Sade appeared "even more calm," according to Commandant de Launay. The commandant also informed the Comte de la Tour of another observation: during the previous week, when Renée was staying at Montmélian, he noticed that Lieutenant Duclos left his post early every afternoon. Sure enough, the commandant's inquiries revealed that "last Friday," March 12, Duclos had gone to Montmélian when Mme de Sade was staying there.[48] It would appear that Sade had been in communication with his wife all week long through Duclos. He would have also obtained some ready cash from her. The escape plan that finally succeeded would require money.

Lieutenant Duclos's misconduct was the last straw for Commandant de Launay. On March 17, he sent Duclos to the Comte at Chambéry for disciplinary action.[49] Sade's expense records show that the last of his almost nightly suppers with Duclos took place on March 16. As we shall see, Duclos did more for Sade than smuggle letters and money. He would be instrumental in

Sade's escape plan. Around the same time that Duclos was removed from the fort, another link in Sade's secret mail service, M. de Vaulx, disappeared from his lodgings at the Pomme d'Or. Sade felt the loss, for he now had to rely on the prison's regular and censored mail service.

Finding a way out of Miolans increasingly depended on desperate chicanery. On February 27, Sade wrote to the Comte to complain about Commandant de Launay's "bad treatment" of him and accuse de Launay of breaking prison rules by permitting the prisoners to gamble. Sade confessed that he had himself lost 12 louis playing cards with the Baron de l'Allée, the very sum "that I wrote to ask Your Excellency to please send me using the pretext of a watch." Sade asserted that, during the same card game, the Baron also won 100 louis d'or from Sade's servant Latour. Sade complained that there was something "quite suspicious" in the Baron's unremitting good luck. This charge of cheating, in fact, was a smokescreen to disguise the close relationship developing between the Baron and Sade, and it was also a way to accuse Commandant de Launay of malfeasance. Hoping for a disbursement for the escape fund, Sade asked the Comte "to pay the note for a hundred louis" and to charge it to him. At the same time, Sade also tried to drive a wedge between the Comte and the commandant by asking the Comte "not to compromise me in the information that I have the honor to provide him. That would be to expose me to new scenes with M. de Launay." Incredibly, Sade was asking the Comte to become his fellow conspirator against the commandant, even to the point of concealing Sade's secret means of communication out of Miolans—the Duclos–Violon–de Vaulx connection. Otherwise, Sade asked, "How could I succeed in informing him [the Comte] of matters of this consequence without any risk, unless I had used this circuitous route?"[50] Ever malleable, ever demanding, ever inventive, Sade pursued the most chimerical inspiration with an almost demonic force. Imprisonment somehow aroused and released his imagination, his cunning, his spontaneity.

The gambling story continued. A week after Sade supposedly lost the 12 louis d'or, de Launay complained to the Comte that Sade was urging the Baron to "inform Your Excellency" about the gambling "in order to incriminate me."[51] In fact, Commandant de Launay was quite unnerved by Sade's tactics, his "caprices and insults," which, as the Comte observed, have put de Launay "in constant fear, knowing the subtlety and power of his imagination."[52] On March 19, the gambling plot blew up into an angry, almost theatrical squabble between Sade and the Baron de l'Allée. According to Commandant de Launay's letter to the Comte de la Tour on March 21, the Baron warned a new prisoner, M. de Battines, "that he must not gamble with these Gentlemen [meaning Sade], who, when they lose, run and complain." Having taken offense, Sade burst into the commandant's room "in a towering rage," accusing the Baron of having insulted him. When the Baron reported to the commandant's office, he was informed that his privileges would be curtailed, according to the standing orders of the Comte de la Tour, which specified this punishment at the slightest sign of any disorder. Hearing this, the Baron flew into a frenzy of anger and despair. "He would rather kill himself," he cried, and rushed off to his room. He soon returned in an even greater rage, a knife in his hand and his clothes stained with blood. The Baron had inflicted many bloody (but superficial) wounds on his stomach. The following day, he was still talking about suicide.[53] It is likely that the whole argument between Sade and the Baron had been contrived by them to divert suspicion from their close relationship.

Strangely enough, a week later, Commandant de Launay was happy to report to the Comte de la Tour "that the Marquis de Sade is beginning to become more human, and that he has agreed with me that his writing too much, and his not having wished to submit to his relatives, have retarded his release." Sade's change of heart, his conciliatory attitude, his confession of his errors, about a month before his escape, all had a useful and a calculated impact on the commandant, who added, "I do not even think that he was planning an escape, although I continue the same precautions." The commandant, moreover, felt so sorry for the Baron de l'Allée that he asked M. Collomb de Battines to try to effect a reconciliation between the Baron and Sade.[54]

Sade's new attitude was evident in his letter to the Comte de la Tour on the same day, March 26,[55] in which he attempted to curry sympathy by portraying himself as an officer and, in effect, as an orphan: "I have been a major for several years, Monsieur; I have, to my misfortune, lost my father, because I would not be here if I still had him; my mother is very old and very ill and is quietly ending her days in a convent, not involving herself in anything." Then Sade offered to promise to do whatever was necessary to appease Mme de Montreuil. Alluding to his affair with his sister-in-law, he said that, if the Montreuils "allege as their sole justification the purpose of breaking up an inappropriate and unpleasant intrigue, they are pushing their resentment too far, because I have most truly sworn that I gave it up." And in case they were concerned that Sade would somehow hinder marriage prospects for Anne-Prospère, he would assure them that such a union was something "that I desire perhaps more than they do." He made the following offer: "I am breaking off all relations [with Anne-Prospère]. I am offering to return all the letters, I am swearing not to come within a hundred leagues of Paris for as long as they require."[56] Sade continued this abject tone in his next letter to the Comte, on April 1, warning that "my health is failing every day in the fort" and offering to do "everything" the Montreuils "could wish."[57]

Sade's good behavior, as reported by the commandant, continued into April. By April 15, Sade even wrote to the Comte to announce "the sincere reconciliation between M. le Baron de l'Allée and me," and he earnestly asked for "the favor of permitting M. de l'Allée to dine with me."[58] The commandant confirmed Sade's "very generous" reconciliation with the Baron, noting that Sade would like to wash away any bad feelings by having the privilege of taking his exercise with the Baron, so as to keep him company. In effect, the commandant was giving the two conspirators permission to study the walls and the defenses of the fort close up. They would make good use of this privilege. The commandant was also charmed by Sade's new "trust" in him, and by his gentler attitude: "Every day," the commandant reported, "he gives me new marks of his esteem," and he saw in Sade a new, "calmer temperament."[59]

The new attitude continued and seemed to Commandant de Launay to be the God-sent effects of the Holy Sacrament. He told the Comte how pleased he was that the Baron and Sade were now behaving themselves, and noted that they were considerably improved for having performed "their religious duty" at Easter. Both of them had sworn off wine in favor of water. Moreover, the commandant had finally come around to Sade's view: that he ought to be released on the payment of a fine.[60] But Sade did not wait to see if the commandant's recommendation would have any good effect, nor did he have long to abstain from wine. That very night, on April 30, Sade, his servant Latour, and the Baron made their escape.

Sade's escape plan depended on gaining access to some room other than his own, for his had a small barred window overlooking a very steep drop. In this, his placation of the commandant had been the key. But de Launay's letter to the Comte on May 4 describing the escape[61] would energetically attempt to shift the blame from the commandant to the Comte himself, who gave permission for the liberties that Sade took advantage of to effect his escape. It was the Comte, de Launay pointed out, who had given approval for the Baron and Sade to eat together and take their exercise together. Allowing both prisoners to exercise in the courtyard of the Bas-Fort favored their communication with outside collaborators. This privilege permitted Joseph Violon, who had earlier assisted Sade in the transmission of letters to M. de Vaulx, to obtain a "secret interview" with Sade in which "they agreed upon the place, the means, and the time of the escape."[62] The privilege of eating together was equally crucial:

> They arranged to have their food brought from the canteen [in the Bas-Fort] to the room of Monsieur de Sade, and after informing me that the dishes became cold, that they were poorly served because of

the distance of the canteen from the donjon, I gave them permission
to go to eat at the canteen.

This would be a reasonable request at the Grand Hotel but not at a high-
security prison. Commandant de Launay appeared eager to please his formerly troublesome but newly cooperative prisoner. There were other favors:

> The canteen owner served them in a room in Monsieur Duclos's
> apartment, adjoining the said canteen. And that is why Monsieur
> Duclos, who would have occupied the said apartment, ate, lodged,
> and slept in a small room in the said canteen owner's house, and the
> latter used his [Duclos's] apartment to store the provisions necessary to
> the canteen, and even kept there some silkworms the previous year.
> And it was from this apartment that they made their escape.

All the attention that Sade had given Duclos (including dinners and probably
money) had finally paid off. During Sade's visits before Duclos had been sent
away, Sade might have noticed or else been told by Duclos that recent construction of a window in the toilet of his apartment had left a window larger
than normal, and also without the usual bars. As it turned out, the weakest
place in the entire fort was Duclos's apartment, which the commandant
described as follows:

> It is necessary to know that it consists of two rooms. The first, upon
> entering, leads to the second, in whose corner there is a small cabinet
> serving as a latrine, in which a window was put, a foot and eight inches
> high by a foot and two inches wide,[63] and through which a man could
> easily pass; we made the experiment, following the escape, with a
> heavyset man of the approximate girth of Monsieur de l'Allée, who
> easily passed through it. This window gives out on the back of the fort,
> opposite the mountain, and is only about fourteen and a half feet
> high, so that a man below, raising his arms, can catch by the feet
> another who was descending by the said window.

Violon was the man below. On the day of the escape, Violon, "foreseeing that
he would have to keep watch" that night, stopped at a cabaret in the neighboring town of Saint-Pierre d'Albigny, "and there slept until four o'clock in
the afternoon." Later, he came to the fort and "placed himself beneath the
window," where he assisted Sade, Latour, and the Baron in their escape and
accompanied them as a guide in their flight.[64]

Commandant de Launay continued his account:

These gentlemen, then, on Friday, the night of the 30th of last month, having come to the said canteen owner's around seven o'clock, to have supper, which they did, and for the execution of their plan, having looked to see the place where the canteen owner put the key for that second room which served him as a storeroom, the servant [Latour, Sade's valet], perhaps in going to get something at the canteen, gained possession of that key and took it at a time when they had foreseen that the canteen owner and his staff were eating and when they would have no reason to go into that second room. With that success, they opened the door and went through that window at around eight-thirty, Monsieur de Sade having left his frock-coat and hat on the seat of the latrine beneath the window. It is believed that the above-mentioned time was when they escaped because, the canteen owner having given the order to clear away the table, they were no longer to be found; it was thought that they had retired into their room as was their custom.

When Latour stole the key to the storeroom, he also stopped at Sade's cell and left two letters for the commandant, one from Sade and the other from the Baron. Latour then also lit some candles, a detail of the plan that would delay pursuit for more than five hours. Had the alarm been sounded soon after they escaped at eight-thirty, the prisoners might have been easily caught beneath the walls of the fort. The commandant tried to explain the delay to the Comte:

> You will also tell me, Monsieur, that the custodian Jacquet was sup-posed to lock Monsieur de l'Allée in his cell after supper: it is true, and such are the orders that I gave. But he was deceived, and this is how. It must have happened that the servant Latour came at this time to light the candles in Monsieur de Sade's room, overlooking the donjon, so as to make it seem that they were in their room. Jacquet, on finishing his supper, looked up at Monsieur de Sade's window; he saw light; he thought that they had retired; he did his chores, and afterward climbed up to Monsieur de Sade's room, which he found closed; and having looked through the keyhole and having seen some light, he presumed that they were playing cards together, which they very often did. He had been considerate in not knocking and in allowing them another moment together, because, as he told me, the night before, Monsieur de Sade had cursed him to the devil when he had come to take Monsieur de l'Allée to lock him in.

One never knew what one would find behind Sade's door. Around nine o'clock, rather than open it and face another scolding, the intimidated Jacquet took a nap on his cot outside Sade's cell, where he usually slept, waiting for the card game to break up. On this night, however, he was guarding an empty but well-lit room.

The commandant described his first news of the escape:

> The said Jacquet having thus fallen asleep on his bed, overwhelmed by sleep, he did not awaken again until around three o'clock, when, having gone to look through the keyhole of Monsieur de Sade's room, he still saw the light and he had suspicions concerning their escape; he came to alert me about it. I immediately arose and, having gone to the said room, I found it locked; I had it broken down; I found no one there. I clearly saw two candles that were going out in their two candlesticks; I also saw two letters addressed to me that I have had the honor to send to you.

Then Commandant de Launay waited four hours, until dawn, before sending out a search party, which pursued the escapees toward the French border. Sade and his companions had almost half a day's head start. They also had Violon as a guide, someone who knew the roads and the obstacles in the dark. When the search party finally reached the border, they learned that Sade had passed through the town of Chapareillan at dawn. A mile and a half to the south, safe in France at Barraux, where Mme de Sade had pretended to write her letters, Sade was able to rent a coach to take them farther south, to Grenoble.[65]

Sade stopped long enough at Chapareillan to pen a farewell letter to the Comte de la Tour at Chambéry, thanking him for his kindness and putting the responsibility for the escape on Mme de Montreuil: "The excessive cruelty of a mother-in-law on whom I am in no way dependent, the lies, the equivocations, the deceptions with which I was lulled to sleep for such a long time, are the sole cause of the perilous step that I am taking."[66] The letter that Sade left in his room for Commandant de Launay was a mixture of charm, humor, and bluster. He said that the only thing that could tarnish his joy at escaping was his fear that the commandant would be held responsible. Sade gallantly offered an escapee's testimonial: "If my testimony, however, can carry any weight with your superiors, I beg them to read this, where they see the authentic word of honor that I am giving them that, far from encouraging this escape in any way, your vigilant attention retarded it by several days, and that, in short, I owe it only to my own maneuvers." Sade's practical interest in this letter, however, was to prevent an aggressive pursuit by concocting a fantastical story and a fantastical persona for himself as an armed desperado at the head of a band of armed men "that my wife sent from my estates": "This help consists of fifteen men, on good horses and well armed, who are waiting for me at the foot of the château and who are all determined to sacrifice their lives rather than allow me to be captured again." If he were overtaken, Sade vowed to fight to the death.[67]

Despite Sade's testimonial for Commandant de Launay, and despite the Comte de la Tour's intercession with the Chevalier de Mouroux on behalf of de Launay's "probity, dedication, and zeal,"[68] the commandant was relieved of his command and placed under arrest.

Sade left the Comte de la Tour a list of his possessions at Miolans that he wanted to have back. They included two locked and sealed bags that contained no manuscripts, only clothes. Most of his furnishings had been rented, but the following belonged to him:

A wooden bedstead;
One of the mattresses of the said bed, labeled with my name, the frame and curtains for the said bed;
. . .
On the walls of my room are six maps that I absolutely want to have back;
A water jug and its basin, of white pottery;
A mirror;
A bidet;
A yellow cup and saucer;
A chamber pot;
A glass;
Two small silver candlesticks;
Two silver table settings and a knife, all bearing my coat of arms.
. . .
In addition, they will return my épée and my pistols, which are in the commandant's rooms.
. . .
A quite new blue frock-coat left at the point of the escape . . . and a pair of stockings;
Two little spaniels, one completely black, the other black with white markings, to which I am deeply attached.[69]

One must now revise one's picture of Sade in prison. One must now imagine a cell with furnishings arranged to his taste, with maps (Sade loved maps— there were many at La Coste), with his personal cutlery, etc., and especially with two spaniel puppies waiting for him to awaken in the morning, frisking at his heels on his promenades about the prison grounds. Ten years later, in a more rigorous prison, Vincennes, he asked for and was refused "a small puppy, so that I may have the pleasure of raising it, either *a spaniel* or *a setter;* I want only one or the other of these two breeds."[70]

If Sade was unable to live in the real world, if he could not head his own family without falling into snares that others of his class easily avoided, if he could not keep from infuriating his powerful and vengeful mother-in-law, then this experience of prison would not be his last. During subsequent, more stringent incarcerations, he would conjure with the whole internal world of demons that tormented his soul. In prison he would turn these demons into the stuff of his fiction.

CHAPTER 9

Wolf-Man

O N THE tenth day after his escape from Miolans, Sade had a brief stay at La Coste. On May 10, 1773, his wife wrote to the Comte de la Tour to say that Sade had spent just "twenty-four hours" there and had immediately left "for a place unknown to his persecutors."[1] Sade and his wife agreed to say that he had gone off to Spain. On July 29, in another letter to the Comte, Renée stated that her husband was then in Cádiz.[2] In fact, Sade was in Bordeaux, where he wrote to Mme de Montreuil asking for money so that he could take refuge in Spain. Not surprisingly, she refused.[3] The Comte de la Marmora, who had been the first to inform her of the escape, reported that she "received this news with the most intense distress and disappointment."[4] Sade, with his mixture of taunting insouciance and his need for some sort of relationship with Mme de Montreuil, asked her to help him flee from the arrest order that she herself had instigated, and after she would not help, he managed to complain about it.

Once Sade and Renée had set a false trail directing attention to Spain, Sade actually lived quietly, in effect secretly, at La Coste during the summer and fall of 1773. Not very many men escape from a high-security prison. Sade could now savor the sheer thrill of the memory—going through the thick wall of that mountain fortress, watching its dark bulk recede into the clouds as he scrambled down moonlit roads to France and safety. Now Renée could finally give him the details of her failed rescue attempt. There was much to talk about. Despite Renée's disappointment in her husband's infidelities, the frightening and sometimes offensive nature of his sexual drive, and his legal and financial brinkmanship, and despite, from his point of view, her frumpiness, her cold and devout nature—despite these obstacles, their trials and sufferings through their first ten years of marriage had brought them closer together, and had indeed made of them a couple. In Renée's *requête*, submitted to the Châtelet in 1774, she recalled this as a relatively happy time, a time when she could "forget her past misfortunes" and hope "that her solicitations finally had vanquished her mother's prejudices."[5] But it was also a time of need. In a civic and financial sense, her husband was dead as a consequence of the contempt judgment that followed his failure to appear at the Parlement of Aix after the Marseilles affair. Sade's annual income of 10,000 livres from his post as lieutenant general of Bresse, Bugey, Valromey, and Gex was sequestered for the same reason. There would be no money for Spain, certainly no money to rehire the actors who, not much more than a year earlier, had been performing in his theaters at La Coste and Mazan. Soon, there would not be money to buy firewood.

The marriage had forced Renée, if not to completely renounce, then at least to suspend, her former self. Earlier, and especially when she sold some of her diamonds to finance her stay at Lyons when Sade was imprisoned at Pierre-Encize, Renée had begun to rebel against her mother's views. She had accepted Sade's explanation of the Keller affair, his need to seek pleasure in Marseilles, and, finally, his running off with her own sister. Once she had come to believe that her lot in life was the same as her husband's, and begun to free herself from her mother's domination, she was no longer her mother's daughter. She had become part of the terrifying myth created by her husband—she had become Mme de Sade. Perhaps all Renée had done was change masters. Her mother, of course, noticed the change and complained to the Abbé that Sade was "holding his unfortunate wife captive, forced to be the agent of his vile machinations." Whatever Renée wrote, her mother claimed, "she writes only what he dictates."[6]

Mme de Montreuil was writing letters too. In particular, she was corresponding regularly with Fage, Sade's lawyer and a resident of Apt. With regard to Fage's disloyalty to Sade (or at best his divided loyalties to Sade and now to Mme de Montreuil), it might be said that he was only trying to do what was best for both his clients, but any attempt to embrace those two was bound to fail. By winter, Sade's money problems and Fage's failure to work miracles had aroused Sade's temper. On December 21, 1773, Fage was so nervous that he wrote to Mme de Montreuil enclosing a copy of a threatening letter that Sade had just written to him. Sade wrote that, although he had nothing to eat, he still had a taste for vengeance. He threatened to jump on his horse and come to Apt to give Fage a sample of it.[7] Worse was to come. On December 16, unknown to Sade, Mme de Montreuil had finally obtained an extremely powerful weapon. On this day, the King of France signed orders for Lieutenant General of Police Sartine to have La Coste searched in order to seize all papers there and to imprison Sade under a lettre de cachet at the fortress of Pierre-Encize.[8] In effect, Mme de Montreuil was renewing the old lettre de cachet obtained following the Arcueil affair, when Sade was removed from the normal jurisdiction of the Parlement of Paris and placed under the personal, privileged arrest of the King at Pierre-Encize. This was exactly the sort of situation for which lettres de cachet had been intended.

It is worth noting that lettres de cachet were rarely used for political purposes. By the eighteenth century, they were no longer sought exclusively by noble families. In fact, Arlette Farge and Michel Foucault, in their study of lettres de cachet in eighteenth-century France, were struck by the wide range of classes and types of people petitioning to obtain them.[9] For example, among the seventy-four lettres de cachet signed by the King for 1758, one was granted Charles-Louis Botot, a bookbinder, against his wife, Catherine, who "now lives such a depraved life that there are no words strong enough to express it."[10] During the same year, the wife of Antoine Chevalier, a mason, was granted a lettre de cachet against her husband, who "frequently returns home at all hours of the night completely naked, without hat, without clothes, and even without shoes, which he left as payment at the cabaret."[11] One woman complained that her profligate husband "has even sold my bed."[12] Two-thirds of the petitions for lettres de cachet involved some economic complaint, often related to the moral issues of debauchery or drunkenness.[13] Lettres de cachet had once been a privilege of the nobility. Now they had become a necessity of the middle and even the lower classes.

The lettre de cachet that Mme de Montreuil obtained on December 16, 1773, was not granted in response to any new provocation by Sade. For the past eight months, ever since his escape from Miolans, he had avoided any scandalous behavior, for the most part living quietly with his wife at La Coste. Nevertheless, the contempt judgment and the consequent loss of his civil rights as a result of the Marseilles affair would continue to dog him. Everyone on Sade's side agreed that there were serious legal errors in that judgment and in the charges of poisoning and sodomy. By means of the *requête*, Sade hoped to reverse the judgment. Mme de Montreuil, however, believed that Sade would have to submit to the Parlement of Aix and be imprisoned until the appeal could be successfully brought.

First came the police assault on La Coste during the night of January 6, 1774. No one who had anything to do with it earned glory. Sade's lawyer Fage had already been suborned by Mme de Montreuil, during the latter months of 1773. By the end of December, Fage was extremely anxious about his double role and about Sade's capacity for violence if his treacherous correspondence should become known. Fage fully understood Mme de Montreuil's plans. On December 31, 1773, he wrote to her and tried to stop the police raid on La Coste. He described how quietly and decently Sade was living there, how much Sade appeared to be in love with his wife, and how difficult it would be for police from Paris to get anywhere near La Coste without Sade's being warned by someone.[14] The arrest party, however, was already on the road from Paris, led by Inspector Goupil.[15]

Mme de Montreuil had anticipated the difficulty strangers would face in crossing Sade's estates and assaulting his château. Goupil's expense account[16] lists "the purchase of 2 complete peasant costumes, as agreed with Mme de Montreuil," for a cost of 76 livres 18 sols. Mme de Montreuil had taken a personal, active interest in the planning of the police raid, whose total cost for archers, policemen, and travel expenses, as well as the above peasant costumes, came to an astonishing 8,235 livres 12 sols. This sum was charged to Mme de Montreuil, who passed the cost on to Sade, who ended up paying very handsomely for the police raid on his own house. Among the charges were ten cab rides to and from Mme de Montreuil's house taken by Inspector Goupil "in order to confer about the affair, before and after the trip." There were also charges for three archers to guard Mme de Montreuil's house for six nights. Did she imagine that, if Sade got wind of the raid, he might come to Paris and kill her in her own bed? There were also extra expenses for the troop's detour to the Abbé de Sade's château at Saumane, after which they would go on to Apt to meet with Fage, "on the orders of M. l'Abbé de Sade."[17]

It may appear surprising the Abbé would lend himself to assisting in an assault on Sade's château. The Abbé, however, had grown increasingly distant from his wayward nephew, whose escapades he had earlier regarded as the vagaries of youth, deserving indulgence until the period of heated passions had passed. On August 21, 1774, the Abbé referred to Sade as "a madman."[18] At seventy-two, the Abbé no longer had the patience or the energy to deal with his nephew. Now he and Mme de Montreuil shared much the same view about how to clear Sade after the Marseilles affair and the contempt judgment. The Abbé believed, as he wrote to Gaufridy on December 13, 1775, that "the sentence and the judgment" were "unjust," but that, whatever legal strategy one chose to clear Sade, "there was one indispensable prerequisite: the appearance or the arrest of the condemned individual in order to purge the contempt judgment."[19] Sade would never understand this logic: that his cause was just but he needed to be arrested before he could be cleared. By now, except for his wife he did not have a friend or a relative in Provence—or anywhere else—who would stand by him.

According to his expense accounts, Goupil spent twenty days in the field masterminding the raid.[20] After clattering around the countryside from Saumane to Aix to Apt, five Paris policemen (two in peasant garb!) and a troop of mounted constables from Marseilles finally arrived at sleepy Bonnieux, less than two miles from La Coste. There Goupil set up his command post. He thoughtfully obtained an "iron bar forged in Bonnieux," which would come in handy later.[21] Everything was ready on the night of January 6, 1774. The troop must have made a good deal of noise as they approached the town of La Coste. Perhaps Sade had sent out spies of his own, or one of his farmers might have sounded the alarm. In any case, Sade did receive a warning half an hour before the raid.[22] He immediately slipped out of the château and went into hiding, leaving his wife to deal with the police.

The purpose of this raid, requested by Mme de Montreuil, was twofold: to arrest Sade and to confiscate unspecified "papers." After the raid, Sade wrote to Ripert stating his belief that the search "was performed only in order to remove" Anne-Prospère's letters.[23] When Sade escaped from Miolans, Mme de Montreuil had immediately stepped up her campaign to retrieve all letters that might have been left there, especially Anne-Prospère's. Renée, coached by her husband, joined the contest to see who would get the baggage left at Miolans. She even made a surprise visit to Chambéry on July 27, 1773, to demand (without success) her husband's belongings. In the end, Mme de Montreuil won. The issue of Sade's effects was settled on February 17, 1774, when she wrote to the Comte de la Tour to give him instructions for sending Sade's baggage in care of M. de Bory, commandant of the fortress of Pierre-Encize at Lyons—but she wanted all letters sent to her.[24] Of course, when Mme de Montreuil was planning the January 6 police raid on La Coste, the question of the letters had not yet been settled in her favor. Consequently, her son-in-law's château needed to be searched. At this time, negotiations were being conducted for a possible marriage between Anne-Prospère and the Marquis de Beaumont, the nephew of the Archbishop of Paris. Sade bitterly complained to Ripert that "the family of the Archbishop of Paris" required the raid on La Coste and Sade's arrest "before consenting to grant permission for his nephew . . . to marry" Anne-Prospère.[25] When Renée went to Paris, she learned more about this prospective marriage, as she wrote to Gaufridy in a letter of July 29, 1774: "It is settled that Beaumont and his family agree to the marriage only on condition that he [Sade] will be imprisoned for the rest of his life, and they want the minister's word on that."[26] This marriage never took place. Anne-Prospère would die a spinster.

In her *requête*, Renée stated that "only the gallows would be sufficient from then on to expiate" her mother's "crimes" for arranging the raid on La Coste.[27] Renée's *requête*, as taken down by Gaufridy and no doubt dictated word for word by Sade, gives a horrific picture of the raid:

> This troop arrived at La Coste on the night of January 6, 1774. The ladders were made ready, the walls of the château were scaled; they

enter, with pistol and épée in hand. It is in this condition that the police officer presents himself to the petitioner. The fury aroused by his exertion painted on his face, with the most dreadful profanity on his lips and the most vulgar expressions, he asks her where her husband, M. de Sade, is to be found, that he would have him dead or alive. Who could possibly depict the situation of the petitioner in such a cruel circumstance? She had savagery staring her in the face; horror and terror overwhelm her by turns. . . . She replies that her husband is absent. This word is the signal for the most frightful outburst. The troop divides; one part keeps watch over the approaches to the château, the other sets about rummaging in every nook and cranny, weapons in hand, ready to attack at the least resistance; their tools had been provided in advance; one of the archers, it was evident, carried an iron bar forged at Bonnieux for prizing open doors and furniture.

The fruitlessness of their searches only redoubles their rage; the Marquis de Sade's study is the object of the final scene; they rip down and slash the family pictures; the police officer especially distinguishes himself by the breaking open of the desks and cabinets of this study; he seizes all the papers and all the letters that he could find there. Some of them, at the pleasure of this officer, become the prey of the flames; he separates out others of them which he takes away without giving to the petitioner the least indication what they contained, without leaving the least account of them. . . . However, what is scarcely credible is that several of his troop were overheard to push savagery so far as to blurt out that they each had orders to put three bullets into the Marquis de Sade and afterward to carry his corpse to Mme de Montreuil.[28]

Even though Sade had escaped arrest or death by hiding out, he now sensed how alone he was. He may not have known about the Abbé's role in the raid on La Coste, but Fage's betrayal was evident.

Sade took immediate steps to fire Fage. In February 1774, Renée wrote to Ripert to tell him to report directly to her and not to Fage.[29] It was at this time that Sade entrusted his legal and financial affairs to Gaufridy, whose father had performed the same service for Sade's father. Gaufridy was about the same age as Sade and had been his playmate in his youth. The lawyer would perform an important role in Sade's life for decades to come. However, he, like Fage before him, was unable to avoid the influence of Mme de Montreuil, with whom he too maintained a clandestine correspondence.

Following the raid, Sade remained in hiding near La Coste. In Gaufridy's files, there is an undated letter from Renée urging him to warn her husband "not to return here" and to stay where he was.[30] Toward the end of February, Sade proposed to go to Mazan—not to his own fine house there, but to stay with his steward, Ripert: "I will come to your house at Mazan without fail on the night on Tuesday, March 1, to Wednesday, March 2; I will arrive by the little garden door that you will leave open as you have said and I will spend a whole week with you in hiding." Sade intended to sneak into Ripert's house in the middle of the night, but Renée would arrive openly the next day. Then, Sade continued, "we will urgently ask you that your door be hermetically sealed to everyone." Hiding out with Renée in his steward's house, Sade gave himself a week to make plans for leaving Provence. He intended to leave Mazan as secretly as he had arrived. He instructed Ripert that, on Friday, March 11, at seven o'clock at night, "two mules or horses will be required to carry me in one night to Pont-Saint-Esprit," a town on the Rhône, about thirty miles to the northwest of Mazan.[31]

In May, Sade wrote to Ripert describing his departure. Not only had Sade left secretly and suddenly at night, he had also disguised himself as a priest and worn clerical garb borrowed from Ripert, whose brother was a priest. Sade joked about how eager Ripert was to get the fugitive Sade out of his house: as Sade rode away on horseback, Ripert "slammed the gate so quickly on his behind that you took off his horse's tail, whose hairs you should have found the next day." The real purpose of this letter was to ask Ripert to send money: "You see me devilishly far from home."[32] On March 19, a few days after Sade's departure, Renée wrote to Ripert, returning a hat and a bag (with Sade's clerical costume). She recounted the following amusing anecdote of Sade's journey, suitable for elaboration in a picaresque novel: "M. le Curé has had an excellent journey, according to the coach driver, except that, the rope of the ferry he was on having broken crossing the [river] Durance on the way to board ship at Marseilles, the passengers wanted to make confession."[33] Did Sade, disguised as a priest, accommodate his terrified fellow travelers?

It is not clear where Sade went after leaving Ripert's house at Mazan. He rode in the opposite direction from Marseilles, where Renée later said he had gone.[34] At times, even Renée did not know where her husband was. On September 3, she wrote to Gaufridy from Paris asking if her husband was back in Provence, as she hoped he would be, "rather than living abroad, at considerable expense."[35] But what foreign land he might be in was never mentioned.[36] Given the continuing failure of Sade's finances and the continuing pressure of his creditors, it is unlikely that he had the money to go very far.

Before Sade went into hiding in March 1774, he put the final touches on the *requête* that Renée would take to Paris that summer. In March, Sade wrote a note to Gaufridy asking him to bring the document to La Coste, ready for

Renée's signature.[37] At first, it had seemed like a good idea to appeal directly to Paris and ultimately to the King, thus avoiding the courts at Marseilles and at Aix, which had already proved themselves hasty and legally faulty in their judgments against Sade. The death of Louis XV on May 10 may have also held out some hope that the previous lettre de cachet would fall into a kind of legal limbo. The new King, however, was persuaded to renew the order. Renée's *requête* would fail, for several reasons. Mme de Montreuil was at the seat of power in Paris and had more influential allies than did Sade, a young provincial nobleman without power or friends, a man who had already disgraced himself. If Paris, the ground on which Sade chose to wage this fight, was distant and controlled by his enemies, he also made the terrain more difficult for himself by focusing his petition and all his energy against Mme de Montreuil—as if he thought that the Paris court had any interest in his complaints about his mother-in-law!

Renée left La Coste for Paris on July 14, 1774, armed with her petition—an attack on her mother, against whom Renée was now in complete rebellion, having tied her fate to that of her husband. In Paris, she wrote Gaufridy on July 29 that she was not even staying in her mother's house: "I am staying at the Hôtel de Bourgogne, rue Taranne, Faubourg Saint-Germain." She had already been infected with her husband's suspiciousness, his feeling that he was in combat with great forces often invisible to others. Renée asked Gaufridy to write to her in care of Sade's tailor, Carlier: "Always address your letters in an envelope to Carlier, tailor, rue Saint-Nicaise, in Paris. This man is reliable, and the furnished hotels are not, reporting everything to the police."[38] It was not quite three years since Renée had come to live at La Coste in the autumn of 1771. In the meantime, her whole world had changed, and so had she.

The *requête* that Renée carried to Paris could have and did have no good effects, unless its purpose was to force a complete break between her and her mother. In Renée's letter to Gaufridy on July 29, she mentioned some painful gossip she had just heard: "I was assured that my mother was madly in love with M. de Sade, and that she was much more angry with me than with him. I replied: 'So much the better!' " Renée also reported on the annoying gossip at the Châtelet: "The King's prosecutor . . . goes to the trouble of telling everyone that I am crazy."[39] By September 3, when she wrote to Gaufridy again, she felt that the King's prosecutor, though appearing to be "a man of intelligence," nevertheless "flits about and is full of sophisms." She was also able to meet "often" with Lieutenant General of Police Sartine, Sade's archnemesis. At first, she was optimistic, believing that she had obtained "a definite promise that the appeal will be presented here in six weeks."[40]

However, the appeal would never be presented, and Mme de Montreuil would never have to answer the extreme charges Sade had lodged in his petition. In the end, Renée had come to accept the strategy devised by her mother: the criminal charges against Sade could be cleared only by the Parlement of Aix. In an undated letter to Gaufridy from Paris, Renée argued that the court would have to rescind its earlier verdicts because "the Spanish fly has not been proved and, on review, the second article [on sodomy] can be set aside."[41] But such a plan would mean Sade first had to surrender himself to the court, and that was unacceptable to him.

Sade never admitted that there was anything criminal in his treatment of the Marseilles prostitutes, which in his "Grande Lettre"[42] he dismissed as "*a party with some girls*, which happens eighty times a day every day in Paris!" No law, he insisted, had ever been broken: "There was only libertinage involved."[43] When Renée was preparing to leave for Paris, Sade insisted that there had been no real crime committed at Marseilles; he ought not be punished for what he may have been thinking at that time. In his philosophical novel *Aline et Valcour*, Sade has the Comte de Beaulé, by no means a libertine, say, "Let us not speak of thoughts, I beg of you; there would not exist a single chaste woman in the whole world if their thoughts were revealed."[44] In a letter to Gaufridy from June 1774, Sade exclaimed, "Does one punish ideas? God alone has the right to do so, because He alone sees them, but the law can do nothing against them."[45]

Sade had come to see himself as a persecuted champion of intellectual freedom, carrying the banner of liberty onto a great, almost a cosmic field of battle; there he was persecuted by the devilish lawyer's wife, Mme de Montreuil, and all her legal allies, all the abusers and misusers of the law, the law that could not, or at least ought not, punish ideas. The state could not, or ought not, punish mental crimes. Only God could do that. In a perfect world, justice would prevail. In a perfect world, Sade's *requête* would prevail. Unlike Sade, however, Mme de Montreuil had no interest in Quixotic campaigns. In a letter to the Abbé on November 22, 1774, she dismissed Sade's *requête* as silly: the King, she said, "had already responded, 'I granted him mercy once, I desire no further involvement.' "[46] Renée's trip to Paris, the Abbé thought, would prove futile, partly because, in his judgment, she was "scarcely capable of handling matters of this nature."[47]

While Renée was in Paris trying to enlist support for Sade's appeal, Sade was enjoying himself at Lyons for some part of August 1774. He was entertained there by a twenty-four-year-old woman, Anne Sablonnière, called "Nanon," whom he would soon employ as a servant at La Coste. Nine months later, on May 11, 1775, at a nearby village, Courthézon, she would give birth, it was said,[48] to Sade's child. For many years to come, Renée, her mother, Gaufridy, and others would be involved with Anne Sablonnière. At Lyons, Sade asked Anne Sablonnière's aunt, a procuress also known as "Nanon," to round up some young women to work as servants.[49] She found five from Lyons and Vienne who were brought to La Coste, some 150 miles to the south. Sade's treatment of these servants became a problem during the winter of 1774–75, when their parents complained and demanded their return. In his "Grande Lettre," Sade tried to excuse his treatment of his new servant girls by claiming that they were prostitutes hired through a procuress. He correctly observed, "It is expressly forbidden in France for any bawd to furnish girls who are virgins, and if the girl furnished is a virgin and if she complains, it is not the man who is accused, it is the bawd, who is rigorously punished on the spot."[50] In fact, in eighteenth-century France, there were heavy penalties for a procurer who took a virgin into a bordello, even with her parents' consent.[51] Sade was trying to say that the girls he hired through a procuress in Lyons were not innocents. In his "Grande Lettre" he told his wife, "I would rather you considered me a libertine than a criminal." He confessed, he said, to "a tiny idiosyncrasy": "loving women perhaps a little too much." In this case, he foresaw no problems, since he hired the servant girls through "a well-known bawd in Lyons." Sade explained what happened next in this way: "I take them with me; I use them. After six months, some parents appear to ask for these girls, assuring me that they are their children. I return them, and suddenly there appears against me a charge of kidnapping and rape!"[52] Sade's defense was that there could have been no kidnapping or rape because the girls were supplied by a procuress, and she "should have been punished," he claimed, "not me." Because "there was no profit to be got from the bawd," Sade asserted, the parents of the girls were trying to blackmail him, "hoping to extract some money from me."[53] The explanation exhales a Sadeian chill, the coldness of the man when acting out his methodical fantasies, the coldness of his explanations and his equivocations.

The house Sade and Renée returned to in the fall of 1774 was not depopulated; it was not in need of the new servants Sade had just hired. Sade was attended, as usual, by his valet La Jeunesse. The housekeeper, Gothon, served at both La Coste and Mazan. There was a servant, Saint-Louis, whose devotion to drink and the new servant girls would get him into trouble with his master. There was also a certain "Jean," perhaps Sade's secretary. The grounds were attended by a gardener and a game warden. Renée was conscious of the need to contain rumors about her husband's past, and also about what might occur inside the house. She gave a standing order that each new servant had to be warned about the need for "discretion." "In the house," Renée explained to Ripert, a servant "will not speak of the [Marseilles] affair, seeing that all those who live there know nothing about it, and on the outside . . . he will say nothing of what he sees happen on the inside."[54] There were other precautions taken during this year. In and around the house, carpenters and masons were repairing the drawbridge and the outer, defensive walls of the château. Later, on April 29, 1777, Mme de Montreuil would complain to Gaufridy not only about the cost of these repairs, but also about their apparently ominous purpose. M. de Montreuil tried to make his daughter "realize to what she was exposing herself by persisting in locking herself up with such a mentality and rendering her own house inaccessible to all help, by means of the precautions that she took to close it."[55] It was to this house, repaired and fortified following the police raid the previous January, that Sade and Renée returned in the fall of 1774.

At the same time that Sade hired Nanon and five servant girls at Lyons, he also sought a young man who would act as his new "secretary." Hiring this servant proved more difficult than obtaining the five girls. The family of the prospective secretary required assurances that their son's new employer was not the same Sade everyone had been talking about, the one who had been convicted at Marseilles and Aix. Engaging this new secretary would require Renée's delicate touch. She wrote from Lyons to Gaufridy, asking him not quite to lie about Sade's identity, but to tell what she called *"un petit mensonge à la jésuite,"* a kind of complicated truth:

> You are going to receive a letter in which someone will ask you if M. le Comte de Mazan, now at Lyons, is the same as the Marquis de S[ade] in legal action at Aix. You will please, I beg of you, answer this with a kind of complicated truth, which, without compromising you, nevertheless confirms that this is not the same one, as, for example, by saying that there are several Sade families, the Sades of Eyguières, and those of Mazan, of Saumane, of Tarascon, but that certainly the Sade of that account, presumably being in a foreign land because of his sentence, definitely could not be he who is now at Lyons.[56]

The parents of the girls rounded up by Nanon were less scrupulous. During the winter of 1774 and the spring of 1775, other women would be brought to La Coste, including a dancer and "two or three other girls, as cooks or kitchen helpers."[57] This collection of young people had but one purpose: to satisfy the lust and the fantasies of the Lord of La Coste.

Even as Sade was enjoying the carnal table he had set for himself, Mme de Montreuil was writing to the Abbé about the need for circumspection. On

November 22, 1774, she expressed guarded optimism, believing that Sade's legal problems would be solved given enough time to erase the old bad impressions. Until the appeal of the judgment against Sade at Aix succeeded, Mme de Montreuil thought that the main thing for Sade was "to behave prudently enough and quietly enough so that one could deny or claim ignorance of the place of his retreat and so keep it secret, in the event of inquiries." The place of Sade's retreat would soon become all too evident to justice officials at Aix, Orange, and Lyons, where complaints against him were about to be brought. As if sensing the periodicity of her son-in-law's scandals, and expecting some imminent eruption, Mme de Montreuil bluntly criticized the Abbé's "philosophical indolence," and asked him to go over to La Coste and put things right: "You are only 4 leagues away!" She urged him "to go and impose and establish order over all of that! and speak firmly! They would listen to you."[58]

On January 23, 1775, Mme de Montreuil's husband wrote to one of Sade's uncles, the Commandeur de Sade. His purpose was to consolidate the support of Sade's relatives for Mme de Montreuil's plan to rehabilitate Sade's name, so that the children could one day have their estate. However, M. de Montreuil argued, "in order to purge the contempt judgment, the appearance of the accused is necessary." It would be better, he said, if Sade were locked up under a lettre de cachet somewhere far from Provence, and he recommended the prison of Pierre-Encize.[59] Mme de Montreuil had also been in contact with another of Sade's relatives, the Comte de Sade-Vauredone, the provost of Saint-Victor in Marseilles. On January 20, 1775, the provost wrote to Renée to report on his recent trip to Aix "in order to see Monsieur de la Tour, the ruling judge," and, indeed, "all the judges and the counselors who are my relations and friends." The provost advised Renée to write to the Abbé "so that we may be united in our way of thinking and speaking . . . in accordance with what your mother has prescribed." Mme de Montreuil, it would appear, had been completely successful in isolating her son-in-law, in separating him from his family, and in controlling his legal as well as his financial affairs. The provost concluded his letter to Renée by advising her and her husband "to behave better in the future and to try to erase by good conduct all the unfavorable impressions he has created."[60]

In the winter, the afternoon shadows lengthened quickly in the valleys around La Coste. Even as the last rays of the sun were blunted on the walls and the tower of the château on the bluff, the great wooden door was closed, the drawbridge was raised, and all was silent. Any guests had long since left. Gaufridy and his wife sometimes visited—early, as Sade insisted in the following letter dating probably from December 1774:

We will expect you, then, on Tuesday, my dear lawyer. . . . I beg you to try to arrive early, at least for dinner, that is, at three o'clock; you would oblige me to follow this same custom whenever you come to visit us this winter. This is the reason for it: we have decided, for a thousand reasons, to see very few people this winter. As a consequence, I spend the evening in my study, and Madame, along with her women, is occupied in an adjoining room until bedtime, with the consequence that, from dusk on, the château is totally shut up, the lights extinguished, no more cooking and often no more food.[61]

There is no sure way to know what Sade got up to after Gaufridy left La Coste, after the château was "totally shut up, the lights extinguished." If there is no direct evidence about exactly *what* happened in the château during December 1774 and early January 1775, correspondence afterward does show that *something* happened. These two months are a blank canvas on which each biographer paints his own picture. Bourdin and Lever believe there were orgies that inspired the scenes at the château of Silling in *Les Cent Vingt Journées de Sodome*.[62] Bourdin calls the orgies at La Coste "a witches' Sabbath," and believes that Sade tortured some of his victims with a knife.[63] Lely resists this idea, considering it an elaboration of the evidently false accusation that Sade had used a knife on Rose Keller. Lely surmises that Sade had recourse to his customary pleasure of employing whips. He also believes that "the complete submission" of Mme de Sade to her husband "leaves no doubt [that] she herself took part in the orgies."[64] Lely speaks of the "progressive erotization" of Renée, how she, "in all likelihood, must have insensibly yielded, particularly during the course of the orgies of the château of La Coste, to the most audacious requirements of her husband."[65] Lever assumes that Renée submitted to her husband's taste for anal intercourse, but thinks that the primary torture for Renée was moral and psychological. He believes that there were limits to her complaisance, and that she would not have accepted flagellation, nor would Sade have subjected her to it.[66] At the other extreme, Alice Laborde accepts Renée's claim that Sade was not at La Coste at all during the winter,[67] so that there could not have been any orgies.

The continuing mystery about Mme de Sade attracted the attention of the Japanese writer Yukio Mishima, who wrote his play *Madame de Sade* because he was, as he said in its "Author's Note," "most intrigued" by "the riddle" of Renée. Ingmar Bergman directed Mishima's play in Sweden. When the production was brought to Brooklyn, New York, in May 1993, the actress who played the leading role, Stina Ekblad, tried to explain what Renée's appeal was for her and for Bergman: "Bergman sees things in her that he sees in me. . . . I don't like the sort of masochism that I have in myself, which I think is quite natural for lots of women. I don't like it, but I can understand it: to stick to this man when he treats you like that and to let the world which is ruled by men treat you badly and to go on."[68] The actress found in Renée a kind of negative feminist role model—the nadir of feminine masochism.

There are more unanswered and perhaps unanswerable questions about Mme de Sade than there are about her husband. Curiously, there is no good biography on this enigmatic woman,[69] who was conventionally raised and religiously educated in a middle-class home, who shared Sade's bed until his long imprisonment from 1777 to 1790. The best evidence of the nature of their relationship is the large correspondence (essentially their only form of communication) during Sade's thirteen years of imprisonment. The letters reveal Renée's devotion to her husband, her sometimes frantic attempts to win his freedom, her tireless efforts in running errands for food, for books, for writing paper, for anything that he asked for, anything that might ease his suffering; the letters reveal that she put up with continual humiliations, sometimes from him, often from her mother and prison and legal officials; they reveal her emotional strength and show the support she gave her husband during his darkest days, when he was suicidal, madly angry, threatening, or insanely paranoid and jealous; they demonstrate her *constancy*, for she was his only connection with the outside world, with his children, with his past, with any hope for a future—in sum, they show her *love* for her husband, which had always informed her life and which gave some meaning to his. The prison letters of Sade and his wife are a very much underused resource for charting the depth, the complexity, and the progress of their relationship.[70]

A few excerpts from Sade and Renée's correspondence may suffice to give an idea of the emotions that bound them together:

Sade to Renée, March 6, 1777:

> My dear friend, you are all that remains to me on the earth: father, mother, sister, wife, friend, you take the place of all of them, I have only you. Do not abandon me, I beg of you.[71]

Renée to Sade, November 24, 1777:

> When you write me even a one-word letter, I am as pleased as I can be, separated as I am from you. . . . Take good care of yourself; I keep repeating it to you because you are dearer to me, without a doubt, than my own life.[72]

In his letter of December 14, 1780, Sade responded to Renée's informing him that she had drawn a money order against her mother's account. He composed the following ditty, in which he also expressed his fear that she had taken a lover:

Song, song.

You say you need a cashier's check
To plump yourself up, my little chick?
Fie! fie! how heinous!

Oh! good God, how fierce she attacks!
Though I well know there is nothing she lacks,
Not even a big, fat [penis].

What! I am wrong?[73]

Renée to Sade, July 11, 1781:

I am not in the least different toward you. I have even more experience, I know my world better, and this knowledge makes the human race odious to me. I see very little, very little indeed, in every sense of the term, of your intelligence and spirit in the world. If your poor head did not sometimes deviate from these virtues by writing unseemly things, you would be the perfect human being; but you will always be so for me. It is not possible for me to stop adoring you, even were you to heap insults upon me; I am too sure that your heart would never be in it.[74]

Sade to Renée, end of November 1783:

Either kill me or take me as I am, because I'll be damned if I ever change—I have told you, the beast is too old—there is no room for hope—the most honest, the most candid, the most sensitive of men, the most compassionate, the most beneficent worshipper of my children, for whose happiness I would go through fire, conscientious to the most extreme degree not to wish to corrupt their morals, or to warp their minds, or to make them adopt in any way my philosophy, adoring my parents (meaning mine), adoring those who are left of my friends, and above all, my wife, whom I desire only to make happy, and with whom I have the deepest desire to make up for much of the indiscretions of my youth—because, in fact, *one's own wife is not made for that.* . . . So there you have my virtues—now as to my vices— arrogant irascibility—extremely hot-tempered in everything, with a dissoluteness of imagination with regard to morals such as has never been seen before, atheist to the point of fanaticism, there you have me in brief. To repeat, either kill me or take me as I am, because I will never change.[75]

The level of passion in this relationship, the level of understanding of themselves and of each other, can have come about only through the long development of love.

Sade did not treat his wife in the same way he treated his servants and prostitutes. In his "Grande Lettre," he wrote: "I am a libertine, but I have never compromised the health of my wife."[76] Above, we have seen him declare, perhaps self-servingly and rather proudly, that his chief vice was mental: "a dissoluteness of imagination with regard to morals such as has never been seen before." Again, in his "Grande Lettre," he admitted that he was a libertine, that he had "conceived everything imaginable in that department." This is a boast he made good in his novels. If he saw himself as a kind of mental adventurer, as a kind of global explorer in the area of sexuality, in his "Grande Lettre" he was quick to add, "but I have certainly not done everything I thought of, and I certainly never will. I am a libertine, but I am not *a criminal* or *a murderer*."[77]

If the parents of the five girls from Lyons and Vienne misunderstood or did not care about the purpose for which their children were hired by Nanon, some of them very soon had reason to change their minds and to demand the return of their children. By the middle of January 1775, some of the parents brought a complaint at Lyons, claiming that their children were either abducted or seduced by Sade. The exact nature and the details of these complaints, and even the precise names of the servant girls, have been swept away by time and chance.[78] However, the charges had immediate consequences. This was precisely the sort of trouble that Sade did not need. On January 27, 1775,[79] he wrote to Gaufridy: "I am preparing for you a formal refutation of everything claimed by the child, and, particularly, of the personal accusations of M. l'Abbé."[80] This nameless "child," who was probably, like the others, fourteen to sixteen years old, appears to have suffered more than the rest during their brief stay at La Coste. Sometime before Sade's letter of January 27, this girl escaped and went to the Abbé's house.[81] It is not clear why she went to the Abbé at Saumane, or if she had been recaptured and sent there. The Abbé could not have been happy to see her. He had long since given up hope of his nephew's reform. Sade did not appear to have learned about the assistance his uncle provided the police a year earlier in their unsuccessful raid on La Coste. Now Sade put his uncle in an unpleasant position by asking him to hold this servant girl prisoner and to hide her from her relatives and possibly from the police. Sade dispatched Gaufridy to persuade the Abbé to help, and in the above letter of January 27, he congratulated Gaufridy on his "very great accomplishment."[82]

Renée had for a time intended to bluff down any and all charges. To return the servant girls would be to admit something wrong had been done to them. Renée had even gone to Lyons, as she wrote to the Abbé in February 1775, and she boasted that she "kept everything quiet." She asked the Abbé to "please do the same" and "destroy all the charges" of the girl locked up at Saumane. "Above all," Renée urged him, "prevent her from returning to Vienne . . . because she everywhere spreads a thousand hideous tales." According to Renée, what the girl had to say was nothing but "lying and calumny." All one had to do, Renée claimed, to prove that the girl "left intact" from the château is "to have her examined."[83] However, on February 15, Renée wrote again to the Abbé to ask him not to let the girl be seen by any doctor.[84]

Next, Renée's letter acknowledged the trouble the Abbé was being put to, and his anger at his nephew, whom "you like so much to inveigh against, to treat as mad." But then she tried to make the Abbé feel guilty by reminding him that her husband had once helped him get over his own scandal with a girl. This brazenness and implicit blackmail indicate that Sade had a hand in Renée's letter. The Abbé was evidently so angered by it that he scratched out portions of the offending paragraph. However, the words that remain make it clear that Sade's plight ought "to remind" the Abbé "that eight years ago" Sade "took" care of "that girl called Rose," whose "silence" the Abbé "owed" to Sade's intervention. Renée suggested that this Rose had "some things considerably worse" to say than anything alleged against Sade. And Rose also had something irrefutable: the "testimony . . . of her pregnant condition." By contrast, Renée insisted that her husband "in fact is completely innocent." Finally, Renée felt obliged to defend her own behavior, especially because the Abbé appeared to believe the charges the servant girl had made: "What dreadful things can a creature like that say against me! and how could you lend credence to everything you told me? You treat me rather cavalierly in your letter, and, to listen to you, would I then be the mistress of ceremonies of my husband's orgies? No, Monsieur, that is not and never was the case." Renée could not possibly have assisted in her husband's orgies: "How could it be true, since it is perfectly clear that for the past year my husband has not set foot at La Coste?" To say otherwise would be slander, "in the first place because I am incapable of it, which you should do me the justice to believe, and in the second place because my husband neither is here nor could be."[85] This argument abc ut her husband's absence is so evidently false that it resembles many of Sade's ironical apologies or irrational arguments that came accompanied by a crowbar to help the reader pry them apart. Sade seemed to enjoy the wreckage.

Although Renée told the Abbé that she had returned the other servants to their parents, saying, "I no longer have any of them in my house,"[86] returning them had not been her first intention, and she had not told the whole truth. Renée had written to her mother for advice, as Mme de Montreuil reported on February 11, 1775, in her first of many letters over the years to Sade's lawyer Gaufridy:

> My daughter has written to me in order to consult over what she should do. I answered her: "send them all back, but take precautions so as to avoid being troubled in the future." She informs me of having to some extent taken these precautions, and of being furnished with certificates of good health for all of them.

Mme de Montreuil also knew the value of "obtaining releases" from the girls' parents. She presumed to advise Gaufridy to "make sure to get from them in advance the nullification of any legal actions already begun." She told Gaufridy "to keep these children within reach and in a secure place, until you obtain agreements with each of the parents who have demanded them back." The news from Lyons, she reported, was very bad: "This story is causing a considerable scandal there." She also alluded to privileged "reports" from Lyons that she had seen only two days earlier, reports that made it clear that her daughter had mismanaged her visit there:

> The Lady [i.e., Renée] has implicated herself in the responses that she gave to the King's prosecutor and to the priests. She has equivocated, talked about convents, said that they would be returned only when she had been reimbursed for their expenses . . . then conceded that one was at her house. All of this caused bitterness, appeared more suspicious, and made a very bad impression.[87]

The matter had reached a crisis. Mme de Montreuil always appeared energized by emergencies. As usual, she managed to impose her will upon her son-in-law, who, once again, appeared feckless and inactive following the trouble he had caused. The threatening, injured, confused letter he had Renée write to the Abbé is an indication of the confusion of his mind when confronted by a crisis. For example, he had Renée tell the Abbé that the gossiping girl in the

Abbé's care at Saumane might well be "prompted by some secret enemy, and that this may well be the very crux of the whole matter."[88] What "secret enemy" was Sade trying to pin his problems on this time? When he was desperate, he said and did things that amounted to a kind of symbolic conversation or debate with imagined antagonists. Mme de Montreuil, unlike Sade always clear-sighted, always the pragmatist, drew a straight line of attack through a problem to its solution: get the releases.

While Mme de Montreuil was writing to Gaufridy behind Sade's back, Sade was writing sometimes pointless, sometimes humorous letters to him. In the following excerpt, Sade displayed a humorous interest in food when he compiled a ludicrous shopping list for Gaufridy upon hearing that there had been a well-provisioned fair at Gaufridy's town of Apt:

> As for us, poor unfortunates, far from the grandeur of cities, all
> we have is a miserable cabbage, and poor Gothon, who says that Apt
> is bursting with excellent things of which you do not want us to
> have any share at all, is prepared to launch a heated assault against you
> if you do not take a little pity on her tomorrow by sending her car-
> doons, cauliflower, asparagus, beans, green peas, carrots, parsnips, arti-
> chokes, truffles, potatoes, spinach, rape, radishes, some endive, some
> lettuce, some celery, some chervil, some watercress, some beets, and
> other vegetables.[89]

Sade sounded happy, playful, even pleased with himself, while those around him were tearing out their hair in exasperation over the mess he had made. "What," he seems to ask, "is all the fuss about?" He forgot it almost at once, forgave himself almost at once. Then he bounced up, cheerful, untroubled, almost innocent.

Other people's tempers, however, were less resilient. The Abbé and some of Sade's relatives were proving to be stubborn and resistant to Mme de Montreuil's advice. Renée told Gaufridy that her mother was "furious" with the Abbé. It was not merely the lack of cooperation that Mme de Montreuil noticed in the Sade family, but a haughtiness or class superiority that evidently hurt her deeply. Sade's relatives, she complained to Gaufridy, "do us the honor to take us for imbeciles."[90] For his part, the Abbé complained to Gaufridy about Mme de Montreuil's demands: he said that he would "certainly not go to Aix," would not "make the ridiculous trip that she asks of me." The Abbé added that the whole Sade family were "appalled beyond expression" at Mme de Montreuil and the way that she "looks upon us as so many automatons made to be moved according to her will."[91] But neither would the Abbé be moved by his nephew any longer. On May 18, he wrote to the minister of the King's household asking for the arrest of his nephew, because his insane acts were disturbing to society and to his family.[92] Of course, Sade was still technically a fugitive, but the unsuccessful police searches of La Coste demonstrated how difficult it would be to arrest him on his own land.

The suggestion that Sade was insane and had committed atrocities upon one or more of the servant girls at La Coste comes from three sources: from Bourdin's otherwise uncorroborated claim that Sade had employed a knife; from the inference that can be made from Renée's denying a doctor access to the girl at Saumane; and from Mme de Montreuil's equally unsubstantiated remark on April 8, 1775, in a letter to Gaufridy: "It is claimed, in fact, that the proofs exist on the bodies, the arms, and are in conformity with the statements of the children."[93] These alleged stab wounds were not part of Sade's repertory. He had offered to whip and be whipped by Jeanne Testard in 1763, but she rejected both offers; stabbing was not an issue. Though this charge was raised by Rose Keller, it was rejected after a medical examination. There was no suggestion that Sade had ever harmed such high-class actress-courtesans as Beauvoisin and Colet, who certainly did not have to put up with abuse, and who stayed with him even though they had many wealthier and more generous patrons. There was no question of any knife employed against the Marseilles prostitutes, and the whipping they received was minor and elicited no complaint. Except for the affair with Rose Keller, it is clear that Sade was far more masochistic than sadistic. His requests were more often refused than acceded to, and he never employed physical force or even much argument to get his way. This is not to say that Sade was a good man, or that he did not take advantage of his rank and his power to do harm. In this case, some young people had apparently got worse than they and their parents had bargained for; they did not deserve to be abused and frightened and later locked away to keep them from talking. The myth of Sade, however, is far more extreme than the truth of Sade. As bad as he was, there are people in the city or maybe even the town or street where the reader lives who are much, much worse.

It may even be said that the sort of girls that Nanon was likely to find, and the sort of parents such girls were likely to have, made Mme de Montreuil's suspicions about blackmail rather more plausible. Of their complaints, Mme de Montreuil had asked Gaufridy, "Are these not some fables fabricated out of previous events in order to make one buy silence?"[94] If the parents or relatives had a legitimate grievance, if there were reasons to suspect mistreatment, the authorities at Lyons would have acted more forcefully. The police or the

courts of Paris and Marseilles had made strong efforts on behalf of Jeanne Testard, a prostitute; on behalf of Rose Keller, a beggar; and on behalf of a group
of prostitutes in Marseilles. At Lyons, the complaints of the parents of the servant girls were dropped a couple of months after they were made. According
to Sade's "Grande Lettre," two of the girls were "returned to their parents."
Possibly some of the other girls had little desire to return to their so-called
relatives. One of them, Sade claimed, "set herself up as a w[hore]."[95] Another,
who had been put into a convent at Caderousse, fled to Lyons in March 1776,
according to Renée's letter to Gaufridy on March 15 of that year.[96] (There
sometimes appear to be more than five girls in this account; it is admittedly
difficult to keep track of them.) Another, a cook named Marie, Sade said in
his "Grande Lettre," "stayed in my service and died of natural causes" at La
Coste.[97]

The fifth girl, the talkative one the Abbé reluctantly guarded at Saumane,
was brought down to the hospital at L'Isle-sur-la Sorgue in October 1775. On
October 17, Renée wrote to the Abbé to say that she would pay for the girl's
expenses on the condition that she be prevented from talking to anyone.[98]
Perhaps her illness was a pregnancy begun nine months earlier, when she was
at La Coste. This may explain why, when Renée had sought to blackmail the
Abbé into keeping her back then, Renée reminded him of his girlfriend Rose,
who was in a *"pregnant condition."* In any case, the condition of the girl in the
hospital had sufficiently improved in a few weeks for her to be moved to a
farm at Mazan under the supervision of Ripert. The girl stayed there through
the winter and spring, until she somehow managed to persuade Sade's young
valet Jean and possibly Ripert himself to let her escape at the end of July. By
July 26, 1776, she reached Orange and made a statement to the judge there.
Renée mentioned the rumor of the escape in a letter to Gaufridy on July 26,
amidst some talk about partridge—she had none and wanted some as soon as
possible—and about chocolate, of which she asked Gaufridy to send "a few
pounds."[99] By August 3, Renée knew about the deposition and the fact that
the girl had remained at Orange "babbling for a week." Renée warned
Gaufridy that there would be "consequences." However, considering the
blinding heat of a Provence August, Renée told him there was no rush: "It is
indeed too hot to aggravate one's mind or body."[100] When Mme de Montreuil heard about it (Paris is rather more cool than Provence), she wrote to
Gaufridy on August 12 to go at once to Orange, "if you have not already done
so," to find out all about it. She also wanted Gaufridy to keep an eye on Jean
and to prevent him from talking: warn him, she advised, that "if any harmful
remarks get out about his masters whom he claims to respect, he will be
locked up like Nanon."[101]

In his "Grande Lettre," Sade would be especially careful to account for the whereabouts of the five girls he had hired from Lyons and Vienne, as well as of the three who came later to La Coste: namely Du Plan, a dancer at the Comédie de Marseilles, who lived there openly, he said, as his housekeeper, and whom he later saw at the Comédie de Bordeaux; a girl named Rosette from Montpellier, who stayed secretly at La Coste for two months, and who, "growing bored," had the man she had been previously staying with at Montpellier come and get her;[102] and finally, a year later, a girl named Adélaïde who was brought to La Coste by Sade in October 1776 from Montpellier on the recommendation of the above Rosette. Adélaïde, Sade said, later left La Coste in the company of the postmaster of Courthézon.[103] By 1781, when Sade wrote this "Grande Lettre" to Renée from prison, the myth attaching to his name had become sufficiently gruesome for him to feel the necessity of defending himself against implicit charges of savagery and even murder. The message virtually shouted by this letter is clear: None of the girls died! The myth was started, Sade felt, by Rose Keller, who "had bruited about all of Paris that I had performed certain experiments and that the garden of my house [at Arcueil] was a cemetery in which I buried the corpses that had been used in my experiments." Sade felt that his "enemies" were charging him with similar experiments on the girls at La Coste during 1775.[104] That is why he was making every effort to prove that all of the girls emerged alive from his estate.

When Inspector Marais, chief of the vice squad, rearrested Sade at La Coste on August 26, 1778, he fueled speculation on the extent of Sade's perversity by shouting at him about "d[ead] bodies."[105] Sade was never charged with murdering anyone. Strangely enough, human bones *were* found in his garden at La Coste, but this was all the consequences of a foolish joke, Sade said in his "Grande Lettre." The bones "had been brought" to La Coste, he explained, by Du Plan when she had visited him during that winter of 1774–75. And anyone who doubted it "can interrogate her." Du Plan must have known something of Sade's macabre taste. One can only wonder what Sade did with the human remains, or why Du Plan thought that it would be an amusing gift for her host. In his "Grande Lettre," Sade continued: "It was a joke, in good or bad taste (I leave it to you), to decorate a study with them. These bones were definitely used for that purpose, and when that joke, or, rather, stupid prank, was over, they were disposed of in that garden." The best he could say for himself was that he was "no more guilty of *tortures*, of *experiments*, or of *murders* in this last episode than in any of the others." What he did, he said, "everyone in the world does": he "met with girls, either already completely debauched or supplied by a b[awd]." "Seduction," therefore, was "not an issue in this case." Nevertheless, he complained, he "is being punished and made to suffer as if he were guilty of the blackest crimes."[106] His escapades during the winter of 1774–75 at La Coste would help send him to jail almost for life.

In his "Grande Lettre," Sade also tried to explain the charges lodged against him by the mother of the young secretary he had hired at Lyons, when Renée had asked Gaufridy to hide the truth of Sade's identity. Around the end of June 1775, Renée had to take the boy to Aix to return him to his mother, who had first made a fuss at Lyons, then at Aix. "What have you to say about all of this new trouble?" Sade asked Gaufridy at the time. The trouble came out of the blue, Sade claimed, because the mother never directly asked him to return her son and because "in all of her letters" she even urged her son "to attach himself to me and to serve me well." This mother, Sade said, "now comes without warning to make a devilish commotion at Aix."[107] She may have learned something she did not like. On May 3, 1775, the Président of the Parlement of Provence, Bruny d'Entrecastaux, informed some of Sade's relatives that the Marquis was performing scandalous acts at La Coste with young people of both sexes.[108] Sade did not blame himself for this result. He blamed the King's prosecutor at Lyons, and saw himself as the focus of a large conspiracy: "It is clear that they are working secretly against me . . . and want this child in order no doubt to make him swear to new lies. This behavior of the King's prosecutor at Lyons is unprecedented." In the next paragraph, Sade expressed the highest praise for the prosecutor for the Parlement of Aix: "M. de Castillon has conducted himself in all this with a prudence and a desire to be useful that deserves our undying gratitude. . . . This magistrate seems quite wise, quite honest, and quite reasonable."[109] Once again, there was a Good Father and a Bad Father. Sade was tireless in imposing such structure on the events and people in his life—even, and especially, when the real events and people bore no resemblance whatsoever to Sade's characterization of them in this way.

Of all the young people at La Coste during the winter of 1774–75, Nanon was the most troublesome to Sade—actually to Renée and to Mme de Montreuil, who had to deal with her. The daughter to whom she had given birth on May 11, 1775, Anne-Élisabeth, was probably Sade's child. The infant had been given by Renée to a woman of La Coste to nurse. On July 30, when the nurse's milk had failed because she herself was pregnant, little Anne-Élisabeth, only two and a half months old, died of starvation. The Curé of La Coste, M. Testanière, who had attended the funeral, made inquiries that alarmed Renée. The Curé, Renée wrote to Gaufridy, "sent for the nurse of Nanon's infant girl" and tried to get her to "admit that she knew, just like those [the Sades] who had given the infant to her, that she was pregnant when she took it."[110] The peasant girl, however, would not admit that she had taken money to nurse an infant when she had no milk and knew she could have none. Nanon would not learn of the death of her infant daughter for almost a year: she had just been thrown in prison by Renée, and on very dubious grounds.

On June 21, Renée wrote to Gaufridy to deny all of Nanon's complaints—for example, that she had not been paid, that she was prevented from quitting her job, that she had been beaten. Renée countercharged that it was Nanon who had fomented the rebellion of the other young servants. Nanon, Renée claimed, was "the cause of all the trouble this winter." Renée considered her "an extremely dangerous creature." Mme de Montreuil agreed, advising "everyone now to work to have her locked up." Renée said that her mother had discussed this in a secret letter earlier in the winter. This plan to lock up Nanon makes Renée's charging Nanon with theft all the more dubious. According to Renée, Nanon "came to tell me a million impertinences, . . . I sent her on her way, and . . . she thereupon went off like a madwoman, ranting on with her insolent arguments." Renée immediately had an "inventory made of the silverware before witnesses," and "there were three table settings missing." She wanted Nanon arrested at once, to "keep her in prison under this pretext until the arrival of the *lettre de cachet*" that Mme de Montreuil would obtain in Paris. By the time Renée was writing to Gaufridy on June 21, her troubles with Nanon had reached the breaking point. The two women had fought, and Nanon had fled the château, down through the village of La Coste to the Maison-Basse, "whence," according to Renée, "she has just written a thousand impertinences and frightful things, saying that she is going to Aix." Renée's plan was to lure Nanon to Gaufridy's house at Apt, where she could be arrested or otherwise guarded. "I am going to try," Renée told Gaufridy, to get Nanon "to go to see you . . . to have you give her her final wages."[111]

Around the same time, Sade wrote to Gaufridy to say that "a truce has been called until the 30th of this month." Sade had placated Nanon for the time being, until "you-know-what" arrived—the *lettre de cachet* from Mme de Montreuil, which was not expected until July 15. In the meantime, Sade said that he was keeping Nanon locked up at La Coste on suspicion of theft. This could not go on for long, lest, "finding ourselves in a predicament, for lack of proof, . . . it would be consequently necessary in a short while to set her free." There were other inconveniences. Sade's servant Saint-Louis, possibly enamored of Nanon, had been behaving badly: "His conduct throughout this whole affair has been horrible, he has constantly supported and backed up this girl, even to the point of impudence and rude remarks, he has gone out over the walls, has got drunk, has used swear words, has cursed, has damned both master and valets." Sade begged Gaufridy to "rid me of Saint-Louis" once and for all.[112]

The lettre de cachet for Nanon arrived in time. The minister of the King's household wrote to Mme de Montreuil on July 5, 1775: "Madame, I have just expedited the orders of the King necessary to have imprisoned Nanon Sablonnière at the prison at Arles, which you have yourself specified. I am directing them to the officer of the constabulary of Apt so that he can execute them."[113] It is strange to see Sade eager to imprison an innocent by means of a lettre de cachet. Nanon would not emerge from the prison at Arles until two and a half years later, in February 1778, exactly a year after Sade was himself imprisoned in Vincennes by a lettre de cachet also obtained by Mme de Montreuil.

On July 6, 1775, Mme de Montreuil wrote Gaufridy to give him her watchwords on the handling of Nanon at Arles: *humanity, but secrecy and security.*[114] The person Mme de Montreuil chose to supervise Nanon's security at the prison for women at Arles was Antoine Lions, Sade's agent on his estate at the Mas de Cabanes, close enough to Arles for him to make frequent trips there. On October 6, three months into Nanon's imprisonment, Lions went to see how she was doing and try to explain to her why she needed to be locked up. He wrote Gaufridy, "She replied with all the horrors that her brain concocted." Lions and Gaufridy were as bad as those who hired them, she said, and those people, not she, "deserved to be locked up." She threatened that, "if she were not released, she would take her life so that the public would learn about everything."[115] Nanon had not yet heard about the death of her infant daughter. On February 25, 1776, Lions informed Gaufridy that Nanon asked him for news of Anne-Élisabeth,[116] but he decided a month later "to wait until Easter to tell her about the death of her girl."[117] There are no letters indicating how the angry and suicidal Nanon took the news of her daughter's death, or what she thought about the cause of death or the fact that it had been kept from her for so long.

Nanon's plight prompted her father to seek her release. Mme de Montreuil was kept informed of his efforts by the minister of the King's household. Indeed, on July 26, 1777, she boasted that the minister had told her that he would "decide nothing without my advice."[118] Nanon's father eventually sought legal advice. He addressed a very lawyerly letter to Lions and Mme de Montreuil on October 20, 1777, demanding the return of his daughter, or at least information about the charges on which she was being imprisoned. "If such outrages are permitted," he continued, "we are no longer in France, where slavery is not allowed." He even threatened to appeal directly to the King: "Our good King, who protects the poor as well as the rich, will deign to hear me." He put emphasis on his poverty: "I am poor, but I will find the resources to prevent iniquity from triumphing."[119] The sound of tumbrels full of aristocrats creaking over cobbled streets to the guillotine is almost audible.

After two and a half years in prison, Nanon finally gave Lions sufficient promises of her silence, and she also agreed not to come within three leagues of Lyons or Vienne. She signed with a cross a receipt for 320 livres, the balance of her wages.[120] Then she disappeared into the provincial demimonde from which Sade had plucked her more than three years earlier, never to be heard from again.

Over the years, Mme de Montreuil had become increasingly involved in, even obsessed by, the life of her son-in-law. Because of her influence on Sade's uncles and her political influence, she was able effectively to project her view of Sade. Her letters and her strategies for dealing with Nanon and the others show her ruthlessness in attempting to preserve the value of the Sade name— for her grandchildren, if not for Sade himself. The following letter from Mme de Montreuil to Gaufridy on June 14, 1775, humorously displays her passion for secrecy. She wanted Gaufridy to go to La Coste and "personally deliver this letter" to Renée. "Manage it in such a way as to deliver it to her alone," and to make sure that she burned it after reading it in his presence. Mme de Montreuil wanted to make sure "*that no one,* including M. de Sade," knew the contents. She appeared to have had some previous experience of her son-in-law's prowess as a spy. She made a special point of warning Gaufridy to arrange his interview with Renée "on a walk outside the château, because, though you may believe you are alone, he could be hidden in some corner, behind a curtain, or in some hiding place, watching and listening. I have seen him get up to these tricks before."[121] She somehow believed he might materialize out of nowhere!

By the spring of 1775, Mme de Montreuil had decided that her son-in-law was insane and that his madness had infected her daughter. Her accounts of the otherwise unrecorded charges of the young servants have greatly influenced biographers. Her version must be studied with great care. For example, the idea that the servants were seriously injured largely depends upon her report of hearsay in her letter to Gaufridy on April 8, 1775, where she spoke about the "proofs" existing on the bodies of the servants. Mme de Montreuil did not know the facts, however. She commissioned Gaufridy to find out: "The statement," she asked him, "is it proved to have substance?" In the same letter, she also said that, though the servants did not "bring charges against"

Renée, "they angrily charge" Sade, and they spoke of Renée "as being herself in danger and as the primary victim of a fury that can only be regarded as madness." Even though the charges remained unsubstantiated, Mme de Montreuil was properly worried: "Can a mother rest easy knowing her daughter is locked under the same roof, and in the uncertainty at least whether if what she is told about the fate of that girl [lodged with the Abbé] is true or fabricated?" Mme de Montreuil said that Sade believed himself invulnerable, omnipotent at La Coste, where Renée somehow favored this delusion: "In his ch[âteau] with her, he imagines himself too powerful, too secure, and so permits himself everything." Sade, she continued, "is too much feared, and this opinion which he has sown gives him his power and his misfortune." She felt that Renée's passivity at La Coste encouraged Sade to increase his "aberrations." "Elsewhere," Mme de Montreuil said, "he controls himself more."[122] Mme de Montreuil was trying to suggest that Sade's sexual acts were growing more perverse, but it must be noted that she had no proof that her son-in-law's "aberrations" at La Coste were any worse than or any different from his behavior with Jeanne Testard, or Rose Keller, or the prostitutes of Marseilles. One might say that, if anything was new or different at La Coste, it was Sade's exposure of Renée to his "aberrations." Sex, like many human activities, frequently requires an audience, generally implicit and sometimes explicit. From the beginning, Mme de Montreuil served this implicit purpose. She knew all about his indiscretions; she cleaned up after them; she heard his apologies. Renée knew about her husband's "aberrations" from the Keller affair on. When Sade brought the servant girls into La Coste, he was bringing the sexual scene closer to Renée. Perhaps his need to shock and to receive punishment was leading him into incautious acts; or perhaps he really did feel omnipotent at La Coste.

Yet it is unlikely that Renée was present during her husband's sexual scenes with others. Her religious devotion, her coldness could be experienced by Sade without her actual presence. She could be teased, humiliated, offended on any number of occasions during the day. Nor is there any evidence that Sade's sexual behavior at La Coste was any different from his earlier behavior. Sade claimed that these servants were no different from prostitutes hired by a madame. He would have corrupted them with money, seduced them with erotic pictures, involved them in arch conversations and arguments about the nature of sexuality, engaged them, if they were willing, in acts of symbolic flagellation (only Rose Keller, of all of Sade's known partners, appears to have been injured by this activity). Sade's other servants, Jean and Saint-Louis, might easily have been involved, just as Latour had engaged in homosexual acts with Sade in Marseilles. Jean and Saint-Louis, we saw, had become attached to two of the girls. It would seem, then, that inhibitions had been lifted from everyone in the house—from everyone, that is, except Renée.

Renée's continuing support of Sade confused and infuriated her mother. In the above letter to Gaufridy, Mme de Montreuil bitterly complained that her daughter "would rather have herself hacked to pieces than to agree to anything that she believed could harm him."[123] On July 26, 1775, Mme de Montreuil wrote to Gaufridy "to take all steps to protect her from her own weakness."[124] She was willing to convey the idea that her daughter, if not as depraved as Sade, was nevertheless a willing participant in his depravity. On November 10, 1775, the Abbé expressed the same view of Renée to Gaufridy, objecting to her proposed trip to Aix to further her husband's appeal of the Marseilles judgment:

> It seems to me that it will not be convenient for Mme de S[ade] to appear at Aix. . . . That Lady [Renée] will toss her dirty laundry into a town where it is known that she was the accomplice of her husband's recent debauches. I know from a good source that that spectacle at La Coste has considerably cooled off the goodwill of most of the counselors and of M. le Procureur Général. . . . I cannot imagine anyone less capable than Madame de S[ade] to solicit a matter of this nature, and thinking as I do, I doubt that she will find anyone in the family who would act in concert with her.[125]

Renée's reputation had been ruined in both the Sade and the Montreuil families. As long as Sade and Renée were together, Mme de Montreuil continued, "there will always be reason to believe the same things" are true of the wife as are true of the husband, and to fear that "he will drag her down along with him into the abyss."[126]

During this last period of freedom, Sade's sexual escapades had increased, had brought scandal directly into his home at La Coste, and had provoked new and damaging contacts with provincial legal officials, who were cast from a narrower mold than their superiors in Paris. Sade's alleged orgies with his newly acquired staff of young servants at La Coste had also implicated Renée. In a letter to Gaufridy in June 1775, with a mixture of bravado and philosophy (the same odd tonal blend to be found in his novels), Sade brushed off the charges made by the relatives of the servant girls, as well as the rumors about his conduct that he claimed were promulgated by the "charming" ladies of Apt, where Gaufridy lived: "They have given out at Avignon that from morning to night I have been running around all the neighboring towns and that I have been frightening everybody. I pass for the *wolf-man* around here. The poor little chickadees with their *panicky* cheeping! But why complain about it? That is human nature, people like to decry what thrills them."[127] The *loup-garou*, the wolf-man, the bogeyman, the myth of "Sade," had already been created, and its creator, Sade himself, took pride in its terrifying capacity.

Sometime in June or July 1775, there was another police search of La Coste, and Sade was obliged to hide out in the attic.[128] In a letter to Gaufridy on July 26, 1775, Mme de Montreuil referred to the raid and disclaimed any responsibility, saying that she "would have to be stupid indeed" to attempt an arrest at La Coste. She understood Sade well enough to know his reaction to such a search: "He will run away or hide, as he has already done, and if he lives quietly, . . . in time it will all be forgotten. But will they both be sensible enough to keep to this behavior? I doubt it."[129] The wolf-man had been run to ground, driven into his lair, and as soon as he saw his chance to get away, he escaped, over the Alps to Italy.

CHAPTER 10

Italy

O N THE AFTERNOON OF JULY 17, 1775, accompanied by his valet La Jeunesse and also the postmaster of Courthézon, Louis Charvin,[1] Sade turned his back on La Coste. He was heading for Italy on a year-long expedition that would become the basis for a lengthy and ambitious manuscript, *Voyage d'Italie, ou dissertations critiques, historiques, politiques et philosophiques sur les villes de Florence, Rome et Naples, 1775–1776*.[2] Like Sade's earlier *Voyage de Hollande* of 1769, this work is addressed to "Madame la Comtesse" (presumably referring to Renée). In it, Sade confidently displays his erudition, his taste in art and architecture, his philosophical views on the morals and politics of the places he visits. Though sometimes tedious and pretentious, the *Voyage d'Italie* nevertheless contains passages sufficiently curious and personal to be considered a Sadeian text of some value.

On the fourth day of his journey, Sade arrived at Briançon, where he observed the two forts perched high above either side of the mountain pass, "completely guarding the route over the Alps." He noted their strategic value with interest. As in his account of his earlier trip to Holland, Sade showed off his military training by commenting on the fortresses he encountered, and often by imagining strategies a general might use to conquer them. In evaluating the natural and man-made defenses of Briançon, Sade concluded that it amply deserved its title as "the Key to France" (118).

The French commandant, M. Audifrey, hearing that Sade intended to cross the Alps over Mont Genèvre, tried to warn him of the dangers of that route. When Sade insisted, M. Audifrey directed him to M. Prat, who agreed to conduct him over the mountain and provided him with twelve porters and eight mules. At dawn the next morning, Sade wrote, the village priest "wanted me to say mass before leaving," not the most encouraging send-off (118). Sade's coach was lightened, the baggage transferred to the mules. Extra horses were ready for the haul up the steep and tortuous road. The porters carried large chocks of wood to wedge behind the coach wheels to keep it from rolling backward off the narrow road and over the precipice. "The drop," Sade noted, "would be nearly three hundred feet." When they finally arrived safely down the other side, M. Prat, "the general of our little army," made a surprising disclosure: "He told me that, concerned about frightening me, he had not wanted me to realize the extent of the danger, but that in fact my coach was the third that he had seen come over this terrifying mountain in the past twenty years" (119). Sade felt rather like a conquering general himself when the location of Hannibal's encampment was pointed out, just to the right of Mont Genèvre, "and you know, Madame Comtesse, it was over this mountain that he entered Italy" (121). The next day, July 23, on passing the Gorge d'Exilles and its strategic fort, as if again to demonstrate his own military aptitude, Sade suggested a plausible way it might be taken by means of foot soldiers supported by artillery (124). Sade saw every situation in adversarial terms and always required an adversary, even if only a hypothetical one, to clarify his own thoughts. Hannibal was on his mind as he climbed and descended the Alps.

Like any travel writer, Sade gave details of the accommodations the reader was likely to encounter, from fine city hotels to simple farmhouses to execrable posting inns. Curiously, he was a complaisant and a sympathetic traveler, not at all like those French tourists, those "gentlemen of fashion," whose haughty and insulting treatment of "foreigners" Sade later ridiculed in his novel *Aline et Valcour*. They did so much harm to the image of France abroad that Sade suggested the government not grant visas to such tourists. As an example, he offered the following anecdote of a confrontation between a French traveler and an Italian innkeeper:

> A coach arriving very late at a hostelry in Italy that had no vacancies, they hesitate to open their doors. The host appears at a window and asks the traveler's nationality.
>
> "French," some of his servants reply with insolence.
>
> "Travel on," the host says, "I have no room."
>
> "My servants are deceived," the master replies adroitly, "these are hired servants; I am English, Monsieur Innkeeper, open up for me."
>
> In a trice, everyone is running, everyone eagerly receives the traveler. Is it not, then, dreadful that the disrepute of the nation was such that it was necessary to disguise it, to disavow it, in order to gain admittance into a foreigner's house, not just in society, but even into a cabaret?[3]

Sade reached Turin early in the morning of July 25, noting that the best inn was the Hôtel d'Angleterre, crowded with visitors come to celebrate the marriage of the eldest son of the King of Sardinia. Understandably, Sade was not inclined to mention in his *Voyage* that he himself had been the King's guest at Miolans Prison two years earlier. As it turned out, the King, Victor-Amédée III, actually had Sade very much on his mind, having just the day before signed an order banishing Joseph Violon from his kingdom for his role in Sade's escape.[4] Sade was not disposed to linger at Turin, and though he praised the handsomeness of the city, his private and bitter feelings may be sensed in his description of the King's palace as "rather vast . . . but of little beauty" (125). Sade chose not to spend the night and departed at once on the road toward Florence, lodging without notable incident at Alexandrie, Voghera, Plaisance, Parma, Modena, and Bologne. A special trip was made to Pietramala to see the two volcanoes there. He remarked on the noxious gases and the hot and blasted aspect of the earth surrounding the crater, and how, if one picked at the earth around the perimeter, one could see the fire underneath. Whatever was thrown into the crater was immediately consumed in violet flames. The gases emerging from the other volcano nearby could be set aflame by a candle. Sade imagined a conflagration and disaster as great as or greater than that caused by Vesuvius (130–31). The things that he chose to see on his journey and to include in his *Voyage d'Italie* reveal his persistent interests. Like the volcanoes, much of what he wrote in his *Voyage* is subversive, subterranean, and explosive.

After lodging at Maschere, Sade arrived in Florence on the afternoon of August 3, 1775. His letters to Gaufridy over the next months were angry and disturbed. He was exasperated to be short on money to continue his trip to Rome, and flew into a rage at Gaufridy when he learned that, "as soon as my back is turned," some builders had persuaded Renée to undertake repairs at La Coste. Jealous even of a building, Sade whined, "I am the one most in need of repair." Renée was a dupe, the builders were scoundrels, Gaufridy was disloyal: "God! how I detest Provence!" He continued: "In truth, I am really tired of being taken for a fool and of seeing that bunch of people, on whom I would do a dance if I wanted to get involved with them, and who have scarcely left their shell or their village, seek to impose on me, to blind me, to make me believe what they wish, me—why, I would make a fool of God himself if I attempted it!"[5] That sentence effectively summarizes Sade: "tired of being taken for a fool," feeling injured, victimized by his inferiors, he could trample them underfoot if he wished to soil his boots; then, aroused to megalomaniacal frenzy, he cried out that he could easily destroy God himself.

Renée wrote to Gaufridy telling him to "pay no attention" to her husband's tirades, citing "the predicament he is in."[6] Sade himself would beg Gaufridy's forgiveness on the same grounds, but just as he could not attack without apologizing, so he could not apologize without attacking. He now blamed Gaufridy for failing to check Mme de Montreuil's malignant schemes: "I have relied upon you . . . , but that wretched creature, with a charm . . . that I never understood and never will understand, seduces everyone she deals with and, as soon as anyone falls under her magic spells, they abandon me . . . and no one dares to stand up for the poor helpless victim of oppression." He continued: "If, during the past year, you had written to this harpy with greater force, I would not now be so vexed." But with his appeal still in legal limbo, and with his reputation blackened, he could not do anything without arousing the darkest suspicions. Until his reputation was "rehabilitated," he told Gaufridy, "there will not be a cat whipped in the province without someone's saying: *It was the Marquis de S[ade]*."[7] Sade's bitter joke was all too true, and quite prophetic.

Despite the complaints that filled Sade's letters to Provence, the summer and fall in Florence were pleasant enough. He was fortunate to have carried a letter of introduction to Dr. Barthélemy Mesny of Florence. They shared a common interest in natural science, architecture, archaeology, history, and the collecting of antique curiosities. When Sade returned from Italy, he sent back to Provence two enormous crates, one of which weighed over thirteen hundred pounds,[8] full of Roman antiquities and other objects. But when Sade's lawyer at Aix, Reinaud, received and examined the contents of the first crate, he said he would not give 12 sols for the lot! Gaufridy was equally unimpressed, and Renée wrote to chide him: "It is very clear from what you say that you are no expert in antiquities."[9] Bourdin gives this account of some of the contents of the second crate:

> It is a veritable ark. Out of it comes, among other things, marble statues, fossils, "a vase or amphora for keeping Greek wine, veined with coral," antique lamps, funeral urns, "all in the Greek and Roman style," medals, idols, rough stones and carved stones from Vesuvius, a handsome funerary urn perfectly intact, Etruscan vases and medals, a fragment carved in serpentine, a piece of nitrous sulphate, seven sponges, a collection of shells, a small Hermaphrodite, and a vase of flowers, "all made of alabaster from Volterre in Tuscany," a marble plate filled with all sorts of fruits "remarkably well simulated," two chiffonniers of marble from Vesuvius, a Saracen bouquerini or cup, a Neapolitan knife, some antique clothes, some engravings and books.[10]

It was an eclectic collection, and Sade relished the bizarre variety with dilettantish delight and indiscriminate enthusiasm. He related to objects perhaps more than to people. They anchored his thoughts. To him, they were like icons onto which he projected his private meanings.

Dr. Mesny, also a collector of some attainment, was kind enough "personally to conduct [Sade] to view all the beauties of Florence" (160). Among the very first was the "famous library for manuscripts, called Mediceo Laurenziana," where Sade found the original Cicero manuscript that Petrarch copied. There was a copy of Petrarch's poems, and adorning its cover was "the portrait of Laure and Petrarch." Sade criticized this portrait of his celebrated ancestor because it in no way resembled the other likenesses of Laure he had seen (139). Her face was etched in his memory, and it would be recalled almost four years later in his cell at Vincennes when, after reading the Abbé's biography of Petrarch, Sade saw her oddly beautiful image in a dream.

Sade's next stop was the gallery of the Palazzo Vecchio, where he found the variety of aesthetic experience particularly congenial. Progressing through the rooms of paintings and sculpture, he came upon Titian's Venus, "a lovely blonde with the prettiest eyes in the world, but with features more pronounced than delicate" (151). Also attracting his attention was a sculpture of Venus, which he declared "the loveliest I have ever seen":

> The proportions of this sublime statue, the charms of her face, the divine contours of each limb, the graceful swellings of her breasts and of her buttocks are masterpieces that can even now vie with Nature. . . . Her posture is that of a woman surprised to be observed in the nude, who immediately deploys her hands to cover her breasts and that which modesty does not permit me to name. [153–54]

Rapturous though his admiration of vital beauty might be, Sade was equally fascinated by its antithesis. In another room he found a case containing wax sculptures of corpses:

> One sees a sepulcher filled with an infinite number of cadavers, each one displaying the different gradations of decay, from a cadaver one day old to that which the worms have entirely devoured. This bizarre creation is the work of a Sicilian named Zummo. Everything is executed in wax and tinted in realistic colors. The impression is so overpowering that one's senses are utterly repelled. One instinctively covers one's nose without realizing it upon viewing this dreadful work, which it is difficult to see without bringing to mind ghastly thoughts

of annihilation and, as a consequence, the more consoling thoughts of the Creator. [152]

These two reactions suggest a critical polarity in Sade's sensibility: he is equally moved by the wreckage of worms and the ideal line of Praxiteles, by hell and heaven, by the terror of annihilation and the consoling, uplifting hand of God the Father, by Laure as corpse and Laure as lover.

In the same museum, Sade stopped to admire a statue of Hermaphrodite. He described this one for his wife:

> You are aware, Madame la Comtesse, that the licentiousness of the Romans dared to seek out pleasure even in these sorts of monstrosities. This one is life-size, lying on its stomach, although very slightly on one side; it is resting on its arms in a posture that permits one to see a beautifully feminine bosom; its thighs are somewhat crossed and thoroughly conceal the other feature of the female sex; while the masculine feature is quite vividly revealed; the body is beautiful and its sublime proportions appear with absolute verisimilitude. [156]

Later, in Rome, Sade would complain of the "mistaken religious zeal" of those who disfigured another, equally perfect statue of this species of anatomical curiosity:

> An Hermaphrodite in which the bosom is beautifully formed; at one time, the masculine part was also very well formed, but the master of the house's piety ordered the breaking off of this lewd part so that the statue, thus having only the feminine attribute, has lost all its value and now looks like nothing at all. [211]

Somewhere, Sade acquired his own Hermaphroditic statue which he sent back to La Coste in one of the crates. Like Sade's occasional bisexuality, the statue had a totemic significance: it was another rejection of the conventions and limitations of reality and of gender.

Sade had been traveling incognito, under the name of the Comte de Mazan. Soon, though, his cover was destroyed by his devotion to the theater scene. Inspector Marais's surveillance of actress-courtesans in Paris gave him power over an extraordinarily mobile sort of spy network, extending well into Italy. Sade's entrance into Florence had been immediately reported to Marais by a male dancer named Pitrot in the Comédie-Italienne, who, according to the list of enemies Sade compiled in a 1785 letter to Renée, had been "commanded by Marais to write if I should appear in a court of Italy where he stayed, and who immediately communicated my arrival in Florence." According to the same list, Sade had also detected "a French comic actress" who was serving as Marais's spy in Rome, and who followed him to Naples.[11] Apparently it would require more than an alias for him to evade the surprisingly far-reaching and efficient apparatus of the French police and the tenacity of his mother-in-law.

Despite these perils, Sade found occasion to enjoy his other customary pleasures. It is not surprising that he found ways to meet some of the actresses of Florence. At a ball or a play, Sade came across Sarah Goudar, reputed to be the most beautiful woman in Florence, renowned "as much for the beauty of her face as for the superiority of her figure and the culture of her mind" (164). She was, in fact, the celebrated accomplice of her infamous scoundrel of a husband, Ange Goudar, both of whom were known to Casanova. Sade may have become her lover.[12]

Sade did have among his Florentine lovers one respectable woman. One of Dr. Mesny's five daughters, Mme Chiara Moldetti, was thirty years old and six months pregnant with her sixth child in September 1775, when Sade won and then broke her heart.[13] Her early letters to the Marquis are filled with a girlish glow. "I love you, *mon amour*," she wrote at the height of their romance, "I await you tonight at my house with a passionate eagerness to embrace you."[14] This ardor would endure even after Sade's departure from Rome. As late as February 1776, even as she lamented "the sadness that oppresses my heart," Mme Moldetti could still write, "I always have your adorable image present before my eyes; it is the only pleasure I have experienced in this world since I had the fortune to know you."[15] Her continuing attachment to Sade, and undiminished tenderness, testify to his ability, given an appropriate subject, to inspire the high romantic passion that was always his ideal. There was not the slightest suggestion of perversion or of brutality in his relations with Mme Moldetti. It was only upon women of a much lower class that Sade felt free to conduct his more deviant sexual experiments. With women like his wife, or Mme Moldetti, or elegant actress-courtesans like Beauvoisin and Colet, Sade proved to be a gentle, considerate lover—indeed, an idealistic, romantic lover. If he is remembered today for his pursuit of the basest passions imaginable, it is worth observing that he could also be possessed by the most sublime.

According to the *Voyage d'Italie*, Sade left Florence on October 21, taking the road south to Rome (183). On the fifth day, Sade put up for the night at a "very poor" inn "twelve or fifteen miles" from his destination, just so that he could have the pleasure of entering Rome, "that capital of the World," by daylight. Thus, on October 27, Sade arose early, eager for the sight awaiting him. From more than six miles away, he saw the cupola of Saint Peter's, and as he came closer, in the fields and by the roadside, he saw the ruins of Roman monuments (188).

Sade's account expresses how deeply moved he was to visit the remains of a great classical civilization. His purpose was to celebrate the Roman past, to decry "modern superstition" (255), as he called Christianity, by seeking the subversive—that is, sexual elements in even the most sacred Christian art-work. Upon beholding Bernini's statue of Saint Theresa, whose "look of ecstasy" and "passion afire in her expression" could easily "confuse" the viewer as to the nature of her feelings, Sade observed, "You have to keep reminding yourself that she is a saint" (205). Similarly, in the Church of Saint Eusebio, he admired the sensuality of a painting by Rossetti "representing an Adora-tion of the child of Mary borne on the knees of his mother." Sade found the Virgin so attractive that he allowed as how he would "willingly become one of Mary's followers." There was, he believed, a pagan sensuality at the core of this goddess whom he archly dubbed "this modern Venus of the Christians" (216). Sade's search for the subversive took him to the caves below the Church of Saint Agnes, caves that once housed "the brothels and public places of debauchery." In fact, "the whole church is directly above this ancient and pro-fane place" (303). Beneath the altar of the church, Sade descended into a "sub-terranean vault" where he delighted to discover an exquisite sculpture of a blushing Saint Agnes, "naked" and "covered only by her lovely hair that, according to the miracle, immediately grew so as to spare her tender and modest temptations from the shame of being leered at." Sade objected that this lovely object was buried in a vault where "the viewer can examine such beauties only by the light of a candle. That divine piece was made to be seen by the full light of day" (304–5).

Sade's journey to Italy became a deepening inquiry into the sources of human nature, even its anomalies. He sought the wellspring not only of the sexual urge, but of its sister passion of aggression as well. Standing amidst the ruins of the Colosseum built by Vespasian, Sade could sense "the power of a people and the magnificence of its leaders" (364). He contrasted the "bar-barity" of the "bloody scenes" of combat in the Colosseum with the refined modern spectacles of contemporary French plays, "when the simple panto-mime of an actor who kills himself throws us into tears." To the objection that the ancient Romans "were fierce," Sade would reply that "they were great and we . . . are more human, but much smaller" (366). Such ceremonial ferocity in the ancient Romans was appealing, but Sade was curious as well about another kind of violence—personal, psychotic, pointless. In the Castel

Sant'Angelo, he examined an arsenal containing "some forbidden weapons," including poison daggers. Even more insidious was a sneaky device for indiscriminate murder, murder for pleasure:

> I saw a sort of very small and powerful bow of a unique design that had belonged to a Spaniard whose singular pleasure consisted in shooting by means of this bow (without any other intention than that of gratuitous destruction) several poisoned barbs in the streets and among the crowds where he happened to be, whether in public places or upon coming out of churches. This bizarre mania to do harm for the sole pleasure of doing it is one of the passions of man the least understood and, consequently, the least analyzed, and that I, however, would presume it possible to include in the general class of the madness of the imagination. [356]

The pleasure of gratuitous violence figured importantly in Sade's fantasies. As in the above paragraph, Sade was beginning to formulate a style of portraiture—the psychosexual miniature—that would play a prominent part in *Les Cent Vingt Journées de Sodome*.

During his stay in Rome, Sade acquired a new friend and guide in the person of Giuseppe Iberti, recommended to him by Dr. Mesny. Iberti's connections facilitated Sade's endeavors, sometimes to his own detriment. When, for example, Iberti tried to oblige Sade's desire for access to scandalous information from the Vatican's secret archives, the young doctor fell afoul of the Inquisition and was imprisoned for four months. "I was afraid of being kept there for ten years," he wrote Sade upon his release at the end of 1776 or the beginning of 1777. Iberti did offer to continue to help Sade with his research, "but as to the details of libertinage, excuse me, I am surrounded by spies, and I fear that my letters can be opened in the post office."[16] Iberti's assistance would not go unappreciated: in the Roman section of Sade's *Histoire de Juliette*, Sade celebrates his friend by name as "the most handsome, the most intelligent, and the most amiable doctor of Rome."[17]

At the end of December 1775, Sade left Rome and traveled down to Naples, armed with an introduction to Jean-Baptiste Tierce, a French landscape painter married to one of Dr. Mesny's daughters. But no sooner had he arrived than Sade was engulfed in a crisis. All the trouble arose, as he informed his wife in a letter, because he chose not to be "presented" at Court before King Ferdinand IV. The problem was that, having come to Naples as the Comte de Mazan, he was extremely worried about being recognized and humiliated at Court before the King. His "predicament," he said, "is

dreadful": "I am dying of fear of committing a blunder at this presenta-
tion."[18] His anxiety was exacerbated as he grew more certain that he was
being spied upon by a French actress who had followed him to Naples from
Rome. And to make matters worse, the French chargé d'affaires at Naples,
M. Béranger, became suspicious of the newly arrived Comte de Mazan, and
somehow got it into his head that this French nobleman who would not present himself at Court was really M. Teissier, a clerk in the salt-tax bureau at
Lyons who had absconded with 80,000 livres. Accordingly, the Comte de
Mazan was called in and was "obliged" to prove his identity to M. Béranger.
The Comte de Mazan "produced the letters of [the Marquis de] Donis [Sade's
neighbor at Goult in Provence] and others." But this evidence was deemed
insufficient, and he was ordered to produce more satisfactory proof or be
arrested. In the meantime, Sade was put under police surveillance, and even
"his landlord was warned."[19] How humiliating for the Marquis de Sade, in
flight from a royal lettre de cachet and under a death sentence from the Parlement of Aix, to be mistaken for some mercenary felon by the name of
Teissier! Could not the French chargé d'affaires tell the difference between a
French nobleman (by whatever name he went) and a mere embezzler?

Sade's letter to Renée in February described "the denouement of my
story." By this time, he had gained mastery over the situation by obtaining a
letter of introduction from the *grand-maître* of the Court of Naples. He was
now able to tame his panic and turn his predicament into an entertaining
anecdote, a story:

> I left you at the letter that the *grand-maître* sent me to show to
> Béranger to convince him of my existence and to show that I was per-
> sonally recommended to him. I brought it to Béranger on Sunday
> morning. The said gentleman received me rather rudely. He told me
> that he did not recognize this letter, neither the person nor the hand-
> writing. He certainly fell into the trap that I set for him and he
> answered exactly as I wanted him to.

Sade, who had fallen into every trap that had ever been set for him, who
had even found traps to fall into that no one had ever set (except himself,
perhaps)—this Sade now surprised Renée with an account of his mastery over
the suddenly gullible M. Béranger:

> "Very well, Monsieur," I told him, "I am going to report at once
> to M. le Grand-Maître that you receive thus what he sends to you
> and that you treat thus a letter that comes from his own nephew in
> Florence."

You may imagine the embarrassment of my man; he went off his head, he stamped his feet, but as for me, totally cool, I banter him, telling him that he wondrously performs the duties of his office and that one could not be too careful in an occupation like his, and, meanwhile, I reached the door, continually assuring him that I was going to inform the *grand-maître* of absolutely everything that he told me. . . . You can well imagine that I did not fail to do so!

"What's all this about this naughty fellow?" the *grand-maître* asked me when I returned the letter and gave the details of the case. "What has M. Béranger done about it? I am going to speak to him about it this morning at Court and teach him how to behave!" He spoke with him so well that the result was a visit to me from Béranger in order to tell me that he was at my service and that he would meet with me any time I wished, but I was not inclined to receive his visit and I told his lackey, who came up to my apartment in order to learn if I was in: "Tell your master, Monsieur, that I am not in, and that I will come to him to conduct me to Court the first day that the King does not go hunting." I will be presented in uniform.[20]

Things worked out well after all. Sade rejoiced in entrapping the annoying M. Béranger, and his confidence in his own abilities was renewed. Not the least satisfaction of the experience was in recounting it, and using the power of storytelling to neutralize painful predicaments by fictionalizing them. This is perhaps the first letter to show the pleasure and control that Sade would derive from integrating fact, fantasy, and fiction. During this, his last year of freedom before his long imprisonment, Sade had begun to write himself into a career, and to create a style and express an outlook that make his *Voyage d'Italie* a Sadeian text, whose hallmarks are irony, philosophical speculation, and brutal realism. Sade's account of Naples displays a much more noticeable freedom of thought and felicity of expression than are to be found in the other sections of the *Voyage d'Italie*. Perhaps this was Sade's response to the almost tropical atmosphere and moral corruption of Naples, or simply a result of his increasing confidence and pleasure in the act of writing. Whatever the cause, in this section Sade is at his most writerly and self-revelatory.

On May 5, 1776, after four months in Naples, Sade headed back to Rome, where he would spend a week. Instead of returning through Florence, Sade took a different route, disappointing Dr. Mesny, and no doubt his heartbroken daughter, Mme Moldetti. The detour seems to have been intentional. Had he been frightened by Mme Moldetti's passionate letters? He crossed the Alps on June 15, reached Grenoble on June 18, and stayed three days, hiring as his secretary a young man named Raillanne.[21] Something about Grenoble appealed to Sade; he would return there within a month. But, like so many things that appealed to Sade, this one would prove unfortunate. By the end of June, Sade was back at La Coste. The wolf-man of Provence was in his den once more.

CHAPTER 11

The Shot

URING SADE'S year away in Italy, little had happened at home to improve his situation. When he returned home at the end of June 1776, the threat of scandal still clung to the château. Nanon was still imprisoned at Arles under a lettre de cachet. In July, the young girl entrusted to Ripert at Mazan fled to Orange, where she made a deposition before a judge. In August, one of the girls Sade had hired for that scandalous winter of 1774–75—little Marie, a cook—died of a fever after having been removed from the château, despite her plaintive requests to stay.[1] Sade's appeal of the contempt judgment at Aix had got completely bogged down.

The young man Sade had hired as his secretary at Grenoble proved uncooperative, and Sade returned to Grenoble to trade him in for a new one. The position itself was redundant, since La Jeunesse did all of Sade's copying work in a very clear and careful hand. Nevertheless, at Grenoble, with the assistance of Mme. Giroud, a bookseller, Sade hired a new secretary, a young man named André Lamalatié, or Malatié.[2] He may have been a more willing "secretary" than Raillanne, but he was quite unlettered; Renée would later say, "He seemed to me such an idiot!"[3] The following is the beginning of a letter written to Gaufridy by this secretary (translation can scarcely suggest the deformity of the original French):

Monsieur Gofredie
lawyer of La Coste
Apt in Provaince

Monsieur
Gofredie I beg you to have the complesance to find me desent place in the village ofApt because I not at all the intension of my returning to my house.[4]

Lamalatié would become yet another loose end in the tangle of Sade's sexual life. Having arrived at La Coste in the summer of 1776, he would be in a position to know all about the new scandals of the coming winter.

During that summer, in his study at La Coste, surrounded by his books and the objects he had collected from Italy, Sade began to write his *Voyage d'Italie*. There was little comfort to be found at home. He was virtually penniless and utterly dependent upon Mme de Montreuil. By November 19, Mme de Montreuil had to send Gaufridy 1,200 livres, prompted by her daughter's pathetic appeal to her, claiming that she was out of food and that she lacked firewood, and even glass for the broken windows in her room. Gaufridy, however, was expected to disburse payments only for Renée's particular needs. She complained to him on November 27 that her mother's "torturous arrangements" would now oblige her to send Gaufridy to the butcher, the baker, etc.[5] Renée's pen was evidently becoming quite sharp.

Despite his money problems, Sade spent a couple of weeks in October at Montpellier in search of amusement.[6] According to his "Grande Lettre," he found there Rosette, one of the servant girls who had taken part in the escapades at La Coste during the winter of 1774–75. He *"saw her there,"* he said, *"in every way imaginable, or, to put it more decently, saw her in the fullest extent of the term."* And she was pleased enough with him to introduce him to another willing friend, Adélaïde, who was promised that she would find nothing at La Coste to complain about "except for the loneliness there."[7] Sade planned to gather a contingent of servants similar to the group Nanon had put together for him from Lyons and Vienne during the winter of 1774–75. This time, he was assisted by a friar in Montpellier named Durand, who spread the word that staff positions were available at a nobleman's château "about fifteen leagues [thirty-seven miles] from Montpellier."[8] Durand was mistaken or else duplicitous, for La Coste is actually more than ninety miles from Montpellier. Two daughters of a Montpellier gardener named Besson told their friend Catherine Trillet about the job for a cook. Catherine, according to her father, was "quite pretty"[9]—"an epithet," Sade would later have occasion to deny, saying that it "does not suit her at all."[10] "Besides," Sade added in another letter to Gaufridy, "her age put me out of danger"[11]—she was twenty-two years old. Catherine and the two Besson girls[12] went to Sade's inn for inspection, where Catherine, "who earned forty écus at Montpellier, asked M. de Sade for fifty, which he promised to her and offered to pay her according to how she would serve him." Catherine's father, a weaver by trade, made inquiries of Père Durand, who assured them that the house of Sade was very much like a convent in its orderliness and in its morals, and that this girl could not find a better place. The next day, Saturday, she entered into service with M. de Sade, and Père Durand conducted her alone by carriage to the château of La Coste. M. de Sade did not leave Montpellier until two or three days later. Père Durand and Bataillet, a carter, on returning to Montpellier, informed Trillet that his daughter had been considerably apprehensive before entering the château, but that Mme de Sade, to whom he brought her, had comforted her.[13]

When Sade returned to La Coste in November, he was well pleased with his new cook, and she with him. He chose to call her "Justine," a name he would make notorious in his libertine novels.

But Sade believed that he required more servants. Around the middle of December, according to M. Trillet's deposition, "M. de Sade wrote to Père Durand to send to him at La Coste a chambermaid, a kitchen helper, a *perruquier*, and a secretary."[14] Sade would later deny that he had "ever asked for them" in view of "the little need I had of them."[15] Nevertheless, they were brought by Père Durand from Montpellier to La Coste. M. Trillet's deposition describes what happened that night:

> After supper on the day of their arrival, M. de Sade shut each of them in a separate room, and during the night, he tried to have his way with them by offering a purse with money in it; which provoked them to leave the next day for Montpellier with the friar and in the same coach driven by the said Bataillet, a carter, with the exception of the kitchen helper [Catherine Trillet], who remained and is still in the service of M. de Sade.

When three out of the four new servants returned to Montpellier, they "warned" Trillet about "what happened," and he "complained about it to Père Durand." The friar acknowledged "having known in the past about M. de Sade's disorders," but he now "believed him returned to his senses and very much better." Trillet claimed that Durand first "tried to put him off going to take back his daughter," then agreed to write a letter to Sade for him. This letter, however, "was opened by the Father Superior," who found that "it was written contrary to Trillet's wishes." Trillet, evidently, could not read, and Durand had only pretended to write what Trillet dictated. Durand's ruse having been discovered, he was obliged to write a new letter, and then he was expelled from the monastery.[16]

When Sade was accused of attempting to seduce these new servants, his response smelled of the lawyer's lamp. First, he said that it was not he but "a servant" who "led them to bed." Rather, "he remained to chat with Madame [de Sade] and Père Durand," while the new servants "shut themselves in their rooms until four o'clock the next morning, when the same servant awakened them for their departure." In any case, Sade claimed, these servants were too old and too ugly to appeal to him: they were "Nature's horror for their age and looks." Yet, even if he had found them attractive, he said, "I would not that same night have violated their modesty." Sade called upon his lawyer Gaufridy to bear witness concerning the charge that he tempted these servants with money: "No one knows better than M. Gaufridy that, at that time, I did not have a sol." In short, according to Sade's dubious, nitpicking defense, all these charges were a pack of "slanders invented" by M. Trillet.[17]

When Catherine Trillet's father heard what these servants had to say after their return to Montpellier, he decided to go to La Coste himself, and he put a pistol in his pocket, even though it was illegal for an ordinary person to carry arms without a permit. Around one o'clock on the afternoon of Friday, January 17, 1777, M. Trillet arrived at La Coste and presented himself at the great door of the château. It was locked. Next to the door was a wire attached to a bell. He rang. A servant appeared. M. Trillet explained that he was the father of Catherine, the cook, and asked to see her. The versions of what happened next vary, but, taken together, they add up to a clear picture of the event.[18]

According to Trillet, when he asked to speak to Sade, a servant told him "that Monsieur was not in":

He asked for Madame, who appeared a moment later; he identified himself as the father of her cook. Madame spoke a few words in private to her servant; they both went and told Trillet to wait, M. de Sade appeared, insulted him, threatened him, told him that his daughter was only too happy to be in his employ, he called her by the name of Justine. At this moment, the daughter appeared, flew in tears onto the neck of her father. M. de Sade quickly drew her away from the arms of her father, pushed her, and with violence locked her up in a room, so that she and her father could not speak to each other, and he also violently pushed the father out of the château, threatened to have him rot in prison if he did not immediately leave his lands, and told him that his daughter had to fulfill the year for which she had engaged herself in his service.

Trillet offered three witnesses to his ill treatment at the hands of Sade.[19] "False," Sade objected in his itemized retort. "At the first meeting, there was no witness at all, unfortunately; I would have very much wished that there had been one."[20] Trillet left another crack in his deposition when he acknowledged that his daughter had given him 12 livres during that first meeting.[21] Sade, quick to detect the slightest discrepancy, wrote the following note on his copy of Trillet's deposition: "If his daughter had had the time to give him twelve *livres*, they therefore had the time to speak to each other." "Thus," Sade concluded rather airily, Trillet's other charges were equally "false."[22]

For his part, Sade called Trillet "obviously a lying scoundrel and a dishonest fellow" and dismissed his deposition as "false and calumnious." Sade also denied using foul language: Trillet, he complained, "is the one who started in with impertinences."[23] Sade had been upstairs in his study, perhaps working on his *Voyage d'Italie*, when, informed of Trillet's presence below, he came down to deal with him: "This fellow came forward with an insolent air and said that he is here to get his daughter, having learned . . . And with that, he disgorges every filthy word belonging to his condition, etc. His insolent manner rather put me off a bit." Sade claimed that he kept his temper and offered to return Justine (as he persisted in calling Catherine)—as soon as he found a substitute cook. Given Trillet's enraged state and his charge that Sade had seduced or imprisoned his daughter, the offer to return her only when a new cook could be found displayed Sade's characteristic misjudgment of the situation he had got himself into. Was the Lord of La Coste to overthrow his household just to please this weaver fellow from Montpellier? A little window is flung open into Sade's egoism by his later question to Gaufridy: "But dare I ask you if, in order to have order reign in my house, I have to cook my soup myself?"[24]

Sade was attempting to conduct Trillet out the great door of the château. Renée was at her husband's side throughout this encounter. If only they could get the heavy wooden door shut! According to Sade, "at the precise moment the rascal's feet touched the threshold of the great door," Trillet turned to face them.[25] According to the inquiry report, "without Monsieur le Marquis or Madame la Marquise noticing it," Trillet then "furtively slipped his hand into his pocket," and "drew out a pistol."[26] Sade had no sympathy for this man's predicament or his state of mind—a father confronted with the man he believed had defiled his daughter. Lacking such sympathy, Sade had no capacity for anticipating what Trillet would do next, as he was propelled from his daughter's presence and out the door of the château. "At that very instant," Sade would tell Gaufridy, "without replying and without warning, he let fly a pistol shot point-blank at my chest, of which, fortunately for me, only the primer fired, and he immediately took flight. You may imagine my fright and that of the whole house." It was, as Sade described it to Gaufridy, "a terrifying event," and one "which had really made me think that I would never see you again."[27]

Trillet, for his part, turned and fled the château into the town of La Coste. He stopped, as luck would have it, at the house of a person whom Sade did not like and who did not like Sade, the village curate, Testanière, the person who had earlier made annoying inquiries that could have implicated Sade and Renée in the death of Nanon's infant. Among other things, the unrepentant Trillet told the curate, "I am extremely sorry that the pistol misfired; otherwise, Monsieur le Marquis would have been killed instantly."[28] Sade, believing that Trillet had fled the neighborhood, was surprised to learn that "this fellow" was still down in the town at Mathieu Béridon's cabaret, "prattling the most dreadful slanders before the whole village." Sade tried to get Gaufridy to come, and he also sent for Blancard, the brigadier of the constabulary of Apt, but both of them, he discovered, would be unavailable for six days.[29]

Trillet was gossiping freely and arousing the villagers below the château. The situation appeared out of control. By early evening, Catherine suggested to Sade that she be allowed to see her father in order to calm him down. Sade sent Bontemps, a mason working at the château, to retrieve Trillet, which effort Trillet resisted, "claiming that they were trying to entice him up to the château only to set a trap for him."[30] Catherine sent Bontemps back down, and at nine o'clock at night, her father finally agreed to come up, but only with an escort, including the two masons, Bontemps and Perrin. According to the inquiry report, when the party reached the great door of the château, "Monsieur le Marquis and Madame la Marquise came to the door; without opening it, they talked for a while, on opposite sides of the said door."[31] The conversation was "extremely heated," Sade wrote, "the fellow continually prosecuting his harangue with abuse and the daughter doing whatever she could to appease and distract her father." There was a small window in the outer wall of the château, blocked on the inside with wooden shutters. The conversation or argument moved to this window, which, prudently, Sade kept shut from inside. Even so, when Trillet thought he could gauge the direction of Sade's voice, he "let fly," according to Sade, "a second pistol shot," through the shutters, "hoping (so he said) to hit me in the courtyard, where he claimed to hear me." Was it a mere oversight, or indifference to their lord's welfare, that prevented anyone in the village from disarming Trillet after his first attempt on Sade's life? Although Trillet's blind shot missed its target, the explosion was stunning. According to Sade, "instead of seizing that fellow," Trillet's escorts on the outside were overcome with terror and "ran for their lives."[32] Trillet also took to his heels, and did not stop until he again reached Béridon's cabaret. Naturally, he would be thirsty after his exertion.

Sade complained to Gaufridy that Trillet had not been arrested even then: these people of La Coste "put my life in jeopardy yet a third time by not arresting that fellow and leaving him at liberty, which I thought was *disgraceful.*"[33] Sade was shocked by the disloyalty of his vassals: "I assure you that, were they all to be roasted one after the other, I would supply the firewood without batting an eye." Sade told Gaufridy that there were larger issues at stake in prosecuting Trillet: "it does not suit me to bend before a fellow who began by insulting me," because that weakness would set a very bad example "on my lands especially . . . where it is so important to maintain in the vassals the respect that they owe and of which they are only too ready to withdraw at any moment." Sade sensed an erosion of his authority as a noble: "Today a stranger comes to demand his daughter with a shot from a pistol, the day after tomorrow a peasant will come to demand his wages with a shot from a rifle. Do they not already demonstrate enough independence . . . ?"[34] It was then twelve years before the Revolution. Sade's libertine lifestyle and his sense of his own prerogatives were teetering on the cusp of a great social and political change that was already well under way. He could feel this change, but he would not, he could not, adapt himself to it.

This January 17, 1777, had already been a long day, and it would be hours before the candles at the château could be snuffed. Around midnight, Sade sent Thomas Paulet "as mediator" down to the cabaret. Paulet took Trillet "to sleep at his place so he would quiet down, stop prating nonsense." The next day, "negotiations were begun." Sade "was in favor of a speedy indictment" of Trillet, but Rayolle, the judge of La Coste, informed Sade that proper form would have to be followed, and this would take time. Meanwhile, according to Sade, "the whole day of Saturday, the *pacific Paulet* was negotiating" with Trillet. The result was that Catherine saw her father one more time "on neutral ground," the cellar of Sade's farmer Chauvin. There, she gave him a louis for his trip and proposed that she return to Montpellier at the beginning of Lent: "The fellow agreed to everything, grumbling through his teeth, however, that he would do better to go and bring his complaint to Aix." On Sunday, Trillet's departure was delayed "because of the bad weather." He was still grumbling about seeking justice at Aix, and on Monday morning he finally left La Coste heading in that direction.[35]

Sade asked Gaufridy to inquire through the Aix lawyer Mouret whether Trillet arrived there and lodged a complaint. If so, he wanted Gaufridy to convey his side of the story to M. de Castillon, the prosecutor for the Parlement of Aix, and to ask for "his advice, assuring him that our complete trust and respect in him will lead us to follow blindly whatever he advises."[36] In his next letter to Gaufridy, Sade insisted on having Trillet arrested for attempted murder: "Otherwise you will prove to me that the only thing they want now is my death."[37] Gaufridy, however, advised Sade to avoid any actions, such as prosecuting Trillet at Aix, that could revive public interest in Sade's previous scandal involving the servant girls during the winter of 1774–75. But Sade, typically, could not see how *that* had anything to do with *this*. In the meantime, Trillet had already filed his charges and prejudiced the mind of M. de Castillon, who now "imagines," Sade complained, that Catherine Trillet was "kept prisoner for every other purpose than in the kitchen."[38] The lawyer Mouret informed Gaufridy on January 30 that M. de Castillon extenuated Trillet's violent behavior because of his fear for his daughter. Taking note of Sade's "unfortunate reputation," Mouret added, "Suspicions and fears of this sort would not be misplaced." Thus, there would be no official response to Trillet's gunshots. Mouret reported that Trillet's "acts of violence" in fact "legitimate" Trillet's suspicions.[39] "I am convinced," Sade replied, "that if this fellow had *killed* me they would still have said that *I was to blame*."[40]

The year 1777 had begun dangerously and dismally, and it would not get any better. Even before Trillet's appearance, Sade had expected trouble. Gaufridy had received an anonymous letter informing him that "ten cavaliers and an officer are supposed to leave to go to arrest him. They expect to arrest him at your fair of Saint-Clair" in Gaufridy's town of Apt on January 2.[41] Sade had written to Gaufridy and asked him to come at once to La Coste and to bring 50 louis, "the warnings being only too clear and the need for my departure only too obvious."[42] Sade had hidden out for a while, only to return to La Coste by January 17 to stare down the barrel of Trillet's pistol. No place was safe for him, and Sade was becoming desperate. A few days before Trillet's arrival at La Coste, Sade had Renée write a long letter to Mme de Montreuil. It arrived in Paris on the night of January 17, just as Trillet was making his second attempt on Sade's life. Even before she learned about this new scandal, Mme de Montreuil was furious, as can be felt in her letter to Gaufridy on January 21: "I received ten large pages of threats and invectives from Madame de Sade, which would have to be seen to be believed. If I wished to seek vengeance or to punish her for it, I would show it to the ministers who better than I know how to judge their conduct and mine and the justice of her complaints and reproaches. Whether she is the author of it or only the scribe, she is no less culpable in my eyes." In an outpouring of righteous indignation, "overwrought by all the infamies and unjust things that I suffer from them," Mme de Montreuil refused to have any further concern for Sade's finances or his creditors, and, she added, "I absolutely renounce getting involved with whatever concerns them."[43] Gaufridy tried to warn Sade that the Catherine Trillet scandal would only further arouse Mme de Montreuil's wrath. "You understand her very badly," Sade blithely rebuked him: "Do not imagine that Madame de M[ontreuil] was angry that there had been at my house some decent person who was nice to me; I assure you that she would be the first to approve of it, provided that this was not a topic of scandal."[44] But it already was a scandal, and it was Sade himself who very badly understood Mme de Montreuil. He was thinking of the time at the beginning of his marriage—the time of his tearful, boyish confessions and the confidences he and Mme de Montreuil shared, his promises of better behavior that he was sure she believed. But she had long since stopped enjoying the role of his confessor and fellow conspirator. Perhaps that had been a flattering, pleasant interlude for her. But Sade had not seen his mother-in-law for almost six years; since then, there had been his affair with her favorite daughter, the scandal at Marseilles, his imprisonment at Miolans arranged through Mme de Montreuil's influence, the police raids on La Coste, and the more recent scandals. Whereas she had once thought to help him, now she flaunted her influence with ministers and sought his arrest, his destruction. Sade was too far out of touch with her and with reality to stop her, or even to see what everyone else could see.

Near the end of January 1777, Sade learned that his mother, long a resident of a Carmelite convent in Paris, had taken seriously ill. On January 30, Sade and Renée left La Coste in separate coaches to visit his ailing mother. Sade traveled with La Jeunesse, and Renée with Catherine Trillet, who, Sade said, "threw herself on the mercy of Madame . . . in order to beg her to take her to Paris, telling her that she absolutely did not want to go to Montpellier."[45] If M. Trillet showed up, Sade advised Gaufridy to tell him that Catherine would be returned to him when Mme de Sade came back to La Coste.[46] Heedless of the legal advice of Gaufridy and others, Sade had in the end done just what he wanted. The rest of his letter to Gaufridy contained the usual complaints of the winter traveler: the roads were "horrible" and so was the weather.[47]

It was extremely dangerous for Sade to go to Paris, the seat of his mother-in-law's power. Even Gothon, Sade's housekeeper at La Coste, thought he was foolish to go.[48]

CHAPTER 12

Vincennes—House
of Silence

ON FEBRUARY 8, 1777, the day Sade entered Paris, his lawyer at Aix, Reinaud, wrote to Gaufridy predicting trouble for their patron. Reinaud said that he would stake his life on his belief that Mme de Montreuil's letter alerting Sade to his mother's illness was "a trap . . . especially coming after a recent failed attempt" by officers to arrest Sade in Provence on January 2—an attempt Reinaud correctly ascribed to Mme de Montreuil. He believed that Mme de Montreuil, "tired of seeing her mines exploded, is plotting a subtle stratagem so as to obtain by guile what had been denied her by force." Now, "without the slightest doubt," he attributed to Mme de Montreuil the letter that lured Sade "like an imbecile" to Paris.[1]

There is something of class rivalry in Reinaud's contempt for the gullibility of the foolish Marquis who was blind to Mme de Montreuil's schemes. Also evident is Reinaud's solidarity with his fellow professional Gaufridy. He warned Gaufridy to keep the records of his dealings with Sade in a safe place: "This is a wise precaution with respect to certain noblemen who no longer know you as soon as they cease having any need of you, and this one can well be placed in that class."[2] A little while later, Reinaud wrote to Gaufridy to learn if his prediction had come true—that is, "if our Priapus is still at large."[3]

When Sade arrived in Paris on the night of February 8 to see his sick mother, he discovered that she had been dead for more than three weeks. Indeed, she had died on January 14, more than two weeks before he left La Coste to visit her. Sade and his mother had not seen each other for many years. There is not even a single letter extant between them. It would appear that Sade, dependent upon his mother-in-law for news of his mother, had been seriously duped by her. There is no other way to explain his actions.

Sade and Renée had agreed not to inform her mother of his arrival for a while. He had also taken the precaution of installing his wife in the Hôtel de Danemark on the rue Jacob. He felt safer lodging separately from his wife, whose whereabouts would become known to Mme de Montreuil. As Renée informed Gaufridy, on February 10, her husband was shocked to learn about his mother's death; he "had raised his hopes on the journey and the blow has been all the more felt." Sade immediately retired to "the house of his friend"—a term generally applied in Sade's correspondence to his old tutor, the Abbé Amblet—who, according to Renée, "welcomed him very kindly and who is giving him the greatest possible attention."[4]

His mother was dead, but the next thing Sade did was write the following letter to an unidentified libertine abbé, obviously an old friend from his past debauches in Paris:

> My mother's death, my dear Abbé, brought me here at the very moment you least expected it, since I wrote to you only a few days ago to renew my pleas for you to come to Provence. The occasion of this death and the situation concerning my parents-in-law, with whom I am still not completely reconciled, oblige me to remain incognito for some time longer. Thus, I ask you not to tell anyone that I am here. But I am burning to see you, to recount for you all my conquests, to listen to yours, and to perform some of them together. The services that I requested of you for Provence can now be performed here, since here I am. Moreover, I will confess to you that, as for myself, I have the greatest need of these services, having found no one who performs them for me like you. But you will be paid back in kind if you require it, so you will not find me remiss in any way. Indicate a rendezvous anywhere in some place not too public, or at your place, and however late at night it may be, I will be there on time, and we will do a bit of hunting. You can send back your reply with the person who delivers my letter, without either asking him any questions or giving him any details about me, for reasons that I will tell you.
>
> I embrace you with all my heart.[5]

Sade offers up the death of his mother as an unforeseen opportunity for a rendezvous. His tone is eager, excited, adolescent. In a kind of secret code, he alludes to sado-masochistic activities—Sade's great need for the "services" only this Abbé can perform. Interestingly, part of the pleasure of this letter is literary, verbal—the conspiratorial tone, its allusions—just as some of the anticipated pleasure of their meeting will be verbal—the recounting of past "conquests." Past "conquests"—that is the romantic term with which Sade encapsulates his sexual escapades for the past six or so years—the affair with his sister-in-law Anne-Prospère, the Marseilles prostitutes, the two winters with various servants at La Coste, the Italian conquests, all the actresses, all the "secretaries," all the prostitutes in various towns: they become verses in Sade's boastful song of himself. Very soon, in a day or two, and for the next thirteen years in prison, all he would have would be himself and words.

On the night of Thursday, February 13, Inspector Marais entered Mme de Sade's apartment at the Hôtel de Danemark and arrested Sade by order of the King, under a lettre de cachet arranged by Sade's mother-in-law. Without delay, Marais drove him under guard eastward across Paris, to the fortified royal château of Vincennes. Sade was familiar with this prison and its peculiar rules and rituals, having spent about two weeks there in the fall of 1763, following the complaint of the prostitute Jeanne Testard. This new arrest could not have been as much of a surprise as Sade would later claim. He had intended to hide his arrival from his mother-in-law, and he would blame Renée for letting the secret out. But if the trip was foolhardy in the first place, and if he had come only to see his sick mother, why did he remain in Paris when he discovered that she was already dead?

Disregarding the danger of his situation, he decided that he could not return to La Coste unless he made some settlement with Mme de Montreuil. He was virtually without funds; the Trillet affair the previous month showed how little influence he had at Aix, where his appeal of the contempt judgment would have to be heard; and during the same month, he had avoided yet another police attempt to arrest him at La Coste. In a sense, he had little choice but to try his luck with Mme de Montreuil once more. Sade later explained his motives to an unnamed official, probably Lieutenant General of Police Jean-Charles Lenoir. He said that he had come to Paris "because of my mother's death." His "intention," he said, "was to make use of this circumstance to plan" his appeal at Aix "with his wife's parents"; "to beg them to pardon me"; and "to beg them to take the place of parents whom death had taken from me."[6] It is difficult, as always, precisely to assess Sade's emotions—for example, how much he was shocked by his mother's death or, as here, to what extent he had consciously anticipated it before he had left for Paris, intending, as he now claimed, to make use of it to curry sympathy with Mme de Montreuil. In any case, he certainly did not want to appear a fool before Lenoir, and he also sought to portray his mother-in-law as unsympathetic during his time of grief. Despite the utter impracticability of Sade's hope for a rapprochement, this was his plan, if that is not too strong a term. He acted, as always, out of overwhelming emotional need, taking pride in not considering the consequences of his actions, as if he believed that spontaneity, even folly, would suggest sincerity, openness of heart, innocence. His great need made him feel that his cause was just and that he deserved to succeed. Thus, he came to believe that he *would* succeed.

In the above letter Sade ruefully acknowledged that Mme de Montreuil did not respond to his overtures for peace.[7] Notwithstanding his intention to remain "incognito" in Paris, he was sufficiently deluded to try to communicate with his mother-in-law, whom he and Renée regularly referred to as "The Hyena" in their correspondence.[8] In a letter to Renée on April 18, Sade claimed that, at the "instant" he was arrested, he had been telling her "not to put any trust in that reassuring letter from your mother."[9] Evidently there had been some attempt at negotiation, some new effort by Sade to woo his mother-in-law with tears, apologies, promises of reformation. But at nearly thirty-seven, he was too old for the part, and she had seen it played too often. She put the matter to Gaufridy in a rhetorical question: "You, who have known everything, virtually seen everything, . . . do you believe that it is wise to rely upon good resolutions?" She wondered how one could "possibly know if they were really genuine." She said that she had received an anonymous letter from Apt that led her to conclude that Sade's "resolutions on leaving" Provence "were not like the repentance displayed here," in Paris.[10] Thus, Sade had indeed tried that same old song, but Mme de Montreuil was past listening.

On April 18, Sade wrote Renée the following account of his arrest at the Hôtel de Danemark: "Your room became filled with *a pack of rascals*—who, without presenting any order from the King, came, they nevertheless said, to arrest me in the name of the King." In retrospect, Sade tried to cast his trip to Paris in a brave light, claiming that, although "surprised" at his mother-in-law's having him arrested, he was not "deceived" by her: "In coming here, I acted like Caesar, who said *that it was better to face the dangers that one feared once in one's life than to live in the perpetual anxiety of avoiding them.* This philosophy brought him to the Senate, where he well knew that the conspirators lay in wait for him. I have done the same."[11] In fact, the event was not as heroic as Sade pretended to his wife. When Marais and his "rascals" burst into Renée's room, as Sade complained to Lenoir, "they dragged me as ignominiously as possible" to Vincennes.[12] Sade put up no struggle, any more than he had done when he had been arrested in Chambéry. In the coach on the way to Vincennes, Inspector Marais explained to Sade, numbed and depressed, "In order to settle my appeal . . . my detention was necessary."[13] Later, in his letter to Renée, Sade ridiculed the notion that he had been arrested for his own good: "It is for my own good, they say. Divine phrase! in which immediately one recognizes the customary language of *stupidity triumphant.* So, it is for a man's own good to put him at risk of going crazy, for his own good to have his health ruined, for his own good that he is fed on the tears of his own despair! I confess that I had never before been so fortunate as to realize and to sample such goodness. . . ."[14]

In the darkness of a wintry night, the coach entered the compound of Vincennes and stopped at the gate of the donjon. The guard cried, "Who goes there?" Marais replied, "By order of the King!" The soldiers averted their eyes; they were not to gaze on noble prisoners detained by royal prerogative. A warning bell was sounded, and the drawbridge descended.[15] The coach crossed over the deep fosse. Entrance through the three iron-reinforced doors in the massive outer wall was complicated, requiring separate keys from the sentries on the outside and the guards within. The doors were so strong that Mirabeau thought only artillery could breach them.[16] Unlike at Miolans, there could be no escape from Vincennes. (Even today, the force and meaning of the donjon are dreadful. During the Nazi occupation, it was used as a torture chamber.) Inside the walls, the horses' hooves rang on the cobblestones of the courtyard. Above, the connected towers of the donjon loomed like a four-barreled shotgun carved of stone. The single entrance to the donjon itself was guarded by another three massive doors, curiously arranged so that only a few persons could enter or leave at a time: opening the first door blocked the second from being opened, and the same arrangement limited passage for the second and the third. The donjon was picturesque only if one had no serious connection with it. Rousseau, happily on his way to pay a visit to the Prince of Saxe-Gotha's country house, felt guilty thinking of Diderot, then imprisoned in the donjon. "As I passed Vincennes," Rousseau wrote in his *Confessions*, "and saw the keep I felt a pang at my heart."[17] He did not, of course, stop the coach.

Mirabeau, who began his own imprisonment at Vincennes a few months after Sade, tried to describe the devastation of the entering prisoner: "Reality weighs upon him: conscious pain rends his heart and forces tears to his eyes."[18] Once inside the tower, Mirabeau described the climb up to the cells: "The iron doors turn on their enormous hinges, and the vaults echo this lugubrious harmony. A narrow, steep, tortuous staircase prolongs the march and multiplies the detours; vast rooms are crossed: the trembling lamp, which scarcely pierces this ocean of gloom and allows one to see everywhere locks, bolts, and bars, increases the horror of such a spectacle and the terror it inspires."[19]

Sade described his cell and his predicament in a letter to his wife: "I am in a tower, locked up behind nineteen iron doors, glimpsing the daylight through two little windows each fitted with a score of iron bars. For about ten or twelve minutes a day, I have the company of a fellow who brings me my food. The rest of the time I spend alone and in tears. . . . That is my life. . . . That is how they reform a man in this country."[20]

Mirabeau depicted the depressing cell in more detail: "The unfortunate finally reaches his cave: he finds there a pallet, two straw-covered chairs and often of wood, a pot nearly always chipped, a table smeared with grease. . . . And what else is there? . . . nothing.—Imagine the effect produced on his mind the first time he glances around himself." All of the prisoner's personal effects were confiscated: "money, watch, jewelry, lace, wallet, knife, scissors, everything is taken from him." Then, Mirabeau continued, the prisoner was paid an official visit by the commandant of the prison, Charles-Joseph de Rougemont, who explained the seemingly endless and extremely onerous rules of the establishment. Prisoners were kept isolated from one another in their own cells and not permitted to communicate in any way at all. They were also forbidden to speak to their guards and turnkeys, or even their physicians, except concerning the most mundane and superficial matters. Before leaving the poor prisoner to his own thoughts, Commandant de Rougemont intoned in a dreadful manner, *"This is the house of silence."*[21]

Within Vincennes's solitary and largely silent confinement, writing letters would become an important consolation for Sade. Like the novels and plays he also wrote in prison, the letters were a kind of discourse with himself, as well as his only means of communication with the outside world, that reality to which he had never been strongly or authentically connected. Furthermore, his letters from prison constitute some of the most important documents in the Sade canon—dramatically revealing an already fragile mentality virtually disintegrating because of its own weakness and the weight of solitude and stone pressing upon it. Like shards of a broken mirror, the letters reflect—sometimes in surprising, or pathetic, or brilliant ways—the mosaic of his fractured psyche. For all their revelatory value, though, these documents proved worthless in the one purpose for which Sade intended them: swaying those who oppressed him.

Except for his wife, Sade had no allies on the outside. When the Abbé de Sade had learned of the arrest, he wrote to Gaufridy on February 23 that he believed that "everyone will be pleased."[22] Renée, of course, was not. Mme de Montreuil had played her daughter and her son-in-law for fools. Immediately after Sade's arrest, Renée tried to influence her mother to obtain his release, but, now and forevermore, she would have no impact on the thinking or decisions of her mother, who regarded Renée as a kind of love-besotted ninny. "How can she be as blind as she seems?" she asked Gaufridy. Mme de Montreuil believed that Renée's personal experience of Sade's offenses at La Coste ought to have convinced her that her husband needed to be locked up: "Because, at last, she should have seen, known, been *convinced* for herself that finally it all is not just slander!"[23]

Mme de Montreuil's clandestine correspondence with Gaufridy during the next few months shows her efforts to destroy evidence at La Coste of what she took to be Sade's extremely serious offenses there. She would try to control the scandal for the sake of her grandchildren, now that their father had been safely locked away. For example, on April 29, she wrote to Gaufridy about "a certain room which it would be good to destroy. This is dangerous evidence to allow to exist."[24] On June 3, she referred to some "discovery" made there by Gothon, Sade's housekeeper, of papers or objects—"traces," she called them—that she feared might be some sort of libertine "mechanical devices." Confusingly, she also used "paper" as a code word to mean the several servants who had taken part in Sade's debauches at La Coste, and who (like Nanon) still needed to be kept in prison or closely watched, lest they make further damaging revelations.[25] Mme de Montreuil was kept very busy. Her son-in-law was in prison and she had all of his former servants to manage, clandestine correspondence to maintain with Gaufridy and who-knows-who-else, ministers and police and prison officials to confer with over strategy, lawyers and judges at Aix to write to concerning the appeal of Sade's contempt sentence, all Sade's writings to hide or destroy. Mme de Montreuil was now in her ascendancy.

Managing Sade's affairs was almost a full-time job for her; she was almost a division of the government. If only she could make her daughter see things as she did. Renée's attempts to get Sade out of Vincennes were "incomprehensible," Mme de Montreuil wrote to Gaufridy.[26] She was offended by her daughter's "obstinacy," which "will force me to speak openly to her" about "the manner in which I have been most authoritatively informed" of Sade's crimes.[27] A year and a half later, on September 15, 1778, Mme de Montreuil wrote to Gaufridy that she was sorry that he had destroyed (following her instructions) the remains of "the small loose sheets and of the two volumes" that had been discovered in Sade's attic at La Coste. It cannot be known now what they contained, but she felt that Renée would not be so angry with her if she could have been shown them: then "she could not deny the dangers from which she was protected and the justice and wisdom of the precautions taken."[28]

After Sade was arrested in her apartment, Renée did not even know where he was taken. Now, as throughout his imprisonment, she was able to write to him only by means of unsealed letters sent to the office of Lieutenant General of Police Lenoir, where he or his assistant, M. Boucher, read and censored them. The same procedure was applied to Sade's letters to his wife. Immediately after his arrest, Renée wrote to her husband: "How have you passed the night, my sweet love? I was rather worried about it, although they told me that you were well. I will not be content until I see you. Rest easy, I beg of you." She had already written to Lenoir to arrange a personal servant for Sade, a luxury that was sometimes accorded noble prisoners (but at this time was not granted to Sade), and she said that she would go to see M. Amelot, minister of the King's household. She also saw Inspector Marais, who assured her that Sade "will be released immediately after the conclusion" of the appeal at Aix. "Count upon me," Renée told her husband, "as the best friend [Sade's notation on her letter: 'a rotten board'] whom nothing could topple."[29] Here, as throughout Renée's letters to him, Sade made interlinear comments on what she wrote. Often these comments refer to what he called her "signals," secret messages that he took to refer to the date of his release. He also pored over Renée's letters for opportunities to make sarcastic comments, seeking perhaps to simulate the intimacy of an actual argument.

In the two days following her husband's arrest, Renée had been busy, and had been told a number of things. And none of them were true. She did not even know what prison he was in. In the above letter, she wrote that she surmised he was in Vincennes, but she soon came to doubt her guess and focused her attention on the Bastille. On February 21, she proudly wrote to Sade that she had discovered "by dint of stratagem" that he was in the Bastille.[30] She proceeded to make a vain trip there, and of course learned nothing. Only on June 4, almost four months after the arrest, could Renée finally report to Gaufridy (who, as Mme de Montreuil's confidant, must have known from the beginning) that Sade was in Vincennes. Renée was excited by her discovery, but she was also bitter: "I know where M. de Sade is, I know it, I assure you, with thanks to no one. If I receive any news, it is like a child's game; these are letters opened by the minister, unsealed. When I write anything that might mean anything, they return it to me."[31]

Renée obtained her first clue to her husband's whereabouts by means of messages hidden literally between the lines of their regular letters. The secret communications were written in invisible ink that she and Sade began to use to evade the censors. He must have instructed Renée in this technique even before his arrest. Perhaps he had learned of it at Miolans. Still, his own first attempt to use the ink was not entirely successful: "Too much lemon juice," Renée wrote back to him, using the same method, on May 12. Despite the care she took with the candle flame used to make the ink visible, Renée could not keep from burning holes in the letter and could not fully make out the secret message. In particular, she wrote that his address had become "entirely smudged." "You say you are in Vincennes," she wrote, incredulously.[32] The letters on which the invisible ink was employed still bear marks of the candle—burns and brownish heat blotches. The lines of regular writing, together with the faint, almost invisible inscriptions running between them, present a paradigm of Sade's predicament and his mentality. He had never been able to control the eruptions of his private, secret, rebellious self into the public sphere. His wife had come to accept his dual nature, had come, in fact, to accept him totally. These letters, with their two kinds of writing—public and private—represent the couple's secret compact amid the ordeal that was thrust upon them—or, in Sade's case, to a large degree sought by him.

From Vincennes, Sade wrote an angry, suicidal, and ostentatiously pathetic letter to Mme de Montreuil. His reference to an earlier, now lost letter written during his week of freedom in Paris indicates that he had indeed tried to effect a reconciliation with his mother-in-law before he was arrested:

> Of all the paths that vengeance and cruelty could have chosen, admit, Madame, that you have indeed taken the most ghastly of all. Come to Paris to glean the last of my mother's sighs, having no other aim but to see her and to embrace her yet one more time if she still lived, or to weep if she were no more, it is this very moment that you chose to turn me into your victim yet one more time! Alas! I asked you in my first letter if it was a second mother or a tyrant that I would find in you, but you have not left me long in uncertainty!

Sade went on to say that his former tutor Amblet had informed him— "doubtless on your behalf—that a *death certificate* was the document most suited and indispensable for hastening an end to this unfortunate business. You must have it, Madame, and I swear you will have it before long." Sade would threaten suicide on many occasions during his long imprisonment. Then he offered the following extraordinary fantasy, prophetic of his dream of Petrarch's Laure, in which his dead ancestor, whom he would also call "Mother," invites him into a deadly embrace. In his letter to Mme de Montreuil, his "second mother," he imagined himself once again upon the breast of his dead one:

> From the bottom of her tomb, my unfortunate mother is calling me: I seem to see her open her bosom to me one more time and beckon me to enter there once again as into the only refuge left to me. It is a satisfaction for me to follow her so soon, and I ask you as a final favor, Madame, to have me buried beside her.

His death would be the final consummation with Mother Earth, whose grave opens as he would have had his mother open herself to him. The prison of Vincennes itself, as Sade wrote to Renée on March 6, was another kind of grave, another kind of "tomb" in which he has been "swallowed alive."[33]

Mme de Montreuil remained unmoved by her son-in-law's appeal. She also disclaimed any responsibility for Sade's arrest, as Renée informed Gaufridy on February 25: "My mother, without anger, without temper, says that it was not her doing and that she is incapable of betrayal."[34] Although Renée did not believe her, by the time of Renée's second visit to her mother, on March 3, she had come to accept the explanation that Sade had to be detained so that the appeal of the Aix contempt verdict could proceed. On March 4, Mme de Montreuil felt pleased enough with her scheme and with her management of Renée to boast to Gaufridy, "Everything is working out the best way possible and the most securely; it was high time!" She added that Renée was "calmer" and had approached some officials in order to find out where Sade was and also "to get permission to visit him, which was refused to her, as I was informed." Mme de Montreuil was informed of everything, controlled everything. All of the reins now firmly in her grasp, she smugly concluded, "All of this is as it should be."[35]

Mme de Montreuil did not want her daughter to see Sade. Try as Renée would, she would not get to lay eyes on her husband at Vincennes until exactly four years and five months after his arrest, on July 13, 1781. Renée had not been entirely duped by her mother, but she was powerless to resist her and the government. Renée saw that she had "no other means" but to act with "the appearance of trust and of resignation."[36] Thus, she was caught between two inexorable forces: on the one side, the all-powerful yet elusive Mme de Montreuil, who presented her daughter with a blank wall of lies and prevarications; on the other, the frenzied, crazed, despairing, suicidal prisoner Sade, who treated her with suspicion and often with angry abuse. If Sade's life had in a sense ended on February 13, 1777, so had Renée's.

In some ways, Renée's dilemma was worse than her husband's. She was in a prison without walls. She was expected to do everything, accomplish miracles, when she was in fact powerless to influence her mother or anyone else. The only thing she could approve in her mother's actions, she told Gaufridy, was the attempt to "work on the larger matter"—that is, the appeal of the Aix verdict.[37] Nevertheless, Renée was bitter about her help, because of "the vexations" that her mother "attaches to" it. "Once free of her claws," Renée told Gaufridy, "I would much prefer to labor in the field than to fall back into her clutches." Renée also expressed her resentment of her younger and prettier sister, Anne-Prospère: as long as her mother "contemplates her beautiful Dulcinée, she is satisfied."[38] For her part, Mme de Montreuil did not bother to hide her contempt for Renée and her devotion to Sade: "Is it some implacable weakness of character that makes her do it? An excessive belief in her duty?" In the end, Mme de Montreuil dismissed Renée's motives as being "unfathomable to everyone."[39] Her mother's disdain and the deaf ear turned to her by officials drained Renée's faith. At the beginning of her husband's second year at Vincennes, on February 16, 1778, Renée wrote to Gaufridy: "Accustomed to being deceived, I mistrust everyone."[40] On March 28, she was even more disheartened: "I am, I swear to you, in a state of discouragement and despair beyond expression to see myself tricked on every issue and forced to put my trust here in relatives who so cruelly deceive me."[41]

Once, Renée even caught a glimpse of Gaufridy's duplicitous role. In April 1777, her father made a conversational slip that threatened to unravel the tapestry of lies that his wife had such a talent for weaving.[42] In the Montreuil parlor in their new house on the rue de Mail in Paris, her father was expressing incomprehension at how his daughter could have locked herself up in La Coste "with such a mentality" as Sade's, after they had made themselves inaccessible behind fortified walls and a new *drawbridge*. Mme de Montreuil immediately noticed her husband's blunder: the building of the new drawbridge had been kept secret and should not have been known to Renée's parents. The moment Mme de Montreuil's clumsy husband revealed that they had a spy down in Provence—Gaufridy, perhaps?—the moment he uttered the word "drawbridge," she observed her daughter's "astonished" expression. After Renée left the room, M. de Montreuil got an earful from his wife. In her letter to Gaufridy, she reduced their conversation to the following summary: "I have asked M. de M[ontreuil] to be more circumspect." To be on the safe side, Mme de Montreuil promised herself (and Gaufridy) that she would "no longer say anything" to her husband "but what is public knowledge."[43] Poor M. de Montreuil! From now on, some lawyer in Apt, Gaufridy, would know more about his family's affairs than he would himself.

Renée took after her father: sincere, generous, a bit dense. She did not act on the clue her father had let slip as to Gaufridy's role. She continued to write openly to the lawyer about her feelings, and even about her plans for Sade's possible escape when he would have to be transported down to Aix for his appeal hearing. Renée needed someone to talk to, and she knew that she could not express feelings of despair to her husband. Throughout his long imprisonment, no matter how she felt, no matter what had just happened, no matter what horrors Sade had just accused her of, including collusion with her mother and acts of adultery with her servants, she had to swallow her own feelings and write only optimistic, loving, encouraging letters to him. In her first letter to him at Vincennes, on February 15, 1777, she had been naïvely hopeful: "Calm your poor head. You know that I have never lied to you. *I give you my word of honor that this matter will come to an end and that you will be released immediately.*"[44]

During the first months of his imprisonment, Renée tried to distract Sade with reports on the children's progress, with news about La Coste and questions about managing business there, with questions and letters from Dr. Mesny of Florence concerning some sort of legal matter he was embroiled in and about which he was asking Sade's advice. Sade sometimes replied rationally and courteously to these requests. His children, then living with the Montreuils—the boys, Louis-Marie and Claude-Armand, almost ten and eight respectively, and the girl, Madeleine-Laure, six—had been protected from the truth of their father's fate. Renée told them that their father was traveling. She would maintain this lie for years to come. Sade was sometimes pleased by Renée's sending him news about their children. On April 18, he told her "how ravishingly I will embrace them, although I cannot—despite my tenderness for them—delude myself to the extreme of not perceiving that it is because of them that I am now suffering."[45] As he correctly understood it, one of Mme de Montreuil's primary goals in keeping him in prison was to preserve her grandchildren from further harm to their reputation by cleansing the Sade family name that she had spent good money to buy and a great deal of effort to maintain.

Sade not only knew that his letters were read and censored by M. Boucher in the office of Lieutenant General of Police Lenoir, he also believed, correctly, that copies or summaries of his letters to Renée were regularly made available to his mother-in-law. Thus the ambivalence he expresses about his children—that he loved them even though they were the cause of his imprisonment. The statement contained emotional truth, to be sure, for Sade *was* ambivalent about them, as he was about everything and everyone else. But the gesture was also a matter of strategy. He wanted Mme de Montreuil to see that she was endangering the relationship between a father and his children, perhaps causing irreparable harm to their future chances.

Many of Sade's letters to his wife have this odd, double-edged design. He was ostensibly writing to her, but he was often looking past her, through her, to other readers. Renée was in fact the last one to know what her husband wrote. There were all those enemies, all those police and prison officials, who read them first. Moreover, both Renée's letters and his own would often arrive with words or whole passages censored, inked over by M. Boucher—"the blotsman," Sade called him.[46] All this furnished fertile soil indeed for the growth of paranoia. Sade could see further into a millstone than anyone. The stone walls of Vincennes were as clear as glass to his eyes—or they were like a screen on which he projected images from his own mind. He could see all of his enemies plotting against him, reading his letters, rejoicing in his humiliations, devising new ones. Sometimes he addressed his rage at these enemies directly. At other times, he treated them with sarcasm, irony, ridicule.

In a different mood, he would offer them contrite confessions, promises of reformation. He would try to elicit their pity by vividly portraying his misery, his despair. Every sentence in Sade's letters has this rhetorical instability, this multiple valence, intended for the gamut of perceived readers—including Renée, who was sometimes the least of his addressees, if the only explicit one. For example, in the middle of a particularly strong letter to Renée, Sade paused to say that he doubted that the letter would pass the censor and be delivered to her. "No matter," he added, "it will be read anyway [by the censors and his enemies], and who knows if, of all those who are obliged to read it, you or they are the one I am most directly writing to?"[47] There are layers upon layers of meaning, often with quite opposite intentions, directed at the "cabal," as Sade called them, of his enemies reading over Renée's shoulder.

On March 6, 1777, just three weeks after his imprisonment, Sade wrote plaintively to Renée:

> Oh! my dear love, when will my frightful situation come to an end? When will they—great God!—let me out of the tomb where they have swallowed me alive? Nothing can equal the horror of my lot! Nothing can express everything I am suffering, can portray the anxiety which torments me and the desperation that is devouring me! Here, all I have are my tears and my cries, but whoever else may be around does not hear them. . . . What happened to the time when my dear love shared them? Now I have no one. I feel as if all nature is dead to me![48]

By the middle of June, however, his self-pity had turned into a frenzy of rage. Now, when he wrote to Renée, he blamed her inactivity and called his children "worthless brats."

> If you knew, Madame, how completely exasperated I am by your letters, and how, after four months of the most detestable of all situations, it is cruel to read absolutely the same platitudes, the same stupid maunderings, and the same excuses that you used at the very beginning! If, from the comfort of your easy chair, where you contentedly digest your supper, if you could, I say, see their effect, you would truly spare me your six letters a month, or at least you would fashion them in a style that avoids producing the effect they have on me, which, I assure you, is inexpressible, since, from the moment they arrive, the fever resulting from rage and indignation holds me continually in its grip for three or four days, so that nothing can calm me and I can get no rest at all. Is my fate not already horrendous enough without being

tortured by your insulting epistles, which like clockwork coincide with the six visits of the commandant, who does not fail to speak the same things that you wrote, and which thus plunges me once more into the same pain?

Sade is engulfed in paranoia: noting similarities between the contents of Renée's letters and the commandant's comments during his visits, Sade concludes there is a conspiracy involving his wife and de Rougemont:

What would you all have me understand by your stupid, evil turns of phrase? That I am to be here for a long time, or not—or that they only want me to think so? Make up your minds quickly, then, and do not keep me any longer in this cruel suspense, which completely upsets my mind and boils my blood, so as to thrust me into a thousand new extravagances the minute I get out of here.

Sade argues that prior imprisonment, far from rehabilitating him, only inspired him or angered him to commit even worse "follies" when he got out. Despite the exaggeration of Sade's argument, it nevertheless appears true that his crimes or infractions were a form of discourse or argument with his mother-in-law and with others. His letter to Renée continues:

Begone! you, her, and your children. I swear you will repent of what you have made me suffer here on account of these worthless brats, whom I hate as much as you and all your relatives. . . . Your vile treatment will end by killing me. Once again, tell me the precise day of my release. Only that can calm me. You can tell your mother that I wish never to see her or to hear from her, and that her infamies will end only in my death. She is a sneaky bitch, that is all I can say about her. The day of my release, or, once again, I am not responsible for the consequences of my despair. My future attitude toward you depends on your compliance. If you deny me this, I will never see you again, neither you nor your children, for whose sake I am offered up as some kind of scapegoat. Remember: I will certainly never write to you again if you do not perform what I am asking of you. You will doubtless deny receiving this letter. I know that you receive all of them, and that you deny receiving whichever one you choose, and in so doing, you are a monster, the spitting image of your execrable bitch of a mother.[49]

During these early months of his long imprisonment, Sade's moods fluctuated between love and hate for his wife and children, hope and despair that his mother-in-law would relent. As much as he might try to influence Renée and his enemies, he nevertheless had to try to adapt to the graveyard of Vincennes. Prison, both as womb and tomb, acts as a powerful engine for regression. Everything is taken from the prisoner, even his name. From now on, Sade was called "No. 11," his room number, just as later, in a new room, he would be "No. 6." Everything about his life was now regulated—what and when he ate, what he might say or write, what privileges he might have. The Marquis de Sade now had to submit his enormous pride and his very irregular habits to the strict rules of Vincennes; he had to submit to what appeared to him the whimsically perverse orders of Commandant de Rougemont and his staff of soldiers, guards, and turnkeys—people so far beneath him socially and intellectually that it would be impossible for him to stifle his rage, his ridicule, his scorn. The Lord of Mazan, the Lord of La Coste, the lieutenant general of Bresse, Bugey, Valromey, and Gex, was now sent to his room and told to stay there. But it would not be for a few months, as he thought Renée had promised. This was only the beginning of a very long detention.

CHAPTER 13

A Surprise at Aix

T HE APPEAL of the Aix contempt verdict was slowed by Mme de Montreuil's efforts to manipulate the process. For one thing, she did not want Sade to be present as the Parlement of Aix heard the arguments for an annulment. She was concerned that his appearance might reignite the scandals she hoped had been forgotten, and she did not want her wily son-in-law to have any chance to escape at Aix or on the journey there and back. Even if Sade were to be exonerated at Aix, she had no intention of letting him go free: he was in prison not because of the Aix verdict, but because of the royal lettre de cachet that she had obtained. Her secret plan was to annul the Aix verdict on legal technicalities, thus cleansing the Sade name for the sake of her grandchildren, but without removing the idea that Sade would be dangerous if the lettre de cachet were also lifted and he were set at large.

In June 1777, Mme de Montreuil tried to enlist the Abbé's support for her plan to keep Sade in prison while the appeal went forward at Aix. Noting that she had written to him "in a much gentler style" after a long silence, the Abbé correctly surmised, "Mme de Montreuil has need of me." Nevertheless, he had to decline her request that he go to Aix to try to influence the court. He was suffering from "indispositions,"[1] and in fact had but six more months to live. Although he approved of her plan, he seems to have considered the venture hopeless. In a letter on July 24, he expressed astonishment at Gaufridy's willingness to make the same trip "during this weather," the blast-furnace heat of a Provençal summer, "to solicit a favor that you knew you would not obtain."[2]

Meanwhile, Renée had been trying to think up a plan for her husband's escape. One scheme was devised by Sade's friend Vidal, the Chanoine, or Canon, of the village of Oppède.[3] On June 4, 1777, Renée wrote to Gaufridy in some detail about her hopes for an escape at Aix. It was the resolution she most desired, even more than a favorable verdict, her reasoning being, "It is better to have your freedom than to have to ask for it." If Sade should have to go to Aix, Renée urged Gaufridy "to spare no cost" to arrange an escape. She instructed him on how to inform her secretly in the event the scheme succeeded: "You will write a letter to me in which you will simply indicate that he has left with his guard for Paris and the signal would be that the address would not be in your handwriting."[4] Renée was becoming clever about signals, but Gaufridy, to whom she was sending these escape plans, was still Mme de Montreuil's confidant.

As the summer of 1777 grew warm, then hot, Sade began to make increasingly importunate demands on Renée to run errands for him. On June 9, he complained to her that he had nothing to wear but the winter clothes in which he had been arrested.[5] Subsequent requisitions included everything from books to eel terrines to hemorrhoidal cream, the last of these proving a particularly difficult order to fulfill: Renée was forced to wander in the oppressive heat searching for the one apothecary whose formula Sade favored. But her effort was acknowledged only by complaint. On August 5, she assured him that the one she sent "is indeed the same cream" and "it is the heat that made it soft."[6] On October 30, Renée's list of items sent included, among other things, an alpaca suit, two jackets (one embroidered, the other plush), six pairs of cotton stockings, two hair bands, a pair of trousers, eight pounds of candles, a jar each of beef-marrow pomade, apricot marmalade, apple jelly, and cherries, six undershirts, six vests, a pair of slippers, a stick of pomade, two pounds of powder, a bottle of eau de Cologne, and a waistcoat.[7] But no sooner had she furnished all his summer requirements than it was time for her to worry about Sade's winter clothes. Her life was now organized around running the errands to fill the boxes with all the things her husband demanded.

On December 31, 1777, during his first winter at Vincennes, Sade lost the uncle who had raised him and had stood by him almost to the end. The Abbé died at age seventy-two at his farm, La Vignerme, at Saumane, leaving his estates in confusion and encumbered by debts.[8] There was also a problem with the farm itself, which he had sold to his Spanish mistress just before his death. Litigation over his estate would go on for years.

As the new year of 1778 dawned with no end to his suffering in sight, Sade actually opened a vein and wrote a desperate letter to his mother-in-law literally in his own blood: "Oh! you whom I once called my mother with such pleasure, . . . may your heart be softened by these tears and these words written in blood."[9] He presented himself at her knees and in tears, begging her to tell him the date of his release. On January 19 and 20, following the anniversary of his imprisonment, Sade wrote a very long, suicidal letter to Renée, begging the "cruel monsters" to kill him at once, rather than "flay my wretched body bit by bit as they now do": "I implore their mercy, their humanity, their pity; my wretched head can no longer bear the abominable horror of this inconceivable torture . . . which, I dare say, has no match, nor could ever have had one since the beginning of time." Following this grandiose claim, Sade demanded to be told the legal basis of his arrest: "What are these crimes?" Quite legitimately, he insisted, "A man should not be made to suffer without understanding why; we are neither in Spain nor in the Inquisition." He demanded to know the extent of his sentence: "Tell it to me, then, tell it to me, then, or I am going to break my head against the walls that hold me." "My despair," he warned Renée, "is explosive, it is violent." He concluded the letter by again threatening suicide if his demands were not met: "I swear to you on my honor that I will end my life at once."[10]

When Mme de Montreuil saw that she might be unable to prevent Sade's appearance before the Parlement of Aix, she began to tie up any loose threads that might unravel and cause trouble. Having earlier asked Gaufridy to destroy any incriminating evidence remaining at La Coste, she now used the pretext of the need to find documents relevant to the Abbé's will to have Gaufridy break into Sade's locked study at La Coste to search for incriminating writings.[11] In direct connection with the appeal, she asked Gaufridy about the progress of his investigation of the Marseilles prostitutes whom Sade had been convicted of poisoning.[12] In Gaufridy's files there was a "Report" on the whereabouts of each of the prostitutes, information supplied *"by a Madame who knows all the nymphs."*[13] Finally, on February 28, 1778, Mme de Montreuil was able to inform Gaufridy that she had reached a complete understanding with M. de Castillon, the chief prosecutor, and M. de La Tour, the chief justice of the Parlement of Aix, concerning how to handle the appeal, and she instructed Gaufridy to follow their advice.[14] By April 14, the Marseilles prostitutes had been coerced or bribed to testify favorably at the appeal. Mme de Montreuil expressed "full confidence" in Gaufridy's ability to act in concert with the above magistrates and police officials over "the arrangements to be made concerning the girls."[15] All was in readiness.

Even so, Mme de Montreuil wanted to try one last scheme to keep Sade away from Aix. For a time, she actually tried to argue the utility of his pleading insanity and absenting himself from the appeal. On January 20, 1778, she explained to Gaufridy: "An absent person causes no trouble, even less when insanity provides a motive for acts of libertinage that cannot be explained in any other way."[16] In February, she instructed Gaufridy to make inquiries at Aix about how to go about having Sade declared insane, arguing that Sade, "who had already been insane off and on, . . . now is completely so."[17] But even if this scheme failed, she hoped that it would have at least one useful effect. If Renée could be deceived into believing that the trip to Aix would not take place, she might then give up planning to help her husband escape from there, an "escape that would ruin everything," Mme de Montreuil told Gaufridy.[18] As she was waiting for events to play out, Mme de Montreuil felt satisfied that she had considered every angle. Even if Sade were vindicated at Aix, she sanguinely wrote, "no matter *what* happens," he would not be free of the law or of his mother-in-law. He would still be bound by the lettre de cachet. "He is too intelligent," Mme de Montreuil concluded, "after all *that has happened* . . . to expect that his vindication will be followed by his release."[19]

On June 2, 1778, Sade observed, though did not exactly celebrate, his thirty-eighth birthday. He had but one hope, and that was to escape. Renée also understood this, having finally realized that, no matter what the decision of the Parlement of Aix, her husband would be returned to Vincennes. She was counting on a detailed plan she had proposed to Gaufridy in February for her husband's escape at Aix, where his appearance was now a certainty. She felt that the best time would be after the hearing, "immediately before the officer takes custody of him to take him back to Vincennes," and she proposed that Gaufridy, Reinaud, and others arrange for Sade to "escape through some door of the palace." Or, Renée suggested, Gaufridy could bribe "the cavaliers of Aix so that they dampen the rifles and pistols of their colleagues who will guard him, so that they cannot fire at M. de Sade or at those who will help him to escape by waiting for him along the route." Money was no object: "I will most gladly reimburse all the expenses if it succeeds."[20] But there would be no reimbursement. Gaufridy was not about to help Renée engineer an escape.

Meanwhile, the weather turned warm. Spring had come again, and in May, Sade's housekeeper at La Coste, Gothon, wrote her master a letter, hoping to cheer him up: "Yes, Sir, it is a pleasure to be at La Coste at this lovely season, but the most precious thing is missing: he who would be its ornament. Everything proclaims it is springtime." Gothon took walks through Sade's lovely park with his dogs, Thisbée, Dragon ("who is lovely"), and Grandodu ("who has but one fault: which is to eat the turkey cocks; though, despite his faults, I love him"). The only thing missing, Gothon said, was Sade himself. "Come," she wrote, "and enjoy the beautiful days that still await you here."[21]

It did not seem likely that Sade would ever see La Coste again. However, the appeal process had finally begun to move forward. On May 27, the King granted him *lettres d'ester à droit*, permitting Sade to appear at the Parlement of Aix despite the lapse of the five-year period that had been given for him to answer the contempt judgment. The King's order also acknowledged that the legal grounds for Sade's appeal were just—the charges against him had not been sufficiently demonstrated and the actions of the court had been "infected by several absolute and even fundamental illegalities."[22] On June 14, 1778, Sade began his journey to Aix, escorted by Inspector Marais and Marais's brother Antoine-Thomas. As the coach crossed the drawbridge of Vincennes eighteen months after Sade had entered, the air seemed purer, freer. Despite the humiliation of the journey under police guard down to Provence, Sade hoped for exoneration and perhaps liberty. As for escape possibilities, however, Mme de Montreuil, taking no chances, kept her daughter in the dark about Sade's trip. Otherwise, "who knows what her anxiety would have made her do?" "Even the minister," she added, concurred in this secrecy, without which Renée "would have been *ordered* into a convent in order avoid any problem."[23] Thus, unaware of her husband's transfer, Renée continued to write letters to him at Vincennes, complaining, as she frequently did, about his silence.

There would be no escape on the way to Provence. In his "Histoire de ma détention," Sade noted that he and his guards arrived at Aix on the night of Saturday, June 20.[24] Because it was too late to arrange for Sade's admission to the prison, Marais put up at an inn, the Auberge Saint-Jacques. The next day, Sade was conducted to a cell in the Conciergerie, where he remained, except for court appearances, until July 15. Gothon, having just sent Sade her spring letter, heard from Gaufridy that Sade was at Aix, and immediately wrote to him that she "felt inexpressibly joyous" at his "proximity" to her. She begged for a word from him and said that she missed him: "I cry very often in thinking about your predicament." At the same time, she sent with Gaufridy "some flowers from your terrace, some apricots, and two pots of your own jam."[25] Two days later, she sent Gaufridy a package of clothes that Sade requested: "two brown dress-coats, . . . two jackets, two pair of white breeches, a green-and-white-striped taffeta jacket," as well as some linen she thought he would need, and a pot of apricot marmalade. If Sade wished it, Gothon offered to catch a hare and to cook it for him.[26] For his part, Sade settled in at the prison at Aix. The regimen was more lax than at Vincennes, and he began to make quite a pest of himself. In a letter to Lieutenant General of Police Lenoir on July 1, Inspector Marais complained that Sade "incessantly annoys me with a thousand requests . . . , in spite of the fact that he is treated as well as a man of quality can expect in prison." Moreover, Marais grumbled, in order to display his generosity and his bonhomie, Sade "would bestow his largesse upon all the prisoners." Marais tried to prevent him, but, knowing Sade, he found it "necessary to give in to him from time to time."[27] In fact, Gaufridy's records show that Sade ran up a bill of 72 livres with the prison caterer.[28]

Among the other prisoners at the Conciergerie at Aix, one in particular,

Mme Doyen de Baudoin, attracted Sade's attention and his benevolence. He called her his "Dulcinée au Miroir," his Dulcinea at the Mirror. A few months later, he would delight in giving Gaufridy an account of how he had employed the lawyer Reinaud of Aix to pass her a letter. When the letter was "intercepted," and Reinaud was "publicly named the Messenger of the Gods," Sade took pleasure in the lawyer's embarrassment: "It is enough," Sade crowed, "to make one die of laughter."[29] It is possible that Sade's providing treats for prisoners and guards—as he had done at Miolans—bought him and his Dulcinea some privacy. Whatever went on between Sade and Mme de Baudoin in the Conciergerie, she remembered him fondly. In fact, Gaufridy's files contain two letters written years later, in August 1781 and February 1782, with which Doyen de Baudoin tried unsuccessfully to re-establish contact with Sade. In the first, she wrote, "I am and I will be for the rest of my life your sincere friend,"[30] and was trying to find out if he was alive or dead, or imprisoned for life. In her second letter, she said that she was in "torments of anxiety" about his fate, provoked, she said, as he should well understand, by her "gratitude and the desire to share your misfortune or your happiness."[31] The correspondence between Sade and his Dulcinea was clearly not favored by the gods. Gaufridy did not forward her letters, and her longing to hear again from her friend is a plaintive air, sealed in time and muffled in a lawyer's filing cabinet.

If Sade could find pleasure in the unlikeliest of places, this was, nevertheless, a serious trip, and there was work to be done. On Monday, June 22, two days after he arrived at Aix, one of his lawyers, M. Gabriel, appeared before the Parlement to present the royal *lettres d'ester à droit*, and to argue that "there were no proofs whatsoever" of the "nonexistent crimes" of pederasty and poisoning, and that, moreover, the legal proceedings of 1772 "had been corrupted by extreme defects" that warranted annulling the original verdict.[32] The court agreed to hold a formal hearing on June 30. In the meantime, Sade's remaining uncle, the Commandeur de Sade, at the instigation of Mme de Montreuil, was busy writing letters to members of the court. On June 25, he wrote to Chief Justice de La Tour, thanking him in advance for restoring the honor of the Sade family name. "I feel a double happiness," he continued, "in learning that the libertine, of whom we have so many reasons for complaint, will no longer be, through your justice, regarded as the most criminal of men." On the same day, he wrote to another judge very much in the same vein, adding this distinction between public and private offenses: "Libertinage deserves punishment, but not that belonging to crime."[33] Three days later, he wrote a circular letter to various Aix magistrates, stating that the family had already dealt with their wayward relative in a private way: "The family has punished the libertine as soon as it was able. He will no longer trouble society."[34] Sade would have been better off having to deal only with the law (which in this case was on his side) than with "the family" as organized by Mme de Montreuil (who definitely was not).

Tuesday, June 30, was the day for Sade's formal hearing. Inspector Marais wrote about the details of the events in a letter to Lieutenant General of Police Lenoir the following day.[35] At eight o'clock in the morning, Marais appeared at the Conciergerie to escort Sade in a sedan chair fitted with dark curtains over the windows to the Couvent des Jacobins, where the Parlement held its sessions. In the street, a crowd of "at least two hundred persons" had gathered to see the notorious Marquis de Sade come face to face with his judges. They were foiled, Marais was pleased to say, by his "precaution" of the dark curtains. Inside the chamber, the judges were at their benches. Mme de Montreuil's preparations had rendered their verdict as certain as such things could be. When Sade entered, he placed himself on his knees before this august body. Was this the Ultimate Tribunal of his dreams? As Sade knelt, the chief justice, embarrassed, signaled with the palm of his hand and bade him stand up. Then Sade's lawyer Siméon made his speech, as Marais reported, "with a good deal of energy." Next, the King's prosecutor, M. d'Eymar de Montmeyan, also spoke strongly in favor of annulment. The chief justice and almost the entire court appeared willing to dismiss all of the original charges. However, one member rose to say that a sweeping revocation would leave a stain of suspicion "both against the accused and against the Parlement, which would appear too favorably disposed to him." Thus, in the end, the court annulled only the charge of poisoning as being unfounded, but ordered a new investigation into the charges of libertinage and of sodomy. The Marseilles prostitutes would now have to appear before the court to give testimony; the ordeal at Aix would be prolonged by a few more weeks. This was far from the sublime event that Sade had imagined. The session had lasted two hours; he was still a prisoner; there would have to be another appearance, yet more humiliation; even if it went well, he would probably still be a prisoner. Marais observed, "The Marquis did not seem very moved by this first session." On the way back to prison, Sade, slumped in the gloom behind the heavy curtains of the sedan chair, passed through the same crowd, still eager to catch a glimpse of the wolf-man of Provence.

Marais reported to Lenoir that Gaufridy was immediately taken aside by both the chief justice and the chief prosecutor and instructed by them to go at once to Marseilles and to tell the prostitutes to eliminate any reference to sodomy in the testimony they would give the court. Marais's observation of Gaufridy in action drew high praise from the police inspector: "This

M. Gaufridy is a capable man, strongly attached to the house of Sade, and a lawyer who seems in this affair to have the complete confidence of Mme de Montreuil; and this secret alliance could not be in better hands." At Marseilles, according to Bourdin, "Gaufridy spent money hand over fist, which Mme de Montreuil repaid him" from the money obtained from the sale two months earlier to the Comte de Sade-Eyguières of Sade's post as lieutenant general of the provinces of Bresse, Bugey, Valromey, and Gex. As always, Mme de Montreuil used Sade's own income to pay for his room and board in prison, just as she billed him for the police raid against him at La Coste. As for those Marseilles prostitutes—how many times would they have to be paid for that day or two in June of 1772! Gaufridy, Bourdin continued, "paid to wine and dine the girls," and also to coordinate the testimony of the surgeons and apothecaries.[36] Marais himself left for Marseilles the next day, July 1, "to assist [Gaufridy] behind the scenes, if he has need of it." Marais guessed the whole affair would be over in ten or twelve days; he already was aware that M. de La Tour had "the royal orders necessary to transfer him [Sade] from the prison at Aix to Vincennes."

For the next week, the witnesses, including Sade, gave their depositions. On July 7, Sade was interrogated by M. de Bourguet, an officer of the court. The word "interrogate" had a special, even a magical meaning for Sade. During his many months in Vincennes, he had wanted to be interrogated in order to demonstrate his innocence. Sade complained to Renée that, when Lieutenant General of Police Lenoir had paid him a formal visit in his cell at Vincennes on October 16, 1777, Lenoir had merely chatted nonsense with him: "He was supposed to interrogate me, there are many ways of learning if a man is guilty, why did he not employ them? In short, I want to be interrogated at all costs."[37] Perhaps now, at Aix, Sade would at last meet the Supreme Catechist! On July 8, Mme de Montreuil, taking no chances, wrote to several of the chief magistrates of the court, urging them, "with the greatest insistence," to permit "absolutely no stigma" to remain on the Sade family name.[38] On July 10, there was a formal confrontation between Sade and the witnesses. The King's prosecutor made his recommendations to the court. Their decision to dismiss the charges of libertinage and sodomy had already been made when the court reconvened on the morning of July 14. Once again, Sade was brought from the Conciergerie to the Couvent des Jacobins, this time for a public hearing. Shortly afterward, he was brought back to hear the court's verdict. The court dismissed all of the remaining charges against Sade and ordered his release once the following conditions were met: he was to make a contribution of 50 livres for charitable work in the prison, he was to be "admonished in private in the presence of the King's prosecutor in the future to put more decency in his conduct," and he had to promise to stay away from Marseilles for three years.[39] At the same time, Sade's civil rights were restored to him. He was a free man!

Except for one thing. Though he was a free man in the eyes of the law, he was still bound to his mother-in-law, who, as we have seen, knew he was "too intelligent" not to know what would happen next. On the very day of Sade's happy verdict, July 14, Marais received an order from the King dated July 5 commanding Sade's return to Vincennes.[40] The lettre de cachet under which Sade had first been arrested on February 13, 1777, was still in effect. Sade's family name had been cleansed (that was all Mme de Montreuil had wanted and intended); Sade had been declared innocent of all crimes by the court (how sublimely fair were the scales of justice!). After hearing a lecture by the King's prosecutor about the need to behave decently and to keep up appearances, Sade was once more escorted by Marais back to the Conciergerie. Marais had the King's orders in his pocket.

CHAPTER 14

The Golden Dawn of a Beautiful Day

O N July 14, 1778, at Aix, Sade had proved his innocence, but he remained a prisoner. He did not get very much sleep that night. At three o'clock in the morning on July 15, Inspector Marais came to his cell in the Conciergerie and awakened him.[1] They were to begin their journey back to Vincennes.

In the cool darkness before the Provence sunrise, a coach was waiting outside the door of the Conciergerie for Sade, Marais, and Marais's brother Antoine-Thomas. Marais had also hired two guards for the trip. He decided to take the road toward Tarascon, "in order not to come near" Sade's estates, just to the north.[2] By this longer route, they also avoided Avignon.[3] Then, finally turning north, they put up for the night at Valliguières. Sade studied the road, the inn, the habits of his guards: "I noticed," he later wrote to Gaufridy, that the guards' "attention diminished the farther we went."[4] It had been a long day, and it would prove another unrestful night: years later, he complained about Marais and his guards, who got drunk "in my room every night" so that "it was never possible to sleep."[5] Sade also wrote of this stop at Valliguières in his "Histoire de ma détention": "There, I sought to accomplish the escape that I had been thinking about, but it was impossible."

The next day, July 16, Sade and his guards continued to travel north, crossed the Rhône at Pont-Saint-Esprit, passed through Montélimar, and finally, at nine-thirty, put up for the night at an inn, the Logis du Louvre, on the outskirts of Valence. The room they rented overlooked the high road from Marseilles to Paris, and there Sade sat, looking out the window, until supper was served at around ten o'clock. Marais bade him join them at the table, but Sade replied that he was not hungry and would eat nothing. He paced the room while the others ate. At ten-thirty, Sade interrupted Antoine-Thomas, claiming a "pressing need," whereupon he was escorted to the toilet, which Antoine-Thomas had previously inspected in order to satisfy himself that it had but one exit, down a flight of stairs, where the guard took up his post. Sade climbed the stairs and entered the toilet, a lit candle in his hand. He was inside for five or six minutes; then, leaving the candle burning inside, he was able to tiptoe down the stairs in the darkness. Antoine-Thomas did not notice his prisoner until, at the last moment, he looked up and discovered Sade almost upon him. At that instant, Sade pretended to stumble on the stairs, and Antoine-Thomas rushed up to assist him, whereupon Sade, "with the greatest agility," slipped through his arms and raced across the dark court-yard and out the unlocked carriage-gate.[6] This was Sade's second escape from a toilet! In 1773, he had left a candle burning in his room at the fortress of Miolans to distract his guard while he crawled through a toilet window to freedom.

Antoine-Thomas immediately conducted a search of the nearby houses and gardens—without success. Marais made a close search of the entire inn. He alerted Commandant Thyais of the local constabulary. Then Marais sent his brother and one of the guards south on the Marseilles road, toward Mon-télimar, and the other guard north on the same road, toward Tain. At dawn of the next day, July 17, Commandant Thyais supplied officers for a widening search. Horsemen investigated surrounding farms and the roads and paths along the Rhône.[7] Later, Sade would write to Gaufridy, mocking their futile efforts: "Their searches, do you not find them amusing? To spend the first night searching the inn! Was it plausible that is where I chose to hide? . . . This is a farce to make you die of laughter!"[8]

That first night of his escape, Sade headed for the open fields. A quarter-league (around half a mile) from Valence, he hid for a while in a shed where peasants threshed wheat. Before dawn, Sade found two peasants who accom-panied him farther south, in the direction of Montélimar. Along the Rhône, Sade found a "small boat which carried me down to Avignon for 1 louis."[9] Sade's account in his letter to Gaufridy of July 18 is picturesque:

> At dawn, I saw several small boats belonging to fishermen, none of whom would risk taking me down to Avignon. Finally, by dint of entreaties, and the hope of compensation, the owner of one boat even more decrepit than any of the others I had seen, full of holes and leaky, taking on water everywhere and piloted by only one fellow, agreed to take the risk, as he put it, of drowning the both of us. . . . I risked everything, my dear lawyer, and for the simple reason *that whatever God watches is well watched.*

Yes, God watched over Sade on his voyage down the Rhône to Avignon, the City of Popes, where he safely disembarked at six in the evening of July 17, only nineteen hours after his escape the night before. Meanwhile, on July 17, Marais had made his deposition and vowed to continue to beat the bushes around Valence despite the approaching darkness.

But Sade was by then resting at the house of his friend M. Quinaut in Avignon. Mme Quinaut provided a good supper; Sade had not eaten his the night before. M. Quinaut arranged for a coach, and after dining, Sade traveled through the night, arriving at La Coste at nine the next morning, July 18.[10] Following a year and a half in prison, Sade was home once more. As he entered the château, he gave quite a shock to Gothon, his excitable housekeeper. As soon as she could be quieted, Sade retired to his study and wrote the following brief note, which was then sent to Gaufridy by messenger:

> I arrived exhausted, dying of fatigue and of hunger; I gave Gothon a dreadful fright. I will tell you all; it is a novel. Come and visit, I beg of you, as soon as possible.
>
> Send, I beg of you, by return messenger, some lemons and all my keys. You will also bring me, I beg of you, the two packets of papers that I sent you for safekeeping, especially the large one. I am now going to eat and to sleep, and I embrace you with all my heart.
>
> I believe that you were right when you said: *They will not follow you.* I do not know anything for certain, but I rather doubt that they did follow.[11]

Sade felt safe. But what did he mean when he praised Gaufridy for having said that his escape would not provoke any real pursuit? Had Gaufridy aided in Sade's escape? Had the whole thing been set up in advance? Had Gaufridy actually said, *"They will not follow you"*?

The idea that Marais conspired in Sade's escape comes from the above letter (on which Gaufridy jotted a note: "Received July 18") and from the other letter Sade wrote to Gaufridy, a few days later, and antedated July 18. In the second letter, Sade pretended that this was the first communication he had had with Gaufridy after his escape and his return to La Coste. He also offered the elaborate and preposterous explanation that at the inn at Valence Marais himself suggested that Sade escape:

> The inspector charged with escorting me gave me to understand in the strongest terms that my return to Vincennes was only a matter of mere formality and that, if I chose to escape without giving the impression that my flight was colluded in, I was free to act; that, for their part, following this escape, they would give their activities the appearance of a

rigorous pursuit, and that, these two things being accomplished, by maintaining at home a behavior such as naturally would keep me from the misfortunes I have suffered, then I would have nothing to fear.

In his letter, Sade fulminated a good deal against "such an imbecilic plan," how inappropriate a course of action it was for "a man of honor," exonerated as he had just been by the court, and guilty at most of "merely a simple youthful indiscretion." Sade claimed that Marais made him realize that Mme de Montreuil did not wish his ruin. In this plan for his escape, Sade said that he was able to see her benevolent hand, was able to see "the machinations of a woman as shrewd as she is intelligent and wise, and as clever as she is a compassionate and good mother." The irony in these statements is more complicated than mere sarcasm. Sade went on to say that, after everything that he owed to Mme to Montreuil and to the members of the Sade family, he could now unfetter the feelings of his heart, which would "dissipate the fears of this worthy mother," would "bring calm to the breast of my relatives," and would prove "that I have always been more unfortunate than guilty." Now, at last, Sade could look forward to "the golden dawn of a beautiful day so longed for after so many storms."

Besides the irony in Sade's flattery of Mme de Montreuil, there is also strategy in it and in his explanation that his escape had been condoned by his mother-in-law and the authorities. During the day-long boat trip down the Rhône and a night's journey by coach to La Coste, he had the time to contrive this story: They let him escape! Mme de Montreuil, and Marais, and Gaufridy too! By publicizing this absurd version of his escape, Sade hoped to confuse Mme de Montreuil. Perhaps she might be willing to accept the fiction and leave him in peace. Sade wrote the above letter to Gaufridy for wide circulation. Later, Sade mentioned that he himself had sent copies of the July 18 letter to all of his aunts at Avignon, and he threatened to send a copy to Mme de Montreuil if Gaufridy would not do it for him, telling Gaufridy "it would be infinitely better" if it "came from you." Sade also wanted Gaufridy to display Sade's letter containing his version of the condoned escape: "Show it to anyone who asks you for details." He wanted it widely read: "Let it be public, then. Give it the publicity I ask around Aix and Paris, I beg of you."[12] Sade, who had never paid much attention to public opinion before, was now beginning to try to manipulate it.

Sade kept harping on this version of events. In another letter to Gaufridy, probably dating from the beginning of August, Sade claimed that in all that had happened, including the condoned escape, he could see "the hand of Madame de Montreuil, who acts in everything." He added "that Madame de

Montreuil did not hate me, that she wanted to help me, but that she evidently was not able to, and that, in order to better accomplish her goal, she was forced to hide behind the appearance of hatred and vengeance; rest assured that I am not in the least deceived." Here, once again, is Sade's characteristic formulation of opposites, the Bad Mother and the Good Mother, in this case curiously combined into one creature whose goodness he alone could see beneath her mask of evil. Sade further claimed that Mme de Montreuil's devious strategy extended to her engineering Marais's failure to recapture him after the escape, for Sade claimed to have been given the wink by the commandant of Vincennes, Mme de Montreuil's "tool," who plainly told him in prison, *"If you escape on the return journey they will not pursue you."* This, of course, like everything else that Sade was professing, was an enormous bluff. Sade's torturer at Vincennes, M. de Rougemont, would not have suggested an escape, and Marais would not have risked his job by assisting it. Nevertheless, in this letter to Gaufridy, Sade insisted, "I have thus unassailably established . . . that they have absolutely no desire to recapture me, and that I run no risk whatsoever as long as I behave myself."13

Sade underlined the following points he wanted Gaufridy to convey to Mme de Montreuil: that *"my presence on my estates is absolutely necessary"* to manage business affairs; that, once he was proved innocent at Aix, a new arrest *"would cause a scandal in the present circumstances when it would seem so essential to manage public opinion"* (he knew all Mme de Montreuil cared about was public scandal); that a new arrest would produce a bad effect among Sade's relatives, *"following the letters that I have written to all of them to announce the final settlement of my legal affairs."*14 Sade had worked it all out in advance: the letter-writing campaign to manipulate his family and public opinion, and the big lie that Mme de Montreuil—so clever, so kind!—had allowed her son-in-law to escape, or at least not to be pursued. All of Sade's communications to her through Gaufridy were coated with such irony that she must have been as puzzled and as infuriated as Sade's father had been when he had received just such a communication in a similar style. What *could* that slippery boy be up to?

Beyond simple audacity and utility, there is a wishfulness and a sort of paranoia in the myth Sade concocted about his escape. There is wishfulness in Sade's fantasy of an organized state conspiracy, involving Commandant de Rougemont, Inspector Marais, and Mme de Montreuil, focused solely on him and on allowing him, somehow, to go free. This is the obverse of his paranoid fantasy in prison, in which he imagined that these same individuals—and others—were plotting to kill him. Alone and without influence or real friends, Sade took comfort in imagining himself the object of a conspiracy to help him. His big lie about the condoned escape was a bold and tantalizing bluff. Would Mme de Montreuil let herself be outwitted? Would she be cowed into accepting Sade's version of reality, his assertion that she did not mind his escaping? And would she therefore not push to have him arrested as long as he behaved himself down in Provence?

Sade's above letter to Gaufridy, dating from the beginning of August, also reveals that Sade had learned of his lawyer's secret correspondence with Mme de Montreuil. Sade put an odd, ironic twist on this shocking discovery by praising Gaufridy for his diplomacy in not having informed Sade of this treachery himself: "You have always had too much tact to reveal to me your dealings with Madame de Montreuil." Gaufridy must have blushed to read that sentence, even though he may have believed that, in acting as Mme de Montreuil's confidant, he was trying to do his best for everyone involved. Then Sade added an ironical turn to the explicit threat that he would eventually see Gaufridy's correspondence with Mme de Montreuil: "What a satisfaction it would be for me when someday . . . she will reveal your letters to us all and then we will recognize in them, my wife and I, the kind attentions of your friendship, and the evident proof of your sincere loyalty."[15] Instead of exploding in a rage, Sade appeared to be enjoying this odd minuet of false smiles, of delicate footwork that brings the combatants close and then apart.

Instead of firing Gaufridy, as he had his previous lawyer, Fage, for a similar betrayal, Sade would claim that Gaufridy assisted in his escape. In this way, Sade eventually got him into difficulty and to some extent destabilized the relationship between Gaufridy and Mme de Montreuil. On November 3, Mme de Montreuil wrote to Gaufridy that she had heard, through various "individuals in the administration, that it was you who helped him to escape at V[a]l[ence] by providing him with the means."[16] In another letter, she warned Gaufridy that there was a "little cabal" at La Coste trying to discredit him. She informed him that someone at La Coste had written to her that there was "proof" that Gaufridy was a *"rascal"* and a *"traitor."* It made her wonder if Gaufridy was telling her everything he knew.[17] Sade had caught the lawyer, and he enjoyed teasing him on the line without reeling him all the way in. Gaufridy, however, was but the pilot fish to Mme de Montreuil's shark.

And what of Renée? Her mother had kept her in ignorance about the progress of Sade's appeal at Aix. In fact, Renée believed her husband was still in Vincennes. On July 14, Mme de Montreuil informed Gaufridy of her plan to keep her daughter in the dark until around "the end of the month," when, presumably, Sade would have been safely returned to prison at Vincennes.[18] Renée had been formulating various schemes for her husband's escape and forwarding the details to Gaufridy. She had prepared a letter for her husband in the event of his escape. In Gaufridy's files, this letter bears the note *"This letter is to be delivered to M. le Marquis de Sade after he is safely beyond the grip of the policeman from Paris"*:

> Do you now believe that I love you, my good little love whom I adore a thousand times? Take good care of your health, do not let yourself want for anything. Arrange to have some letters written to me [i.e., by Gaufridy or others] that are not in your handwriting, and between the lines and on the blank sheet you will write to me with the secret ink.
>
> I will do the same. I will come to you when I can and I will explain many things to you. . . . Gaufridy will give you some money;[19] whatever you want.[20]

Not until the third week of July did Renée learn from her mother of Sade's trip to Aix. Mme de Montreuil, herself yet unaware of her son-in-law's escape, saw fit to inform her daughter of the appeal at this time. On July 27, Renée wrote to Gaufridy about this interview: "I had a terrible scene with my mother on the day she told me the result of the appeal." Renée's joy at the news was cut short, however, when her mother also told her that Sade would not, despite the judgment, be given his liberty. This news was conveyed, according to Renée, with "a revolting haughtiness and despotism that put me beside myself." Renée gave vent to her shock and disappointment in an outburst that irritated her mother, especially because it made Mme de Montreuil see that "my ideas and words come from me, and not from M. de S[ade], who she believes has trained me to speak like his parrot." On this same day, July 27, believing that there might still be time to see her husband on his journey back to Vincennes, Renée wrote to the lawyer Reinaud of her intention to "rush to the road" to intercept him.[21] Within a few days, however, Renée and her mother had learned that Sade had escaped and was at La Coste.

Sade was annoyed that Renée did not immediately come to him. On August 8, he complained about the delay to Gaufridy: "It does not appear that Madame de Sade is going to come, since she pretends not to receive my letters." Sade told Gaufridy that Renée's "presence" was "extremely essential for a thousand reasons."[22] Sade by now understood that Gaufridy could be used as a conduit to Mme de Montreuil. However, with regard to allowing her daughter to assist Sade, Mme de Montreuil was adamant: "If she wants to be of use to him, so be it. But let her stay in Paris." Writing to Gaufridy on August 1, Mme de Montreuil vowed that she "will never permit" Renée "to expose herself and to be further disgraced and compromised as she had been by rejoining her husband, at least until a *long* experience of good conduct should prove that there is safety in doing so." If Renée disobeyed and tried to go to La Coste, "if her love or her blindness lures her there, the government will lend us all assistance in a such an honorable and just cause."23 Mme de Montreuil threatened to have her daughter arrested by a lettre de cachet. Renée believed her. She asked Gaufridy to inform Sade that her mother "is like a lioness over that": "When I speak to my mother of going to join him at this time, she breathes fire and flame and quite seriously threatens to have me arrested if I go."24 On August 13, Mme de Montreuil concluded a stern letter to Renée repeating the above threat in the most chilling tone:

> Above all, do not forget what I have told you: Your honor belongs to your family; as your mother, I must be vigilant to keep you from falling once again into the dangers which are apparent to us. And if you wish that his liberty not be disturbed, do not risk making him worry about your own. You should understand my meaning, and the proof of my word is as easy to accomplish as it would be dangerous for M. de S., if one were forced to do it.25

Renée stayed in Paris.

At La Coste, Sade continued to try to influence Mme de Montreuil through Gaufridy and by means of two letters he wrote her, one mailed to her directly, and one sent to Renée. Mme de Montreuil read the first one. However, as she informed her daughter in a letter of August 13, "The style made me wish not to receive others, and I will certainly not accept any. If any arrive, they will be kept or returned without being opened." Of the other letter, which Renée had cleverly left on her mother's desk, Mme de Montreuil replied to her daughter:

> I discovered on my desk, Madame, the letter that I am returning to you. It was pointless to leave it there. You ought to have considered that, if I allowed myself to be vanquished into opening it, it would have been at the moment when you were at my knees, and not afterward out of some motive of curiosity, my refusal being entirely coolheaded and reasoned.

Mme de Montreuil gave the following reason for not opening any more of Sade's letters: "Is it appropriate for me, when M. de S. evades the authority of the King, to be in correspondence with him and suspected of having assisted him?" Sade had thought it a clever ploy to claim that Mme de Montreuil and others had assisted in his escape at Valence. Now she turned the argument against him, defying his attempt to implicate her in criminal matters and vowing that she would not communicate with a fugitive. Renée, on her knees, in tears before her mother, was trying to get her to lift the lettre de cachet. But Mme de Montreuil replied that it would be inappropriate for her to ask the King to rescind this order "when it has just been violated"—as if Mme de Montreuil were not the sole reason for the very existence of this lettre de cachet in the first place. Then she went through a litany of complaints, how her virtues, her "easy indulgence," her "generous credulity" had been abused by Sade, by his "many repeat offenses," by "all his maneuvers, abuse, insults, etc." Her tirade reached a crescendo: "Why, he accused me of having betrayed him! I, betray him!"[26] It was obvious that she was done with him. Sade had hoped that his escape might have given them both a way out. He could stay quietly at La Coste, and she would eventually lift the lettre de cachet. Now Renée, at least, knew that her mother was implacable and that her husband was on borrowed time.

Renée tried to warn Sade. By "the most tortuous route," she sent an anonymous letter to Reinaud, who recognized the handwriting and tipped off Gaufridy. But in a letter to Gaufridy, Sade dismissed his wife's warning as "banal rubbish" and "just another prank." "They have no more desire to recapture me," Sade scoffed, "than I have to drown myself."[27] But then he received another warning, which he also communicated to Gaufridy: "*The latest information from the same source assures us that there will be yet another expedition to the château;* it is therefore essential to go into hiding." Sade wanted Gaufridy to go to Aix "to discover the truth of all this. Do they want to capture me or not? As for myself, I continue to think not."[28] Gaufridy wrote that he had heard Marais was distraught to the point of tears over Sade's escape. Marais in tears! Sade assured Gaufridy that police inspectors never cry. They might vent their rage in "blasphemies but not tears!" It was all "a comedy," Sade joked, "a farce."[29] Once again, Sade preferred cloud nine to reality.

Sade, of course, was happy at La Coste. One of his greatest pleasures during these magical weeks of summer was the presence at the château of Mlle Marie-Dorothée de Rousset. Because of the depth of their friendship, begun during this summer of 1778, and because of their remarkable correspondence over the next few years, Mlle de Rousset deserves special notice. She was four years younger than Sade, having been born in Provence, at Saint-Saturnin-d'Apt, in 1744. Earlier, it was seen how fondly Mlle de Rousset recalled participating as a girl of nineteen in the festivities at La Coste in April 1763, when Sade was welcomed onto his estate just before his marriage. Now, in the summer of 1778, she was thirty-four years old and admittedly not particularly attractive. Even so, it was Mlle de Rousset whom Sade invited to La Coste soon after his escape. "I had a beautiful young lady to dinner," Sade teased Gaufridy. "But, for not having come, you do not deserve to know her name."[30] Mlle de Rousset had come to stay. In a short time, she won a place in Sade's heart. By September 1, Sade commended her to Gaufridy as "a very dear and respectable friend," and added, "Her honest and sensitive soul is truly made to make one savor all the charms of pure friendship. I am and I will be for the rest of my days extremely attached to her."[31] She was constantly with Sade during the end of July and almost all of August, taking care of the house, offering him, as he wrote to Renée in September, "all the services that her friendship could suggest."[32] The following year, in May of 1779, when Mlle de Rousset was returning to La Coste from Paris, Sade wrote her a letter from Vincennes that drifted off into a reverie as he imagined her returning to the places that had meant so much to them both during the summer of 1778:

> You will sit down on the bench . . . you remember that bench? . . . yes . . . and when you are there, you will say: "A year ago he was here beside me . . . yes, I sat here . . . and he sat just over there . . . he opened his heart to me with that candor and that innocence that were evident in all his dealings with me. . . ." . . . And then you will go into the little green parlor . . . and you will say . . . "That is where my table was . . . that is where I wrote all his letters, because he kept nothing secret from me . . . sometimes he sat down in the armchair . . . you remember that armchair? . . . and from there he said . . . 'Write . . . *we will make . . .*' But Monsieur, *we?* 'Yes, my dear friend, *we.* Our phrases should be like our hearts. Write *we.*' " Next, you will go and wind the clock. . . . Then you will take two or three turns around the great hall and you will say . . . "If I had utterly lost him . . . how dear to me would be all these places! . . ." . . . I will wander with you on all these little promenades and through all these recollections. . . . Perhaps I will fly to you. I will hold your hand once more. . . . Are you aware of the force of illusion upon a sensitive soul? You will think you see me, but it will be only your own shadow. . . . You will think you hear me, but it will be only the sound of your own heart. . . .
>
> Adieu, Mademoiselle . . . yes . . . adieu . . . I am not crying, at least not while writing this. . . . No, in truth, I am not crying. . . .[33]

During the summer of 1778, Sade needed a friend. He opened his heart to Mlle de Rousset, and she became a member of his "little cabal." She was able to evoke all of the pent-up feelings that Sade could express to no one else. He felt more comfortable with her than with anyone in displaying his tender emotions. She was (by her own description as well as Sade's) a mixture of "saintliness" and "coquetry."[34] He had a number of nicknames for her, each suggesting some feature of her appeal: she was "my very dear and very kind saint" or "Saint Rousset"[35] (even Renée affectionately referred to her as "the Saint"[36]), or "Milli Printemps"[37] (Miss Springtime), or "my little beast,"[38] or "my dear Fanny"[39] (possibly after John Cleland's notorious English novel *Fanny Hill*); she also called Sade "my dear Saint,"[40] or "my dear little Saint,"[41] and Sade styled himself as "your Lovelace"[42] (the satanic and doomed rake in Samuel Richardson's *Clarissa*, which they both enjoyed discussing).

Mlle de Rousset was everything that the dour, humorless, priggish, conventional Renée was not. It was Mlle de Rousset's remarkable openness, her wit, her intellectual tolerance, and her pleasure in playing with ideas and words that made of her a soulmate for Sade and allowed him to open his mind as well as his heart to her. When he recalled this summer of 1778, he remembered their long discussions: "I listened to you for more than two consecutive hours when you talked reason to me."[43] When she talked reason, she could be harsh with Sade, saying things that no one else dared tell him. She expressed herself bluntly when she thought that he was wrong. "If I love you," she wrote to him on December 29, 1778, "I cannot spare you from telling you the little truths that others hide from you. You know that I am not frank by halves."[44] Her letters displayed such a wildness of mind and humor that one particularly lively turn of phrase in one of them made Sade "die of laughter for a quarter of an hour." When she complained that Sade had criticized her writing style, he wrote back in astonishment, vowing to "search the entire planet, if you want me to find support for the idea that your style is not delicious!" Then he offered the following fantasy about such a pilgrimage: "My little beast, like a new Don Quixote, I will go to break my lances at the four corners of the world to declare that my little beast is, of all the little female beasts breathing between the two poles, she who writes the best and who is the most lovable." Renée, Sade continued, did not have the Saint's writing talent, for his wife's letters were filled with such "stupid and boring absurdities" that "I would rather she copied the *Mercury;* at least I would get the news."[45]

During that brief summer of 1778, had Mlle de Rousset become Sade's lover? Sade's previous biographers tend to think not, or avoid the question.[46] Certainly, there was a good deal of sexuality in their conversation and in their letters. From prison in May 1783, Sade concluded a letter to his Saint with this passage:

> Adieu, beautiful angel, occasionally think of me when you are in bed, your thighs open, and your right hand busy with . . . looking for fleas. Remember that in such a matter a partner is also required, otherwise one has but half the pleasure.
>
> One hand should be . . . like that, and the other where La Présidente shoves her signals.[47]

One of Mlle de Rousset's charms for Sade was that he felt that he could say *anything* to her. And she responded almost as audaciously. She could express herself quite racily with others as well. This is how she began a letter on April 27, 1779, to Chanoine Vidal, another member of the cabal in the summer of 1778: "The honor of your silence constipates me to such an extent that I take the liberty to assure you of my perfect looseness!"[48] On June 30, 1782, Mlle de Rousset wrote to Gaufridy that this same Vidal had "so well confessed his housekeeper that the result was a nine-months' swelling."[49] Strangely enough, the grave Gaufridy later became the object of Mlle de Rousset's affection and flirtatious banter. While she was in Paris, Gaufridy may have considered staying overnight in her bedroom at La Coste, and then thought better of the idea. She teased him about this in a letter of March 12, 1779: "You were wrong to refuse to sleep in my bed, Monsieur. What lovely thoughts, what lovely dreams, what sweet sens[uality] would you not have enjoyed!"[50] On many occasions in Mlle de Rousset's correspondence with Gaufridy, she professed her passion for the somber lawyer. For example, on November 9, 1779, she assured Gaufridy she was not joking when she said "I love you."[51] But then, on February 7, 1780, she told him that she had "countless lovers," and that she played at love "to pass the time."[52] The question then returns: Was Mlle de Rousset's love talk with Sade merely another such diversion? Was she one of those spinsters (she died without marrying) who were all talk, all gossip, all words, and no action? Probably not.

Mlle de Rousset's attachment to Sade throughout the rest of her short life was profound. It began with sensual love in that summer of 1778 and grew into something more. As for Sade, he had no one else that summer, and it is doubtful he would have avoided a physical relationship with his love-struck, lonely, and fascinating houseguest. Eight months later, on April 27, 1779, she wrote about it to Vidal, their constant companion at La Coste: "You know how much I love him. You have read all the love letters that I wrote to him when he was with you! Well, then! I loved him then in that way, and now I still love him even more strongly in another."[53] It was an affair of a few weeks, a month perhaps; pleasures stolen during those brilliant sunny days of August in Provence, while storm clouds gathered—Gaufridy's betrayal, Renée's unexplained absence, Marais's possibly imminent appearance at the head of a troop of soldiers and policemen, the uncertainty of Mme de Montreuil's plans. It was remarkable that Sade and Mlle de Rousset, having loved each other "in that way," grew to love each other "even more strongly in another." This relationship supports a point mentioned earlier but worth repeating. Sade's sexual activities with prostitutes, characterized by frenzied libertine experimentation, were different from those he indulged in with women he loved. Sade was capable of being a lover and a friend, a man worth loving even after the sexual relationship had ended.

There were signs enough of the bad weather that was coming. When Gaufridy visited La Coste on August 5, he felt a distinct chill toward him coming from the "little cabal" of Mlle de Rousset and Chanoine Vidal, who seemed intent upon discrediting him.[54] By the time Sade wrote to Renée in September, he had learned enough about Gaufridy to call him a "knave" and a "monster." For one thing, after examining Gaufridy's accounts of the estate's rents and leases, Sade concluded that the lawyer was cheating him by letting Sade's farmland go at a loss, while accepting a bribe for himself "under the table."[55] And then there is the question of Gaufridy's possible implication in Inspector Marais's discovery of human bones at La Coste. After briefly visiting La Coste around August 5, Gaufridy had spent almost the rest of August at Aix. There, according to Mme de Montreuil's letter of September 15, he had "the opportunity to see Mar[ais]." Mme de Montreuil was angry (and suspicious) about how information concerning human bones at La Coste had come to Marais. She asked Gaufridy if Marais "spoke to you about these things, and from whom he could have learned about them."[56] It is strange enough that Gaufridy was meeting with the police officer while his client was hiding out at La Coste. But could Gaufridy himself have passed along the secret evidence about the bones that he discovered during his own searches at La Coste? Could he somehow have aided in Sade's arrest?

Sade's summer holiday was about to end. On August 19, he was strolling in his park in the cool of the evening with the Curé Testanière and Mlle de Rousset. Suddenly from the woods nearby came the sound of running footsteps. "Much alarmed," Sade shouted for the intruder to declare himself. There was no answer. Then from out of the woods stumbled Sambuc, the guard of La Coste, "his head rather muddled with wine." Upset and frightened, Sambuc warned Sade to flee, for down in the village "the cabaret was beginning to fill up with some very suspicious-looking characters." Sade dispatched Mlle de Rousset to investigate. After an hour, she returned, "assuring me that she would bet her life that these fellows were actually what they claimed, that is, silk merchants." But they were not silk merchants. Later, Sade would blame Renée for not having been with him at La Coste: if she had been, and if he had sent her down to the cabaret (a rather unlikely errand for the Marquise!), she would have recognized "one of them" as being "of the gang that arrested me" in her apartment in Paris in 1777.[57] Despite the reassuring report of Mlle de Rousset, Sade decided not to spend the night at La Coste. He went to stay with his friend Vidal at Oppède, about six miles to the west. This was Wednesday, August 19. Mlle de Rousset kept Sade informed about events at La Coste by sending him two letters a day. Her news was not good. By Friday, August 21, Sade went deeper into hiding, spending the night in an abandoned farmhouse a few miles from Oppède. He remained there Saturday night. By Sunday, August 23, he heard reports that sent him "into a sort of anxiety so violent that anyone with the slightest foresight would see in this cruel situation the grave of my ill-fated liberty":

> The woman whom the Chanoine [Vidal] sent to me was so alarmed by my condition that she ran to warn the Chanoine of it. He came.
> "But what's wrong with you?" [he asked].
> "Nothing. I just want to get out of here."
> "Is it making you ill?"
> "No, but I want to leave."
> "And where would you go?"
> "To my place."
> "You are mad. I definitely will not go with you there."
> "I don't require it. I will go perfectly well by myself."
> "Think it over for a moment, I beg of you."
> "Everything's thought over. I want to go to my place."
> "But you are just closing your eyes to the danger, to what people are writing to you! . . ."
> "Fine, fine, it's just tall tales, that's all. There's no danger at all. Let's go."
> "But let's at least wait four days (alas! the poor devil said the exact number of days that it had been necessary to wait!)."
> "I don't want to, I tell you, and I want to leave now."[58]

He did. Accompanied by Vidal, Sade returned to La Coste Sunday night, August 23. This was a busy Sabbath, for Sade felt the need and found the time to masturbate twice on this day, as he would later note in his

"Almanach illusoire," or his record of masturbations. The first occurred at Vidal's house. Years later, Sade recalled that it was "with his cook,"[59] and he also remembered that the ejaculation arrived *vipériquement*—viperlike. Sade recorded his further exploits at La Coste with the follow-ing cryptic and indecipherable abbreviations: "at night pr ↓ rr Hélène."[60] Oppressed by anxiety and danger, Sade resorted to masturbation not merely for pleasure, but as a way of drifting into a private world of factitious power-relations that made him feel omnipotent and in control—for the moment. It was in just such a desperate and dreamy state of mind that he had gone to Paris in 1777 and arranged a tryst with the unnamed Abbé—on the very eve of his imprisonment. Sade was a person who could not bear frustration. He had no patience for navigating troubled waters. Now, as on his trip to Paris, sex could provide an escape. But now, also as then, rather than rig his ship for stormy seas, he chose impulsively to end the suspense and his troubles by throwing himself overboard.

On Monday, August 24, Sade's friends begged him to go back into hiding. He stayed where he was. Although nervous, Sade was still acting upon the illusion that he himself had created—that Mme de Montreuil would not have him rearrested, causing a new scandal after she had gone to so much trouble to have his name cleared, and after Sade had informed all of his relatives of the restoration of his freedom and his reputation. Sade also felt paradoxically encouraged by two letters that arrived from Renée on August 25. In one, she informed her husband of the sale almost four months earlier of his post as lieutenant general of Bresse, Bugey, Valromey, and Gex. Hearing this for the first time, Sade was "stupefied" by the news.[61] However, he managed to twist this shocking turn of events into a hopeful, magical signal. "It was impossible to imagine," he wrote his wife later, "that one would tell me such dreadful news the day before one was preparing an even more horrendous blow." This was mere superstitious thinking and paranoia. Sade imagined, wished, that he were the focus of rational, benevolent forces. He was then also able to say that what happened next was all Renée's fault: "You are, therefore, the sole cause of what happened to me, and I slept at home on the night of the 25th to the 26th."[62]

Inspector Marais's "silk merchants" had been watching the château for some time. They were aware of Sade's return, and they may have obtained the assistance of someone on the inside. Perhaps Gaufridy, then at Aix, had oblig-ingly supplied information about a secret way to enter the walled château. In the darkness before dawn of Wednesday, August 26, Marais assembled his troop of ten policemen, and they entered the château at 4 a.m. Sade slept on. The noise, however, awakened Gothon, the housekeeper. According to Sade,

Gothon, "naked and all in a rush, flings herself into my room." "Run for your life," she screamed. "What an awakening! I flee in my nightshirt wherever I can . . . , instinctively climbing the stairs to a place that was in no way made ready, despite the orders that I had given about it." He then flung himself into a storeroom and locked the door, hearing "such a frightful commotion on the stairs that for a second I thought it was thieves who were coming to cut my throat." Mlle de Rousset and Chanoine Vidal were, along with Gothon, in the château that night. The assault of the policemen set them to shouting "Murder! fire! thief!" Sade listened in his hiding place. "In a minute the door is broken down and I am seized by ten men at once, some of whom put the points of their épées on my body and the rest the muzzles of their pistols at my face." Sade was shocked at this arrest made by a sort of rabble who could be easily mistaken for thieves, who broke down doors, and who had the insolence to insult the person of a marquis with their weapons. That was not all. Inspector Marais then spewed upon Sade "a flood of outrageous nonsense."[63] Marais had been closely involved in guarding and surveilling Sade since 1763. In the past, Marais had always acted with complete professionalism. But Sade's escape still rankled. Now Marais gave vent to his anger, gloating over Sade's capture, shouting in Sade's face, and, even worse, addressing him by the familiar pronoun *tu:* "Speak, speak, little man, you who are going to be locked up for the rest of your days for having done such-and-such things in a black room upstairs, where there were dead bodies!"[64] Marais had learned about the bones.

Marais's obnoxious behavior and words were reported by Mlle de Rousset in a letter of August 28 to Mme de Montreuil. Sade's mother-in-law thought, "It is inexcusable to use such language in such a situation." She said that she was "lodging a complaint about it," and that Marais would be punished.[65] But, of course, she was mostly concerned about the bones; she had not wanted that story to go beyond Gaufridy. Marais was indeed punished. Mme de Montreuil had registered "complaints," and on November 27 boasted to Mlle de Rousset: "I have employed sufficient influence upon the matter to be confident that he is cashiered." Mlle de Rousset warned Gaufridy, "You see how vicious women are!"[66] Poor Marais! A career spent compiling the sordid details of the lives of courtesans and noble rakes, of being discreet about the indiscreet, came to an end through one intemperate outburst. In the fall of 1778, Marais was still trying to get paid for escorting Sade to and from Aix, and Renée was refusing to reimburse the 4,200 livres in expenses.[67] A few years later, Sade was still thinking about Marais. On January 22, 1781, Sade asked his wife, "Let me also know now what has become of that rascal Marais; I no longer find him in the Almanach. Has he been racked on the wheel or hanged? He certainly deserved it."[68] In fact, Marais did not live long after the scandal that broke his career. He died in his apartment on the rue Montmartre in Paris on January 17, 1780.[69] There is a darkly comic novel in Marais's amphibious journeys between the upper and the lowest social worlds of eighteenth-century Paris. Unlike Sade, Marais was careful, meticulous, discreet in every way. He had cautiously navigated the bureaucratic shoals, avoided making enemies, been useful to a succession of department heads. However, like Sade, Marais, too, fell prey to the implacable vengeance of Mme de Montreuil. In this cruel and humorous way, fate combined the destruction of the wolf-man of La Coste and the chief of the Paris vice squad.

When Marais arrested Sade during the early morning of August 26, he ordered that the prisoner be tied up and conveyed to a coach. Sade looked back. It would be the last time he saw his château intact. One thing was certain: given Marais's precautions, there would be no escape this time. According to Sade, Marais kept up his "abuse" all the way to Valence, the scene of Sade's escape less than six weeks earlier. There were other indignities en route: he was "dragged, bound and gagged, across the breadth of his whole province." Would it not have been better, Sade asked Renée, if his persecutors in Paris had acted straightforwardly—that is, "if they had quite simply given the order to come to my house and blow my brains out?"[70]

The chance to see the captured Lord of La Coste drew large crowds. "At Cavaillon," Sade wrote, "we had the whole population out." Even worse, at Avignon, where Sade's aunts lived, there was a crowd of "more than three hundred people": "and what distressed me there is that at that very moment I had my poor aunt the Abbesse de Saint-Laurent at death's door. She had just sent me a letter through my cousin, charming and full of congratulations. What a reversal!"[71] (Sade apparently chose to exaggerate her condition, for she died in 1783.) She learned of her nephew's capture the very day he passed through Avignon. She immediately wrote to Gaufridy to say that the arrest "does not surprise me": the escape, she thought, "made no sense," because the lettre de cachet was still in effect. What did it matter that Sade had written letters to her during his six weeks of freedom, promising good behavior? "I do not attach much credence to it," she wrote Gaufridy, "accustomed to his fine promises and constantly deceived by his behavior and by the consequences."[72]

On September 1, Sade, Marais, and the police escort had reached Lyons, where they all rested for two days. From here, Sade wrote a letter to Gaufridy, who had conveniently returned from Aix to his home at Apt just in time to miss the arrest of his client. Sade began, possibly with some irony: "You will surely be surprised by the news, my dear lawyer." The rest of the letter, however, was all business: leases for the farms, an authorization for extra money for Gothon to maintain the park, a request for Gaufridy to "draw up a general inventory of all the furnishings of the château," advice to Gaufridy on settling the Abbé's estate at Saumane—especially for saving the Abbé's library and his natural-history curios.[73] Sade wrote about business as if such matters required immediate attention during the short time he would be away. He did not yet realize what had happened to him, could not imagine that this new imprisonment would last eleven and a half years, or that he would be fifty years old when he would next breathe the air as a free man.

CHAPTER 15

Vincennes, Again

O N THE way back to Vincennes, Marais and Sade were on the road thirteen days. Sade was sullen and depressed, and his humor was not improved by the noise and the drinking of his guards. Marais, however, had reason to feel ebullient, and even tried to cheer up his prisoner, telling him that he would be in Vincennes "for only six months."[1]

On September 7, 1778, at journey's end, Sade could see the white towers of Vincennes rise above the horizon. By the time he reached the outer walls, night had fallen. Just as last time, there was the humiliating search of the prisoner and the confiscation of his personal effects. Sade received a new name, "Monsieur No. 6," after the number of his new cell—his old one, No. 11, being occupied. Sade was home. Here he would be for the next five and a half years, until he was transferred to the Bastille on February 29, 1784.

Renée, as usual, had been kept in the dark. She had just written a letter to Gaufridy announcing that her spirits, as well as her health, had been restored by her husband's freedom.[2] Mlle de Rousset, who had witnessed Marais's raid at La Coste, suffered a physical setback: "I am really ill," she wrote to Gaufridy on September 5.[3] On September 7, 1778, the very day Sade re-entered Vincennes, his wife, who had finally learned of his fate, wrote of her shock and "heartache" to Reinaud: "I am tired of being the plaything and the victim of all the vagaries of my family."[4] On the same day, Renée wrote to Mlle de Rousset: "My God, what a shock this is for me! Into what an abyss of sadness I have been thrown once more! How to escape it, whom to trust, whom to believe?" Certainly not her mother. Renée could not even speak to her: "Ever since this catastrophe, I no longer see her." Renée was approached, not by her mother, but by a "third party," who "swears to heaven above" that Mme de Montreuil "knows nothing." Renée tried to talk with officials of the government. Her frustration produced, for her, an unusually picturesque expression: "The ministers are stone walls." Her despair called to her mind the same image she had used that day in her letter to Reinaud, "I am tired of being everyone's plaything." More isolated and hopeless than ever before, Renée had no one to help her, no one to whom she could even talk. She understood that Mlle de Rousset was planning to come to Paris, and she was grateful for the company of this friend of her husband's: "I have," Renée told her, "a great need of your advice and your insight to disentangle me from the frightful chaos where I now am."[5]

As for Sade, he was being reacquainted with the rules of Vincennes. A prisoner can be made to feel grateful for very small favors—like Sade's first shave and some fresh linen nine days after his return, or for some books brought to his cell, or for the first letter permitted from his wife. On October 19, he was delivered his trunk and personal effects. By December 7, he was allowed to have pen and paper and two promenades per week. Sade's new accommodations, however, were not satisfactory: "In No. 6," he complained, "I was much worse off than in 11."[6] In his first letter to Renée from prison, he wrote: "I do not have even a quarter of the meager comforts I had before." For one thing, he said that he was "suffocating" in a room "where all ventilation is closed off, and in which it will be impossible for me to make a fire this winter."[7] When he tried to make a fire in the stove, his cell filled with smoke. Renée suggested that the "secret" was "to paste some gray paper around the pipe to envelop it completely."[8] This "secret" did not work, and Sade continued to complain of his cell: "It is extremely damp and unhealthy, . . . you can hardly see the sky."[9] He dubbed the faulty stove "the pneumatic air-extractor"[10] and attributed his migraines to lack of ventilation. The smoke, he added, "is making me totally blind."[11] Sade did in fact develop a painful, chronic eye inflammation that required frequent medical attention. In the winter, the wretched stove would become a constant source of complaint.

Nor did the room itself give Sade much consolation. Today, visitors to the donjon marvel at the soaring ceilings of the throne room, explore the royal kitchen of Charles V, read the printed plaques in the smaller rooms that once housed noble visitors to the Court of France, and in the eighteenth century held such prisoners of state as Diderot, Mirabeau, and the Marquis de Sade. Picturesque, perhaps, but it is another thing entirely to have to spend years behind the locked door of such a room. Sade called it "a hovel fit only for a dog."[12] There he slept, ate his meals (carried up usually cold from the kitchen below), read, wrote, kept his possessions, his books, the extra food and delicacies his wife sent in her fortnightly dispatches. Sade described himself as living "amidst filth and grime neck-high, bitten by bedbugs, by fleas, by mice, and by spiders."[13] He complained to his wife that the rats and mice "do not leave me in peace for a single moment all night long."[14] He could amuse himself by romanticizing these little beasts, by imagining, as he teased Mlle de Rousset, that she was a sorceress who visited his cell in the form of a mouse:

Admit that you come here every day and that it is you who are this witch of a mouse that I regularly engage in combat every night and that is disinclined to fall into any trap I set. . . . It is you, isn't it? Tell me the truth, then, lest I use too much force in getting rid of you! so then it will be my bed I will open for you, instead of the mousetrap. . . .[15]

He could occasionally make fun of these rodents when he wrote to Renée. At the very moment he was writing her a letter, he told her, "here are six white ones passing by":

When I ask as a favor that they put a cat into the next room in order to kill them, they respond by saying that *animals are prohibited.* To that, I reply: "But, imbeciles that you are, if animals are prohibited, the rats and mice ought to be prohibited too." They answer me: *"That's different."*[16]

Sade could sometimes neutralize the horror of his situation by narrating it.

Wit, sarcasm, satire: these were Sade's defensive weapons against the dreadful reality of Vincennes. When he could formulate his fury into a narrative gem in his letters to Renée or Mlle de Rousset, he felt some satisfaction. On December 2, 1779, he dramatized the following scene in a letter to his wife:

Would you like me to tell you a small example of the compassion of the administration of this place? Last night, having felt rather more ill for a few days, I thought to write a note to the surgeon, in which I asked him for a different medicine, from which I hoped for some relief. I go to bed and sleep a bit easier in the expectation that they are going to bring me what I asked for. . . .

"Well, now," I say [to the turnkey] upon arising the next morning, "do you have what I requested?"

"Not at all," he replies, "I am returning your letter."

"My letter?"

"Yes, Monsieur, your letter. You addressed it to the surgeon, and that is a violation. You have to address it to the commandant."

"And my medicine?"

"Oh! the medicine. When your address is done properly . . ."

Someday, Sade promised, he would reveal all of the abuses he had suffered: "Oh! I will reveal them, all the horrors, all the whole despicable system, all the schemes contrived by greed and rapacity! I know them all now. I learned them at my own cost. Now all of France must know them too."[17]

Earlier, in February 1779, Sade asked for a knife but was told that it was against the rules. The knife that was brought for his meals was taken away when he was finished eating. But what if he wanted a snack, what if he wanted to cut into some of the extra food Renée was sending? "If I am hungry at night, no more knife."[18] If Sade found the rules of society uncongenial and irrational, the discipline and the logic of prison rules appeared even more unbearably surreal. He dramatized an example of another infuriating dialogue he had with a prison guard. He wrote to Renée on December 2, 1779, that he had been taking advantage of his privilege to exercise in the garden when he was informed that the surgeon had finally come to see him:

> "Very well!" I say, "let him come to the garden."
> "Monsieur," I am answered, "he certainly won't do that. That's something expressly forbidden to him. Choose, Monsieur: either lose the surgeon's visit, or lose the promenade."
> "Alas!" I reply, "but both of them would have done me some good."
> "That may be, Monsieur, but it's not your good that's wanted here, it's the rule. . . ."[19]

Doubtless there is pleasure in turning one's misfortune into an anecdote. This is an art form that Sade would have ample time to perfect, and it is one of the motifs of his most interesting letters from prison, as well as the novels, short stories, and plays that he wrote there. The eighteenth-century English novelist Laurence Sterne best expressed the curative power of narrative in *Tristram Shandy.* Uncle Toby, depressed and on the point of death as a result of a war wound, is restored to health by recounting the complete details of when, where, and how he received his injury. "The history of a soldier's wound," Sterne says, "beguiles the pain of it."[20] The same may be said of Sade. Throughout his life, he found more consolation and meaning in the world he narrated than in the real world, in which he was so ill-equipped to survive. In fact, he tended to inhabit the private realm of his own narratives in a variety of ways, from acting out sexual scenarios with prostitutes, to imagining completely impossible outcomes to his dilemmas (as when he thought he could safely go to Paris in 1777 or safely return to La Coste in 1778). Of course, the price Sade paid for expecting the real world to conform to the logic of his narratives was, inevitably, serious trouble. In prison, he would discover that the only real way to actualize his internal world and avail himself of its consolations was with the tip of his pen.

If, occasionally, Sade could hew narrative gems out of the dark mine of his cell, he still did not know how long he would be confined there, and he still had to get through each miserable, infuriating, depressing day. "They get me up," Sade complained, "every day *at five o'clock* in the morning."[21] The turnkey even opened Sade's door "at four in the morning to find out if I had escaped! Like Polyphemus, this monster must count his sheep every day. What rapacious, greedy villains they are!"[22] This was an outrage to a man who went to bed at midnight, who had letters and books to write and to read, calculations to make, whose mind was filled with rage, with fantasies that kept him awake. Mlle de Rousset worried about his late hours: "You have written to me very far into the night; you should doubtless sleep. Why do you stay up like that? You will make yourself sick."[23] And sick he would become. Over the years, he would suffer pulmonary complaints—possibly tuberculosis.[24] Sometimes, especially when driven to a frenzy of rage by his guards, he would experience a kind of seizure and cough up blood. After one such scene, he wrote Renée, "The blood vessel that I had burst in my chest has reopened and I have again been coughing up blood worse than before. How must your horrible witch of a mother be in her glory!"[25] He also suffered from migraine, gout, chronic eye inflammation, hemorrhoids, nosebleeds, and "frightful dizzy spells," from which he sometimes fell into a swoon of unconsciousness. He told Renée that these seizures could kill him: "One of these days, they will find me dead here, and you will be responsible, warned as you have been."[26] His sufferings were real enough, yet he felt that they were not always taken seriously by the prison staff or treated properly by the prison doctors.

Alone and lonely, Sade craved human contact in the House of Silence, where prisoners were kept locked in their rooms, forbidden to communicate with one another, where they were allowed to take their exercise—their promenades, a special privilege—only individually in the walled courtyard below. The guards were under orders not to speak with prisoners except on matters of the most mundane business. Sade was angered by these restrictions and by his oafish and taciturn turnkeys. When he became violent, they would isolate him completely: "They now confine me to my room, never entering, and they serve me through a trapdoor as they do lunatics."[27] No, this was not at all like Miolans, where Sade hosted special lunches and late suppers for his fellow prisoners and even for the officers of the guard. Here was the bread of affliction. Here was solitude and pain, the deprivation of any human relationship. Let the guard grant me, Sade begged, "a half-hour or three-quarters of an hour of perfectly ordinary conversation."[28] The turnkeys, however, "scurry out of my room as soon as they have brought me my food."[29] When Sade got into trouble for trying to engage his turnkey in conversation, he jokingly asked his wife to send him "*a set of laws* governing the matter," that is, "a small catalogue of things that I am permitted to say."[30]

Trapped in silence and rage, Sade sat in his cell and plotted violent revenge against his guards. If they would not allow him to take exercise in the garden, Sade threatened to "punch" the first guard who entered his cell: "That will be some exercise anyway."[31] When he put this threat into practice by striking an impertinent turnkey on June 26, 1780, the obvious consequence was that all of his privileges were withdrawn. But then he had something new to be angry about, some new reason to argue with prison officials. Sade's motive was to get these silent turnkeys, these remote officials to speak to him, even if he did not care for what they had to say. Prison intensified the essential state of his entire life, a profound emotional and intellectual isolation, which he desperately sought to break by brazenly defying the rules.

If the turnkeys would not talk to him, Sade tried to simulate conversation through his letters, as in the following passage from his New Year's letter of 1780 to his valet Carteron, called La Jeunesse or, as here, Monsieur Quiros:

And what are you doing for fun, Monsieur Quiros?

> Which one, Bacchus or Eros,
> Today for glory vies?
> What! . . . you'll praise 'em both
> And seek to win the double prize?

I believe you quite capable of it, for the wines of Meursault, of Chablis, of the Hermitage, of Côte-rôtie, of Lanerte, of the Romanée, of Tokay, of Paphos, of Sherry, of Montepulciano, of Falerne, and of Brie lubriciously titillate your loins for the unpolluted thighs of the misses Pamphale, Aurore, Adélaïde, Rosette, Zelmire, Flore, Fatime, Pouponne, Hyacinthe, Angélique, Augustine, and Fatmé. Splendid, Monsieur Quiros! Believe me, that is how one ought to pass one's days. And when the author of nature on the one hand created wine and on the other c[un]ts, you can be very sure the intention was that we enjoy them.

As for me, Monsieur Quiros, I also have my little pleasures, and if they are not so heady as yours, they are not the less refined. I am constantly stamping my feet to keep warm; I have, for amusement at supper (and that by way of a great favor), a fellow who regularly and with no exaggeration takes ten pinches of snuff, sneezes six times, blows his nose twelve times, and spits *phlegmy gobs* at least fourteen times, and all that in a half hour. Do you think that is not perfectly *generous* and entertaining, especially when I am to leeward? . . .[32]

Thus, the slovenly and uncommunicative turnkey takes his place in what would become an alternate world, a better world for Sade—the world of words. Against his enemies, Sade vowed, "my pen will be my weapon," and he added the proverb that appears more than a few times in his letters: "Patience . . . patience! He laughs best who laughs last!"[33]

Sade's only regular correspondent during his imprisonment was Renée. Again, she inevitably became the focus of his rage against his mother-in-law, his sufferings, his fate. Renée was powerless to help her husband on the most material matters: the date of his release, or even the extent of his sentence. It was not for want of trying, however. On September 7, 1778, she wrote to Mlle de Rousset about how she was trying to establish her own influence outside her mother's sphere: "I am making use of a friend of the minister whom no one suspects in order to obtain the lifting of the lettre de cachet."[34] However, nothing could happen without Mme de Montreuil's approval. Renée had tried to keep up her husband's spirits, and in return he cruelly rebuked her. She longed for a friend, and Mlle de Rousset would become one. Mlle de Rousset was preparing to come and stay with Renée at the Carmelite convent on the rue d'Enfer, where Sade's mother had lived. Her arrival in Paris on November 6, 1778, was not propitious. She was, as she wrote to Gaufridy, "greeted with a rainstorm that resembled the Flood."[35]

One person who certainly was not looking forward to Mlle de Rousset's arrival was Mme de Montreuil, who wrote to Gaufridy, "I fear that the arrival of Mademoiselle Rousset, if she is vexatious and clever, might ruin everything."[36] In fact, after Mlle de Rousset wrote a long letter to Mme de Montreuil about Sade's arrest at La Coste, Mme de Montreuil wrote back a letter that "made her understand, with courtesy" (this courteous letter, alas, is lost), "that she was meddling in matters that did not concern her and that she was passing judgment on me without knowing me. I doubt that she will visit me."[37] But Mlle de Rousset was made of stronger stuff. On November 26, she was granted an audience with Sade's mother-in-law. The following day, the impressions very fresh in her mind, Mlle de Rousset described this "most satisfactory visit" in a letter to Gaufridy, depicting the tension of the confrontation in the following language:

Imagine for yourself, Monsieur, two individuals who wish to get to know each other, or two cats who seek to enter into combat, the aggressor at first hiding his claws, then from time to time exposing them to toy with and excite his adversary. The battle having been once joined, without appearing to come to grips, we sparred until the moment when I intended to launch my attack.

During the interview, Mlle de Rousset portrayed all of the horrors of Sade's earlier imprisonment at Vincennes. But Mme de Montreuil was not moved:

> "He is much better off," she said, "than the first time; he has company, all the facilities for writing, and all possible comforts. But what can we do? It does not depend upon me."
>
> "Oh! I am well aware of that," I told her, "I am asking you only how to go about it."
>
> . . .
>
> "Oh! if you knew, Mademoiselle, everything that he used to promise me! Here, in this very room, what promises he made!"
>
> "I believe it, he intended to fulfill his promises. But man is weak, Madame, you know it. Age and his misfortunes have wrought enormous changes."
>
> "I wish it! But tell me, Mademoiselle, *will you take full responsibility for him?*"
>
> Ah! Monsieur Lawyer, fortunately I had foreseen that question. With neither too much eagerness nor too much reluctance, I humbly replied: "Yes, Madame."[38]

Mlle de Rousset came away from this visit unaccountably optimistic, as she wrote to Sade on the following day: "I estimate at the worst that your detention will not last beyond the spring."[39] She appears to have been dazzled by the wily Mme de Montreuil: "She has made a conquest of me," Mlle de Rousset wrote to Gaufridy, and then gave him the following picture of the woman who held the keys to Sade's cell:

Madame de Montreuil is a charming woman, pleasing talker, still very much in her prime, rather smaller than large, with a pleasant face, a seductive laugh, and brilliant eyes, a puckish imagination, the wisdom and ingenuousness of an angel, although sly as a fox, but likeable and seductive in her way.[40]

On December 8, Mme de Montreuil also reported on this meeting to Gaufridy, and what she recalled she had said to Mlle de Rousset was more harshly blunt than what Mlle de Rousset thought she had heard, or wanted to hear:

> I have only once seen Mademoiselle R——, who, as you may imagine, deployed all of her eloquence. I had but one reply: "My daughter has no better advocate with me than my own heart. The particular or personal complaints that I might have against M. de S. do not figure at all in his *present* predicament, about which I am very disappointed, but for which I have no remedy at the present time. I *stand in the way of no one else's attempts.* I make none myself because I perfectly well know the pointlessness of them."

Mme de Montreuil professed no objection to Renée's trying to obtain Sade's freedom. She simply observed that "much lesser things" requested by Renée "have consistently been refused." The government's "policy is not for me *to explain*," she observed, and added: "In general, I believe that this is a wise *precaution* against the *transgressions that have disgraced him* so many times."[41]

In a letter to Renée on December 7, 1778, Mme de Montreuil repeated this same pretense of helplessness in the face of ministerial opposition to Sade's release. However, she insisted on speaking "plainly" on the question of Sade's sexual depravity:

> If it was done calmly and with all his faculties, he certainly deserves at least to be prevented from doing it again. If he was led to it by an excess of which he was not the master, by an *uncontrollable impulse,* . . . it is, then, necessary (for himself, more closely concerned than anyone) that a few years serve to calm his blood, to cool his imagination, and, in short, to obviate the dangers of his release.[42]

Mlle de Rousset thought that Sade would be imprisoned for a few months. Mme de Montreuil here spoke of years, but she was really thinking of life imprisonment for a man who did what he did either out of mental derangement or a kind of cool, perverse libertinism (to her, it did not matter which). She appears pragmatic, deliberate, absolutely settled and confident in her view of the matter. Not her daughter's tears, not Mlle de Rousset's eloquence, nothing was going to move Mme de Montreuil.

Even if Renée allowed herself to see her mother's intentions clearly, she tried to push this knowledge from her own mind, and she knew that she certainly could not reveal it to her husband. She felt her duty was to cheer him up, and this involved telling him half-truths, which, to some extent, she also wished to believe. But Sade possessed a paranoid's built-in lie detector. He could sense every ambiguity of her style, and he twisted what she said to prove that she was holding back information about the exact date of his sentence. But even his belief that such a date existed was actually a pleasant delusion, a wish that, however far into the future it might be, there was a preordained end to his imprisonment. He did not want to face the truth of his situation, that lettres de cachet involved an open-ended, indeterminate sentence. So he chose to berate his wife for not telling him the exact date of his release, and she chose not to confront herself or him with the harsh truth she had learned from her mother. He adopted a pattern of shouting at her over really quite irrelevant things, and she ended up explaining these small matters in the disingenuous way parents sometimes use with children, speaking with apparent patience and candor, but really oversimplifying everything, withholding everything that really matters. In general, Renée simply tried to be cheerful. "Tell him something to make him laugh," she advised Mlle de Rousset, "some dirty joke, any nonsense, whatever you like."[43]

As the New Year approached, Sade's first since returning to Vincennes in September 1778, he received holiday greetings from his sons—Louis-Marie, aged eleven years and four months, and Donatien-Claude-Armand, aged nine and a half. The boys were being educated at the Montreuils' house at Vallery. Sade had never seen his daughter, Madeleine-Laure, now seven years and eight months old. Renée had just informed Sade that "your daughter calls herself Laure," after Petrarch's beloved muse and inspiration, "although she does not support this name by her beauty." Renée hoped that when the girl grew up "she will not be quite so ugly."[44] When Sade finally got his first look at her in 1790, he was able to see that "she is a fine stout farm-girl," and "is quite as ugly" as he had been led to believe.[45] In 1779, she was too young, or possibly too slow in her progress, to be able to write. The boys' letters, written on December 29, appear somewhat formal and obviously supervised by their tutor, the curate of Vallery. The elder boy's letter contains sentiments that are enough to break one's heart: "Ah! my dear papa, how I wish to be before you to have the joy of embracing you, to call you my father, and to have the honor to be called your son. The first of my cares, my dear papa, is to pray to God that He grant all of your wishes and that He give you success in all of your enterprises."[46] The children had been told that their father was traveling on business. Over the years this excuse would wear pretty thin. The younger boy's letter is even more touching: "I hope, my dear papa, that you will be pleased with my writing. I have written this letter to you myself. I can do no better, my dear papa. But when I will be able to write better, I would not be able to tell you any better that

I love you."[47] When Sade wrote to Renée on January 9, 1779, he covered his feeling with sarcasm: "Let me know something of the footman who wrote that." The boys' penmanship, he declared, was worse than a year ago, and he exclaimed: "Long live progress—Zounds!—and rural education!"[48] Sade wrote to Gaufridy a week later and quipped that, if "my children are being willfully ruined, so much the worse for them." As for himself, he had decided "to drink, to eat, to sleep, to trouble myself not at all, and to laugh at everything."[49]

In many ways, Renée's life was harder than her husband's, and she was beginning to show signs of the intense emotional strain she was suffering. As before, her days were organized around running errands in the attempt to gather all of the things her husband requested—and as before, her efforts were repaid much more frequently with complaints than with thanks. On October 26, 1778, she sent him "some quince pâté" that she was able to find, and she assured him that, "if the orange liqueur is not good, I will look for a better." Answering his complaint about the last shipment, she explained: "Because of the humidity, the pâté does not keep so well."[50] On November 20, 1778, Renée said, "I have run all over Paris for the sausage. They assured me that they were from Bologna: I thought I had made the most marvelous lucky find in the world."[51] A small victory. Renée tried to do anything to please her husband in such matters, because she knew that she could not please him with the only news that really mattered. Here is the conclusion of a longer list of things Renée sent in the middle of December 1778: "a half-roll of colored paper; a half-bottle of vulnerary water; a pound of chocolate; a pot of strawberry jam; a pot of apricot marmalade from the Hyena [i.e., Mme de Montreuil]; a stewed fowl."[52] When Sade immediately complained that Mme de Montreuil's marmalade was too dry, Renée promised to find him some elsewhere.[53] It was endless and very tiring work, and it took its toll on Renée, whose appearance worried Mlle de Rousset when she came to lodge with her in Paris in November 1778. "I found Madame de Sade quite emaciated," Mlle de Rousset wrote to Gaufridy on November 27: "I will get her to eat."[54] Though Renée was afraid of getting fat, she did eat, because her husband asked her to and because Mlle de Rousset watched over her: "She makes me eat," Renée wrote to her husband on January 14, 1779; "she makes me laugh."[55]

For her part, Mlle de Rousset soon had to renounce her earlier optimistic estimate of Sade's release. Further experience allowed her to see through Mme de Montreuil. On January 26, 1779, Mlle de Rousset wrote to Gaufridy about a letter she had just sent Mme de Montreuil, urging the release of Sade on the grounds of "the pressing nature of his business affairs, the danger of a long imprisonment, and finally the poor health of her daughter." What reply did Mlle de Rousset get? "A very short letter in which bad temper is displayed throughout." Mlle de Rousset continued her account of Mme de Montreuil:

> She is as quick with her arguments as a cat on hot coals and, as I always told you, the most evident bad temper is as obvious as the nose on your face. . . . Her hatred is hidden with great art. Her daughter ill, indeed seriously ill (this was before I arrived), she came to visit her, stayed a moment with her, went from cellar to attic, saw the chamber-maid, who is an old servant from the time of the marriage with M. de Sade, and to whom she said with her mean little air:
>
> "It is unfortunate for my daughter that she is so much in love with her husband. . . ."
> "Upon my word! It is perfectly natural that she loves a husband who has always treated her with courtesy."
> This reply incurred the indignation of the dowager: then she criticized her over everything: "This is not well swept; that box is not arranged properly; this pot is not clean; adieu, and take care of my daughter."
> I offer you all of these tiresome little details to give you a hint of her character. I do it rather awkwardly, as you see; the style is so different from my own.
> I suspect and I believe that this lady's plan is to leave M. de S. inside for a long time.[56]

Eventually, Mlle de Rousset also became disillusioned with Sade and with Renée. When Sade learned of Mlle de Rousset's plans to return to Provence, he concluded, as he wrote to Renée on March 22, 1779, "It all too clearly shows me how much my detention is likely to be long, because, if it were only a matter of a few months, she would honor the promise she made to me to wait for me."[57] If she did leave, he vowed, "I will never see her again as long as I live."[58] For her part, a week later, Mlle de Rousset wrote to Gaufridy that she and Sade were now "at odds." "If he is angry," she added, "he has angered me."[59] By May 29, Mlle de Rousset was complaining to Gaufridy about how Sade "is ruining everything by his continued insults." Moreover, "he tried to compromise me very badly," she claimed, "by revealing to the ministers that I was writing to him and gave him secret messages. I received reprimands about it." Mlle de Rousset became so dispirited, she said, that "there are some times when I am tempted to give up on everything."[60]

Mlle de Rousset went on to paint a very gloomy picture of life with

Renée at her apartment in the Carmelite convent: "We maintain an angelic monotony. I see few of my acquaintances." However, there was a surprise visit by M. and Mme de Montreuil. Mlle de Rousset prefaced her interesting account of it by observing, "All her family are uneasy with regard to me, and consider me a friend of M. de S. They are on their guard, as if I were the bogeyman." Mlle de Rousset's account showed how thoroughly she had become disillusioned with Renée, whom she described as nervous and ineffectual, especially in the presence of her mother:

Madame de S., whom a fly unnerves, was face to face with her: "My dear mama, this, my dear mama, that." This display of cheerfulness was inappropriate at that time. She had written, two days earlier, a very sad letter. My serious demeanor brought her back to herself. Her mother did not know very well how to take my demeanor. M. Gaufridy, you are going to better know and judge this lady's character:

"And your health, Mademoiselle?"

"You honor me, Madame; (with a slight display of distraction) I am very well."

Some minutes later: "You would not be sick, Mademoiselle?"

"No, Madame, I am perfectly well, I think."

The conversation continuing with her daughter about some papers and some financial settlements, her daughter went to look for them in an adjoining office.

"I have done much for M. de S. [Mme de Montreuil continued] by occupying myself in his affairs (note that this is said with a syrupy tone, a confidential and informal air, etc.). He has spent thus-and-such against his principal . . . his foolish expenditures here . . . there . . . thus-and-such, etc."

"Madame," I told her, "it is necessary to forget the past, occupy oneself only with the means for repairing everything for the future; they are your children, they should be dear to you; you feel, despite yourself, that you are their mother."

"I love my daughter," she said, "I feel my maternal instincts for her, and that is all."

The fable was about to be resumed. I made a movement on my seat which was not ambiguous. (It was one of indignation.) She hesitated for a moment; her daughter entered, wished to speak. Her speech was so convoluted that neither of them, I believe, was able to understand very much of what she wished to say. I adroitly made my exit; a few moments later, she called for me.

"I have no secrets, Mademoiselle, I had but one word to say to my daughter."

"It was quite proper," I told her, "that you tell it to her in absolute freedom, etc."

. . .

Before she took her leave, I permitted her to take every opportunity to kiss me. Madame de S. was terrified. When she was gone, I told her: "This is the way, Madame, that I pay my court. Your mother is not unaware of my feelings. I have sufficiently expressed myself on every possible topic. Perhaps I am pleading a very poor cause. My pride makes me maintain my firmness until the end."[61]

Mlle de Rousset had come to feel that Renée's weakness of character was to blame for the lack of progress in Sade's case. In the above letter, Mlle de Rousset told Gaufridy that "gold makes everything move here," as did influence, but when it comes to such matters, Renée "is like a newborn babe." Mlle de Rousset, it would appear, believed that she would make a better wife to Sade than the easily frightened, naïve Renée. She played such an active and sometimes every effective role that government officials began to discuss Sade's case with her. She was told, for example: "Oh! he is better where he is; to give him his freedom is to expose him to new troubles!" When she tried to present Sade's case before them, she found they were "set against him." Sade's past, already mythologized, had begun to haunt him. Mlle de Rousset was regaled with tales of the Keller affair of 1768: "Stories from a dozen years ago, and containing nearly nothing in principle, yet magnified by malice, are as fresh today as if they happened yesterday." Sade's name caught in the throat even of those who loved him. "You cannot speak of him," Mlle de Rousset discovered, "without the pavement's threatening to swallow you."[62]

When Mlle de Rousset arrived in Paris in November 1778, she had high hopes for Sade's release. As experience dashed her hopes, the best thing she could do was to try to cheer him up. In a letter on January 18, 1779, she mentioned that before she left La Coste she had searched for a book Sade had asked her to find in his library. It was Samuel Richardson's *Clarissa*, the novel about a virtuous young woman who was raped by an impassioned libertine, Lovelace, and who found her final reward in heaven. Sade so much admired Richardson that he parodied Richardson's plot in his own novels. Mlle de Rousset found Lovelace to be "a mixture of good and loathsome evil" and said, "I would have come to hate men had I continued to read." She added, "I have never understood the thrill of victory you men extract from duping women." However, she asserted that she was not subservient to men. Which of us, she asked Sade, "will be the most adept at subjugating the other? We shall see." She knew herself, she trusted herself: "I will never be beaten," she told him, and even though she knew that he wanted to lead her around by the nose, she warned him, "you will very much risk having your own broken." In fact, Sade was about to receive a thump from her. He had been trying to explain his philosophy of life to her. She said that she could not make sense of it, but it was not her fault: "I am brave," she wrote to him, "and big talk has never frightened me."[63]

Mlle de Rousset understood Sade's personality, understood that, for him, all human and intellectual endeavors, including sexual relations, were competitive and aggressive, that one either subjugated or was subjugated, that one was either the source of power or the object upon which it operated. The power struggle in sexual relations had its obvious role in Sade's scenarios with prostitutes. But it can also be seen obliquely in his challenging relationship with Mme de Montreuil. Indeed, every relationship that Sade entered—even his relationship to ideas and to the act of writing—had this palpable, sexual valence that could fluctuate either way: between domination and subjugation. Quite often, it did not matter to Sade which side he was on, whether he came out on top or on the bottom, whether he whipped or was whipped, whether he was engaged in active or passive sodomy, whether he defied God or was struck down by God, whether he charmed and deceived Mme de Montreuil or was in tears at her feet begging her forgiveness. Both extremes powerfully engaged his emotions and made him feel, for the moment, that he was alive. His trouble was that he possessed no internal mechanism to control the flux of his feelings. Mlle de Rousset believed that she understood Sade, believed that, in spite of the wild swings of his temperament, he was at heart gentle, even sweet. She opened her heart and her mind to him.

As Mlle de Rousset discovered, an acute mind could be a disadvantage for a woman in society. She reported the following anecdote to Sade in a letter of May 7, 1779: "Last week, I went to visit a good sort of woman whom I had seen many times before. Before her husband arrived, she equally found me to be a good sort of girl and saw me with pleasure. But ever since her husband told her that I was intelligent, she no longer wants to see me without him." In the future, Mlle de Rousset humorously asserted, if her female friends felt threatened by her mind, she would cultivate the reputation of a dunce: "I want only to be stupid."[64] Sade replied, "Is it only now that you discover that people fear intelligence?" He continued: "Nothing can make you more enemies, and the reason is simple. With intelligence you more readily recognize the ridiculous, with intelligence you cannot stop yourself from laughing at it, and quite naturally the result is that those who are ridiculous and without intelligence enormously fear you and end by hating those who see through them so well and can paint them in their true colors." Sade identified with Mlle de Rousset. They were both intelligent. They were both satirists. Their laughter at and ridicule of hypocrisy set them at odds with most of the world. He acknowledged that, as a conformist, "one is perhaps less happy, because a wicked wit is a great pleasure." But he added that at least "one is more tranquil, and *tranquillity is worth more than pleasure.*" At this moment, Sade was comically interrupted in his discourse on the nature of happiness in society by his turnkey. "Ah! my little beast," Sade closed this letter to Mlle de Rousset, "here is someone to bring me my oats; I must leave you now to go eat. I will get back to you for my dessert, I will have you for my little compote. Adieu."[65]

This was Sade's first spring since his return to Vincennes, and the news that arrived from La Coste was redolent of revival. "The park," M. Paulet, consul of La Coste, wrote on April 9, 1779, "is in very good shape; all the plantings that you desired there have been done." The gossipy Paulet also reported to Sade on other sorts of plantings in and around La Coste aimed at "increasing the number of your vassals." In particular, "The gallant Guillaume has worked the field of your kitchen maid and has made her produce a little Guillemet."[66] Three days later, Sade's housekeeper, Gothon, also wrote with news of the season's fecundity: the "lovely chickens" and the "charming turkey hens" were doing very well in the lower courtyard, and one of the dogs "has brought forth ten pups."[67] The season put thoughts of sex in every mind. That same month, Renée wrote to her husband about having to reprimand their servant La Jeunesse once again for sneaking off. "And sometimes," she exclaimed, "he stays out all night!"[68] In *As You Like It*, Orlando cries, "O, how bitter a thing it is to look into happiness through another man's eyes."[69] Sade had not seen his wife for more than two years. Now he asked her for a sexual favor. In Renée's reply to him, on April 14, she noted his request: "You ask for a little piece of our petticoats in order to make relics."[70] In prison, Sade came to rely upon sexual fetishes and other devices.

As we have seen, virtually every one of Sade's letters to Renée made demands that re-created in discourse—do this, don't do that, do this—a sexualized power-relation between husband and wife. "Just once in your life," he wrote to her, "get everything on my list right!"[71] On her, he imposed his enormous needs and demands—precise, sometimes arcane, expressing the whole force and power of his connoisseurship. And she dutifully scoured Paris to satisfy him and suffered his complaints, sometimes his withering sarcasm, when she failed. By contrast, Sade's letters to his valet La Jeunesse (also called Martin Quiros) could be extraordinarily lively and entertaining. Beginning on September 14, 1779, La Jeunesse sent Sade three letters about the eruption of Vesuvius the previous month. Sade and La Jeunesse had visited Vesuvius in 1776, on their trip to Italy. Now La Jeunesse quoted newspaper clippings describing the devastation. Sade replied to his valet with a torrent of humorous abuse in a letter of October 4, 1779. The peculiar extravagance of the style is worth savoring. Here are the opening paragraph and a middle one:

> Martin Quiros . . . you are becoming insolent, m'boy. If I were there, I would give you a good thrashing. . . . I would snatch off your f[ucking] fake poof of hair, which you annually refurbish with the nether hairs that fall from the nags you hire on the road from Courthézon to Paris . . . and then, the next morning, with a dab of powerful glue you'd attach them to your old scabby head in such a way that it wouldn't be any more noticeable than a crab louse on a w[hore]'s "honey pot." Isn't that a fact, m'boy? Do try . . . try and keep your trap shut, I beg of you, because I am weary of being insulted for so long by the rabble. It's true that I act like a bulldog, and when I see all that pack of curs and bitches yelping around me, I just lift a leg and I piss on their noses.
>
> . . .
>
> Why, you old monkey-fucker! Weed-face bedaubed with berry juice. You old prop pole from Noah's vineyard, fishbone from the back of Jonah's whale. You filthy old flint matchstick . . . old rancid candle at 24 the pound, stinking harness off my wife's mule. . . . Ah! you old pumpkin, pickled in bug juice, third horn on the devil's brow, face of a codfish with oysters for ears, you old worn-out shoe off a bawd, you reeking piece of Milli Printemps's [i.e., Mlle de Rousset's] *bloody linen.* If I get my hands on you, how I would rub your face in it.[72]

A few days later, on October 8, 1779, Mlle de Rousset wrote to Gaufridy, concluding that Sade was well, based on "an extremely whimsical letter he wrote to La Jeunesse."[73] Mlle de Rousset sounded envious of the intimacy and the high spirits Sade displayed to La Jeunesse. Sade had not written to her since the previous spring, when he quarreled with her over her having led him to believe in an early release. He had written her "some insults" and had told her not to write to him any more. Despite Sade's rebuff, she said that she would continue to support his cause.[74] Even if Sade's anger could not drive away Mlle de Rousset, the Saint was mortal after all: on November 12, she mentioned to Gaufridy that she had been "sick for a week now."[75] This was the first sign of the consumption that was to kill her. To Gothon she wrote with more candor: "I have coughed up blood this week."[76] By March 3, 1780,

she bravely reported to Gaufridy, "I am not dead yet, but not far from it!"[77]
She nevertheless persisted in her effort to free Sade. In fact, by July 24, as she
informed Gaufridy, she had sufficiently annoyed various officials, including
Minister Amelot, that they had agreed to review Sade's case: "The reasons for
imprisonment are currently being examined and judged at Versailles. The first
minister has ordered another minister, his subordinate, to lay all the evidence
before him."[78] Finally, Mlle de Rousset felt that she was getting somewhere.

As for Sade, each day was another battle between rage and despair. When
he wanted to discuss his promenades and his smoky stove with the commandant, he was told that M. de Rougemont was away and would not be back
until night. Writing to Renée in April 1780, Sade ridiculed de Rougemont as a
debauchee running off to his *"early-morning delights."* Knowing that the commandant would see the letter, Sade continued, addressing him directly: "And
do not clear out at six in the morning so that no one knows where you are for
the rest of the day. All of this so as to go *clandestinely* to purge your filthy little
member." Sade even imagined de Rougemont and Mme de Montreuil in bed
together, and he called them "two accomplished and well-tried *bed-hoppers,* in
which activity your pious mother works up quite a sweat."[79] The following
month, Sade imagined that the commandant was sending him messages by
having the jailer post "signals on the garden walls for several days." In a letter
to Renée on May 31, 1780, Sade compressed his feelings about de Rougemont
into an epitaph that he posted on the same garden wall:

> Here lies the jailer of Vincennes,
> Small, base, surly, cuckolded,
> Who took his pleasures from the pains
> And the tears of the unfortunate.
>
> The earth reclaims him whole.
> Traveler, observe him here below:
> Don't bother looking for his soul,
> Because this prick didn't have one.[80]

M. de Rougemont, who had taken over the command of Vincennes in
1767 from the well-respected M. Guyonnet, made many changes designed to
maximize his income. He scrimped on food and firewood for the prisoners.
The food was so bad that, when the turnkeys tried to sell some of it in town,
the people of Vincennes coined the proverb: "As rotten as donjon grub."[81] In
a fit of brilliant insight, Sade saw the whole prison system as a corrupt part of
the national commerce: "We prisoners are a species of *property* whose earnings

buy the officers *pretty women*. We are *joints of beef!*"[82] Mirabeau made the same complaints about the profiteering, and he, like Sade, deeply disliked de Rougemont. "This fellow," Mirabeau called the commandant, "has all the bombast of the most self-important stupidity: he is a balloon full of hot air."[83] Sade, in a letter to Renée on May 21, 1781, attacked de Rougemont's greed, immorality, and hypocrisy: "It is not for this little bastard Rougemont, for this repulsive personification of vice . . . to try to set himself up as an enemy of vice, and of the very same vices that he exhibits to an even more scandalous degree, because . . . it is not for the gimpy to laugh at the lame, or for the blind to lead the one-eyed."[84]

During his imprisonment at Miolans, Sade had tried to cast Commandant de Launay as the Bad Father and the Comte de la Tour, the governor of Savoy, as the Good Father. In Vincennes, Sade attempted to do the same thing with Commandant de Rougemont and Lieutenant General of Police Lenoir. In a letter to Renée on April 30, 1781, Sade had only praise for Lenoir, calling him "a very honest, wise, and considerate magistrate," someone Sade thought "incapable of deceiving me."[85] Of course, he expected that his letters would be read by Lenoir. During this same month, in a letter to Lenoir, Sade complained about his persecution by the government, which "ought to have served as father."[86] Sade's own father had treated him dismissively, and yet Sade had looked up to him with exaggerated awe. Even now, Sade longed for his "beloved father," and recalled him as "one who would not have let me suffer for such a long time."[87] So strong was Sade's need for a father who could make sense of the world for him that he credited Lenoir with magical, prophetic powers. Lenoir's visits to the prison, Sade believed, were his way of "indicating" the "halfway mark" of Sade's sentence."[88] In the end, Lenoir had no magical powers, nor could he be manipulated by the flattery Sade planted in his letters home. Eventually, Sade gave up the attempt, and Lenoir was duly enrolled in the list of enemies and betrayers. Sade came to ridicule him as "an *homme noir*."[89] Writing to Renée from the Bastille, Sade complained that Lenoir no longer had the time to visit prisoners: rather, "Madame Jeanne's ass has enticed him away from all that, is that not so? And he would much rather feast upon the putrid c[un]t of a whore than to do his duty to an unfortunate person in pain."[90] Even if these temporary father-saviors failed, Sade could always put his faith in the King: he wanted "to go and throw myself at the feet of the King, in order to demand justice."[91]

Sade sought a perfect savior, but every candidate proved to be morally and sexually corrupt. He never accused himself of anything worse than youthful indiscretions with prostitutes, of "not having shown a proper regard for a whore's backside," he wrote to Renée in 1781. He had been "shut up like a madman in a cage of iron" merely because "he has the misfortune of being persuaded that nothing is less respectable than a whore and that the way one makes use of them should be no different from the way one moves one's bowels." Sade then launched into a fanciful and sarcastic attack against the supposed universality of Christian sexual morality. He cited "the King of Achem, who makes use of seven hundred strumpets who are given three or four hundred lashes every day for the least infraction." Sade also mentioned "the Emperor of Golconde, who never goes for a ride except upon twelve women arranged as an elephant, and who sacrifices twelve of them with his own hand each time a prince of his blood dies." Sade wondered what these rulers might have said about his own cruel persecution by the French system of justice:

> If, I say, one went to tell these gentlemen that there is in Europe a tiny patch of land where an *homme noir* [Lenoir] daily bribes three thousand strumpets in order to discover the way in which the citizens of this little patch (people who call themselves *very liberated*) give discharge to the spermatic material; and that there are dungeons made ready, scaffolds put up for those of these *very liberated* people who have not yet been able to understand that it is a high crime to open the sluices toward the right rather than toward the left; and that the slightest overexcitement during a crisis like that, when nature yearns to let it fly and when the *homme noir* wants to keep it in, was punished by death or with twelve to fifteen years in prison; if, I say, one went to tell this to the kings I just mentioned, acknowledge that they would be perfectly right to have the speaker locked up as a madman. . . . But because those people are entirely uncivilized, because they do not have the good fortune to be enlightened by the flame of Christianity, they are slaves, and we, on the other hand, are *most Christian, most civilized, and most liberated.*[92]

This is Sade's bitterly humorous argument for sexual freedom, based upon his own peculiar understanding of cultural relativism: because sexual matters are arranged differently in the kingdom of Achem and just about everywhere else, it follows that there is no universal rule about sexuality, so you might as well do as you wish. Sade appears to have enjoyed his argument, but, of course, he was French, not a subject of the kingdom of Achem, and he was now in a French prison.

In his letters and also in his fiction, Sade was argumentative and confrontational. One of the advantages of prison is that a man does not have to look far for opponents. On June 26, 1780, he got into a dreadful row with a fellow prisoner, the future orator of the Revolution, Mirabeau. It all began, Sade explained to Renée, when his jailer treated him, Sade thought, with discourtesy: "I expressed some reproaches to him about it. He replied with insolence." Sade claimed that he did not actually strike the jailer; he merely "conveyed the impression of wanting to strike him." Sade's fits of temper had always been theatrical, operatic, and self-destructive. Immediately, the jailer "ran to report that I had hit him." Sade appeared surprised that Commandant de Rougemont sided with his turnkey. Following the dispute, Sade "collapsed" and remained "totally unconscious" for "a quarter of an hour at least." Then, from four o'clock the next day, June 27, until the moment he was writing to Renée, at nine o'clock on the morning of June 28, he said, "I have not stopped coughing blood."[93] He was coiled for attack when, that afternoon, de Rougemont dispatched the captain of the guard to inform Sade that his promenades would be suspended until further notice. According to de Rougemont's letter to Lenoir on June 30, Sade exploded with a torrent of "dreadful and filthy language" that "resounded throughout the whole donjon and château." In this account, one can hear the howl bursting from Sade's throat, echoing up and down the stone passages. At the beginning of the month, Sade had just turned forty. He had been in Vincennes for more than three years. There was no end in sight. His explosion may appear childish, but he had used his tantrums against the authorities and other inmates to good effect at Miolans Prison. Perhaps he thought he would be lucky again. According to the commandant, Sade shouted to the other prisoners, urging them "to support each other" and thus provoking them to "rebellion." The commandant added, "This is not the first time that M. de Sade has attempted to arouse the prisoners." Once, upon passing M. de Whyte's door, Sade had shouted, *"Comrade, watch out what you eat, they are trying to poison you."*[94] Sade had a knack for the insane *mot juste*. On the eve of the Revolution, he would be transferred out of the Bastille for inciting the mob below his window by shouting the absurd but effective lie that the guards were slaughtering the prisoners, among whom was the above M. de Whyte.

But Sade's tantrum was far from over. Having been informed that his promenades had been canceled, Sade, as chance would have it, glanced out his window and saw that Mirabeau was just then enjoying a promenade in the courtyard below. Immediately, he began hurling curses. According to Mirabeau, Sade called him "the commandant's punk" and "countless filthy remarks of that sort," and told him to "go kiss the C[ommandant]'s ass" to thank him for being given Sade's promenades. Mirabeau recorded the following exchange:

SADE: Answer me, you f[ucking] b[astard], tell me your name if you dare, so that I can cut your ears off immediately I get out of here.

MIRABEAU: My name is that of a man of honor who has never dissected or poisoned any women, who will gladly inscribe it on your shoulders with his sword if you have not already been broken on the wheel before he can accomplish it, and in whom you can inspire but one fear, and that is that he will first be obliged to attend your execution at the Place de Grève.

Mirabeau's threat, and the "biting" tone in which he delivered it, shut Sade up.[95] However, Sade merely redirected his rage and paranoid fantasies onto Renée. The commandant informed Lenoir that Sade imagined that Renée and Mme de Montreuil were trying to poison him. As a consequence, "all his letters to his wife" were "filled only with horrors, threats, and filthy language."[96] It was at this inopportune time, when Sade was behaving so badly, that Mlle de Rousset chose to wage her campaign to free her friend.

In July 1780, Mlle de Rousset informed Gaufridy that she had provided "nearly all the ministers" with petitions and letters, and she had even persuaded "some princesses" to put the matter before Jean-Frédéric Phélypeaux, Comte de Maurepas, "who is examining the evidence." More or less on her own, the indefatigable Mlle de Rousset seemed to be making real progress. Sade, however, was not helping himself, because he "is behaving very badly and because in his letters he is writing ridiculous and frightful things about us which are read to us or told to us." Mlle de Rousset, who was "apostrophized as wh[ore]" in Sade's letters, sadly had to admit, "One must have a brave soul to persevere in trying to help him."[97]

A month after the violent scene with the guard, Sade was still feeling the consequences of his tantrum. Denied his promenades, which he considered essential for his health, he had been "completely unable to eat or to sleep," as he wrote to Renée on July 27, 1780. He had been so ill, so tormented, so harassed, that for the past seventeen nights he had not slept a wink. The surgeon came to find out how Sade was:

> *"My looks will tell you better than I could,"* I reply.
> "But no . . . not at all. In fact, you look wonderful," he says.
> Good, I say to myself, that is all I need to fully convince myself that this fellow sees me exactly like the surgeon of the Inquisition who takes the pulse during the torture in order to determine if one can bear it longer, and who invariably says: "Continue."

According to Sade, the prison officials lied about his situation in order to increase his torment and their profits. The voice of truth, Sade wrote, was stifled "with gold or with pretty girls. Everything is fine, all is well, everything is the best possible when there's a girl in your bed and money in your pocket. Gold and c[unts], there you have the gods of my country."[98]

Renée tried to reply to her husband's tirades with optimism and good cheer. In the middle of such a letter on August 29, 1780, she included this poignant reminder about their children:

> Your daughter has asked me for news of you and where you are. I have told her that you are traveling in Spain.
>
> To your sons, I no longer know what to say; I have exhausted every reason for why you do not answer their letters.[99]

Outside the thick walls of Vincennes, Sade's children were growing up without their father. They had only lies about him—very threadbare, virtually transparent lies.

At long last, Mlle de Rousset's campaign for the reevaluation of Sade's case had succeeded. However, when she pressed officials for a full investigation of the reasons for his imprisonment, she was given an explanation she did not want to hear. On October 21, 1780, she wrote to Gaufridy:

> Matters are still in the same situation and *they will be, I believe, for a long time.* After considerable delays and vague promises, I had hoped to see and to put Madame de S. in a position to see for herself the reasons for the imprisonment. . . . We have discovered from this brave stroke that the dear Présid[ente] was not so blameworthy as we thought. He has even more powerful enemies.[100]

Two days later, Mlle de Rousset elaborated. She had succeeded in getting some influential people to question the imprisonment. These people, including "M. and Madame de Maurepas, two princesses, and some others," had been shown "a dossier," no doubt designed to silence their inquiries. When they finished reading, this is what they said: "He is well where he is; his wife is crazy or as guilty as he to dare to ask for his liberty." This dossier, containing "the whole life of M. de S.," is now lost, but it then held "some horrifying depositions" made by "the various policemen who had been at the château." These must refer to the stories about the human bones. Whatever they were about, Mlle de Rousset said that these stories "are believed." Poor Sade, "the man is to hang!" she exclaimed. "There are grave reasons, very grave," she ominously explained, "that make me fear a long captivity."[101]

More than a year earlier, Mlle de Rousset had discovered that the myth of the satanic Sade was so powerful that she could not even mention his name without the pavement's threatening to open up and swallow her. In eighteenth-century France, as today, the myth of Sade was larger than the reality of the man and his life. To a great extent, he himself fostered the mythologizing, for he sought to live in a world of absolutes. He could not accept the sort of everyday, imperfect, rough justice that actually governs human nature and human society. Rather, he aspired to challenge the world and to position himself in a grandiose way against what he took to be the most powerful myths of human experience—the myth of the meaningfulness of the world (represented by our belief in God), the myth of the fixed dualities of our sexuality (the myth of masculinity and femininity), the myth of limitation (represented by the rules of family life and of society). So powerful was the impression he created that his myth turned out to be a prison whose walls were far stronger than the stones of Vincennes.

In one sense, however, it may be said that prison liberated Sade, redirecting his anger and intelligence to narrative purposes. Largely deprived of the freedom to act out his anger and his sexual fantasies, he had been forced to put them on paper. If "Sade" was already a myth before he entered prison, in Vincennes he began the process by which he would inscribe his name on human consciousness.

CHAPTER 16

Signals

A FEW MONTHS after his imprisonment at Vincennes, Sade commented in a letter to Renée on the regression induced by the prison system and by all of the petty rules and "trivial annoyances" enforced by the guards. At first, Sade said, "I believed myself transported to the island of the Lilliputians, where the people, being but eight inches tall, behave in proportion to their size." "It made me laugh at first," he said. "Next, it annoyed me." Soon, he said, he retreated into childishness as a means of coping with the harsh, quasi-parental rules of this prison house, and also as a means of protecting his pride from the insult of having to submit to the Lilliputian tyrants: "Finally, I concluded by imagining myself twelve years old, . . . and this idea of being returned to childhood sweetened a bit the disappointment a man would otherwise have suffered to see himself thus dominated."[1] When Sade was in fact twelve years old, he was a student in the Collège Louis-le-Grand, where the Jesuit fathers, even more than prison guards, kept up an intense observation of their charges. Throughout his life, this early experience of close scrutiny, of both his behavior and his thought, engendered in Sade an acute sensitivity to being watched and spied upon, one that manifested itself in his writing in frequent references to the idea of the Inquisition. The Jesuit academy, the prison system, and particularly the mental hospital at Charenton, in which Sade was later to find himself, were all institutions shaped by a revolutionary idea that swept through the eighteenth century and into modern life: that, with the expansion and celebration of individualism, society would increasingly require new protections against its possibly dangerous and extreme manifestations. In *Discipline and Punish: The Birth of the Prison*, Michel Foucault has charted the rise in the eighteenth century of the means, the technology, and the perceived need for close surveillance and discipline in such institutions.

In his letter to Renée, Sade tried to coat with humor the bitter pill he was being made to swallow—the fact that his life, his very self, was now in the power of Lilliputians, the little men of the police and prison bureaucracy, that his every gesture was being watched and reported. "One completely amiable thing which I forgot," he wrote to Renée, "is the swift fashion with which they pounce on you here for the slightest facial gesture, in order to report it immediately to the authorities."[2] Sade said that he quickly learned his lesson: "Now I compose my face so that I give the greatest difficulty in deciphering my feelings from my expression."[3] Today, we have become so accustomed to submitting to every manner of institutional probing and recording—whether in the form of school or medical records, credit reports, files of employers or the various branches of the police and government, etc.—that we have grown insensitive to the intrusive power of those practices. But they were invented in the eighteenth century as a reaction to the same ideal of individualism that produced the American and French Revolutions.

Sade told Renée that he first noticed the scrutiny, which inflamed his paranoia, when he reacted "incautiously" one day to a letter from her "that gave me pleasure." He imagined that it was reported that one of his wife's letters made him visibly happy and that an instruction was then given to Renée not to write anything that might please him. For Sade, these suspicions were confirmed by the unpleasantness he thought he detected in her succeeding letters: "Oh, how quickly the letters that followed made me see my folly!"[4] He therefore vowed to disguise his true feelings. There is a germ of truth in Sade's fantasy. Renée's letters were censored, and she may indeed have been informed—or she certainly learned from experience—what was acceptable to the censor. She complained to Gaufridy about the censors: "When I write anything that might mean anything, they return it to me."[5] But if there was any good news for Renée to report, she could always have used the invisible ink. As usual, Sade's suspicions were a displacement of his anger at Renée for not having got him out of prison, for her pointless letters about nothing in particular. In fact, the parts of Renée's letters written in invisible ink were no different in content from the parts written openly. In a list of "Reproaches" Sade compiled against her, the third complaint is that she had written "thirty letters to me in invisible ink only to inform me" of "tiresome drivel."[6] The use of invisible ink had been discovered early, apparently after only thirty attempts. But Sade's anger about Renée's vapid letters continued unabated. Once, when she had protested that the censor had prevented her from writing openly, Sade replied angrily: "But when you were able to speak, when you wrote *thirty letters with invisible ink*, why did you say nothing? And why were these secret letters even more stupid than the others? What? What do you have to say to that? Other than your wickedness or your docility?"[7] What could she say? Caught between Sade and the power of her mother and the state, she was helpless, unable to tell him what he wanted to hear. But

Sade needed to believe that he possessed an ally among the cabal that was controlling his life, so he included Renée in their number and blamed her for not helping him when, in truth, she was utterly powerless herself. After only a few months in prison, driven back into himself, Sade had become quite paranoid, imagining improbable, intricate, but for him very vivid scenes of conspiracy.

Paranoia is only superficially an exaggerated *fear* that others are talking about you, plotting against you. The true grip of this affliction upon the mind comes from its power to satisfy a *wish* to have others talk about you and plot against you. A paranoid is never alone. This wish for a relationship, even with enemies, is inevitable in the solitary confinement of a prison like Vincennes. There are other features of wishfulness in paranoia as well. It gratifies your pride to imagine yourself as the focal point of powerful beings, even if they are all for the moment arrayed against you. Furthermore, attributing your predicament to a conspiracy provides at least some explanation for your suffering. A paranoid's fear always leads to the pleasure of a great discovery of the principles of order and power that can account for his condition and that might one day be redirected to free him from his torment. If the paranoid's discovery and its attendant pleasures appear ludicrous to us, if his explanation about plots and schemes seems absurdly unfounded and incommensurate to us, it must be understood that his pleasure and his explanation refer to some deeper quest for meaning whose actual goal may be hidden even from himself.

One of the most interesting manifestations of Sade's capacity to imagine more intention and order in his situation than actually obtained was his belief in "signals," by which he referred to the hidden meanings he imagined were being sent to him in Renée's letters and in his conversations with prison officials. Anything could be seen as a symbolic act: if, for example, he lost one of his privileges on a particular date, he then took that number to have special significance. Some of his calculations are simply unintelligible, others incredibly ingenious. Almost all of these signals represent Sade's attempt to discover the date of his release from prison. Although his sentence was in fact indeterminate, he insisted that his enemies (including his wife) knew the exact date it would end.

The first indication of Sade's mania about signals came two months into his imprisonment, when, on April 18, 1777, he revealed to Renée the beginning of his practice of making "calculations"—predictions about the date of his release based on arcane computations: "Of six calculations that I worked out on my own and upon which I based a hope of an early release, there remains, praise God, not a single one."[8] Later, when Sade noticed a number 3 at the top of one of Renée's letters, he asked her if it had anything to do with his release date. When she ignored his questions, he became enraged: "Tell me the *exact day*, and *tell it to me* clearly, because it is fixed, I know it, and tell it to me without further tricks, as you did before with your vile number 3 at the head of your letter about the breeches, of which you have never deigned to offer me any explanation."[9] In December of the following year, Renée began a letter with this wish: "Do not be angry, my good friend, I beg of you, but you have so unique a talent for dissecting my sentences that I no longer recognize the idea that I had intended to give them."[10] A week or so later, she renewed her plea: "I ask you in all kindness, because that deeply affects me, not to strain your mind to discover such baroque and ridiculous twists in what I write."[11] Sade was not to be diverted.

Sade's letter to Renée on February 22, 1779, noted the passing of "another anniversary," the second, of his imprisonment. Consequently, this letter contains some particularly devilish conundrums designed to plague Renée. First, he took her to task for failing to comply with his request "for a notebook composed of thirty sheets." Instead, she had sent him "a folio of two or three hundred pages!" From this he concluded, "It is exactly as if you would tell me: *Oh! you will have plenty of time to fill it up.* But what kind of cruel, tactless way of speaking is that, then?" Bitterly, sarcastically, Sade flung the book back at Renée: "I am sending you back your rotten notebook, extremely rotten, covered, moreover, with very rotten paper, filled with coarse, rotten, worthless paper, and, in a word, abominable in every way. So here is yet another errand which I acknowledge with a thousand thanks!" Sade scoured Renée's letter that arrived that day and discovered an enraging "contradiction" between two of her sentences on separate pages. He wrote back:

> In just one letter, today's, see how many contradictions there are! *Your belief that June is the month* [of his release] *is not delusory,* and on the following page, *Do you want me to ask to see you?* But if my belief in June is not delusory, it would seem to me that it is rather with *trunks, post-chaises, and packing cases* that you should be busy than to request visiting privileges. . . .
>
> Oh well! since I must reply to your question, I will still say the same thing. If I must remain here for a long time, certainly ask to see me, whatever the difficulty: this could only be a great consolation to me. If I am not going to be here for a long time, do not ask for it, because the pleasure that I would have in seeing you here could only be mixed with an infinity of impatience on my part. Do you understand me now?[12]

Sade put Renée in a position of making impossible choices. If she were to apply again for visiting privileges—something that he wanted but which would not be granted for another two and a half years—then he would conclude that his imprisonment was to continue for a long time. Thus, more outbursts of despair and rage. But her failure to apply for a visit would only send the unintentional signal that he was to be released in the very near future.

A few more examples will help illustrate the play with words and numbers that constituted Sade's private code. Note that the number itself is the crucial piece of information, supplying the means, Sade believed, with which to calculate his release date. The context in which Renée embedded the numbers was the "signal." In April 1780, he complained to her bitterly:

> The other day, because you required a 24, a scoundrel sent to impersonate M. Lenoir in order that I write to M. Lenoir, *came* [*vint*, meaning "came" and also a pun on *vingt*, meaning "20"] on the 4*th*: and there you have the 24.
>
> Recently, because you needed a 23, the promenade was curtailed, now only from 2 [o'clock] to 3, and there you have the 23. But how lovely that is! how sublime! What sprightliness of genius! what brilliance!

Sade suggested that she try to arrange some signals that would have a positive effect:

> When I would like to form a 16, since, according to you, *sixteen* and *cease* are one and the same thing [these are puns on French near-homonyms *seize* (sixteen) and *cesse* (cease)], and since you take upon yourself the right to pervert the sound and the meaning of the language for this purpose, when, I say, I would like to form a 16, of the thirty or forty perfectly ridiculous restrictions that M. de S[ade] has here, I would remove one of them, and there you have a "cesse"-ation. . . .
>
> When I would like to form a *nine*, I would tell him some news [in French *neuf* means "nine" and "new"], or offer him some pleasure of any kind. The same goes for the other numbers. Do I want a 24? On the 4th I grant him the pleasure of chatting with someone on the 2nd. Do I need a 33? I give him three hours of exercise, and he writes: on the 3rd I had 3 hours of exercise, and there you have the 33.[13]

On March 1, 1783, Renée wrote that she was, "as usual," sending him "a dozen small cakes."[14] Sade annotated her letter by writing the following signal above her words: "These are the twelve months remaining at Vincennes."[15] Also in her letter, Renée mentioned in passing that she had seen "the woman who you said was the friend of Amblet."[16] Nine months later, Sade penned this note and signal between the lines of Renée's letter: "The husband of this lady is dead. There you have the idea of 16 attached to 9, indicating the 9 months remaining. Opinion of December 9, 83."[17] Sade went a long way to extract this "signal." First, to Renée's simple statement that she had seen Amblet's woman friend, Sade added the fact that the husband of Amblet's woman friend had died, thus arriving at the unwritten statement: "There is news of that man's death." Sade then punned on the word "news" (*neuf*, again, means "new" and the number 9) and on the word for the husband's death, *décès*, which suggested both *de seize* ("concerning the number 16") and *de cesse* ("concerning a cessation," i.e., of his imprisonment). Thus, Sade arrived at the signal, "There you have the idea of 16 attached to 9, indicating the 9 months remaining." Also observe that this interpretation was concocted by Sade on December 9, 1783, nine months after he received his wife's letter of March 1, 1783. This delay gives some indication of Sade's habit of poring over old letters to read meanings or "signals" into them. On January 18, 1781, Renée expressed her frequent exasperation with her calculating husband: "With regard to the signals, once and for all, I have never sent any."[18]

In a letter to Renée on September 19–20, 1783, Sade proudly suggests a signal *"invented by me, Christopher de Sade,"* an identification we shall consider presently. Believing that a cut or a tear on one of Renée's letters had been meaningful, he offered her a better signal: "The first cut or tear that you use to signal me, you must cut off the b[alls] of the Cadet de la Basoche [i.e., Sade's former servant, now Mme de Montreuil's secretary, Albaret] and send them to me in a box. I will open the box, I will exclaim with delight, I will say: 'Oh my God! what do we have here?' " In this fantasy, Sade imagines he is told, *"Don't you see that it's clearly a 19?"*[19] This he decodes as follows: a 19 consisted of a 1 (*un*) and a 9 (*neuf*); *un neuf* has the same sound as *un oeuf*—that is, an egg, a slang reference to Albaret's testicle! A tear is always a cut, and a cut is always a castration, and a testicle is always an egg, and an egg is always a 19. By means of these sorts of associations, puns, and transformations, turning words into numbers and numbers into words, by means of his obscure but powerful dream logic, Sade tried to prove that his world and his mind were really connected, that the tragedy he was suffering had some meaning and perhaps some end.

To follow Sade's "logic" in his calculations is to swim with him in the dream-sea of unconscious thought process, where images float free and attach and form strange chains of secret, personal meaning. The "logic" here is the logic of the poetic imagination, of dreams, of wit, of madness—equating and joining together things and ideas that resemble each other in perhaps no other way but the one insisted upon, as with the nearly perfect homonyms *un neuf* and *un oeuf.* Imagination joins things; reason separates things that really do not go together. The sound mind strikes a balance between the two activities, but Sade's had never been strong in the middle register.

When he insisted upon equating *un neuf* with *un oeuf,* when he made them interchangeable, he was simulating a blunder that almost every child has made when learning to speak, a process that requires the mind to equate sounds that are the same, and to discriminate between ones that are ever so slightly different. Out of the stuff of childish missteps, Sade willfully made a symbolic system. If Sade's "calculations" undo the mastery of both language and numbers, which is the major intellectual achievement of early childhood, they represent yet another instance of the regressive influence of his virtually solitary confinement in prison, where, he said, he felt like a twelve-year-old. The subversion of his education reflected in his prison "calculations" certainly refers back to a childhood rebellion against the disciplines of knowledge. Sade's first formal schooling, from age ten to fourteen, occurred at the Jesuit Collège Louis-le-Grand. His regression at Vincennes, however, carries him further back, to the time when he lived with his mother at the Palace de Condé in Paris and his character received its formative stamp. There, at his mother's knee, he learned his numbers and his language. There, his precocious intellectual and sexual curiosity was aroused. There, he felt the urgency of his mother's ambition that he attach himself to the older boy, the Prince de Condé. There, his rage burst forth, and he punched the Prince. He was punished and sent away, and at this critical juncture his emotional development was arrested. He would forever be caught between rage and punishment, between fantasies of murder and retribution. His mind would also be fixated at a level of sexual curiosity that is decidedly infantile and perverse. The demons and fantasies of early childhood would haunt his mind, unexorcised, for the rest of his life.

There are a few as yet unexplored details of the *un neuf / un oeuf* fantasy that allude to the most primitive sexual sources of Sade's mentality—his sexual curiosity and, in particular, his childhood inquiry into the question of where babies come from. If the reader wondered above at the childish and odd way that Sade introduced the story of *un oeuf, "signal invented by me, Christopher de Sade,"* the reader may now see Sade as he was as a very young boy, in the role of Christopher Columbus, discoverer of new and unknown territory. The box with the egg inside contains a good deal of information relevant to what a boy of four or five would know about sex. Some of its meanings look back toward earlier, more primitive speculations; others are more or less accurate and look forward to what might become a mature acceptance of sexual facts and roles. In a sense, Sade himself is in that box, because he never quite got out of it.

Various meanings can be revealed if we understand the box with the egg in it to be a condensed narrative of where babies come from. The man puts his sperm, his "egg," inside the woman's box, her vagina, and when the box is again opened, a new thing, *un neuf,* appears. Except for the egg, this sounds plausibly like what a young boy might know or have heard, perhaps from the older Prince de Condé. It also displays an awareness that a woman does not have an external sexual organ, as he does, but, rather, a box. The idea of castration, which is the pretext for inventing this peculiar signal, is of course present in the image of the woman with the box, Renée, who cuts off Albaret's testicles. On the surface, the motive for the castration of Albaret is revenge. But in the primitive narrative of sexuality that we are trying to reconstruct, the mother keeps the father's testicle inside her box, effectively castrating him. The moral of this childish explanation of the sex act is that there are risks in approaching a woman from the front.

Homosexuality and anal intercourse can represent a retreat from the menace of the castrated and castrating woman. In his adult sexual life, Sade displayed a decided interest in, and perhaps even a preference for, anal intercourse, to which his letters to Renée from prison make teasing allusions. In this humorous example, written to Renée in July 1783, Sade imagines Mme de Montreuil displaying Renée's naked buttocks to Lieutenant General of Police Lenoir and other officials:

It was a question of knowing if the said ass had not been deeply violated in any way,—because La Présidente claimed that *I violated asses.* As a result, she wanted *an expert opinion.* She was present, they say, and she said: *Look you, Gentlemen, you know he is a little devil* [referring to Sade], *packed with lechery; he very well might have . . . who knows? He has so much libertinage in his mind!* . . . And then you raised your skirts. Magistrate Lenoir put on his spectacles, Albaret held the candle, Lenoir's officers took notes. And they drew up a report on the situation in these terms:

Item, we, being brought to the said Hôtel de Danemark at the request of *Marie-Magdeleine Cordier, wife of Montreuil,* we arranged the trussing up of the skirts of the said *Pélagie du Chauffour,* her daughter, and, having performed our examination with all due care, we acknowledged the said *du Chauffour* as being well and duly supplied with two buttocks, most wonderfully white, most wonderfully beautiful, and most wonderfully intact. We approached and we bid our assistants to draw as near as we to the said member. At their risk and peril, they cracked, spread, sniffed, probed, and when they had, like us, observed only the purest components, we issued the current certificate to be used as need be, and being willing, moreover, in view of the aforementioned display, to grant to the said *Pélagie du Chauffour* to be enrolled in the Tribunal and in the future to be taken under our potent protection.

    Signed: Jean-Baptiste Lenoir, lamplighter of Paris and born protector of the whorehouses of the capital and surroundings.

Later in this letter, Sade continued in the same vein:

I screw you fully up your ass and I am going, or the devil take me, to use my hand to good effect in honor of them! Now, do not run and tell that to your mother. . . . She claims that [her husband] *M. Cordier* never *stuffed* it except into *the vessel of propagation*, and that whoever deviates from *the vessel* ought to boil in hell. And as for me, who was brought up by the Jesuits, I, whom Father Sanchez had taught that one must *swim in the void* as little as possible, because, according to Descartes, *nature abhors a vacuum*, I cannot therefore agree with *Mama Cordier*. But you are a philosopher; you have a strikingly lovely *counterargument*, whose manipulation, whose narrow focus in this *counterargument*, and whose very heat in *the rectum* all constrain me fundamentally to take your part.[20]

The first passage, of course, is fantasy, although the focus on the buttocks is relevant. Renée was not an exhibitionist, and it is very unlikely that she participated in Sade's orgies, even though she tolerated them. It is also unlikely, however, that she could have avoided her husband's taste for anal intercourse, as the second quotation (among others) suggests. With telling humor, Sade characterizes the vagina as a vacuum, a dangerous void, abhorrent to nature, a hole where a swimmer can be sucked under.

    Anal intercourse, in denying the site of procreation, also denies the difference between the sexes. If the vagina is dangerous, do not go near it. Pretend it is not there. Pretend the evidence of female castration does not exist. Retreat to a more infantile explanation of where babies come from—the anal-birth theory that is so common among very young children. Sade's *un neuf/un oeuf* signal also contains the remains of this more primitive theory. *Un oeuf*, an egg, in Sade's mind is also a turd, as in *Les Cent Vingt Journées de Sodome*, when a libertine, probing a whore's rectum with his finger, exclaims, "The hen is ready to lay, for I have felt the egg!"[21] Young Sade's precocious sexual curiosity was cut short by his discovery of the true state of the female genitalia and of their use. The implicit threat of castration forced him back on earlier, nongenital—that is, anal—sources of sexual pleasure and induced him to find additional, nongenital versions of sexual congress that he would eventually collect and enshrine as even more valuable alternatives to the one that had frightened him.

CHAPTER 17

Sex in Prison

S ADE'S SEX life, as peculiar as it may have seemed before his imprisonment, could only be made worse by the virtual solitary confinement he suffered in Vincennes and later in the Bastille. He did what
any bored animal in a cage does: he masturbated.

Sade kept a kind of scorecard in which he counted up his daily, monthly,
yearly sexual activities. He called it his "Almanach illusoire"—that is, his calendar of illusory pleasures. This is not a diary, but a statistical accounting of
the various types of physical practices that he employed daily in prison to
achieve sexual gratification. The reckoning is stupefying and very puzzling.
For example, here is a statistic that Sade jotted down on a letter from his valet
La Jeunesse dated December 1, 1780: "3,268 + 3,268 = 6,536, nearly six thousand six hundred introductions since the return."[1] That is, in the two years
and three months since Sade's return to Vincennes, he had performed 6,536
"introductions." These are not acts of masturbation concluding in orgasm, as
Lever suggests.[2] That would suggest an average of eight such acts a day for
two years and three months, and Sade was simply incapable of such glories. In
the important letter he wrote to his wife in 1784, the "Vanille et Manille" letter, Sade described the difficulty and pain of his ejaculations. Even before his
imprisonment, he needed strong mental and physical stimulation—perhaps
even physical pain—to bring about climax. In Marseilles, Sade had counted
a total of 859 blows he received from the prostitutes. In prison, in addition
to masturbating, he also required the stronger stimulation produced by
introducing dildos—or, as he called them, *prestiges*" into his anus. This is
what Sade meant by 6,536 "introductions" in two years and three months—
averaging eight a day. Sade's accounting practices in his "Almanach illusoire"
are difficult to follow, and his notes employ symbols and abbreviations not
easily deciphered or translated. This, for example, is his summary of masturbations for the year from September 7, 1784, to September 6, 1785:

débrouillements   42
   sur quoi

avec prestiges	3
avec celui de 8 pouces et demi	0
débrouillements dûs au sterc.	11
sur quoi	
en le m.	7
en le s.	4
dans l'idée ↓	3 pr Hél.
pr F.	5
pr G.	3
a V: dec.	9
étant b.	0
pr Hél.	5
le rest simple.[3]	

Sade referred to his simple masturbations and to those above accompanied by various sex tools and even ideas. It is unknown what idea "↓" represents. The *"sterc."* may be an abbreviation of the French word *stercoral,* meaning "referring to excrement." Sade regularly recorded a number of sexual events relating to *"sterc."* Among statistics for his "Fifth Year" in prison, Sade recorded this intriguing one:

Sterc. aval   217[4]

Aval may be an abbreviation for *avalé,* meaning "swallowed, eaten." If sexual relief was problematic for Sade in the first place, prison exacerbated his problem, and he appears to have been driven to a kind of desperate experimentation.

When Sade recorded the size of his *prestiges,* the most common measurement was eight and a half *pouces.*[5] Taking into account the difference between ancient and modern measures, that comes to nine inches in circumference. Sade specifically mentioned *pourtour,* "circumference."[6] There was also one of nine *pouces* or nine and a half inches in circumference.[7] These devices were ordered by Renée at a glassblowing factory according to the precise dimensions supplied by her husband. In a letter to his wife at the end of June 1781, Sade mentioned the need to return a "flask" that was "useless" because it was "much too small." This one was too short, "although, in fact," Sade noted, "the circumference is the crucial measure." He informed his wife that his "current *prestige*" should be used as the model for the dimensions that he wanted Abraham, the glassblower, to copy. This, he thought, should not be a problem: as he reminded Renée, Abraham "had assured me of having supplied some of this same size to the Archbishop of Lyons: ask him if he remembers that." Until this one could be made, Sade asked Renée to send him "a pocket flask," which could be smaller: namely, "six *pouces* in circumference by eight or nine in height."[8] A few days later, on July 2, 1781, Renée replied: "I have ordered the flask, but I do not understand how you could put a flask of six *pouces* in circumference in your pocket."[9] Renée was not as naïve as she sounded. A week later, on July 11, 1781, in discussing the flask, she refused to mention the *prestige:* "I will say nothing of *prestige* . . . *fantasies* . . . etc., because I am fully convinced that our happiness will return."[10] In the meantime, however, Renée did run these sexualized errands for her husband, visiting glassblowing shops and factories where she special-ordered the so-called pocket flasks and larger bottles in shapes and dimensions that made Renée blush and the work-men laugh and leer. "I have been all over Paris," she wrote to her husband on July 24, 1781, trying to order the desired objects. Someday, she said, she would tell him about her adventures and "I will make you laugh."[11]

One other sort of object that Sade used for anal masturbation was an *étui*, a cylindrical wooden sheath meant for holding rolled-up drawings or small objects, such as pins. In April 1783, Sade complained about the new sheath Renée had sent. He instructed her how to order the next one, insisting that it should be "six *pouces* unopened, and that at the tip of these six *pouces* should be the part that opens, of about two *pouces;* which gives about eight in all for the sheath"—that is, about eight and a half inches in modern measures. He warned her that the cap must be "firmly screwed on," so that it would not open or fall off. (The one Renée sent had the wrong cap.) Sade's language is marked by double entendre: "You well know that when a sheath comes open in the pocket, one is in danger of losing all his pins, and that is unpleasant. Because they could sometimes prick when they are scattered about in a pocket or in a purse." The last sheath Renée sent, moreover, suffered from a "large inconvenience," being too small: "It is loose in the pocket, that is, it is not shaped just right."[12] The shape, of course, told the whole story. Renée sometimes pretended that she did not know what these odd objects were for, but the workmen knew, and they naturally thought that they were meant for her use! She complained to Sade that they "do not want to make them and take me for a madwoman and laugh in my face."[13]

In this same letter, Renée mentioned one of the consequences of her hus-band's method of sexual excitation: his hemorrhoids were constantly and painfully inflamed. Salves and creams for this condition became a frequent topic. For some time, Sade had also been asking for a cushion, and in fact sent Renée a sheet of paper cut out to the exact proportions for the necessary item to be "made with feathers and horsehair."[14] For Sade, no specifica-tion, no requirement, was too small to mention. He appears to have been a connoisseur of everything. In whatever mattered to him, regardless of how small, he had the most demanding personal standards. In one sense, such connoisseurship was an exercise of power, an attempt to extract from physical nature only its purest, perfect forms. But it was also an attempt to control other human beings, in this case Renée, constrained to adopt the connoisseur's exacting standards.

The wretched sheaths and flasks became the objects of Renée's continuing quest. Sade would not permit her to drop the search, as she had begged him in her letter of November 23, 1783: "Do me the pleasure to charge someone else with this."[15] He appeared to enjoy Renée's humiliation and embarrassment. "You must tell your merchant," he facetiously, teasingly explained, "that this is a sheath for shoving in tails—I mean, for storing the tailpieces of books." Here Sade is punning on the French word *cul,* meaning "ass," and the technical word *cul-de-lampe,* meaning "tailpiece," the concluding bit of artwork in a printed book. In the absence of a proper sheath, Sade explained that he has been "obliged to use something else" (what it was, he did not say), "which ruins, tears, and hurts my tail . . . -pieces, and that is extremely disagreeable." With mock charity, Sade explained to Renée that he was doing her a favor: "It is *out of modesty* and so as not to frighten you that I am willing to ask for a sheath of 8½ [*pouces*] in circumference, because, in truth, it should be 9, as measured directly from my tail . . . -pieces.—But I tell myself, *nine* is just going to scare off people who are frightened by anything; so have it ordered at 8½."[16]

On and on these discussions went. Sade insisted upon his specifications. Renée made excuses and begged to be relieved of her commission. Even from prison, he forced her to become implicated in his peculiar sexual fantasies. Despite herself, she entered into his scenario, and her humiliation became part of his pleasure, possibly the best part.

Renée could not escape Sade's demands, but she could get even with him in small, annoying ways. When she sent her husband a flask according to his specifications, she got everything right—except for two small details. "The flask is worthless," Sade complained in a letter of April 1783. One of his objections should be familiar by now: the flask "needs to be much larger." The other complaint is unique: the flask also needed to be "without facets."[17] Was this mistake Renée's way, perhaps unconscious, of obtaining revenge for all of her husband's demands and reproaches? A similar example concerned Sade's occasional requests for a piece of her clothing. Among items in a list of things Renée was sending Sade on December 10, 1780, for instance, she noted without special comment, "I will send you the taffeta from one of my dresses, that is to say, a piece of it."[18] She must have been aware of her husband's purpose in requesting this bit of her clothing with her scent on it. But Renée was a prude, and she did not like fulfilling these peculiar requests. So she sent him a piece from a new dress. A week later, on December 18, 1780, she claimed not to understand why Sade "would prefer" a piece of a dress "that I had worn." Otherwise, she wrote, "I would have sent you some taffeta that was cleaner and neater."[19] Her naïve teasing here is part of their long-distance flirtation, a kind of partly conscious rejection of and accession to her husband's perverse tastes.

Sade, of course, liked to tease Renée. Writing to his wife in a letter of November 23–24, 1783, he pretended that her request for his old linen (she supervised all of his clothes) was really evidence of her coming around to his own tastes: "Delightful creature, you want my old linen, my soiled linen? Do you realize that this is a truly sophisticated refinement?" Sade swooned into a fantasy, imagining his joy at being able to obtain her soiled linen:

> Oh, good heavens! if, by such a short and easy way, it were possible for me to get *all sorts of your things*, soon devoured, if I got my hands on them, how happy I would be! how I would fly! what a fortune I would pay! how eagerly I would say: Give it, give it to me, Monsieur, it comes from the one I love! I will breathe in the scents of her life; they will enflame the vital spirits that course through my nerves; they will carry some whiff of her into the very heart of my being, and I will consider myself happy!

Also, in the above letter, Sade apostrophized his wife with such ironical expressions as *"Mohammed's delight," "heavenly pussy," "fresh pork of my thoughts," "shining paintbox of my eyes," "mirror of beauty," "spur of my nerves," "violet of the Garden of Eden," "seventeenth planet of space," "discharge of angelic spirit," "rose fallen from the bosom of the Graces," "my baby-doll."*[20]

This long, interesting, humorous letter also contains a version of a story that would find its place among Sade's collected stories, *Anecdotes françaises*, under the title "Attrapez-moi toujours de même," that is, "Always Catch the Same Sort for Me."[21] *"Heavenly pussy,"* Sade wrote in his letter to Renée, "listen to a rather amusing little story that happened when I was in Rome." It is an anecdote about a cardinal who one morning is provided, not with the customary girl for sodomy, but with a young boy dressed up as a girl:

> In Rome there is a cardinal, whom I will not name because I am discreet, who takes it as a rule that the nervous fluid activated every morning by the corpuscles emanating from the charms of a beautiful girl encourages a man's mind toward study, toward cheerfulness, and

toward health. As a result, a matron, favored by Monseigneur with this interesting task, each morning has a pretty young virgin sent to His Eminence's private rooms; a gentleman receives her, inspects her, and presents her. One day, Signora Clementina (that was the matron's name), not aware of that ceremony, and believing that the prelate, full of respect for a virgin, never offended her beyond a certain point, and limited himself with her to several customary examinations that were able in the strictest sense to render both sexes exactly the same in his eyes, not having available the daily goddess, thought to make up the deficiency with *a lovely boy* dressed up as a girl. The child brought in, the lady withdrew and the gentleman entered for his inspection. "Oh! Monseigneur, what treachery!" he exclaimed. "Lady Clementina deserves . . . ! An experience such as you perform!" The Cardinal approaches, puts on his spectacles, verifies what he was told, then, smiling with kindness and having the child shown into his room: "Peace, peace, my friend," he says to the gentleman, "we shall fool her in return: *she will think that I was fooled.*"[22]

Sade was beginning to arrange his sexual knowledge in the form of narratives, often humorous or ironic narratives, whose humor readers still misunderstand when they experience it in *Les Cent Vingt Journées de Sodome.*

Sade's sexual letters to his wife were candid, teasing, even taunting. He wrote a very angry one on Easter Sunday, 1783, in which he complained about her "treacheries, both yours and those of your b[it]ch of a mother." But, considering the sacred day, Sade was sure his hypocritical wife and mother-in-law would consume Christ's flesh in the form of the sacramental wafer: "Go right ahead," Sade urged them, "munch on your tasty little God and so assassinate your parents." The reference to the communion wafer, toward which so many of Sade's own fantasies had run, prompted this characteristic thrust at religion and sanctimoniousness: "As for me, I am going to f[rig] myself, and I am quite confident that in the end I will have done much less harm than you."[23]

Religion is again joined to sex in Sade's letter to Mlle de Rousset concerning the carillon belonging to the Sainte-Chapelle, a beautiful jewel of a building within the Vincennes compound.[24] He was about to answer her last letter—"I had the pen in my hand"—when, suddenly, he was interrupted: "a cursed carillon . . . set up an infernal racket." The sound of the bells, their melody and rhythm, made him think of masturbation. Sade continued:

As a prisoner always takes everything personally, and is always imagining that whatever is done is directed at him, that whatever is said is a

conspiracy—I got it into my head that this wretched carillon was talking to me and that it was telling me—but very distinctly,

> Oh you I pity—oh you I pity
> the only end for you will be
> in dust—in dust

    I jumped up in a fury beyond expression, and I was ready to rush
out and kill the carillonneur, when I sadly realized that *the door of
vengeance* is not always open. So I sat down again—I took up my pen
once more—I thought it was necessary to reply to this rogue in his
own style—and in his own melody,[25] since I was not yet able to do
otherwise, and I wrote,

> To keep me from joy, from pleasure
> you'd first have to dismember
> my heart, my heart.

> Oh monk, oh priest
> won't you shake the hand, at least,
> that f[rigs]—that f[rigs]

> But here—m'dear,
> the only hand that's near:
> my own, my own

> So hurry—so hurry
> relieve with your p[ussy]
> my pain, my pain

> My wife, my wife
> she'll treat me nice in the afterlife
> the tease, the tease

> Destiny, destiny!
> what a trick you've played on me
> I'm a goner, I'm a goner

> Lack of love kills the foxglove
> won't you come at least to remove
> the seed—the seed

What a martyr—what a martyr
I see too well I am born to suffer
without end, without end.[26]

Free or imprisoned, Sade always created through sex a symbolic relationship featuring himself as the rebellious, satanic, deeply needy outsider posed against the laws of God and man. He was aware of how thoroughly he differed from almost everyone else he knew, and he prided himself upon this difference that made an outlaw of him. Sade's sexuality was the most essential constituent of his identity, his very nature, his temperament, which he had received at birth. He could do nothing about it even if he had cared to. He had come to see himself in opposition to the whole world, a Promethean martyr, born to suffer for the hypocritical sex-conscience of the so-called normal world. Sade wrote to his wife on March 26, 1783, "Do you think that the history of the entire globe can offer an equal instance of such tyranny and blatant stupidity?"[27] Even before the Revolution, Sade portrayed himself as a "citizen overwhelmed by despotism and abuse of power."[28] If Sade often pitied himself, his other stance was aggressive and rebellious—defiance toward the world. "In the midst of the most frightful scourging," he boasted to Renée in a letter on September 15, 1783, "I swear to you that nothing in the world will be able to make me give up *either my way of living or my way of thinking.*"[29]

Prison, Sade insisted, could not and would not reform him. "This dog is too old to learn new tricks," he wrote to Renée in 1782, "so take my advice, give over trying to train him." In an explanation of sexual orientation that sounds very familiar to modern ears, Sade insisted, "The ways we think and act do not depend on us, they depend on our constitution, on our nature." He claimed that it is no more in one's power to adopt so-called normal sexual practices "than it is to become straight when one is born crooked, no more in one's power to adopt such-and-such an idea into one's way of thinking than to make oneself a brunette when one is born a redhead."[30] Certainly, he insisted, there was no reason to throw a gentleman in jail for decades because he found sexual pleasure in ways somewhat different from those adopted by the rest of the world. In a letter to Renée in July 1783, Sade flaunted his defiant temperament in an almost comical display of childish petulance: "If you do not want me to become better than I am, keep it up! As far as I am concerned, goodness is a state of pain and unpleasantness, and I ask for nothing more than to sit undisturbed in my mud puddle; I like it there."[31]

During this time in Vincennes, Sade had begun to find a very flexible writing style (or styles) for storytelling and letter-writing that expressed various versions of himself, especially his obsessive fantasizing about sex. His need to satisfy his problematic sexuality in solitary confinement prompted him, from time to time, to take up his pen. In many ways, the pen would become his most constant sexual fetish.

CHAPTER 18

The Visit

AMONG THE prison privileges most desired by Sade was a visit from his wife. Renée was Sade's only connection with the outside world, and he believed that, if only he were able to see her, he would be better able to effect his release, or at least to discover the extent of his sentence. Renée, however, knew very little of the real situation. Mme de Montreuil had prevailed, and Renée saw that she would never succeed in altering her mother's mind. In fact, she stopped trying. On July 6, 1780, she wrote Gaufridy, "It has been more than a year since I talked to her about M. de Sade."[1] The hopelessness of her own situation and her helplessness to change it alternately depressed her and drove her to grasp at straws.

Living with Renée in Paris as her companion and friend, Mlle de Rousset closely sifted Renée's character and found it sad, pitiable, even somewhat contemptible. Mlle de Rousset prided herself on being a realist and was infuriated by Renée's dreamy hopes. There were arguments between them. Mlle de Rousset described them to Gaufridy on October 21, 1780: "I have put her through all sorts of storms and a thousand and one million arguments," but nothing she could say could stop Renée "from constantly hoping and maintaining a total illusion about the present and the future." Mlle de Rousset thought there was something wanting in Renée's education, in her intellect, in her courage, and even blamed her for Sade's indiscretions: "I am no longer so surprised that the unfortunate man committed so many follies; he would have required a woman who had some nerve." Perhaps a woman like Mlle de Rousset herself. But Renée, she concluded, "is only made of strands or filaments woven or webbed by spiders."[2] Three weeks later, in another letter to Gaufridy, Mlle de Rousset complained that Renée "is constantly deluding herself; such is her mania." Concerning Sade's release, she offered Renée "the most appropriate and the most prudent thoughts," but Renée "stupefies herself so completely against them that she daily tells me with the greatest *composure:* 'When M. de S. is released we will do such-and-such, we will say thus-and-so, etc.' Each idea crazier than the others! I laugh or I shrug my shoulders."[3]

As time went on, Mlle de Rousset began to suffer increasingly from the symptoms of the consumption that would eventually take her life. She informed Renée of her wish to return to Provence for the sake of her health— a journey she planned for the spring of 1781. At the beginning of the year, Mlle de Rousset forced Renée to go over the accounts. She informed Gaufridy, "Madame de S—— has spent a good deal during the past year." Like her husband, Renée could not be made to comprehend financial reality. "I will replenish my purse," she said, "to the extent that Gaufridy sends me some." The ever-logical Mlle de Rousset replied, "Yes, but where will Gaufridy get it? Your expenses (daily and others) are always increasing and M. de S.'s whims increase endlessly." Mlle de Rousset, defeated and ill, threw up her hands: "My friend," she wrote to Gaufridy of Sade and Renée, "these two minds, taken together or separately, are not worth that of a twelve-year-old schoolboy."[4]

As the weather warmed and the dungeon air became even more fetid and stale than usual, Sade wrote Renée at the beginning of March that he was "very powerfully" affected by the coming of spring, and he begged her to get his promenades increased, and also to try to obtain visiting privileges, especially a private visit. If Renée could visit regularly, he imagined that she could "rent a little house for the summer at Vincennes." With her nearby, he would not have to rely on her fortnightly deliveries of his books and delicacies: "You could quite easily send me daily everything I would need for each day."[5] But if this was Sade's dream, it was not Renée's.

Visits had to be authorized by Lieutenant General of Police Lenoir, and were conducted in the Council Room under the supervision of Commandant de Rougemont or one of his officers, generally M. Boucher (the censor of Sade's correspondence). Sade could not understand what kept Renée from arranging things quickly, and he complained to her: "Despite what you say, it seems to me that your eagerness to come see me is not very great." He imagined that she was waiting for some particular day whose date would communicate some "signal." So Sade teased his wife and flirted with her over the idea of a private visit: "Get permission to see me alone, as you had promised to ask for, and you will see that I can convey to you a signal infinitely more moving than all those sent by La Présidente's cabal!"[6]

Renée, however, had not been as dilatory as Sade believed. She had persuaded Gaufridy to write her mother that Sade's presence at La Coste was now absolutely necessary to handle the business of his estates. Renée and Gaufridy were also behind a petition drawn up by the elders of La Coste and signed by a great many of the villagers, begging for the release and return of the Marquis. "The Marquis de Sade," the elders petitioned, "was more their father than their lord. The poor found in him a sure defender, the others a protector, and each day was marked by some sign of beneficence."[7] When Mme de Montreuil heard of her daughter's efforts, she wrote an angry letter to Gaufridy, appearing flabbergasted that Renée would want Sade released from prison: "How can she wish it? This is an enigma impossible to comprehend." It was even harder for Mme de Montreuil to imagine how her ally Gaufridy could assist in such a scheme: "Knowing, even more certainly than I, what you *know* so *conclusively*, how could you without trembling for himself promote this liberty?"[8] But Mme de Montreuil would soon receive even more alarming news.

It turned out that Renée had not been entirely ineffective. She had engaged the influence of Sade's mother's first cousin, the Marquise de Sorans, to obtain permission for Sade's transfer from Vincennes to a royal prison at Montélimar, some forty miles north of Avignon. Renée argued that at Montélimar Sade would be closer to his lands, and his lawyer Gaufridy could easily visit him and assist him in the restoration of this noble family's estates, which were now virtually in ruins. When Mme de Montreuil learned about her daughter's successful maneuver, she was surprised and angry. Writing to Gaufridy to describe her mother's reaction, Renée could scarcely disguise her own deep satisfaction: "My mother is nettled, quite put out, over what I have accomplished without her."[9]

However, when Renée told her husband the good news of the transfer approval, Sade thought this was another of Mme de Montreuil's tricks. In fact, he thought it was an April Fool's joke. On April 1, 1781, Sade wrote to Renée: "There is always something dignified about the amusements of the most high and most exalted Lady Montreuil! Lackeys and flunkies are tricked on April 1, so her son-in-law must also be made the butt of a jest. My God, what nobility of character, what greatness of soul, what grandeur of sentiment!" Sade said that he was "absolutely certain that there never was a fort at Montélimar," and that, if they intended to send him to "some ancient tower, the haunt of owls or screech owls," they could forget about it.[10] He also refused to write and thank Mme de Sorans. He did not see what he had to thank her for. Of Renée's request, he snarled, "It must take a good deal of impudence to dare to write to an unfortunate who has been suffering for nine years . . . to ask him to very humbly thank someone who won him the astonishing favor of changing his lock!"[11] Thus, Sade vetoed the transfer that his wife had worked so hard to get. On May 1, he wrote to Renée congratulating himself on his acumen in avoiding this trap of Montélimar: "What pleases me, at least, is that you will not have had the glory of congratulating yourself for having turned me into your dupe for a single moment. Tell La Présidente de Montreuil from me that if she would catch someone like me she needs to use a finer net."[12]

But Mme de Montreuil had more pressing concerns at that moment. Inside the Montreuil house in Paris, her favorite daughter, the young lady Sade had seduced during the theatrical season at La Coste in 1771, Anne-Prospère, lay ill of smallpox. In a matter of a few days, on May 13, 1781, she was dead. "They say that Madame de Montreuil is inconsolable," Mlle de Rousset wrote to Gaufridy. And Renée, she added, "cries and grieves."[13] In the midst of Renée's grief, Sade's letter to her on May 16 must have hurt her. It was full of vituperation against her failure to visit and against her "whore of a mother."[14] Renée's letters to her husband at this time gave no indication whatsoever of the death of Anne-Prospère, who had been so closely involved with him. It must have been difficult for Renée to conceal her emotions. Six years later, in answer to Sade's questioning her about Anne-Prospère, Renée wrote that "the silence" that she had "imposed" upon herself about Anne-Prospère was for his own good.[15]

Renée had worked hard for permission to visit her husband, and also for his transfer to Montélimar. She had approached Amelot, minister of the King's household, and paid Lenoir frequent calls. At the beginning of April, Lenoir paid a visit to Sade at Vincennes to inform him of the plan to transfer him to Montélimar. On April 12, 1781, Sade wrote a strong letter to Lenoir complaining about Mme de Montreuil's persecution of him, and demanding his freedom, not a transfer.[16] Lenoir visited Sade a second time on April 18. "I have seen Monsieur Lenoir, my dear love," Sade wrote Renée on April 20, "and I could only have good cause to be very pleased with everything that he told me." Lenoir, Sade added, "has flattered me with the hope of seeing you soon."[17] The same day, Sade wrote again to Lenoir, this time tearfully begging to be released onto his estate so that he could be with his wife and children. He vowed that he was a changed man. Finally, he tried to appeal to Lenoir not as the lieutenant general of police, but as the Good Father: "You permitted me to think, the day before yesterday, that I was speaking to a father or to a friend."[18] It soon became clear that flattery would not work on Lenoir. By May 16, Sade was calling him "a scoundrel."[19] Renée replied two days later, defending Lenoir. She told her husband: "Your misfortune is to be at the extremes in everything and not to have trust in anyone."[20]

At this time, as Mlle de Rousset departed for Provence on May 19, Renée was left to deal with her husband alone. In her loneliness, Renée would keep up her friendship with Mlle de Rousset by letter, and occasionally would also write to Gaufridy. But in June, permission for Renée to visit was finally granted. Sade must have learned the news on his own, because, in the middle of one of her typical letters to him, written on July 11 and received by him on July 12, Sade excitedly added the note, "VISIT TOMORROW."[21] This would be the first time the couple would be together in four years and five months—ever since Sade had been arrested in his wife's presence on February 13, 1777.

When Sade was called down from his cell to the Council Room on July 13, 1781, however, he saw that he was not to be granted the private visit with Renée that he had hoped for. Officer Boucher was awaiting him there. The rules required some official to be present to overhear the conversation. Whispering was forbidden. There were to be no secrets transmitted, no escape plans. On this first visit, Sade doubtless asked Renée when he would be released. No doubt she said that she did not know. The visit, after so much anticipation, could not but be a disappointment. It was, in fact, worse than that. Whatever Renée said, even the way she looked, almost everything about the visit irritated Sade. To begin with, there was the matter of her clothes. In an undated letter Sade wrote soon after the visit, he vowed that he would not see her again "if you are again dressed like a w[hore] like last time." He also objected to her fancy "hairdo." "Tell me," Sade continued, "would you go to take communion at Easter in that getup, looking like a Gypsy or a mountebank?" Whatever may be the current fashion, and "however younger you may be," he wanted Renée to dress like "women of sixty."[22] She was thirty-nine. They talked about her clothes, about her servant Lefèvre, about her apartment. Sade had just learned that Renée had moved a year earlier, during the summer of 1780, from the Carmelite convent on the rue d'Enfer to an apartment on the rue de la Marche, in the Marais section.[23] Sade became inflamed with rage and sexual jealousy, and he kept returning to these same topics with increasing violence for months afterward.

Two weeks after the visit, Renée wrote to Mlle de Rousset down in Provence that Sade was "jealous." "Ever since I saw him," Renée wrote, "he has tormented me with a thousand delusions." For one thing, Renée went on, her husband was "jealous of Madame de Villette because I told him that she suggested I go live with her."[24] Renée had mentioned her distant relative as early as December 1778, when she wrote to Sade in Vincennes promising to ask Mme de Villette about the cost of Voltaire's works. Like a character out of one of Sade's libertine novels, the cousin, "the daughter of a poor gentleman living near Ferney," had been raised in a convent. "She is tall," Renée continued, "with her figure well molded; she is not at all a beauty, but she has a sweetness and a naïveté suffusing her face that make one prefer her to a pretty

woman; her graces are natural, she is intelligent." As Renée reported, the girl
had earned the attention of Voltaire, who "kept her at Ferney and said that it
was a pity to bury such a one in a cloister." Later, "on his deathbed," Voltaire
promoted the marriage between this young woman and his friend the
Marquis de Villette. Alluding to the Marquis's notorious pederasty, Renée
quipped, *"Villette got a dowry for his conversion."* Such a bawdy reference was
unprecedented in her letters to Sade, and perhaps she was trying to appear as
lively a letter-writer as Mlle de Rousset. Renée had been to visit the Villettes
in Paris: "The two times that I had dined with them," she told Sade, "I saw
there the Wits, *Lalande*, etc."[25] She was dropping the name of the notable
astronomer Joseph-Jérome Lalande. He was a member of the Académie des
Sciences and also a writer on many topics of culture as well as science. Four
months later, on April 30, 1779, she wrote, "I have been at her house several
times."[26] When Sade finally got the chance to see his wife on her first visit, he
was quick to note from her dress and from what she said that she seemed to be
having too much fun.

Sade obliged his wife to promise never to visit the Villettes in the country.
He went so far as to write out an oath for Renée to sign and return to him: "I
give you my word of honor upon all that I hold most sacred in the world that
I have never lodged at Mme de Villette's, that I do not lodge there, and that I
will never lodge there." As if this were not enough, Sade made Renée swear
that she would also give up her apartment: "I join to this promise that of
immediately quitting the place where I now live, in order to go live within the
walls of a convent and to see there only those people who would be useful to
you, and to remain there until the time of your release, when I will be
reunited with you forever."[27] "Remember," he urged Renée, "you have given
me your word not to go to the country, and above all not to your precious Villette's, who I assume to be a great fucker and perhaps even a bit of a *Sap-
pho.*"[28] Renée was shocked by Sade's attack and wrote back, "I am not living
nor will I live with Villette. I have never lived there."[29]

In his rage over her new apartment and her new way of life, Sade compared Renée to Mme d'Olonne, a notorious seventeenth-century female-lib-
ertine, for which Renée thanked him and replied, "I would be mortified if
even only one person suspected me of resembling her." She added that, if he
found her new apartment "ridiculous," as he claimed, then he ought to know
that the Marquis de Villette and his wife "have for the past month been offering me lodging with them."[30] But Sade would never permit such an arrangement. His sexual jealousy was understandable, yet ambivalent, for he also felt
a perverse wish to see Renée sexually debased. After her visit, when he angrily
wrote that he would prefer her not to see her mother, he added that he

"would much prefer" to see Renée at a famous Paris bordello, "Mme Gourdan's."[31] At the beginning of the year, on January 22, 1781, Sade had written to
Renée that he dreamed of her "perhaps five hundred times," and it was always
the same dream: Renée has "a secret to tell" that she does not want to reveal—
namely, that she is "always unfaithful, *in every sense of the word.*"[32]

Ever since Sade found his wife provocatively dressed on her visit in July,
his suspicions focused on his former secretary, now his wife's servant, Lefèvre.
Sade began to pore over Renée's old letters, seeking clues to her infidelity and
annotating his bizarre findings between the lines of her writing. For example,
in one of Renée's letters to him from the previous year, April 16, 1780, he
found the following innocuous phrase signifying that she was sending him a
warm undergarment for his weak chest: "A chest warmer of which we think
the cords are too long." A year later, Sade concluded that this was a damning
remark and added the following note to her letter: Renée "wishes to say that it
is Lefèvre who serves as her chest warmer and who has a very long one. Surely
that is clear."[33] Sade made a feverish, sad joke of Renée's August 5 letter, marking it with bloodstains, crossing out some of her words, adding some of his
own, as if his words could reveal her true thoughts. Sade's additions are set off
below in italics within brackets. "Good God," Renée wrote, "how do you
conclude that I am making a mockery of my feelings, me, who loves you *[my
dear Lefèvre]*." She tried to reassure her husband: "I love you, I have never
stopped loving you, even for a second. Calm yourself, eat, sleep *[while I
f(uck)]*." And when Renée mentioned that she owed nine months' rent on
her apartment, Sade naturally concluded that she had become pregnant.[34]

Following Renée's visit, Sade confronted her about the presumed affair
with Lefèvre. "They have succeeded in providing you with a lover," he
charged. Everyone, he felt, was "laughing" at him.[35] Indeed, Mlle de Rousset
had a good laugh about Sade's delusion when Renée told her about it in a letter on July 27, 1781.[36] However, it soon became clear to Renée that her husband was seriously out of control. A few weeks later, on August 18, in another
letter to Mlle de Rousset, Renée had to concede that Mlle de Rousset had
been right all along: the "visit caused more harm than good." Renée added
that she had to go see Lieutenant General of Police Lenoir, who informed her
that "they are holding back" Sade's letters to her because "they were full of
frightful things." "I am despondent, I am in despair," Renée moaned. Lenoir
also told her that her husband was demanding a second visit, but only "in
order to kill" her, and that Sade "keeps harping" about an individual named
Lefèvre; Lenoir was hoping that Renée would help explain who this person
was. "Imagine," Renée exclaimed to Mlle de Rousset, "imagine how pleasant
it was for me to have to listen to such questions!"[37]

On the same day, August 18, Renée wrote to inform her husband that Lenoir "no longer wants to give me your letters." She was deeply upset, telling Sade that his suspicions and accusations "have struck a wound in my heart that will never be healed." She continued: "Your way of thinking with regard to me overwhelms me, destroys me, humiliates me; me, who lives and breathes only for you, to see me suspected and degraded! . . . I have done nothing at all requiring vindication. My conduct is open and known to the whole world. No, it is not possible that, knowing me as you must know me, you actually believe everything that you write." Here is Sade's interlinear note to Renée's plaintive defense: "How trite—great God!—how trite!"[38]

Renée's spirit was at the breaking point. "I am fully determined," she wrote to Mlle de Rousset on August 18, "to put myself into a convent," just as her husband had demanded; within a month, she was lodging in the Convent of Sainte-Aure on the rue Neuve-Sainte-Geneviève. "I am ensconced here with the rest of the old folks," she wrote to Mlle de Rousset.[39] By this time, however, nothing could placate Sade. On September 12, Renée wrote to say that she was "truly tortured" by his continuing suspicions of her. "My heart," she went on, "is profoundly affected by your trying to convince yourself that I have sinned."[40] "Does your fit of anger continue, my dear love?" Renée asked in another letter.[41]

Sade would not calm down. His moods alternated between rage and fits of self-humiliating, abject contrition. He desperately begged Renée to visit him again: "Just let me cry for a moment at your feet, let me embrace your knees one last time, to hear my verdict from your own lips, and then I will die content."[42] In another letter from this time, Sade again flung himself into the same humiliating fantasy: if only she would visit, he promised, "I would be happy to come before you with a dagger in your hand, . . . I would sprawl at your feet, and . . . I would savor your punishment."[43] On October 20, Renée wrote, "I have just seen M. Lenoir again" about getting her visiting privileges restored. But she did not get a satisfactory answer. When Sade read Renée's letter on Sunday morning, October 21, he was ready to explode. Later, he noted on this letter that it was received "in the morning of the day of the scene."[44] The "scene" involved an altercation that turned physical between Sade and his turnkey. Six days later, Sade mentioned it in an offhand manner, as if his breach of the rules was of no moment: "Regarding the fellow I beat, he can rest easy. I give my word of honor not to touch him again."[45] De Rougemont punished Sade by denying him all privileges. "They refuse to shave me or to sweep out my room," Sade complained to Renée on October 27. Even "the beasts of the *Ménagerie*," Sade wrote, are washed every week, "themselves as well as their cage. I demand to be treated no worse."[46]

Sade could not quell his rage and jealous frenzy. "They report that you are writing things that prevent them from permitting me to see you," Renée informed her husband on December 13, 1781.[47] The next day, she told her husband: "M. Lenoir will not give me permission to see you unless you calm down. So calm down, I pray you."[48] The following day, Renée pleaded with Lenoir: "Do not judge him from his writings, but rather, judge him by his deeds."[49] On December 31, Renée wrote to her husband to say that the "rancor and passion" in his letters "incense the ministry against you." She assured the authorities, she said, "that you do not think of what you write." Wonderful apology! And surely one that Sade would not much appreciate. The authorities, however, told her, "that they can judge you only by your writings."[50] It would, in fact, be Sade's writings more than his deeds by which he would be judged, then as now. In his letters from prison, he had been perfecting the writing style that would make his novels famous, even immortal.

CHAPTER 19

Writer

 F SADE'S letters to his wife were irksome, full of accusation, paranoia, jealousy, and cranky demands for this and that, those he
wrote to Mlle de Rousset display his delight in the act of writing.
Here is the beginning of his New Year's letter to her of January 26,
1782, written after five years in Vincennes:

> In whatever climes you may be, Mademoiselle—near or far, with
> Turks or Gallileans, with monks or comedians, with turnkeys or hon-
> est folk, with cryptographers or philosophers—even so, friendship can
> scarce permit the neglect of those sacred rituals that the renewal of the
> year imposes upon me—after which, still observing the ancient cus-
> tom, I will give myself over to pleasing you with some random
> thoughts, nevertheless bearing directly upon the subject at hand.
>
> If my situation has some thorns, it must be admitted, however,
> that it often inspires ideas of a rather pleasing sort of philosophy.[1]

The following, from the same letter, is an example of Sade's philosophical and
rhapsodical style:

> Miserable creatures flung for a second on the surface of this little pile
> of dirt—is it, then, written that one half of the herd must be the perse-
> cutors of the other? Oh, mankind, is it for you to say what is good—or
> what is evil? Is it for a puny individual of your species to presume to set
> the limits for nature—to decide what she will permit and to proclaim
> what she prohibits—you—who cannot understand her most trivial
> operations—you—who cannot explain the smallest phenomenon, is it
> for you to define for me the origin of the laws of motion—of the laws
> of gravity? Explain for me the essence of matter, is it inert or not?—If
> it is not in motion, tell me how nature, which is never at rest, was able
> to create something which would be always at rest, and if it is in

motic a . . . if it is the authentic and manifest first cause of the perpetual creation and alteration of things—tell me what is life—and explain what is death; tell me what is air—explain clearly its different effects, tell me why I find seashells on the tops of mountains and ruined cities at the bottom of the sea, you who rule on whether something is a crime or if it is not—you who hang someone in Paris for what is given the highest praise in the Congo, resolve my views concerning the action of the stars, their suspension, their attraction, their motion, their essence, their orbits—confirm Newton over Descartes, and Copernicus over Tycho Brahe—just explain to me why a stone falls when it is thrown from on high—yes, just clear up for me this utterly simple effect, and I will tolerate your being a moralist when you are a better scientist.

This would become one of Sade's favorite sophistical ploys: if you cannot explain nature's laws—gravity, for example—then do not presume to criticize the impulses nature placed in me when I was born. He continued:

You want to analyze the laws of nature, yet your heart—your heart, where she inscribes them—is itself an enigma for which you cannot offer any solution. . . . You want to plumb, philosophize upon mankind's aberrations, you want to make laws concerning vice and virtue, even though you cannot tell me which is which, or which is the more advantageous for men, which is most in harmony with nature, and if perhaps there does not spring from this contrast the profound harmony that makes them both necessary. You want the whole universe to be virtuous, and you do not see that everything would perish in a second if there were only virtues in the world. . . . You do not want to understand that, since vices are necessary, it is as unjust of you to punish them as it would be to make fun of a one-eyed man. . . .

Virtue of any sort is merely a local prejudice in favor of one sort of values and behaviors. Vice has at least an equal claim, and can even more reliably be founded in nature and in our human nature. In any case, Mother Nature inspires vice as much as she does virtue. She needs both. Thus, Sade concludes, "seek out pleasure, my friend, seek pleasure and do not judge."[2]

Mlle de Rousset replied to the above letter on March 22, 1782, with a tone of humorous criticism, but criticism nevertheless. She patiently exposed the absurdity of Sade's enthusiasm for the idea of cultural relativism: "We are born French, we are in France; the laws, the customs are such as we know them and not as we would sometimes wish them." If he found the customs and laws of the Congo in some respects more to his taste, "the noose," she pointed out, is given "in Paris to every violator of our laws who has the folly to believe he is living in the Congo." And then, most effectively, she demolished his argument that no one should formulate moral laws without first explaining the physical laws of nature—like gravity. "What does it matter to me," Mlle de Rousset replied, "to know the cause of a stone's falling from on high, as long as I do not experience its painful effect on my head!"[3] Mlle de Rousset understood her friend very well. When Sade threw his stones, they tended to fall on himself.

Mlle de Rousset had her own close call with a stone. While she was trying to recover her health, living quietly in the village of La Coste, suddenly, "on the eve of the fair," her peace was disturbed by "the riotous activities" of inebriated townspeople who behaved like "wild wolves." As they caroused through the narrow streets, one of them burst through Mlle de Rousset's door, dislodging a stone "weighing more than thirty pounds," which she "dexterously" avoided.[4] When she moved up to the château to look after the place, she found new reasons to complain about Sade's servants and tenants. The servants neglected their duties, tolerated vandalism, and were insolent. As she informed Gaufridy on June 30, when she remonstrated with Sambuc, the guard of La Coste, because the rabbits were not being fed, he shouted such vile and filthy abuse at her that she had to leave the field of battle.[5] On September 6, she complained to Gaufridy, "All of the grapes have been stolen, and the vines below the château have been vandalized, uprooted." Hunters and poachers prowled the grounds. Moreover, the locks to the doors of the château had still not been repaired: "The first madman can come and strangle me in my bed."[6] The imminent danger, however, was from the building itself. During a "frightful storm," Mlle de Rousset was terrified by "the thunderous music of falling roof tiles and plaster. . . . Cracks gape in every corner."[7] In fact, the plaster and beams of the ceiling in one of the rooms suddenly collapsed. Sade chose to profess indifference to Mlle de Rousset's reports. As he wrote to Renée in August 1782, "I will certainly make no response to Milli Rousset's stupid chatter."[8] However, his ancestral home was indeed falling into ruins. The collapsed ceilings, the tileless roof, the cracked walls would never be repaired. Sade would be the last Lord of La Coste. Everything was changing, even the tenants and the peasants. It was seven years before the Revolution.

As Sade's château was crumbling, he was building a wonderful imaginary castle in the air—actually, a Culture Palace. He had been sketching out a "plan" for an extraordinarily ambitious architectural project, which he sent to Renée in May 1782.[9] Sade wanted her to have his sketch executed by a professional draftsman. An architect was consulted, who offered to draw up formal plans at a cost of 25 to 30 louis. The architect's analysis of the plan gives some idea of Sade's design. Sade imagined an enormous circular theater some 240 feet in diameter. Radiating from this central structure were to be twelve alleys leading to twelve pavilions dedicated to the Muses of various forms of art. Sade was flattered to read the architect's praise of his proposal ("This is a vast idea, ingenious and well conceived"),[10] but he did not want to spend 30 louis to see what the architect could do. In August, he told Renée that he knew that "the idea of my plan is lovely," but admitted that it could never be achieved in stone and mortar: "There would not be a country or a king in all Europe rich enough to accomplish it." As strong as was his interest in theater, he did not mean to try to realize his plan in any practical way. His was an idealistic daydream. "My idea is exquisite," he wrote to Renée, "and so sublime that it is completely unattainable. . . . It is but a pleasing fantasy."[11] Such was Sade's dual nature: on the one hand, he could embrace a materialistic view of the world that reduced life to matter and dismissed all religions and moral value systems as mere prejudice and superstition; on the other hand, he could dream of ideal Temples of Art. He dwelt at once in both a brutally material and an immaculately ideal world.

Sade's divided mentality continued to be a source of great volatility, and in July 1782, there was another serious outburst. Sade wrote to Renée that the commandant had decided to have the garden wall of the prison repaired expressly "in order to again deprive me of my promenades."[12] On July 31, Sade vented his rage on his guard by abusing him verbally and perhaps also striking him in the face.[13] As punishment, he was confined to his cell, and all of his books, manuscripts, and writing materials were confiscated. Renée wrote to her husband on August 6 that Lieutenant General of Police Lenoir had told her "that they have taken away all your books because they inflamed your mind and made you write inappropriate things that were not proper." She urged her husband to maintain "an honest manner of thinking, so typical of your true character, and especially neither write nor say all those aberrations that come to your mind." Renée preferred to see the best side of Sade. "Refrain from writing, I beg of you," she told him.[14] But it was too late for that.

Sade had begun a highly intense period of literary activity. He began writing plays. More correctly, he continued writing them: one of his earliest plays was *Le Philosophe soi-disant*, which he staged at La Coste in 1772. By 1780, in Vincennes, he was working on *Le Capricieux* (*The Man of Caprice*).[15] This is a light comedy about a man who cannot make up his mind about anything—which clothes to wear or whether to have tea or chocolate. In a letter to Renée, Sade called this play "the least unsatisfactory one I have written in my life,"[16] and he insisted in his introduction that he was creating "an absolutely new character" for the stage.[17] Using an image even more appropriate for the truly peculiar and perverse characters in his fiction, Sade explained, "The human heart is a kind of terrain suitable to the cultivation of all sorts of plants."[18] If the main character is rather zany, there is also a darker element in the play, for the man of caprice, like Sade himself, has a penchant for philosophizing about his personality. He declares,

> Happiness is a god of our own construction;
> He who would seize it finds only illusion.[19]

In differentiating his play from Philippe Néricault Destouches's *L'Irrésolu*, Sade argued that, though the irresolute man cannot make up his mind which object to choose, he nevertheless believes that the choice is meaningful, that happiness depends upon the choice, and that "this happiness is something very real to him." On the other hand, Sade's man of caprice "regards happiness only as a chimera that eludes whoever would seize it." There is a tinge of bitter wisdom in his folly, for he knows "the despair of having been deceived." He has seen beneath the surface "illusion" of happiness the dreadful inner vacuum, "the void," that can never be filled.[20] Therefore, he flits from object to object, not because he cannot decide which one will make him happy, but frenetically, madly, because he senses that nothing will. This manic frenzied dance over the abyss foreshadows the sexually perverse characters in Sade's erotic novels—characters who are driven to a programmatic, obsessive experimentation in the hope of discovering a happiness that always eludes them.

Sade had begun his regular practice of sending the drafts of his plays to Renée for her opinion and sometimes for that of his former tutor Amblet, who was still attached to the family. In April 1781, he actually sent Amblet a detailed questionnaire on *Le Capricieux*. Here are a few examples of the list of topics upon which he wanted Amblet's judgment:

> If the plot has the degree of interest required in this sort of work.
> If the work is in a style suitable for good society, which is essential.
> . . .
> If the moral and the maxims are good.[21]

As the above questions suggest, Sade's approach to writing plays was conventional and practical. He wanted a product that could be performed in public; eventually, two of his plays would be produced. These works may be conventional in appearance, but occasionally they contain allusions to the powerful and dangerous fantasies that Sade felt greater freedom to unleash in his novels.

Les Jumelles (*The Twins*) is an example of a conventional play that was so "respectable" Renée felt it "could be played in a convent."[22] In this love comedy, Damis, a Parisian lover who has in his wake left many broken female hearts, is sent into the country by his father to choose a bride from between two twins, Adélaïde and Julie. Damis decides on Adélaïde, whom he saw first, but he soon mistakes Julie for her twin. He refuses to believe Julie's protestations that she is not Adélaïde, and he persists in wooing her as if she were. The girls offer to employ a rose to distinguish one from the other, but they slyly pass the rose back and forth and continue to fool him. The goal is to ridicule and humiliate the proud Parisian (the expert on love), who continues stubbornly to boast of his ability to distinguish (although wrongly) his true love. In talking to Julie, he mistakes her for Adélaïde, and claims,

> Love is my guide, it cannot lead me astray.
> It's you I prefer; it's you I adore.[23]

In the end, everyone is sorted out, and love reigns.

Sade mentioned two additional plays in his March 26, 1781, letter to Renée (the beginning of his fifth year in Vincennes): *L'Égarement de l'infortune* (*The Vagaries of Misfortune*) and *Henriette et Saint-Clair*.[24] In *L'Égarement*, Sade portrays a couple—Derval and his wife, Cécile—who flee to London from France for the sake of love. Starving and desperate for food, Derval robs the Chevalier de Merville. He is arrested at once and sent to prison, thus exposing Cécile to the obnoxious seductions of the libertine Chevalier, who promises to help her, but at a price: "If I offer a fortune, it is clear enough that I expect some return. . . ."[25] Cécile is placed in the kind of moral dilemma—either to submit sexually or to see her husband executed—that in Sade's erotic novels usually ends in a humiliating orgy. But in the play, a happy ending is contrived when the Chevalier's good father arrives to thwart his rakish son, who at first tries to minimize his plot against Cécile: it was but "a peccadillo . . . I admit it . . . a mere amusement."[26] This sounds like one of Sade's own bewildered apologies when he found himself caught out.

Saint-Clair, the hero of *Henriette et Saint-Clair*, gives his aunt the same sort of worries that young Sade gave his relatives. Saint-Clair's aunt describes him as "young, impetuous, headstrong." She knows, however, that "the innate nobility of his soul will never let him lay aside the maxims of honor."[27] The problem is that Saint-Clair has fallen in love with a poor newcomer to the neighborhood, and his father disapproves of the match. As if that were not enough, there is a further complication: incest. It turns out that Saint-Clair's beloved Henriette is his long-lost sister. Saint-Clair refuses to accept the reality of the blood relationship and asks Henriette to accompany him to some foreign land where they can be free to love. This is a favored belief of Sade's: taboos are merely local prejudices, and by relocating, one can choose more favorable rules. Saint-Clair cannot accept that his love is illicit, since it was inspired in his breast by nature. Henriette, however, refuses to agree to his specious arguments, and instead proposes a suicide pact. In the end, it is revealed that no blood tie really exists, and the young lovers, who followed the voice of their hearts and of nature, can wed without any obstacle. But for a moment, the play flirts with the taboo against incest and with the kind of freethinking philosophizing in which Sade would fully indulge in his erotic novels.

Sade felt inhibited by the theater, and complained about the decencies required by the stage, particularly in the dramatic representation of love, wherein "the only thing I like and value is *the fucking.*" "As soon as I am free," he said that he would "very eagerly" look forward to devoting himself entirely to his "unique talent," fiction, which, then as now, paid better. Plays, he said, were not worth more "than a fart in the capital of Guyana." But fiction can pay for "six months of my luxuries in one of the premier cities of the realm."[28] He would later find, when he was desperate for money, that he could live on his prose. And in his fiction, usually published anonymously, he could feel free to please himself, and to please and shock his equally anonymous readers.

A kind of intermediary work between Sade's plays and fiction was his *Dialogue entre un prêtre et un moribond* (*Dialogue Between a Priest and a Dying Man*), written during the summer of 1782. The dying man begins by admitting that he is repentant—but not about what the priest expects. In fact, he is repentant not for having committed so many sins, but for not having committed more of them. He is sorry "only for the very modest use I have made of the faculties (criminal, according to you; perfectly pure, according to me) that she [Nature] gave me to serve her."[29] In this dialogue, the priest becomes more and more scandalized by the witty reprobate's attacks. When the priest is shocked by the dying man's atheism, the latter explains that "it is utterly impossible to believe in what one does not understand." "Prove to me," he challenges the priest, "that Nature is not sufficient in herself, and I will permit you to posit a Lord over her."[30] Furthermore, the dying man points out, "There are more gods than there are countries, more ways of serving him than there are different heads and different inclinations."[31] The priest first tries to tempt the dying man with the hope of an afterlife. Then he tries to frighten him with the threat of punishment in hell or with the prospect of the mere oblivion of death. Heaven and hell, the dying man replies, are ridiculous fictions. And oblivion does not frighten him; he reasons that death is "neither terrifying nor absolute," for we have in Nature our own kind of immortality: "Today a man, tomorrow a worm, the next day a fly—is this not eternal life?"[32] It is the dying atheist who brings enlightenment and consolation to the priest: "Leave off your prejudices," he tells the priest, "be a man, be human, without fear and without hope." Even though the dying man feels the approach of death, he invites the priest to join him in savoring the best consolation life has to offer; "sensual pleasure."[33] It is his intention to die as he lived: in the bosom of delight. He then asks the priest to share the pleasure of the six attractive women who are at this moment in the next room. In the end, it is the priest who is converted.

As the years passed in Vincennes, and as Sade grew accustomed to his fate, he used more and more of his time to write his plays and stories, and to conduct his extremely varied research. Almost all of Renée's letters to him concerned lists of books that Sade wanted her to borrow or buy. He especially liked to read travel books; they provided ammunition he could use to attack the idea of a uniform morality. He recorded his thoughts in commonplace books, only one of which has survived, his "Quatrième Cahier de notes ou réflexions," written between June 12 and August 21, 1780. He also kept various journals: his above-mentioned "Almanach illusoire," concerning his masturbation; and his journal concerning his eye inflammation and its treatment.[34] "I will soon be half blind," he wrote to Renée at the beginning of 1783.[35] Shortly after February 4, 1783, Sade informed her, "I have completely lost the use of my eye."[36] Renée made inquiries at Vincennes and was told, as she informed Mlle de Rousset on February 7, that "this was a ruse on his part."[37] However, the authorities did send M. Grandjean, the King's oculist, to visit Sade. Sade described the muddled doctor and his visit in a letter to Renée on March 4, 1783:

> You would laugh so much if you saw his confusion when I complained. He goes round, he goes round, never did a carrousel pony go in circles like that; not even to sit down, or to take my pulse, or even to look at me directly, except yesterday, when he betook himself to examine my eye. If I were not in pain, I would have been tempted to laugh like an idiot, so amusing was it.[38]

The doctor prescribed a powder made from the iris plant—a kind of superstitious, magical treatment: irises for irises. On May 22, Sade informed the brothers Grandjean (elder and younger), both of whom were oculists, of the failure of their medicine, which "caused an extraordinary irritation; it has considerably inflamed all of the small vessels in the white of the eye and has made that area entirely red."[39] As a consequence, Sade wrote to Renée, "I read less, I work less, and my mind wanders to something else"—sexual day-dreams. He was proof, he said, of the theory he had often heard "that to deprive us one of our senses triples the force of the imagination." He was inspired to extend the theory "to create an unusual law of pleasure": "I am quite persuaded that one would succeed in attaining the highest and strongest possible degree of pleasure in love by deadening one or two of the senses, or even more, each time that one makes love."[40]

The idea of blindness comes up in Sade's "Quatrième Cahier" in a philo-sophical discussion of free will and culpability:

> Let us imagine an egg placed on a billiard table and two balls shot by two blind men. One ball, in its route, misses the egg; the other breaks it. Is it the fault of the ball? Is it even that of the blind man who shot the ball harmful to the egg? "The blind man is Nature," say the philosophers partial to the view that man is not free; "the balls, they are us; the broken egg, that is crime." Now you see what sort of justice there is in laws![41]

Sade later gave this passage—almost word for word—to Zamé, the uto-pian tribal king in the novel *Aline et Valcour*.[42] Zamé's philosophy also depends upon the continuation of the above passage in the "Quatrième Cahier":

> The laws punish an infinite number of crimes that entail only the most slender consequences, and that, properly understood, are only very mild infractions against the well-being of society. Among these are primarily those that concern morals, whereas, on the other hand, they say nothing against crimes that are considerably more tangible and whose consequences are frightful, such as avarice, treachery, ingrati-tude, swindling, etc. A man rapes a girl: he is hanged. Now, that is no doubt a bad thing, but one whose consequence, properly understood, is merely to place this girl in a category she must needs come to sooner or later. But a miser stands by as his neighbors, an unfortunate family, perish, of whom perhaps half hasten to their graves so as to avoid the dreadful suffering of poverty, and the rest keep it at bay by means of all the aberrant crimes prompted by the squalor into which they have sunk: what a chain of horrors, what a complication of crimes results

from the aid denied by that miser! But what can be done to him? *Not a thing.*[43]

If we can judge by the one surviving commonplace book that Sade kept at Vincennes, much of what he read and wrote in prison would eventually find its way into his more famous works. His erotic novels are constructed on a pattern of sexual scenes followed by passages in which the characters argue about the philosophical, moral, and cultural implications of whatever they had just done or had done to them. As in the above passage, it is not clear where Sade himself stands in these debates. Did he really believe, for example, that the raped girl had less to complain about, and the law less to concern itself with, than when a family is bilked by a swindler? Sade's method of thinking is to run at once to the extreme. His thoughts are ironical, provisional, hypothetical. The logical operator is, What if? What if human prejudices and emotions—in this case in favor of the raped girl—were expunged from the law, and instead rules were written based solely on the measurable amount of suffering a particular act inflicts on the greatest number of people? Sade plays with this hypothesis, teases out of it whatever arch, ironical pleasure he can extract. In his argument, the element of special pleading is also very evident. After all, he is the one in prison on a morals charge, and his mother-in-law is free, even though, in his view, she is the swindler who stole his money and destroyed his once noble family.

Sade made an impassioned defense of his philosophy, his way of thinking, in a letter to Renée at the beginning of November 1783:

My way of thinking, you say, cannot be condoned. But what does that matter to me? Quite mad is he who would adopt his way of thinking to please others! My way of thinking is the product of my thoughts; it is bound up in my very existence, in my very nature. It is not in my power to change it; and were it possible, I would not do it. This way of thinking that you condemn is the sole consolation of my life: it lightens all my suffering in prison; in the world, it heightens all my pleasures, and I am bound to it more than to my very life. It is not my way of thinking that has caused my misfortune, it is the way others think. The man of reason who ridicules the prejudices of fools inevitably becomes the enemy of fools; he must expect it and disdain it.

This sounds remarkably high-minded and brave. But then Sade immediately offered the following autobiographical parable, and the reader must wonder what is wrong with it: "A traveler treads a fine road. But it is laid with traps.

He falls into one. Do you say that it is the fault of the traveler, or of the scoundrel who set the traps?" Sade's problems were never his own fault, always someone else's, some scoundrel out to get him. Sade's "traveler" may be entitled to one mistake. His road seemed "fine" until he fell into some villain's trap. But now that the traveler knows there are traps, ought he continue down that same road in the same unwary way? Yes, according to Sade. Thus he insisted on his view:

> If, then, as you say, they set my freedom at the cost of giving up my principles and my pleasures, we can then bid each other farewell forever, because, rather than those things, I would sacrifice a thousand lives and a thousand freedoms, if I had them. These principles and these pleasures are carried by me even to the point of fanaticism, and the fanaticism is the product of the persecutions of my tyrants. The more they continue their abuse, the more they entrench my principles in my heart, and I explicitly state that they do not need to talk to me of liberty if it is offered only at the cost of their destruction. I tell it to you. I will tell it to M. Lenoir. I will tell it to the whole world. Even on the scaffold, I would not change.[44]

We have seen that by this year, 1783, Sade had formed the literary persona that we recognize in all of his later works. His subject matter is sexuality. His style is radical assault, so extreme that the narrative seems ironical, unstable. Yet, quite often, the focus is philosophical, serious, as if there is meaning there that ought to make sense. Sade was already at work on a major novel, *Aline et Valcour, ou le roman philosophique,* which is usually dated during Sade's imprisonment in the Bastille. He certainly referred to the progress of his writing in November and December of 1786, when he was imprisoned there. He kept asking Renée for information about Spain and Portugal for the novel.[45] However, this large work also owes its inception to Sade's fertile period in Vincennes. Renée referred to one of its topics in a letter on March 5, 1781, when she mentioned having read the passage concerning the Otahitiens.[46] On May 6, 1781, Mlle de Rousset also commented on these noble savages, led by their philosopher-chief Zamé: "I have read the four chapters on the Otahitiens. These people are happier with their simplicity of pure nature than we are, ruled by our laws and customs."[47]

Sade was also beginning to work on the short stories that would form his *Anecdotes françaises.* His first reference to this work occurs in a letter to Renée on November 4, 1783, in which he sought her opinion of a sample story out of the "nearly two hundred similar" he had written. He also requested a notebook large enough for the whole collection.[48] A few weeks later, he included in a letter the anecdote about the Cardinal, which became the story "Attrapez-moi toujours de même" of the *Anecdotes françaises* (see above page 296). The style of this and many other stories in the collection also remind the reader of Sade's masterpiece, *Les Cent Vingt Journées de Sodome.* In June 1783, Sade wrote to Renée that he was about to "begin a great romantic work which should occupy me until the autumn."[49] It is possible that he was here referring to *Les Cent Vingt Journées,* the final draft of which he completed in the Bastille. Certainly everything that Sade was writing during the early 1780s at Vincennes—in letters, plays, stories, and novels—indicates a mind and a pen already aimed at his highest achievements.

On March 26, 1783, Sade wrote his wife a letter presenting her with a second draft of his historical tragedy, *Jeanne Laisné,* and a short comedy, *Le Boudoir.*[50] The latter is a slight play about M. Delcour's extreme jealousy of his wife and her young relation M. Sérigny, who are closeted every night in her boudoir, studying "ethics"—or so the husband is told. The wife is made aware of her husband's scheme to hide in her boudoir to see for himself, and she and Sérigny conspire to teach him a lesson about the folly of unfounded jealousy. Whether or not the wife had been conducting an affair with her young philosophy teacher is left ambiguous. She and Sérigny stage a performance for the husband's benefit, in which she sermonizes against adultery and declares her love for her husband. Sérigny announces his friendship—his Platonic friendship—for the wife. The husband, overwhelmed by this display of purity, bursts from his hiding place, falls at his wife's feet, and reports on the error of his false suspicions. Sade's letter to Renée accompanying this play tried to deal with its moral ambiguity and its failure to follow the rules of poetic justice, which he called "an ancient error": the resolution of a dramatic action, he argued, "in no way needs to depend on vice's being punished and virtue's being rewarded." His play "would have been detestable" if he had sought to punish the wife for her bad behavior; "but, even left unpunished, who would want to be like her?" Sade was trying to change the laws of the drama, just as he had tried to argue that all laws were biased, local, and nugatory. In this case, he first tried to say that poetic justice was not even a law but, rather, a mistake, an ancient error. Even if it was a law, it was not a good law, for the dramatist's art "consists not in punishing vice in comedy, but in painting it in such a way that no one wants to be like it; and in that case, there is no need to punish it."[51]

Ironically, Sade very nearly became a victim of nature's poetic justice. In a letter to Renée, he had sworn, if he ever made any calculations or signals regarding the restoration of his promenades, "may lightning blast me to dust."[52] His oath soon came very close to being fulfilled. On July 8, 1783, Renée wrote to her husband to express her great relief at finding him still alive—"My God! how lucky you are"—after "the accident at the donjon."[53] The tower had indeed been struck by lightning. Sade immediately wrote to Renée to dismiss the importance of this event, but it made a deep impression on him. If he had been struck by lightning, he told his wife, "of all possible deaths, this is the one I would love the best." Lightning, he added, never frightened him: "I do not even think it is necessary to keep one's windows shut during such a time, and it has never aroused in me that natural fear that it excites in animals."[54] Death by lightning stuck in Sade's imagination and became the final blow added to all the other insults and injuries suffered by the perfectly virtuous Justine in his novel *Les Infortunes de la vertu* (*The Misfortunes of Virtue*).[55] After Justine has experienced every sort of misfortune possible, she is finally saved from execution by her perfectly libertine and vastly more successful sister, Juliette. When Justine is finally safely recuperating at Juliette's magnificent château, the sisters plan to take a "promenade" because of the "excessive heat" of the summer's day. This plan is thwarted by "a terrible storm." Justine is asked to shut the window, and when she attempts to do so, she is struck dead by a bolt of lightning which "entered at her right breast . . . and came out through her mouth," cruelly disfiguring her entire face.[56] Thus, the seed for the conclusion of this novel was planted in the thick walls of the donjon of Vincennes.

If it were not for Sade's writing, prison life would not have been very much life at all. To be sure, from time to time he caused disturbances, struck a guard, wrote very angry letters. For example, as the new year of 1784 dawned, he began a bitter letter-war when he learned that his elder son, Louis-Marie, following Mme de Montreuil's wishes, planned to take advantage of the Montreuil family's connections and enlist in the infantry regiment of Rohan-Soubise, whereas Sade wanted him only in the Carabiniers, an elite regiment under the command of the Comte de Provence, the King's brother. Even though Sade had long neglected his children, he chose to make Louis-Marie's choice of regiment a struggle for control. Throughout the month of January 1784, he laid on with full guns. "No motive in the world," he wrote to Renée at the beginning of the month, "will make me consent to my son's being a second lieutenant in the infantry, and he will not be one. . . . I want him to serve nowhere but in the Carabiniers. As soon as he was born, I formed this plan for him, and I will definitely not change it." As a postscript, Sade added, "I beg you to forbid him to write to me until he swears to obey me."[57] At the same time, Sade wrote a note to Louis-Marie demanding his compliance: "I have no son capable of entering against my wishes a regiment where I do not wish him to serve. He could be the son of Mme de Montreuil, but he is not mine."[58] Moreover, anticipating that Mme de Montreuil might even try to marry the boy off, Sade wrote another letter to Renée insisting "that most definitely I will not grant my approval of any marriage until he is twenty-five years old."[59] In January and February, Sade renewed his ultimatum: "Your son will not enter the Soubise."[60] But of course he did. And all of Sade's shouting and threats came to nothing; indeed, the affair could have ended no other way.

It is puzzling why Sade chose to draw a line here. He had not been actively involved in any other aspect of his children's lives, and had even stopped replying to their annual New Year's letters. Sade knew he would lose the battle over Louis-Marie's choice of regiment. In a letter to Renée, he acknowledged, "I cannot stop him, since I am in prison." Why, then, continue so stubbornly in a clearly losing cause? Sade was acting out his father's role—the father who could bully his son into line. "The head of a family is the master of his children," he informed Renée in the same letter.[61] Sade himself had always followed his father's wishes, had allowed himself to be forced into marriage at the age of twenty-three (relatively early for a man of his rank in the eighteenth century) merely to pay off his father's debts. His totally unfounded suspicion that Mme de Montreuil was about to marry off Louis-Marie at the age of sixteen and a half suggests that Sade was thinking about his own situation in being made to marry Renée. If Sade was now playing out the heavy-handed role his own father had played with him, it is likely that he was also identifying with Louis-Marie, who, unlike the young Sade, would not be bullied by his almost comically blustering father. Did Sade (the rebel in principle, if not in deed) secretly wish his son to rebel against him, as he had failed to rebel against his own father? Yes, for Sade certainly chose to fight over an obviously futile cause.

The wheel of Sade's life had turned. His children were growing up and away from him. And he was growing older. He would be forty-four in June. He had already spent seven years in Vincennes, and he saw no chance of getting out. Moreover, the new year would begin sadly. On January 25, 1784, Mlle de Rousset died of tuberculosis at La Coste. She was forty years old. At the beginning of February, Sade also learned of the death of one of his aunts, Gabrielle-Laure, the Abbesse de Saint-Laurent at Avignon. On February 3, he wrote to instruct Gaufridy to divide her pension between the two surviving religious aunts.[62] We do not know Sade's thoughts on the death of Mlle de Rousset, his "Fanny," his "Milli Printemps." Sade had composed a very lively eulogy on Gothon's death, particularly celebrating her backside. "Immediately one begins to mourn the death of someone," he had written, "it is the physical qualities, the very features of the person, that fling themselves, willy-nilly, beneath one's pen."[63] But that charming letter had been written to Mlle de Rousset. Renée was not a correspondent likely to evoke a tribute to Mlle de Rousset's "physical qualities." More and more, Sade's deepest feelings and his pen had become united, devoted to the liberation of his fantasies and his art. Despite the horrors of prison, there was still something congenial about it for a writer. In his *Confessions*, Rousseau commented on his own artistic sensibility: "It is a very strange thing that my imagination never works more delightfully than when my attention is the reverse of delightful. . . . If I want to describe the spring it must be in winter; . . . if ever I were confined in the Bastille, there I would draw the picture of liberty."[64] Sade best described his own artistic liberation when he wrote to Amblet about his play *Le Capricieux* in April 1781. "Prison is good for something," Sade wrote. "It well serves the imagination."[65]

In February 1784, a curious literary event occurred in the Council Room of Vincennes, where Renée and Sade had a visit, supervised by the major. Sade entertained the two of them with a reading from his tragedy in verse, *Tancrède*, now lost except for twelve lines in one of Sade's letters to Amblet.[66] On February 14, Renée informed Sade that reading the whole play in manuscript was not as pleasing as hearing "the piece of it that you read to me." Amblet also did not approve of the play as written. But "in your mouth," Renée added, it "gave me the greatest pleasure and favorably impressed the major, as you must have noticed."[67] It was a poignant scene. Inside the donjon, the prisoner recited his poetry, Renée was thrilled, and the major was struck with admiration. Outside, the winter had turned bitterly cold.

Somehow, Sade had got it into his head that the King had been persuaded by Mme de Montreuil to let Sade out of prison to live on her estate at Vallery, or else to allow him to accept an ambassadorship in some foreign land. Sade thought it was just another plot of "the sneaky bitch," and his imagination produced this intriguing image: "Your plan is to remove me from here like a *balloon* and to waft me to Vallery."[68] The image of a balloon was much on people's minds. Today prisoners dreaming of escape conjure up helicopters. In 1784, at the very dawn of aviation, it was balloons. The previous June, Montgolfier had ascended in his hot-air balloon from the Champs-de-Mars before three hundred thousand spectators.[69] On October 15, 1783, Pilâtre du Rozier amazed a crowd in Faubourg Saint-Antoine with his balloon.[70] And in October and November, according to Thomas Carlyle, the Montgolfier brothers launched balloons from the Tuileries Garden, creating another sensation. Carlyle captured the poetry, and the bombast, of it: "Beautiful invention; mounting heavenward, so beautifully,—so unguidably! Emblem of much, and of our Age of Hope itself . . . —So, rising on windbags, will men scale the Empyrean."[71]

Sade would indeed make a journey, but it would not be to Vallery, and it would not be in a balloon. On February 29, 1784, he was surprised by Inspector of Police Surbois, who came with orders to transfer him to the Bastille. It was a complete shock, as Sade informed Renée, "to find myself taken away by force, without expecting anything, without any warning, with all this mystery, with all this ridiculous secrecy."[72] But there was nothing sinister or personal in the transfer. It was a question of economics: there were few prisoners left in Vincennes, and the structure of the prison had been allowed to decay.[73] Finally, it was cheaper to close it. Also transferred to the Bastille from Vincennes were the Comte de Solages and the Comte de Whyte de Malleville, the latter insane, the former incarcerated under a lettre de cachet by his family because of his presumed incest.[74] Earlier in February, before the transfer, Sade had threatened Renée that, if he were moved to Vallery, "I would rather throw myself beneath the coach."[75] But on this journey, there would be no bluster, no threats. Sade went off to the Bastille as quietly as he had entered Vincennes seven years earlier. In one important respect, he left a different man. He had fed his rage and his fantasies on the profound isolation of prison. He had made himself a philosopher of sorts, and certainly he was now a writer. Naturally isolated and solipsistic, he had been driven further into himself by prison. Yet he would rise—like Carlyle's emblematic balloon, "so unguidably!"—on the force of his inspiration.

CHAPTER 20

The Bastille

HE BASTILLE was a royal citadel of stone overlooking the Seine
and guarding the entrance to Faubourg Saint-Antoine. Construction had begun in the fourteenth century, and over the next four
hundred years, it had become more massive, more complex, more
forbidding. Among its famous prisoners can be counted La Rochefoucauld,
Richelieu, Voltaire, the Man in the Iron Mask, and now the Marquis de Sade.
Only individuals who were detained at the King's pleasure under a lettre de
cachet, or who had somehow become enemies of the state, were kept in the
Bastille. Here Damiens, who had stabbed King Louis XV in 1757, was interrogated before being slowly put to death in the Place de Grève, his tortures
more hideous than any Sade imagined, because Damiens's torments were real
and were witnessed by thousands.

By the time Sade entered, the Bastille had ceased to be used for prisoners
as often as it had been in previous reigns. Imprisonments reached a peak of
2,320 under Louis XIV. Under Louis XVI, there would only be 306.[1] It was
becoming too expensive even for kings to keep every wayward son of the
nobility under lock and key. The Bastille had a capacity of forty to fifty prisoners. Generally there were far fewer, and only a few of those stayed for more
than a year.[2] Sade's long term, first at Vincennes and now in the Bastille, was
highly remarkable for its duration.

The coach that carried Sade from Vincennes on February 29, 1784,
approached the portcullis of the Bastille toward nine o'clock in the evening.
The sentries at the entry gate gave challenge and rang a bell to summon the
major. Inspector of Police Surbois presented the order signed by the King and
by the new minister of the King's household, Breteuil.[3] Sade was then conducted to one of the four towers, La Tour de la Liberté, the Liberty Tower.
There were two massive doors, each requiring a separate key. Up the spiral
staircase Sade followed the turnkey, who opened another iron gate. The tower
rose almost eighty feet above the ground. At the lowest levels, there were dungeons designed for special punishments. At the top, there were other punishment cells. Above them were ramparts armed with cannon and patrolled by

the military sentries. The turnkey stopped at the second floor and unlocked the double doors. Sade entered his cell.

Voltaire, during his first imprisonment in the Bastille, in 1716, wrote a poem about the fortress. His jailer, opening the doors to his cell, gestures at the heavy doors, the iron bolts, the barred windows:

> "Phoebus," he says, "in his journey bright,
> Never troubles here to shine his light:
> Notice the walls fully ten feet wide,
> You will find it somewhat cool inside."[4]

The cells in the towers were octagonal, perhaps twenty feet wide and rising as much again to vaulted and plastered ceilings. The floors were of brick. The stone walls were whitewashed. The interior was not much lit by the single, triple-barred window. The air was foul, and often made worse by the sewage in the fosse or moat below. The smoke from the heating stove aggravated Sade's eye problem. The furnishings consisted of a table or two, some chairs, and a bed.

"I am as naked, praise God, as on the day I was born," Sade wrote to Renée on March 8, 1784, his first letter to her since his transfer. When he left Vincennes, he had tried to take some of his clothes, but Commandant de Rougemont, Sade claimed, began "to shout himself hoarse," so Sade left everything. Among the long list of clothing, food, and drink that he wanted Renée to send, he gave paramount importance to "the two mattresses for my bed and my large pillow," which he had been obliged to leave at Vincennes. Sade would not let go of this pillow. In the same letter, he recounted its importance to him because he suffered "dizzy spells" and "nosebleeds" when he did not sleep with his head "extremely high." He told Renée that, when he tried to take his favorite pillow with him from Vincennes, he caused a sensation: "They savagely tore it from my hands, arguing that actions of this magnitude were never allowed. And I came to the realization that some secret motive of the government was much concerned that a prisoner sleep with his head flat." Sade continued in this humorous vein:

> There was an official inquiry, and confirming that I was, indeed, very badly bedded, the judgment was reached that *it was not the practice* to be otherwise. I tell you in all honesty that you need to see these things to believe them, and if they told us that they happened in China, our sensitive and compassionate Frenchmen would immediately cry out: *Ah! the savages!*
>
> In addition, they claim that I must make my bed and sweep up my

room. As to the first, fine! because they did it very badly and because doing it amuses me. But as to the second, unfortunately, I understand nothing about that; it is my parents' fault for not having had this particular skill included in my education. That is because they did not foresee . . . *a great many things*. If they had foreseen them, there would not be a better tavern-sweeper than me in the whole realm. In the meantime, I ask you to get them to agree to give me some lessons. Let the man who serves me sweep it out just once a week for four or five years: I will observe him, and you will see that afterward I will manage it quite as well as he.

Despite the humor, Sade felt extremely bitter. At the Bastille, he told Renée, "I am a thousand times worse off and a thousand times more uncomfortable than in the miserable place I left."[5]

On March 21, Sade wrote to Lieutenant General of Police Lenoir to complain about the rudeness of the turnkeys in this "infamous hovel." Among the other "frightful humiliations," Sade listed the "filth" of the place, the inedible food, the smokey stove. He threatened suicide if he was not transferred.[6] In another letter in March, Sade wrote again to Lenoir and tried, as he had tried before in Vincennes and Miolans, to drive a wedge between Good Father and Bad Father—in this case, between Lenoir and the governor of the Bastille, Bernard-René Jourdan, the Marquis de Launay. Sade was trying to argue that the agreement about his treatment and privileges made by Lenoir and Minister of the King's Household Breteuil was being ignored and violated by de Launay, who "came yesterday to assure me that nothing of what you had asked him on my behalf could be done."[7] The prisoner wanted his promenades, his baggage from Vincennes, his linen. This last was a sensitive subject for prison officials. Linen had been strictly controlled ever since Latude, the only person to escape from the Bastille in the eighteenth century, accomplished this feat by means of a ladder he made out of his linen.[8] Sade also wanted to keep his candle burning past ten o'clock at night.[9] As always, he was trying to see what he could get away with. For the time being, Sade cast de Launay as the monster and Lenoir as the good magistrate, who, unless he did something to stop de Launay, would be revealed as "a weak magistrate who only toadies to power."[10] First Sade tried to bend the rules. Then he tried to foment a quarrel between those in authority. When that failed, he tried to wheedle some advantage in a different quarter: he wrote to Major Antoine-Jérôme de Losme of the Bastille. Sade agreed to abide by the rules governing the promenades, but asked de Losme to let him have them at the same hour each day: "An hour after noon each day will doubtless be the time most convenient to me." The reason had to do with accommodating the rhythm of his writing schedule. "I beg Monsieur the Major," Sade wrote to de Losme, "please to note well that it is impossible for someone who is working to cut short his work today at one time, tomorrow at another."[11] Sade the nihilist, the anarchist, needed order in his life. In time, Major de Losme, too, would fall under Sade's censure. On September 4, 1784, he told Lenoir that de Losme was "a man dishonored and cashiered from the Gardes du Corps for embezzlement."[12] Once again, Sade was surrounded by spies and operatives in the pay of Mme de Montreuil.

In the meantime, life went on. In the Bastille, meals were served at seven and eleven in the morning, and then at six in the evening. The midday meal might consist of a soup, an entrée, and a meat dish of mutton, salt pork, sausage, or veal, plus one pound of bread, and a bottle of wine. Supper consisted of two dishes, including a meat dish, perhaps of roast chicken or calf's liver.[13] "They are clearly starving me to death here," Sade wrote Renée in April 1784. Sade found the dinners "such as one would not dare serve to your footman."[14] That is why he demanded money to purchase food on his own. "I insist on being fed," he continued, "on their furnishing me, as at Vincennes, *with pâtés, hams, jams*, etc., and let them be quite certain that I will then allow the cook to send me at his convenience all *the vomit* that he wants."[15] On September 4, 1784, he wrote to Renée again about the food: "If you saw the *foul and disgusting slop passing for vittles* that is served here, you would easily understand how someone accustomed to a refined table would need to spend his own money to supplement it."[16] With extra money, Sade could order in special foods. The prison financial records show that, for June 1784, Sade was weekly provided with cut flowers, and daily with strawberries.[17] And of course there were the fortnightly dispatches in which Renée sent her pâtés, terrines, jams, etc. Sade was as precise and as demanding as ever in the tasks he set for his wife. He insisted on the chocolate "that I am accustomed to get from my regular shop."[18] Renée sometimes had to search far afield for her husband's favorite delicacies. On November 28, 1787, she wrote to Gaufridy asking for a few pots of a specialty of Provence, a jam made of small green oranges: "M. de Sade passionately desires some *petits chinois*, a superb jam of which he is much enamored."[19] Even amidst the darkening clouds of revolution, on February 25, 1789, when food was scarce, when rioters at Aix chased magistrates through the frightened streets,[20] Renée remembered her husband's craving for "some truffles from his estate, all put up in oil." Sade had been asking for them. Could Gaufridy send some?[21] After consuming such rich food and taking very little exercise, Sade put on weight. As Renée expressed it in a letter to Gaufridy on May 25, 1787, her husband had grown "very fat."[22] By November 1788, Renée wrote that, because of her husband's obesity, "it is impossible for him to change his shirt alone"—that is, without the assistance of his servant in prison, Mérigot.[23]

Renée continued to handle business affairs at La Coste through Gaufridy, supervised the rearing of her children, ran errands for her husband, tried to keep him in good spirits. She did not always succeed. "Brighten up your style," Sade urged her on August 14, 1787. "The dullest thing could be written gaily."[24] Humor, however, was not Renée's strong point. She also tried to keep secret any unpleasantness in her own situation. Now that Mlle de Rousset was dead, the only person Renée could confide in was Gaufridy. To him, but not to her husband, on September 12, 1784, she revealed her annoyance at having to change apartments in her convent. The replacement that was being offered was much inferior—"It is a hole in the wall," she admitted—yet, she noted with irony, "we have three châteaux that are falling apart for want of being lived in."[25] Renée knew that she could not express this kind of self-pity to her mother. Mme de Montreuil's sharp tongue would have soon put an end to any pipe dreams. This is how Mme de Montreuil bluntly expressed her final view of her son-in-law: "The situation," she wrote to Gaufridy on March 17, 1785, "is still the same. I cannot foresee when it will change." She would never allow Sade to be released. "I have heard it said," she continued, "that the excitability of his character remains exactly the same, and that it is to be feared that the same results it produced until now would follow upon his release." It is almost possible to see Mme de Montreuil rubbing the side of her nose and winking as she told Gaufridy, "You know what you know, Monsieur, and there is nothing more to add except to do what is for the best."[26] It was over. Renée would get nowhere with her mother. It was best not even to talk to her or listen to her.

Nor could Renée talk effectively to her husband about business. For example, on August 17, 1784, Renée had to confess to Gaufridy that she was "at an impasse in settling" the debts against the Abbé's estate, because her husband was "continuing not to want to reply to matters of business."[27] Some matters could not be delegated or assumed by others. When Renée's aunt the Marquise d'Azy died on May 20, 1781, and left Renée an inheritance of 25,000 livres, Renée asked her husband in a letter on June 16, 1781, for the power of attorney needed for her to receive the payment.[28] Ten months later, on April 13, 1782, Renée was still pleading with Sade: all of Mme d'Azy's other relatives were hounding Renée for the power of attorney, and "they say that it is my fault that you do not give it."[29] But Sade believed that one of the purposes of his imprisonment was to permit his mother-in-law to steal his fortune. Therefore, he stubbornly refused to conduct business while he was imprisoned. As a consequence, Renée was often without money to pay bills, as she patiently explained to him in a letter on November 10, 1783: "I must pay for the candles, the confectioner, the bookstore, since they will not give me credit any more. So do not make light of it by turning a deaf ear." Of course, these were bills she incurred buying supplies for Sade. She asked him, "Send me a draft on the interest on my dowry," or else "allow me to receive the share from the sale of Mme d'Azy's house."[30]

As the children grew older, they required more money. They were running up debts, Renée informed Gaufridy on May 24, 1785. La Jeunesse's last illness, Renée said, also "cost me a good deal." La Jeunesse, Sade's valet, copyist, and sometime correspondent, was a member of Renée's household, and she attended him at his deathbed. "He died," she wrote Gaufridy, "with his faculties intact and with God on his lips." Renée was touched: first Mlle de Rousset, and now La Jeunesse. "Despite his faults," she continued, "I deeply miss him, because he was attached to me." Renée felt more and more alone. "Everyone seems to be dying," she moaned. The person who carried this letter down to Provence for Renée was probably the lawyer Reinaud, whom she said she saw "with great pleasure." Renée's loneliness, bordering on despair, had led her to enjoy a curious fantasy when Reinaud came to see her in the visiting room of her convent. "When I was chatting with him," she told Gaufridy, for a moment "I enjoyed the illusion and almost believed that I was in Provence and that M. de Sade was there."[31] It was a pretty illusion—that at any moment her husband might look in on them from the door as he went off to inspect the new plantings in his park.

During the summer of 1786, another attempt was made to get Sade to sign a power of attorney so that business on his estates could be conducted in his absence. The following year, Mme de Montreuil finally succeeded in gaining legal control over her son-in-law's property. On June 24, 1787, Renée informed Gaufridy that she was certain her family, "instead of trying to get" her husband "released," were seeking to establish a "trusteeship." Renée added that she "did not consider it proper to oppose" the plan, since "real harm" had been done to her husband's estates through "this lack of administration."[32] In fact, the family had already met to name a conservator—Sade's paternal uncle, Richard-Jean-Louis de Sade, Commandeur of the Ordre de Saint-Jean de Jérusalem. At the same time, M. de Montreuil was given the right of approval over expenditures, and Gaufridy was authorized to continue his administration.[33] Just two months later, the Commandeur confessed to Gaufridy that he was "already weary" of the responsibility.[34]

There had not been anyone present to stand up for Sade at the legal proceedings that removed his estates from his control. M. de Montreuil was there, along with a few of Sade's relatives, including his cousin the Comte de Sade-Eyguières, the same one to whom Mme de Montreuil had sold Sade's royal post of lieutenant general of Bresse, Bugey, Valromey, and Gex. The Commandeur sent his approval of the conservatorship by proxy. This may explain why his given names, Richard-Jean-Louis, were recorded in the official decree as Joseph Gaspard Balthazar, although no one present noticed the mistake. Sade had been in prison for more than ten years. His absence from his estates was the very reason the Châtelet was being petitioned to appoint a conservator, yet he did not even know about this legal proceeding. He was forty-seven years old and had effectively lost his money, his lands, his family.

Renée had been cowed into submission. When she needed money on August 24, 1787, she had to ask Gaufridy to discuss it with the Commandeur.[35] A year later, her husband ran up extra expenses redecorating his new room higher up in the Liberty Tower. On October 22, 1788, Renée wrote to Gaufridy: "I am supposed to bring him another ten louis on Monday, which I will have to borrow." She could ask her parents, she admitted, but she preferred not to, "because they will only say that these are pointless expenditures."[36] Renée had lost this argument to her mother a great many times over the years. Her spirit broken in the conflict between her husband and her mother, she lived a life that appeared more and more tragic. "Sometimes," she wrote Gaufridy on April 21, 1788, "I would like to have wings in order to fly to see how everything is," to change her perspective and see if anything made any sense. Normally subject to melancholy, Renée drifted deeper into depression and religious fatalism. She had come to accept her helplessness: "As for me," she said, "I will spend my life without the power to rule on anything."[37]

The sad winds that dispirited Renée blew over the towers of the Bastille as well. Locked in his cell, Sade raged on about bad food, injustice, signals, turnkeys, etc., etc. His eyes continued to cause him great distress. "The pains in his feet, which frequently torment him," Renée wrote Gaufridy on December 30, 1786, had been diagnosed as either rheumatism or gout.[38] Sade did find some brief consolation in a fellow prisoner named Villeman, with whom he conducted a secret correspondence. Major de Losme's report for December 11, 1787, related the discovery of this correspondence when Sade tried to smuggle a letter to Villeman inside a Royal Almanac.[39] The turnkeys were specifically trained to prevent this sort of conspiracy. However, Sade's neighbor Villeman was very adept at passing messages. According to a contemporary, Villeman had tried to sneak messages out of the Bastille inside a guitar that he had broken on purpose, so that it would have to be sent out for repairs. Villeman also "sometimes hid small notes in the hollowed-out cork of a bottle."[40] On December 11, 1787, Major de Losme wrote to inform

Lieutenant General of Police de Crosne that "the Marquis de Sade engages in a daily dialogue with M. Villeman, across their partition, and against which I have vainly employed with both one and the other my strongest arguments." This illicit correspondence, de Losme added, "could have a dangerous outcome, because the Marquis de Sade every fortnight receives a visit from Madame his wife, and whatever precaution we take with him, there is always a part of their conversation in a whisper, which would be of little concern if the above correspondence had not existed."[41] Sade wrote a courteous letter to his "dear neighbor" Villeman, explaining that he was obliged to give his "word of honor" to the authorities to "break off all sort of conversation with you." Sade concluded his letter: "I beg you to be absolutely confident that I will always be grateful to you and that you will have my eternal affection."[42]

Another neighbor in the Liberty Tower, however, was a continuing source of irritation. Around Easter 1784, Sade wrote to Renée about him:

> They have ensconced three feet from my pillow a fellow who sleeps the whole day and who, from midnight to eight in the morning, gallops, smashes, breaks, throws, howls, and performs other such pleasantries, and all that so that I could not close my eyes, a torture so cruel for my pitiful existence that I am very sure I will not last a month if that goes on that long. . . . This is a barbarous and petty treatment for which there is not, perhaps, an equal in the whole world.[43]

Sade, not surprisingly, believed that his noisy neighbor was part of a conspiracy against him headed by Mme de Montreuil and including officials of the Bastille. "It is," he wrote to Renée in April 1785, "the very devil's workshop!" He charged that Renée's "execrable mother," in order to convey the number 37 as some sort of signal, had kept him up for thirty-seven nights in a row "by paying a police informer that they lodged not six feet from my head to create an uproar all night long."[44] By August 1785, this noisy neighbor had grown worse, as Sade explained to Renée: "A small inconvenience has just occurred here, quite pleasing to the staff, though not as much to me, which results in making this room as insupportable as it is uninhabitable. My neighbor has gone mad and is making an infernal racket." Sade suggested that this was the actual purpose of the Bastille, "to drive insane everyone who has the misfortune to live in this hellish place." He imagined that Governor de Launay must be delighted: "I am convinced that there was quite a celebration over at his place."[45] The worst of it was that this neighbor's early-to-bed, early-to-rise habit was interfering with Sade's own night-owl writing schedule. Sade complained about it to Major de Losme on January 16, 1787: "I go to bed at midnight, my head burning and fatigued from work; the result is that I cannot fall asleep before four o'clock in the morning. Now, I leave you to imagine what it is like to be awakened at *six o'clock* to a man who fell asleep only at *four*."[46]

Sade's "work," the activity that kept the candles lit in his cell in the Bastille, was the writing of some of the major works of his literary career. What Sade wrote to Amblet in April 1784 about his plays is even more true of his fiction: "It is absolutely impossible for me to stand against my genius; it carried me onto this road despite myself, and whatever they may do, they will never turn me out of it."[47] It would not be in verse drama but in prose that Sade would project himself into the world. His letters from prison contain some of his strongest ideas and his strongest expressions. His sufferings would find release, his injuries vindication at the tip of his pen. On November 2, 1786, he asked Renée to bring him on her next visit "two packets of those excellent pens from Griffon at two sols apiece and cut very flaringly but with the point *sharp* and *hard*."[48]

If Sade's letters caused trouble, there would be a real problem with his fiction. As soon as Renée began visiting her husband in the Council Room of the Bastille, she contrived a very feminine means of avoiding the prison censorship: she carried secret letters to Sade hidden in her muff. On April 18, 1787, after using this method for some years, she expressed her wish to stop: "I am not wearing my muff any more, because I must take care that they do not discover the letters, and above all not cause any difficulty that would deprive us of my visits."[49] Sade, however, insisted that she continue. For example, on December 29, 1788, Renée smuggled into the Bastille a hidden letter that was a "response to your secret letter given at my last visit."[50] Sade had also been trying to find a secure way of getting his manuscripts out of prison without having them read by the censor. He had asked Renée to get official permission for such a delivery. In a hidden letter on August 22, 1786, she told Sade that, although she "pleaded" with the authorities, "their response has always been that nothing could leave the Bastille without being read."[51] Despite this rebuff, and despite her anxiety about breaking the law, she kept on smuggling letters in and out of the Bastille. She also managed to sneak out some of Sade's manuscripts. In the hidden letter of December 29, 1788, she reminded her husband of her loyalty over the years: "I have taken all the papers and secret packets; those you have said to open, I have opened; those you wanted me to keep hidden, they are to be returned to you upon your release."[52]

Some of the prose works that Sade wrote in the Bastille and that Renée smuggled out were his philosophical romance, *Aline et Valcour*; a draft of a novella, *Eugénie de Franval*, which was the seed for his later novel *La*

Philosophie dans le boudoir; and the first draft of *Les Infortunes de la vertu.* These are the central works of Sade's canon. But his most important work was not smuggled out of the Bastille. It was *Les Cent Vingt Journées de Sodome;* and the story of what became of this manuscript is as interesting as anything else in Sade's life.

CHAPTER 21

Sodom

ADE WROTE *Les Cent Vingt Journées de Sodome* in his prison cell in the Bastille. As he noted at the end of the manuscript, it "was begun on October 22, 1785, and finished in thirty-seven days," on November 28.[1] He cleverly and carefully prepared the paper to receive his finest and most dangerous work, gluing together thin sheets almost five inches wide until he had a scroll nearly forty feet long. Tightly rolled up, the scroll could be hidden each day in his cell. Indeed, it survived the various searches of the guards. In the quiet of the Bastille night, Sade began to write, his constantly painful eyes protected from the candles' glare by his special eyeshade. He selected a sharp quill and wrote the first sentence in his tiny, clear hand:

> The considerable wars that Louis XIV had to endure during the course of his reign, in depleting the treasury of the state and the energy of the people, nevertheless revealed the secret for enriching a horde of those leeches always on the prowl for general calamities that they rather nurture than alleviate with an eye to profiting from them all the more. The end of this otherwise sublime reign was perhaps one of the epochs of the French Empire singularly noted for the sort of dubious fortunes that flaunt a luxury and debauchery as sordid as they are themselves. [19]

In this stately way, in this context of history, sociology, and economics, Sade began what must be the most radical novel ever written, if such a distinction is to be measured by the violence of the feelings a narrative can arouse. The incredible corruption of the major characters is attributed to the weakness displayed by the nobility of the blood in the face of a new money-making nobility. Sudden vast wealth, the leisure to spend it, and a lack of character to control what it was spent on—all of these features, according to Sade, produced the spoiled, childish species of sociopathic perverts exemplified by the four main characters of the novel. These characters—the Président de Curval, the financier Durcet, and two brothers, the Bishop of ——— and the Duc de Blangis—are fellow orgiasts in a private sex-crimes club. The word "pervert" is not chosen lightly, for Sade's characters are not just concerned with sexual calisthenics or sexual preferences, but with a sexuality predicated on torturing their victims to death, as happens over and over and over at the end of this novel.

These are not the young, handsome, marble-shafted studs of ordinary erotic fiction, which for Sade was tame, stylized, conventional, and uninteresting, because it earned its way by *not* exciting any other feelings than a dreamy, unreal sexuality. Sade's characters are brilliantly particularized personifications of unexpected traits and ordinarily submerged impulses. The Bishop, for example, in addition to being a thorough atheist and scoundrel, is described as a decidedly girlish man of forty-five:

> . . . a small, wispy body, quite dainty, in rather delicate health, emotionally extremely sensitive, overrefined and fussy in his acts of pleasure, with a rather mediocre endowment and a very modest member, small, to be honest, but managed with such proficiency and self-control that his imagination, thus kept in continual flame, endowed him with as much capacity for pleasure as his brother; indeed, such rarefied sensations upon a sensitivity as responsive and as nervous as his often precipitated him into a swoon at the moment of his discharge and he nearly always lost consciousness. He was forty-five years old, with a very delicate countenance, rather pretty eyes, but rotten teeth and bad breath, with pallid skin, a hairless body, a small but shapely ass, and a prick five inches in circumference and ten long. A devotee of both active and passive sodomy, but with a decided preference for the latter, he spent his life having himself buggered. [31]

All of the four main characters have achieved their wealth and power by crime and murder. The Bishop's brother, the Duc de Blangis, has killed his own mother, his sister, and his first three wives—and all this even before the novel begins. Similarly, the financier Durcet has already poisoned his mother, his wife, and his niece for their money. Like the Bishop, he cannot be mistaken for a leading man, and is, in fact, entirely impotent. He is also, with one notable exception, homosexual. He has such a supreme detestation of "cunts" that "just the sight of one would have unstiffened his prick for six months." The sole exception was when he slept with his sister-in-law, and that was merely to "produce a child who could someday provide him with the pleasure of committing incest" (38). Sade's peculiar method of characterizing the financier (as with the others) emphasizes physique and sexual tastes:

> Durcet is fifty-three years old, small, short, fat, very broad, with a pleasant, open face, very pale skin, and his entire body, but especially his hips and buttocks, absolutely like a woman's; his ass is full, plump, firm, and well shaped, although excessively spread by continual sodomy; his prick is incredibly small: it is hardly two inches around by four long; it no longer gets hard at all; his discharges are rare and very difficult, scanty, and always preceded by paroxysms that hurl him into a sort of fury that propels him into criminal acts; he has bosoms like a woman's, a sweet, musical voice, and in society impeccably decent, while at the same time his mind is as depraved as his three friends'; an old school friend of the Duc, he and the Duc continue to amuse themselves each day, and one of Durcet's great pleasures is to have his anus tickled by the Duc's monstrous member. [37–38]

Sade later describes Durcet's tiny penis as a "nasty little anchovy" (134).

The Duc de Blangis is the most formidable of the four perverts. The murderer of all his own female relatives appears such a "terrifying colossus" that it is suggested "his immense size was what doubtless killed off his wives." Unlike the other perverts, the Duc is in excellent health and frightfully alive—actually more animal than human, a "centaur" or a satyr:

> In addition, he had a proud, masculine countenance, large, piercing dark eyes, full, dark eyebrows, an aquiline nose, handsome teeth, a general air of health and vigor, with broad shoulders, a powerful build, although perfectly balanced, with strong haunches, superb buttocks, the most eligible leg imaginable, with a temperament of iron, the strength of a horse, and a tool that would make a mule proud, incredibly hairy, endowed with the prowess to shoot its fuck as often as desired each day, even at his current age of fifty, a virtually constant erection whose size measured eight inches in circumference by twelve long.

If the Duc de Blangis is frightful at rest, so to speak, Sade invites the reader to picture how he looks when sexually aroused:

> He is no longer human; rather, he is an enraged tiger. Unfortunate indeed is the person who then serves his pleasure: from out his

powerful lungs are hurled frightful roars and appalling blasphemies, flames appear to shoot from his eyes, he foams at the mouth, he brays, he seems, for all the world, like the very godhead of lubricity. At any moment, in whatever way he happened to be satisfying his lust, his hands would inevitably stray, and he has on more than one occasion choked a woman to death at the moment of his heinous discharge. [29]

When the frenzy of lust was over, the Duc de Blangis, far from feeling the slightest remorse for his evil acts, displayed that "indifference," that peculiar "apathy," from which immediately spring those new "sparks of lechery" and the need for increasing infamies that are the hallmark of the true libertine (29). Once, on a bet, he killed a horse by crushing its ribs with his powerful legs. And yet, for all his manly prowess, when he went to war as a young man, he disgraced himself so badly that he was obliged to leave the military. This dangerous, proud, vengeful, libidinous beast, whose crimes, tortures, and perverted pleasures will sicken any reader brave enough to read to the end of the novel—this paragon of orgiastic violence was a coward. The colossus could have been frightened off, Sade tells us, by "an intrepid child." A fair fight, or one that involved even the slightest risk of injury, would have "made him flee to the farthest ends of the earth" (30).

The final member of the foursome, the Président de Curval, at sixty years old, is a hideous, macabre cartoon of a man:

He appeared hardly more than a skeleton. He was tall, thin, sour-looking, with sunken, deadened eyes, thin lips and foul breath, a chin that pointed up and a long nose that pointed down. Covered with hair like a satyr, with a flat back, with slack and hanging buttocks that resembled nothing so much as two filthy rags dangling over the tops of his legs; this slack flesh had been so withered by the lashes of the whip that you could twirl it around your fingers and he would not even notice. Dead center, and without your having even to spread them, appeared an immense orifice whose truly enormous diameter, stench, and hue put you in mind more of a septic pit than an asshole; and to crown the glory, this Swine of Sodom included among his little customs that of always leaving that very spot in such a state of filthiness that surrounding it there was always a wad two inches thick. Below a belly as creased as it was slack and sallow could be seen amid a forest of hair a tool which, in the erect state, might come to around eight inches long and seven in circumference; this state, however, was now but extremely rare, and to achieve it required a furious chain of events. Nevertheless, it occurred at least two or three times a week, and the Président would then indiscriminately slip into any hole at all, although the one in the rear of a young boy was infinitely the more preferable to him. [33–34]

Curval is literally a dirty old man, dirty in his own body and in his peculiar obsession of being attracted to whatever is, like himself, befouled, offensive, disgusting.

These four bizarre heroes, having grown bored with their usual criminal meetings and orgies, propose a kind of libertine winter retreat at Silling, Durcet's romantically isolated château, where in absolute secrecy and security they can study every sort of perversion imaginable and perform it without the slightest constraint. Their plan is methodical, scientific, philosophical. "It is not at all appreciated," Sade writes, how infinitely various and how minutely differentiated are human sexual acts, perversions, manias, fetishes, tastes (45). We are all human, but our sexual styles, ranging from the smallest oddity to the absolutely, impossibly grotesque transformations of the act, yield a great puzzle. The person "who could fix and classify these deviations would perform perhaps one of the finest and most interesting works one could have on manners" (46). It is a typically eighteenth-century idea—like founding new religious and political organizations, like studying alien cultures in far-off lands for their secrets, like assuming that truth, whether philosophical or scientific, is obtainable, and that all truth reflects the general meaningfulness of the world. Admittedly, it is odd that Sade should entrust such a lofty, utopian purpose to the likes of the four *philosophes* described above. But Sade's style, in all of his best writing, whether in his letters or here, is notable for its irony, its tantalizing playfulness, even and especially on the most troubling topics. The château of Silling in *Les Cent Vingt Journées* is, therefore, an odd sort of utopia, or dystopia, and the reader is left to decide for himself where Sade stands in relation to the characters and to the narrative. The answer will confirm either Sade's humanity or his depravity. The difficulty of this test keeps alive the myth of Sade and also engages and probes the reader's own humanity.

The scheme for this brave new world of libertinism at Silling naturally requires a population of subjects for the experiments, a collection of trusty servants and executioners, and a group of sex experts. First among the victims is a group of four young women, daughters of the four perverts, who had been raised and trained for incest. Eventually, their fathers married them off to or shared them with the other members of their quartet. The four libertines also required for their experiments "a considerable number of erotic objects of both sexes." However, they had to limit themselves. There would be eight young girls, eight young boys, eight "fuckers" or "fellows endowed with monstrous members suited to the pleasures of passive sodomy" (50). The libertines planned every detail: the fuckers' penises were to be at least "ten or twelve inches long by seven and a half in circumference." There would also be four servants and an excellent kitchen staff. The libertines were as insatiable about food and drink as they were about sex. The young girls and boys, as well as the fuckers, were all to be selected by the unanimous vote of the libertines in a beauty contest following a massive talent search by the most adept pimps and bawds throughout France. The young girls and boys had to be between twelve and fifteen years old: "Anyone above or below was rejected without mercy" (51). They also had to be virgins and of good families. Necessarily, these young people had to be kidnapped from convents, from schools, from their families' estates. The terrified captives were examined, prodded, probed, sniffed by the libertines, who for the moment controlled themselves so that passion would not sway their rational judgment. Finally, eight perfect girls were chosen from the 130 who had been kidnapped, and eight perfect boys from 150. Some of the rejects served to amuse the libertines for a time after the balloting, but finally all the losers were disposed of: into houses of prostitution, or into slavery in Turkey.

The personnel at Silling also included four sex experts: experienced women who acquired their knowledge of the perversions firsthand in their long careers as prostitutes and keepers of bordellos. After all, who should know more about perversions than prostitutes? The women were meant to give a full account of their experiences, whereupon the libertine philosophers would be able "to analyze them, expand upon them, catalogue them, arrange them in a progression, and situate them within an engaging story." Over the 120 days at Silling, the four months from November to March, each of the four whore-narrators would be daily responsible for reciting five anecdotes about various perversions. Thus, each whore would narrate 150 perversions during her month of duty, and the total number of perversions described for the four months would be six hundred. Each of these whore-narrators would have the following literary task:

> . . . to situate within the adventures of her life all the most unusual perversions in her experience of debauchery, and narrated in such order that the first storyteller, for example, would include in her autobiography one hundred fifty of the simplest, the most ordinary, the least complex of all the passions; the second, employing the same method,

an equal number of more complex perversions, involving one or several men with several women; likewise, the third in her narrative would include one hundred fifty of the most criminal perversions contrary to law, to nature, and to religion; and, as all these excesses lead to murder, and as these murders in the name of libertinage are as infinitely various as the inflamed imagination of the libertine contrives new tortures, the fourth narrator shall include in her autobiography a detailed account of one hundred fifty of these various tortures. [46]

The whore-narrators are all fifty and older, and it seems appropriate that the most hideous, Madame Desgranges, comes last and has the most experience in the delights of torture leading to murder. Here is Sade's portrait of her:

> As for Madame Desgranges, she was the personification of vice and lust: tall, emaciated, fifty-six years old, looking gaunt, indeed cadaverous, with dead eyes and pale lips, she was the image of crime on the verge of expiring for lack of vigor. She had once had brown hair; it was even said that she had once had a beautiful figure; soon enough, she had become no more than a skeleton that could inspire only disgust. Her ass, withered, worn, scored, tattered, more closely resembled mottled paper than human skin, and the asshole draped open and hung so wide that the most immense tool could plunge in totally dry without her feeling a thing. To crown these charms, this self-sacrificing athlete of Cythère, wounded in several contests, was missing a breast, as well as three fingers; she had a limp, and she lacked six teeth and one eye.

Whatever the cause of her injuries, her sufferings did nothing to reform her. On the contrary, Sade tells us:

> Her soul remained the repository of every vice and the most heinous crimes. Arson, parricide, incest, sodomy, tribadism, murder, empoisoning, rape, theft, abortion, and sacrilege, one could swear with absolute veracity that there was not a single crime in the world that this jade had not committed herself or arranged to have committed. [49]

With the device of the four whore-narrators, Sade found a way of opening up what could otherwise have been a very claustrophobic and lengthy orgy. Within the locked fortress-prison of Silling high on a mountain peak in the middle of the Black Forest, these women bring onto the narrative stage an entire class of people, libertines, fetishists, perverts, criminals—an entire sub-culture of Paris society.

But far from being merely a device, the whores' stories are central to the meaning of the novel, and are, in fact, its engine, and a very powerful one. The perversions for each month have a common theme, and month by month, this theme increases radically in its repulsiveness. The last month, the reader knows (although he often wishes to forget it is coming), will be devoted to tortures leading to murder. This is made clear from the beginning, and it is this dreadful expectation that inexorably drives the narrative forward. Furthermore, it is also made clear that each of the six hundred perversions will be a unique part of a progression, forming a great chain of being running from simplest and least offensive to most complex and inexpressibly horrific. The fundamental dynamic of this book, therefore, is crescendo. Beginning with snickers (one of the five perversions narrated on the first day concerns a priest whose sole pleasure is to suck the snot out of a girl's nose [102]), the tale will end in horrors and endless, ineradicable screams. To begin reading this novel with this expectation is to display some bravery. To finish it may be more than every reader can bear. It may be enough just to try. And it ought to be tried. For *Les Cent Vingt Journées de Sodome* is one of the most radical, one of the most important novels ever written.

Sade perhaps takes some pleasure in warning "every pious reader to drop the book at once if he would not be scandalized, since it is obvious that the plan is none too chaste, and we dare inform him in advance that the execution will be even less so" (47). But if Sade has scared off the God-fearing reader, he still has the rest of us to deal with. As the narrative of the first of the 120 days is about to begin, he flings his arm over our shoulder, as it were, and addresses us familiarly: "Now, reader-friend, prepare thy heart and mind for the most impure tale that has ever been written since the world began, a book whose like is not to be found either among the ancients or the moderns" (78). This is no idle boast.

Eventually, the libertines' vast entourage, as well as an enormous supply of luxury items and food sufficient for a stay of four months, is transported bit by bit to Durcet's walled fortress-château of Silling. The route takes them through Basel, across the Rhine, and deep into the Black Forest. They then climb a towering mountain by a difficult and dangerous path (reminiscent of Sade's description of his own perilous ascent of the Alps on his trip to Italy in 1775). The peak of this mountain has another defensive feature: it is split by a wide crevasse that plunges more than a thousand feet below. There is a wooden bridge that connects the first peak to the second, on which the château stands. When everyone has crossed over, Durcet orders the bridge destroyed: "From this moment, there existed not the slightest possibility of anyone's communicating with the château of Silling" (63). The château, moreover, has thirty-foot-high walls, a deep moat, and an additional interior wall. As if that were not quite enough, on the last day of October, the day before the 120 days of Sodom are about to begin, Durcet also walls shut all of the doors to the château. When a blizzard strikes, the libertines awake on the morning of November 14 to find themselves isolated in every sense. "It is not to be imagined," Sade writes, "how much licentiousness is favored by such security as this, and what it means to be able to say: 'Here, I am alone, I am at the end of the world, removed beyond every eye and beyond the ability of any creature to come at me; no limits, no barriers' " (225).

Unlike the Bastille, where Sade shivered in the cold and dreamed his dreams, the château of Silling boasted every convenience: private apartments for the libertines, separate dormitories for the young people, a dining room, a semicircular assembly room or auditorium intended for the daily recitations of the whore-narrators and for whatever orgies they might inspire, a chapel (which the libertines convert into a public lavatory for water sports), and beneath the altar of the chapel, reached by raising "a fatal stone" in the floor, a spiral staircase leading down into the bedrock to three iron doors that guarded a vaulted dungeon decorated with a vast assortment of instruments of torture. The isolation inspires this rhapsody: "What tranquillity is there! How secure must feel the villain drawn by crime to this spot with his victim! He is in his own house, he is beyond the borders of France, in a safe country, in the depths of an uninhabitable forest, in a secure haven within this forest which, through the measures taken, could be reached only by the birds of heaven, and there he was in the very bowels of the earth" (66).

This torture chamber recalls the inner room hung with whips and crucifixes to which Sade had taken the prostitute Jeanne Testard in 1763, just as it also recalls the locked room in which Rose Keller claimed Sade had tortured her with a knife in 1768. An isolation cell in a dungeon is the pre-eminently Sadeian space. Sade had spent ten years in various dungeons. Now, in the Bastille, he was writing in a vaulted dungeon room; it recalled the secret places of his own youth in his uncle's fortified château of Saumane, its subterranean cells; it recalled all the other prisons in his life. The Sadeian space is a place beyond civilization, beyond the reach of the law, buried even beneath the sight of God. It is a satanic place where, like Milton's dark hero, Sade could roar rebellion as much as he liked. In prison, as he had been for much of his life, Sade was left alone with himself. He sexualized isolation and peopled his cell with his fantasies. *Les Cent Vingt Journées de Sodome* is a reflection of his distressing circumstances, his sexual preoccupations, his loneliness, his rage. Indeed, it expresses the quintessence of his nature.

For all the rebelliousness of the libertines, it may come as a surprise that the first thing they do when they arrive at Silling is to promulgate "a code of laws" (67), seven pages long, under the unlibertine general heading "Rules." Although most of the regulations specify the absolute deference required of the slaves, some also limit the libertines' freedom. For example, they agree to declare the kitchen staff absolutely out of bounds. Any of them who "breaks this law will pay a fine of a thousand louis" (74). That makes sense: they may be libertines, but they know how difficult it is to find a good cook. Almost all of the other rules are aimed at establishing an absolutely rigorous schedule of daily events. A schoolboy in a Jesuit college or a prisoner in the Bastille would not have had his day mapped out in greater detail.[2] Here is the schedule condensed from the "Rules":

10 a.m.	libertines awakened by four fuckers and four boys.
11 a.m.	libertines take breakfast in girls' dormitory; inspection of their persons and chamber pots.
12 noon	inspection of boys' dormitory, etc.
1 p.m.	chapel—to witness defecation of those girls and boys who have permission to relieve themselves.
2 p.m.	libertines retire to the salon, while dinner is served boys, girls, etc.
3 p.m.	dinner is served the libertines and eight fuckers by the four wives, all naked.
5 p.m.	coffee in the salon, served by naked boys and girls.
6 p.m.	whore narrates five perversions in the assembly room, where the libertines are free to imitate what they hear.
10 p.m.	supper with four fuckers and four boys.
11 p.m.	orgies: everyone present, everyone naked; promiscuous sex *"à l'exemple des animaux."*
2 a.m.	bedtime, each libertine with his fucker, his wife, and anyone else. [68–74]

This program is a joke both on those who conventionally impose schedules in the real world (like schoolmasters, governors of prisons, etc.), and on these anarchistic, nihilistic libertines of *Les Cent Vingt Journées*, who would rebel against everything. Ironically, they try to make anarchy run on time—rather like the way the Nazis ran their death camps. The Italian director Pier Paolo Pasolini found this comparison so compelling that he set his film version of Sade's novel in Italy under the Nazi regime. In *Salo, or The 120 Days of Sodom* (1975), Pasolini turns Sade's libertines into the Gestapo. Their victims—innocent children and anti-Nazi freedom fighters—are all forced to participate in perversions and somehow made to feel pleasure in them. Pasolini's movie is a case of special pleading, arguing that everyone harbors unconscious perversity and that, given the proper inducements, everyone can be made to act in perverted ways. For Sade, however, perversity is not a feature of brainwashing (a modern idea), but of temperament, a genetic quirk. In his view, a pervert is not something one becomes. Perversity is a feature of one's "constitution" at birth; it is the way one is. Pasolini's film is interesting, but ultimately does not capture the power of Sade's novel.

If Silling seemed like a Gestapo outpost to Pasolini, for Sade it was more like school, a symbol of everything orthodox, conventional, and confining that he had always rebelled against. The first whore-narrator, Mme Duclos, in her autobiography on the first day of the 120, jokes that she was in a sense "born into the Church," because her mother had been allowed by the good monks of a monastery in Paris to eke out a living by begging in their church: "But since she looked young and fresh, she soon caught their eye and, step by step, from the church below she ascended to their rooms, from which, in due time, she descended a mother." The first perversion that Duclos narrates concerns a Père Laurent of that same monastery, whose sole passion, one she herself experienced at the age of five, is to introduce a girl of her age to his "monstrous prick," which he then masturbates onto her face (94). Little Duclos earns a tidy allowance in return for satisfying the simple perversions of the priests. The second perversion concerns Père Louis of the same monastery. He gives her a drug to drink and has her squat on two chairs, one foot on each, while he sits on a little stool beneath and masturbates as her urine flows over his penis (95–96). The third perversion concerns Père Geoffroi, who gives little Duclos (she is now aged seven) the same drug to drink and then struggles to arouse his "poor little shrunken member," which produces results only when he signals her to urinate into his mouth (99–100). The fourth example on this first day deals with old Père Henri, whose ecstasy is provoked by the simple act of placing his mouth over her nose and sucking the snot out of it (102). The fifth and final narrative concerns Père Étienne, who gives the catechist Duclos (she is now nine years old) lessons in how to masturbate a man, and he returns the favor, so effectively demonstrating the function of the clitoris that she gratefully swoons with delight (102–4). Thus ends the first day's narratives.

The force that drives the plot, such as it is, of this novel is not so much the activities of the libertines as the relentless narrative imperative generated by the whore-storytellers, who are obliged to relate in increasing order of intensity five examples of perversions each day. These vignettes—some are longer than Sade's short stories—provide the continuing, unifying interest. The reader is always aware that, as offensive as the page he is reading now may be, the next one and the others later on will only be more and more offensive. The lectures take place in the assembly room, a very curious, Sadeian structure. In fact, it is, as Sade says, a theater, semicircular in shape. Against the flat wall of the diameter are several broad steps forming a platform stage, richly carpeted in black velvet with gold fringes. On these steps the libertines' slaves are displayed. Above them, against the back wall, on a throne, sits that month's whore-narrator. On either side of her are two tall columns destined for use in the "punishments," on which hangs every conceivable instrument of torture. Opposite the stage, built into the curved wall, are four mirrored alcoves or niches, one for each of the four libertines. At the back of each alcove, a door leads to a private room in which the libertine may perform acts in seclusion. The novel reveals an obsessive concern with every detail of decor, furniture, and the arrangement and dress of the personnel. The goal is a tableau vivant, a theatrical, stunning, sensual image. The quartets of children are variously garbed in Greek, Asian, Turkish, and Spanish costumes. The whore-narrators are fitted out like the most elegant Parisian courtesans. The libertines' wives are entirely naked, but the four fuckers on duty are colorfully presented in vests and tights of pink taffeta. There is a quartet of two boys and two girls attached to each niche: "Each child in the quartet will have a chain of artificial flowers attached to his arm and going to the niche, so that, when the proprietor wants this or the other child of his quartet, he has only to pull on the garland, and the child will run to sprawl at his feet" (71). This could be a scene out of the Folies-Bergère or the Ziegfeld Follies—theatrical, kitschy, overblown, almost funny, if you did not know what was about to happen next.

The days pass according to the schedule. Each morning the young people are given instruction (another parody of school), and receive tutoring on a practice dummy in the art of masturbating a man. The boys are naturally quicker studies in this aspect of the curriculum than are the girls, at first. The young people are also inspected each morning. Infractions are recorded in a book for later punishment. The most common transgression is the unauthorized use of the chamber pot during the night, thus depriving the libertines of the pleasure of watching and participating in toilet activities in the chapel. Gluttony at mealtime adds to the licentious atmosphere. There is the indiscriminate sexuality of the orgies, as well as the private sex acts at night in the bedrooms.

Mme Duclos, continuing her life story, says that, after the monastery, she entered what turned out to be a not dissimilar institution, Mme Guérin's bordello. There, she observed through a peephole before participating in all of the activities she is about to narrate. On the third day, she describes a client whose sole passion is to suck the saliva out of her mouth (132). Here, as often happens, one of the libertines becomes excited by the narrative and imitates the particular perversion with one of his slaves. Another regular client, an elderly abbé, arrived three or four times a week to suck and pump Duclos's anus with his tongue while he masturbated himself. The act always caused Duclos to swoon with pleasure, but she observed that the Abbé did not seem to be interested in or even to notice her own orgasm. "Men are so peculiar," she muses, "who can say whether he might not have even been displeased to find out?" (133). Another client savors drinking a bidet-full of champagne he first used to cleanse the nether parts of a whore, fore and aft, who had been asked not to wash or even wipe herself for six weeks. The old sot swirls the now brownish cocktail in a glass, samples it, pronounces it superb, and then knocks back half a dozen brimming glasses before masturbating on the whore's buttocks (150). "I understand perfectly," says Durcet, offering a theory of the perversions frequently advanced in this novel: "Boredom alone accounts for all these sorts of infamy." Ironically, it is satiation that provokes libertinism: "One grows bored with simple things," Durcet explains; "the imagination champs at the bit, and the insufficiency of our powers, the weakness of our faculties, the corruption of our soul, all lead us to the perversions" (151). There is something tragic, desperate, even pathetic in this law of the imagination. Sade puts it succinctly in a proverb: *"L'appétit vient en mangeant"* (343); literally, "Appetite increases from eating," or, even better expressed, "Feasting makes you hungry for more."

The principle that the sexual life of the libertine is essentially unsatisfying is inherent in the very structure of the novel. The libertines at Silling imitate the perversions as they hear of them, and each perversion is followed by one slightly more complex, slightly more disgusting than the one before. A cruel economy is seen to operate: for some of the libertines, orgasms are problematical, even impossible, but whatever the case, the next orgasm (if one is possible at all) will require slightly more stimulation, slightly more complexity, slightly more spice than was required to provoke the previous one. Sade portrays the libertines as on an endless quest, really a doomed quest. The real sex organ in *Les Cent Vingt Journées de Sodome* is not the genitalia, but the imagination, which incessantly makes new and greater requirements before it allows the body to obtain the same quantum of pleasure it obtained yesterday with less effort. The libertine must continually run faster merely to stay in place. His situation is like that of the pharaoh who built the pyramid in Samuel Johnson's novel *Rasselas:* "It seems to have been erected," Johnson wrote, "only in compliance with that hunger of imagination which preys incessantly upon life, and must be always appeased by some employment."

The pyramid, "this mighty structure," is to be regarded "as a monument of the insufficiency of human enjoyments."[3]

When commonplace, conventional pleasures lose their charm, when even perfect beauty comes to bore the palate, Sade's libertines are driven to invent new stimulations and to claim as beautiful things no one else would ever think to place in that category. Curval argues, "A certain salt, a certain pungency, is always needed for any sort of pleasure, and this pungency is to be found only in a bit of filth." A mouth that smells of childhood and milk has no appeal, Curval insists: "A mouth that has no odor at all gives no sort of pleasure to kiss." However clean a mouth may be, Curval continues, "the lover who sucks it certainly is performing an unclean act, yet there is no doubt but that it is this very uncleanness that gives him pleasure" (267). Freud regarded kissing as an interesting "point of contact between the perversions and normal sexual life," because even though kissing "is held in high sexual esteem among many nations (including the most highly civilized ones)," strictly considered, "the parts of the body involved do not form part of the sexual apparatus but constitute the entrance to the digestive tract."[4] Most people in the act of kissing are sufficiently aroused by the activity and its ultimate goal that they never think of the mouth as one end of the intestinal tract. Freud rather humorously points up the incongruity in human nature: "A man who will kiss a pretty girl's lips passionately, may perhaps be disgusted at the idea of using her tooth-brush."[5] In kissing, most people can deny the mouth's commonplace function, or indeed idealize it as one of the loveliest and purest sites of the body. In fact, every part of the body is susceptible of this kind of denial or idealization. Sex, for most people, would not be possible if they remained fully mindful of the complaint so well expressed by Yeats:

> But Love has pitched his mansion in
> The place of excrement.[6]

Sade's libertines, however, perversely focus on and celebrate these very elements that most people ignore or find disgusting. As Curval states, "It's always the filthy thing that attracts our fuck: and the filthier it is, the more voluptuously it flows." Durcet agrees: "These are the salts that, emanating from a lubricious object, excite our animal spirits and set them in motion; and who doubts that whatever is old, filthy, or rank does not have a very considerable quantity of these salts, and consequently a greater faculty to provoke our fuck?" (170). Duclos offers examples of clients who cannot be aroused unless they eat vomit (158, 160), swallow farts (161–64), eat menses, eat stillbirths (168), and so on and on and on.

Sade appears to enjoy the considerable possibility for humor in the perversions. For example, he has Duclos relate the following anecdote about Aurore, an otherwise attractive blonde in Mme Guérin's establishment, who had a lovely mouth except for this fault: "Whether for lack of education or due to a poor stomach," she continually let fly "a gale of belches forceful enough to run a windmill." As it turns out, this very fault attracts an ardent admirer:

> He was a learned and serious professor of the Sorbonne who, grown weary of trying to prove to his students, without any success, the existence of God, sometimes showed up at the bordello to convince himself of the existence at least of this charming creature. On that day, he would alert Aurore to eat until bursting. Intrigued by this pious tête-à-tête, I rush to the peephole. The lovers are in the room, and after a few preliminary caresses, all aimed at the mouth, I see our Rhetorician gently pose his dear companion upon a chair, seat himself directly opposite her, and, entrusting his withered, utterly pitiable jewels to her hands, command, "To work, my little beauty, to work: you know what you must do to liberate me from this state of languor. Go to it at once, I implore you, because I feel ready to let fly." Aurore with one hand takes up the doctor's limp tool, with the other she pulls his face to hers, glues her mouth to his, and promptly disgorges sixty belches down his throat. Nothing could describe the ecstasy of this man of God. He was in the clouds, he inhaled, he swallowed down everything she could blast at him. Indeed, he would have been in despair, or so it seemed, had he lost even a single whiff. In the meantime, his hands wandered over her breasts and under my friend's petticoats. These caresses, however, were merely digressive: his primary and singular goal was that mouth brimming with eruptions. Eventually, his prick, swelling from the voluptuous reverberations inspired in him by this operation, discharged at last in my friend's hand, and he hastened away, protesting that he had never had so much pleasure.

Duclos prefaced this story about the burping girl with an aphorism: "There isn't a blemish that doesn't find its admirer" (157).

The professor at the Sorbonne spends his days blowing so much hot air over the drowsy heads of his students, attempting to prove the existence of God with mere words. Humiliated by his impotence as a man and as a teacher, tired of life itself, he obtains a thrilling humiliation by breathing in the inspiring breath of a whore's belly. His fetish—or, to use Sade's word for it, his passion—is a parody of his own life's work, his inquiry into the nature of things. It also recalls what Freud dubbed "the first, grand problem of life," namely, *"Where do babies come from?"*[7] This inquiry is perhaps the source of all intellectual curiosity and science.[8] A puff of wind from the interior may bring a tantalizing hint, a whiff of what mysteries take place within. One may laugh—indeed, Sade tempts one to laugh—at the incredible variety of ways the sex drive takes aim at seemingly nonsexual and apparently disgusting activities.

Sade's sense of humor, like his prevailing mentality, is hyperbolic and parodic. Given a pure, virtuous, gracious, masculine, shining God, Sade will automatically depose him and instead enthrone Mother Nature, goddess of the cloaca and the mere amoral, material world, bedaubed in matter and presiding over randomness and chaos. This extreme vacillation between conscience and id reflects, no doubt, Sade's own weak ego, his own weakness in understanding and dealing with the world as it is. In his life, as in his art, his habitual way of thinking is to reduce things to absurdity by parody. *Les Cent Vingt Journées de Sodome* is a parody of utopian fiction's customary retreat. Sade's heroes, far from being the usual romantic idealizations, are mundane and grotesque parodies of such perfect creatures. Except for the frightful Duc (who is a coward when confronted), the others are ugly old men, suffering from various forms of decrepitude and sexual impotence. Sade's style of portraiture focuses ridicule on their withered penises and flaccid buttocks. His narrow focus on the sexual body is serious, of course, for this is a novel rigidly constructed to elaborate a single issue. But it is also humorous, to reduce the philosophical novel to a catalogue of perversions and to people it with freaks such as these. It is not that Sade is a monomaniac on this subject and does not realize or intend the humorous effects he produces. Certainly there is humor and irony in his solicitously addressing his audience as "dear reader" and "reader-friend." A good deal of his diction and metaphoric language is humorously parodic of romantic style, as when a sixty-year-old tax commissioner prefers to perform 69 with "an old witch" of a whore more than seventy years old—"Daphnis" and "Chloë," as Duclos refers to them. He hauls open the hag's buttocks—"two wrinkled ass-wipes," Duclos calls them, concealing a "repulsive cloaca"—and repeatedly thrusts his tongue in as far as it will go, inspiring Duclos to this romantic description: "The honeybee pumping nectar from a rose does not suck more voluptuously" (176–78). Sade plays with language and metaphor, shifting the context in a surprising way between the clouds and the cloaca.

If Sade is playing against the expectations and conventions of romance, he is doing the same thing against those of pornography. Although Sade is often dismissed as a pornographer, it is worth examining the differences between that genre and Sade's novel. For example, the characters in pornography are idealized, fictionalized, sanitized. Their compliance with the predictable needs of the simple plot is taken for granted. When a person buys such a book or movie, he knows he is getting what he paid for, a reliable commodity with no surprises. The product is desired precisely for its dreaminess, its lack of connection with the lives of real men and women. Whereas pornography tries to allay anxiety, *Les Cent Vingt Journées* seeks to arouse it. Reading *Les Cent Vingt Journées de Sodome* is like staring at a deformity, arousing both horror and fascination. The hundreds of creatures who populate the novel bear no resemblance at all to the virile studs and moaning beauties of pornography. Sade's creatures are parodies of these carefree idealizations. They are highly particularized and realistic, especially in their ugliness and their deficiencies. In this respect, *Les Cent Vingt Journées* is more like a raree show than a sex show. The extremes Sade's characters have to go to in order to get any satisfaction at all (and it often turns out to be a few dribbles of sperm from a still-flaccid penis) are far removed from the readily surging gratifications of pornography. So is Sade's plot. A pornographic work in any medium is generally repetitive, with the same or basically similar acts performed by the same or similar characters over and over, as though in a continuous loop. Sade's plot, however, is deliberately progressive, not repetitive. If the plot and characterization in pornography are conventionalized with the aim of allaying anxiety, *Les Cent Vingt Journées* succeeds in achieving the opposite effect. Sade provokes anxiety. He dares the reader to read on.

Finally, a work of pornography seeks to satisfy the largest possible number of consumers, and thus, except for a limited degree of novelty, offers little variation upon conventional sex acts. Sade's work, again, is different. He warns his reader-friends that, far from arousing them, "many of the perversions that you are going to see depicted here will doubtless displease you." He suggests that the reader consider the book as "a magnificent banquet" with six hundred different dishes. "Choose" the ones you like, he advises, "and leave the rest, without declaiming against that rest solely because it has not the ability to please you. Think that it will please others, and be philosophical about it" (79). Sade's advice will hardly please the consumer of pornography. Georges Bataille, though admiring *Les Cent Vingt Journées*, also understood that the book could not bring much erotic pleasure. "Nobody," wrote Bataille, "unless he is totally deaf to it, can finish *Les Cent Vingt Journées de Sodome* without feeling sick: the sickest is he who is sexually excited by the book." Bataille was right about the novel as a whole, but he probably overstated his point. Sade's mentality is devoted to exaggeration, and his chronicling the perversions in increasing intensity straight through to number 600 is ample evidence of this. Sade does not recommend every one, or even any one, of them. His mission is more an exploration of the depths of the mind, traveling, as Bataille said, "as far as the imagination allows." For Bataille, *Les Cent Vingt Journées de Sodome* is the only book "in which the mind of man is shown *as it really is.*"[9] Two of the Duc's comments perhaps best summarize this point: his statement that their purpose was an "inquiry into the human heart" (117), and his exclamation, "Oh, what an enigma is man!" (298).

Though horrific and unrelenting in probing the depths of the human psyche, the journey on which Sade leads us does have, as we have already seen, frequent touches of humor in language and in the characterizations of the libertines and the other perverts. Humor allows the author to gain a critical distance from the matter he is narrating. Is Sade the monomaniacal sex fiend of myth, merely writing down his own masturbatory fantasies in the Bastille? Or is he bravely and purposefully attempting to write the only book that will show the mind of man as no one acknowledges it to be, but *as it really is?* The answer must be yes to both questions. Sade is the man who felt compelled to conduct sexual experiments with prostitutes and with the servants of both sexes at La Coste, who kept a detailed record of his masturbations and sex fantasies in prison. Of course, some of his own experiences and tastes inspired the creation of the six hundred perversions catalogued in *Les Cent Vingt Journées,* whether they were acts Sade in fact performed or ones he was merely alleged to have performed. But Sade's actual perverse activities represent only a rather tame subset of the perversions and the truly horrifying bloodshed and savage murder whose depiction constitutes the majority of the text. Sade was singularly open to thoughts that almost all the rest of us keep hidden, even from ourselves, and possessed an almost scholarly curiosity about their meaning and origins. (Recall Dr. Iberti, arrested for doing forbidden research into libertinism in the Vatican at Sade's request.) From the beginning, Sade was constantly gathering information that would prove useful in writing his magnum opus. His own experience of the Paris sexual demimonde yielded a wealth of information. He must have liked to listen to stories told by the whores and their procurers, for the pleasure is evident in his decision to organize his novel around the talks given by the four whore-narrators. In that sense, then, the work is autobiographical, an autobiography of the imagination—as is every novel ever written. *Les Cent Vingt Journées* draws on Sade's situation as it was when he composed it, on the experiences of his previous life, and on his fixed mental preoccupations. But to read the work as merely an inscription of the author's own life and impulses is to deny the literary elements in the text that clearly indicate his distance from and his control over the material. Those finely managed elements of humor, parody, and

irony (features typical of his best letters, from the earliest ones on) suggest
that he could not have been the drooling, out-of-control sex maniac of myth
and legend. Sade was, in fact, an author of serious, urgent purpose and considerable creative discipline.

Sade's artistry is evident from the beginning. Some of the perversions that
Duclos narrates are little short stories, displaying a mastery of characterization, plot, and dialogue, in which the technique is as elevated as the subject is
base. Here is a rather comical, and surreal, account by Duclos of her visit to a
shit fetishist:

> Sometimes I used to visit clients in town, and since these trysts were
> usually more lucrative, La Fournier [the procurer] tried to arrange
> them as often as she could. One day she sent me to the house of an
> aged Chevalier of Malta, who opened a sort of cupboard fitted with
> cubbyholes, each containing a porcelain vase in which there was a
> turd. This antique debauchee had made an arrangement with a sister
> of his who was the Abbess of one of the most important convents in
> Paris. This charming woman, at his solicitation, every morning sent
> him containers full of turds from the prettiest of her lodgers. He then
> ranked them and put them in order, and when I arrived, he required
> me to take down one marked with such-and-such a number, which
> was the oldest and ripest one. I presented it to him. "Ah!" he
> exclaimed, "this one comes from a sixteen-year-old, the prettiest girl in
> the world. Frig me while I eat it." The whole ceremony consisted of
> my frigging him and offering him a view of my buttocks while he
> dined with relish, then of dropping on the same plate a turd of my
> own in place of the one he had just swallowed. He watched me do it,
> cleaned my asshole with his tongue, and discharged while sucking my
> anus. Then, the cupboard closed once more, I was paid, and our man,
> to whom I made this visit rather early in the morning, went back to
> sleep as if nothing at all had happened. [227]

The details are humorous, exquisitely organized, and meaningful: the social
position of the "Chevalier of Malta" (Sade's uncle was the Commandeur of
this order), the unwitting providers of his feast being the prettiest young girls
of the best convent in Paris, the connoisseurship involved (numbering, aging,
classifying feces as if they were fine wines), the ritualization, the "ceremony"
attached to this unclean event, the blithe, blissful, almost childlike falling
back to sleep of the satisfied pervert—all display Sade's narrative control and
sense of humor.

Sade's portraits frequently play on the incongruity of the age, high profession, and noble status of the libertines and the degradation and infantilism of their chosen perversion. Such incongruity is the soul of both humor and metaphor. Sade often uses metaphor for humorous effect, as with his comparison of the ass-sucker to a "honeybee pumping nectar from a rose." An elderly chaplain to the King requires Duclos not to move her bowels for at least thirty-six hours before his arrival. Like many of the libertines described, he cannot bear the sight of female breasts and genitalia. (On another occasion, when Duclos's breasts accidentally fall out of her dress—against specific orders—an ancient financier, M. Dupont, who is there to swallow farts, flies into a rage: "The devil take your tits!" he cries. "Who asked to see your tits? That's exactly what aggravates me about all of you creatures: you all have this brazen compulsion to show off your tits" [162].) The King's chaplain above also requires Duclos to be scrupulously covered in front, but otherwise exposed. His pleasure is to masturbate his "minute tool" ("you'd almost need spectacles to assure yourself of its existence") while watching Duclos shit sitting on a commode built to his specifications. But first, to verify that she is ready, says Duclos, "he shoves the middle finger of his right hand into my anus. . . . This augering digit did not have far to go. . . . 'God's balls!' he shouts, 'she's right, the hen is ready to lay, for I have felt the egg!' " (193–94). Sometimes in *Les Cent Vingt Journées*, feces are idealized as "treasure" (202), often as "marmalade" and "jam" (240). Sometimes the humor is numerical, as in the forty-second perversion of the third month: "He sees thirty women a day, and he has each shit in his mouth; he eats the turds of three or four of the prettiest ones. He enjoys this feat five days a week, which comes to 7,800 girls a year" (371). The seventy-year-old libertine has been doing this for fifty years. Sade leaves the reader to do his own multiplication to arrive at the astronomical sum of 390,000.

Sade's style and humor distinguish and separate him from the four libertines of Silling and the hundreds of perverts to be described by the whore-narrators. So sensitive are these four libertines to the incongruity inherent in their perversions that among "the most serious" infractions they list in their "Rules" promulgated on the first day, and one that will be "most cruelly punished," is betraying "the slightest laugh" (73). The reader, of course, not liable to such penalties, may laugh if he feels like it. Camille Paglia, in *Sexual Personae*, enjoyed Sade's humor: "Properly read," she says, "he is funny."[10] Of course, the potential for entirely humorless discussion of the perversions certainly exists. To be convinced of this truth, one has only to read Krafft-Ebing's *Psychopathia Sexualis*, a catalogue of perversions compiled more than a hundred years after Sade wrote *Les Cent Vingt Journées de Sodome*.

Krafft-Ebing gives case studies of some truly horrific sadists and masochists. But there are also milder cases of shoe fetishists (one requires "a prostitute's shoe that was elegant and *chic*"), ladies'-handkerchief thieves ("*Lovers of female handkerchiefs* are frequent, and, therefore, important forensically," Krafft-Ebing observes),[11] and hair-despoilers (one, like the Baron in Alexander Pope's comic poem *The Rape of the Lock*, "when he touched the hair with the scissors . . . had erection, and, at the instant of cutting it off, ejaculation").[12] Krafft-Ebing, who regarded Sade as a "sexual monster,"[13] wrote his book for the use of judges to combat "the decay of general morality," due in part, he felt, to "the present mildness of the laws punishing sexual crimes."[14] But Sade's ability to see humor in the perversions indicates some degree of separation from the humor-fearing perverts he describes, and also from his own perverse tendencies. This humor is a sign of greater mental health than he is often thought to have possessed.

Sade's humor also provides an important insight into the nature of the perversions. A perversion can be seen as an alternative to or, if you will, as a parody of so-called normal genital coitus. The pervert's celebration of and idealization of his particular fetish or his particular manner of obtaining sexual pleasure always contains an implicit reference to genital sex, against which he is rebelling. The incongruity between his particular method and the normal method is always capable of producing surprise and, in a suitable context, laughter. Even in the relatively mild examples already cited from *Les Cent Vingt Journées*, the reader may easily feel wonder and amusement at the sheer idiosyncrasy and inventiveness of the imagination in arriving at a particular variant for sexual satisfaction. It may provoke the same kind of amusement with which grownups greet very young children's explanations of where babies come from. Because these children do not yet really know, their imaginations have a vast variety of possibilities to work with as they formulate their interesting theories. The same is true of perverts. For them, anything at all can become a sexual object and sexual act—just as long as it does not involve the joining of a penis and a vagina. For Sade's perverts, normal sex acts and objects are regarded with the same horror, or amusement, or contempt a normal person feels for the perverts' peculiar solutions.

Perverse sex acts may appear as parodies of genital coitus, but they actually have their source in a period of infancy that precedes any possible knowledge of mature genital sexuality. What is called perversity, then, is every infant's and every very young child's ordinary disposition. Perversion in an adult, therefore, indicates a stunting or a disturbance in normal psychosexual development, in which a child is in effect shipwrecked at an infantile stage of development and can go no further toward normal adulthood. In a very evocative statement, Freud said that it would therefore not be accurate to say that a child has developed into a pervert—that is, "has *become*" a pervert— but, rather, "that he has *remained* one."[15] The residue of perverse infantile sexuality remains in every adult. Janine Chasseguet-Smirgel, the best psychoanalytic authority on the perversions, calls this buried trove "the pervert core, common to us all."[16] Freud himself was far more tolerant toward this subject than is commonly understood. "Even in the most normal sexual" activities, Freud acknowledged, can be seen "rudiments" or features of foreplay such as looking, touching, etc., "which, if they had developed, would have led to the deviations described as 'perversions.'"[17] Freud accepted a certain degree of "uncertainty" with regard to "the boundaries of what is to be called normal sexual life."[18] Who among us will presume to set himself up as the standard for normalcy in this matter? The emotion of disgust, which protects one from a sexual aim that one regards as being perverse, is "often purely conventional"[19]—that is, contingent upon a certain time and a certain culture. It was in this context that Freud mentioned the example of a man's willingness to kiss his lover's mouth though he might nevertheless disdain to use her toothbrush.[20] Freud also pointed out that homosexuality was not only tolerated "but was actually entrusted . . . with important social functions" by the ancient Greeks. He therefore urged a degree of tolerance and humanity on this subject—"We must learn to speak without indignation of what we call the sexual perversions"—and he noted, "The sexual life of each one of us extends to a slight degree—now in this direction, now in that—beyond the narrow lines imposed as the standard of normality."[21] Though it might be tempting to ascribe "severe aberrations of the sexual instinct" to "insanity," even that "cannot be done," for "many people are abnormal in their sexual life who in every other respect approximate to the average."[22] Since sexual perversity, therefore, is a common feature of everyone's mental life, more or less superseded eventually by so-called normal sexual goals, there is in every reader extremely powerful motives to respond to Sade's imagination on this subject—whether through identification, laughter, titillation, horror, anger, or disgusted rejection. These are emotions intimately suited to Sade's subject, and probably experienced universally by readers.

To return to Sade's technique, it is well to take special note of the elaborate, obsessive numbering and cross-referencing of the narration in establishing a continuum of values. Sade makes lists, and it is important that he get his calculations right. Sometimes, he gets them wrong. For example, in the second month's account of the complex passions, Sade skips from number 68 to 70. There is no 69. At the end of the month (December), he finishes with number 151, when there should have been 150, and he adds this reminder to the manuscript: "Ascertain why there is one too many" (384).[23] At the very end of the manuscript scroll, Sade left further editorial reminders for himself. The first calls attention again to the "outline": "Do not deviate in any way from the outline: everything in it has been thought through many times over and with the greatest precision." In another note, he reminds himself: "Do not forget to put in December the scene of the little girls serving supper, squirting liquor into the friends' glasses out of their assholes; you announced it but have not at all included it in the outline" (450). He reminds himself also to reread carefully all of the perversions cited "in order to avoid duplications" (451). And, in case he should need them, Sade adds two "Supplementary Tortures":

> By means of a tube, a mouse is introduced into her cunt; the tube is withdrawn, the cunt is sewn shut, and the animal, having no exit, devours her entrails.
> She is made to swallow a snake, which sets to devouring her in the same fashion. [450]

Thus, although Sade wrote the manuscript of *Les Cent Vingt Journées de Sodome* in thirty-seven days in October and November of 1785, it is clear that he had worked for quite a long time before on his "outline," cutting each piece like a gem, carefully weighing it, and fitting it into its proper setting. The almost hypnotic self-absorption of this kind of activity is evident in the text. The reader can almost see Sade in his cell, with his notes and calendar, arranging his little bits of perversity in graduated progressions.

In one sense, this activity seems humorless, anal, obsessive. But it is a measure of Sade's flexibility and sense of humor that he can also make fun of his obsession. For example, the plan of *Les Cent Vingt Journées* would prevent the narrator, or anyone else, from discussing a perversion until its proper place in the outline. Even at the beginning of the novel, at the orgy on the night of November 5, Curval performed countless "horrors, . . . which, however," Sade regrets to say, "the essential order that we have set for ourselves does not at this time permit us to reveal to our readers" (153). The orgy period on November 7 was given over to inflicting punishments on young people who had committed infractions of the rules, but Sade once more has to admit that he cannot describe these punishments for us. He apologizes fulsomely and ironically, "We are in despair that the order of our plan prevents us from describing these lubricious punishments at this time, but our readers ought not blame us" (171). On November 20, the libertines whisper to each other about a perversion even worse than the one they have just heard Duclos narrate. Again,

Sade will not tell us what was said. It is not because this revelation would be out of order (though it certainly would be). No, this time Sade ironically explains that he is keeping this secret out of consideration for his reader's sensibility: "There are a great many things that one should only allude to; a prudent circumspection is necessary; one can come across some very innocent minds." An author has to look his own conscience in the mirror:

> In the end, whatever one may say, everybody has his own soul to save. And what punishment, in this world or the next, would he not deserve who, without any moderation, pleased himself, for example, by divulging all the caprices, all of the odd tastes, all of the secret horrors to which men are subject in the throes of their frenzy? This would be to reveal secrets which ought to remain buried for the good of humanity. [276]

Marvelous irony, delicate parody of the eighteenth century's intense concern for the morality of art—especially for the new genre, the novel, with its seductive capacity to lure its reader into a close identification with the realistic characters and situations it depicts. Roland Barthes correctly observed that Sade is not erotic: there is "no striptease."[24] However, in *Les Cent Vingt Journées*, where Sade progressively reveals more about sex than most readers would want to know, he frequently does tease the reader by promulgating moral concerns that he obviously does not believe; this same teasing is behind his excuse that the strict plan of the work requires him to withhold information about certain perversions. Sade's metaphor for this ironical self-censorship is drawn from the theater, which, because it was public, was always held to a higher standard of morality. The requirements of his plan "oblige us," he says, "to draw the curtain on what went on" in the private rooms behind the alcoves of the auditorium (303). Each perversion must be carefully fitted into the matrix of the text, must be given its proper place and value. This insistence upon the orderliness of the text is especially at odds with the libertine ethos that says that rules are meant to be broken, that the laws of religion and society are artificial limitations without intrinsic value, and that the only law is the law of nature that authorizes any action for the sake of pleasure. On the one side is this libidinous wildness, this chaos of the polymorphously perverse, and on the other the strict imposition of order, and not simply on the narration, but on the perverts themselves—what they can and cannot do from one month to the next. This incongruity borders on the ridiculous. On the one hand, the chaos of perversion; on the other, extreme narrative tidiness. It is almost a recipe for comedy—a very dark comedy.

Ironically, Sade's narrator is fanatically devoted to a rigid order and a strict control over the flow of the text. The narrator's frequent editorial discussions with his reader about his "plan," about what he is obliged to leave out, and his own notes to himself all call attention to the narrator and to the act of narration. Sade often humorously portrays his narrator's obsession with control. The text itself becomes a straitjacket against which the narrator (and the reader) perversely wishes to rebel. One might say, then, it enacts its own subject: the eternal struggle between order and chaos, reason and madness, mind and body, the head and the genitalia, law and transgression, God and the devil. Yet, for all the rigidity of the narrator's sacred "outline," *Les Cent Vingt Journées de Sodome* is a very volatile text, a very unstable attempt to rationalize and control extremely explosive material.

Sade's theory of sexual perversions that underlies the rigid structure of the novel may not even be correct: namely, that the perversions are progressive. He believed that the disposition to libertinism was a congenital or what he called a "constitutional" endowment already determined at birth (60). The libertine, moreover, is someone for whom sexual release is more problematical than it is for the average person. He immediately becomes bored, jaded, or impotent if he must repeat the same activity that provoked his orgasm the time before. Even to obtain the same quantum of pleasure as he obtained the last time, he must set himself the task of creating a new and more intense sexual perversion by means of variation, experimentation, invention. In this sense, Sade's libertine is a kind of creative artist or poet of eroticism, doomed either to grow and create, or to wither. *Les Cent Vingt Journées* is not just another sex book describing six hundred positions. What is operating in Sade's novel is not even eroticism or pornography, that all-too-repetitive, utterly conventional manipulation of familiar and anxiety-allaying symbols, but, rather, a kind of frenetic, anxious, ultimately tragic *poesis* of the sublime. Simply to remain in place, to keep himself whole, the artist must destroy his old creation and invent a new and better one. If he cannot sustain this spiraling, upward glide of creativity, if his imagination weakens, he dies.

The metaphoric nature of Sade's depiction of the perversions can perhaps best be seen in his probably mistaken portrayal of the perversions as inherently progressive. An individual's sexual style (that is, an individual's sexual object, whether it be the genitals of another person, or the anus, or the mouth, or some fetish, and an individual's method of dealing with that object) is a very conservative structure of his personality, not very liable to change or to therapeutic treatment. One has only to glance through all of the sexual self-help books in the psychology section of any bookstore to realize that changing or varying one's sexual style is a universal wish for which no expert can provide an effective strategy. So, when Sade insists upon the progressivity of his libertines' sex manias, he is either describing an extremely rare kind of mentality or using the idea of sexual progressivity as a metaphor for something else.

The text of *Les Cent Vingt Journées de Sodome* is strange in another important respect. To most readers, it appears unfinished because the full narration of the 120 days ends after the first month, November.[25] Each of the days of November contained a full narrative account of the four libertines' activities, highlighted by their listening to, discussing, and imitating the five fully narrated perversions of the whore-narrator. However, this fully realized narrative treatment is abandoned for the rest of the novel—the next ninety days, in December, January, and February. Instead, Sade merely provides the date with which he is concerned and five numbered, extremely short summaries—until he reaches the 150 required for that month. Occasionally, he adds a brief commentary about what the libertines say or do. But normal narrative is abandoned, revealing the bare-bones outline which would have been the basis for a full account. The effect is shocking and may remind the reader of one of those modern buildings like the Beaubourg Museum in Paris, in which everything is made transparent and turned inside out, so that all of the usual inner workings—the escalators, stairways, pipes for plumbing, electricity, and ventilation—are now on the outside of the structure. After the first month in *Les Cent Vingt Journées*, the reader is suddenly bereft of whatever comfort he had taken in the somewhat companionable, somewhat humorous, somewhat ironic narrator. Now even the voice of the whore-narrator Duclos would be a comfort. She told her stories with narrative skill, some humor, and often some humanity. But when the reader is left entirely on his own, he finds himself in what will progressively become a bare, unconsoling, nightmare landscape of horror. No literary device could more powerfully suggest the dreadful loneliness and interiority of Sade's vision.

In December, we have left the "simple" perversions behind, and we move on to the "second class," or "double" perversions. Here are some examples from this month:

5. He wants to deflower three girls in sequence, one in the cradle, one five years old, the last seven years old. [367]
46. He requires girls A and B to shit; then he forces B to eat A's turd, and A to eat B's turd; afterward, they both shit, and he eats their two turds. [372]
65. He smashes crucifixes, statues of the Virgin and of the Eternal

Father, shits on the debris, and burns the lot. This same man has the passion of taking a whore to church and of having himself frigged while listening to the Word of God. [374]

79. He has himself whipped by his wife while fucking his daughter, and then by his daughter while fucking his wife. This is the same man mentioned by Duclos who prostituted his daughter and his wife at the bordello. [375]

102. He has six girls lie on their stomachs on his dining table, each with a lit candle up her ass, while he dines. [378]

125. He spreads glue on a toilet seat and sends a girl in to shit; as soon as she sits down, her ass is glued fast; meanwhile, a brazier of hot coals is set beneath her ass; she jumps up and leaves a circle of her skin stuck to the seat. [380]

147. He whips only on the breasts; he likes them very big, and pays double when the women are pregnant. [384]

This brief selection represents the odd mixture of taboo, childish prank, and sadistic fantasy that is typical of December's "complex" perversions.

Throughout December and January, the four libertines will celebrate mock (unconsummated) marriages between their young slaves, with the boy "dressed as a bride, and the girl as a groom" (166). The four libertines create a detailed schedule, a "Table," to allocate to themselves the taking of their slaves' double virginities, vaginal and anal (126–27). January's "criminal" perversions, given the progressive design of the work, are devoted to sodomy, bestiality, necrophilia, cannibalism, and mental and physical tortures falling short of murder. Here are some representative selections:

15. He embuggers the priest saying mass, and when the latter consecrates the Host, the fucker pulls out for a moment while the priest shoves the Host up his ass, and the fucker drives in behind. [389]

38. He has a trained snake put up his ass to embugger him while he embuggers a cat held tightly in a basket so it can do him no harm. [391]

58. He shoves a sheaf of fireworks up her ass; the flames fry her ass when they go off. [394]

79. He ties a naked girl stomach-down on a table and eats a very hot omelette off her buttocks with a very sharp fork. [398]

91. He gives her an enema of boiling oil. [399]

98. He draws blood from her arm and does not stop until she faints. [400]

105. He breaks one of her fingers, sometimes more. [401]

121. He makes a eunuch of a boy between ten and fifteen years of age. [403]

141. He cuts off her buttocks after having embuggered her and whipped her. He also eats them, it is said. [405]

146. He chains a mother and a daughter at their wrist; for one or both to live, one has to cut off her hand. He amuses himself watching their debate to see which one will sacrifice herself for the other. [405]

During this month, similar tortures are to be performed on the four libertines' young slaves.

The last month, February, is devoted exclusively to the "murderous passions." The whore-narrator for this month, Desgranges, warns that most of them deal with "extreme cruelty" and very painful deaths (425). The four libertines also ask her to provide details about her murdering perverts' earlier, simpler tastes that led them to their ultimate crimes (412):

1. At first, he liked to amuse himself with a beggar woman who had not eaten for three days; now his passion is to let a woman starve to death in a dungeon, without giving her the least aid; he frigs himself while he watches her, but he does not discharge until the day she dies. [413]

14. At first, he liked to frig clitorises, and now he has one of his servants frig a girl's clitoris until she dies. [414]

21. His earlier passion was bestiality, and now he sews a girl into a freshly skinned donkey hide, with her head sticking out; he keeps feeding her and he leaves her in there until the animal's skin shrinks and squeezes her to death. [415]

35. He used to like to watch a candle stuck in a woman's anus burn down to the end; now he attaches her to the end of a lightning rod and watches her blown up by a thunderbolt. [417]

44. Formerly, he loved to burn a girl with fireworks up her cunt; now he straps a young girl, who needs to be pretty and also rather slender, to a large rocket; she is sent aloft and crashes to her death. [418]

105. A great lover of incest brings together two sisters he had embuggered; he straps them to a machine, each with a dagger in her

hand; the machine is activated, the two sisters are driven together, and they impale each other. [431]

109. . . . He shoves a shotgun charged with grapeshot up a boy's ass he has just fucked, and he fires while discharging. [432–33]

122. After having completely cut off a young man's prick and balls, he gives him a cunt with a red-hot tool that in the same process makes the hole and cauterizes it; he fucks him in this orifice and strangles him with his own hands while discharging. [435]

While Desgranges narrates the murderous February perversions, the four libertines, as before, imitate them on their young slaves. Possibly the worst example, that of Augustine, ought to be given in some detail. After the Duc and Curval torture her excruciatingly (it is impossible to imagine how anyone can still be alive), this is how they finish:

A hole is made in her throat, through which her tongue is threaded; her remaining breast is burned, then a hand with a scalpel is shoved into her cunt and the wall that separates the anus from the vagina is severed; the scalpel now set aside, the hand is thrust in once again, groping amongst her intestines, forcing her to shit through her cunt; then, through the same opening, her stomach is ripped open. Then they return to her face: her ears are lopped off, the inside of her nose is burned, her eyes are blinded and burned with hot sealing wax, her skull is banded with metal, she is hanged by her hair with stones attached to her feet so that she falls and her cranium is ripped open. When she fell, she was still alive, and in this state the Duc fucked her in the cunt; he discharged, but it left him even more inflamed. They cut her open, they burned her entrails in her own stomach, and they thrust in a hand armed with a scalpel to prick her very heart. It was only then that she gave up the ghost. Thus perished at fifteen years and eight months one of the most celestial creatures engendered by nature, etc. Her eulogy. [437–38]

This surgery is an imitation of infantile sexual thought process and rage against the mother. Her breasts are removed; her hidden penis is discovered at her throat; her stomach and womb are proved to contain excrement. Nothing is what is seems to be or what it should be. Throughout the novel, the libertines treated the anus as if it were a vagina. Now, in this final frenzy, it proves possible to deny the vagina and literally to turn it into an anus. The purpose of the experimental surgery is to deny the specialized biological functions of the body and to make them do double service, thus refuting the normal meaning of the two genders and their functions.[26] This hideous example may stand as a paradigm of the sexual confusion of the novel and of the author.

Only one more narrative remains. The last perversion of February is a complicated tour de force; Desgranges calls it "the hell passion" (443). This noble pervert's story is a summary of the entire novel. He has a secret pleasure-house outside Paris where every two weeks he is supplied by procurers with fifteen girls between fifteen and seventeen years of age. Ugly ones are refused. He brands them with numbers indicating the order in which he will receive them for torture. First, he sees each one, deflowering each vaginally and anally (without discharging), whipping each, stabbing each, and tying color-coded ribbons around each one's neck to indicate the final torture he will perform, before kicking each down a trap into the torture chamber below. His devilish assistants have already begun the tortures (much like those of February) when their master descends. He watches the scene from his plush armchair while two of his demon assistants frig him until he finally discharges. Any girls still alive are quickly dispatched by the servants, who then bury their bodies (443–47).

It is over.

There is no novel more scarifying than *Les Cent Vingt Journées de Sodome*. It is certainly a test of the reader's humanity, his stomach, and the absolute limits of his curiosity. Sade's rebellion against the image of God the Father, against the idea of Authority, against his own father and all fathers, against the fact of sexual gender, drove him to invent images and arguments in support of the amoral, perverse, hedonistic Goddess-Mother of merely material nature and mere materialism. Plunging from the grown-up world of meaning, coherence, and compromise, Sade ends by wallowing in an incoherent slurry of body parts and the infantile, primal, inchoate ooze of urine, feces, and blood. *Les Cent Vingt Journées de Sodome* is a transcendent, darkly sublime novel, the most extreme evocation of disillusionment and disappointment, the most unconsoling exploration of the most irredeemable aspects of human nature.

In a letter to Renée on January 22, 1781, Sade wrote of Icarus' fall: "Ever since I saw the rock upon which he had been shattered, I have had a horrible dread of his fate."[27] In the Bastille, with his candle lighting his scroll, and the endless darkness looming above him in his vaulted cell, Sade had stopped writing his tame plays. He had given up pushing yet another star-crossed, kin-crossed pair of lovers onto the conventional stage. Instead, he embraced the radical new eighteenth-century invention, the new genre—the novel.

And, most important, he accepted his own tormented sexual nature and turned it into art and into a metaphor for the unattainable. In *Les Cent Vingt Journées de Sodome*, Sade had soared further downward than anyone had gone before or since. He was right to fear rock. He had become Icarus. And under the rocks of the Bastille, he had been buried alive.

CHAPTER 22

The Revolution

HEN SADE finished copying *Les Cent Vingt Journées de Sodome* onto the manuscript scroll, he rolled it up and hid it in his cell. Penning "the most impure tale that has ever been written since the world began" produced no thunderbolt from the heavens. Life in the Bastille went on in its usual way. Had history not intervened, Sade would have died there.

When Thiroux de Crosne replaced Lenoir as lieutenant general of police in the summer of 1785, Sade wrote him an angry letter minimizing his own sexual "trifles" and portraying himself as the victim of the oppression of the corrupt Montreuil family, composed, he claimed, of "Messalinas," "Sapphists," "committers of incest," "sodomites," "thieves," and "bankrupts."[1] Around the same time that Sade wrote to de Crosne, a new and celebrated prisoner, Cardinal de Rohan, was brought to the Bastille over the scandalous affair of the Queen's necklace. Sade did not mention this event from the summer of 1785, but he might have heard some of the commotion as a crowd gathered beneath the walls of the Bastille to sing derisory ditties about the new prisoner and his fellow conspirators.[2] The disturbances went on for quite some time. By December, Renée expressed impatience: "The affair of the Cardinal," she wrote to Gaufridy on December 2, 1785, "keeps me from visiting the Bastille." She lamented the interruption of her visiting privileges as another instance of her helplessness, sounding a theme that had become increasingly familiar over the years: "It is quite disagreeable to spend your life as the plaything of other people's fantasies."[3]

In June 1786, Renée petitioned Minister of the King's Household Breteuil for increased visiting privileges. However, the governor of the Bastille, de Launay, wrote de Crosne an angry letter on July 7, pointing out that Renée's visits invariably disturbed the prisoner. De Launay characterized Sade as "extremely difficult and violent." Sade refused to follow prison rules during visits and insisted upon speaking in whispers to his wife. When reproved, he made "scenes." When told to speak aloud, "he threw himself with the greatest violence upon Monsieur de Losme," the major of the Bastille. That wasn't the half of it. Governor de Launay pointed out that the police files were "full of letters full of horrors committed upon his wife, his family, and us." The governor recommended visiting privileges be suspended, or at most limited to once a month. He explained that, during times when visiting was denied, Sade was "more reasonable." The governor went so far as to imply that Renée did not really want to visit her husband more often. He suggested that it was only her "goodness and kindness" that prompted her to "ask to see him."[4]

The visits, however, were permitted to resume, and Sade, as de Launay predicted, reacted badly. Once again, in an angry, jealous fit, he attacked his wife. On her visit to the Bastille the following month, she smuggled past the censor this anguished letter to her husband, dated August 22, 1786:

> You are worried, you say, about my conduct. What would you have me do when I love only you in the world? I think constantly of you. I would give a thousand castles in Spain for the moment of your release, for the things we do together, and finally for everything that could contribute to your happiness. The rest of society bores me and I would reproach myself for the slightest satisfaction that I might take without you.[5]

To be sure, Renée's conduct was irreproachable. She lived alone in her poor room in her convent. She saw no one. She had no friends, almost no money. Yet she was changing, even as Paris was beginning to change.

On October 17, 1787, the English poet Arthur Young recorded the conversation going around the dinner table on his visit to Paris: "One opinion pervaded the whole company, that they are on the eve of some great revolution in the government." Everyone understood that the country's finances were in a shambles with apparently unmanageable deficits, and that there was no minister capable of controlling the economy or the government. Meanwhile, Young continued, there was the taunting spectacle of "a court buried in pleasure and dissipation." There was violence in the air, a great sense of "ferment" among the people, "who are eager for some change, without knowing what to look to, or to hope for." Add to this combustible atmosphere "a strong leaven of liberty, increasing every hour since the American Revolution," and Young concluded that any spark could ignite a revolution.[6] Returning home that night, Young remarked with some disdain on the stark contrast between the ill-lit, dirty streets and the frenzied gaiety of Paris night life: "Coffee-houses on the boulevards, music, noise, and *filles* without end."[7] As Young passed beneath the great walls of the Bastille, he thought of the "state prisoners" inside.[8] He was not aware of Sade, but he would have found him an example of the faults of an aristocracy "buried in pleasure and dissipation." The day before Young made these observations on French dissoluteness and financial waste, Sade was upbraiding his wife for the "disgusting" wine she had just brought: "As soon as this letter arrives, despite the rain, Madame de Sade should return to take back the sixteen bottles of the vinegar that she brought yesterday."[9] Long-suffering Renée, like the French people, was also eager for some change.

France was changing—into what, no one yet knew. On June 15, 1788, Renée wrote to Gaufridy about "the present situation." Some people were beginning to go hungry: "The lower sort of people are dying of starvation; which is a great pity." She feared for her son in the military at Rennes: "Until now, nothing has happened to him." The future was alarming. There are only rumors, and "people say so many things!"[10] On September 12, 1788, she wrote to Gaufridy about the worsening financial situation and the turmoil "of crises, of fear, of banknotes and bankruptcies, of joy, of revolt." Indeed, she continued, troops had employed "guns and sabers against the people" to quell a disturbance. It had been too much to bear. Renée told Gaufridy that she had left Paris for the Montreuil château of Échauffour, where she had fallen ill. Now back in Paris, she saw that the city roiled with uncertainty: "The truth is that people say a great many things and that they do not know the truth. The currency rises or falls depending solely on rumors." Her effort to describe these events, her inability to make sense of them, and her own physical weakness were evident in her abrupt conclusion to this letter: "I am stopping now, because I can no longer see clearly since I am so tired; to have been sick has put me behind in many things. Do not worry about me, because I am really much better."[11]

Renée, however, was not better. In a letter to Gaufridy on October 22, 1788, she sounded both distressed and depressed: "I can no longer go out," she said. "The coach tires me." She had seen her husband only two days before, the first visit in a long time: the year before, Sade's privileges had been withdrawn after another row with a guard. Even though that visit depleted Renée, she intended to go again the following week to bring him money that she did not yet have: "I am supposed to bring him another ten louis on Monday, which I will have to borrow."[12] She did go, but she suffered from the exertion. When she sent three vials of eau de Cologne to M. Cauchy of the police for delivery to her husband, she displayed a surprising lack of decorum about her situation: "I offer a thousand apologies for my scribbling," she told the policeman; "I am in bed, where one does not write properly."[13] On November 21, she wrote to Gaufridy: "I have completely lost the use of my legs by pushing too hard, I think." She added, "They say it will improve, but I do not believe it at all."[14] Renée had lost faith in herself, in her husband, and in her world. Although she would recover from this illness, and although she had a long time yet to live, she somehow knew that she would never see her husband again.

An interesting early sign of Renée's disaffection came in the fall of 1786, when Sade had been asking her repeatedly for help with research concerning Spain and Portugal, where he intended to set some of the scenes of *Aline et Valcour*. His first reference to this work, in a letter to Renée on November 9, 1786, suggests that she had long been ignoring his requests. He was "in great need," he told her, "of the Spanish answers," and he begged her to send them "at once."[15] By December 2, Sade had lost patience, and scolded his wife: "In what language is it necessary to tell you that I need for *Lisbon*," among a list of other things, "the name of an inn, of the innkeeper of said inn, of the street where it is situated, and of the neighboring buildings," etc., etc. Renée, it would seem, did not appreciate the importance of the task Sade was giving her. So he explained: "Everything that elaborates the details in a novel, everything that characterizes the setting, adds enormously to its interest. This is a kind of decoration that one could compare to that of costume and scenery in the drama." Such details contribute to "that honesty, that truthfulness, that pathos" that Sade admired in the novels of Samuel Richardson, "who does not take one step in *Clarissa*, in *Grandison*, or in *Pamela* without indicating the street they are crossing or the building they are entering."[16] Sade's admiration of Richardson went beyond a mere interest in realistic details. In *Aline et Valcour*, Sade copied Richardson's eccentric but popular epistolary format. He also imitated Richardson's enormously successful formula of the virgin in distress in *Aline et Valcour* and in *Les Infortunes de la vertu;* in such works as *Juliette* and *La Philosophie dans le boudoir*, he parodied the same formula with his portrayal of brazen female libertines. So it happened that the most sentimental and moral of eighteenth-century English authors had a profound influence on Sade.

But to return to Sade's quest for his Spanish answers. By December 14, he imagined that "this saucy and pretty little *mutiny*, this delay of the Spanish answers," was part of a conspiracy fomented by Renée and her *"allies"* to discover "yet another way of giving Monsieur de Sade fits."[17] Renée must have made an attempt to answer Sade's questions, for on December 24, 1786, Sade insisted on receiving a *complete* answer, and he ended his letter with this embarrassing apostrophe:

One kisses you on both cheeks and appendages, adjoining parts, and abutments.

One asks pardon for the pain that this is going to give Monsieur de Losme in transcribing this letter.[18]

Renée had frequently expressed disapproval of her husband's style in his letters and literary work. As she had written to Gaufridy on July 22, 1785, "With M. de Sade, it is always the same thing: he cannot hold his pen still, and that does him unbelievable harm."[19] In her current mood, she was not inclined to appreciate his rather public private joke about kissing her private parts. Nor did she like the idea of being asked to do research for a novel of which she probably could not approve.

In the past, Renée had sometimes withdrawn into a state of passive resistance to her husband's unpleasant requests. Increasingly, however, her letters displayed overt disapproval, especially on the subject of religion. When Sade criticized her for her inability to obtain his release from prison, she fought back in a letter on April 18, 1787: "Your release is certainly not a matter of indifference to me, because I would give my life to be sure of your happiness"—adding, rather ominously, "in this world and in the next." Renée had never preached religion before in her letters to her husband. But this time, he had said something about Easter, which made her respond that she found the Lenten diet actually restorative: "I am never sick during that time." She accused him of having fallen into "another error" when he had referred to "piety" as being "sad." "You will see," she warned him, "I will not abandon my duty to religion when you are released." At that happy time, he would discover from her example that "true piety is not at all sullen or somber." Perhaps Renée was herself surprised by the strength of the religious fervor she had just expressed, because she immediately moderated her statement: "I will not at all press you to adopt my way of thinking, although I do not cease nor will I cease praying for that, because a forced or unwilling homage cannot please God."[20] Softened as her final thought was, it nevertheless sent a shiver through the man in the Bastille who was thinking through his next novel, *Les Infortunes de la vertu*, whose simple heroine suffers every possible indignity while still absurdly preserving her faith in God. On July 8, 1787, Sade finished copying out a 138-page version of this work, which would later undergo two enlargements.

Sade noticed something new in Renée's character. He complained to her that she seemed different: "You have changed, m'love, during the time we have been apart." Then, as if to tease her, he mentioned that he was at work on another piece of fiction. This was news Renée was unlikely to hear with pleasure. "Adieu," Sade bade Renée, "this evening I am to be busy writing like a beast, like an ass, like a Spanish stallion: so I bid you farewell."[21] His evident pleasure in his work could only frighten his wife.

Sade had been thinking over a novella about incest; in it, a libertine by choice and philosophy educates his young daughter to his own tastes and ideas by depriving her of any contact with religion. He is rewarded with her willing compliance, in heart, mind, and body. Sade wrote this novella, *Eugénie de Franval,* in six days of hard work beginning on March 1, 1788. When the father, Franval, is told that incest is against the law, he exclaims, "What folly! A pretty girl ought not tempt me just because I made the mistake of bringing her into the world?"[22] Then Franval enters into a philosophical argument with a priest, Clervil. Whereas the priest argues the clear moral injunctions of both the scriptures and our conscience, Franval considers these imperatives merely provisional, accidental, and therefore unreliable. If conscience were a sure guide, Franval argues, "would not mankind have an unvarying conscience? from one end of the earth to the other, would not every act be regarded by it in the exact same way?" These are nice questions. Franval continues: "Does the Hottentot tremble at what terrifies a Frenchman? and the latter, does he not every day do what would get him punished in Japan?" Cultural and moral relativism raises a cacophony of voices to drown out the one voice of the one God. "No, Monsieur, no, there is," Franval concludes, "nothing that deserves praise or blame, nothing that is worthy to be rewarded or punished, nothing that, unjust here, is not lawful five hundred leagues from here, no real bad, in short, no reliable good." The priest replies to these sophisms with good common sense, just as Mlle de Rousset had once replied to one of Sade's similar arguments by saying that you do not have to be a physicist to know that if you throw a stone into the air it may hit you on the head. Sade had understood her argument, for he has the priest reply that breaking any local law brings local and reliable misfortune.[23] In the end, Franval suffers for his crimes and kills himself on his wife's coffin amid a thunderstorm of suitably Gothic proportions, thus pointing to the "sole motive" Sade claims for this romantic tale—"to instruct mankind and correct their morals." He hopes, he says, to "be pardoned for the monstrous details of hideous crime that we are bound to describe" in this novella, and he asks the question that may properly be applied to all of his shocking works: "Is it possible to raise detestation for such aberrations if we lack the courage to lay them bare?"[24]

Renée, however, was now more than ever unlikely to be receptive to these matters or to the philosophical arguments they inspired in her husband. When Sade completed *Aline et Valcour,* she dutifully smuggled the manuscript out of the Bastille for him. Then she read it. In the spring of 1789, Renée wrote a long critique of this novel and sent it to him enclosed in a letter on June 14. It is a remarkable document. Strongly, even bravely written, it displays Renée's full understanding of her husband's ideas and of her objections to them. She noted that it was "unfortunate" that there were so many immoral and criminal characters in the novel. She knew how he would answer that objection: "It is necessary, you will tell me, that they should be made known in order to guard against them and to despise them."[25] "That is true," she acknowledged, but she insisted that, if an author sets about describing such characters, he ought merely to allude to their crimes, not describe them in detail; he ought to aim for "a certain deftness of style" to protect a potentially unbalanced or naïve reader, "to deprive a deranged mind of the means of corrupting itself still further." The novel, she admitted, "has some charming and virtuous characters, some thoughts and maxims superb, proper, true." It was all the more "a pity," she insisted, that the "corrupting details make it unreadable by respectable men."[26]

The question of Renée's adequacy as a reader of Sade's work had come up in their recent discussions of this novel. "You reproach me," she noted, "with blinding myself with my principles," to which she replied, "What would you have me use to judge a work which is a product of the human spirit?" She imagined his rejoinder: "One cannot do it, you will tell me, except by rational consideration which weighs the arguments from both sides."[27] Sade, as we know, loved to consider things like incest and murder in the abstract, and he delighted in finding arguments that justified them—in the abstract. "But you well know," Renée countered, "that one can prove with sophisms whatever one likes."[28] In *Aline et Valcour*, Sarmiento, the philosopher of the hedonistic African kingdom of Butua, argues that "virtue is merely relative": "it is false that there are any other virtues than those based upon convention: all are local."[29] Since there is no universal law, no universal right or wrong, you might as well do whatever pleases you. However, Renée insisted that crime "is a reality, and it is because of this reality that the law opposes it in order to restrain it." She refused to have the commandments of her religion and the laws of her nation undermined by invidious comparison with the so-called laws of "savage peoples." They could not, she argued, have real laws: "Laws cannot exist among savage peoples; they ought to change the name, because they do not have the same principles, the savage has no other law than his needs and passions."[30] In *Aline et Valcour*, the libertine Blamont argues with his moralistic wife that the savages walk around "entirely naked."[31] "There are countries," he tells her, "where your duties are illusory, and your crimes are excellent deeds."[32] Renée perfectly understood her husband. She knew he would say that "sodomy and theft were permitted in Greece," as if that fact made such acts acceptable in modern France. As advanced as ancient Greece was, Renée replied, their laws and their religion were nevertheless "faulty."[33] Her husband could adduce contradictory laws and customs from whatever tribes he chose. For Renée, "the variety of the contrasts cannot be an argument in their favor."[34] She believed in one God and one universal law of human nature. "Sodomy is a crime against nature," she wrote, and "theft is a crime because it takes away what belongs to another."[35] It is as simple as that. "Laws made in favor of these things," she said, "cannot deny or change these principles."[36]

As we know, religion had become increasingly important to Renée. It was much on her mind as she wrote her critique of *Aline et Valcour*. Of religion, she acknowledged that "we do not agree,"[37] but she made the case for religion as simply as possible: our religion, she said, asks "us to love God with all our heart and our neighbor as ourselves. He who precisely fulfills these two precepts performs his duty."[38] Finally, she offered a powerful analogy, one that demonstrated that she understood her husband very deeply. She was referring to his habit of sophistical, equivocating argumentation—whether it is to prove that God did not exist or that sodomy was a virtue instead of a crime, or that the incest taboo was merely a local custom. Renée had no patience for these prevarications: "A door," she said, "must either be open or shut. One believes or one does not believe. In the first case, it is not natural to challenge hopelessly what is stronger than oneself. In the second case, one does not passionately argue against what one does not believe exists."[39] She ran straight at the heart of the matter. All of Sade's writing, like all of his behavior, was one side of a dialogue with the God he claimed did not exist. It was all designed to call forth a response, a final answer. *"If you are God, avenge yourself,"* Sade had bellowed before the startled prostitute Jeanne Testard. Just as Renée had developed renewed confidence in her own faith, she now knew that her husband wanted to believe in God. She accepted that religion was based on faith and not the imminent, transcendent certainty that her husband craved. "We would be wise," she advised him, "to submit to Him who made us and not to try to go beyond the limits that He gave to our intelligence."[40]

Renée was finally able to articulate what she had felt through her own experience of her husband, the man who had created a national scandal with prostitutes, seduced her own younger sister, foolishly created another scandal with young servants in her own home, lost his estates, his civil rights, and finally his freedom, yet who had all sorts of peculiar arguments to prove that he was right and everyone else was wrong. He could prove that the state of nature was devoid of limitations and rules and that the social contract was a fraud promulgated by the weak to fetter the strong. He could enshrine a kind of godless, meaningless materialism as the only rule of nature, and he could use cultural relativism to destroy any universal meaning in human nature— all in order to justify his own eccentric, selfish, alienated, and ultimately selfdestructi e feelings and behaviors. He had made a mockery, a parody, of the very idea of coherence—of authority, of meaning, of law, of family life. Essentially, he had destroyed the world and its peoples, their accumulated history of meanings and beliefs. He stood outside experience and reality, and he set everything that was not himself at nought. Even today, and perhaps for all time to come, Sade's name and myth represent a categorical rejection of every value and belief that holds society together. But Renée experienced the man and the myth directly and personally. She saw to what his way of thinking led. She saw the madness of his "signals," his attempts to extract meanings where none existed—a bizarre parody of his specious philosophy that sought to empty the world of meanings that everyone else naturally trusted. Finally, she refused to be swept away into the anarchistic void. Instead, she found her own ground and stood firmly on it.

Renée's critique of *Aline et Valcour* displays not just an understanding of her husband, but a new attitude toward him and toward herself. At the very end of 1788, on December 29, she found the courage to reply honestly to the painful accusations he had made against her in a hidden letter he gave her on her previous visit. His letter, she now told him, "broke my heart." She called him "the most unjust of men."[41] She had finally given up humoring him, treating him like a spoiled and dangerous brat who might throw a fit if she crossed him. For the first time, she said what she thought. As in her critique, her new straightforward honesty suggested that a complete revolution had occurred in the way she saw herself and her relation to her husband. Just as he had feared, she had changed. In the isolation and misery of their long separation, she had grown up, and she had grown apart.

To some degree, it was illness that evoked Renée's religious sense and her courage. She had been ill during the fall and winter of 1788. During the following spring, she continued to suffer. "I begin to be old and disabled," she wrote to Gaufridy on May 11, 1789. She was forty-seven years old, and now needed a servant. "I can no longer go out without someone," she explained. As a consequence, she had grown "fat for want of exercise."[42] On June 22, she wrote again to Gaufridy: "I am in my bed. Do not be worried, that happens frequently now and much hinders me from going about my business."[43] Her physical problems and her religious faith were reflected in her critique of *Aline et Valcour:* "The soul is immaterial and does not die when it separates from the body: it is the body and the organs that grow weak." She repeated this idea, which must have been much on her mind: "Our body weakens by illness, etc., but not the soul."[44] If Renée had found moral courage, she would certainly need it. The world was about to be turned upside down, and she would need all of her strength and her wits just to survive.

On the eve of this tumultuous new year of 1789, Renée wrote to the

Marquis de Launay, the governor of the Bastille, to beg him to provide her husband with "all possible relief and amenities." She asked the governor to "try to watch and see that he stays out of the cold," and to change his room to a warmer one if possible: "The excessive cold must be even worse in his tower."[45] Hippolyte Adolphe Taine noted that this was the worst winter since 1709; by the end of December, the Seine was frozen solid from Paris to Le Havre, and there had been serious damage to crops; a third of the olive trees had been destroyed in Provence.[46] But it was not just the weather that was on Renée's mind. She feared her husband might take his own life, and she told de Launay that it would give her "great peace of mind" if Sade "could have someone nearby to keep an eye on him." On her recent visits, she said, "I find him sad, melancholy. I fear that the length of his detention will throw him into despair, and that something dreadful will befall him in that tower where he is all alone."[47] Some improvements in Sade's living conditions had been made the previous year. He moved to, and redecorated, a better room higher up in the Liberty Tower, on the sixth floor, and he was granted permission to have a personal servant, Mérigot, an invalid soldier. Sade's promenades had been increased to one hour every day on the ramparts of the tower, in addition to his regular one in the courtyard. His visiting privileges were also made more liberal. For the first time, moreover, he was allowed to have newspapers. In the spring of 1789, Sade made a note of the tally of delegates to the États-généraux that was about to convene:

Clergy	134.
Nobility	180.
Commons	191.[48]

Now Sade was able to sense the political turmoil on the other side of the Bastille walls.

The failure of the harvest and the harsh winter added to the suffering and to the political ferment. Sade would have read about the riots in February 1789 at Aix, where he had suffered his own humiliations. Renée kept Gaufridy abreast of the events and the rumors swirling around Paris. On February 25, she wrote: "They say that all is in readiness for the États-généraux. May God grant this and that the general good be done. A rumor is going around that M. de Mirabeau is in the Bastille."[49] Back in Provence, Gaufridy was considering standing as a deputy in the États-généraux. For a change, Renée was able to give *him* some good advice: "It is not propitious to be named a deputy," she wrote to him on April 3, "given the current situation." She very well summed up the danger of the situation: "The great evil is that they have given too free a rein to their imaginations. Too much has been written on both sides. They have gone too far. Can they stop this disease? God only knows."[50] Gaufridy had enough trouble of his own in Provence. On April 15, Lions, the farmer on Sade's Mas de Cabanes, wrote to Gaufridy about violence and about houses burned. "Inform Madame de Sade of this disaster," he told Gaufridy.[51] Mme de Sade, however, would soon be an eyewitness to larger disasters.

On Monday, April 27, 1789, in Faubourg Saint-Antoine, in the very shadow of the Bastille, a riot began at the house and wallpaper factory of Jean-Baptiste Réveillon. On the night of April 28, soldiers quelled the mob by firing into the crowd, injuring nearly a thousand and killing three hundred.[52] Réveillon's neighbor Henriot placed the immediate blame for the riot on a cabinetmaker named Mutel, who the week before had lost to Henriot in the election for delegate to the États-généraux. Afterward, Mutel had threatened and abused his rival in such an irrational manner that Henriot believed him to be the instigator of the riot.[53] One member of the mob, Jean-Thomas Leblanc, twenty years old, said after his arrest that he had merely been swept up by the crowd pushing into Réveillon's street on the afternoon of April 27. He admitted that they all drank the wine from Réveillon's cellars and threw his furniture out the windows. As justification, he explained that he had been informed that Réveillon had said that workers could live handsomely on fifteen sols a day. Leblanc was sentenced to the pillory, to branding, and to the galley for life.[54]

Renée's letter to Gaufridy at the beginning of May[55] described the riot in unusually vivid detail:

> If, dear lawyer, you are alarmed in your province, Paris this week affords a no less distressing tableau. The Faubourg Saint-Antoine and that of Saint-Marceau, where I live, have been the theater of revolution.
>
> The matter or pretext: a man named Réveillon who, as they claimed, supported an ill-considered proposition at the Assembly of the Third Estate. The crime for which they reproached him was having said that a worker could live, despite the dearness of provisions, on fifteen sols a day, both him and his family, and still have a watch in his pocket.
>
> A mob of rascals without jackets or shoes, on most of whom were found marks of the whip and branding iron, had come to force the factories to let out their workers under durance or voluntarily. They [assembled] here in this suburb, armed with large sticks, tools, even

boards. The first day, they charged into Faubourg Saint-Antoine to the house of Réveillon, who had fled, and, despite the guard, too weak to resist three thousand people, they broke, smashed everything, drank the wine, the liqueurs, even including the paint spirits, which poisoned some of them. They burned the notes from the cash boxes, out of altruism, claiming that they were not thieves. But on other days, later, they pillaged, robbed the houses, attacking and overturning carriages, forcing people to give them all their money.

In order to get them to leave you in peace, you had to say that you were of the Third Estate and to accept the staff that they gave you. Their numbers increased to eight thousand. They appeared extremely powerful to me, while the troops, the watch, the constabulary were too weak; what they needed was to call in two regiments of cavalry.

Shots were fired at them; a great many were killed; several hanged; and many locked up in jail. More innocents than the guilty perished: among the swarm of curious onlookers, with everyone looking out their windows. With the rioters above ripping up the roofs, throwing down the tiles, stones, upon the troops, the soldiers hid themselves against the walls and opened fire. So much the worse for those who became targets. There was nothing else to be done. They [the rioters] no longer come into the city. There are still a great many of them outside Paris, but everything is guarded so that they are no longer feared. The soldiers remain on duty to come to the aid of any quarter where they might appear. . . .

At this very moment, someone is repeating to me the words bruited about the streets, incredible as much for their absurdity as for their irrationality and their boldness. The soldiers are always at fixed bayonet, doubled everywhere, and with a reserve force ready to march wherever the riot begins again. Heads are in turmoil for the reasons you mentioned. The Estates will still open on Monday—that is, they will reassemble in order to make their procession to hear the mass of Saint-Esprit, of which there is a great need to restore order to their minds.[56]

Renée sounded frightened. She put her hope in God. Réveillon, for his part, fled from the rioters into the refuge of the nearby Bastille, where he remained for a month, and where he penned his "Exposé justificatif," which begins, "I am writing from the depths of a sanctuary which was the only haven I could find from the fury thrown against me by a frenzied mob."[57]

Réveillon's involuntary companion inside the Bastille, the Marquis de

Sade, viewed the event only as it concerned himself. Réveillon's presence was interfering with Sade's promenades, so Sade penned this "humble request" to Major de Losme on May 29:

> Because the numerous visitors to M. Réveillon require me to spend my hour of promenade in my room, I ask Monsieur the Major to try, until M. Réveillon returns to his store, to allow that my hour in the courtyard be changed for one on the ramparts of the towers, which seems to me to be absolutely the same thing, since no one goes there and it would suit me better.[58]

At this time, Renée had a larger vision and a more sensitive soul. Her heart was in pain for those who suffered: "What is most piteous is the extreme misery of the poor," she wrote to Gaufridy on May 11. "There are many people dead of starvation." Although "the revolt here is completely quelled," she continued, "soldiers are everywhere." It was unclear what would happen next: "People spread a thousand rumors; it is impossible to discern the truth." She reported on the tumultuous session of the États-généraux. She apostrophized the French character that shouts for liberty and vengeance, yet in the same breath whimpers for a leader: "O! Frenchmen, how fickle you are! You display the rope, but you end by wanting to be led! What will come of all this? God knows, but not a single Frenchman."[59] Renée's commentary on *Aline et Valcour* contained a sentence illustrative of her good common sense and prophetic of the bloodbath that would occur one month later, on July 14, 1789. She argued that it would be impossible to re-establish perfect equality among individuals in the real world: "Equality is illusory, doubtless, in a state long in existence, and to re-establish it there after a number of years passed under different forms of government, . . . a sea of blood would be necessary, and they will not achieve it in the end."[60]

In her above letter to Gaufridy of May 11, Renée enclosed a note given to her by her husband that very day, on her visit to the Bastille. This is what Sade wanted Gaufridy to send him from La Coste: "The two small vases of painted metal which are on my desk, intended for flowers; they are on either side of a small painted cartouche. They must be packed in wool or cotton and placed in a small box." Renée urged Gaufridy to act with haste, "since you know him to be always in a hurry and impatient."[61]

When Sade wrote to Major de Losme on May 29 about restoring his promenades on the ramparts of the tower because Réveillon had disrupted them in the courtyard, he did not realize, or else chose to ignore, that the cannon on the towers were being readied for firing. In writing to Major de

Losme, Sade ridiculed the governor's preparations for the defense of the Bastille. Sade mocked the "thousand airs and affectations, one more ridiculous than the other," displayed by Governor de Launay when he "supervised the parade" of his ragtag troop of soldiers in the courtyard of the Bastille. Sade had been to war. He knew the character of soldiers. He saw what would soon prove all too true: de Launay was "afraid," he told the major. It had been obvious "for a month now."[62] But Sade returned to his own problems concerning the promenades, as he asked the major, "Must I suffer for [de Launay's] terrors?"[63]

On June 8, a week after her husband's complaint to the major about Governor de Launay, Renée visited the Bastille, carrying a hidden letter. She promised her husband that she would go see Lieutenant General of Police de Crosne. In the meantime, she urged Sade to be more polite to the officers: "Abstain from telling them things that displease them; you see what that leads to."[64] It is surprising that Renée braved the streets at this time. Arthur Young noted that on this date Paris was in "a ferment." A day later, he wrote, "Everything conspires to render the present period in France critical; the want of bread is terrible."[65] Renée had indeed seen de Crosne, who at this time was under intense pressure. In a letter on June 14, Renée patiently explained to her husband that, though de Crosne had in fact visited the Bastille, the official, because of "the great deal of business that he has," could not make time "to go speak with you."[66] It was in this letter that Renée enclosed her long critique of Sade's novel *Aline et Valcour*. She visited her husband on the following day, June 15. On June 20, the Commons, having declared itself the National Assembly and thus having effectively destroyed the États-généraux, met at the Jeu de Paume to take the Tennis Court Oath. Renée wrote to her husband the next day to explain that her "usual indisposition"—hemorrhoids—would force her to miss her visit.[67] On June 22, the day she would have gone to the Bastille, she wrote more honestly to Gaufridy about the political crisis. She described things as "pretty calm on the surface," but only because of the presence of "the soldiers who enforce" order. However, the National Assembly, she added, "are firing the people up with their harangues." For the first time, she used the word "revolution." Some provocateurs, some "scoundrels," she said, were arrested for cutting down the wheat "prematurely."[68] This was her last letter to Gaufridy until after the Revolution.

Events now moved quickly. On June 24, Arthur Young wrote, "The ferment at Paris is beyond conception; 10,000 people have been all this day in the Palais-Royal."[69] "At Versailles," he added, "the mob was violent," attacking members of the nobility and the clergy.[70] On June 26, he saw that revolution was inevitable: "Every hour that passes seems to give the people fresh spirit."[71] Riot was now a common occurrence. The normal garrison at the Bastille, consisting of sixty men from the Hôtel des Invalides, was strengthened. There were fifteen cannon charged and ready on the towers and three more in the courtyard. This was the very moment Sade chose to kick up a fuss over no longer being allowed to have his regular promenades on the ramparts of the tower.

On July 2, 1789, Governor de Launay was "obliged" by "the current circumstances"—as he reported the next day to M. de Villedeuil, minister of the King's household—to order the suspension of Sade's promenade privileges. "It is impossible to allow him promenades on the towers," de Launay explained; "the cannon are loaded, and that would risk the gravest danger." Sade flew into a rage at Lossinote, the turnkey who conveyed de Launay's new orders, and he rushed to his window. It was noon. A mob had been gathering all morning beneath the walls of the Bastille. According to Governor de Launay's letter to M. de Villedeuil, Sade "appeared at his window and shouted with all his strength, and was heard by the entire neighborhood and by passers-by, that they were slaughtering, they were assassinating the prisoners of the Bastille, and that people ought to come to their aid." Even when Lossinote tried to explain to Sade that he could still "take his exercise in the morning and at night in the courtyard," Sade was not appeased and threatened "to renew his shouting."[72] Additional details are reported by a contemporary writer, Pierre Manuel, who claims to have learned them from Lossinote. Sade, according to Lossinote, "swore" that he would "cause a dreadful uproar" if the turnkey did not immediately return with "a favorable reply" from the governor. When de Launay refused to change his orders, Sade ripped off a pissing tube from the wall. This implement, consisting of a tin tube with a funnel attached, was used for dumping waste into the fosse, which functioned as both defense and sewer. Sade used the pissing tube as a megaphone to shout his "invectives against the governor." It was a perfect Sadeian emblem, this pissing tube: like his novels, it served to exaggerate discourse and to connect language to the lower depths. Sade's violent rhetoric "gathered quite a crowd" on the rue Saint-Antoine. He "called upon the citizens" to come to the aid of the prisoners he claimed were being slaughtered.[73] A year later, in 1790, Sade recalled in a letter to Gaufridy that he had caused "a bit of trouble" at the Bastille "over the annoyance they gave me there": "From my window, I inflamed, they said, the minds of the people, I gathered them below this window, I warned them of the preparations being made at the Bastille, I exhorted them to rise up and throw down this monument of horror. . . . All that was true."[74] After the Revolution, Sade would turn this moment of rage into the selfless, patriotic act of a victim of one of the ancien régime's most despotic powers, the lettre de cachet. This was the sort of story a citizen in revolutionary France might embellish and live on for a great many years.

However, on July 3, 1789, Governor de Launay had more to worry about than his troublesome prisoner in the Liberty Tower. He wrote to M. de Villedeuil, "This is a time when this man would be very dangerous to keep here." The governor argued that it was "absolutely necessary" to transfer Sade, "whom nothing can restrain, and over whom no officer can gain any control."[75] He suggested a more suitable institution for dealing with the sort of person he understood Sade to be: Charenton, the insane asylum run by the Brothers of Charity. In eleven days, de Launay would be dead, his head paraded through the streets of Paris on a pike.

On July 3, 1789, Minister Villedeuil at Versailles transmitted the King's order to move Sade to Charenton. For a few moments at Versailles, the name of the Marquis de Sade fluttered across the royal consciousness. How much thought had been given to the man who had been locked away behind the walls of royal prisons for more than twelve years? The order was signed; the seals were affixed. On the same day, at twelve midnight, the turnkey Lossinote and six soldiers entered Sade's cell in the Bastille. They were accompanied by Commissaire Pierre Chenon and Inspector Asmodée Quidor, who were in attendance, as they explained in their report, for "the purpose of affixing our seals to the door of his room the moment he left it to be transferred to Charenton" in order to "safeguard his property in the aforementioned room." These two officials duly reported: "We affixed our seals on a band of paper which crossed the opening and the aforesaid Monsieur de Sade affixed his seal beside each of our seals."[76] Then Sade was hustled into the dark night by six soldiers who conducted him by coach to Charenton. "In accordance with the ancient practices of ministerial despotism," as Sade described the event to Gaufridy in the spring of 1790, "they did not allow me to take anything with me. I left naked as a babe."[77] Up on the ramparts of the Bastille, the nervous sentries watched the streets below. The cannon were primed and loaded with shot. On the sixth floor, the two bureaucrats had been busy affixing their seals to paper strips across the door. How quickly would these strips and that door yield to the mob ten days later, when they plundered the Bastille and took away Sade's possessions!

Almost a year later, as Sade wrote to Gaufridy in the spring of 1790, the bitterness of this loss still burned in his memory: "All my possessions, that is, more than a hundred louis of furniture, of clothes, or of linen, six hundred volumes, several quite expensive, and, what is irreplaceable, *fifteen volumes of my works in manuscript,* ready for the press, all these things, I say, were put under the seal of the Commissaire of the Bastille, and Madame de Sade *ate dinner, went to the toilet, took confession,* and *went to sleep.*"[78] On October 1, 1788, Sade had drawn up a detailed catalogue, his *Catalogue raisonné,* of the works in various genres that he had already written, as well as those he planned to write. He expected they would come to fifteen volumes: they included two volumes of plays, four for *Aline et Valcour,* four for his stories, one for his short novel *Les Malheurs de la vertu,* four for a miscellany of essays, stories, and his travel books on Holland and Italy that he called *Le Portefeuille d'un homme de lettres.*[79] Sade did not think fit to list the manuscript he had hidden in his cell, *Les Cent Vingt Journées de Sodome,* but it too was left there when Sade was removed to Charenton. These were works that during his imprisonment, he said, "had consoled me in my isolation, and which, by easing my loneliness, had allowed me to say: 'At least I have not wasted my time!' " Over their destruction, he said, "every day I shed tears of blood."[80]

Sade, of course, did not know and would never guess the bizarre fate of his manuscript scroll containing his best novel, *Les Cent Vingt Journées de Sodome.* After the mob had carried off the more obvious plunder from the Bastille, one Arnoux de Saint-Maximin purportedly discovered the scroll hidden in Sade's cell. It was kept for several generations in the family of the Marquis de Villeneuve-Trans and then sold to a German collector. A German psychiatrist, Sade's first modern biographer, Iwan Bloch, published a faulty limited edition of 180 copies in 1904 under the pseudonym "Eugène Dühren." Finally, in 1929, the Sade scholar Maurice Heine was authorized by Vicomte Charles de Noailles to purchase the manuscript. Heine carefully edited the text and then published it in three volumes from 1931 to 1935. This text forms the basis of all subsequent editions.[81] How pleased Sade would have been! But in 1790, writing about his loss to Gaufridy, he said that the pain was too much to bear: "It tears my heart so cruelly that it would be better for me to try to forget this misfortune and never speak of it again to anyone."[82]

Sade would not get over his anger at his wife for allowing the loss to occur. In another letter to Gaufridy in the spring of 1790, he repeated his lament over the loss of his "manuscripts, six hundred volumes of books, two thousand livres' worth of furnishings, valuable portraits, all torn up, burned, taken away, pillaged, without my being able to find a shred; and all that through the sheer negligence of Madame de Sade." Sade's voice rises off the page in a cry of anguish: "My manuscripts, for whose loss I cry tears of blood! . . . One can get back beds, tables, bureaus, but one cannot get back ideas. . . . No, my friend, no, I can never express to you my despair over this loss; it is irreparable for me." Sade could not understand why Renée did not collect his belongings after he had been moved out of the Bastille on July 4. "She had had ten days to get my things out of there; she could not doubt that the Bastille, which for these ten days was being crammed with weapons, powder, soldiers, was being readied either for *attack* or for *defense*. Why, then, did she not rush to remove my things?"[83]

What had Sade expected of Renée? By July 1789, the streets of Paris had become very dangerous. Mobs formed in an instant. The most incendiary speeches were made and believed. Sometime in June, Renée fled Paris for "the country," as she explained to Gaufridy on July 23. Perhaps she had gone to her parents' château at Échauffour, or to one of her uncles' houses closer to Paris. In any case, she made the mistake of returning to Paris "on business" on Monday, July 12.[84] It was a bad day. There had been disturbances throughout the night. Lieutenant General of Police de Crosne barely escaped with his life when his *hôtel* was sacked.[85] There was rioting the next day, July 13, when the Saint-Lazare Convent was pillaged and burned by a mob in search of wheat.[86] In Charenton, Sade was anxious about his possessions and manuscripts. On July 9, he had written a legal document to Commissaire Chenon, giving Renée the power to unseal his cell and obtain his belongings.[87] "Unfortunately," as Sade sarcastically expressed it in one of his letters to Gaufridy in the spring of 1790, "the day she decided to awaken from her lethargy was the very one when the people marched in a mob against the Bastille."[88] According to a manuscript written by former Lieutenant General of Police Lenoir, on the morning of this fateful day, July 14, 1789, Renée appeared at the door of Commissaire Chenon. However, the outbreak of hostilities prevented their leaving his house, which doubtless saved their lives.[89] The mob went on to storm the Hôtel des Invalides without opposition and to take away thirty thousand rifles and ten cannon stored there.

At the Bastille, Governor de Launay, believing he had negotiated safe conduct for himself and his staff, lowered the drawbridge. A massacre ensued. De Launay, already wounded, Major de Losme, and Aide-Major de Miray were dragged and beaten through the streets to the Place de Grève, where they were killed. A young man, Desnot, tried to cut off Governor de Launay's head with a saber but failed. However, since the lad was an assistant cook and knew a bit about butchery, he produced a small knife and finished the job. One of the mob rifled the pockets of the headless corpses, but, being an honest man, turned in what he found. The records show that, among the gold watches, purses, keys, there was also a "gold box engraved with scenes of gardening."[90] Governor de Launay had denied the Bastille garden to the prisoners and kept it for himself and his fruit trees. The gold box with gardening scenes, it would seem, had been his.

If only Sade had kept quiet ten days earlier, he too would have been freed and glorified by the revolutionaries, along with the seven remaining prisoners in the Bastille on July 14. These included four embezzlers imprisoned since 1787, as well as the three transferred with Sade from Vincennes: Tavernier, who, imprisoned since 1759, had become insane; the Comte de Whyte de Malleville, who was insane; and the Comte de Solages, who had been committed by his family for incest. Unlucky, that shouting through the pissing tube. Locked in a cell in Charenton, Sade would have envied the other prisoners' celebrity and freedom. As soon as the four embezzlers had been liberated, they naturally disappeared. De Whyte and Tavernier, being quite mad, soon proved to be not of much use to the revolutionaries. They followed Sade to Charenton, de Whyte on July 15 and Tavernier five days later.[91]

During these days of revolution, after Renée suffered her narrow escape on the morning of July 14, she remained in her convent. As she wrote to Gaufridy on July 23: "I went three days without closing my eyes. There is no image to describe everything that was said and done. You had to have seen it to believe it, and our descendants will think that that was exaggerated." It was not until July 19 that she felt the streets safe enough for her to leave Paris. Even then, she left "without any baggage and with but little money, because with those I would have been brought to the Hôtel de Ville." Renée did not long stay away from her convent. When she returned, she learned that Sade's uncle, the Commandeur, had suffered a fit of apoplexy in his house at Toulouse at the end of July. She also learned that Sade's aunt the Comtesse de Villeneuve had immediately gone to the Commandeur's château at Saint-Cloud to bring back to Mazan two cartloads of the dying man's possessions. He died on September 20, leaving M. de Montreuil, his fellow executor of Sade's estates, now in sole control. Provence, like everywhere else, was in turmoil. On August 21, Ripert's son, writing to Gaufridy, reported, "At Mazan, the populace are beginning to cry out against the lords and the priests."[92] Arthur Young, who had fled Paris and was then passing through Besançon, decried the violence there:

Many châteaux have been burnt, others plundered, the seigneurs hunted down like wild beasts, their wives and daughters ravished, their papers and titles burnt, and all their property destroyed; and these abominations not inflicted on marked persons, who were odious for their former conduct or principles, but an indiscriminating blind rage for the love of plunder. Robbers, galley-slaves, and villains of all denominations, have collected and instigated the peasants to commit all sorts of outrages.[93]

When Young arrived in Avignon on August 27, he paused to pay homage at the grave of Petrarch's Laure at the Church of the Cordeliers. Without displaying any recognition of the fate of the current possessor of the title, he noted that on the wall adjoining the grave was a stone "with the armorial of the family of Sade."[94]

The summer of 1789 saw the Declaration of the Rights of Man and the abolition of all privilege. On September 1, Renée wrote to Gaufridy from Paris, "People here are in a constant frenzy": "They are in a state of perpetual fear; they are terrified by the intemperance of writings and of words and of the daily papers that are circulated. . . . One dares not speak or even think out loud until decent folk take over. We have twelve thousand rogues in the Bois de Boulogne."[95] Nobles who fled the country, she thought, "would be wise not to return until all is calm." Among them was the Prince de Condé, Sade's old playmate whom he had punched all those years ago. The force of these historic events, as well as Renée's growing sense of independence from her husband, produced a new vibrancy and candor in her letters to Gaufridy. Here is one in its entirety from September 17, 1789:

Here, one is in constant need of bread. It is the confusion of the Tower of Babel. Everyone wants to be the master. One must hope that the frosts of winter and hunger will set people's heads straight; the babble will be seen as serving no good purpose.

You can be sure only of what you see with your own eyes. You must listen to everything and say nothing. The harvest was excellent and there is wheat for three years if it is not squandered. . . .

Banditry has been more prevalent here than anywhere else, with the consequence that the peasants do not dare bring in the harvest for fear of being shot in the back. Complaints have been made which were received and heard. The King himself—shots have been fired beneath his windows and at the game he himself was hunting.

I look upon this as a river over its bank or as a watch whose mainspring is broken. All the arguments in the world, all the calculations will not make it work; it is the mainspring that needs replacing.

Everyone here is armed, and many people have gone over to England. . . .

M. de Sade is well. . . .

I perceive that I am losing my memory, tired out for the past two months listening to everything that is said, thinking, reflecting, replying, scheming; the mental tension of guarding against compromising oneself, of distrusting everyone one meets, of not knowing with whom one is living, of hearing forceful arguments, yet not daring to repeat them or to applaud them, it would truly be much better to be in the galleys; at least there one knows what one has to do. I have, however, taken a resolution that I follow as much as possible, not to read or to hear read any of the pamphlets that are sold.

The poor are increasing in number; commerce is ruined; no or very little appearance of taxes. All this is too harsh to last; the chaos, such as it is, will bring back order.[96]

By October, Renée decided to leave Paris for her parents' château at Échauffour. As on July 14, October 5, the day she moved, proved to be a very bad one to go out. Political frenzy and lack of food drove the women of Paris to riot that day. The women broke into the Hôtel de Ville, set it on fire, disrupted the National Assembly, then, gathering momentum, marched to Versailles, whence they led the King back to Paris on October 6. Renée described the events and her flight in a letter to Gaufridy on October 8:

I am safely out of Paris with my daughter, a chambermaid, without a lackey, following the general flood in a hired carriage so as not to be caught up by the female revolutionaries who by force were taking all the women out of their houses to go and seize the King at Versailles and to make them march on foot through the rain and the mud, etc. I have arrived safe and sound; I threaded my way through back streets and I am now here. The King is at Paris; they led him into the city, the heads of his two bodyguards on lances in front, and from there to the Louvre. They are drunk with joy in Paris because they believe that the King's presence will bring them bread. What is the province going to do? It will, like everyone, open its eyes and see the consequences. God alone knows what will happen, because mortal understanding could never comprehend it!

On October 24, Renée again wrote to Gaufridy, explaining her reasons for leaving Paris—not cowardice but hunger:

I am in the country, not that I am afraid of the lantern [i.e., of being hanged from a lamppost] or of the man with the large beard [i.e., the state executioner] who cuts off people's heads, but so as not to die of hunger, and also because I do not have a sol, which makes me await with impatience hearing from you.

. . .

My elder son has arrived on a leave of absence. I will keep him by me as long as I can, so that he does not go about, for fear of roving brigands, etc. A baker has been killed. He went through horrors that make one shudder; some of the culprits have been hanged. That will not give life back to the others. If only this could stop the scoundrels! They are so numerous as to make one tremble. It is said that a devilish plot has been uncovered.[97]

By November 26, Renée was back in Paris, where daily life was, if possible, even more precarious than before, as she explained to Gaufridy:

> We are continually threatened with slaughter. . . . Going to bed, one is not certain about the morrow. Two days ago at the Palais-Royal and at the market, they were stealing shoe buckles and earrings, they were making you turn your pockets inside out on the pretext of bringing everything to the Treasury. . . . In the future, no one will ever believe what happened here. . . .[98]

The danger continued. On December 15, Renée wrote to Gaufridy again, but disguised her handwriting and left the letter unsigned. "This is the way," she lamented, "in which decent people have to behave."[99]

When Arthur Young returned to Paris on January 3, 1790, he found the citizens obsessed with a "devotion to liberty" that he characterized as "a sort of rage."[100] He was shocked to see the King under guard and the Queen followed around by a "mob."[101] On February 4, the King attended the National Assembly for the Swearing of the National Oath. At night, outside the Hôtel de Ville, Mayor Bailly led the citizens in reciting the oath. There were fireworks and celebrations. Renée described these events to Gaufridy with a sense of humor that had not been evident in her before:

> Now they pray to God in the streets and they cry *"Vive le roi!"* in the churches. They will chant a *Te Deum* on Sunday; the Assembly will attend. The King has been to Notre-Dame; do not ask me why, because I know nothing about it.
>
> They swear a new oath in the middle of the squares; on the ramparts they light torches; and all for the same reason. Several members of the Assembly are refusing to swear the new oath. They would like to have it explained; they are told that what has been decreed has no need of explanation.
>
> One woman, in the enthusiasm of having sworn, this was a woman of the people, someone asked her what she had said. She retorted: "I raised my arms to heaven, and I said: *'Vive notre bon roi!'*" Another

man raised his hand to the same quarter and said that, if it was required that he lift his leg, he would have done it. Then he saluted his masters, declaring that they were no '*istocrats*. At a public speech, there was a proposal to make M. de La Fayette general of the entire kingdom and M. Bailly mayor general of the entire kingdom.[102]

On March 11, 1790, Renée wrote to Gaufridy about the almost random terror: "The watchword for doing harm is to say: 'This is an aristocrat; he wants to free the King,' and he is immediately hanged without due process!" There was a man in prison in the Châtelet confined by just such an accusation. He seemed to enjoy the prospect of being hanged. He said "in all seriousness that it was not six thousand men that he enlisted" to free the King, but "six hundred thousand." Ever since this man had witnessed M. de Favras hanged in the Place de Grève, Renée explained, "he conceived an incredible wish to be hanged, which appeared to him the greatest pleasure that could be given." This anecdote could easily have found a place in *Les Cent Vingt Journées de Sodome*. "This is an extraordinary lunacy," Renée concluded.[103]

Renée's letters to Gaufridy during the aftermath of the French Revolution display her humanity, her religious faith, her sense of humor, and her courage. She had come through great sufferings in her life. Finally, at the age of forty-eight, with her children grown, she had made peace with herself and with her religion. She had become an interested and interesting observer of her world. She had also decided what to do about her husband. A few days after her letter about the lunatic who wanted to be hanged, the National Assembly would vote to abolish lettres de cachet, one of the last vestiges of royal authority. Her husband would soon be free.

"Amidst Madmen and Epileptics"

F SADE had found the Bastille inconvenient, he was in for a very unpleasant shock when he was transported in the middle of the night of July 3–4, 1789, to Charenton, to "languish," as he wrote to Gaufridy, "amidst madmen and epileptics."[1] The Brothers of Charity had run an asylum there from the middle of the seventeenth century. Some of the rooms, or cells, were worse than anything Sade had experienced in the Bastille or imagined in *Les Cent Vingt Journées de Sodome*. Cages, iron collars, manacles, chains were common forms of restraint. There were also wickerwork cages approximating the human form into which patients could be locked. Violent or obnoxious inmates were chained in cells below ground level, where there was no ventilation or light, and where the walls dripped with humidity and excrement. As Sade wrote to Reinaud, his lawyer at Aix, "I have yet to understand how I did not die there!"[2]

The asylum at Charenton stood on the southern edge of the Bois de Vincennes, high on a bluff overlooking the Marne River. On the other side of the *bois* was the château of Vincennes. The prison and the madhouse. Metaphorically and in fact, that is where Sade lived the greater part of his mature life, almost twenty-nine years.

In 1785, Minister of the King's Household Breteuil had appointed a committee to examine the hospitals of Paris. One of its members, Jacques Tenon, published his findings in *Mémoires sur les hôpitaux de Paris*. "Hospitals," he pronounced in his first sentence, "to some degree, are the measure of the civilization of a people."[3] In general, Tenon concluded that the hospitals were sorely wanting, including Salpêtrière, the Hôtel-Dieu, the Hôpital de la Charité at Versailles. He found them unsanitary, poorly run, and overcrowded. The hospital at Versailles had 182 people in eight rooms.[4] There were often four to six people in one large platform bed.[5] Of some of the latrines, he said, "It is necessary to see these horrors in order to be persuaded to believe them."[6] Tenon took special note of the insane. Writing even before the Revolution, he pointed out the potential abuse of administerial imprisonment of the supposed insane: "Before removing the insane from society, one owes it to them, one owes it to oneself, to take the trouble to determine if their illness is or is not incurable. It is only after having exhausted all possible resources that it is permissible to submit to the sad necessity of depriving a citizen of his freedom."[7] In 1788, Louis-Sébastien Mercier in his *Tableau de Paris* described the usual inmates of Charenton as "madmen, imbeciles, libertines, debauchees and spendthrifts." However, he noted, "The place is pleasantly sited."[8] Everyone remarked on the beauty of the spot.

In the eighteenth century, with its obsessive emphasis on reason and rationality, madness was the universal bogeyman. Ladies and gentlemen paid visits to the asylums of Bedlam in London or Bicêtre near Paris to gape at the madmen and so to reassure themselves of their own sanity. Philippe Pinel, often called the father of modern psychiatry, ended this practice when he supervised the hospitals of Bicêtre and Salpêtrière. In his influential treatise, *Traité médico-philosophique sur l'aliénation mentale ou la manie* (1801), he noted the harmful effects of "the thoughtless jests and barbarous provocation of idle and unfeeling visitors."[9] Pinel refused to regard lunatics either as amusing freaks or as men beyond the reach of rational influence. In particular, he rejected the "very general opinion, that mental derangement depends upon lesions of the head, and especially upon irregularities and disproportions of the cranium."[10] Rather, he believed that many forms of madness were not organic and could be susceptible to what he called his "moral treatment."[11] He sought to humanize the treatment of the insane and to rely on controlled and careful conversation with his patients to get at the sources of their torment and to bring them as much as possible to reason. When he first began to treat the insane, he noted that "the furious and extravagant maniacs were perpetually chained down in their cells," and their "cries, howlings and tumults echoed, at all hours, throughout the melancholy mansion."[12] Although Pinel did not rule out organic treatment, he did try to minimize its use. "My faith," he wrote, "in pharmaceutic preparations was gradually lessened."[13] He also criticized "the usual routine of baths, blood-letting and coercion."[14] A member of the committee of the school of medicine charged with inspecting Charenton in 1796–97, Pinel noted the presence of "a reservoir of cold water for what is called the bath of surprise."[15] At Charenton, the patient to be treated with this shock therapy was strapped into a chair. He was suddenly inundated with a jet of very cold water under great pressure. The physician who took control of Charenton in 1826, Jean-Étienne Esquirol, preferred to call "the bath of surprise" a "terror bath."[16] He came to see that "insanity was curable in many instances, by mildness of treatment and attention to the state of the mind exclusively."[17] With regard to bleeding, the common eighteenth-century remedy for just about any disorder, he wrote: "The blood of maniacs is sometimes so lavishly spilled, and with so little discernment, as to render it doubtful whether the patient or his physician has the best claim to the appellation of a madman."[18]

If the often barbarous treatment of the insane reminded Sade of some of the tortures he had invented in *Les Cent Vingt Journées de Sodome*, the asylum at Charenton was no fiction. Whatever prison Sade entered, he always found ways of testing the resolve of his keepers, of finding the limits and trying to manipulate the system. At the Bastille, the governor had certain restrictions to his powers when dealing with a noble guest of the King. However, the Brothers of Charity and their staff had more latitude in dealing with Sade's outbursts. At Charenton, no doubt, Sade experienced some of their harsher measures. His knowledge of these measures is revealed in a letter he may have intended to publish.[19] In it, he warned his fellow citizens that "they deceive themselves . . . when they imagine they have buried the Hydra of despotism under the debris of the Bastille!" Sade charged that, when the government really wanted to get rid of someone, they did not send him to the Bastille, "they entombed him in the catacombs of Charenton." Sade envisioned something like the Stalinist subversion of the psychiatric profession. The honor of the career soldiers who had administered the Bastille had put some limit, Sade argued, on crimes against the prisoners. However, there were no such limits on the monks at Charenton, those "befrocked scoundrels." He described the subterranean rooms: "Four bare walls, damp, infested with insects and spiders undisturbed for a century at least; a miserable chair and a rotten table." There was a trapdoor in the wall through which the guard could feed the inmate without having to enter the room. Those who made the slightest complaint about the accommodations or the wretched food were beaten. Sade called upon his fellow citizens: "Come, throw down the ungodly walls of these menacing retreats; come and set free the miserable creatures imprisoned there."[20] If only part of what Sade complained about were true, it would appear that he was much worse off at Charenton than at the Bastille. This letter is very much like his shouting out the window of the Bastille. It was becoming increasingly clear to the staff at Charenton that Sade was trouble.

Six months after Sade's transfer there, Eusèbe Boyer, the Prior of the Brothers of Charity, sent the National Assembly a detailed list of the ninety-three inmates committed to Charenton by "royal order"—that is, by lettre de cachet. They had been variously diagnosed as "imbeciles," "madmen," "sporadically mad," "dangerously mad," "maliciously mad," "furibund madmen," "demented," and "mentally deranged."[21] On January 12, 1790, the Prior explained to the president of the National Assembly why he had omitted a detailed account of "the reasons for the detention of M. le Comte de Sade": "because the enumeration of them would have been too long and because he is generally known to the National Assembly." Perhaps it was Sade's reputation, more than any actual misconduct, that appeared so threatening in the churchman's mind. In any case, the Prior continued, "I earnestly solicit" the National Assembly "to be so good as to relieve me of this sort of person or to authorize me to keep him locked up, so as to protect this institution from the dangers that threaten it."[22] Prior Boyer's urgent request came at a time when the National Assembly was debating legislation to eliminate lettres de cachet. With regard to Charenton, Mercier complained in 1788 that, although the asylum "was not intended to be a state prison," it had nevertheless become one, "as people are imprisoned there by lettre de cachet." "It fills one with anger," Mercier continued, "to see the friars of the Charité turned into jailers and their hospitals transformed into petty bastilles."[23]

In March 1790, the National Assembly abolished lettres de cachet and set up procedures for deciding on the fate of those who were then in custody. There were three options: criminal charges; recommittal to a hospital for the insane; or outright freedom. All of Mme de Montreuil's efforts were in danger of being undone by the Revolution. On March 23, 1790, she wrote to Gaufridy about the recent decree of the National Assembly. Gaufridy should not be surprised, she told him, by her own silence on matters of estate business, and by Renée's evident "indifference" to these same matters. They had much more urgent concerns on their minds. The mother and daughter had grown closer, to judge from Renée's trips to the family estate at Échauffour during the revolutionary troubles. They had discussed the impact of the decree of the National Assembly and agreed on a course of action. Mme de Montreuil understood that the wording of the decree "can provide for exceptions." That is, "in certain situations," families could petition to have their wayward relatives formally committed. However, with regard to her son-in-law, she and Renée had decided "to remain neutral and to let the administration, or the public, decide how the case should be judged."[24] Mme de Montreuil did not want to create a special case concerning her son-in-law, because that would only reopen old scandals and cause new publicity. But she would not have given up control over her son-in-law were she not absolutely sure from her discussions with Renée that her daughter had no intention of being reunited with him once he was free. Indeed, Mme de Montreuil and Renée must have already begun making the legal arrangements for the separation decree that was granted by the Châtelet a few months later.

In March 1790, Sade's two sons, Louis-Marie, now over twenty-two years

old, and Donatien-Claude-Armand, now almost twenty-one, informed Mme
de Montreuil of their intention to visit their father at Charenton to tell him of
the change in the law concerning lettres de cachet. Mme de Montreuil told
them, "I hope that he will be happy, but I very much doubt that he knows
how to be."[25] Sade's sons came to see him on March 18. According to Sade's
account of the visit in a letter to Reinaud, they walked around the grounds of
the asylum and had dinner together. Sade reported that one of his sons
"decided to ask the Prior one day by what right and what authority he kept
me there." The Prior fumbled for an answer, mumbling something about the
request of the family, "not daring to cite the orders of the King, whom no one
any longer acknowledged." Perhaps overdramatizing this encounter for Reinaud's benefit, Sade reported that he then told the Prior, " 'Oh, then these
orders, Monsieur, are even much worse today than those of the minister. I
recognize them no longer! . . . *I command you to open the door.*' The rascal did
not dare resist; the double doors opened, and I bade him good night." Sade
had been in Vincennes, the Bastille, and Charenton for more than thirteen
years, since February 13, 1777. He concluded the anecdote about his release
with a literary flourish: "There, I think, you have exactly our maxim: *There
isn't such good company that you never want to leave.*"[26] He was free.

CHAPTER 24

"Free at Last"

SADE left Charenton on April 2, 1790—Good Friday. "A good day, a good deed," he quoted the proverb in a letter to Gaufridy on April 12. Sade promised his pious friend that he would commemorate this holy day and "sanctify it" for the rest of his life with "moaning and weeping": "Each time that the forty-fifth day of Lent brings us a Good Friday once again, I will get down on my knees, I will pray, I will offer up thanks. . . . I will make a resolution to mend my ways, and I will keep to my word."[1] His charm was such that his friend may have almost believed him.

To be sure, Sade was happy to be free after being locked up for more than thirteen years. But to whom should he be grateful? To what should he dedicate the rest of his life? He was almost fifty years old, and he felt older than he was. Both angry and depressed over having wasted the prime of his life in prison and over the loss of his manuscripts, he wrote plaintively to Gaufridy sometime after April 14, 1790:

> In prison, I have lost my eyes, my lungs; but I have gained, for lack of exercise, a corpulence so enormous that I can scarcely move; all my senses are deadened; I no longer have appetite for anything; I love nothing; the world that I was foolish enough to miss so much, now seems so tiresome to me . . . so dreary! . . . There are times I feel driven to become a Trappist monk, and I do not guarantee not to disappear one fine day without anyone's knowing what has become of me. I have never been so misanthropic as when I came back to live among men, and if, in coming among them again, I seemed alien to them, they can be quite sure that they are producing the same effect in me.[2]

It was with mixed emotions that the Marquis de Sade entered Paris on the evening of April 2. Everything was the same and yet totally different. The world he had known had been overthrown, and it would continue to revolve and change almost daily. It would be an interesting question—really a matter of life and death—whether a noble of the blood, now virtually impoverished and tainted not just by scandal but, more importantly, by class, could adapt himself to the new conditions and survive.

Sade's situation was desperate indeed, as he wrote to Gaufridy on April 12: "I have fallen in the middle of Paris with one louis in my pocket, without knowing where to go, where to sleep, where to eat, or where to get some money." He went directly to the rue du Bouloir to find the house of M. de Milly, the lawyer who had managed his business affairs in Paris for the past twenty-six years. M. de Milly was "kind enough," Sade wrote, "to offer me a bed, board, and six louis." But M. de Milly's Eastertide compassion lasted only four nights. By April 6, Sade was forced to fend for himself. With the 3 louis that remained, he "was obliged, so as not to be a burden, to find an inn, a servant, a tailor, a cook, etc."[3] He found lodgings on the same street, in the Hôtel du Bouloir. That same day, April 6, he wrote to Gaufridy to announce his freedom—"I am free at last"—and also to take control over his estates from M. de Montreuil. Sade made this clear to Gaufridy: "It is only with me that you will have any business." Sade's most pressing concern was money, for "the main thing is to eat." He urgently asked Gaufridy to advance him "a thousand écus at least," which would see him through July.[4] Food was scarce and expensive. "The storekeepers," Renée had written to Gaufridy on March 11, "refuse to sell" for the devalued banknotes.[5]

As soon as Sade arrived in Paris, he tried to see his wife at the Convent of Sainte-Aure, but she refused him admittance, as she wrote to Gaufridy the next day, April 3.[6] She understood that her husband wanted money, but she "informed" him that it was to Gaufridy "that he must apply in order to get some money." By now it was absolutely clear to Sade that his wife was serious about seeking a divorce. "He wants to see me," Renée wrote to Gaufridy, "but I replied that I was still intending to separate, that it could not be otherwise." Her determined tone and her refusal to permit Sade a visit (she knew how persuasive he could be) showed that her mind was made up. She asked Gaufridy to send her belongings from La Coste to her mother's house in Paris.[7] The marriage in which she had endured so much heartache was over. In some ways, it had been easier to deal with her husband in prison, as an object of compassion, or as a very demanding child who wanted this sort of sweet or that package of books. Finally, she had had enough. She was forty-eight years old, and she had come to value her privacy and her solitude in the convent. She did not want to see her husband again.

When Sade wrote to Gaufridy around this time, he professed not to be surprised by Renée's decision. "Quite a while ago," he wrote, "I noticed something in the way Madame de Sade behaved when she visited me at the Bastille which caused me anxiety and some pain." Now he chose to blame his wife's decision on the convent: "I clearly descried the instigations of her confessor and, to tell the truth, I also plainly saw that my freedom would bring a separation."[8] In the past, Sade had indulged in jealous and irrational sexual fantasies about Renée and his servant Lefèvre. Now he imagined a priest had come between them. Sade railed at his wife for choosing, as he put it, "to *languish pleasantly* in a convent where some *confessor* doubtless consoles her, smooths the path before her of sin." Sade's anger went deeper than his hurt pride and injured feelings. The separation would strike at his wallet. He would have to repay his wife's dowry, "one hundred and sixty thousand livres," Sade exclaimed to Gaufridy. "Alas, great God!" he cried out against the Montreuils, "this separation is going to ruin me, and that is exactly what these monsters want."[9]

Sade, however, swallowed his pride and applied to "these monsters" for assistance while he waited for money to arrive from Gaufridy. Through M. de Milly, Mme de Montreuil agreed to advance Sade 1,200 livres to pay his bill at Charenton and to defray additional loans from M. de Milly.[10] Sade preferred to hide the extent of the loan from Gaufridy, telling him that it only amounted to "several louis." He once again urgently asked Gaufridy "not to permit any sort of delay" in the forwarding of the 1,000 écus he had requested earlier.[11] His almost continual badgering of Gaufridy for money would become the main feature of their correspondence and of their relationship. For example, prompted by a letter from Lions, his agent on his estate at the Mas de Cabanes, containing excuses but not money, Sade exploded in a letter to Gaufridy on June 23:

> I get, along with yours, a letter from M. Lions, who tells me that the *sheep have not been sheared.* . . . F[uck] the sheep, my dear lawyer! Do you think my butcher and my baker will settle for being told: "Messieurs, my sheep have not been sheared"?
>
> Yes, yes, laugh, lawyer, laugh! . . . I am deeply delighted to make you laugh, but still send some money, or you are going to put me in the most troublesome situation and the most cruel financial straits. It is impossible for me to wait more than two weeks.[12]

Sade would always need a scapegoat on whom he could focus his rage and frustration.

In preparing for the legal battle over the separation agreement, Sade tried to bring Gaufridy firmly onto his side against that "abominable family" the Montreuils. "You have no idea at all," Sade told him, "of the *infernal* and *cannibalistic* dealings those people have had with me." Now he also included Renée among his persecutors. "The sensitive and refined Madame de Sade no longer wants to see me," he lamented. The separation, he said, would "ruin" him—financially, to be sure, but also in terms of his reputation, for the charges against him in her suit would "validate all the slanders spewed against me."[13] In another letter to Gaufridy, Sade complained that Renée's petition was full of "horrors, lies, and prattle" that could only do him harm: "All of the disgraceful things bruited about me in the cabarets, in the guardroom, compiled in the almanacs, in the stupid newspapers, form the basis of this lovely document; the most atrocious and shameful things are scandalously invented in it . . . slanderously related."[14]

Sade told Gaufridy that he had been given advice, which he had followed, not to contest the separation. Renée had displayed a very strong determination to "hold" to her decision, as she explained to Gaufridy on June 13, a decision that "was made after hard and carefully weighed thought by me for a long time." She adopted a very firm and clear line of attack (possibly suggested by her mother): if Sade contested the separation, Renée would be obliged to reveal his past sins. As for the "notoriety," she told Gaufridy, "I will only say what he will force me to say in order to justify myself. *But I will say it if he forces me to it.*"[15] The uncontested separation agreement filed at the Châtelet on June 9, which obliged Sade to pay back the dowry of 160,842 livres, did indeed contain references to the Marseilles affair and its legal consequences.[16] "I will be condemned by default," Sade acknowledged in the above letter to Gaufridy, "but not utterly ruined," he hoped. He agreed "to pay back the money drawn upon the dowry," but he was confident that "they cannot touch my property." With Gaufridy's help and management, he said, "my affairs in Provence will always be in such a state that I will not be obliged to beg alms."[17] As always, Sade was more hopeful than realistic in his reading of the separation agreement.

Sade's letters from this time reveal his mental and emotional confusion. As would become increasingly plain, he had utterly misunderstood the financial details of the separation agreement. In some letters he appeared overly confident; in others, he poured out his anguish for Gaufridy's benefit: "Oh! Madame de Sade, what a change in your heart! . . . What horrible treatment! . . . My friend! . . . My dear lawyer! If you knew the humiliations this woman caused me! . . . I write with tears in my eyes, I can say no more for now!" In another odd emotional appeal, Sade said that he would come visit Gaufridy in Provence, and then, he said, *"I will be ready to die where I was born."*[18] Sade, of course, had been born in the Hôtel de Condé in Paris. Wouldn't Gaufridy have known that? But the rhetorical flourish, the gesture of expiring on Gaufridy's native soil, was too appealing for Sade to resist. His attempts to manipulate, to charm, always contained a fairly obvious trip-wire that could blow the whole thing up. Sade always left a clue to indicate that he knew that the target of his charm knew he was being bamboozled. This was his way of retaining his honor in the midst of a humiliating exercise, flattering Gaufridy, buttering him up.

Sade had not yet seen his wife since his return to Paris. He was reduced to communicating with her indirectly through his sons. In April, he sent them a list of requests to pass on to Renée. He also wanted an accounting of the linen she had sent to him, "because I perceive that they have stolen a good deal from me at Charenton." He wanted the small watch in her possession that might have been his. Sade's lack of money and even of clothes can be seen in his inquiry about "the three coats that I had at Amblet's." Very much on his mind were the manuscripts Renée had smuggled out of the Bastille for him, his plays in particular, from which he now hoped to earn fame and fortune.[19] Renée was not helpful. Sade complained to Gaufridy, "She refuses to give them to me." She had informed him that she was "fearful that these works (too strongly written) should cause . . . harm at the time of the Revolution." Renée, Sade explained, had "entrusted them to individuals who burned some of them!" Of course, the most painful loss was the scroll of *Les Cent Vingt Journées de Sodome*, presumably destroyed in the sacking of the Bastille. Sade told Gaufridy that he had found out where the refuse from the Bastille had been taken: "I did find a few items in the places where the papers from the Bastille were thrown out, but nothing important . . . some wretched things, but not a single work of any consequence. Oh! I give up all thought of it, I give it up! Just God! This is the greatest misfortune that heaven could have devised for me!" It is a memorable image. The Marquis de Sade, enormously fat, enraged, and mumbling execrations against his wife and his fate, rummaging through a garbage dump. Some of his prison habits died hard, he told Gaufridy: "I still sometimes talk to myself when there is no one there at all."[20]

On May 19, 1790,[21] he wrote to the Aix lawyer Reinaud in an attempt to repair relations and to impose his own view of his long imprisonment. He blamed everything on the Montreuils, "these rascals, these scoundrels." Most significant is Sade's description of the current political situation, and his explanation of why he could not soon return to Provence:

> Some matters essential to settle here, and also the fear of being hanged in Provence from *democratic gallows*, will keep me here until next spring. At that time—that is to say, at the beginning of March— I expect to go to Provence with my children. Those are my plans,

Monsieur, those that I will perform, if God and the enemies of the nobility permit me to live. At these words, however, do not go and take me for an *enragé* [i.e., a radical]. I declare to you that I am merely impartial, sorry to have lost a great deal, even sorrier to see my sovereign in chains, confused by what you Messieurs in the provinces fail to understand: namely, that it is impossible that good can come and continue, so long as the authority of the monarch will be coerced by thirty thousand gawking soldiers in arms and twenty cannon; but, moreover, regretting very little else of the ancien régime; certainly it had made me too wretched for me to cry over it. There you have my profession of faith, and I make it fearlessly.

You ask me for some news: the most important today is the Assembly's refusal to allow the King to meddle in issues of war and peace. It is the provinces, moreover, that provide the news that occupies us the most: Valence, Montauban, Marseilles are the theaters of horrors where the cannibals daily perform bloody dramas, in the English style, that make your hair stand on end. . . .

Ten months after the Revolution of July 14, Sade's "profession of faith" made him appear a political moderate with very strong sentimental ties to the idea of the monarchy. He broke off his invective against the bloodthirsty revolutionaries as if the danger of such statements had just dawned on him: "But enough of that," he told Reinaud. "It is necessary to be prudent in one's letters, for despotism never unsealed them as much as liberty does." Sade also ended his letter by noting that he was purposely making no reference to being Reinaud's most humble servant, etc., such a formula being considered unrevolutionary: "That is a vestige of our centuries of slavery which liberty ought to banish."[22] Thus, in a single letter, Sade tried to navigate between the two extremes of French politics. There was good cause to be prudent. On the same day that Sade wrote to Reinaud, May 19, Ripert's son wrote to Gaufridy about the fighting that "still goes on continually in this province and in the city of Avignon." Ominously, he added, "Even as I write to you, I hear the drum beating to call the people to perform some farce or other." Just sending such a letter could be dangerous, and he urged Gaufridy to be "circumspect" with the servant delivering it.[23]

The previous month, Sade had been depressed enough about his situation to want to join a Trappist monastery, but he soon came to see that he would have to make his own way in the new world following the Revolution. He had always been able to charm women. He knew his way around the theaters of Paris. Despite his somewhat exaggerated claims about his lost manuscripts, he nevertheless had in his possession a number of plays that he hoped would be put on stage. And he had also acquired an influential lady friend. As he wrote to Gaufridy, there were "at least a few roses among so many thorns." That is, he informed Gaufridy, "I am lodged at a charming lady's." She was Marguerite Fayard des Avenières, La Présidente Fayard de Fleurieu, "forty years old," a married woman, but "separated from her husband," who was head of the department of finances of Lyons. Sade described her as a woman of "intelligence" and "talents." Sometimes he stayed at her country house. "She inundates me," Sade claimed, "with kindness." She also rented him a small apartment "for one hundred écus a year" opposite her house at No. 7 rue Honoré-Chevalier, in Saint-Sulpice Parish. "I can scarcely turn around in it," Sade said, "but I am decently and agreeably housed: pretty view, good air, good society." Sade also tried to improve things with some relatives on his mother's side of the family, "Madame the Comtesse de Saumane, first lady in waiting to Madame Élisabeth, the King's sister," and also "M. and Madame the Comtesse de Clermont-Tonnerre (a name celebrated in the Assembly)," who, Sade claimed, "shower me with kindnesses and courtesies."[24] Sade was happy to impress Gaufridy with the mention of such luminaries.

Sade had begun to adjust to the new world. He had begun to pay and receive visits: "I have found several acquaintances, several lady friends." But he was quick to add that these relations were strictly Platonic, that "absolutely no other sentiment than friendship is involved in our relationship." There would be, Sade assured the pious family man Gaufridy, "no more impure pleasures, my dear lawyer, no more heterogeneous pleasures." His new morality, he claimed, had come about as a result of his suffering in prison and from the continuing physical ailments he contracted there: "The exhaustion from all that does not leave me enough energy, thank God, to think of anything else, and I find myself four times happier." Sexuality, he claimed, "disgusts me now as much as it formerly inflamed me." However, as will become evident, Sade did not take up chastity, nor is it likely that his sexual nature had undergone any profound transformation. Sade was probably trying on a moral persona for his religious lawyer (who was also Mme de Montreuil's confidant). The financial negotiations over his separation were much on his mind. If, as it turned out, he would not have much money, there would be no *petites maisons*, no extra funds for actress-courtesans. Nevertheless, he had begun to enjoy a social life. "I feel that I need to open up," he told Gaufridy; he recognized that "society is necessary" to him. He felt that his "misanthropy," developed during his long years in prison, was finally "remitting somewhat." He now felt that "the Trappist monastery will no longer suit me."[25]

Sade had already begun to go to the theater. His reference to becoming a monk put him in mind of a play he had just seen by d'Arnaud "which is set in the Trappist monastery," he told Gaufridy in the above letter. "The only actors are monks," he continued, "the only setting a cemetery and some crosses. They are murdered onstage, so much have we become Engishmen— what am I saying? savages!—cannibals!"[26] It is more than a little strange to see the author of *Les Cent Vingt Journées de Sodome* inveighing against the bloody English style of drama, but the times themselves were bloody, and the former Marquis who now prudently called himself "Louis Sade" was worried about his own neck. He would be lucky to keep it.

CHAPTER 25

Citizen Sade

O N JULY 1, 1790, Sade filled out his citizenship card, signing himself "Louis Sade." He delivered it to his section of the Place de Vendôme, later called the Section des Piques, one of the most radical of all the revolutionary sections of Paris and the spawning ground of Robespierre himself. Sade made himself right at home, telling everyone who would listen about his having suffered thirteen years of imprisonment as a victim of "ministerial tyranny" under the hated lettre de cachet. As he gained confidence in his ability to move in the new world, he learned the new courtesies, the new code words, that would enable him to get by.

In particular, he alluded frequently in his speech and writing to the harangue he delivered to the mob on July 2, 1789, just before the taking of the Bastille. He needed to remind everyone of his revolutionary credentials, and this became a story he told over and over, improving the narrative until he had it just right. He even wrote to Minister of the Interior Paré for a copy of the July 3, 1789, letter in which Bastille Governor de Launay described Sade's actions for Minister Villedeuil and demanded Sade's transfer.[1] Sade would refer to his copy of this letter on many occasions when his loyalty to the Revolution was called into question. The Bastille and Sade, Sade and the Bastille. He wanted those names firmly joined in people's minds.

"In Paris," Sade explained to Gaufridy, "it is a great honor to have been" in the Bastille; "you boast of it, you publish it, and that brings you a kind of respect."[2] Gaufridy, whose sympathies lay with the monarchy, had been forced to flee his town of Apt to hide out. Sade urged him to take courage, to return, and to follow his own example by staring down the slanderers: "I have done the same here. They wanted to gossip; I made them shut up by showing myself everywhere and by not retreating."[3] Bravado, perhaps. But these were dangerous times. Sade appears to have enjoyed inventing his new persona of revolutionary hero. It was like playing a role in one of his plays, swearing to ideas he did not believe in, embellishing events into things they were not, denying things that had actually happened.

On July 14, 1790, a few months after his release from Charenton, Sade felt confident enough to attend the first-anniversary celebration of the Revolution. For months, workers had been preparing a vast amphitheater in the Champ-de-Mars, capable of holding four hundred thousand people.[4] The volunteer workers marched to the site each day singing *"Ça ira,"* a kind of macabre revolutionary anthem:

> *Ah! ça ira, ça ira, ça ira,*
> *Les aristocrates à la lanterne!*
> *Ah! ça ira, ça ira, ça ira,*
> *Les aristocrates, on les pendra!*

> [Oh, it will be done, it will be done, it will be done,
> To the lamppost with the aristocrats!
> Oh, it will be done, it will be done, it will be done,
> The aristocrats will hang!]

The Marquis de Sade might have trembled, but what had Citizen Sade to fear? On Wednesday, July 14, he found himself a protected seat in the amphitheater—a prudent choice, since this summer day was chilly, the sky dark and threatening. The delegates to the National Assembly were present, as well as the King and his family. General La Fayette sat astride a white charger. All swore allegiance. The cannon thundered. And so did the heavens. As Sade wrote to Gaufridy on July 17, it rained "for six full hours," prompting some wags to say "that God had just then revealed himself and that he was an *aristocrat.*" Sade must have been worried that there would be some turmoil in such a vast gathering. He noted, however, that there were only three casualties: "One man killed and two wounded by the cannon, and only by accident, that was all."[5] Among the celebrants was a delegation from Provence, some of them friends of Gaufridy, whom Sade treated to a dinner at his house.[6] The hero of the Bastille now felt very much in his element.

On Sunday, July 18, there was an additional celebration on the grounds of the Bastille. Most of the vast edifice had already been demolished, stone by stone, carted off as souvenirs. This was the sacred symbol of the ancien régime, rendered all the more awesome to the imagination by the now truncated walls of stone which provided a bizarre setting, strung with lanterns, for the first Bastille Ball. A banner invited the visitor to enter: "Dancing Here."[7]

During the summer of 1790, Sade regained his spirits and his strength. He set about trying to get his plays put on. His new friend and landlady, Mme de Fleurieu, would be of help with valuable introductions, and perhaps it was at her house that he was introduced to the celebrated actor Molé. She also arranged a reading of Sade's verse play *Jeanne Laisné*, the tragic story of a young woman who dies a hero's death, torn between divided loyalties to her father and to her patriotic lover. On June 16, the actor Saint-Prix wrote to apologize to Sade for not having yet read *Jeanne Laisné:* "I am just now come back from the country in order to perform Macbeth tonight." But he promised to hear the play read on the afternoon of the dinner that Mme de Fleurieu "has done me the honor to give for me."[8] Sade was beginning to make useful contacts. It was possibly Molé who arranged a reading of Sade's *Le Boudoir* at the Comédie-Française on August 17, 1790.[9] The next day, Sade wrote to the actor Naudet, who had been present at the reading, asking him to use his influence with the other members of the jury. Sade conspicuously dropped Molé's name into the letter and, as a further inducement, mentioned that his home was "opposite" that of Mme de Fleurieu.[10] No matter how many names Sade dropped, this slight comedy about a woman who bamboozles her jealous husband was not to succeed at the Comédie-Française. On August 25, Naudet informed Sade that the play could not be performed in its present state.[11] But there was some good news. The Théâtre Italien read Sade's play *Le Suborneur* on August 3, 1790, and accepted it.[12] Then, on September 16, the Comédie-Française accepted *Sophie et Desfrancs;* this, however, would never be performed.

Sade tried other measures to get his plays put on. He had never been shy in the presence of actresses. Now he courted them for their influence in the theater. He promised the leading role of *Jeanne Laisné* to the actress Mme Vestris, but when he came to her home one morning very early to visit her, he was sent away by a servant. On August 8, 1790, she wrote to apologize (after all, what actress is awake very early in the morning?): "I am truly mortified, Monsieur, that my usual wretched laziness kept me in bed until nine-thirty, and for this reason I was deprived of seeing you. I assure you that I was looking forward to the honor of your visit, but I must also admit that I was expecting it rather a good deal later." She professed to be honored by his offer of the leading part, "if I am still the one for whom you intend the leading part." Mme Vestris's doubt about Sade's intentions was well founded, for he had also offered the part to her colleague Mlle de Raucourt.[13]

On August 25, 1790, Sade met the woman whose loyalty and affection would remain a constant throughout the rest of his life. Marie-Constance Renelle, the abandoned wife of one Balthazar Quesnet, had also once been an actress. She was thirty-three, and she had a six-year-old son, Charles.[14] Sade described her to Gaufridy: "Her society is gentle; she is pious, utterly respectable, quite reserved." Sade thought that he and Mme Quesnet would visit Provence, and he wanted Gaufridy to find decent lodging for them in

Avignon. Perhaps for this reason, as well as Gaufridy's own moral reserve, Sade added that she was bound to him "only with ties of friendship."[15] In another undated letter that was also written in 1792, Sade again asserted to Gaufridy the lady's respectability: "This lady friend, who most definitely is nothing but a friend, is moreover most assuredly a very decent woman. There is not the slightest suspicion about either her behavior or my manner of living with her."[16] Sade nicknamed her "Sensible," a word in French suggestive not of common sense and rationality but of sensitivity, tenderness, delicacy of feeling, sympathy. Their relationship would survive the terrible ordeals that lay ahead, and would end only with Sade's death in 1814: twenty-four years, almost as long as Sade's marriage to Renée had lasted.

Sade's marriage to Renée was legally dissolved when he signed the articles of separation on September 23, 1790, at the Châtelet. Instead of having to repay Renée's dowry of 160,842 livres (or francs) at once, he was allowed to send her the annual interest on that sum, agreed at 4,000 livres. In fact, he would never pay her a sol. He soon came to see that his income from Provence would not be enough to support him, much less pay back Renée. When she complained about not receiving her first installment, Sade instructed Gaufridy to tell her that her husband had been deceived by the accounting of his income that had been presented to him at the time of the agreement. He had since come to see that these accounts were "false" and that the agreement therefore was illegitimate. Sade now claimed that he had been led to expect that he would be able to keep the first 10,000 livres of his income for himself "free and clear," and that he would pay Renée her 4,000 from the surplus. On closer inspection, it appeared that there would not be enough income for Sade to get 10,000 out of his estates. Even if there were a surplus, Gaufridy was instructed to inform Renée that her husband would not send any part of her payment until she fulfilled her "responsibility to him concerning what is due him from the inheritance of his mother,"[17] who had died just before his imprisonment at Vincennes in February 1777. Sade's countersuit against Renée would drag on for a long time. His behavior must have infuriated Mme de Montreuil.

Renée responded to Sade's prevarications forthrightly and clearly in a letter to Gaufridy on March 15, 1791: "He can have no grounds at all to reopen that agreement. . . . If his estates do not produce enough to give him ten thousand francs of income for his expenses, that is not my fault."[18] By the end of the year, on December 5, 1791, the two sides had worn themselves out with their legal maneuvers, and Sade was able to inform Gaufridy that "our discussions with Madame de Sade are about to conclude." Renée paid him a lump sum from his mother's inheritance, and Sade agreed to abide by the original separation agreement (which he nevertheless failed to do). Sade's money problems would continue. In the above letter, he described himself as "a poor devil who scarcely has any clothes to wear," and as someone "who is obliged to write comedies for a living."19

Sade did not mind appearing a dupe of the Montreuils. "It is the lot of honest people to be dupes," he told Gaufridy on November 26, 1790.20 How could Sade have been so easily fooled into believing that he had more income than he had in fact, and why would he sign an agreement that he could not afford? Did he plan from the beginning not to pay Renée? He was never interested in the details, and when reality finally obtruded, he always thought that he could find some way of slipping around it. When he ordered Gaufridy to sell one or all of his properties in Provence, he conveniently forgot that his estates could not be sold until he paid back Renée's dowry, for which they stood as guarantee. Money, money, money, was his constant refrain to the lawyer, as in this typical and very sarcastic demand: "This is what I am asking you for, *it's money*, this is what I want, *it's money*, this is what I need, *it's money*." Sade did not care how Gaufridy got it. Sell some land, sell anything. Just as long as he sent the money: "Oh! do it! . . . do it, in the name of God, do whatever you please with Saumane, with Mazan, with Arles, with La Coste! Chop, cut, lease, sell, to hell with it, to the devil with it, but just send me some money, because I need it at once, or I am at the end of my rope!"21 Sade's needs were greater than anyone else's. Had he not suffered enough already? Had he not already lost his life, his fortune, his wife to the Montreuils? His sense of his own injury, his sense of his own entitlement, allowed him to adopt whatever role was needed to get what he believed he deserved, even if that role made him appear something of a fool or a knave.

Sade's Machiavellian selfishness and his desperate need for money can be further seen in his efforts to worm an inheritance out of one of his relatives. In the fall of 1790, learning that Mme de Villeneuve's daughter, Mme de Raousset, was ill and possibly near death, Sade informed Gaufridy of his plan to send his son Donatien-Claude-Armand, the Chevalier, down to Provence "to settle the inheritance of Madame de Raousset." Sade believed that she "has a good deal of gold," and he could not imagine anyone more suited than his younger son to get some if not all of it: "I could not send her anyone who pleases me more than the Chevalier, no one better suited to *truly* attack the place. I leave the *pillaging* to his discretion, fully confident that he will give me a handsome share."22

Sade needed 1,200 francs a year for the house he had rented for himself and Mme Quesnet at No. 20 rue Neuve-des-Mathurins, on the fashionable Chaussée d'Antin. The famous Mirabeau lived just up the street. Sade asked

Gaufridy to hasten the shipment of the cases of household goods that he had requested from La Coste in order to furnish his new home. He made his situation appear pitiable, calling the house his "little shack" and his *"final refuge,"* good enough, he added dramatically, "to receive in the end my last sighs!" Yes, he would expire without his furnishings and without any comforts. And although the house had a nice garden, that was where, Sade insisted, "I will be buried": "They are already building my tomb there."[23]

All the same, Sade sounded quite cheerful about his middle-class ménage, which he shared with Mme Quesnet and her son:

> To give you an idea of my present situation, imagine a fat country priest in his parsonage. My little house . . . looks very much like a parsonage. I am there with a good housekeeper, who, at the very moment I am writing to you, is raising a frightful din throughout the house because someone has made off with her key to the cellar, either a cook or a footman; that is my entire entourage, all my livery. Is it too large?[24]

As the new year of 1791 dawned, he could hope for a better life. After so many years in prison, he finally had a home, a few servants, and a woman who cared for him. Sade described his happy new life with Mme Quesnet in a letter to Reinaud on June 12:

> Nothing so virtuous as my little household! First, not a word of love; she is in every way a completely good and decent bourgeoise, pleasant, quiet, intelligent, who, separated from her husband, a trader in America, was pleased to take charge of my little house. She gives me the modest allowance her husband gives her; I provide her lodging and food. That is the only pleasure that she currently obtains there. Indeed, if she is attached to me in order to try to prolong my life, *every five years* I will give her a small gift, as a clever means by which I will make her concerned about my life and by which, out of mere selfishness, she will try to preserve it, but of *dalliances* not a bit. Was I supposed to live alone, beset by two or three valets who would *rob* me, perhaps *kill* me? Was it not essential to place a *reliable* person between these scoundrels and myself? Am I in a position to skim my cookpot, to check my butcher's accounts, when I am ensconced in my study in the midst of Molière, Destouches, Marivaux, Boissy, Regnard, whom I respect, value, admire, and whom I will never reach? Besides, do I not need someone to whom I can read *hot from my pen*? Well, then! my companion fulfills all of these purposes; may God preserve her for my

sake, in spite of the flaming cabal that tirelessly labors to deprive me of her! What I most fear is that, tired of so many stupid *Montreuil-ish* tricks, the poor woman will grow sick and tired, and so leave me.[25]

Because Reinaud, like Gaufridy, had some connection with the Montreuils, Sade played down the sexual part of his relationship with Mme Quesnet. He feared that the Montreuils would somehow wreck his happiness. Happiness there was, with Sade in his study at his books and manuscripts, while his soup bubbled on the hearth and young Charles played in the garden. It is good to picture Sade in this small rented house, relatively happy at last in a comfortable domestic scene.

Sade's almost suburban peace was disturbed at the end of March, when lines of carriages and a multitude of pedestrians filled his street. Mirabeau, the great patriot and orator, lay gravely ill. Pierre-Jean-Georges Cabanis, the physician who attended Mirabeau during his final days, described the scene in front of the patriot's house: "His door all day long was besieged by a numerous crowd of men of all classes, all parties, all opinions. The street was already choked with people."[26] Bulletins on Mirabeau's worsening condition were issued from his windows and carried from mouth to ear. Day and night, the street and the city were in a state of morbid crisis. Within three days, on April 2, 1791, Sade's distant relative and old enemy from the time they were both prisoners at Vincennes was dead. At the moment of his death, cannon were fired and church bells rang out. Suspicions that Mirabeau had been poisoned prompted an immediate autopsy, which was performed the next day.[27] Sade wrote this stunning news to Gaufridy. His tone was ironic and bitter regarding the operatic national grief displayed over the death of his relative, the "Liberator." Sade was rather cavalier about this autopsy: "The *liberator* had been opened up in order to verify whether or not there was any poison in his gut." Suspicions had been cast far and wide—falling upon, among others, Mirabeau's physician, Cabanis—and the crowd in front of Mirabeau's door would not disperse until they heard the autopsy results. Sade was especially annoyed that grieving patriots "march en masse to the theaters and interrupt the plays." The funeral, held on Tuesday, April 4, was magnificent. The cortège was a league long and comprised dignitaries, delegates to the National Assembly, contingents from the patriotic clubs, military units, and ordinary citizens. "All the bells of Paris were striking," Sade wrote to Gaufridy, and he admitted grudgingly, "The funeral procession was superb."[28]

While the name of Mirabeau was on everyone's lips, a few doors away, Mirabeau's cousin Sade continued his literary labors in obscurity and deprivation. Many of his plays had been rejected by the theaters, and those few that had been accepted had not yet been produced. Meanwhile, the last shipment of his possessions from La Coste arrived in May. Opening the boxes, Sade discovered that a pot of preserves had spilled over the blue tapestry and had also stuck the pages of his books together.[29] Later that month, he had been hoping to receive some income from his farm, the Mas de Cabanes, near Arles; when Gaufridy's letter arrived in Paris on May 20 with no money and only the lawyer's assertion that he had "written forcefully to Arles," Sade replied with withering sarcasm:

> I showed this line to my butcher and to my baker. These creatures—utterly stupid, as you will see—replied that *they did not understand what was this Arles.* "If the writer of the letter," they told me, "had instead written: 'You will have your money on such-and-such a day,' then we would continue to supply you on credit, but since he had done no more than to write to Arles, which Arles may be no more than some rogue, some bankrupt, you will accept that we can no longer supply you."

All the money he had in the world, he added, was an *assignat* for 50 livres, which no one wanted to accept because this note was worth only 21 percent of its face value. "It is extremely painful," he told Gaufridy, "to starve to death here with one's wallet full of banknotes."[30]

With money a constant problem, Sade suffered another unpleasant meeting: "new scenes," as he put it, with Reinaud's representative, a M. Baguenaut, whom Sade described as "undoubtedly one of the least honest and least obliging men there ever was in Paris." Sade had asked to be paid in cash rather than in *assignats,* and M. Baguenaut told him to take his business elsewhere, for Sade had proved "tiresome" to him. The world had changed. Sade was profoundly insulted that M. Baguenaut conducted this interview while eating his lunch. Sade complained to Reinaud, "In all decent society, either one waits until the person who is talking to one has finished before sitting down to gobble, or one invites him to join in."[31]

Money, Sade told Reinaud, was also the motive behind the publication of his novel *Justine, ou les malheurs de la vertu (Justine, or the Misfortunes of Virtue).* Jacques Girouard was then printing the manuscript at his establishment on the rue du Bout-du-Monde. The title page, however, would disguise the place of publication as "Holland." Whereas Sade had promised Reinaud a copy of *Aline et Valcour,* he refused to do the same with *Justine,* which he deemed "too immoral to be sent to a man as pious as you, as decent as you." If Reinaud chanced upon a copy, Sade advised him to "burn it, do not read a word of it." For himself, Sade said, "I repudiate it." In fact, he would always deny authorship of this novel. He had written it, he said, according to the advice of his publisher, who "asked me to make it rather *spicy.*" Sade obliged: "I made it capable of corrupting the devil himself."[32]

Justine is an enlargement of an earlier manuscript, *Les Infortunes de la vertu,* written in the Bastille and smuggled out with Renée's help. Sade had tried without success to get his plays performed. And his true masterpiece, *Les Cent Vingt Journées de Sodome,* was still lost. So he enlarged and spiced up his next-best work and turned it into *Justine.* If Sade's motivation was pecuniary, the original work and the revised novel he brought to the press were nevertheless genuine expressions of his mentality. *Justine* is a parody of the moral and rational world exemplified in Samuel Richardson's international bestseller *Pamela, or Virtue Rewarded,* in which a young servant girl preserves her virtue against the blandishments and the assaults of her titled employer and is finally rewarded by marriage to the chastened and reformed rake. Sade was charmed by Richardson's skill as a novelist, but found the Englishman's optimistic morality at odds with his own view of the world. In Sade's novel, Justine, who is twelve, and her older sister, Juliette, who is fifteen, suffer the bankruptcy of their father and the death of both their parents. The two girls are expelled from their convent to seek their fortunes in the harsh world outside. Juliette, utterly without moral principles, lands on her feet—or her back. She earns her living first in a bordello, then as the mistress of rich and powerful men. She eventually marries a count and murders him. At every turn, she is rewarded for her crimes and sins with more wealth and influence, proving, as Sade says, "that prosperity can accompany the worst sort of behavior."[33]

As the story opens, fifteen years after the girls' abandonment, Juliette is in the company of her latest and devoted lover, M. de Corville, a rich and influential counselor of state. They are at a country inn, on the way to his estate, when a coach stops, carrying a bedraggled female prisoner under sentence of death for murder, robbery, and arson. As an amusement, Juliette invites the poor woman to tell her story, little realizing that the prisoner is her long-lost sister, Justine. From here on almost until its end, the novel consists of Justine's sad tale of a virtuous woman in an unvirtuous world. Wherever she turns, either to seek assistance or even to give it to others, she is always disappointed, betrayed, raped, or tortured. When she humbly and feebly protests her ill treatment, her persecutors always offer her a philosophical harangue demonstrating the folly of virtue and the good sense of vice. Here, as in Sade's other erotic novels, the sexual scene, the rape, is sandwiched between a kind of intellectual rape or assault upon the victim. The libertines want Justine to agree that she is wrong and they are right. Here, for example, are some of the arguments of M. de Bressac, who is trying to enlist Justine's assistance in poisoning his aunt for her inheritance. Acts of murder, M. de Bressac argues, are actually in the service of Nature, "reinvigorating her force." Nature is indifferent as to whether this primal energy takes the form of a human being or a pile of worms: "What does it matter to Nature's ever-fecund womb whether a particular mass of flesh in the shape today of a human biped tomorrow assumes the aspect of a thousand divers insects?" Since Nature herself inspires the so-called criminal passions within human beings, since Nature herself requires a constant flux of destruction and creation, then all crimes, including murder, are necessary to Nature's plan.[34]

Justine is raped, tortured, defiled in every part of her body by the various scoundrels and perverts she encounters on her luckless journey. M. Rodin, a perverted vivisectionist who runs a school, cruelly tortures and sexually abuses his pupils, yet he defends his practices by attacking the very idea of a universal good, or a universal standard of morality: "There are not," he lectures Justine, "two nations on the face of the globe who are virtuous in the same way; thus virtue has no validity, no intrinsic value, and in no way deserves our respect."[35] With such sophistries, Rodin justifies incest and infanticide.

The church is also a venue for debauchery. When Justine seeks refuge in a monastery, she is imprisoned as a sex slave by four monks who have an elaborate underground seraglio occupied by kidnapped girls of good family. The whole arrangement, including the color-coded ribbons and the division of sexual labor, the rules, and the alternation of perversions and philosophical discourse, is reminiscent of *Les Cent Vingt Journées de Sodome*. Brother Clément tries to persuade Justine that perversions are good: "Doubtless, the most ridiculous thing is to seek to quarrel over man's tastes, to oppose them, censure them, or punish them if they do not happen to conform either to the laws of the country where one is living or to social conventions." Our sexual tastes are stamped at our birth. Even if we could somehow change our nature, ought we try? Ought we become, Clément asks, "other than what we are?"[36] Justine is doomed to suffer, not only sexual assaults, but also a continual verbal barrage of sophistry and cynicism. Finally, when Justine's bad sister, Juliette, recognizes her, saves her from the gallows, and sets her up in her own country estate, the reader may hope for a happy ending. But no: a massive thunderstorm erupts, and Justine, shutting a window, is struck dead by a lightning bolt.

Justine is constructed in a conventional manner. It belongs to that popular eighteenth-century species of novel the philosophical romance, which includes works like Voltaire's *Candide* and Johnson's *Rasselas*. The main character is serially exposed to a variety of individuals standing for various philosophical theories or stances. After a suitable number of didactic episodes, the main character has acquired wisdom and the author may conclude his labors. *Justine* parodies the same pattern: an episode followed by rational discourse. Sade, as guide, likes to point out the freaks and oddities along the way. He likes to tease us, challenge our assumptions. His style is erotic, but not mindless; meaningful, but not entirely serious. In dedicating this novel to Mme Quesnet ("at once the paragon and glory of your sex"), he claims that "the design" is "undeniably new," a kind of negative example, the display "throughout of Vice triumphant." He argues, however, that this spectacle will provide "one of the most sublime lessons in morality ever offered to mankind," albeit achieved "by a heretofore untrodden route."[37] A year after its publication, one reviewer gave it a serious reading, bestowing upon it a kind of thoughtful condemnation, and in language that is still appropriate and accurately captures Sade's extremism: "Everything that the most deranged imagination could possibly conceive in the way of obscenity, of sophistry, and, indeed, of loathsomeness, is discovered indiscriminately heaped in this bizarre novel." The reviewer warned impressionable young people to "fly from this dangerous book," but he acknowledged that "mature" individuals could read this "rich and brilliant" novel "in order to see just how far the derangement of the imagination can be carried."[38] This is a remarkably perceptive understanding of Sade.

While Sade pursued his literary careers—public and clandestine—he also regularly attended the meetings of his section of the Place de Vendôme. He had to act cautiously. Public disturbances were frequent. In February 1791, a mob marched out of Paris to the château of Vincennes, which they began to demolish, just as they had the other royal prison, the Bastille. Only La Fayette was able to save the structure from their fury. Terror then struck Sade's own family. In May, he learned that his aunt Mme de Villeneuve, while traveling from Carpentras to Orange in Provence, had been arrested by the revolutionaries and taken off to prison. "At eighty years old," Sade exclaimed to Gaufridy, "that poor woman! That is truly an abominable horror and fully worthy of those sorts of brigands!" He asked Gaufridy to write Mme de Villeneuve to offer her the haven of his château at La Coste upon her release: "She would be safer there."[39] Sade also enclosed a letter for his aunt that he asked Gaufridy to forward to her. A few weeks later, on June 12, Sade was very glad that his lawyer had prudently held back that letter, having now realized that it might have fallen into the hands of those who had arrested his aunt, whom he had rather too freely abused as "brigands." Sade added, "One must show respect for the bear when one is in his claws."[40]

That same June, there was a great political crisis. Paris woke up on the morning of June 12, 1791, to find that King Louis XVI had escaped and fled to Varennes, leaving his written complaint, his "Déclaration." Sade answered these royal complaints with a pamphlet, *Adresse d'un citoyen de Paris au roi des Français,* printed by Girouard, who was just then putting the finishing touches on Sade's *Justine.* In the *Adresse,* the first of Sade's extant political writings, he defended the current behavior of the Revolution against the King's charges of divisiveness and factionalism. "Frenchmen wish to be free, and they will be," Sade assured the sovereign. "Twenty million men are not factious: . . . *liberty* is the national cry; the desire to enjoy it, and to enjoy it eternally, is unanimous."[41] If the King had sought to flee the country in order to return with a counterrevolutionary army, Sade warned him that such a plan would have resulted in a bloody failure: "Do not doubt it, Sire, there is but one Frenchman, all speak here through my mouth, and not one of them who would not have preferred death to the return of the abuses of your former despotism."[42] Sade's description of these former abuses has a personal ring, a strange kind of special pleading for those victims of ministerial prosecution. "Deign for a moment," he asked the King, "to contemplate" the suffering "of the former victims of your despotism," of "those wretched individuals who, merely by your signature, as a consequence perhaps of bribery or inattention, were ripped from the bosom of their family in tears, to be thrown forever into the dungeons of those dreadful Bastilles with which your kingdom bristled."[43] Sade portrayed himself as an important figure in revolutionary politics. "You perhaps take me," he concluded his pamphlet to the King, "for an enemy of the monarchy and of the monarch: no, Sire, I am not that at all; no one could be more thoroughly persuaded than I that the French Empire can be governed only by a monarch; however, this monarch, chosen by a free nation, must faithfully submit himself to the law. . . ."[44] Yes, Sade was always a tantalizing mixture of extremes. In this one essay, he was both a radical and a monarchist.

Sade himself experienced difficulty when Gaufridy asked him to define his political philosophy. On December 5, 1791, he wrote the following statement of his belief:

It is not, in truth, for any of the parties, yet is a composite of all of them. I am an anti-Jacobin, I hate them to the death; I love the King, but I detest the former abuses; I love the vast majority of the articles of the Constitution, others of them revolt me; I would like the nobility returned to their glory, because taking it away from them accomplishes nothing; I wish that the King were the head of the nation; I do not at all want the National Assembly, but two houses as in England,

which gives the King a mitigated authority, balanced by the concur-
rence of a nation necessarily divided into two orders; the third [i.e.,
the clergy] is unnecessary, I want nothing of them. There you have my
profession of faith. What am I now? Aristocrat or democrat? Please tell
me, lawyer, because, as for me, I do not have the faintest idea.

If Sade was describing an attempt to steer a middle course, this was not a
course typical of his mentality. Strangely enough, the revolutionary politics of
the nation, and of his section of the Place de Vendôme in particular, suited his
extremist mentality. Because he served his section "in the capacity of a man of
letters," he explained to Gaufridy, "the obligation I am daily under here to
work sometimes for one side, sometimes for the other, entails a mobility in
my opinions, which has an effect on my private way of thinking."[45] In one
sense, Sade was apologizing for having to shift his private political views
according to the direction of the political winds at any given moment; he
acknowledged that this shifting had a corrupting influence on his "private
way of thinking." But this same statement is even more true when read the
other way: lacking a strong central way of thinking, generally, in fact, enjoying "a mobility in my opinions," Sade found the sudden surging of revolutionary politics, the violent sweeps from one extreme to the other, very
familiar, very similar to his own mobile, volatile way of thinking.

One thing is certain. Sade did not anticipate the political cost when he
professed himself a constitutional monarchist in his *Adresse*—a reasonably
acceptable stand in 1791, but one that could get a citizen guillotined in 1794.
In was during this dreadful Terror that Sade wrote to the Comité de Sûreté
Générale (Committee for General Security) to claim that he had personally
"thrown" this pamphlet into King Louis XVI's carriage "as it crossed the Place
de la Révolution" on June 25, 1791, when the King was returned from his
flight and was paraded through the streets.[46] Such an extraordinary attack
upon the King was expressly forbidden and would have caused a scandal at
the time. It may be that, although the pamphlet was Sade's, the method of
delivering it was a product of his imagination.[47]

Everything is political, one may say, especially during a revolution. Everyone's politics are situational, one may say, especially during a revolution.

On July 13, 1791, Sade's elder son, Louis-Marie, not quite twenty-four,
submitted his resignation as an officer in the infantry and fled the country,
thereby seriously compromising his father's position. Having children who
fled the Revolution, possibly to take up arms against it from another country,
could cost a parent his head. In a letter to Gaufridy on October 4, Sade mentioned the flight of his elder son, calling him a "troubled" individual. Sade

said that his younger son, Donatien-Claude-Armand, was in garrison at Lyons.[48]

For the next few months, Sade was occupied with schemes to obtain some money from the estate of Mme de Raousset, his cousin, who had died on October 7. He was also concerned about losing the estate of her aged mother, Mme de Villeneuve, whom he told Gaufridy to work on: "Could you not labor, both with body and mind, to see that the above-mentioned funds do not evaporate until I have had a chance to twitch the sleeve of the said aunt? She is swarmed over, she will continue to be swarmed over, can you not unswarm her, speak to her, speak to her constantly of me, of my attachment, *totally sincere,* for her?"[49] Sade hoped to be able to use any inheritance, or a loan guaranteed by the prospect of an inheritance, to buy the house he was renting in Paris. It "would be lovely," he wrote to Gaufridy on November 14, if he could thus "obtain the eighty thousand francs for the house." Sade was worried that Mme de Raousset's legacy would get snapped up by her lover. If this individual was "a certain Virette from Bonnieux," then there would be little concern: "I know him," Sade reassured Gaufridy, adding that this lover "would have been perfectly able to forgo my cousin's money." Sade summed up Mme de Raousset's lover thus: *"Fuck her, yes; but fleece her, never."*[50]

Mme de Villeneuve's prospective death and legacy were still on Sade's mind when he wrote to Gaufridy on February 6, 1792. Sade had learned that Claude-Armand had been conducting his own scheme to get the legacy for himself. Claude-Armand, according to his father, "sneaked out of the garrison" in order to lay siege to Mme de Villeneuve. Sade suspected that the Montreuils were behind this trick, and also that they wanted Claude-Armand "to look into the revenue" from Sade's estates in order to gather evidence to sue Sade for the annual income he owed but never paid to Renée. Sade was really in a high fury with Claude-Armand: "I will never forgive him as long as I live." In a chilling summary of his second son, Sade concluded, "I do not like swindlers or spies."[51] A week later, believing that his son "is now in possession of Madame de Villeneuve's legacy," Sade instructed Gaufridy to visit Claude-Armand, to offer him his father's ironic compliments on his success, and to inform him that he would be written out of Sade's own will. But when Sade learned that all Mme de Villeneuve had promised Claude-Armand was 300 francs, he wrote to Gaufridy that such a paltry sum would not even cover Claude-Armand's expenses for the trip. "The dear aunt is not generous!" Sade cried, seeming to cackle with delight over his son's wasted efforts.[52] In a few more months, Claude-Armand would desert his post as aide-de-camp to the Marquis de Toulongeon and, like his older brother, flee to Germany. In the worsening political storm, the sins of the sons would be visited on the father.

By that time, moreover, the house that Sade wanted to buy with Mme de Villeneuve's money had been bought by a courtesan. "It is always the whores who have money," Sade grumbled.[53]

Perhaps Sade would meet with success in the theater, as "a poor devil . . . who is obliged to write comedies for a living."[54] In October 1791, Sade was looking forward to having his first play put on in Paris, *Le Comte Oxtiern, ou les effets du libertinage*. It had been accepted the previous summer by M. Boursault-Malherbe of the Théâtre Molière. This play was a toned-down adaptation of "Ernestine," a short story he had written in prison. But even a toned-down version had been rejected earlier by the Théâtre de la rue Feydeau, because, as they informed the author, they "did not think that a play could be put on with success based upon the most odious atrocity."[55] The play concerns a rich and powerful libertine, Oxtiern, who falsely imprisons his rival, Herman, and then kidnaps and rapes Ernestine. Like Samuel Richardson's character Lovelace in *Clarissa*, Oxtiern cynically suggests that, if need be, he can eventually marry Ernestine and so make an honest woman of her. But, like Clarissa, the noble and virtuous Ernestine will not compromise, and her suffering even wins over some of her persecutor's confederates. Oxtiern's friend Derbac asks him if he does not fear the law. "Works of man . . . applied by man," Oxtiern replies; "I have never seen them resist the force of gold." But what about the persecutions of his soul? What about his guilty conscience? "Calm . . . perfectly calm," Oxtiern assures him.[56] Like the libertines of *Les Cent Vingt Journées de Sodome*, Oxtiern is a willful deviant, a conscientious and philosophical defier of morality. He has labored hard to corrupt his soul. He boasts of it to his friend: "That is what I have worked for, my friend; I have seen much, experienced much; if you only knew what sensations derive from having experienced too much!"[57] Oxtiern finally plots to rid himself of the sullen Ernestine and her revenge-seeking father by causing the two of them to duel each other, each believing the other to be Oxtiern. Fortunately, Herman is freed from prison, appears just in time to save all, to kill Oxtiern, and to claim his ravished Ernestine for his wife. The slapped-on moral ending, however, did not disguise the libertine extremism of Oxtiern's views.

Some members of the audience at the Théâtre Molière were not kind when the play debuted on October 22, 1791. Sade could not contain his excitement after the performance—"I have finally appeared in public"—and he found ways to extenuate the play's mixed reception, blaming "cabals," "factions," and "women I spoke badly of." There would be another performance in a week, he told Gaufridy, "with some changes."[58] These changes and M. Boursault-Malherbe's objections to them caused an additional week's postponement. The second performance thus took place on November 4. The review in *Le Moniteur*, though acknowledging that "there is some interest and energy in this play," nevertheless complained that "the role of Oxtiern is of a revolting brutality." The review compared him unfavorably with Richardson's libertine: Oxtiern is "more of a scoundrel, more vile than Lovelace." The review also commented on a disturbance that interrupted this performance. At the beginning of the second act, one spectator, described as "displeased or malevolent," began shouting for the curtain to be lowered. A stagehand had actually lowered the curtain almost all the way when the rest of the audience made him raise it again. There were shouts against the spectator who had started the ruckus, cries of "Out with him!" The audience, for a time, divided into factions. "A very small minority," the reviewer noted, "produced some timid whistles, for which the author had been amply compensated by the strong applause of the majority." At the end of the performance, the audience called for Sade to come out onstage and take a bow.[59] Sade described the performance to Gaufridy in much blunter terms. There had been, he reported, "a frightful uproar." He would have to withdraw the play. "They slaughtered it," he moaned.[60]

Eighteenth-century theater audiences were more active and vociferous than modern ones. Indeed, they could become violent, as happened on March 5, 1792, during the premier performance of Sade's comedy *Le Suborneur* at the Théâtre Italien. This disturbance was more political than critical. The climate had been steadily growing more volatile. On March 26, Sade informed Gaufridy that "it was my distinction to be the first victim" of the patriotic disturbances at the Paris theaters, when "the Jacobin faction succeeded in vanquishing a play of mine . . . solely because it was by a *ci-devant*"—that is, by a former aristocrat. "They showed up," Sade continued, "wearing their red wool caps. This was the first time anyone saw anything like this."[61] The *Journal des Théâtres* noted that there was a scent of trouble from the very first scene, when a "whispering" and then a "chattering" arose in the stalls "as if the curtain had not gone up." The noise increased. By the fourth scene, the din was so loud that the actors, unable to make themselves heard, withdrew from the stage. One of the demonstrators, wearing the cap of liberty, called upon all true patriots to rally at the playhouses "where the aristocracy would be ceaselessly assailed by the friends of liberty."[62] The political disturbances, Sade wrote Gaufridy, "went on for two weeks, at the end of which the mayor succeeded in putting an end to it, but it was my distinction," he added, once again attaching his pride to humiliation, "to be the first victim."[63]

There was also bad news from Provence. Sade was informed that the local

patriotic club of La Coste had voted to order the demolition of the fortifica-
tions of Sade's château, despite the long letter he had just sent them testifying to his "attachment" both "to the Revolution and to the Constitution."[64]
Sade's troubles in Provence would only increase. His revenues were down and
his taxes were up. Violence was always in the air. He was becoming a bit
alarmed, as he wrote Gaufridy on April 28, because Ripert, "in a dreadful state
of panic," had just written to Sade "without signing his name and in a disguised hand." "The devil take me," Sade exclaimed, "if you have not all gone
mad in Provence!"[65] In another letter dating from this time, Sade informed
Gaufridy that he had finally received assurances from the municipal authorities at La Coste that they would "place my *properties under their safeguard*"
and protect them from the radicals who were putting châteaux to the torch.
The authorities had warned Sade that he needed to submit a residence certificate, which he now enclosed.[66] Sade would spend a good deal of ink and anxiety over the next few years trying to prove to various officials that he had not
emigrated and that he was a resident of Paris, even though it would be difficult to mitigate the suspicions that fell on him after his sons had fled. Any act
of his could be misinterpreted. For example, when Sade learned of the plan to
demolish the church in Avignon where Petrarch's Laure was buried, he
thought about giving "an inviolable haven" to the corpse of "this celebrated
lady" that he had embraced so fervently in his dream thirteen years earlier, in
his cell at Vincennes. However, could such an act be politically dangerous?
This is what he wanted to know from Gaufridy: "Would it be viewed as aristocratic by the patriots?"[67]

On June 19, 1792, at the Place de Vendôme, the genealogical records of the
aristocracy were burned, as provided by the new law abolishing such titles.
The next day, Sade wrote to Ripert, asking him and Gaufridy to take good
care of Sade's own genealogical records: "This sort of madness could spread
into your district; take good care of my papers, I beg of you."[68]

And then, in July, a woman of La Coste, whom Sade described only as
Soton's daughter, traveled up to Paris from La Coste and arrived at Sade's
door. She was seeking to settle old scores—with Gaufridy, with the former
curate, and with several others. Her plan was to denounce them all before the
National Assembly. Sade teased Gaufridy about his enemy: "She is in a fury
over you." She also told Sade about Gaufridy's betrayal of him, but this Sade
said he refused to credit. According to Sade, Mme Quesnet "tried to do everything to calm her down; she had dinner with her; she gave her some of her
own clothes in order to take her on walks and to plays; nothing could placate
her; her refrain is always: *Off with M. Gaufridy's head!*" One of the things the
woman accused Gaufridy of was double-dealing with the Montreuils behind

Sade's back. "I do not believe it," Sade assured Gaufridy. But about the Montreuils he added, "If with a single word I could have them hanged, I would do it; but I take pity on them, I treat them with disdain and indifference for all the harm they have done me."[69] Sade may have been writing humorously, but such threats would soon seem tame.

Soton's daughter would not go away. One day, she appeared at Sade's door and put on a tearful performance. Two days later, she was back, having had an interview with Mme de Sade. "That *Soton woman* is still causing an uproar here," Sade wrote to Gaufridy, adding that she seemed "extremely dangerous": "At this very moment, this girl is at my door with a soldier whom she has with her but without wishing to explain why. I had them both sent away."[70]

Gaufridy had become an active figure in counterrevolutionary royalist politics. At times, he felt sufficiently endangered to go into hiding. Sade teased him for his cowardliness, as in this letter of July 16, 1792, concerning the third anniversary of the storming of the Bastille: "I am not as craven as you, my dear M. Gaufridy," Sade told his lawyer. "Instead of hiding out during the national celebration for fear of some disturbance, as you have done, I have, on the contrary, attended all of the ceremonies and the patriotic supper held here last night."[71]

A month later, Paris underwent another revolutionary convulsion. The radical Paris Commune was created and demanded Louis XVI's forfeiture of the throne. On August 10, 1792, the King submitted to the legislature to avoid bloodshed, but his Swiss Guard and his servants at the Tuileries were butchered by the mob. The palace was looted and the bodies of the slain were stripped, mutilated, and put on display in the courtyard. Years later, Sade, writing from prison and trying to re-establish his revolutionary credentials, claimed that he had taken part in this day's bloody events, even declaring that, when they all reached the Place du Carrousel in front of the Tuileries, "my friend was wounded next to me." Sade added this emotional detail: "I boiled with rage that the tyrant and his vile wife did not immediately suffer the penalty for their crimes."[72] If Sade had actually stood face to face with death during that day's fierce fighting, he mentioned it to no one else. He did, however, take note of the naked corpses of the Swiss Guard. Writing in Charenton, more than ten years later, he commented that, just as the noble ladies of the Court of Catherine de Médicis came out of the Louvre to look at the naked bodies of the murdered Huguenots, "on August 10, the women of Paris came in the same way to look at the bodies of the Swiss scattered about the Tuileries."[73] In Sade's mind, this beginning of the Terror resolved itself into an image of the bloodthirstiness of women.

The day was a tragic one for Sade. His relative Comte Stanislas de Clermont-Tonnerre was brutally murdered by the mob. A political moderate and an admirer of the English form of constitutional monarchy, the Comte had evidently been targeted by the mob. He was dragged out of his house. He tried to make a speech, defending his position to the crowd. He was wounded, yet managed to escape to a friend's house, where he was pursued, cornered, and flung out an upper-story window. His corpse was mutilated and finally dragged through the streets to be shown to his wife, who fainted dead away. These were scenes of which Sade had only dreamed. He was in no mood to sympathize with Gaufridy, who had once again been obliged to flee his home down in Provence and go into hiding because of the political turmoil. "Do not accuse me of not fully appreciating your predicament," Sade wrote to him on August 25. Referring to his own "cruel situation" and particularly to the emigration of his sons and the slaughter of Clermont-Tonnerre on August 10, Sade continued: "I am here alone, absolutely alone now. The day of the tenth has taken away everything from me, relatives, friends, family, protection, assistance; three hours have totally ripped away everyone around me, I am alone. . . ." Sade's voice trailed off into vague fears. Just a month earlier, he had teased Gaufridy for being afraid on the anniversary of the overthrow of the Bastille. Now he saw his own situation drastically changed. He could not even flee, because "we, as relatives of émigrés, as if that were our fault, under the surveillance of the law, both are prohibited from leaving Paris and are on the eve of perhaps even much harsher measures!" Sade returned to the main point of his letter: if Gaufridy did not immediately send some money, Sade would have to go *"begging for my bread."* "Now you see the situation in which you have abandoned me."[74]

Sade was correct in believing that things would only get worse. At the end of August, Dr. Guillotin's new invention was installed at the Place du Carrousel, where it received its first political victim, Collot d'Angremont, accused of a royalist conspiracy. Sade prudently began to prepare his defense against the charge that he had conspired with his sons to help them flee the country. He concocted three self-serving exculpatory letters to his sons, to M. de Montreuil, and to Renée. Combining the revolutionary rhetoric of his section meetings with his own old complaints against the Montreuils, Sade criticized Mme de Montreuil as an "ambitious" social climber and a would-be aristocrat who was willing to "sacrifice everything, betray everything, in order to try to give new life to the rotting skeleton of the stinking robinocracy [i.e., the rising aristocracy of lawyers and judges] and to the pestilential claws of administrators of lettres de cachet."[75] He addressed Renée from an equally lofty soapbox: "I am a citizen and a patriot myself, Madame, and I always have been."[76] He did not send these letters, but they constituted a paper argument in case he had to justify his political propriety.

Sade worked hard to maintain his revolutionary orthodoxy, becoming secretary of his section. He also had surveillance duty to perform, and military service as a member of the National Guard. War having been declared between France and Austria, aristocrats and counterrevolutionary suspects were rounded up and imprisoned throughout France. Now that Gaufridy was in hiding, Sade was penniless: "I am ill, I am taking medicine, and we are so greatly overwhelmed in our section that I do not even have the time to regain my health. Today, I am at the same time on guard at the Tuileries and on surveillance duty at the section, sick as a dog and without a sol." Moreover, there was new trouble from Soton's daughter. She had been an amusing topic in Sade's letters just a month or two earlier, when her charges were primarily leveled at Gaufridy and when the political climate was much milder. Now Sade was worried about his own safety. That "hussy," he wrote to Gaufridy, "had a letter sent to me from her mother full of threats and outrages," concerning "some supposed confidences offered her by Gothon, which she intends to reveal." It would be extremely inconvenient for Louis Sade, the secretary of the Place de Vendôme section, to have to explain away "false slanders" brought by the servant girls at La Coste against their master, the Marquis de Sade.[77]

The news from the war front was becoming increasingly alarming. Longwy fell on August 23, 1792. Verdun was reported lost on September 2. Bells were rung throughout the city and cannon were fired to sound the alarm. Tents were pitched on the Champ-de-Mars, where the volunteer army frantically drilled. The hysteria was explosive. More than a score of nonjuring priests on their way to Abbaye Prison were massacred by a mob, and more than a hundred met the same fate at the Prison des Carmes. Thus began the September Massacres. Aristocrats and suspected aristocrats in the packed prisons were given summary justice inside or by the mobs outside. More than a thousand, many of them children, were killed during the four terrible days following September 2. In a letter to Gaufridy on September 6, Sade understandably appeared carried away by the horror of events: "Ten thousand prisoners perished on the day of September 3," he wrote. There must have seemed to be that many, as the carts carried the bodies through the streets. "Nothing equals the horror of the massacres that were committed," Sade went on, and then, possibly thinking that his letter might fall into unsympathetic hands, he added between the lines, "but they were justified." He described in some detail the horrific fate of the Princesse de Lamballe, the Queen's friend: "The Princesse de Lamballe had been among the victims; her head carried on a pike had been paraded before the King and the Queen, and her poor body dragged for eight hours through the streets after having been defiled, they say, by all infamies of the most ferocious debauch."[78] Sade may have been alluding to the report that her breasts had been cut off, as well as her vulva, which one of her butchers wore as a mustache.[79] History had begun to invent perversions that exceeded Sade's fictional fantasies.

The bloody pikes of the September Massacres inspired the new name for the Place de Vendôme, Place des Piques, as well as for the section located there. As the secretary for the Section des Piques, Sade took the minutes and conducted the correspondence. Strangely amphibious as he was, he wrote like a royalist in his letters to Gaufridy, yet was still able to inspire the trust of his fellow citizens in one of Paris's most radical sections.

Even as blood poured onto the stones of Paris, elections were being held to replace the Legislative Assembly with the National Convention. When it convened, its first task was to establish France as a republic on September 22, 1792. The rights of man would be proclaimed throughout Europe at the mouths of French artillery. All of France was in turmoil. Down south, Gaufridy and his son, involved in royalist plots, were forced into hiding at Lyons. On September 13, Sade wrote to Gaufridy to express his concern over the loss of his primary conduit of funds out of Provence: "Your sudden departure threw me into the most frightful apprehension." Sade selfishly suggested to his friend that it was perhaps impolitic to leave—"to flee always makes one appear culpable"—and offered Gaufridy and his son a room and reasonable board in Paris, if only they would come. He warned Gaufridy not to sign any communications he sent.[80] It would not do for the secretary of the Section des Piques to receive letters from a royalist in hiding.

A month later, Sade was again writing to Gaufridy. "With tears in my eyes" and "in the name of God," he begged, "return to Provence." There was no real danger, Sade assured his friend in hiding: "These great disturbances are actually quite transitory." As he was in the midst of impugning Gaufridy's manhood and minimizing the dangers down in Provence, Sade was brought a letter from Reinaud, informing him that La Coste had been sacked. For Gaufridy's benefit, Sade dramatically re-created the moment when he received news of this disaster: "A dreadful letter was just now brought in to me. . . . I unseal it, trembling. Alas! it foretells my doom! . . . It contains the frightful details of what occurred at La Coste! . . . No more La Coste for me! . . . What a loss! It is beyond expression. There was enough there to furnish six châteaux! . . . I am in despair!"[81]

There had been looting and burning of châteaux throughout Provence. On the morning of Monday, September 17, 1792, some ringleaders came into the town of La Coste, after having razed houses at nearby Lauris. Paulet, a municipal official of La Coste, wrote the details to Sade on October 21.[82] He had learned about the riot around one o'clock in the afternoon, and immediately left his farm and went to the château, only to find a "scene of horror," the house already pillaged, and everyone gone. The riot had begun at ten in the morning. When the municipal officials of La Coste heard of a disturbance in progress, they took some of the National Guard and went up to restore order. On their arrival, they found "approximately eighty individuals, men, women, and children," rioting in the courtyards of the château. The elders tried to disperse the crowd. The rioters moved on to demolish the dovecote, then returned their attention to the house. Their revolutionary enthusiasm would hear no reason, partly because, as Paulet told Sade, "they were already drunk on your best wine." What they could not carry away, they smashed. The pillagers took "everything," throwing most of it "out the windows" in order to speed their work. "In less than an hour," Sade's lovely château, where he had sent the treasures he had collected from Italy, kept his manuscripts, stored the scenery for his little theater, kept so many objects important to his family and to his own taste—in less than an hour, it had been entirely "devastated and pillaged."

To obtain the return of Sade's goods and to prevent renewed riots, the municipal authorities gathered the villagers together in the parish church. A visitor from nearby Apt, one Ange Raspail, who may actually have been an instigator of the riot,[83] was asked to speak to them. The villagers responded by returning only a very few of Sade's belongings. The authorities deputized a dozen men to conduct searches in the village and in the surrounding area. They also put a guard on the château. However, at 5 a.m. on September 19, Raspail was called to the château to quell another riot, this time consisting of approximately fifty men and young people. With "threats" and "reproaches," he dispersed the mob. Two hours later, all the villagers were again summoned to the parish church to hear Raspail inveigh against disorderly conduct. This exhortation succeeded. "Throughout the day," the municipal report noted, a great many of Sade's possessions "were seen carried along, or were found lying about the streets." The next day, on September 20, Sambuc, the mayor, who had conveniently been absent during the rioting, returned and addressed the entire village in the church at dawn, forcefully expressing "his great surprise and indignation" at their behavior. He ordered a new and comprehensive search, which turned up a great many additional possessions "in streets, in courtyards and gardens, in grottoes, and in open fields." Sade, however, was not destined to see the return of his goods. Four carts arrived with orders to remove the goods to Marseilles in support of the army.

Sade's château had been gutted through and through. The mob had even torn out the floorboards and the roof. There are a few more curious details worth noting. On September 23, the municipal authorities of La Coste met to hear a denunciation of one of their own members, Jean Gardiol, for having instigated the riot. After the council found Gardiol guilty, his petulant response was "that he was not alone, and *that he did only what he saw others doing.*"[84] The sacking of La Coste, it would appear, had little to do with any animus against Sade in particular, but was, rather, an expression of the almost random violence, envy, and opportunism that were unleashed by the destruction of the old order. For example, the municipal records indicate that, on September 30, at three in the afternoon, two officers received a tip that "new devastations" were taking place at the château. When they arrived on the scene, they discovered Charles Béridon of the nearby town of Goult, who had "torn down the great entrance door" to the château and "had broken it up in order to carry off all the ironwork." When they remonstrated with him, explaining that he was committing a criminal act, he simply "ran off." The two unarmed officers did not feel strong enough to apprehend the culprit, and they contented themselves merely with collecting the "iron fittings" and putting them "in a safe place."[85] The ardent friend of the Revolution far off in Paris, or wherever he had gone (some believed he had fled the country), would not mind if the furnishings of his château went to the army (or wherever they did go), or if his great entrance door lay in pieces in his courtyard.

At the same time, an event occurred in Sade's Section des Piques that he told Gaufridy "will make you laugh":

As you were aware, in Paris they have made a general inspection of all the houses. During this visit, the Montreuils not being found at home, a seal was put on their house. They are now asking that it be removed; however, as they are lodged in my section, and as I am about to be named commissioner for the removal of seals, I assure you that, if I find them to be of the aristocracy, as is not improbable, I will not spare them. Did you laugh a little, lawyer?[86]

What a remarkable irony, what a delightful freak of history! The former Marquis, now an official of the Section des Piques, finds himself in a position to condemn the social-climbing Montreuils as aristocrats!

"Do you realize," Sade went on to ask Gaufridy, the royalist still in hiding, "that I am now highly esteemed by my section? Not a day goes by when I am not at work." Sade enclosed in his letter a "short piece," his essay entitled "Idée sur le mode de la sanction des lois" ("On the Method for Approving

Laws"), which, he boasted, "has been greatly relished." Furthermore, he told Gaufridy, he had just been given the honor of being "named by my section to serve as a commissioner to the Administrative Assembly of Hospitals." Each of the forty-eight sections nominated two commissioners. Their charge involved "a complete reorganization" of the hospital system, "a very difficult task," he assured Gaufridy: "I scarcely have an hour to myself."[87] The report, drafted by Sade and the other commissioner from his section, Sanet, was read by Sade before the Administrative Assembly of Hospitals on October 28, 1792. Sade read his other essay, "Idée sur le mode de la sanction des lois," before the general meeting of his section on November 2. It, too, was approved for printing and distribution to the other forty-seven sections. In it, Sade forcefully made the radical point that the new Constitution ought to be ratified not by elected legislators but directly by the people, in their own cantonal meetings. Sade's language was dangerous, passionate, radical. He recalled the bloody uprising of just a few months before: "Men of the Tenth of August," Sade reminded his fellow citizens, "you did not shrink from ripping the despot from his proud palace"; now was the time to consolidate and preserve "the power obtained by your exploits."[88] Sade was supporting a direct democracy, far more radical than the English bicameral limited monarchy that he had previously favored. "Sovereignty," he cried, "is *one, indivisible, inalienable,* you destroy it by sharing it, you lose it by conferring it on others." Power lay with the people. The people, he declared, were "rays of pure sunlight," whereas their elected representatives were merely "the magnifying lens," containing nothing but "the illumination that you choose to shine through them."[89] Sade exhorted his fellow citizens to find the means "to preserve that liberty which was obtained only by a tide of blood."[90]

In casting doubt on elected representatives, Sade identified himself with the sans-culottes, the most radical of the revolutionaries, the very people he had earlier decried as brigands. Now he declared that these people, the lowest of the low, ought to have a direct vote, "since it is them that the law *strikes* most frequently," and "thus it is for them to choose the law by which they consent to be *struck.*"[91] He then shifted to a more intimate tone of voice: "I know how far the abuse of power can go; I have experienced all the machinations of despotism." "I love the people," Sade cried, and he referred, rather disingenuously, to his prerevolutionary writings: "My works prove that I foresaw the present system long before the cannon which toppled the Bastille startled the entire world." Sade was referring to his novel *Aline et Valcour,* which, though written in the Bastille, was still with his publisher, Girouard. Sade had gone through the manuscript, adding passages and footnotes on Sartine, on ministerial despotism, on the Revolution—all designed to estab-

lish his revolutionary credentials before 1789. He concluded "Idée sur le mode
de la sanction des lois" on a personal note: "The happiest day of my life was
the one when I believed I saw the rebirth of the sweet liberty of the golden
age, when I saw the tree of liberty spread her beneficent boughs to efface the
wreckage of scepter and throne."[92] Sade's aim in his essay was to solidify his
story and his position in his section. As he declared to Gaufridy a few days
earlier, "I am, mind, heart, and neck, in the Revolution."[93]

Four days after Sade delivered his speech at his section, he found himself
performing regular guard duty outside the National Convention. "I work
every day" to make "myself better known in the Revolution," he told Gaufridy, adding that, without even running, he received ten votes in his section
for a municipal post.[94] The following day, under heavy guard, Louis Capet, as
the King was now unceremoniously termed, made his first appearance at the
Convention to hear the reading of his indictment for capital crimes against
the French people. During this tumultuous time, as Sade later explained to
the Committee for General Security, he went about "the daily business" as his
section's representative to the commission on hospitals, and he "personally
stood guard duty"; he added, "I never missed a single one, all the times that
Capet was in Paris for his trial."[95] In fact, Sade spent Christmas Day on guard
duty. The penalty for not appearing, he had been informed, was a day in
prison.[96] The trial of Louis XVI continued. The day after Christmas, Sade
wrote to Gaufridy: "This morning, the 26th, the King appeared for the second time at the bar of the Convention. I will try to send you the details."[97]
But the rest of his letter, like so many others at this time, was concerned only
with pleas for Gaufridy to send him some money. A few days later, he
informed Gaufridy that he was reduced to borrowing "at the rate of one louis
interest per day!" Far more terrifying, however, was Sade's discovery that his
name had appeared on a list of émigrés at Marseilles. He would forward
Gaufridy an official certificate of his residence. In the meantime, he asked the
lawyer to spread the word that Sade was indeed the secretary of the Section
des Piques in Paris.[98]

Sade's residence certificate, issued on March 7, 1793, described "Louis
Sade, man of letters," as "five feet six inches tall," with "blue eyes," a "round
face," and "hair nearly white."[99] He was almost fifty-three years old. Of his
sexual temperament, he used to like to say that you could not teach an old
dog new tricks. But he had certainly learned the trick of how to get by in
postrevolutionary Paris. He was, in fact, making progress in his section. At
the beginning of 1793, he was named by his section as its commissioner on
charity and health. On January 17, he was selected, along with two others—
one Désormaux, a man-midwife, and Carré, a lemonade seller, as delegates to

a new commission on hospitals, orphanages, and other charitable institutions, including the orphans of the Mère de Dieu and Les Filles Saint-Thomas de Villeneuve. If it is surprising to see the author of *Les Cent Vingt Journées de Sodome* inspecting a girls' orphanage, it is equally difficult to imagine the conversations he had with his fellow commissioners, the lemonade seller and the man-midwife. Indeed, the former Marquis was in the Revolution "mind, heart, and neck."

On Monday, January 21, 1793, as Sade prepared to attend his first meeting as a health commissioner at eleven in the morning, a momentous, even world-shaking, event was about to take place at about the same time in the Place de la Révolution. The streets bristled with soldiers. At ten o'clock, the enormous contingent guarding Louis XVI arrived at the square under a lowering sky that pressed heavily on the truncated pedestal from which the statue of Louis XV had been toppled. Across the square now stood the guillotine. Speedily, the King was fastened to a board, his neck beneath the blade. The rope was pulled at 10:22 a.m. A moment later, the executioner held up the bloody head by the hair for all to see. A roar of approval went up from the vast crowd packed into the square. The sound was echoed throughout the city. A year and a half later, when Sade was trying to authenticate his revolutionary credentials from prison, he said that he had been among the throng in the Place de la Révolution. "I saw his head fall like a true republican," he claimed. "Could I love a despot who had kept me for so many years behind bars?"[100]

During the winter and spring of 1793, Sade continued his committee work for his section. But more and more he was embroiled with Gaufridy over losses in his income and over loans to carry him over until the next payment. He still tried to have his plays produced, even going so far as to offer the Comédie-Française his previously rejected short comedy *Le Boudoir* free of charge, renouncing, as he put it to Citizen Delaporte, the theater's secretary, "all rights and emoluments of authorship."[101] It would be useful for Sade to support his title, "man of letters," with literary as well as political works. After two weeks, when he did not hear from M. Delaporte, Sade wrote him a curt, sarcastic note asking what was the delay over his offer on March 1: "I had not thought it possible that one had to suffer the same delays for what is freely *given* as for what is *sold*."[102] The minutes of the Comédie-Française indicate that Delaporte was instructed to return the manuscript and to inform this would-be playwright that the Comédie-Française "is not accustomed to accept any play without paying its author."[103] Characteristically, Sade backed down and wrote a groveling letter, saying that it would be "very unfortunate to quarrel" over a gift. He professed his warm feelings for the Comédie-Française: "I love it, serve it, and defend it." Then Sade dropped that famous old name: Delaporte could even "ask M. Molé to confirm this." Sade begged Delaporte to patch things up with the management, and repeated his previous proposal: "I want nothing for this play." If that offer was unacceptable, then he would make another, a patriotic gesture that could not be refused: "I donate to the war effort whatever profits this trifle produces."[104] The Comédie-Française was not moved.

If Sade found that he could not bully the Comédie-Française, he felt free to discharge his frustrations on Gaufridy. At the beginning of the year, Sade wrote, "You must be taking one hell of a shit (knowing the straits I am in) to delay so long this money from Sulleau [a moneylender]."[105] By April 6, 1793, he described his financial "crisis" as "frightful," and begged Gaufridy: "My money, my money, I implore you." Sade concluded the letter with a threat: "My money, my money, my money, or, on my word of honor, I am leaving to go and take up lodgings at your house!"[106] On May 5, Sade wrote, "*I am starving to death,*" and explained, "I have survived only by cadging dinners here and there."[107]

Naturally, he resented any expenditures. On April 6, for example, he wondered why he was still paying a pension to his old relative M. de Murs. If he still had to pay, he asked Gaufridy, "at least try to see that I inherit something for it." Then came the following not very subtle question: "Anyway, how is this man doing? Is he a hundred yet?" Money and spiraling inflation were not his only problems. In the same letter, Sade made it clear that he felt the increasing political tension: "You cannot conceive how the ex-priests and ex-nobles are now persecuted. They are even denied their citizenship card (without which one can be thrown into prison twenty times a day) if they cannot give proof of their birth, their good citizenship, their payment of taxes, etc., etc., etc."[108]

In the above letter of April 6, Sade also informed Gaufridy of an extraordinary meeting he had had with his father-in-law, M. de Montreuil, who "came to our section meeting, of which," Sade added, quite unnecessarily, "I am the secretary." He was enjoying the reversal of fortunes. Sade was an official in the revolutionary government, and his father-in-law was in some danger as a former judge in the old system. "As pleasantly as possible," the two men "chatted for one hour." Sade "savored the moment."[109] In a couple of days, Sade himself would be appointed a judge in his section, charged with adjudicating indictments against counterfeiters of *assignats*, and he teased the lawyer about this surprising piece of news, telling him that he would never guess what it was, not in a hundred tries. "I am a *judge*, yes, a *judge*!" he cried. "Who could have imagined it?" Sade, who had so often stood at the other side of the bar of justice, was puffed up with pride: "You may well believe that I have matured and that I now begin to grow wise." "So congratulate me," he bade Gaufridy, and then added this humorous but chilling threat to the royalist lawyer: "And above all, do not forget to send some money to Monsieur the *Judge*, or the devil take me if I do not *sentence you to death!*"[110]

Sade's quip contained a shiver of prophecy. By March and April 1793, the country was in disarray, France's armies were in retreat, there was a bloody royalist uprising in the Vendée, and the National Convention was divided in bitter disputes between the radicals (Montagnards) and the moderates (Girondins). By the middle of March, revolutionary tribunals had been set up in Paris and throughout France to provide summary military justice for anyone suspected of being disloyal to the Revolution. April 6 saw the creation of the Committee for General Security, the instrument of the Terror that was soon to come. The roiling political divisiveness was fueled in Paris by food riots, brought about by the severe devaluation of the *assignat* and by the scarcity of bread. By June 2, the Convention was besieged by sansculottes and section men armed with weapons and cannon. The Girondins were defeated and forced to give up their leaders, who were immediately imprisoned.

During this tumultuous time, Sade continued to badger Gaufridy to get his name removed from "that damned list of émigrés."[111] He succeeded in accomplishing this in May. However, when the department of Bouches-du-Rhône was divided in June, Sade was horrified to find his name on the list in his new department of the Vaucluse. A bureaucratic error like this could spell the difference between life and death. He set about once more to write letters and to supply certificates of residence and good citizenship. Meanwhile, he continued to work for his section. On June 15, 1793, he was designated one of four delegates to present objections to the decree establishing a standing army in Paris. On the following day, he read before the National Convention the address he had written, "Pétition des sections de Paris à la Convention nationale."[112] He argued that a mercenary army would become a kind of "Praetorian guard," subject to political misuse and exploitation. Sade favored a civilian militia. Patriotism, alone, he maintained, was sufficient to protect Paris: "Those who toppled the walls of the Bastille, those who broke the scepter of the despot, had neither wages nor salary; only the pure love of their country inspired their souls, and absolute liberty was their only reward for victory."[113] Voices of reason, however, would soon be drowned by a sea of blood. On July 13, 1793, one of the voices that called loudest for blood, that of Jean-Paul Marat, the Friend of the People, was silenced forever by Charlotte Corday's knife. Jacques-Louis David's famous painting confirmed Marat as an icon, idealized his plebeian features, now chiseled and perfected by David and death, as he reclined in the bloodied waters of his bathtub (a treatment against his severe psoriasis), his writings neatly weighted beneath his arm, his inkwell ready beside him, his pen still clutched in his lifeless fingers. In a few months, Sade would write a superheated and perplexing eulogy on Marat for the memorial service.

Marat's assassination may have cast a pall on the July 14 celebrations the next day, but Sade, "the man of letters," was busy at his section work. At the July 16 meeting, Sade read his report as a delegate to the Commission on Charity and Health. Members of the commission had thoroughly inspected the Hôtel-Dieu and the Hôpital Saint-Louis, and found nothing to support the rumor that the plague was rampant in the Hôtel-Dieu.[114] The following day, July 17, Charlotte Corday, having been speedily convicted and sentenced to death, was taken from the Conciergerie through curious crowds along the rue Saint-Honoré to the waiting guillotine at the Place de la Révolution.

By July 23, 1793, Sade had become president of the Section des Piques. In this capacity, he learned that he had been called to testify for the defense in a criminal trial at Versailles. A locksmith from his district was the accused. On the same day, Sade informed Gaufridy about the news of his "promotion": "I am president of my section," he crowed. Three months earlier, he had threatened to sentence Gaufridy to death if the lawyer did not send him his money. Now, in even more desperate need of money, he complained about Gaufridy's "silence." Sade was at the peak of his influence in his section, and could really have made trouble if he had wished. Indeed, he was given a perfect opportunity to do so. At the meeting of his section on July 22, he looked down from his chair as president and once again saw M. de Montreuil, "Papa Montreuil," among the audience. "I had him where I want him," Sade told Gaufridy.[115] More would come of this.

On August 1, President Sade informed all the landlords and tenants in his district of their obligations concerning the upcoming celebrations on August 10 for the Festival of Unity, marking the first anniversary of the bloody overthrow of the monarchy and also commemorating the new Constitution. In particular, Sade informed his fellow citizens that they were obliged to paint in large letters the following motto on the fronts of their houses: "UNITY, INDIVISIBILITY OF THE REPUBLIC, LIBERTY, EQUALITY, FRATERNITY, OR DEATH."[116] Already, the patriotic duty to sacrifice one's life for one's country had been turned into a threat: join the Revolution, or die.

During Sade's tenure as president, his father-in-law came once more to see him about having the seals removed from his vacant house. Believed to be royalist sympathizers who had fled the country, the Montreuils had been added to a long list of suspects. They were in serious trouble. A wrong step might seal their doom as well as their house. Miraculously, their son-in-law was now the president of their section. "Papa" Montreuil, as the one of the family least likely to rub Sade the wrong way, was dispatched to ask for his help. Would the former son-in-law, now that he had the upper hand, exact vengeance for all of the infamies he felt he had suffered from this family? This is how he described his decision to Gaufridy on August 3: "During my presidency, I caused the Montreuils to be moved onto a list of exculpated persons. If I had said a word, they would have been roughly handled. I held my tongue; there you see how I avenge myself!"[117] It was a scene right out of a melodrama, and Sade clearly enjoyed the role.

Sade's kindness to the Montreuils perplexes those who know him only from his novels or from the myth of the savage fiend that for years grew like a fungus over his name. To be sure, during his long years in prison, he often indulged in elaborate fantasies of revenge, particularly against his mother-in-law. Only the previous year, on July 10, 1792, Sade had written to Gaufridy that he despised those "notorious scoundrels" the Montreuils, "whom I could get rid of with a word if I so desired." Sade was far more a fiend in fantasy than in reality. Indeed, whether in his letters or in his fiction, he may have imagined savagery so systematically and so deeply that he was not easily surprised into actual brutality when the opportunity arose. With the Montreuils, he seemed to enjoy playing a superior role. He told Gaufridy, "I take pity on them, and I repay them with contempt and indifference for all the harm they did to me."[118] It may be that it was in Sade's own interest to save the Montreuils: if they fell, it would have been revealed that M. de Montreuil's grandsons—that is, Sade's own sons—had emigrated.[119] But Sade's decision was more than pragmatic, as is evidenced by the emotional force of his exclamation, "There you see how I avenge myself!" Sade flung himself dramatically into his role. All his life he threw himself into his roles with an extremism and a theatricality that make them seem fictive, almost delusional: the perfervid lover of the actress-courtesan Colet, the tearful penitent begging "Mama" Montreuil's forgiveness, the imprisoned martyr, the president of the Section des Piques; there was no end to it. And there was no hypocrisy in these performances. Part of Sade's charm was that, for the moment, he truly felt and truly was what he seemed to be. At this moment, with a trembling M. de Montreuil before him, he was magnanimity personified.

Indeed, Sade appears to have been overcome by his emotions and by his sense of honor. Seated in the president's chair at the turbulent meeting of August 2, Sade was forced to admit that his "conduct of the meeting was so stormy" that he could "no longer do it!" For once, words failed him. He had "been compelled to retire twice" from his chair. Finally, as he told Gaufridy, "I felt obliged to leave my chair to my vice-president." The reason for the tumult and his resignation? "They were seeking to make me give assent to a horror, an inhumanity. I never intended to let that happen." The exact nature of the proposition and the specifics of the riotous debate are unknown, but Sade's passion and his principled stand against an unnamed "horror" are evident. Perhaps his description of his role in the meeting was slanted for the benefit of his religious and royalist correspondent, for he concluded his letter to Gaufridy with a very unrevolutionary exclamation: "Thank God I am free of it now!" Sade may have known that his theatrical stand was made on very shaky ground. He may have saved the Montreuils, but he himself was in danger. "In despair" and "exhausted," as he said, he went directly home and became physically ill: "I am spitting up blood."[120]

A month later, the process of denunciation, imprisonment, and execution received an important judicial implement. On September 17, 1793, the National Convention enacted the Law of Suspects, under which revolutionary committees in sections throughout France were empowered to arrest, try, and execute all suspicious persons. Treason was so broadly defined as to include gestures, laughter, and even presumed thoughts. The Terror now had a powerful machine with countless blades that would purge the nation, or so it was claimed, of its bad blood.

At this time, Sade chose to compose a memorial speech, a kind of panegyric on two luminaries of the Revolution, Marat and Lepeletier. Marat had been assassinated two months earlier. Michel Lepeletier, a reformer of the legal and educational systems, and an active member of the National Convention, had been stabbed to death in a café by a royalist the day before Louis XVI's execution. Sade's section proposed to honor these patriots with a memorial celebration on October 9. He submitted his speech to the section meeting on September 29. This time he was applauded for "the principles" and "the energy" of his speech, and the assembly voted to have it printed and distributed to the National Convention, to all of the departments, to the armies, to the forty-seven other sections, and to the *sociétés populaires.*[121] On October 9, 1793, a solemn processional took place as Sade's section, augmented by delegations from the other sections, musicians, and a large crowd, marched from the Place des Piques to the Place de la Révolution, from there to the Place de la Réunion, and finally back again to the Place des Piques. Ominously, at the Place de la Révolution, one speech was drowned out by the noise of the guillotine nearby.[122] At each stop in the march, there were speeches, poetry, or music. This kind of peripatetic street-theater was a modest imitation of the truly grandiose spectacle devised by David for the Festival of Unity and Indivisibility two months earlier, on August 10, 1793, designed to march a huge throng from one historic location to another for speeches, music, poetry, and vast theatrical displays. This secular iconography was the Revolution's alternative to religious festivals and ceremonies.

On October 9, when the Marat-Lepeletier procession returned to the Place des Piques, it was Sade's turn to make his speech. "Citizens," he began, "the most cherished duty of hearts truly republican is the recognition owed to great men." Sade exhorted his audience, "Always admire and honor your great men: this precious rapture will increase their number among you." (Perhaps Sade was thinking of his own reputation, his failed plays, especially the one that had been hissed off the stage, or of his having been shouted out of the president's chair.) *Marat! Lepeletier!* he cried. "Sublime martyrs of liberty, already lodged in the Temple of Memory, whence, forever revered by men, you soar above them like the beneficent stars that light their way." Sade hailed Marat (rather improbably) as the embodiment of "consummate altruism" and benevolence. He pictured Marat writing selflessly in his wretched garret, "deprived . . . of all the luxuries of life, buried . . . alive in a kind of tomb." Indeed, Sade portrayed Marat as a version of himself: a fellow writer and a victim of despotism. How many times had Sade told his fellow citizens in his section that story of his own political and literary awakening in the bowels of the Bastille, of his own battle with royal despotism? As the Revolution turned to Terror, Sade hoped to connect himself with one of its most rabid exponents. Sade evoked a Marat persecuted for wanting to cleanse the earth of all tyrants. There are some people—"slaves," Sade called them—"who accused you of loving blood!"[123] Yes, Sade himself had been misunderstood in this very same way!

Sade's speech then shifted to ridicule Charlotte Corday. He complained about the illustrators who portrayed her as beautiful. In fact, she was a comely young woman, twenty-five years old, and possessed a principled, resolute character; her interest, in addition to ridding the world of Marat, was to demonstrate that women "are capable of firmness."[124] The prosecution was unsuccessful in its attempts to force her to admit that she had merely been the tool of a masculine conspiracy. "I have killed one man to save a hundred thousand," she replied, and added, "I was a republican well before the Revolution and I have never lacked energy."[125] Her sense of honor and her courage were evident even as she climbed the steps to the guillotine. Sade, however, toed the revolutionary line, which held that women were pure, gentle, nurturing spirits. He called the women in his audience the "timid and soft" sex. A normal woman, he said, could not have committed Corday's brutal act. He expressed outrage at artists who present "her likeness to us, as they dare to do, in the enchanting image of Beauty." Sade preferred to ridicule Corday as a monstrous androgyne, a freak of nature, neither male nor female, "like those mixed creatures to whom one can assign no particular sex, spewed forth from hell to the despair of both sexes."126

It may be wondered what Sade's intentions were when he deified Marat, and how far Sade's politics had moved from his support for a constitutional monarchy toward Jacobin extremism, whose rhetoric he seemed to adopt (or parody) in this speech.127 Far more interesting than the question of whether Sade's speech accurately reflected his true politics are the autobiographical and self-referential allusions in it—very private allusions to his own thwarted quest for renown in the theater, to his own isolation and his own literary activities in the state prisons, and to his own ambiguous sexuality. The surprising anger that he pumped into his tirade against the man-woman Corday was the extreme voice of rage and disgust always heard inside his own mind. Now, at the age of fifty-three, he seemed disturbed by his own sexuality, by his own baffled ambitions, by writing political tracts and hospital reports for his section, and by the prospect of his own death. Two months earlier, he had suffered another pulmonary crisis, spitting up blood. And now the Revolution had itself taken a very bloody turn indeed.

On October 16, 1793, a week after Sade's speech, Marie-Antoinette, her hair ignominiously clipped short for the blade, was carted off from the Conciergerie for her appointment with "Monsieur Guillotine." Later, when Sade was imprisoned as a moderate, he would claim that he had been one of the patriotic mob at Marie-Antoinette's execution: "I was also there when the Austrian submitted to her just punishment."128 Privately, however, he identified with the Queen during her own bitter imprisonment. In his notebook, he recorded these words that he imagined her speaking at the Conciergerie: "The ferocious beasts who surround me each day invent some humiliation that adds to the horror of my fate; drop by drop they infuse into my heart the poison of adversity, count my sighs with delight, and, before fattening themselves on my blood, they slake their thirst with my tears."129 At the end of the month, on October 31, the twenty-two imprisoned Girondin deputies were guillotined. On November 7, Philippe-Égalité, the Duc d'Orléans, met the same fate. On November 19, it was the turn of Sylvain Bailly, the first mayor of Paris. And, of course, there were countless others. By this time, arrests and executions were so common, and the prison system was so vastly overcrowded, that buildings like the Luxembourg Palace had been commandeered as places of detention. Executions were not confined to Paris. The brutal reconquest of the rebellious Vendée resulted in the systematic slaughter of as many as a quarter of a million civilians, one-third of the population.130 At Nantes, Jean-Baptiste Carrier relieved the backlog at the guillotine by an expedient he called "vertical deportations"—sinking barge-loads of bound and naked citizens in the icy river Loire.[131] This atrocity prompted Carlyle to exclaim, "Cruel is the panther of the woods, the she-bear bereaved of her whelps: but there is in man a hatred crueller than that."[132] Sade was already on a list of émigrés. Could he see them now preparing a place for him in the tumbrel?

In November, Sade believed that he might escape the guillotine. He had been appointed vice-president of his section, and in that capacity, on November 7, he presented to his section meeting a proposal to change some of the street names in the district that bore "proscribed, disreputable, or inconsequential" names. For example, the rue Saint-Honoré would now be called the rue de la Convention; the rue Neuve-des-Mathurins would be the rue de Caton; the rue Saint-Nicolas would be the rue de l'Homme-Libre; the courtyard that had been called Henri IV would be Cour de Junius Brutus, "who," Sade added, for those who might not know, "drove the kings out of Rome." The proposal was unanimously adopted.[133] Thus, all references to the monarchy and to religion were to be obliterated. This was a time when churches were looted and religious images were defaced. To this sacrilegious frenzy, Sade added his own voice, writing his final tract for his section, his "Pétition de la Section des Piques aux représentants du peuple français." This antireligious tract was approved by the section, and Sade was part of the delegation that carried it to the National Convention on November 15, where he read it to cordial applause. His argument was that royalty and religion (which he called "superstition") propped each other up and imposed an equal tyranny on the minds of the people. With the monarchy gone, it was time to finish off religion as well and install "the reign of philosophy." An enlightened people could now finally cast off "the frivolous toys of an absurd religion" for a worthy divinity: "Reason replaces Mary in our temples, and the incense that burned at the knees of an adulteress will now be kindled only at the feet of the Goddess who broke our chains." Then, in a passage rich with autobiographical significance, Sade recalled the fate of enlightened thinkers (like himself) before the Revolution: "In the past, the philosopher laughed in secret at the monkeyshines of Catholicism; but if he dared speak out loud, it was in the dungeons of the Bastille, where ministerial despotism knew how to compel his silence."[134] It was time now to progress "from idolatry to wisdom." Sade called for clearing out churches and using them to inculcate the people with revolutionary virtues, the new secular religion, based on man's innate morality, "that precious organ which Nature always places in the heart of man." The new secular religion would indoctrinate the people in virtues useful to the state: courage, equality, love of country. One of the pleasures this essay afforded Sade was the opportunity to utter blasphemies: Jesus was "a Jewish slave of the Romans"; Mary was an adulteress and "the whore of Galilee."[135] Sade was right. Blasphemy and sacrilege had now become politically correct discourse. His sacrilegious words and acts with the whore Jeanne Testard in 1763, which had got him into so much trouble then, were now commonplace statements to be greeted with applause. Words that could not be uttered in 1763 were now published at government expense.

The applause, however, would not sound long in Sade's ears. The Revolution lurched from one extreme to the other, and woe betide the citizen who did not jump quickly enough. Robespierre, it happened, had been offended by the de-Christianization movement and worked to rein in its excesses. Sade's anti-Christian speech, read at the National Convention, turned out to have been ill-timed. Moreover, Robespierre, who was after all a member of the Section des Piques, would also have remembered the tract written by Sade and recited by him before the National Convention on June 16; in it, Sade had spoken against the idea of a mercenary revolutionary army, an army that Robespierre happened to favor. Perhaps the former Marquis de Sade needed reindoctrination. The surgical tool for this mind-altering operation stood in the Place de la Révolution, and it was working overtime.

CHAPTER 26

The Guillotine Beneath Our Windows

*I*T WAS Sunday morning, December 8, 1793, and Sade was at home with Constance Quesnet at 20 rue Neuve-des-Mathurins. There was a knock at the front door. It was Jouenne Juspel with an arrest order issued by the police department of the Paris Commune. Earlier that morning, at ten o'clock, Juspel had stopped at the Section des Piques to obtain assistance, and he was assigned Michel Laurent, a member of the section's Revolutionary Committee. When they were shown into Sade's apartment, they informed him that he was to be arrested "as suspect" according to the Law of Suspects enacted on September 17. During the Terror, this dreaded pronouncement was virtually the same as a sentence of death. Sade did not even blink. According to the officers, he calmly replied "that he recognized nothing better than to obey the laws, and that we had to do our duty."[1] Had Sade rehearsed his stoical and apparently innocent-sounding reply? He knew that his response and his demeanor would become part of his dossier. He did not appear surprised by the men at his door.[2]

When Sade told Juspel and Laurent to perform their duty, the two men set about it. According to their report, they had Sade open up all his cabinets and drawers, and they conducted the usual search for incriminating papers. In particular, they carefully went through his study—a peaceful room "overlooking the garden," they noted. Sade made a special point of asking the two men to allow him to keep in his possession "eight pieces," his political tracts and speeches for his section. Sade watched as the two men read over his eight essays. He was getting along well with Juspel and Laurent. When they were done reading (had Sade finally found the appreciative audience he craved?), they let him keep his papers. "Finding nothing in them but patriotism," the officers reported, "we did not believe it was our duty to refuse." This was an interesting victory for Sade, who was staring the messengers of death straight in the face.

In the past, whenever Sade had won some concession from prison authoriti s, he had immediately tried for another one. Encouraged by Juspel and Laurent's flexibility, he now asked them "to forward to the Citizen Girouard, Publisher, rue Bout-du-Monde, three sheets of a manuscript with the title *Aline et Valcour*, which sheets the Citizen Sade had asked his publisher to return to him for corrections." Sade's pushing for this additional favor turned out to be a serious blunder, since it divulged his connection to someone who was already under investigation and would be guillotined exactly one month later. Sade was being arrested as "suspect," and that charge could have meant anything. An enemy in his own section could have denounced him. Possibly Robespierre himself had taken a dislike to his politics. Eventually, however, specific crimes would have to be offered into evidence at Sade's hearing before Fouquier-Tinville, the dreaded prosecutor of the Revolutionary Tribunal. But now Sade had just given the prosecution evidence of his relationship to a royalist who was the publisher of his, until now, anonymously published erotic novel *Justine*, and when Girouard's offices were searched three weeks after Sade's arrest, copies of *Justine* were discovered. Robespierre, "the Incorruptible," though in favor of freedom of the press, had no use for pornography. Under interrogation, Girouard implicated Sade.[3] On January 8, 1794, Girouard climbed the steps to peer through the republican window, as the guillotine was called. Sade, instead of wheedling favors, would have done better to say nothing at all.

Mme Quesnet was present during the search of her friend's rooms. If Sade was calm and affable, even to the point of foolishness, she was visibly upset. Juspel and Laurent asked him if she was his wife. He said no, explaining that she lived on the floor below. The officers, however, "observed that there was some sort of affection between them because of the interest she took in the arrest of said Citizen Sade." Juspel and Laurent therefore went down to her rooms and rummaged through all her papers, but found "nothing suspicious." Finally, they all went back upstairs, and Sade watched as Juspel and Laurent secured both his study and his bedroom by attaching white strips of paper across the doorways with dabs of red wax. Even then the machine of state Terror had its many functionaries, rituals, and officious bits of business. While the two officers affixed their seals into the soft wax, Sade and Mme Quesnet said their farewells, very much dreading that, the way things were going during those dark days, they would never see each other again.

Sade was immediately taken to the Madelonnettes prison, previously a convent for wayward girls and reforming prostitutes. Like all of the other prisons, the Madelonnettes was vastly overcrowded with a constantly renewed supply of "suspects." The prison records list the entrance of "François Desade," François being his third given name, which was recorded by mistake at his baptism as Donatien-Alphonse-François, whereas his parents had intended him to be named Donatien-Aldonse-Louis. After the Revolution, Sade had begun to call himself Citizen Louis Sade. Did he mislead the jailer at the Madelonnettes into recording his Christian name incorrectly? Or was it just a bureaucratic error? The jailer looked at the new prisoner and entered the following formal description: "Height five feet six inches, hair and eyebrows gray-blond, forehead high and broad, eyes light blue, nose medium, mouth small, chin round, face oval and full."[4] No one could tell Sade exactly for what he had been arrested, and on the day he entered the Madelonnettes, he began a very short letter to the Section des Piques: "I was arrested without being told the reasons for my detention; I throw myself into the arms of my fellow citizens, fully hopeful that, my patriotism being known to them, they would not want to leave me to languish in chains." He then gave the short form of his usual recitation of his sufferings under ministerial despotism—just a phrase or two. Though he appeared too depressed to rouse his prison muse to the usual heights of outraged innocence, he did muster a bit of bravado: he told his fellow citizens that he trusted they would come to his aid but he would accept it "only on the condition that I am in no way guilty; if I am, let me be punished, that is just; however, citizens, I am not, I swear it to you, and in this certitude you will not refuse to take an interest on behalf of your unfortunate fellow citizen."[5] The citizens of the Section des Piques simply ignored the plea of their former president.

Sade was, of course, familiar with imprisonment and prison life, but nothing could have prepared him for the psychological and physical horrors of Paris's prisons during the Terror. There were more than fifty such institutions in operation, some of them quite makeshift and inadequate to deal with a population that had swelled to around seven thousand in December, when Sade was arrested.[6] As always, even during the Terror, conditions could be improved for individual prisoners if they had the means to bribe the right officials and jailers. Sade got no special treatment. He did not get a cell. He did not even get a bed in a dormitory. "For six weeks I slept in the toilets," he wrote to Gaufridy.[7]

Three weeks into his imprisonment at the Madelonnettes, on December 29, Sade composed a letter to the Committee for General Security:

> Legislators,
>   Ten years a victim under the chains of ministerial despotism from which only the Revolution freed me, how could I have imagined that the beneficent hand of a nation that broke my chains was on the verge of giving them back to me? Attached as I am to the new order of things

both philosophically and out of gratitude, was it not likely that I would eternally cooperate with all my strength for the support of the Revolution? Legislators, what my heart feels, my actions demonstrate with the same ardor that I called out to the people on July 3, '89, for the destruction of the Bastille, where the infamous despots locked me up: I possess in this connection one of the best claims to good citizenship that any republican could possibly furnish; I will prove it to anyone it pleases the committee to name for the examination of my conduct. Yes, indeed, with this same ardor I have ever since continually demonstrated the deepest attachment to this Revolution, which for so many reasons I called my liberating goddess. Constantly honored with the most important posts in my section, charged with all of the petitions it addressed to the representatives of the people, fulfilling, in short, all my duties with zeal, alacrity, accuracy, imagine my shock at finding myself put under arrest last 18 of Frimaire[8] and conducted to the Madelonnettes without any kind of explanation, without anyone's being able to tell me the reasons for such an act of violence! Legislators, error or vengeance alone has woven this devilish plot, and it behooves your sense of justice not to allow it to drag down innocence. . . . None of the articles of the Law [of Suspects] can apply to me; my heart is pure, my blood is ready to be shed if necessary for the good of the Republic. I implore you therefore to name someone to examine my conduct; I wish to be punished if I have merited it, freed if I have done no wrong. I cannot even obtain the lifting of my seals; my enemies, who very well know how much justice is on my side for regaining my liberty when it will have been seen that there is nothing suspicious at my house, are delaying this inquiry as much as they can.

This was an all-too-familiar role for Sade. He had "enemies"—possibly in his own section, possibly in the very Committee for General Security to whose sense of justice he was appealing. It may seem strange that, with life and death in the balance, he made a fuss about the lifting of the seals placed on his apartment when he was arrested. But he wanted action, anything to break the suspense of those dreadful first three weeks in prison. He wanted an officer of the Committee for General Security to go to his study and read the patriotic essays in his bookshelf. As he wrote, it was as if he could hear the tumbrel wheels. Perhaps his petition was already too long. Perhaps the members of the Committee (if they read it at all) were already rolling their eyes. More anxiously than when he began to write, Sade came to the point deferentially: "Legislators, in short, and knowing how much it is improper to waste your time, I limit myself to asking you with the greatest urgency to bring me to my house in order to lift the seals there, to send me back to prison if I am guilty, to leave me at my hearth if I am innocent."[9]

One of Sade's wishes was granted with surprising speed. Late at night on January 12, 1794, he was taken to witness the search of his apartment. Was this the Ultimate Examination that he had requested—the one, it may be said, he had sought throughout his whole life, the one that would determine his guilt or innocence in an absolute sense? Hardly. Sade and his guards must have startled Mme Quesnet. When Juspel and Laurent had gone over the rooms on December 8, he had been able to distract them with his calm manner and by having them read through his patriotic essays. This time, however, the inspectors were thorough. At around midnight, when they were done, they had found and taken as evidence fourteen letters, some of them Gaufridy's. About a year later, Sade mentioned these letters to Gaufridy, "which the imbecilic members of my Revolutionary Committee found to be suspect."[10] Sade had asked for this search, which then turned up his correspondence with a known and hunted royalist in Provence. The committee sent him back to prison, but not to his toilet in the Madelonnettes. They sent him to an even worse place, the Prison des Carmes, another former convent, where more than a hundred priests had been brutally murdered during the September Massacres of 1792. He stayed there only a week, but he had been crammed into a cell "with six persons suffering from malignant fever, of whom two died right next to me."[11] On January 22, 1794, he was transferred to Saint-Lazare, which had been first a leprosarium, then a convent, and finally a vast revolutionary prison; Sade (this time registered under the name François Aldonze Sade) was among its first prisoners.

On March 8, the Committee of Surveillance in the Section des Piques filled out the printed form supplied by the Committee for General Security. A case was going to be made against Sade. Under the printed heading *"His relations, his associates,"* his colleagues at his own section noted that he was "by all reports a very immoral, a very suspect man, and unfit for society"—that is, they added, "if one believes" what had been published in *L'Espion anglais* about the Marseilles and Arcueil affairs, and also by Jacques-Antoine Dulaure in his pamphlet on the corruption of the nobility; he considered Sade a counterrevolutionary and compared "this monster" to Gilles de Rais, Bluebeard.[12] Someone in Sade's section had gone to a lot of trouble to dig up these ancient and totally spurious accounts.

Under the same heading, Sade's section also exploded the story he had tirelessly recited to them ever since he had become a member. The committee wrote, "He prides himself on having been imprisoned at the Bastille under the ancien régime in order to emphasize his patriotism." However, the committee easily disposed of Sade's claim that he had been a political prisoner. They noted that, during those days, "he would necessarily have suffered a different, a very severe punishment if he had not been of the noble class."[13] The committee asserted that they had sniffed him out from the start: "Ever since he appeared at the section, he has not ceased, from August 10 on, to counterfeit the role of patriot, but those there were not deceived by it." Sade was first "unmasked," they continued, by his pamphlet against the standing army, which revealed him to be an "enemy by principle of the republican system, in his private conversation constantly making comparisons drawn from Greek and Roman history in order to prove the impossibility of establishing a democratic and republican government in France."[14] Sade was a learned man. He did draft the petition for the renaming of streets in the district, and many of them were to be given Greek and Roman names. That might be enough to point him toward the guillotine.

The next charge, however, had some basis in fact. They accused him of attempting in 1791 to obtain posts for himself and his sons in the proposed constitutional army for the King under the command of Louis-Hercule-Timoléon, Duc de Cossé-Brissac, in whose regiment Sade had long ago served as an officer (see above, page 39). Sade would spend a lot of ink trying to explain this away. And, finally, there were the confiscated letters from Gaufridy, "which prove" that Sade "had correspondence with the enemies of the Republic." To be sure, this whole indictment was a shabby patchwork of rumor, gossip, and catchphrases. But in Robespierre's France, much less would be enough to get a man executed. Someone on high, possibly Robespierre himself, wanted to get rid of Sade, and in the political climate of the Terror, where "Purge or be purged, suspect or be suspected" was the rule of the day, the sections blew this way or that, as the winds from above directed. The meanness of Sade's colleagues was evident not only in their trumped-up charges against their former president, but also in the way they answered the question about the accused's "profession before and after the Revolution": "Former Comte," was their curt reply. They did not even get his age right. "Around sixty years old," they said.[15] He was fifty-three.

On March 8, 1794, from the bowels of Saint-Lazare, Sade wrote his defense to the Committee for General Security. In it, he repeated the story of his revolutionary activities at the Bastille in July 1789, his subsequent transfer to Charenton, his gratitude to the Revolution that finally set him free. He retold his participation in the events of August 10 that effectively ended the monarchy, how his friend was wounded beside him. He recalled his having been given important positions in his section, how he witnessed the executions of the King and of Marie-Antoinette, how he had been honored to deliver the eulogy for Marat and Lepeletier. Even if he had now been wrongly imprisoned, he told the committee, in setting him free they could rest assured that he bore the Revolution no ill feeling: "I am attached to it philosophically and out of gratitude. And whatever inconvenience it made me experience by incarcerating me for three months for no reason at all, I am and I will always be ready to spill the last drop of my blood in order to maintain it." He added that the only thing that could possibly be held against him was that he had written "a letter or two to Brissac." But Sade insisted that Brissac had rejected his application. If Sade had committed any error, it was that of an "excess of zeal," but, he added, "I would rather be guilty of too much ardor than of moderantism." This was the first time Sade mentioned that dangerous charge. Ironically, his whole mentality had been the opposite of moderate. He had adopted the revolutionary rhetoric and found in it a kind of heady effervescence, a mind-tingling elixir. But the Revolution had suddenly leapt to new excesses, leaving Sade in the no-man's land of the middle. "I swear," he vowed to the Committee for General Security, "no one will have cause to reproach me with complaints of this type ever again."16

Around the same time, Sade also filled out a printed form for the committee. Prison had "obliged me to acquire," he later explained to Gaufridy, "the unfortunate habit" of "writing petitions." He wrote them, he said, "as much for myself as for my comrades in misery, all of whom generally applied to me" for this favor.17 On his own form for the committee, he answered the first question with yet another version of his name: "My name is Aldonze Sade." Still believing that his problems came from the emigration of his sons, Sade continued to take pains to distance himself from them. He made this blunt declaration: "I declare that for the past twenty-two years I have not seen my children, that I do not know where they are, that, if they have emigrated, I consign them to public execration . . . to the nation's vengeance."18 Sade's answers to the questions on this form contained much the same information as in his letter to the committee cited above, but some details were new and interesting. For example, he described his quiet home life:

> I live very privately, I busy myself a great deal with literature, I have relations only with my section, my printers, the various theaters where I have plays, and my agent in the department of Bouches-du-Rhône [i.e., Gaufridy]. Citizen Quesnet, at whose house I live, an excellent patriot, constitutes my only society; I am pleased to raise her son, and the patriotic principles that I inspire in him, and about which he can be interrogated, will prove that the purest good citizenship has always

been the true passion of our household, as it will always be; the true patriot knows how to suffer without complaint when it is for the good of the country.

Answering questions about his income before and after the Revolution, Sade claimed it was about the same; no one could say that he was bitter about the loss of his revenue. "The Revolution," he said, "has not cost me anything, I owe it only my gratitude."[19] To the question about his profession before and after the Revolution, the question to which his own section had brusquely answered "Former Comte," Sade said that his ancestors had been "farmers and merchants," and he boldly asserted, "I have never been a noble, I can prove it whenever one wishes."[20] Sade amplified his denial of any noble blood in a paragraph he added to the letter he sent to the Committee for General Security on May 7.[21] Born and for a time raised in the Palace de Condé, in whose family connection Sade's mother had invested such great pride and such great hopes, Sade here denied any noble title or connection: "I am accused of being a noble. This is false. . . . My ancestors had nearly always performed the honest work of farmers, my father was a man of letters, I have followed the same career after serving six or seven years in the military during my youth. I retired twenty-six years ago, and I have never set foot in Court."[22] In all of these answers and petitions, it is clear that Sade was arguing for his life. Given the way things had gone and were going, it is surprising that he had survived as long as he had. But now he truly was in the jaws of the beast.

On March 27, 1794, Sade was once again transferred, this time "because of illness," to Eugène Coignard's *maison de santé*, newly opened in a former convent in Picpus.[23] This so-called hospital Sade later described to Gaufridy as "a terrestrial paradise: beautiful house, superb garden, choice society, pleasant women."[24] Citizen Coignard's establishment, in fact, was a very profitable scam, a protection racket by which wealthy and influential prisoners could escape the unhealthy, unpleasant, and almost inevitably deadly consequences of detention in the other revolutionary prisons. Like all ideals, the *égalité* celebrated by the Revolution did have its exceptions. Coignard's hospital, similar to one run by Citizen Belhomme, was an extremely lucrative business. The fee for a bare room at Belhomme's started at a princely 1,000 livres a month. Food, furnishings, and heat were extra.[25] In addition, influence high up or carefully arranged bribes to officials would be required to contrive the transfer in the first place. The difference was not just in standard of living, but between life and death, for prisoners tended to be lost or forgotten in these hospitals. Picpus was indeed a "terrestrial paradise," as Sade said. But how could he have afforded it? How could he have been so lucky?

Details are scanty, but such as they are, they point only to Mme Quesnet. Once again, Sade's condition in prison depended on the remarkable loyalty and resourcefulness of one woman. Fittingly, when he drew up his will on January 30, 1806, his bequest to Mme Quesnet appeared first. He would leave to her all of his "furnishings, effects, linen, clothes, books, or papers," as well as the generous sum of 24,000 livres, in "my extreme gratitude for the care and for the sincere friendship" she showed him. In particular, "under the Terror," he said, "she plucked me from the revolutionary scythe most certainly suspended over my head."[26] It took more than a little courage during the time of the Terror to try to help a former noble imprisoned as suspect of antirevolutionary acts and attitudes; fortunately, Mme Quesnet was a person of some fortitude, in addition to being "acquainted with some deputies."[27] Sade would offer these contacts—including a member of the National Convention, Philippe-Charles-Aimé Goupilleau de Montaigu[28]—to help Gaufridy with his own and his son's legal problems over their flight to avoid arrest. Contacts were useful, but money was essential. While Sade was being transferred from one wretched prison to another, Mme Quesnet (to whom he had given his power of attorney in financial matters) struggled to arrange new loans. Sade variously estimated the cost of his detention at 6,000 and 10,000 francs.[29] One thing is clear, as he told Gaufridy: *"At whatever it cost,"* Mme Quesnet personally assumed "the *terrible burden* of getting me released" from prison.[30]

Despite Sade's gratitude for his transfer, he was not free by a long shot. To be sure, at Citizen Coignard's country-club "hospital," he was infinitely more comfortable than he had been before. There were the lovely gardens, the choice society, the pleasant women—an ambience almost recalling the time before the Revolution. Sometimes, it almost seemed as if the world had not changed. Almost.

Beyond the quiet, suburban walls of the former convent, the Terror machine of the Revolution increased its speed and efficiency, its fury consuming even its leaders. While Sade was in Picpus, the celebrated orator Danton was guillotined, on April 5, 1794, along with Hérault and Desmoulins. The prisons were crammed as Robespierre cleaned house of the Indulgents on one side and the Ultras, the extreme revolutionaries, on the other. On April 22, d'Eprémesnil was executed, along with Malesherbes, who had the hideous misfortune to stand on the steps of the scaffold and watch his daughter, his granddaughter, and her husband guillotined before him. In May, it was the turn of the chemist Lavoisier. In one of his last letters to his wife from prison, he wrote with courage and some humor, noting that, at the age of forty-nine, he had lived a "tolerably long" life, and he trusted that his "memory will be accompanied by some glory. What more could I wish? The situation in which

I am now involved will probably spare me the inconveniences of old age."[31] Whole sections of Paris society, in the business, financial, intellectual, professional communities, were scooped up, imprisoned, judged, and sentenced virtually in batches, and then trundled in carts through indifferent or, worse, jeering crowds to the scaffold.

The wheels of even this speedy justice system did not turn quickly enough for Robespierre. The Revolutionary Tribunal, which passed judgment on the prisoners, was proving to be a bottleneck, but that would be remedied on June 10, when the National Convention passed a decree forbidding suspects to call witnesses in their defense or to have counsel. Moreover, the range of capital offenses was broadened to include almost anything. Beneath and around the guillotine, the river of blood overflowed the ditches that had been dug to receive it, producing a genuine inconvenience for the executioners and citizens who lived near the scaffold. Around the time of the Festival of the Supreme Being, held on June 8, another pretentious celebration organized once again by the painter David for Robespierre, the guillotine was moved from the Place de la Révolution to relative suburban obscurity at the end of the rue Saint-Antoine. However, the odor of blood and of decaying corpses quickly brought protests from the guillotine's new neighbors. Within three days, the apparatus was moved once again, this time outside the Barrière du Trône, at that time called the Place du Trône Renversé (now called the Place de la Nation).

The guillotine's new location turned out to be exactly on the other side of the walled garden of Citizen Coignard's hospital at Picpus. If Sade and the privileged "guests" inside believed they had escaped harm, the sounds of workmen breaking into their garden wall to create a gate for the corpse cart rang as terrible and as hollow as a shovel of dirt on a coffin lid. The Great Terror had followed them; death had entered paradise. Sade described this awesome event in his November 19 letter to Gaufridy: "All of a sudden, the place of execution was moved exactly beneath our windows, and the cemetery for the guillotined into the exact center of our garden. My dear friend, we had eighteen hundred buried there in thirty-five days, of whom a third came from our unfortunate prison."[32] As a concession to the complaints about the rivers of putrefying blood, the constructors of this guillotine added a lead-lined wheelbarrow beneath the scaffold to catch the effluvium. Sade would later report to Gaufridy the execution of "poor Dolci, my close friend."[33] He would also say that being so close to this scene of horror had affected his health: "My *national* detention, *the guillotine before my eyes,* did me a hundred times more harm than all the Bastilles imaginable had ever done."[34] The stench of decaying flesh and blood horrified the entire neighborhood.

Each morning, throughout the vast prison system of Paris, turnkeys would search out the prisoners on their lists designated for transport to the Revolutionary Tribunal, where the only two possible verdicts were death or, more rarely now than ever, acquittal. After trial, the condemned were taken to holding cells in the Conciergerie for execution, usually the following day. Soon it would be Sade's turn. On July 24, 1794, the charges compiled by the Section des Piques against "Aldonze Sade, ex–noble and Comte, man of letters and officer in the cavalry, accused of conspiracy against the Republic," were transmitted to the Revolutionary Tribunal.[35] Two days later, on a list of twenty-eight people called to appear for trial, number eleven was "Aldonze Sade, age sixty." "Ex-noble" is the most common identifier among those on the list, although there were military officers, a chemist, a florist, a former priest, a bailiff, a carpenter, and a lemonade vendor, among others. Also on the list was Perrine-Jeanne Leroux (the Comtesse de Maillé), a relative of Sade's mother. Number four on the list was François-Désiré-Mathieu Courlet-Beaulop, who called himself Vermantois, age thirty-one.[36] Courlet may have met his doom because, as a prison snitch or *mouton* (sheep), he knew too many of Fouquier-Tinville's embarrassing secrets.[37]

These were the charges lodged against Sade as one of "the enemies of the people" and as an active participant in "counterrevolutionary machinations and conspiracies":

> Sade, ex-Comte, captain in the guards of Capet in 1792,[38] engaged in communications and correspondence with the enemies of the Republic. He has constantly attacked the republican form of government by arguing in his section that this form of government was impracticable. He revealed himself to be a partisan of federalism and an advocate of the traitor Roland. Finally, it appears that the proofs of patriotism that he sought to provide were merely his way of eluding the investigation into his complicity in the conspiracy of the tyrant of which he was the vile satellite.[39]

The business about the "traitor Roland" was one of the accusations the Section des Piques had lodged against Sade in their report to the Committee for General Security on March 8, 1794: "At the time of his appearance in the section in October '92, he immediately opposed the decree voted by the Assembly that charged that Roland had lost the confidence of the section and was unworthy of that of the French People." Sade, they claimed, defended Roland, "using the specious pretext that he did not have any material evidence" of Roland's misdeeds, and "that it was necessary to wait before judging a man of such virtue."[40] Sade never responded to this charge against him, and nothing more is known of the Roland affair, which must have created quite a stir in his section. If it was true that, when Sade first entered the section, he had stood against the radicals and had insisted on proof before a citizen received revolutionary justice, then he would certainly appear to be guilty of "moderantism"—a capital crime now, on the eve of his appearance before the Revolutionary Tribunal.

As to Mme de Maillé, Sade's relative on the same list, it was her fate to follow her son, age sixteen, into the courtroom three days after he had been sentenced to the guillotine. She had originally been summoned from prison on the same date as her son, July 24. Through a mix-up, however, instead of Mme de Maillé, a woman named Mayet had been brought to the court by the harried bailiffs, among a group of seventy-four prisoners. A small mistake. No matter, the busy Tribunal quickly found Citizen Mayet guilty, along with the seventy-three others, and they were all sent to the guillotine outside Sade's walls at Picpus. Among them was the lad Maillé, accused of participating in the supposed counterrevolutionary conspiracy among the prisoners of Saint-Lazare. His actual crime, it appears, was to have recited an angry speech "replete with poetry" to his jailer.[41] The mistake about Mme de Maillé's name would be rectified on July 27, when she, along with Sade, was summoned for judgment before the Tribunal. Still in shock and grief over her son, she sat numbly on one of the wooden benches provided for the accused, and when her name was called, she suffered convulsions and a complete nervous collapse. She was removed to the Conciergerie until her health could be restored. By a strange turn of fate, her reaction to her son's death saved her own life: on that very day, Robespierre himself was overthrown, to be guillotined a day later. The others who were tried with Mme de Maillé, with the exception of a farmer who was acquitted, were all sent to their death.

But what of Sade? How had he missed the tragic fate of the others on the list with him for trial on July 27, on the very eve of Robespierre's execution? Quite simply, Sade was not at the trial. Against his name was marked the gracious word "Absent," a blessing he shared with four fellow prisoners. Could he not be found? As in the case of the unfortunate Mme Mayet, mistakes were possible. Carlyle mentioned the following freakish escape: "One prisoner's door happening to be open, the warder carelessly put the chalk mark for the next day's death consignment on the inside, which did not show after the door was shut!"[42] Lely believed that Sade escaped the guillotine "thanks to the multiplicity and the overcrowding of the prisons": the bailiff from the Tribunal, in visiting the various houses of detention to collect the other prisoners on the list with Sade, may have become confused because of Sade's various transfers from one prison to another, and when the bailiff finally got to

Picpus, he may not have known that Sade was there.[43] Mistakes did occur, but Lely's explanation seems unlikely. At Picpus, the bailiff did collect one prisoner, Béchon d'Arquien. Why did he not find Sade? Lever suggests that the bailiff did not even call Sade's name, and that Sade was spared "neither by chance, nor by error": it was because he paid the price.[44] The same means Mme Quesnet employed to get Sade safely tucked away in Picpus could also have been used to spare him on that final day of the Terror. But if Sade was saved from the guillotine by a relatively obscure person like Mme Quesnet and the relatively modest sum of money she could borrow in his name, why were so many individuals with truly vast fortunes and with more important friends not spared? Bribery, influence, error, Providence—the exact explanation for Sade's good fortune in this instance may never be known.

The news of the Thermidorian coup d'état of July 27 (9 Thermidor, in the revolutionary calendar) ran through the prisons, a giddy rumor, a Godsend. Robespierre had been denounced and temporarily arrested at the National Convention. At the Hôtel de Ville, where he, Couthon, Hanriot, Le Bas, and Saint-Just had taken sanctuary, troops loyal to the Convention that night arrested these five. When they entered the room, they found Robespierre's face and jaw a bloody mess, apparently the result of his poorly aimed pistol shot in a failed suicide attempt. During the early morning of July 28, the guillotine was returned to the Place de la Révolution. Later that day, Robespierre and a group of his close supporters were executed. There would be over a hundred put to death in three days. Sade perfectly well understood how close he had come to being one of the last victims of Robespierre, but, fortunately for him, "the blade of justice mightily fell that night on the new Silla of France."[45] Throughout the prison system, there rose a great sigh of relief. The Terror was over.

The Thermidorians now in control of the National Convention enacted measures to free political prisoners. "Everything became easier," Sade wrote to Gaufridy.[46] Once more, Sade eagerly turned his pen to writing petitions. In considering his case, the Committee for General Security made inquiries at the Section des Piques, which responded on August 25 with a brief declaration in praise of Sade's "zeal and intelligence" in his work for the section, asserting that they were aware of nothing that could cast doubt on his patriotism or his "good citizenship."[47] The Thermidorian purge had already changed the personnel and the attitudes of Sade's and Robespierre's old section. On September 30, in another petition to the committee, Sade wrote, "I was a patriot even before the Revolution."[48] With a happier step, Mme Quesnet now walked out to Picpus to visit Sade and to collect his petitions. On October 11, she wrote to Citizen Bourdon, a member of the National Con-

vention, asking for his help in freeing Sade, "a man of letters" and "an excellent patriot."[49] Sade credited his release to her, to "the attentions as passionate
as they are devoted of the amiable companion who has won my heart and
who has shared my life for the past five years."[50] Finally, on October 15, 1794,
after 312 days, Sade once again walked out of prison a free man.

On My Knees,
Dying of Hunger

HE LITTLE house on the rue Neuve-des-Mathurins was much the same as when Sade had left it more than ten months earlier. In the study overlooking the garden, he wrote at once to Gaufridy, informing him, for the first time, of the fact of his detention, of his release, and of the ruling of the Committee for General Security permitting him to remain in Paris and to have the sequestration of his income lifted, and he sent copies of this decree to the relevant offices in Provence. He also complained about Gaufridy's "silence for the past ten months."[1] Sade expected his money to start rolling in. His detention had put him deeply in debt.

At the end of October 1794, Sade wrote to Esprit Audibert, his farmer at La Coste, informing him that rents could now be sent, and asking him to convey regards to Gaufridy, "wherever he may be."[2] Receiving nothing from Gaufridy, who was still in hiding, he again wrote to Audibert, warning that, if he did not immediately receive his rents, "I will take my complaints to the Committee for General Security," a strange threat for one who had himself barely escaped the committee's clutches. He also said that, if a certain Citizen Payan of La Coste did not mend his ways, he too would be "referred by me to the Committee for General Security."[3] Sade liked repeating the name of the Committee for General Security. It had an orbicular sound.

Sade tried to encourage Gaufridy by offering his own and Mme Quesnet's political contacts to help with his lawyer's legal problems. "Take courage," he wrote on November 19, "everything will return to normal bit by bit, and we will think no more of our troubles except to make our nephews tremble."[4] His principal concern, however, was his own financial predicament. He warned Gaufridy that the next year, because of inflation, he would require 14,000 rather than the usual 10,000 francs from his estates. Where would Gaufridy find the additional money? Sade had the answer: "Not one of my estates," he complained, "is leased out at its value," an assessment supposedly made by an unnamed man from Provence he had met in prison, and meant to imply that Gaufridy was indolent at best, and perhaps even a cheat. By means of this obvious fiction, Sade hoped to shame Gaufridy into somehow finding the difference. He further instructed him to sell off whatever furnishings were left after "the pillage of La Coste," and to use the money to send him basic commodities, "such things as oil, jams, candles."[5] Very soon, people would begin to go hungry in Paris.

On January 21, 1795, Sade received a visit from a man who turned out to be a nephew of Mlle de Rousset. That "recommendation" alone would have been enough to elicit his sympathy: "I was delighted," Sade told Gaufridy, "to see a relative of that amiable former friend." The memory of that golden August at La Coste in 1778 with Mlle de Rousset after his escape from police custody rose in his mind like the dream of a former existence: the sunny walks in the park, the herbal fragrance of the Provence summer in his nostrils, Mlle de Rousset beside him. How the climate had changed since those lovely days: "You cannot imagine how cold it is; and we are in need of everything. Even water is more expensive now than wine was before." Now his thoughts were of death, aging (he was fifty-four), illness, deprivation, and money. He still saw, he told Gaufridy, *"the guillotine before my eyes."* He ended this letter with news of another death; "Madame de Sade has just lost her father."[6] Morbid thoughts oppressed him: "In past years I had friends who exist no more, I had money that exists no more, and letters of credit that are no longer sent."[7]

The winter of 1794–95 was one of the coldest in the century. Sade wrote to Gaufridy, "My ink *freezes* in writing and I am obliged to keep it in a bain-marie."[8] He also complained about having to bundle up and walk all the way to the post office to collect a letter in which Gaufridy had sent him some money—which Sade sarcastically described as "the exorbitant sum" of 200 francs. "In the name of God," Sade exclaimed, "do not send me such paltry sums as that."[9] Throughout this harsh season, Sade continued to be called by the Section des Piques to serve in the National Guard one day a month. But he no longer took part in the business of the section, nor did he hold any office there. His experiment in revolutionary politics and rhetoric was definitely over. For one thing, he, like almost everyone else, felt safer. He now devoted his attention to what really mattered—money. He badgered his agents in Provence for money, money, money. Of course, he could have gone down there to live on his estate. That would have been far more economical, but then he would have had no one to blame for the insufficiency and mismanagement of his income. No, he would stay in Paris and try to live on what Gaufridy sent. He would try again to live as a "man of letters." Soon after he was released, on December 5, 1794, he wrote to ask the new administration to give him the partially printed copies of *Aline et Valcour*, which had been impounded in Girouard's office. Girouard's widow was asking to have the seals on the establishment lifted, and though Sade admitted that Girouard had already paid him for the book, he argued, "I nevertheless have the greatest claim upon the copies." He said that he looked forward to the pleasure of seeing it properly published.[10]

If Sade liked to dwell on his own misfortunes, his own losses, he had little patience for those of others. Just ten days after his reverie about Mlle de Rousset, he wrote to Gaufridy to console him over the death of his eldest son, Elzéar. Sade's letter began well enough: "I understand your sorrow, your grief, and I very sincerely sympathize with you over the terrible loss that you have suffered." But a sentence later, Sade's own problems took sudden precedence: "However, my dear and good friend, in lamenting the dead, do not suffer the living to perish, and yet that is exactly to what your terrible negligence is reducing me. My money, I am begging you for it."[11] Ten days later, still desperate, Sade imagined he could rouse his lawyer by writing to Mme Gaufridy. Referring to the death of her son, Sade told her, "I have the greatest sympathy for the misfortunes that have befallen you." However, he explained, "your husband's dismaying silence obliges me to appeal to you to please send me news of him. For the past two months I have been starving to death and I have not been able to extract either a sol or even a response from him."[12] The grotesque intertwining of sympathy and importuning in these and later letters reveals how deeply disturbed and bereft Sade had become. But we must also allow that it was never his way to resolve his feelings internally; he always acted out his impulses, however contradictory, more or less in public.

Death and money would remain Sade's fixations. For example, in February 1795, having discovered that his aged relative M. de Murs had finally died "five months ago," Sade upbraided Gaufridy's "cursed negligence" in having done nothing to wrest the inheritance from the natural heirs, who, as daughters of an émigré, could not legally inherit.[13] Sade appeared equally crass in his attempts to extract money from his aunt Mme de Villeneuve, who Sade's agent Quinquin had suggested might wish to rent Sade's house at Mazan for the flat fee of 15,000 livres for the duration of her life. Accordingly, Sade sent Gaufridy to "go see her at once" and "*take her pulse*, and if you think that she cannot live beyond two years, conclude the deal at once."[14]

Nothing came of the chimerical hopes Sade pinned on Mme de Villeneuve and on M. de Murs's legacy. A year later, when he tried to get the silverware that his uncle the Abbé had left, Mme de Villeneuve would write him a stern letter, insisting that it belonged to her and that she had her own problems: "Believe me, my dear nephew, you are not the only one in financial straits."[15] Sade, however, deemed his own need greater than anyone else's, particularly considering the extravagance and duration of all of his misfortunes. He concocted his schemes in a kind of egocentric frenzy, and pushed them to embarrassing extremes. Perhaps part of him needed a witness to his desperation, an audience for the pitiful drama of his neediness, his fear of poverty and old age.

Forced to economize, Sade lived a quiet, sober life: "stew from my section, bread from my section, vegetables five times a week, not one play, not one extravagance, just my companion, a cook, and me."[16] On August 26, he warned Gaufridy that the rate of inflation was such that he would need 60,000 francs for 1796.[17] Because of the high cost of commodities in Paris, he asked Gaufridy to send him "a hundred bottles of wine," "fifty one-pound pots of fruit in syrup," "ten boxes of dried fruit"—"but not sugar-coated," he added—"some candied fruit, such as lemons, orange peels, figs, apricots, walnuts, etc. etc. etc., a pot of anchovies." From whatever furnishings remained at La Coste, Sade wanted "the best armchairs in the yellow or crimson damask, the best of the little writing tables," the objects in his natural-history collection, and "the best writing case in Morocco leather."[18] Writing implements were much on his mind.

Sade concluded this letter to Gaufridy by announcing the publication of his novel *Aline et Valcour, ou le roman philosophique*, the first publication to appear under his name (*Justine* having been published anonymously four years earlier). "I beg you to let me know," Sade asked Gaufridy, "the best way of sending you postage-free two copies of a work in 8 volumes that I have just published, one for you, the other for your best friend. This work, from which they expect, they claim, a great deal, perhaps may interest you."[19] Did his publisher really expect "a great deal" of this long and cumbersome epistolary novel? Sade had hopes. He spared no effort to promote its success. A day after he wrote to Gaufridy, he composed a publicity release to be sent to booksellers in Provence. "Copies are going with such a rapidity that it behooves you to act quickly," Sade told the merchants, and gave them instructions for ordering copies.[20] Pleased as he was to see *Aline et Valcour* in print after so many years, he had been occupied writing another, more interesting novel, which would also be published at the end of this year, *La Philosophie dans le boudoir*, identified on the title page as "A posthumous work by the author of *Justine*," in an effort to capitalize on the notoriety and popularity of his earlier book.

Sade completed *La Philosophie dans le boudoir* during the summer of 1795. Its title suggests its characteristic marriage of argumentative discourse (the philosophy) with extremely erotic and bold sex scenes (the bedroom).

Comparatively short and tightly focused, *La Philosophie dans le boudoir* may be the most clearly realized, purest example of Sade's literary technique. The story concerns Eugénie de Mistival, her sexual awakening and education into the principles of libertinage. Eugénie is a very willing fifteen-year-old virgin fresh out of her convent. She will have three instructors, the first being the voluptuous Mme de Saint-Ange, twenty-six years old, and thoroughly devoted to libertinism of every sort with both sexes. "I am an amphibious creature" (383),[21] she tells her brother, the Chevalier de Mirvel, twenty years old, also a libertine and bisexual, with whom she has been conducting an incestuous affair. He is also the lover of Dolmancé, the third instructor, who, at age thirty-six, is, according to the Chevalier, "the most celebrated atheist, the most immoral man, . . . the most wicked and the most depraved individual who ever lived." A libertine by philosophy, a sodomite by preference and principle, Dolmancé loves men but will occasionally have sex with women if, as the Chevalier expresses it, "they are so kind as to change their sex for him" (385). The education of Eugénie will take place in Mme de Saint-Ange's bedroom in her isolated country château. This setting is far removed from the coercion and the murderous perversions of the nightmare dungeons of the château of Silling. The beauty, the handsomeness, the air of courtesy and the ready compliance of the participants, as well as their general cheerfulness, suggest, if not a happy fantasy of the ancien régime, then perhaps a happy fantasy of the Thermidorian thaw following the atrocities of the Reign of Terror.

The philosophical Dolmancé acts as the chief tutor, directing the discourse and the sexual scenes. For Sade, they are virtually the same activity. A scene in which Mme de Saint-Ange and Dolmancé suck Eugénie's vagina and anus arouses, in due course, the questions of virtue and the existence of God. "Virtue is nothing but a chimera," Dolmancé asserts, and adds: "Can Nature urge something that offends her?" (404). As for God, Dolmancé dismisses Him as "that abominable phantom" (406). Dolmancé prefers to consider the prime force in the universe as matter in motion:

> If matter acts and moves, by a system yet unknown to us, if movement is intrinsic to matter, if it alone is capable, by reason of its energy, of creating, producing, preserving, sustaining, balancing in the immense plains of space all the orbs whose view astounds us and whose uniform and invariable course fills us with respect and admiration, what need is there to look for a power foreign to all that, since this active principle is inherent in Nature itself, which is nothing but matter in action?

To try to explain the mysteries of the universe by supposing a mysterious God as first cause is to introduce unnecessary difficulties. Dolmancé asks, "How do you expect me to accept as the cause of something I do not understand, something that I understand even less!" (407). And what kind of a God did man invent? A ridiculous and base creature, according to Dolmancé: "for, since man *fucks*, he wanted his God *to fuck* too." That's how Christ came to be in "the belly of a Jewish whore." Dolmancé ridicules Christ as a demented swindler, liar, and trickster (408).

Dolmancé, of course, is preaching to the converted. Even the teenage Eugénie is so eager, is such a star pupil, that during the first lesson, when Mme de Saint-Ange is demonstrating masturbation on Dolmancé, Eugénie begs Mme de Saint-Ange, "Oh! my dear friend, please let me frig this magnificent member." To which Dolmancé, losing control of his lecture, replies, "I can't resist! Let her do it, Madame: this artless innocence makes me stiffen prodigiously." Mme de Saint-Ange, however, will not allow the deviation from the lesson plan. "Be prudent," she counsels Dolmancé; "the discharge of this seed, by diminishing the activity of your animal spirits, would retard the force of your lectures." Dolmancé then resumes his lesson on terminology, defining, appropriately enough, testicles, since, all the while, his have been in Eugénie's hands (397). The novel progresses through alternating passages of "theory" and "practice," the *philosophie* and the *boudoir* of the title, beginning with mild sexual scenes and progressing through masturbation, oral, genital, and anal sex, in orgy scenes or "tableaux" carefully staged and directed by Dolmancé or Mme de Saint-Ange. Many of the features of this novel will be familiar to readers of *Les Cent Vingt Journées de Sodome*, including the frequent touches of humor. There is a complex scene in which Eugénie fellates Augustin (Mme de Saint-Ange's doltish but extremely well-endowed gardener) and simultaneously is sodomized by the Chevalier, who is whipped by Mme Saint-Ange, whose backside Dolmancé kisses, slaps, and bites while inhaling her farts. After the orgasms, Dolmancé asks Eugénie: "I would like you to place in my mouth what the Chevalier has left in your ass." Swallowing, Dolmancé enthuses, "Ah! there's nothing quite as good as the fuck that flows out of the bottom of a lovely ass! . . . It's a dish worthy of the gods" (543). Now comes Sade's joke about a mystery perversion. Dolmancé has become so heated that he asks permission to do something with Augustin in private:

DOLMANCÉ: Ladies, I beg your permission to retire for a moment into the next room with this young man.

MME DE SAINT-ANGE: Can you not, then, perform here whatever it is you wish with him?

DOLMANCÉ, *low and with an air of mystery:* No, it is one of those things that absolutely require privacy.

EUGÉNIE: Oh, but at least tell us what it is.

MME DE SAINT-ANGE: I won't let you leave otherwise.

DOLMANCÉ: You really want to know?

EUGÉNIE: Absolutely!

DOLMANCÉ, *drawing Augustin to him:* Very well, ladies, I am going to . . . but, truly, it cannot be spoken.

MME DE SAINT-ANGE: Is there, then, a single infamy in the whole world that we are not worthy to hear and to perform?

LE CHEVALIER: Dear sister, I will tell you. (*He whispers to the two women.*)

EUGÉNIE, *with an air of revulsion:* You're right, that is horrible. [543–44]

What it is that Dolmancé and Augustin perform in the next room we are never told. As in *Les Cent Vingt Journées,* we are shown more than we want to know, and yet teased into wanting to see something even worse.

In the middle of the novel, Sade introduces a forty-six-page essay of his entitled "Français, encore un effort si vous voulez être républicains" ("Frenchmen, Another Effort If You Would Be Republicans"). Dolmancé reads the essay aloud to the group following a complex scene in which Eugénie was deflowered fore and aft to her infinite delight. "A bit of theory ought to follow practice," Dolmancé says, taking out the pamphlet. Before he can start reading, however, Mme de Saint-Ange sends Augustin, her young gardener, out of the room: "This is not for you," she tells him (489). She can fuck the servants, but she would not want to politicize them. The pamphlet makes some very modern suggestions for the new Constitution that would be debated and passed during the summer of 1795, even as Sade was writing *La Philosophie dans le boudoir.* For example, he attacks the "atrocity" of capital punishment, and he argues that "it has never retarded crime, because it is committed daily at the very foot of the scaffold" (505–6). He is for the liberation of women: "Why should the more ravishing part of humanity submit to the other's chains? Oh! break them, for Nature wishes it; accept no other restraint but that of your own proclivities, no other laws but those of your own desires, no other morality but that of Nature" (518). Sade defends a woman's right to an abortion: earlier, Mme de Saint-Ange asserted, "We are always the mistress of what we bear in our bodies, and we are no more wrong to destroy this sort of matter than we are in evacuating, by means of purgatives when necessary, the other sort" (444). Sade also champions the rights of homosexuals (522).

Moreover, the Chevalier de Mirvel earlier declared that, though he preferred women, he certainly did not mind if a handsome man propositioned him. He rejected that "ridiculous and hollow vanity that prompts our young blades to think that they must reply to such a proposition with blows of their cane" (385). For Sade, it is impossible for tolerance to go too far. Dolmancé, having been told about a rather disgusting perversion, calmly replies, "It's all in Nature" (423).

Sade's essay quickly becomes more radical than his characters' behavior. He is soon defending incest, rape, theft, infanticide, and murder of every sort. Sade asks whether "theft, whose effect is to equalize wealth, is a great harm in a government whose goal is equality." Why should a citizen obey laws against theft when the original social contract was unfairly stacked in favor of the rich in the first place, thus "requiring him who has nothing to respect the property of he who has everything" (508)? The initiative shown by a thief may be of use to the state (509). Sade goes further, arguing that a certain degree of immorality, especially sexual immorality, is essential to sustain the "perpetual" state of "insurrection"––a kind of continuous revolution—that he claims is appropriate to republics (510). Furthermore, incest "should be the law of every government whose basis is fraternity" (520). How seriously should the reader regard these sorts of arguments? Sade states that murder should be decriminalized: "It is a horror, but a horror frequently necessary, never criminal, essential to tolerate in a Republican State" (534). He may be recalling his own horror, imprisoned in the shadow of the guillotine. Now he brazenly asserts that murderers, like thieves, ought to be prized by the state; "Republican pride requires a bit of savagery." If the patriot "goes soft, if his energy grows weak, he will soon be subjugated" (529). Sade asks, "Is it not thanks to murders that France is free today?" Does he really believe this? And what, he asks, is so special about the crime of murder? Whatever lives must die. It is only man's anthropocentrism, his "pride," that criminalizes his own early death (526). Nature makes no such distinctions. In fact, Nature requires the "perpetual movement" of life and matter through death and change (527). Sade concludes with a kind of ode to infanticide, describing the practice of killing unwanted children as common throughout the world and throughout history. In the Greek republics, infants judged unable someday to defend the republic were immediately killed. "In those days," Sade observes, "they did not think it was necessary to build richly endowed charitable institutions to preserve this vile scum of human nature" (531). Sade describes abandoned children in China, their little corpses clogging the rivers. "One cannot deny," he concludes, "that it is extraordinarily necessary and extremely politic to erect a barrier to population growth in a republican government" (532). For a moment, you do not know whether you are reading *Mein Kampf* or *A Modest Proposal*. Is Sade serious or is he a satirist? The purifying and regenerative aspects of the bloodletting during the Reign of Terror had been common topics of political discourse. Was Sade now making a mockery of such inhuman ways of thinking and behaving (as we saw, he had expressed horror at the time), or was he here asserting an absolute, inhuman kind of freedom? If so, it is a freedom based upon Nature's laws that are indifferent to man. Reduced to the significance of a fruit fly in the vast scheme of generation and death, man is ridiculed for his pretensions. On the other hand, rendered insignificant, he is freed to behave as the fruit fly does.

In Sade's vision, there are two extreme versions of the modern world. In the most obvious version, the one most commonly associated with Sade, there is a theoretically unlimited personal freedom, regulated, like a free market or a red-light district or an orgy, only by the materialistic laws of Nature, whereby any individual's life is rendered rather cheap. The opposite version, something like a wish—a representation of the ancien régime, perhaps— offers an ideal matrix of meanings and laws restricting an individual's freedom, but also giving some coherence and dignity to life. All too easily, Sade appears to lend himself to being read merely as an exponent of sexual freedom and anarchy—that is, as an exponent of the modern world, drained of meaning and value, and reduced to the materialism of matter and the sexual body (is not an orgy like Nature, "nothing but matter in action"?). But to read him only in this way is to miss the humor in his exaggerations and the irony in his style. As we have seen in his life and in this text, there is a longing (profoundly disappointed, to be sure) for high meaning, for philosophy. If there is a philosophy in the boudoir (namely, Sade's materialism and sexual freedom), there is also a boudoir in philosophy (namely, his yearning after true meaning, his pleasure in satirizing ideas and playing with them). It is a mistake to reduce Sade to one version or the other. If he can be read as an anarchist, he can just as profitably be read as a satirist of anarchy.

The trouble with Sade in his writing, as in his life, is that he does not stay in one configuration long enough to develop a consistent or reliable personality. It may be tempting to call him a satirist. As we have seen, he is certainly at times satiric. But a true satirist bases his aggression on a consistent set of moral values. There is no such stability in Sade. Indeed, part of our problem in understanding him is that his mind runs to extremes, as we have just seen. It is as if he straddles two worlds of meaning, but can find no solid place between them on which to construct his own life. This has been Sade's problem all along, both as a writer and as a human being. He can be idealistic one moment, nihilistic the next. He can be sweet one moment, and then horribly greedy and totally selfish the next. He can be a free man for a time, but then he must turn himself into a prisoner. Whether one tries to look into Sade's mind or to read his fiction, one is struck by a stroboscopic, dizzying fluctuation between extremes.

Engaging though he found his literary efforts, Sade's chief concerns continued to be food and rent. On October 7, 1795, he complained that Gaufridy had not yet sent any of the foodstuff Sade had requested, or any money.[22] He also mentioned the brief but bloody skirmish on October 5 between rebellious section members and government troops (led by Napoleon Bonaparte). The sound of cannon rumbled throughout the night. "There are a great many wounded in the streets adjoining the Convention," Sade reported, fearing that his son Louis-Marie might be among them.[23]

At the beginning of 1796, it became clear that Sade would have to economize further. In March, he gave up his little house and rented one with Mme Quesnet at Clichy-la-Garenne, near Paris. Sade's letters to his agents in Provence became more heated, more desperate, and the patient Gaufridy, finally losing his patience, gave over much of the business correspondence with Sade to his son Charles. The hyperinflation was made worse by the creation of the *mandat*, the new paper money that replaced the *assignat* in February, though Sade hoped he might pay off his debts with the new deflated *mandats* but still receive his income from Provence in silver. On April 19, he admitted to Charles that he had "not paid a sol" of the money he owed Renée, which, after six years, came to 24,000 francs. Money, money, money—that is all Sade wanted to see in Charles Gaufridy's letters, and he told him that he did not care how he got it, or even if the method of obtaining it would ruin his estate for his children. He said that he never saw his daughter (still living with Renée), for whose sake, he said, "I do not wish to make the slightest sacrifice." He complained that his younger son, at Malta, never wrote to him. And as for Louis-Marie, there was no point in preserving an estate for him, an artist who "wants to be a citizen of the world."[24]

Throughout the winter and the spring, Sade also suffered from gout. On June 24, 1796, he got his doctor, Jean-Baptiste-Joseph Gastaldy, to write a note, seemingly for the benefit of Charles Gaufridy, whose letters to Sade contained unwelcome truths and no money. The doctor stated that Sade was suffering from "a grave and complicated illness" requiring "a long and costly treatment," which "ought to induce those individuals who are associated with him and who take care of his business not to allow him to suffer the slightest delay in the dispatch of his revenues."[25] On the same day, Sade wrote to Gaufridy bitterly complaining about the lack of money or any response to his pleas. Sade portrayed the dour Gaufridy as "frisking about the fields with your country maidens," while Sade was "sick in bed, surrounded by doctors and medicines." "Some money, some money, some money," Sade demanded, "or I ask the doctors to finish me off!" Then he shifted the blame for his illness onto Gaufridy: "My doctor says that all my sufferings come only from the dreadful anxiety that you keep me in." It was all Gaufridy's fault: "All the afflictions, all the worries that you have given me since April 3, 1790, have done more to disturb my health than my twelve years in the Bastille. I even miss my stay there; at least there I was certain of my dinner, and I am never so with you." Sade ended with more ranting: "Some money, some money, some money! You are driving me to despair."[26]

Sade's letters about money display a bizarre and operatic range of emotions: there are outrageous arguments and schemes, bathetic appeals for pity, flourishes of imperious sarcasm, antic comical verbal riffs. Gaufridy, being used to Sade's manner, must have got a good laugh out of some of them. His son Charles, however, took offense at Sade's violent criticisms, and Sade had to retract (as he invariably did when challenged). Sade wrote to Charles: "It is very wrong of you, permit me to tell you, to try to make me say something I never had in my mind. I swear that I never thought of accusing you, neither you nor yours, of robbing me." Sade was a master of self-detonating apologies. This was how he concluded: "Adieu, my dear Charles. For God's sake, do not get angry when I am angry, because, if we are both angry, who will reconcile us? I want to feel free to shout and to rage as if I were being flayed alive when you do not send me money, and your sole response to that ought always to be a money order."[27] That was a very pleasant division of labor: Sade could yell at Charles, and Charles could send money. But really there was almost nothing to send.

During the summer of 1796, Sade personally arranged the sale of his estate at La Coste. He announced this surprising news to Gaufridy in a letter on September 11, blaming the lawyer for his slowness in selling Mazan. Sade also asked Gaufridy to hide away any of his valuable possessions that might remain at La Coste, for in ten days they would belong to the new owner, Joseph-Stanislas Rovère,[28] an elected deputy from Provence who, with his brother Simon-Stylite Rovère, had greatly prospered from the Revolution. Sade and Deputy Rovère had come to terms on September 9 in Paris. Understanding that it would be natural for the new owner to continue to employ Gaufridy as agent for the estate, Sade congratulated Gaufridy on his new employer, but warned him not to ruin the sale by revealing anything unpleasant "in order to ingratiate yourself to your new client." If the deal fell through, Sade threatened "to go and drown myself in the river." In particular, he was worried that Renée might upset the sale. At the time of his separation, all of his lands had been legally encumbered as a guarantee for the repayment of her dowry, which, with the unpaid interest, had grown to nearly 200,000 livres. "As for Mme de Sade," he assured Gaufridy, "her rights are preserved in the contract" for the sale of La Coste, which was true as long as Sade used the proceeds of the sale to buy a new property. Even so, Sade urged Gaufridy, "do not tell her anything."[29]

Rovère had no illusions about La Coste. "The château is a ruin," he wrote to his brother Simon-Stylite in Provence, adding, however, that "the park could make a rabbit warren." For Rovère, the primary value of the estate lay in "the famous spring that waters the Maison Basse."[30] The Rovère brothers were very slick operators and land speculators. For his part, Sade always treated any transaction as a test of his mettle in an absolute sense, or, more pragmatically, to see how much he could get away with. On January 11, 1797, Rovère warned his brother that Sade had probably moved a lot of furniture from the château after the agreed date.[31] Before the final payment, there was also a dispute concerning a sum of money bequeathed long ago by one of Sade's ancestors, the income of which, amounting to 90 francs a year, was designated for the poor of the town of La Coste. Nine months after the sale agreement, Rovère was still embroiled with Sade, this time over the question of who got the profits from the harvest. Rovère called Sade "the most vile creature, the most contemptible, the most loathsome that I know." Rovère very clearly summed up two extremes in Sade's character: the wheedler and the tyrant. "If he needs you," he concluded, "he will act the charmer, the wheedler," but "he is nothing but a paper tiger when he knows he is the weaker one." Rovère understood that there was only one way to handle Sade: "Stand firm."[32] On the other hand, when Sade felt powerful, he could dismiss his inferiors with peremptory disdain. Displeased with Charles Gaufridy, Sade coldly forbade him to conduct business for him ever again. "It is unbecoming to discuss my misfortunes with a child like you," Sade wrote. "You, Monsieur, do not please me in the least, and I ask you to write to me no more. Limit yourself to sending me money."[33]

Sade used the money from the sale of La Coste to buy two farms, Malmaison and Grandvilliers, in the Chartres region. Renée's dowry money would be protected by mortgages against these two properties. On March 5, 1797, Renée wrote to Gaufridy to express her opposition to the sale of La Coste: "My goal," she insisted, "is to preserve as much money as I can for my children, and toward that end, not to give up anything that is due me."[34] She sent Louis-Marie down to Provence to make sure her interests were protected. Sade thought his son's meddling would ruin his plans.[35] But the deals went through, and Sade also managed to use some of the funds to help purchase a middle-class country house at Saint-Ouen, near Paris, giving a down payment in October 1796, when he sold La Coste, and paying the rest in April 1797.[36] This house, No. 3 Place de la Liberté, cost 15,000 livres, and Sade bought it for Mme Quesnet, put it in her name, and thereby managed to move a significant part of his money out from under Renée's legal control. By the spring of 1797, Sade, Mme Quesnet, and her son Charles were living in their new house. But as soon as they were settled in, the three suddenly departed for Provence on a visit Sade had been threatening to make ever since he had been freed from Charenton in 1790. He was very secretive about this trip and went out of his way to mislead Gaufridy: "No, no, no, a thousand times no," he insisted in a letter on April 9, "I will definitely not go this year."[37] However, by the middle of the next month, Sade was in Provence, with the intention to check up on his income and also to sell a bit of land.

Whether at Gaufridy's house in Apt, or at his own at Mazan or Saumane, Sade found utter disorder, and worse. Farmers had not paid their rents. Sade, it turned out, had not paid his taxes. His involvement with the truly wealthy and very lucky speculator Rovère may have given him the notion that he too could make a quick killing down in Provence and then return to Paris miraculously wealthy. But Sade was so disappointed with the reality that within a few weeks he vastly overplayed his hand, falsely accusing Noël Perrin, the registrar at Carpentras, of having robbed him of some of his income. Perrin then accused Sade before the court at Avignon, alleging that on June 18, 1797, Sade had written him a libelous letter calling him a "knave" and accusing him of confiscating some of Sade's income for his *"own pocket,"* instead of depositing it in the national Treasury, where it should have been placed as belonging to a presumed émigré.[38] The issue concerned nine years' rent and late fees at 3 francs 6 sous a year, coming to the trivial sum of 29 francs 14 sous, that Marianne Paradis had deposited with Perrin instead of paying directly to "the émigré Sade."[39] Only at this point did Sade ask for Gaufridy's legal help. Perrin, Sade complained to Gaufridy, was "the most obstinate man in the world; he absolutely refuses to listen to anything."[40] But it was Sade who had to back down. On July 12, he replied to the complaint, stating that, although he had never emigrated, his name may have appeared "in error" on a list of émigrés in the department of Bouches-du-Rhône, and that Perrin had not stolen his money. He admitted that he had acted "rashly" and acknowledged Perrin to be "an upright and honest man."[41] The matter was settled when, on July 13, Perrin agreed to drop his complaint on the following conditions: within twenty-four hours, Sade would pay Perrin's expenses, deposit sufficient funds for the printing and the posting of his retraction throughout the province, and pay 24 francs in alms for the Hospital of Carpentras.[42]

During the course of this debacle, Sade was trying to raise money by any means: a bit of his land would be auctioned off to the highest bidder. "That is why," he told Gaufridy, "I am leaving on Monday and why I want to see you on Sunday."[43] Amid all this bustle and business of deeds, taxes, rents, and Perrin, Sade did not fail to indulge his love of sweets. "Please do not forget," he reminded Gaufridy concerning the Sunday visit, "to bring the chocolate."[44] Sade told Gaufridy that he expected to be away on business at Arles for three weeks.[45] Sade's business had to do with his scheme to sell some land by lottery at the fair at Beaucaire, for which he enlisted the help of Charles Gaufridy. But when Sade arrived there on July 23, he found that Charles had failed to sell a single ticket. Sade then went to Arles with Gaufridy's other son, François, in order to try to sell the Mas de Cabanes. In this, he was no more successful than he was in trying to collect the back rent from his farmer there.[46] From this fruitless voyage Sade returned to Apt, where he had left Mme Quesnet in the care of Mme Gaufridy.

Toward the end of September, Sade decided that it was time to return to Paris. He had given Gaufridy an extensive list of provisions he wanted his lawyer to gather: olive oil and pickled olives; preserves of apricots, lemons, plums, cherries; dried fruit; barrels of anchovies; fifty pounds of chocolate; fifty pounds of sugar.[47] Sade would take what he could carry with him; an additional cartload of foodstuffs would follow the coach on the road to Paris; the rest Gaufridy would send later.

There had been an unnerving incident at Mazan, when a group of young people invaded the château and threatened to raze it to the ground.[48] Sade's entire trip had been disappointing, even humiliating. When he turned to leave Provence, he may have sensed that it would be for the last time. The château of La Coste was his no more. Ironically, its new owner, Rovère, would get no pleasure out of it. That very month, as a consequence of the coup d'état of September 4, 1797, Rovère was arrested and deported to Guiana, where he died a year later.

From the moment Sade returned to his house at Saint-Ouen in the fall of 1797, he found that things were going from bad to worse. Soon, he would have to pawn every one of his possessions just to stay alive. He tried to play on Gaufridy's feelings for "Sensible," Sade's nickname for Mme Quesnet: "Poor Sensible, who loves you so much, sups on a glass of sugar water. . . . Will you still continue to allow such a sweet, such a lovely creature, and one who loves you so much, to go without a skirt and supper?"[49] Still on a list of émigrés, Sade was earning no income from Provence. He could not sell any land because of Renée's prior claims. He still owed money to the former owner of the farm he had bought at Beauce. The income from this farm was, in fact, seized by the former owner's agents, who also showed up at Saint-Ouen to seize Sade's furniture. "In despair," Sade told Gaufridy that he was obliged to flee his own house: "I am going into hiding for a few days." As if the shame were too much to bear, he exclaimed, "Damned children! Cruel and cursed wife! My predicament and my despair are infinitely beyond the torments of the unfortunates plunged into hell." To make matters worse, Sade's old eye trouble had returned. "I am about to lose an eye," he said; "I can no longer make out what I am writing to you." And he cried out, "Some money, in the name of God, some money!"[50]

On July 31, Sade threatened Gaufridy: "If I do not receive any money here within a fortnight, *I am determined to blow my brains out.*"[51] By September 2, Sade, "in tears," begged him for "a little money": "I have nothing left to pawn," he explained, "and when I am done with what was borrowed yesterday by poor Sensible, we must starve to death."[52] He had cried poverty and threatened suicide countless times before; Gaufridy filed these letters with the others. This time, however, Sade had told the truth. He had no money, and nothing left to pawn. Hounded by creditors, he and Mme Quesnet surveyed the empty rooms of their house at Saint-Ouen and faced the bitter truth. If they did not wish to starve to death together, they would have to separate; on September 10, 1798, they did so. Mme Quesnet, as Sade later explained to Gaufridy, sought "bed and board with her friends," and Sade went into hiding with a farmer on his land at Beauce.[53]

A good deal of Sade's financial troubles had come about because his income had been sequestered by the government after his name had appeared on a list of émigrés of the newly created department of the Vaucluse, even though his name had been cleared from the list of émigrés in his former department of Bouches-du-Rhône. It accomplished nothing to cite this earlier clearance—or "radiation," as it was called—as well as to provide countless certificates of his continuous residence in Paris from his section, and even records from the various prisons he was in during the Terror in 1793 and 1794. He had used so many different versions of his given names that officials in Provence and Paris professed to be uncertain whether they all referred to one and the same person. For example, on March 7, 1798, the minister of police in Paris wrote to the department of Bouches-du-Rhône about his confusion over whether the Sade in Paris who had provided such a large packet of certificates of continuous residence was the same Sade that the department of Bouches-du-Rhône had removed from the list of émigrés under the name "Louis Sade" on May 26, 1793. "In these certificates," the minister of police wrote, Sade "is identified by the name Aldonze François Sade, in others François Sade, and in yet others François Aldonze Donatien Louis Sade." These inconsistencies required further "investigation to determine if this is the same individual" who had been cleared under the name of Louis Sade. The minister found an additional difficulty in that the Section des Piques had certified Sade's continuous residency, even though, for the same period, Sade had supplied prison records showing that he had been incarcerated for part of that time. These "contradictions," the minister concluded, would have to be cleared up before any action could be taken.[54]

"What, then, can he do more to establish his identity?" Sade wrote to the government on September 5, 1798.[55] He was caught in a curiously modern quandary: he had become a nonperson. His frantic petitions met with a bureaucratic shrug. Papers were reshuffled and sent around once again to the various departments. If he could not get himself cleared, if his income remained sequestered, he *could* very well starve to death.

Sade had certainly tried to earn money as a writer. His efforts only led him deeper into misfortune. He had revised and enlarged *Justine, ou les malheurs de la vertu*, again publishing it anonymously, this time under the title *La Nouvelle Justine, ou les malheurs de la vertu, suivi de l'histoire de Juliette, sa soeur.* This work—in ten volumes, with a hundred obscene engravings—was supposedly printed "in Holland" in 1797, although it was actually set in type in Paris by Sade's publisher, Nicolas Massé.[56] More than half of this massive undertaking consists of the six-volume autobiography of Justine's incredibly successful libertine sister, Juliette. The story of the happy whore, of course, was alluded to in various versions of Sade's account of Justine. The *Histoire de Juliette, ou les prospérités du vice* is the exact inverse of *Justine, ou les malheurs de la vertu.* The opposites are rigorously delineated. The Machiavellian, amoral, active libertinism of the courtesan Juliette is constantly rewarded, whereas the Christian, passive, sensitive, sentimental, virtuous Justine had been everywhere abused and defiled. Camille Paglia, championing Sade's importance in her book *Sexual Personae: Art and Decadence from Nefertiti to Emily Dickinson*, regarded *Juliette* as Sade's answer to Rousseau's *Julie.*[57] According to Paglia, "Justine is Rousseau" and "Juliette is Sade."[58] But really they are both Sade, who, in his fiction as in his life, embodied irreconcilable extremes as no one before or since.

The farmer at Beauce with whom Sade had sought refuge finally refused to continue providing him with room and board. On December 9, 1798, Sade described his pitiful existence to Gaufridy as he wandered day by day, begging bed and board from anyone willing to help him. The orthography itself is pathetic: except for one paragraph, the letter is written by Mme Quesnet's son, Charles, since Sade's old eye problem had flared up once more. Sade asked Gaufridy to write back using "the largest letters possible."[59] As the new year dawned, having worn out his welcome everywhere, accompanied by

Charles Quesnet and a servant, Sade ended up living in miserable circumstances at Versailles: "We eat a few carrots and some beans, and we keep warm (not every day, but when we can) with a few sticks we get on credit most of the time." Mme Quesnet, who was staying with friends in Paris, went to see various officials, trying to get Sade's name off the émigré list so that he could receive his income. When she could, she went to Versailles and brought news of her efforts; more materially, "in her pocket she brings us something to eat from her friends' houses."[60] Sade was now happy to live on table scraps.

For a time, Sade lodged incognito at No. 32 rue Satory at Versailles; later he moved to No. 100, where he had room and board with M. Brunelle, the proprietor of an eating house. On February 13, 1799, he asked Gaufridy to address him there as "Citizen Charles," as a means "to elude my creditors." Using this name, he had also found "a small job" as a prompter in the town's theater. It was his first and only job. His salary was a joke: "I am earning *forty sols a day*," he told Gaufridy, "and on that I am feeding and bringing up the child," Mme Quesnet's son, Charles. During this cold weather, Mme Quesnet ran errands for him in Paris "in order to appease the creditors and to obtain the radiation" from the list of émigrés. "In truth," he added, "this woman is an angel whom heaven has sent me so that I should not be completely overwhelmed by the scourges hurled at me by my enemies."[61]

Among Sade's enemies, he now counted his eldest son, Louis-Marie, whose treatment had been "frightful" and "barbarous": "Not only has he not lifted a finger to help, but he has even impeded as much as he could the efforts of Mme Quesnet." For example, Sade's lawyer in Paris, M. de Bonnières, had succeeded in persuading Renée to meet with Mme Quesnet at his house so that Mme Quesnet could make her aware of "the total horror of my predicament." However, Louis-Marie, "this scoundrel who calls himself my son," roundly scolded M. de Bonnières for his interference and then went directly to his mother's house "to prevent her from going to the meeting."[62]

In the fall of 1799, Sade tried once more to make some money from his plays, writing to Goupilleau de Montaigu asking help in arranging for him to read *Jeanne Laisné* at Goupilleau's house before a small gathering of influential persons. Sade hoped that the government would order it performed "as a patriotic play."[63] Although nothing came of this scheme, Sade did have the satisfaction of seeing his play *Oxtiern* (first performed in 1791) put on by the theater at Versailles on December 13, 1799. For this occasion, Sade gave the play a new subtitle, *les malheurs du libertinage*, and played the role of Fabrice, the good innkeeper who helps save Ernestine from the libertine Comte Oxtiern. As Fabrice, Sade spoke the last lines and the moral of the play: he refused any reward for his good deed, saying, "I have put my money to the best use. . . . To punish crime and to reward virtue . . . Let anyone tell me if it is possible to place it at a higher interest!"[64]

The theater at Versailles must have reminded Sade of happier times long ago, of his own theaters at La Coste and Mazan, of the plays he put on there in the spring of 1772 with Anne-Prospère, and even earlier, of those he performed with Renée, Mme de Montreuil, and his new relatives at the château d'Évry in 1764. Those tableaux painted in memory, the manners, the wealth, the privileges associated with those châteaux, now seemed quaint and antique miniatures, observed through the wrong end of time's telescope. Fabrice might well disdain money, but Sade could not. He was in debt to everyone, including his landlord, M. Brunelle. In truth, he had not even a roof over his head. At the dawn of the new century, on January 3, 1800, Sade wrote to Gaufridy from the Hôpital de Versailles, where he had finally been obliged to beg a bed and a bowl of soup: "Here you see me, thanks to your attentions, reduced to the lowest depths of misery."[65]

Even though Sade was able to leave the almshouse and return to his wretched room on the rue Satory, worse was yet to come. He was in his room with Mme Quesnet on February 20, 1800, when he received an urgent visit by M. Cazade (also known as Laloubie), a commissioner of the district of Clichy, in which Sade's house at Saint-Ouen was situated. Earlier, when Sade was attempting to get his name off the list of émigrés, Cazade had been assigned to investigate his case. The two men had got along very well, and Cazade had been helpful. On August 5, 1799, Cazade had officially certified that, "from the commencement of the Revolution until the present, Citizen Sade has constantly manifested the principles of a good and sincere patriot."[66] Now Cazade had rushed from Saint-Ouen to Versailles to warn Sade and Mme Quesnet that two bailiff's men had been stationed at Sade's house for non-payment of taxes. Even as Cazade was conveying this alarming news, another bailiff entered the room to arrest Sade for nonpayment of two bills to M. Brunelle. It was fortunate for Sade that Commissioner Cazade was in the room: otherwise, Sade would have found himself in debtors' prison.[67]

On February 20, Sade wrote to Gaufridy's son Charles and accused him of purposely holding back Sade's rents and using them for his "own profit."[68] Sade had Commissioner Cazade write to Gaufridy for a clarification of the finances. Sade was not satisfied with Gaufridy's reply to Cazade, which he characterized, on April 5, as "a monument of equivocation, of Jesuitical carping, of lies, of sophistry, and of bad faith."[69] Sade directly accused Gaufridy of cheating him, and on May 1, 1800, he threatened Charles with a lawsuit if he did not get his money.[70] Gaufridy sent in his resignation. At the end of the month, Sade wrote Gaufridy a mollifying letter, telling him that he was not fired and begging him to remain in control of his affairs.[71] Gaufridy, however, was serious about ending the relationship. In June, Sade sent Mme Quesnet and Cazade to Provence to see if they could make sense of his affairs.[72]

The abrupt falling out with Gaufridy thus ended (with a few later exceptions) a correspondence that is an invaluable source of information about Sade's life and feelings. His feelings toward Gaufridy had been a mixture of amity and hatred, of tenderness and lordly disdain, of almost childlike dependency and operatic rage. Sade had turned what was essentially a business arrangement into a continuing psychodrama whose wild swings of often inappropriate, incommensurate, and contradictory emotions upset Gaufridy, but satisfied a deep need in Sade. A sensible person would have paid more attention to his interests, and would have found a better business agent when he became dissatisfied with his current one. But even from his earliest years, Sade discovered there was satisfaction in blaming others for his own faults. Dogged by misfortune, he nevertheless always found ways to court more bad luck. Humiliation was a state he somehow found congenial; victimization was one that justified and allowed the expression of his powerful emotions. His forlorn condition placed him at the center of his universe, a screaming, crying, outrageously demanding, vengeful primal being, striking out against a world of uncaring, unreliable, even pernicious humans. One never knew where one stood with Sade, because, whether one was a whore suffering his fantasies, or the governor of the Bastille, or the reader of *Les Cent Vingt Journées de Sodome*, one ended up feeling like a screen upon which Sade was projecting some inscrutable interior drama. But there was also, perhaps, something attractive in the immense energy and meaning that Sade extravagantly pumped into any situation or relationship, no matter how banal, a kind of flattery in the way he focused his attention on one so powerfully, even if only to berate. His superheated passion, the sense that any sentence Sade wrote contained some transcendent argument quite beyond the literal context and meaning, remains an attraction in his writing. But whatever his attractions, the living Sade was, in the end, utterly exasperating. Gaufridy, who had been drawn into Sade's powerful orbit, who for twenty-six years as his business agent suffered his attractions and repulsions, finally found Sade's accusation of theft too much to bear. He broke free, dropped beneath the Sadeian horizon, and ended his days peacefully in his home at Apt in 1818.

Despite his grinding preoccupation with financial matters during these years, Sade somehow found the time to write. In addition to *La Philosophie dans le boudoir*, *La Nouvelle Justine*, and *Juliette*, his literary production from 1795 to 1800 may have included other works in manuscript now lost, among them *La Théorie du libertinage* and *Vénus dévoilée*. In March 1801, the police would seize three other manuscripts now lost: *Les Délassements du libertin, ou la neuvaine de Cythère;*[73] *Mes Caprices, ou un peu de tout;* and a collection of stories, *Le Boccace français.*[74] There may even have been additional works written during this period.[75] In 1800, Sade also published his play *Oxtiern* and *Les Crimes de l'amour*, a four-volume selection of eleven of the novellas and short stories he had written in the Bastille. He put his name on the title page and added the phrase "by the author of *Aline et Valcour*," thus associating it with the only one of his novels that he ever publicly acknowledged.

If the public or conventional aspect of Sade's literary career brought him neither fame nor fortune, his anonymous, underground works were beginning to arouse ominous attention. For example, the journal *Le Cercle* announced the death of the writer de Langle and identified him as the author of *Justine*, of which the journal said the following: "If anything could inspire belief in the existence of Satan, it would be this most disgusting and immoral work of libertinage. It is not possible to have written such a work and to remain human."[76] On April 15, 1798, de Langle's friends got the *Journal de Paris* to print a correction, asserting that de Langle was not dead and that "a certain Monsieur de Sades" was the author of *Justine*. So much for Sade's anonymity. He wrote an angry reply to the *Journal de Paris*, published April 18, stating "that it is *false, absolutely false*, that I am the author of the book entitled *Justine, ou les malheurs de la vertu*." He threatened legal action if he was again identified as the author of "that evil book."[77] A year later, on August 29, 1799, the journal *L'Ami des lois* announced the death of Sade, whose "name alone . . . exhales a cadaverous odor that kills virtue and inspires horror: he is the author of *Justine, ou les malheurs de la vertu*."[78] Sade again sent letters to several journals insisting that he was neither dead nor the author of *Justine*. Around the same time, a two-volume collection of literary gossip, *Le Tribunal d'Apollon*, declared Sade dead and the author of *Justine:* "One does not know which one deserves more to be burned, the work or the author; both of them fully deserve to be annihilated." The article went on to offer a garbled version of Sade's affairs with the prostitutes in Marseilles and with Rose Keller, who, the writer claimed, died as a result of the "cruel experiments," the "incisions," and the "bites" inflicted upon her by the "cannibalistic Comte."[79]

On September 24, 1799, in a letter to the journal *L'Ami des lois*, Sade replied to the above article. "No, I am not dead, and this will be made evident," he threatened the writer of *Le Tribunal d'Apollon*, "by means of a stout cudgel." His only hesitation, he said, was "the fear of infecting myself by approaching your putrescent cadaver."[80] On October 19, the author of *Le Tribunal d'Apollon* answered Sade in a letter to *L'Ami des lois*, but his invention failed him and he was reduced to copying Sade's own language. It is Sade's pen, he lamely retorted, that "exhales" a "putrescent odor," and he said that if anyone was to get a cudgeling it would be Sade. "Wretch," he asked Sade, "how could you lift the thick veil that hid your abominable existence?"[81] It is a good question. Sade's clandestine writings were never really completely secret. In 1798, Restif de la Bretonne published his *Anti-Justine*, which was devoted to an attack on "the vivisectionist" Sade, whom he called "Dsds," for "Desades." "No one was more scandalized than me," Restif wrote, "by the filthy works of the infamous Dsds, namely, *Justine, Aline, Le Boudoir, La Théorie du libertinage*. . . . This scoundrel portrays the pleasures of love as accompanied for men only by torments, and for women, even by death itself."[82] Why did Sade answer his literary opponents? Perhaps he believed that his threats could compel silence. He tried to wrap himself in what he thought of as his safe works, *Aline et Valcour, Oxtiern*, and *Les Crimes de l'amour*. He regarded himself as a man of letters, perhaps even as a man of genius. If there was any strategy behind his contributions to the paper war over *Justine*, it did not succeed. His replies to his attackers could only lead to further publicity.

Great changes were about to take place in France. The coup d'état of November 9–10, 1799, brought Napoleon Bonaparte to power with a mission to re-establish central authority and order in the nation. His minister of police, Joseph Fouché, sought to rein in the license of the press. On August 18, 1800, the police raided a bookbinding establishment and confiscated copies of *Justine* as they were being bound with obscene illustrations.[83] The publication, around this time, of *Les Crimes de l'amour* may have earned Sade enough money to feel comfortable for a while. In any case, he had returned from Versailles to his house at Saint-Ouen. But Sade's two literary careers, overt and clandestine, collided when, on October 22, 1800, in the *Journal des Arts, des Sciences et de Littérature*, Alexandre-Louis de Villeterque, reviewing *Les Crimes de l'amour*, alluded to Sade's authorship of *Justine*. Sade had prefaced his *Les Crimes de l'amour* with an essay entitled "Idée sur les romans" in which he offered a brief history of the genre and his defense of his own method of writing novels. He also pointedly rejected the attribution to him of *Justine*: "I have never written such works, and I most certainly never will; only fools or knaves, despite the authenticity of my denials, could still suspect or accuse me of being its author, and henceforth the most sovereign contempt will be the only weapon with which I will combat their calumnies."[84] Villeterque called *Les Crimes de l'amour* a "detestable book by a man suspected of having written an even more horrible one"—that is, *Justine*.[85] This attack was the final and most destructive salvo of the paper war over Sade's work.

Sade immediately wrote a twenty-page pamphlet characterizing Ville-terque as a "hack writer." If Sade sometimes showed vice triumphant, he now argued that he had done so only to render virtue's defeat all the more poignant.[86] The arguments in this pamphlet, the learned references to classi-cal and contemporary literature, even the contemptuous references to Ville-terque as an imbecile and a turd[87]—none of it would make any difference. "I have never written any *immoral books*," Sade declared, and added, "I never will write any."[88] But it was too late for such oaths. Too many people knew about *Justine*. And times had changed. Within weeks, Sade's writings would cause him to be arrested for the last time.

CHAPTER 28

Charenton

O N FRIDAY, March 6, 1801, Sade had come to Paris from his house at Saint-Ouen to meet with his publisher, Nicolas Massé, who had recently brought out Sade's only publicly acknowledged works, his pamphlet against Villeterque and his *Crimes de l'amour*. But Massé was also the publisher of Sade's clandestine works that were now causing a journalistic controversy: the ten-volume illustrated edition of *La Nouvelle Justine, ou les malheurs de la vertu, suivie de l'histoire de Juliette, sa soeur*. Sade's secret career was about to sink his public one. Once again, he had blithely walked into a trap, this one laid by Prefect of Police Dubois, under the direction of Minister of Police Fouché.

Sade would claim that he was at Massé's only because of some business concerning *Les Crimes de l'amour*, a fairly unobjectionable work.[1] But Dubois later said that, from the very beginning of the new year, he had been working to set a trap to catch Sade.[2] "I had been informed," Dubois explained, that Sade, "known to be the author of the infamous novel *Justine*, intended to publish immediately a still more frightful work under the title of *Juliette*." Who had been Dubois's informant? The lenient treatment accorded Massé suggests that it was very likely Massé himself who betrayed Sade. "I learned," Dubois explained, that Sade "was to be found along with his manuscript" on March 6 "at the house of the bookseller-editor of his work." Dubois's police officers raided Massé's establishment on the rue Helvétius, arrested the startled author, and confiscated his manuscript of *Juliette*, along with other manuscripts in his own hand that are now lost. For the sake of appearances and to apply additional pressure on the publisher, Dubois also had Massé brought in for questioning. Under police guard, Sade was then conducted to an address on the rue Trois-Frères to fetch the key for his house at Saint-Ouen from Mme Quesnet. According to Sade, she immediately became "very worried and very upset." She turned over the key, and as Sade was being dragged off, she embraced him and "promised not to abandon" him. He was then taken to his house at Saint-Ouen, where the officers "conducted the most exacting search, which yielded," according to Sade, "only the seizing of a few pamphlets, my three paintings, and the tapestry from my bedroom." Dubois, however, indicated the nature of this artwork: "large pictures representing the principal obscenities of the novel *Justine*." Sade did not mention this, but the police also confiscated some obscene statuettes.[3] Sade's rooms, like his novels, were a kind of projection of his passions and his sexual tastes. Now, at the age of sixty, he stood in the center of his room in a house he would never see again, and watched the policemen rifle his possessions, saw their smirks, heard their comments, as they discovered and confiscated his pictures, his tapestry, his indecent plaster-of-Paris sculptures.

Following the search, Sade was brought to the Prefecture of Police, "where," he said, "I was held for two days and two nights in secret." As was his habit in custody, he immediately tried to gain a favor. He asked if he could be kept under guard at his house at Saint-Ouen. Corpulent though he was, perhaps he imagined another daring escape. His request, however, was refused. From two to four, during the early morning hours of the next day, March 7, he was interrogated by Commissioner Moutard, and again from eight to ten in the evening. There was another interrogation on March 9, when he was confronted with the seized manuscripts. He readily admitted that they were in his handwriting, but insisted, as Dubois reported, "that he was only the copyist and not the author." Since Sade stuck to this improbable story, the police kept asking him to name the real author. According to Dubois, Sade replied that "he was not in a position to know the individuals from whom he received the originals." Dubois expressed irritation at this charade: "It was difficult to believe that a man who enjoyed such a considerable fortune had become the copyist of such dreadful works merely for money." While Sade continued with his stubborn bluff, Massé proved entirely cooperative. Although the police now had the author and the manuscript in their possession, Dubois wanted to obtain all the copies of the already printed ten-volume illustrated edition of *La Nouvelle Justine* and *Juliette*. These had not been found in the search of Massé's establishment. According to Dubois, "Freedom was promised to the editor if he gave over the printed copies. He conducted our agents to an uninhabited place that he alone knew, and they removed a sufficiently considerable quantity of copies for them to believe that this was the entire edition." However, the one thousand copies confiscated in this raid proved to be only the beginning of a clandestine publishing history that extended well into the twentieth century, spreading a lopsided version of Sade's literary activities and thereby supporting the mythical and scandalous version of Sade's life and career.

While Sade sat in jail, Mme Quesnet tried to see him but was turned away. A week into his incarceration, he learned that his complete dossier had been sent on to the minister of police. On March 16, he was told that his case would be settled the next day. However, two days later, Mme Quesnet wrote and told him to get a lawyer. "How vexatious!" Sade exclaimed. "How can they behave in this way to a man in torment?" On March 19, he was allowed to see M. Jaillot, a lawyer from Versailles. Two days later, Sade was taken out of his dungeon cell and permitted to mix with the general prison population. On March 26, he was interrogated again, and on his way back to his cell, he chanced to see Mme Quesnet. This brief meeting may have been a favor she obtained from the prison guards, or she may have haunted the place waiting for just such an opportunity. "I embraced Madame," Sade wrote, "in passing." A week later, on April 2, 1801, Sade was transferred without explanation to the prison of Sainte-Pélagie, where he would languish for almost two years.

During the time that Sade had been at the Prefecture, Prefect of Police Dubois had several conferences with Minister of Police Fouché. They discussed, as Dubois later described it, "what steps I had to take to succeed in punishing a man so profoundly perverse." Dubois's memorandum is a chilling example of arbitrary justice under Napoleon. Fouché and Dubois reached the conclusion that a trial "would cause an intolerable scandal that would in no way be justified by an equivalent punishment." Arbitrarily deciding that Sade deserved a much more severe punishment than the pornography laws provided, they sent him to Sainte-Pélagie "in order," as Dubois put it, "to punish him administratively." Bureaucratic tyranny infects the very language. As with the lettre de cachet, Sade had been thrown into a legal limbo, without indictment, without trial, without hope of regaining his freedom. Dubois found that Fouché was "already familiar with all the offenses that Sade had committed before the Revolution." Seeing no point in a trial, Fouché decided simply "to bury" Sade "for a long time in the prison of Sainte-Pélagie." Sade had managed to be persecuted by Louis XVI, by Robespierre, and now by Napoleon.

On April 3, 1801, a day after his abrupt transfer to Sainte-Pélagie, Sade was in a depressed and confused state of mind when Mme Quesnet paid him her first visit: "I saw Madame for the first time in the parlor of Pélagie; she appeared anxious about the cabals of my family. She had obtained permission to visit me three times every ten days. I observed in her conversation many contradictions, and from then on, I came to understand that the system of signals was being used against me just as in the Bastille." Mentally, emotionally, Sade was back in the Bastille. His mind again filled with numbers, dates, calculations, discoveries of plots, cabals. His detention was outside the boundaries of legality. Once again, he tried to find clues to the identities of his persecutors, clues to the date of his release. In his *Notes littéraires*, he said that what his persecutors wanted from their "system of signals and number codes" was to drive him crazy by "obliging" him "to confuse true events with events contrived by the imbecile wickedness of the scoundrels" who imprisoned him. There is deception and unreliability in the very surface and flow of reality. Some aspects are "of nature," he said, but others are "arranged," "fabricated" by his enemies. It is difficult to tell which is which, a true event or a contrived signal. The solution, he said, was "not to put my trust in anything and to keep myself indifferent to everything."[4] His paranoid distrust of reality was exacerbated by imprisonment. But the truth is, Sade had never been able to trust reality.

Once again, Sade was behind bars and dependent upon a woman for emotional support, for food, for truth itself. Mme Quesnet assumed the role that Renée had put aside. From the very beginning of his time at Sainte-Pélagie, Sade discovered in Mme Quesnet's ordinary conversation enough contradictions and clues to indicate that she was the willing or unwitting conduit of signals from those who were intent on ruining his life. Renée had patiently suffered through all this before, along with Sade's demands for books and food, and along with his endless and often vicious complaints. Mme Quesnet, however, was different: at once stronger and more resilient. On October 31, 1801, during one of her visits to Sainte-Pélagie, Sade tried to make a complaint about something she had brought—probably food, for his enormous corpulence could not have been sustained on prison food alone. Sade's paper arguments with Renée over food had been a substitute for other forms of passionate intimacy. Possibly, he was now trying to start just such an argumentative relationship with Mme Quesnet. He described the event in his *Notes littéraires:* "One day I blamed my friend for forgetting my tastes concerning something that she was giving to me and that I did not like." That was a promising beginning for an argument. *"You are wrong, she told me, to reproach me for forgetting your tastes."* To be contradicted was even more promising, if Mme Quesnet had not paused, smiled, and added this charming acknowledgment of Sade's love of her: *"What is beyond a doubt is that I will never forget the one that you have for me."*[5]

Very little is known about how Sade passed his time at Sainte-Pélagie. It is unlikely that his prison habits and consolations had changed much over the years. As before, he must have spent part of the day reading and writing, and masturbating with the aid of a very large dildo. A search of his room in March 1803 turned up, according to the report, "an enormous instrument that he fashioned out of wax and which he used on himself, since the instrument retained some traces of its shameful intromission."[6]

There are two letters extant in which Sade tried to obtain justice from the government. One, on December 26, 1801, to an unspecified minister, possibly of the interior, begins, "Imprisoned for the past nine months at Pélagie as one accused of having written the book *Justine*, which, however, never came from my pen, I suffer in silence, each day relying upon the justice of the government."[7] Five months later, on May 20, 1802, Sade wrote to the minister of justice: "I am accused of being the author of the infamous book *Justine*. The accusation is false, I swear it to you in the name of all that I hold most sacred." Sade hammered home the irony that he, who denied all connection with the book, was still in prison, while the publisher, Massé, "who printed, who sold, and who continues to sell" it, was a free man. Sade presented himself as a victim and a patriot: "What, then, is this arbitrary partiality that unchains the guilty and that crushes the innocent? Was it to come to this that for the past twelve years we sacrificed our lives and our fortunes?" Sade wanted action: "I have been moaning for the past fifteen months in the most frightful prison in Paris, while, according to the law, they cannot imprison an accused person for more than ten days without judging him."[8]

Prison life at Sainte-Pélagie, however, was not as "frightful" as it could have been. Sade even joined a literary club—limited to nine members, after the Muses—called the Dîners de Sainte-Pélagie. They met every five days for dinner and recitations of their own literary works. An account of this club and some of its productions was given by one of its members, Hurard Saint-Désiré, in a small volume, *Mes Amusements dans la prison de Sainte-Pélagie* (1801). Almost as soon as Sade entered the prison, he became a member and its president.[9] The beginning of one of his poems suggested that happiness could indeed be found anywhere:

> Since fate brings us here together,
> Let us not increase our pains.
> In this hovel, 'tis far better
> To sow some roses 'midst our chains.[10]

Poetry, friendship—and there would be another diversion, one that would force his transfer to an even worse prison in the middle of March 1803. According to the report of Prefect of Police Dubois, Sade "made use of every means that his depraved imagination could devise . . . to seduce and corrupt the young men whom unfortunate circumstances caused to be locked up at Sainte-Pélagie and whom chance had placed in the same corridor as him." In fact, a disturbance at the Théâtre-Français had resulted in the arrest and detention at Sainte-Pélagie of a number of young men. According to Dubois,

Sade—almost sixty-three, enormously fat, and with long white hair—thought he might seduce these young fellows. "Their complaints," Dubois stated, "forced me to have him transferred to Bicêtre," probably around March 14.[11]

Almost thirty years after the event, Charles Nodier in his *Souvenirs de la Révolution et de l'Empire* described Sade's transfer. To be sure, Nodier, who was in Sainte-Pélagie but after Sade left, placed the event in a different prison, the Temple, and he also was mistaken about the time of the transfer, placing it in the autumn of 1803. Perhaps he made up his anecdote from what he had heard from other prisoners. In any case, his account is highly suggestive of Sade's appearance and bearing. Of Sade's manners, Nodier wrote "that he was polite to the point of obsequiousness, affable to the point of unctuousness, and that he spoke respectfully of all that is respected." Nodier's portrait of Sade's physical appearance is full of pathos: "At first, the only thing I noticed about him was an enormous obesity that so hindered his movements as to prevent him from displaying but a trace of the grace and elegance of which faint evidence was found in his manners and in his language. His weary eyes nevertheless retained that nuance of brilliance and clarity that flared from time to time like a spark on a dying ember."[12] Nodier, who had no sympathy for Sade's novels, nevertheless considered him "the prototype of the extra-legal victims of the imperious justice of the Consulate and of the Empire."[13] After two years in prison without a trial or a hearing, Sade was indeed a bewildered, grotesque figure, displaying the quaint manners of an era long past, yet nursing a flame of radical passion and wit that the government still found threatening.

Although no sexual scandal had been associated with Sade's name for almost thirty years, whatever Sade had said to the young men at Sainte-Pélagie sufficiently aroused Prefect of Police Dubois to make him conclude, "This incorrigible man was in a perpetual state of libertine dementia." Sade's fate was sealed. Dubois and Minister of Police Fouché would neither bring him to trial nor let him go free. Sade suffered in the hellhole of Bicêtre for six weeks, while Dubois, in consultation with Sade's family, worked out a permanent solution. Sade would be sent to the insane asylum at Charenton, where his family would pay his expenses (3,000 francs a year), and where the family "wish him to remain," said Dubois, "for the sake of their reputation."[14] So it would be the madhouse for the rest of his life, because he was an embarrassment to his family and because the government did not want to risk the public scandal and a possible acquittal by formally trying him for writing an obscene novel.

On April 27, 1803, Sade was conducted to the asylum at Charenton, just outside Paris, where he had spent nine months at the time of the Revolution. There had been great changes. The asylum, previously run by the Brothers of Charity, had been closed in 1795. Two years later, the Directorate authorized its reconstitution under the management of François Simonet de Coulmier, a former friar who had distinguished himself in the administration of charitable institutions for the church. Coulmier was an individual of considerable vision and energy. Pinel characterized him as "a gentleman of great intelligence and of pure and disinterested philanthropy."[15] As soon as Coulmier took control of the dilapidated asylum, he began an ambitious construction program. When Sade entered in 1803, work was under way on a new women's wing. In 1806, construction was begun on an infirmary that was eventually used as a grand ballroom. In *Mémoire sur la maison nationale de Charenton*, Charles-François Giraudy, a doctor associated with the asylum, praised its buildings, its spacious tree-lined promenades, its thirty-acre garden, its lovely views stretching away "across meadows, washed by the waters of the Seine and the Marne. Nowhere does nature enjoy a richer, more superb or more varied setting."[16] The setting was, and remains to this day, idyllic. Dr. Giraudy may be excused, perhaps, for his rhapsodic praise of the institution, "the first of its kind in France to have been solely intended for the treatment of the insane; the first . . . where the patients are not systematically considered to be totally lacking in judgment; where they are not subjected to brutality, ridicule, barbarous manacles nor to any other inhumane treatment; . . . in a word, the first establishment where the new principles of mental health can be put into practice in a precise manner."[17] Structurally and spiritually, the asylum at Charenton under Coulmier's direction was well on its way to becoming one of the important mental institutions on the continent.

Coulmier had gathered a willing and enthusiastic staff. In addition to Giraudy, there was Gastaldy, Sade's physician in Paris, who was originally from Provence and had worked at the asylum in Avignon. Later, L.-J. Ramon, a young intern, would be added just to attend Sade at his deathbed. Coulmier's vision and effectiveness as an administrator would eventually attract some criticism, specifically over his allowing Sade to put on plays as a therapeutic device, employing some of the patients as actors. In 1867, Dr. Ramon, recalling his career at Charenton, still stood in awe of Coulmier's strong but humane character. Coulmier, he wrote, "reigned despotically over all, but this despotism had nothing harsh or severe about it." Rather, he "was cherished by all under his care, employees and inmates alike. In short, his was a paternal government, but somewhat lax."[18] Dr. Ramon was referring to Coulmier's allowing Sade to put on plays and balls for the inmates. An odder couple could not be imagined—Coulmier and Sade.

If Sade had not been warned in advance what to expect, he would have been surprised indeed on his introduction to the head of the Charenton asylum. For one thing, Sade, even at five feet six inches, towered over Coulmier, who was described as a dwarf, deformed in body and face. In her *Mémoires*, Mlle Flore recounted her shock when, as a young actress in Paris, she first realized Coulmier's disfigurement. Like many other notables from Paris, she had been very happy to obtain a ticket to see one of Sade's productions at Charenton. As usual, Coulmier sat in his special place in the auditorium, basking in the success of his new therapeutic method and enjoying the presence of his interesting visitors from Paris. In attendance on this occasion was the famous singer of the Opéra-Comique Mme Saint-Aubin and a group of her friends. Mlle Flore had not noticed anything unusual about Coulmier until the intermission:

> During the intermission, M. Coulmier, desiring to go and greet Madame Saint-Aubin and her friends, arose, but when he stood up, he disappeared from view.
>
> I looked for him among the throng, when, chancing to lower my gaze, I discovered him beside us.
>
> Imagine my surprise! This man, whom from the appearance of his large head and his large chest I had taken to be very tall, had been sitting on a chair raised especially high, and when he stood on the floor, he turned out to be a dwarf four feet tall, whose short and crooked legs supported an enormous torso.[19]

Sade may have appeared equally strange to Coulmier. Another visitor to the plays at Charenton, Auguste de Labouïsse, composed these awkward and unflattering verses on Sade's appearance and on his acting ability:

> This actor is very large, very fat, very stiff, very clumsy;
> He's a huge mass, a short fellow and ugly,
> Whose face offers a ruinous mess;
> Yet in attendance many a booby
> Gives him applause nevertheless,
> Although his lines he forgets unduly.

Labouïsse added that he found something unsettling in Sade's appearance: "I could not explain that unaccountably extraordinary and sinister quality that I read on that strange countenance." He questioned another member of the audience and discovered that the actor was Sade. For his memoir, Labouïsse tried to re-create the shock he felt at the time: "O Heavens! Dare I say it? It was . . . yes . . . it was . . . the Comte de Sade! *The Comte de Sade!* . . . that infamous villain!!!"[20]

Coulmier, however, did not seem to mind Sade's appearance or his unsavory reputation. And Sade never mentioned the asylum director's height. By overlooking each other's obvious liabilities, they were able to discover what was truly valuable and interesting in each other. In fact, they appeared to like and to respect one another. This was an unusual development for Sade. For his part, Coulmier bridled at the idea that he was being put in the position of a jailer and quickly decided to allow Sade considerable freedom in the institution. He was frequently at odds with his superiors, including the minister of the interior, who expected him to keep Sade away from pen, paper, and ink, essentially confined to his room and segregated from the regular patients. But Sade—with his almost antique manners and courtliness, his charm, his vast reading in ancient and modern literature, his knowledge of philosophy, psychology, anthropology—was a very interesting person. And although their roles as director and inmate sometimes brought them into conflict, frequently over the nonpayment of Sade's pension, Sade's anger never escalated into those bitter, obsessive, and overdetermined feuds he used to wage against those in authority who, he believed, were engaged in a conspiracy against him. In the past, Sade had turned those authority figures into mythical, all-powerful beings, and he responded by playing the enraged child or the wily rebel. Now, for the first time, there was a genuine connection between him and a person in authority. For one thing, Sade and Coulmier were contemporaries (the latter was two years younger). For another, Sade had outgrown the childish need to define himself in opposition to some imagined Absolute Authority. Coulmier was too pathetically small to fill that role, and perhaps Sade found something genuinely brave about the way the asylum director had overcome his disability. Dr. Ramon and others considered him to be at once a powerful force and a humane, sympathetic person. Sade's ability to participate in this relationship suggests, perhaps, that he had finally come to be at peace with himself.

Even so, there were disputes. On July 16, 1803, Sade wrote to complain about Coulmier's inquiry concerning the 3,000 francs a year that Sade's family was slow in paying. "You speak to me about money," Sade protested, apparently using the phrase with which Coulmier had reproached him, *"as if I were born to make you a bankrupt."* With sarcasm, Sade observed, "This tone, I confess, is very new to me, but, happily, after some time here, I see that it is necessary to put up with anything here, even with insults and slander." Sade airily dismissed the question of payment, telling Coulmier that it was to Sade's son Louis-Marie that he should complain. There was one phrase in

Coulmier's letter that especially hurt Sade. Coulmier had written *"that there are many people who do not believe themselves to be crazy but who are."* "Oh, Monsieur," Sade exclaimed, "what a truth!"[21]

For his part, Sade did not think he was insane, even if Coulmier had—perhaps imprudently, perhaps teasingly—suggested that such a belief was itself sometimes a feature of insanity. Among those who thought Sade needed to be locked away were Minister of Police Fouché, Prefect of Police Dubois, and Napoleon himself, who continued to endorse his confinement at Charenton. Sade's family—actually, his sons, Louis-Marie and Claude-Armand—were determined to retain control of Sade's estates and were socially embarrassed by the reputation of their father. The diagnosis of insanity was sheer flummery, a pretext for his continued and extralegal punishment. Governments had come and gone. The very way time was counted changed when, on January 1, 1806, the old Gregorian calendar was reinstated, ending the revolutionary experiment. But for Sade, nothing changed. Or things went from bad to worse, as when his friend Dr. Gastaldy died on December 22, 1805, and was replaced as chief medical officer at Charenton by Dr. Antoine-Athanase Royer-Collard on January 13, 1806. Royer-Collard, as he reported to the minister of police on August 2, 1808, had no sympathy for Sade, "that abominable man," who was given "far too much freedom" at Charenton, where he directed the other patients in plays and amusements unsuitable for them, where he entertained "individuals of both sexes" in his rooms, and where he preached "his horrible doctrine" to anyone who would listen. He asked that Sade be sent to a real prison, which "would suit him far better than an institution devoted to the treatment of the ill." If Royer-Collard was shocked by Sade's immoral reputation, he did not think that Sade was crazy: "This man," he stated bluntly, "is not insane."[22] The actress Mlle Flore, even though she saw Sade at Charenton, understood that "he was, however, not crazy." Rather, she believed that he was "only too fortunate not to be in some other prison, to which he had not been sentenced in order to avoid the most scandalous revelations."[23] "As for me," Sade had written to Coulmier on July 16, 1803, "I assure you that I desire but one thing, and that is to be (and, in fact, as soon as possible) as far from Charenton as I am now near to it."[24]

Nevertheless, Sade's situation in Charenton was better than in any prison he had been in before, and his pension there allowed him far more luxuries than were afforded the average resident. He lived, not in a cell, but in a small apartment on the third floor, with windows overlooking the gardens and the Marne River. He had a bedroom and a vestibule with a closet and an alcove containing his library. The furnishings, however, were ordinary. Over the years, he had pawned everything he loved. Now, instead of decorating his rooms, as had been his custom, he merely furnished them. The inventory taken of his effects just after his death lists his few possessions and appraises their value. There is "an old bureau of blackened wood, three francs"; "a wing chair in yellow velvet from Utrecht with its cushion, with an old screen and two chairs stuffed with straw, eighteen francs"; "in a cupboard to the left of the fireplace: an old cotton workshirt, two pairs of shoes, a shaving dish, and an amount of old linen, six francs."[25] The list goes on in this way. Sade paid more attention to the books he collected, including *Histoire de Don Quichotte*, *L'Homme au masque de fer*, *Le Château mystérieux*, the works of Rousseau, the works of Tacitus, *Mémoires du cardinal de Retz*, copies of his own acknowledged works (*Les Crimes de l'amour*, *Aline et Valcour*), *Le Pornographe* by Restif de la Bretonne, a book on Isaac Newton's theory of physics, the complete works of Voltaire, a rhyming dictionary, Cicero's selected letters, *Contes de La Fontaine*, *Histoire des Indiens*, and so on.[26] To be sure, Sade's library at Charenton was nowhere near the truly massive collection of volumes he had acquired in about an equal length of time in Vincennes and the Bastille. At the time of his death, the inventory indicates that what he owed the *pâtissier* and the *fruitière* in the town of Charenton (Sade loved cakes and fresh and candied fruit) came to more than the appraised value of his library and all of his clothes and furniture.[27]

The inventory reveals what must have been his most cherished possessions. First, there is "a large unframed painting" of Sade's father, and four miniatures: Sade's mother; his elder son; his cousin Mlle de Charolais; and, surprisingly, his sister-in-law, Anne-Prospère de Launay.[28] Her image recalled that season at La Coste in 1771–72, when she had become his lover and he had put on plays there and at Mazan, that dreamy season in Provence of playhouses, actresses, and the Marseilles prostitutes. Imagine Sade's joy when he persuaded Coulmier to allow him to put on plays at Charenton, and not just with inmates of both sexes, but also with professional actors and actresses hired in Paris. Sade, now well into his sixties, managed in some degree to re-create in the asylum at Charenton that happier season of his former life.

The first of Sade's plays at Charenton was probably performed at the end of 1804 or the beginning of 1805. During that early period, Coulmier had come to understand Sade's personality and interest in the theater. He himself had been formulating a new idea that theatrical performances could be a therapy for curing insanity, both in the patients who performed the plays and in those who witnessed them. He also must have realized that Sade, committed to an insane asylum for administrative rather than medical reasons, would become an unhappy and possibly a disruptive inmate if he had nothing to distract him from his predicament. So Coulmier's therapy would work on the proposed director of these plays as well as on the players and the audience. Indeed, after the early confrontations between the two men over money,

Coulmier had come to adopt a very liberal, a very humane approach to his difficult prisoner.

From the beginning, all of Sade's attempts to regain his freedom had been thwarted or ignored. On April 13, 1804, Mme Quesnet had written a short letter to the minister of justice. In her simple style, she asked the minister to grant Sade his liberty since he had now been imprisoned for three years "under mere suspicion." Ironically, the next thing that happened was that, on May 1, Prefect of Police Dubois ordered Coulmier to search Sade's room for papers and to warn Sade that if he did not behave he would be sent back to Bicêtre.[29] On June 20, Sade himself wrote a petition to the Senatorial Commission on Individual Liberty. "It has been forty months," Sade wrote, "that I have groaned under the most unjust and cruel irons," arrested, he reminded the tribunal, as being "the author of an immoral book that I swear to you I never wrote." Sade claimed that the real cause of his "arbitrary" imprisonment was not the book but "a hideous alliance of relatives" whose "actions and views during the Revolution" Sade, as a good republican, refused to share. Sade claimed that it was his "constant and sustained attachment as much to my country as to those who govern it" that made these relatives "furious," and determined them to exact their unjust vengeance "upon their return to France."[30] This appeal, like Mme Quesnet's, was quietly shelved. Possibly it was in recognition of Sade's disappointments in trying to get free from his illegal imprisonment that, during August 1804, just before the plays began, Coulmier allowed Mme Quesnet to move into a room adjoining Sade's.[31] To keep up appearances, Sade always referred to her as his illegitimate daughter.

If Sade got nowhere with the officials of the national government, at least his life at Charenton was improving. He threw himself into play production. Mme Quesnet was at his side and could assist him and even resume her former profession of actress. Coulmier gave Sade space in the Notre-Dame ward and funds to construct a theater capable of seating nearly two hundred people. Conventional plays of the Paris theater were selected by Coulmier; Sade arranged all the details of production and publicity, selling tickets, acting as master of ceremonies, organizing the actors, whether chosen among the inmates or hired from Paris, and directing them in their rehearsals. There was a new production once a month, as well as other entertainments, including ballet, opera, balls, and a fireworks display on Coulmier's name day. On that occasion, Sade would also compose some additional verses in praise of his mentor, to be added to the play for that evening. For one such day, he wrote an allegorical play, *La Fête de l'amitié,* in honor of Coulmier.

News of the plays at Charenton quickly spread, and tickets were avidly sought after. Tours of madhouses had been a bizarre diversion in the eighteenth century. Going to see how the insane might act in familiar plays could provide the same amusement with less guilt, perhaps, since the whole enterprise was claimed to be therapeutic and productive of remarkable cures. "Charlatanism," cried Hippolyte de Colins, in a confidential report he sent to the minister of the interior in June 1812.[32] Colins, a former cavalry officer, had been sent to study veterinary medicine at the nearby school at Alfort, where for some reason he took it upon himself to make a critical investigation of the asylum at Charenton. According to Dr. Ramon, Colins made contact with a worker at Charenton who may have had some "malevolence" in revealing the secrets of the establishment. These two men, Dr. Ramon felt, hatched "a plot to shake up this institution." Even so, he had to agree with Colins's criticism of the lax morality at Charenton, and in particular of the performances, which he admitted "were far from being in accord with the appearance of discretion that ought to obtain in an institution of this sort."[33] The famous alienist Jean-Étienne Esquirol, who followed Pinel at the Salpêtrière, condemned Coulmier for having claimed to discover "in theatrical performances and in dance a sovereign cure for madness." In his *Rapport statistique sur la maison royale de Charenton* (1818), Esquirol bluntly stated his opinion that this new therapy "had no curative value." Moreover, he claimed, "the performances were a fraud," because (as he wrongly insisted) "the insane did not act at all." Coulmier, he said, "deceived the public, and everyone was taken in by it; the great and the lowly, the learned and the ignorant, all were eager to attend the performances put on by the madmen of Charenton. For several years, all Paris ran to Charenton." According to Esquirol, the whole thing was just a tawdry show. Even the insane individuals who were part of the audience were harmed by becoming "the object of the curiosity of a frivolous, thoughtless, and sometimes wicked public. The bizarre posture and behavior of these unfortunates provoked the derisive laughter and the insulting pity of the audience."[34] Esquirol's criticisms, especially about the publicity Coulmier's experimental therapy attracted, may have come from professional jealousy. Coulmier intended to use the theatrical performances as a means of diversion and as a form of expression for some of the more stable patients. The social nature of the performances also raised the spirits of the entire institution. "It was by these means," Colins reported, "that the Director's enraptured adulators claim the madmen are gradually restored to reason, that their imagination is withdrawn from delusion, that little by little they are brought into contact with reality."[35] Even though Colins and Esquirol tried to debunk the method, Coulmier's regimen was a far cry from the overcrowded cells and the barely custodial care that were the norm at other places. Besides, Esquirol may not have had any direct experience of what was going on at Charenton: his descriptions, his criticisms, and indeed often his phrasing closely follow Colins's presumably confidential memo to the minister of the interior.[36]

At the age of sixty-four, Sade embarked on his new career as impresario with a great deal of energy and imagination. According to Colins, three-fourths of the seats in the theater were reserved for "elegant ladies and outsiders." At the back of the auditorium was Coulmier's private box, into which were admitted his special guests. On either side of the box were seats ranged in tiers: those on the right designated for fifteen or twenty female patients, and those on the left for twenty or thirty male patients, "selected from among the convalescents and the tranquil melancholiacs."[37] From the wings, with his troupe of professional and insane actors behind him, Sade could look out on his equally singular audience of elegant ladies, visiting dignitaries, privileged guests like the mayors of the towns of Charenton and Carrières, and the tranquil melancholiacs. "The maniacs, the violently insane, the idiots," Colins noted, "are necessarily excluded."[38] Until Sade and Charenton, a more unusual audience and acting troupe had never been gathered in the history of theater. Before the signal commanding the audience's silence (a mallet thumping on the floor of the stage), a great deal of preliminary work had taken place.

For one thing, according to Colins, the audience had been attracted by Coulmier's having assiduously "distributed in Paris and in the surrounding countryside a great number of invitations signed by him and written in a manner designed to pique curiosity."[39] Sade always cleared the guest list with Coulmier. One such list, dating from 1810, indicates that, of a total of 186 places, thirty-six were reserved for "employees of the institution," sixty for "patients," and ninety for invited guests. Of those in the last category, Sade saved fourteen seats, a significant proportion, for himself and Mme Quesnet. Among the other names on the list were M. Deguise, the chief surgeon at Charenton; M. Finot, a lawyer in the town of Charenton; and Mme Urbistandos,[40] who was probably the mother of a young and beautiful patient whose acting Mlle Flore praised highly. This young Spaniard was "ravishingly dark, with ebony hair, with large almond-shaped eyes, with the face of a melancholiac." This sad beauty very charmingly recited "the couplets written by the Marquis de Sade for the Director of the institution" in honor of his name day.[41] Another person on the list, Mme Louise Cochelet, was lady-in-waiting to Queen Hortense of Holland. Sade wrote the following flattering invitation to her on May 23, 1810:

Madame,
    The interest that you appeared to take in the dramatic performances

of the pensioners of my institution prompts me as a regular practice to offer you tickets to each of their presentations.

Spectators like you, Madame, have such a great effect on their pride that they find that merely the hope of having you and pleasing you is all that is needed to elevate their imagination and to foster their talent.[42]

Sade behaved as if he were in his own château, not a prisoner of state locked away in a madhouse.

It may be that Sade himself was the first success for Coulmier's new therapy. During these years of play production, he was generally reasonable and relatively happy. There was much work for him to do, organizing the music and musicians for the performances, the stage scenery, the costumes, the printing of tickets, the auditions, the rehearsals. The *Journal* Sade kept at Charenton gives some information about his problems as an impresario. Only two notebooks survived the police searches of his room, one journal dealing with 1807–8 and one covering the final year of his life, 1814. Sade's daily entries are usually sketchy and frequently employ code names for individuals. Here are some entries relating to the plays:

1807

July

30, he [Coulmier] changed the time of rehearsals and by this change ruined everything I had prescribed.[43]

October

2, M. de C[oulmier] stopped at M[a]d[ame] Q[uesnet's] to say that he does not want performed the play that had been in rehearsal for the past month and that I had written for him. That somewhat raised tempers. (I wanted to rip the work up.) Léon was to be sent out to perform *Les Chasseurs*, which was to be put on instead; and my verses, which I was asked to rewrite into a new setting, were to be recited.[44]

December

13, a large company at the concert . . . M[a]d[ame] [Quesnet] sang 3 verses of mine at this occasion.[45]

1808

January

7, M. de C[oulmier] sent for me to delay the performance until the *17th*. But that was merely a lovely joke to send me a 17 and a 23.[46]

29, C[oulmier] sent for me to attend, he said, a drama committee, the result of which was that, following what we were going to put on, we would then perform *Claudine et le chaudronnier* and then, in April, *Les Folies*, etc. . . . and a play that would be selected to suit the talents of the new actors I was being asked to develop, but that *Ambroise* would not be performed, although he had given me his word of honor about it, which caused me considerable trouble since the part was supposed to go to Md [Quesnet], who was in tears over it all night long, and all of that made it clear that the chronicle of my vexations would never end; in one way or another, I must always be the victim.[47]

February

15 at night, although the evening performance had gone as well as possible and although I had taken a good deal of trouble over it, he [Coulmier] had plenty of unpleasant things to say about it. He bade me go and tell Descamps that he did not want him to perform; I told him. The next day, the 16th, the said Descamps left in a fury and did not return to sleep.[48]

20, . . . Chaprot came to tell me that Coul[mier] had absolutely forbidden Md. Quesnet to sing at the concert and he told me this with rude words and in an unpleasant way.

22, I saw him [Coulmier] concerning this matter. He took it upon himself to give her this unhappy compliment. He told me to send Md. [Quesnet] to him. She went to him that night, but he did not say a word to her about it.[49]

It would appear that Coulmier could be too tenderhearted. Sade was left on his own to break the distressing news to Mme Quesnet.

Sade's entry for July 31 was more pleasant: Mme Saint-Aubin, the actress, "presented me with two white turkeys that she brought me herself."[50] The turkeys would be useful, for Sade often provided the actresses and other special guests with a supper in his rooms after the performances. On one occasion when Mme Saint-Aubin performed at Charenton, Mlle Flore was in the audience and saw Sade for the first time. This is how she described him in her *Mémoires*:

This man, whom I looked upon as a sort of curiosity, like one of those monstrous creatures put on display in cages, was the infamous Marquis de Sade, the author of several books that it is impossible to name and whose very titles are an insult to good taste and morality, which ought to make you aware that I have not read them.

It seemed that his face was the emblem of his mind and his character. I can see it still in my mind's eye, for I can remember faces as well as I do names.

He had a rather fine head, a bit long, an aquiline nose with flaring nostrils, a tight mouth, with the lower lip projecting. The corners of his mouth curled down in a scornful smile.

His small but brilliant eyes were shadowed beneath the strong arches of his thick eyebrows; his heavy eyelids, like a cat's, folded down over the corners of the eyes; his forehead, high and open, rose in an oval shape. He was coiffed with his hair put up in a tuft, in the style of Louis XV, the sides lightly curled, the whole perfectly powdered, and this was his own hair, even though he was then seventy-four years old.[51]

His figure was straight and lofty, his noble bearing was that of a man of high society.

One will pardon me for going on at length over the portrait of a man who had enjoyed an infamous celebrity.

He had retained his grand manner and a good deal of wit. It was he who wrote the divertissement and the verses from M. de Coulmier's celebration.[52]

Mlle Flore expressed surprise "that the verses written by this man of the most frightful morals exuded such absolute grace and were written in praise of virtue!"[53]

Mlle Flore also gave an account of how, during a performance, one of the inmate-actors suddenly dropped out of character:

A madman was playing the part of a valet, and he was reciting not badly when the person who played his master gave him a letter and told him to go and deliver it.

The latter, forgetting his role, looked at him with haughty pride and said: "What do you take me for? Am I your servant? Run your own errands."

And he left the stage, without anyone's being able to make him go back.[54]

This was not a lucky day for Sade. He had trouble with another patient, who, even though he was playing the part of a noble, refused to wear a peruke. "Since they insisted," Mlle Flore reported, "he maliciously let them put it on, but as soon as he was onstage, he threw it into the prompter's pit." This unscripted outburst put an end to the scene. "They had to lower the curtain," said Mlle Flore.[55]

If moving between the worlds of the asylum and the stage sometimes had amusing consequences for the inmate-actors, the results could be harmful, as in the case of a dancer named Trénis or Trénitz, cited by Hippolyte de Colins (and later by Esquirol). This Trénis had been a well-known dancer in Paris until he succumbed to delusions of grandeur, believing that he was the king. He was sent to Charenton, where, according to Colins, he "was regarded as incurable." However, Colins continues, "at least he was calm; he even experienced some glimmering of reason every night, for only in the morning was his delirium full-blown." Without naming them directly, Colins blames Sade and Coulmier for cajoling Trénis into giving a dance recital:

> They flattered his delusions of grandeur, they addressed him by the name of Prince, they gave him fancy clothes, and they hung a sword at his side. Thoroughly beguiled, Trénis did all that was asked of him and danced with a grace and lightness that evoked extraordinary applause for him; his joy, however, was short-lived. The fashionable admirers gathering around him appeared to him to be his own royal court; the admiration that his performance had excited was attributed by his mind solely to the expressions of the respect and the love of his subjects for him; and when it was time to divest him of this delusion of royalty, to have him give up the presumed ornaments of that station, and to return to his tiny cell just as he was before, he plunged into the most violent outburst of rage. Force had to be employed to deprive him of the sword and the fancy clothes; but that made his fury all the more frightful.[56]

Possibly Trénis was made worse for a time by his stage experience. But Colins's complaints had more to do with morality than with therapy, with how the patients would become overly excited and would be harmed by "the denouements, the surprises, the *coups de théâtre*, the dances, the lascivious situations."[57]

Sade answered some of the criticisms in his allegorical masque, *La Fête de l'amitié*, written to celebrate Coulmier, identified by the anagram "Meilcour." The inmates at Meilcour's country asylum put on a masque to honor him by relating the happy cures at an asylum outside ancient Athens. Orphanis, a young woman driven insane by love but cured, describes the treatment as involving "decent" and social "pleasures," such as "dances," or "a play performed by themselves."[58] Thus did the inmates of one asylum portray those cured in another, ancient one, their smiling faces simple and happy, their hair crowned with garlands. These are lovely moments Sade created, frozen in the amber of the past. Sepia images. Trénis pirouettes in his regal costume. Outside, Sade arranges a fireworks display over the gardens of Charenton. A half-century earlier, when he was a young cavalry officer, he had set off fireworks to celebrate a victory and had almost burned down a house. Now the bright lights explode in the darkness and shine on the faces below, illuminating the pale, melancholy face of the beautiful girl with the almond-shaped eyes, the ravishing Mlle Urbistandos. On the theater stage, Mme Quesnet plays a part much too young for her years. And a fat man with long white hair stands on the stage with a vacant look in his sometimes brilliant eyes. Sade has forgotten his lines again.

If Sade's life at Charenton was often happy, there were also many reminders that he was in fact a prisoner of state. Whenever he began to feel too secure, there would be a search of his room, or a new scandal about his putting on plays, or some complaint about his having too much freedom at Charenton. For example, Prefect of Police Dubois was incensed to learn that Sade had been allowed off the grounds to celebrate Easter Sunday, April 14, 1805, in the parish church of Charenton-Saint-Maurice. On May 17, Dubois wrote to reprimand Coulmier for his surprising and "excessive kindness" to Sade. Dubois explicitly ordered Coulmier not to allow Sade off the grounds. There is no suggestion that Sade was a threat to anyone. Dubois and Dubois's superiors were concerned only with appearances: "How did you not consider," Dubois rebuked Coulmier, "that the presence of such a man could only inspire horror and provoke trouble in public?"[59] A year later, when Sade requested permission for occasional day-leaves to Paris because pressing business required his presence there, Minister of Police Fouché wrote to Coulmier, dismissing the request out of hand and once again stating that the prime consideration was to keep Sade out of the public eye. "The ex–Marquis de Sade is too well known, as well as his execrable works," Fouché wrote to Coulmier on June 10, 1806; "if he were even seen on the outside, it would create a public scandal."[60] There was no real risk of Sade's escaping. He was sixty-six years old. He had no money. And he could not run very far. Indeed, he could scarcely walk.

Sade could still write, however. In 1806 or 1807, he wrote a set of "Notes" for a massive ten-volume erotic novel which, after several changes of names, he finally gave the following title, upon completing the work on April 25, 1807: *Les Journées de Florbelle, ou la nature dévoilée, suivies des Mémoires de l'abbé de Modose et des Aventures d'Émilie de Volnange servant des preuves des assertions.* "La nature dévoilée," nature stripped bare, would be the goal of the narrative sections as well as those sections of argument and philosophy that one would expect in a work by Sade. One can only imagine what might have been the content of the two hundred illustrations Sade had planned for this novel. He at first intended to use the following epigram on the title page:

> 'Tis by stripping vice naked
> That we are to virtue led.[61]

In the end, however, Sade chose this quote from Seneca: "True liberty consists in fearing neither men nor the gods."[62] Sade had made it his life's work to challenge men and the gods. And if the gods did not reply to his challenges, once again the police did. Six weeks after Sade completed his final draft, Minister of Police Fouché ordered Sade's rooms searched. Three policemen, in the presence of Director Coulmier, rummaged through Sade's belongings and confiscated his journals and papers, as well as *Les Journées de Florbelle*, which was discovered next door, in Mme Quesnet's room. Prefect of Police Dubois's report on the raid also noted the seizure of Sade's collection of dildos. Of the novel that was taken, Dubois said that he was disgusted by reading it, and he pronounced it "a collection of obscenities, blasphemies, and wickedness impossible to describe."[63] Later that day, when Sade resumed his *Journal* in a new notebook, he complained that the officer in charge "behaved very rudely toward me." Mme Quesnet was also upset. That evening, Coulmier spent an hour with Sade and Mme Quesnet "to console us." Sade was touched by Coulmier's concern and said he was "very pleased with him."[64]

Sade had once cried tears of blood over the loss of the manuscript of *Les Cent Vingt Journées de Sodome*. Now *Les Journées de Florbelle* disappeared into police custody with nary a whimper from the author. And this work, unlike the other, would not have a charmed life. After Sade's death, it was burned at the request and in the presence of Sade's son Claude-Armand. All that remains today are the seventeen sheets of Sade's "Notes."[65] The "Notes" give some idea of the grand scope and variety of styles that this ten-volume novel had. He must have regarded it as an erotic and philosophical tour de force, a compilation in which he alternated his basic themes and styles, including philosophical exposition, philosophical dialogues, and erotic narrative featuring exemplary and spectacular sexual scenes and punishments. In this respect, the days at the château of Florbelle must have had a multi-genre, three-ring-circus style similar to the one he used for the 120 days of Sodom at the château of Silling.

Les Journées de Florbelle may not have been written entirely at Charenton. When Sade finished the work in 1807, he was almost sixty-seven years old.

Even given his speed of composition, he may not have been up to writing such a large work. Moreover, during this time, as his *Journal* indicates, he was very much involved in producing plays each month. His "Notes" refer not at all to the original composition of *Les Journées de Florbelle* but, rather, to the organization, the problems, the adjustments of a "final draft"—a phrase he consistently used to describe his labors.[66] It is possible that Sade, locked up in Charenton and in need of money, was trying to cobble together out of earlier materials a large publishing venture, with two hundred obscene illustrations, that could earn a good deal of money. On the night of December 31, 1807, eight months after the police confiscated his manuscript and other papers, he had a dream at Charenton: "I dreamed," he wrote in his *Journal*, "that I redis-covered all of my manuscripts in the courtyard along with a very large sum of money in écus."[67]

Money was often on Sade's mind, as is evidenced by numerous references in his *Journal* from June 5, 1807, to August 26, 1808. Although he could not leave the grounds, Mme Quesnet could, and he sent her on frequent business trips to Paris. Sade often mentioned dealing with one of his farmers, Lenor-mand, who sent rent money but then stopped because of legal action by Sade's creditors,[68] an interruption that made Sade "angry and upset."[69] Cour-tois, from Provence, also sent money from time to time. Sade recorded for February 7, 1808, "I received a letter from Courtois containing 300 [francs] and a power of attorney for the cutting of wood at Saumane."[70] Sade was run-ning out of wood for his own fireplace at Charenton. A month earlier, he cal-culated (he was obsessive about counting things) that the wood supplied by Coulmier would run out by March 15.[71] At the beginning of the heating sea-son, on October 30, 1807, he had argued with Coulmier about the amount of wood supplied, and Coulmier, Sade noted in his *Journal* for that date, had "said some harsh and unpleasant things."[72]

Sade also counted and re-counted the years, months, and days of his vari-ous detentions. He had done the same thing long ago at Vincennes and the Bastille. During the period of this *Journal* of 1807–8, he made complete charts of his imprisonments on three occasions.[73] In the final accounting, on May 7, 1808, he reached a total for his time at Vincennes, the Bastille, and his first imprisonment at Charenton of thirteen years and forty-five days.[74] Then he calculated his current imprisonment at Charenton, from his arrest on March 6, 1801, until the present, as seven years and sixty-two days. The grand total yielded the following interesting numbers: "twenty years three months and seventeen days." With "such a lovely twenty-three and seventeen," he "naturally" concluded that he had "reason to base some hopes."[75]

On the interesting May 7, he made the following note in his *Journal:* "In the evening, I was given assurances that someone very frequently entered my room from nine to ten at night."[76] A week earlier, the signals all spoke of death. These are his entries for April 27 to April 29, 1808:

27, the number two was signaled.

On the same day, Mr. Mezange came to see me and spoke of deaths.

28, . . . my son came to dinner and strongly signaled nine and seven. There was talk of deaths and childbirths. . . .

29, all day long, ideas of death were signaled.[77]

In the following example, from January 1, 1808, Sade displayed the pathetic and ludicrous seriousness he devoted to these signals:

1st of January, M. de C[oulmier] visited Md. Quesnet while I was there. Instead of bringing me twenty-four oranges that I had requested, I was brought only eighteen at ten s[ols]. I had Md. offer some to M. de C., who on this first day of the month took only three and left nine of them, which forms the loveliest thirteen and nine imaginable.[78]

Sade paid attention to any unusual event. On July 18, 1807, he recorded in his *Journal,* "at nine o'clock the clock struck twenty-six times."[79] He was aware that, as a result of his attention to the "system of number codes," he was "taken for an object of derision whom it would seem that one could mock with impunity." However, as he wrote in his *Journal* on May 14, 1808, the fault belonged not to him but to the "stupid idiots" who "employ [it] against me."[80] The following account from March 9, 1808, is a touching scene of a proud, witty Sade who was nevertheless disconcerted by the presence of an interesting but disturbing stranger at the asylum:

M. de C[oulmier] had me come to him on the pretext that, going to Paris, he wanted to know if I had anything to ask him concerning the play; there was a tall young man there who did not stop looking at me. C[oulmier] . . . told me that the air of Charenton was good for me, to which I replied I would much prefer that on the outside, and he told me that he would neglect nothing to alleviate my situation, and this stranger kept staring at me.[81]

Sade was almost sixty-eight years old, and if one counted up all of his years in prison, the total would come to twenty-two years, almost half of his adult life. He was reduced to looking for clues to the meaning of his life in oranges, in any odd word spoken to him. He could be unnerved by the gaze of a curious stranger. Sometimes he fell into abject self-pity, as on January 28, 1808, "the anniversary of the death of my father. I occupy myself with him all day, and I lie down only to offer up my tears to him. Ah! if he were alive today, would he have permitted all this nonsense to which I am a prey?!!!"[82] If Sade's father had been alive in 1808, he would have been 106 years old, and he would have to have undergone an equally miraculous change of character in order to satisfy his son's wish for his protection.

At the same time, Sade was having trouble with his own sons. To be sure, they visited him occasionally. His elder son, Louis-Marie, visited on Coulmier's name day, October 3, 1807. As a surprise, he also dropped by for dinner on October 16.[83] They had dinner again a month later, on November 12. "All day long," Sade wrote in his *Journal*, "the number one was signaled." Appropriately enough, Sade added, "my son mentioned his first volume." Two years earlier, in 1805, Louis-Marie had published the first volume (as it would turn out, the only one) of his *Histoire de la nation française*. Forty years old in 1807, Louis-Marie was an unusual mixture of talents: a botanist, an artist, a scholar, a writer, and, unluckily, a soldier. That night at dinner in November, Louis-Marie returned to Sade a book he had borrowed: the first volume (yet another signal for the number one!) of *Les Crimes de l'amour*. He mentioned that his father's name was still a topic of scandal in Paris newspapers, which made the family consider "placing me farther away"—a very chilling threat for a man who had come to regard Charenton as his final home. Sade was made to see very clearly "that it is the family that controls everything."[84] He described the mood of his family with this mordant piece of wit: "The barometer of M[y] F[amily] is stuck on rain."[85] On November 20, his younger son, Claude-Armand, was strolling with him on the grounds when he asked his father, out of the blue, where he intended to be buried.[86]

Real difficulties came to a head during the following spring and early summer of 1808. Claude-Armand had been wooing Louise-Gabrielle-Laure de Sade d'Eyguières, his cousin, and the daughter of the man who, thirty years earlier, with Mme de Montreuil's blessing, had bought Sade's position as lieutenant general of Bresse, Bugey, Valromey, and Gex. Even before Sade heard about the engagement, even before he could oppose it, Louis-Marie lodged his own objections to the match. Perhaps he was concerned about consolidating his own claim to the Sade estate, or he may even have been jealous: many years earlier, he had been considered as a husband for Gabrielle-Laure, who, now thirty-six years old, was certainly no blushing bride.[87] On May 31, as Sade recorded in his *Journal*, Claude-Armand "paid me a surprise visit and said it was to ask my consent to marry" Gabrielle-Laure. "I very strongly approved this arrangement," Sade told his son. Suddenly, Louis-Marie showed up and requested a private discussion with his father. "He informed me," Sade wrote, "that they were setting a trap for me and that this marriage . . . would no sooner be concluded than they would remove me from here in order to put me in a dreadful fortress, such as the fort of Ham or Mont-Saint-Michel." Sade immediately told Claude-Armand that he "would sign nothing." After Claude-Armand left, Sade again spoke with Louis-Marie, who "assured me that he would see to it that nothing happened to me."[88] It was all too easy for Louis-Marie to mobilize his aged father's paranoia. Louis-Marie's feverish activities were mean-spirited and disturbing. Indeed, the scenes over the marriage agreement provoked a serious illness in Mme Quesnet.

On June 1, Mme Quesnet took to her bed with fever, faintness, and vomiting. She was seriously ill for a month, and Sade daily recorded her symptoms, her medications, and her slow progress in his *Journal.* His concern for her is evident throughout, and especially so in this passage:

> During the first week of her illness, my dear friend told me some very painful and indeed heartbreaking things, which, as soon as I found myself alone, made me shed a good many tears. One day, by way of thanking me for my cares, she asked me, "Do you, then, really want me to live?" And on another occasion, "You will not have me for very long," words all the more terrible since they were associated with those of my dream of twelve or thirteen months ago.[89] On another day, she told me, while fixing me in her gaze, "I perfectly well know that you will see me in my grave" (oh! no, no, because I will follow you there).[90]

Much to Sade's relief, by the beginning of July, Mme Quesnet's health was restored. In fact, she would live until 1832, surviving Sade by eighteen years.

While Mme Quesnet lay ill, Louis-Marie visited Sade twice, on June 20 and 21. Louis-Marie wanted to make sure of his father's continued opposition to Claude-Armand's marriage, and he also sought to win his father's gratitude by offering to try to obtain the release of Sade's manuscripts seized by the police.[91] On June 20, Sade formally wrote down his conditions for approving the match: in particular, his son must publicly guarantee that no harm would come to him after the event. However, Renée, Claude-Armand, and his prospective mother-in-law, Mme de Bimard, successfully petitioned to obviate the need for Sade's signature, on the ground that his name had never been removed from the list of émigrés. Theirs was a rather nervy strategy, since Mme de Bimard and her family, as well as Sade's two sons, had all left France during the revolutionary period. This was an unseemly business all the way around. In the end, it was Sade who caved in. On July 20, 1808, a man claiming to be a police officer sent by Prefect of Police Dubois took Sade to the house of the lawyer M. Finot, where Sade signed a document retracting his opposition to his son's marriage. It is not clear who arranged this ruse. Was it "M.F.," "My Family," as Sade called them? Certainly Dubois himself complained about the breach of the rules.[92] Perhaps Sade had been intimidated by the bogus police officer and by the use of Dubois's name. Perhaps he thought that, if he did not sign, Dubois would indeed send him to some horrible prison. Two days later, Sade retracted his retraction. Finally, however, he realized that opposition was meaningless. Accordingly, on September 15, 1808, Claude-Armand and Gabrielle-Laure were married at Condé.[93] Their union and their son, Alphonse-Ignace, kept Sade's blood and name alive even to this day.

Louis-Marie, having lost this family squabble, visited his father for the last time on August 10, 1808. "He was returning to the army," Sade wrote in his *Journal,* and he intended "not to return for a long time."[94] He did not return at all. Less than a year later, on June 9, 1809, Louis-Marie, a lieutenant in Napoleon's army in Italy, was killed in an ambush on the road to Otranto. Sade's other child, the one he rarely mentioned or even saw, the one he called "ugly" and "a fine stout farm-girl," Madeleine-Laure, took care of Renée at the château of Échauffour. In a letter to Ripert on September 20, 1810, Sade described her as "steeped in piety and foolishness, and so utterly deprived of all the qualities necessary to make a mother of a family that she will most likely die as much a virgin as she was born."[95] Indeed, Madeleine-Laure would never marry. She died at Échauffour in 1844, and was buried, as she had lived, beside her mother.

All of the semipublic squabbling over Claude-Armand's marriage may have had some additional unpleasant consequences for Sade. His family may have threatened to have him transferred to a real prison if he did not withdraw his opposition to the marriage. Bureaucratic wheels began to turn in that direction. On August 2, 1808, Dr. Royer-Collard, the chief medical officer of Charenton, wrote a critique of the way the institution was being run by Director Coulmier. Royer-Collard sent his views to Minister of Police Fouché, specifically protesting the presence of Sade, "the author of the infamous novel *Justine,*" a man whose "brazen immorality" deserved "the most severe sequestration." He criticized Coulmier's "imprudence" in allowing Sade to direct plays there, and implied that, "if these details were made known to the public," there would be a "scandal." As if this were not enough, he added that "the rumor" running through the institution "is that he is living with a woman who passes for his daughter." Dr. Royer-Collard asked that Sade be transferred to a prison.[96] On July 3, 1807, Sade noted in his *Journal* that Coulmier warned him that someone had anonymously sent "a frightful letter against Md. [Quesnet] and me."[97]

On September 2, 1808, Prefect of Police Dubois wrote to Fouché, summarizing the results of an inquiry into Dr. Royer-Collard's charges. Coulmier, Dubois wrote, not only defended Sade, but counted himself fortunate to have a man like Sade in his institution, a man capable of organizing the plays, which he insisted were a successful form of therapy. Dubois, however, recognized the potential for scandal in keeping at Charenton a man "who has corrupted public morality by his impious and libertine writings and who has befouled himself with so many crimes."[98] That same day, Fouché signed the order to move Sade to the fort of Ham.

When Dubois revealed this decision to Sade's family, there was a great protest, as he informed Fouché in a letter on September 9. Coulmier had also sent a favorable appeal on Sade's behalf. The family complained that Sade was too old and infirm to be moved, and, perhaps most important, that the transfer would involve additional cost. Dubois acknowledged that these points had merit, "were it a question of anyone else but Sade." Dubois had always treated Sade as some sort of contagion. He suggested the following conditions for Sade's remaining at Charenton, conditions with which he knew Coulmier could not or would not comply: "Unless he is kept under lock and key, unless he is denied all communication inside and with anyone outside except for his family, unless he continues to be deprived of pens and paper, I consider that the decision of September 2 should be sustained."[99] Thus advised, Fouché confirmed his earlier order to transfer Sade to the fort of Ham. However, after further petitions, Fouché agreed to postpone Sade's transfer until April 1809. In March, just before Sade would have been transferred, his relative Mme Delphine de Talaru (formerly married to Comte Stanislas de Clermont-Tonnerre, killed after the Revolution) visited Fouché and also wrote to him, asking him to rescind his transfer order. She enclosed a petition from the family and a supportive medical report from the chief surgeon of Charenton, Dr. Deguise.[100] Mme de Bimard also played a crucial role.[101] By April, Minister Fouché had been persuaded to leave Sade at Charenton.

On June 17, 1809, Sade addressed to Napoleon, "His Majesty the Emperor and King," the following reasonable and moving petition:

Sire,
    Monsieur de Sade, head of his family, in whose bosom he enjoys the consolation of a son who is distinguishing himself in the army, has led

for nearly nine years, in three consecutive prisons, the most unfortunate life in the world. He is a septuagenarian, nearly blind, burdened
with gout and with rheumatism of the lung and of the stomach, which
cause him to suffer horrible pains. Certificates by doctors of the institution of Charenton, where he now is, attest to the truth of these facts
and justify his finally claiming his freedom by swearing that one will
never have cause to repent having given it to him. He dares to call
himself, Sire, with the deepest respect, Your Majesty's very humble and
very obedient servant and subject.[102]

Sade's fruitless appeal to Napoleon is all the more pathetic because in referring to his son Louis-Marie's serving in Napoleon's army, he reveals that he
had not yet learned of his son's death a week earlier.

There would be no reprieve for Sade. His life at Charenton continued as
before, with Coulmier as a beleaguered supporter, with Mme Quesnet at his
side, with journals to write and plays to put on. Following Louis-Marie's
death, Claude-Armand took control over finances. Sade needed money.
On August 14, 1809, he had to borrow 200 livres from Coulmier.[103] On
October 22, 1809, he swallowed his pride and wrote to his former agent
François Ripert. "On my estate," he asked Ripert, "is there nothing that I
could lease or sell—some wood, some land, anything whose lease is due?"[104]
As the new year dawned, it became clear that Ripert (in the absence of
Gaufridy) had become the lightning rod for Sade's violent complaints. On
January 6, 1810, Sade accused Ripert of stealing 144 livres.[105] By January 17,
Sade was forced to beg Ripert's pardon: "I repent what I wrote to my old and
honest friend Ripert."[106]

After Gaufridy ended his long relationship with Sade in 1800, Sade wrote
his old friend two letters. The first, from Charenton, probably in 1806, was
prompted, Sade said, by Gaufridy's "very cordial letter to Madame Quesnet."
Sade asked Gaufridy, "the contemporary of my life, the companion of my
childhood," to make sure that "this dear and honest friend" was fully protected "in her just claims" to Sade's property. At the same time, he added a
complaint against the "ridiculous" and "excessive claims of Madame de Sade."
Sade seemed delighted that the prospective sale of La Coste by Mme Rovère
"is going to result in an enormous lawsuit between the stubborn Mme de
Sade and that respectable lady." Sade knew that questions would be asked
about his apparent misappropriation of some of the sale price. Thinking
about La Coste put Sade in a nostalgic mood. He asked Gaufridy for news of
their mutual friends, and for a report on the state of the ruined château and
his old park. Sade ended, wondering whether Gaufridy ever thought about

him: "Perhaps you would now like a word about me? Very well, *I am not happy*, although I am well."[107] A year later, on December 23, 1807, Sade wrote again to Gaufridy, begging him to make sure that Mme Quesnet's interests in Sade's properties were protected.[108]

Sade, however, was up to his old tricks. When he told Ripert to try to sell some of his property in Provence, he was trying to keep some of the money for himself and thus avoid paying the full price to his principal creditor, his wife. Sade's scheme, as he explained to Ripert, was to sell off Mazan or the property at Arles and to have Ripert "keep back," as he put it, "a *fifth* in a secret payment."[109] Claude-Armand, however, learned of his father's maneuvers and successfully thwarted them. Sade seemed to understand that his attempts to divert money from these land sales away from his creditors were being blocked by his son: "That one," he bitterly complained to Ripert on September 20, 1810, "never has a sol to give to his father, but his pockets are filled with gold to pay his lawyers."[110] Claude-Armand had won. In the midst of all these shenanigans, on July 7, 1810, Renée, attended by her daughter, died at the château of Échauffour in Normandy. Renée had been in ill health for some time. Like her husband, she had grown quite obese. Toward the end, she had gone blind. But in her final years, she had the consolation of celebrating the marriage of her favorite son. After those turbulent years with Sade, she had spent the last twenty in the bosom of her family and her God. Eventually, her daughter, Madeleine-Laure, would be buried beside her. The Marquise de Sade and her daughter, their tombstone reads, "BOTH EQUALLY VIRTUOUS AND CHARITABLE, MAY GOD REST THEIR SOULS IN PEACE."

As for Sade, although he had avoided the government's plan to transfer him to a prison, disturbing changes in the bureaucracy would affect his life at Charenton. In June 1810, both Minister of Police Fouché and Prefect of Police Dubois were dismissed from office. After their departure, Minister of the Interior Montalivet decided to take a personal interest in limiting the activities and the potential scandal presented by the aged prisoner of state at Charenton. On October 18, 1810, he informed Coulmier of new orders for curtailing Sade's freedom within the institution, and he gave the director a week to put them into effect. Montalivet justified the new orders in that Sade, as he put it, "is afflicted by the most serious of all manias; that his communications with the other inmates of the institution present incalculable dangers; that his writings are no less insane than his talk and his conduct; that these dangers are especially threatening in the midst of individuals whose imagination is already weakened or disturbed." This is the order with which Montalivet demanded Coulmier's immediate compliance: "M. de Sade will be placed in a location entirely separate, so that all communication, with the inside or the outside, is prohibited to him." How could Coulmier now conduct his drama therapy? How could Sade, in isolation, train the inmate actors, manage the rehearsals, direct every aspect of the performance? In addition, Montalivet ordered Coulmier to take "the greatest care to forbid him any use of pencils, ink, pens, and paper."[111] Clearly, what most concerned Montalivet was the potential for scandal in the plays that Sade put on and in his writings that might suddenly burst into print. To judge by Montalivet's insistence on solitary confinement, Sade, at age seventy, was still very much a threat to public morality.

As soon as Coulmier received Montalivet's order, he wrote back to say that he could not possibly comply within a week, because it had taken five days for the letter to arrive. But, quibbles aside, Coulmier had been put in a very delicate situation. Though he had to show respect, he also resented Montalivet's presuming to interfere in his own domain. "My birth," he wrote to Montalivet on October 24, 1810, "the various positions and honors with which I have been invested, conferred upon me the honor of being at the head of a humanitarian institution, but I would find myself humiliated to be turned into a jailer." In any case, he insisted that Sade's current room already met Montalivet's new requirements. He added that Sade "is under constant surveillance." To demonstrate that he had control of the situation, Coulmier stated that six weeks earlier, when he was informed that a pornographic work was being sold on the streets of Paris *"in his genre, in his style,"* Coulmier personally made a surprise search of Sade's room at five o'clock in the morning but found nothing incriminating. Perhaps it was once again a book that had brought down the government's wrath. Even though Coulmier insisted that he was not a jailer, he showed that he could be counted upon to be one when he mentioned having searched Sade's room on his own initiative. However, Coulmier complained about having to waste his own valuable time "in persecuting a man who, no doubt guilty, yet for a long time has appeared by his moderate behavior to be trying to make one forget his faults."[112] Coulmier was right. There had been no good reason for Sade's extrajudicial imprisonment. Under the weight of this injustice, he nevertheless behaved well at Charenton. Indeed, its most notorious inmate was perhaps also its most conscientious and active citizen.

Coulmier, however, must have thought it prudent to institute some of Montalivet's new regulations, for, in December 1810, Sade petitioned Coulmier for the reinstatement of his privileges. Sade had even got his influential relative Mme de Talaru to intercede with Montalivet. She reminded Montalivet that Sade's "behavior had been consistently good throughout his stay at Charenton." She also told him he was mistaken to believe that Sade "intendc d to abuse the narrow liberty he enjoyed in order to write any new works and to have his works published at Leipzig." Once again, it would appear that Sade's novels and the fear of scandal played the primary role in the shameful way the government treated him. Mme de Talaru even obtained an interview with Montalivet, as she reported to Coulmier in a letter on December 12, 1810. She had argued that "the frightful state of M. de Sade's health" required him to take exercise, and she reported to Coulmier that the minister had relented and had said that Sade "could take his walks whenever he wished during those times when the inmates were not taking their exercise." Sade could visit with Mme Quesnet as long as "there was no patient with her at the time." In the end, no doubt with Coulmier's assistance, Sade obtained the return of almost all of his privileges.[113]

Sade, at long last, may have found peace within the walls of Charenton, but he also appeared burned out, exhausted, almost submissive. There was almost nothing left in him of the often outrageous, transcendent violence of his angry letters from Vincennes and the Bastille. There were no more petitions for his freedom. Moreover, his efforts to maintain control over his estates had been thwarted by his son. In this matter too, Sade capitulated. He agreed that the money from any properties sold and the income from the remaining estate would go to Claude-Armand to repay the enormous debt of Renée's unpaid dowry, which was now owed to her heirs, Claude-Armand and his sister. The only thing Sade could do was try to protect the 1,600 francs of annual income he had guaranteed to Mme Quesnet. Claude-Armand undertook to furnish his father with 150 francs a month for his personal needs.[114] The only property Sade succeeded in keeping for himself was the land and the château at Saumane. But even this small victory was tinged with pathos; when he wrote to Gaufridy on September 24, 1811, he spoke of his "ardent wish to go there to deposit my ashes next to my dear uncle's."[115] A few months earlier, on June 15, 1811, he had written to Ripert in an equally depressed state of mind. "My hopes," Sade wrote, "must then disappear like the morning dew at the first rays of the sun: must one, then, look forward to nothing at all?"[116]

Given the weakening of Sade's mental and physical health, the ever-increasing governmental pressure to control him appears almost ludicrous. Each change in administration prompted a new inquiry into the aging pornographer in Charenton and brought new restrictions against his socializing with other patients, against his use of writing implements. His room was searched, his papers were taken. In July 1811, and a year later, in June 1812, Napoleon signed orders to continue Sade's imprisonment. From time to time, Sade was interrogated by various officials: on March 31, 1811, by Comte

Jolivet; on November 14, 1811, by Comte Corvietto; on March 31, 1813, by "Comte Appellius, or a very similar name," as Sade put it.[117] Dr. Royer-Collard had written to the minister of police complaining that Sade enjoyed too much freedom at Charenton and that there was potential for scandal in the plays he was putting on. Hippolyte de Colins's report to the minister of the interior in 1812 made the same points. Colins professed himself to be scandalized that "the Director of the plays" and "the elocution teacher" of the actor-patients is none other than "the author of *Justine*."[118] Despite Coulmier's defense of the therapeutic value of the plays and other entertainments, he could not forever resist the easy credibility his critics obtained from nervous government officials. On May 6, 1813, Coulmier was ordered to end all balls and concerts. The plays may have been forbidden even earlier.

Sade was out of work, so he set about writing Gothic potboilers of the sort that even the police who frequently searched his rooms would find unobjectionable. Sometime in 1813, he published anonymously *La Marquise de Gange*, the tragic story of the persecution and death of the virtuous Euphrasie through the evil machinations of her libertine brother-in-law, the Abbé Théodore. The details of this moral and conventional work do not bear close examination. This story of a good woman placed in a series of predicaments is the flip side of *Juliette*. There is one passage in which Euphrasie has been imprisoned in a tower. Sade observes, "One must have experienced the frightful position of a prisoner to be able to describe it." Euphrasie's passionate complaint could have been uttered by Sade himself:

> How cruel it is, indeed, to see all one's days pass in the same manner, to tell oneself, in tears: Tomorrow I will do just what I did today; no change at all for me; it is the darkness of the grave that envelops me already; I am unlike a corpse only in the hideous despair of living; you see me bereft of all the circumstances of life, dead to all the feelings of the soul; all affections are deadened in me, I live a stranger to everyone.[119]

Two other novels that Sade wrote at this time remained in manuscript for a century and a half. *Adélaïde de Brunswick, princesse de Saxe, événement du XIᵉ siècle* received its first French publication in an edition by Lely in 1964, from the manuscript in the Sade family archives. In a note to the manuscript, Sade indicated the speed with which he had composed this short novel: "I began this work on the first of September, 1812; the first draft was completed on October 4."[120] This historical novel concerns the tragic effects of jealousy and Court politics on the marriage of Prince Frédéric and his virtuous wife, Adélaïde, who is treacherously accused of having an affair. Adélaïde escapes imprisonment only to be flung from one misadventure to another. Finally, her husband is killed in a duel, and she ends her days in a convent, where she dies of consumption. The plot and the characters are mechanical and banal. There are predictable devices of the Gothic genre, such as a necromancer and a magic mirror. However, Schinders, the leader of a group of bandits into whose hands Adélaïde and her friend Bathilde have fallen, displays some capacity for psychological torture. He imprisons the two women in "an ancient tower completely surrounded by water." There he leaves them alone to brood while they weave the rope with which he will hang them when they are done—that is, when the rope is forty feet long. "Make the work last as long as you wish," he tells them, "but our vengeance will delight in the knowledge that each of the moments of your life was employed by you only to lead you to your death."[121] Except for a touch here and there, the work is insipid.[122]

The second novel that Sade wrote around this time may hold more interest: *Histoire secrète d'Isabelle de Bavière, reine de France.* This work was also first published by Lely (in 1953) from a manuscript in the Sade family archives. Sade's note in the manuscript indicates that he began the final draft on May 19, 1813, and completed it on September 24.[123] He claimed that his novel was based on original research he conducted at Dijon in 1764 and 1765, when he was twenty-four and twenty-five years old.[124] It is clear why Sade was attracted to the subject. He portrays Isabelle, the wife of Charles VI, the mad King, as a consummate Machiavellian schemer, an "ambitious and vindictive woman."[125] This "monster," as Sade describes her, is a woman "to whom the most heinous treason, infanticide, sacrilege, depravity, incest, adultery, murder appeared to count for so little!"[126] In this respect, Isabelle resembles Sade's most interesting characters, Juliette and also the libertines of *Les Cent Vingt Journées de Sodome.* Sade, it must be remembered, was as interested in portraying dangerous and powerful women as he was in portraying male libertines. Isabelle displays that libertine coldness and total lack of sentiment typical of Sade's major characters. "I value men," she boasts, "only for their usefulness to me."[127]

Some details of this novel have relevance to Sade's own experiences. He portrays Isabelle as a heartless politician, bent on gaining power by setting one faction against another, even to the point of fomenting riots and massacres. The summary executions she instigates sound like the Great Terror during the Revolution, when the "gutters, congested with palpitating innards and still-steaming blood, turned every neighborhood of the city into a vast slaughterhouse."[128] This imagery is so vivid in Sade's memory that he describes another political massacre instigated by Isabelle in the same terms:

This abundance of blood, of tangled and steaming innards, clogs all the streets adjacent to the palace and to the Paris gate; one could not go by without becoming covered with these most revolting objects *even up to one's ankles.* In short, it was only by death itself that one escaped the spectacle of death: one must fall beneath the blade of the executioners if one hoped to avoid seeing those whom their blades slaughtered.[129]

If Isabelle is portrayed as a kind of prototype of Robespierre, Sade also associates her with his old nemesis Mme de Montreuil. When Sade was in Vincennes and the Bastille, he had believed that Mme de Montreuil was somehow poisoning him or driving him crazy with secret drugs. Now Sade argues that Charles VI may have been driven crazy by similar means. He suggests that Isabelle "had employed powders" which she had made her husband "inhale or drink."[130] Sade believes that, by using mind-altering drugs, Isabelle could make her husband as crazy or as sane as she wished. When Sade wrote about the mad King's sad condition, he must have thought of his own unhappy life. The worst aspect of the King's illness was not the madness itself but the alternation between periods of madness and periods of relative sanity, for Sade observes that "the insane individual is not miserable so long as his illusions sustain him." The trouble comes during his lucid moments, when he wakes "only to despair at the state to which he sees himself reduced." Then, indeed, "he becomes the most wretched of men."[131] In all of the hideous hell-holes in which Sade spent so much of his life, and even now at Charenton, he must have frequently experienced this same shock and this same despair.

Even during the last year of his life, as he continued to try to get his plays produced professionally in Paris, there were new disappointments in store for Sade. At the end of 1813, he sent his historical tragedy *Jeanne Laisné* to the Comédie-Française, wrongly stating that it had been accepted there more than twenty years earlier, pending corrections which Sade now claimed finally to have completed.[132] On February 28, 1814, the theater replied with a long rejection letter in which virtually every aspect of the play received harsh, even cruel, criticism. During this winter of 1814, two years after Napoleon's doomed troops retreated from Russia through sleet and snow, Sade shivered near the fire (would there be enough wood to last this season?) and read over again the letter from the Comédie-Française, and the phrases pierced him like the pain in one of his gouty joints: "truly reprehensible," "such a capital fault in a subject like this," "inventions . . . impossible not to find unfortunate," "sheer *melodrama,*" "written in verse that almost never rises to the level of good prose," "very poor indeed."[133] A year earlier, in *La Marquise de Gange,*

Sade had written a paragraph on the seasons. Springtime, he said, "is a flirt who seeks to please," but autumn, "more poignant, more eloquent even than springtime," autumn "is a mother who is bidding farewell to her children," and "the pale colors of the leaves she dons" serve "to warn us of the fate that awaits us all."[134]

Napoleon's fate came a few months later. On April 11, 1814, the Emperor who had kept Sade a prisoner abdicated and became a prisoner himself. On May 3, Louis XVIII entered Paris. The general shake-up of the government brought changes that would affect the ancient prisoner at Charenton. The new minister of the interior, the Abbé de Montesquiou-Fezensac, following the advice of Dr. Royer-Collard (the doctor had won after all), replaced Coulmier with Roulhac du Maupas as director of Charenton. Thus, Sade lost a friend and a protector. One of the first things that the new director did upon taking control of Charenton in June 1814 was to have Sade's rooms searched. Among the papers seized was the *Journal* that Sade kept of his daily activities. What remains, then, of these diaries is the section already discussed (from 1807 to 1808), and the final one, which he began on July 18, 1814. A month earlier, Sade had passed his seventy-fourth birthday.

Sade's final *Journal* opens with an "extremely painful" visit from Claude-Armand. The new director, in order to protect the other patients from Sade's influence, had canceled his promenades. Sade asked his son to get them reinstated immediately, but Claude-Armand "refused with the most excessive heartlessness." Claude-Armand turned to Mme Quesnet and told her that she could go and ask the director herself. The news that Claude-Armand conveyed from the Ministry of the Interior was not much better. The person he normally conferred with, M. Lacroix, was no longer there, and his replacement, M. Biset, professed not to know any M. de Sade at Charenton.[135] Sade had outlived the professional lives of even his most recent persecutors! Ministers of police, prefects of police, ministers of the interior, and their assistants had come and gone, and some of the new ones did not even know who he was.

Sade's *Journal* records occasional events of interest. The former director, Coulmier, paid a visit on July 19, 1814, and again on September 7, when he visited with Sade.[136] With the new director, Sade was no longer a privileged patient. On November 13, Sade wrote, "the Director gave a grand dinner to which we were not invited."[137] Moreover, Roulhac du Maupas was quite energetic in limiting any possibility of scandal that might come from Sade. On September 7, the director wrote to the minister of the interior that he could no longer deny Sade's promenades in view of his declining health, in particular his "extremely violent attacks of colic" following his meals.

However, the director doubted it was the minister's "intention" that Sade should "have the means to communicate with all the inmates of the Institution, that he have pens, ink, and paper, and that he be able to write, to have copies made, and to send his works to the outside."[138] Indeed, some of his old plays were being recopied and carried out to theaters and publishers in Paris. On July 27, Sade recorded in his *Journal* that an individual named Paquet had taken an unnamed work to a publisher who "found it good" but declined to publish it. On August 2, Mme Quesnet saw Béchet, the publisher of Sade's *Marquise de Gange*.[139] She also made the rounds of the theaters with Sade's old plays.[140] So the director was right about Sade's access to the outside as well as to other patients. Sometime in August, Roulhac du Maupas learned from his informants in the asylum that Sade was employing patients to copy out his plays. On August 27, Sade recorded in his *Journal* that *La Tour mystérieuse* (a play dating from his time in the Bastille) had been seized in a patient's room, where it had been recopied for Sade.[141] Roulhac du Maupas read the play and described it for the minister of the interior as a work "without wit, without talent," and "in no respect bearing the taint of perversity and depravity" associated with Sade's other works. However, the danger was, as the director pointed out, if Sade "had this opera copied, he was able to have copies made of anything."[142] Therefore, the director recommended that Sade be transferred to a real prison, and Minister of the Interior Montesquiou-Fezensac penciled in this note: "To the château d'If, if it were possible."[143]

Although Sade suffered some troubles and anxieties during the last months of his life, the subject that would engross almost all of his attention and all of his entries in his final *Journal* was sex. In the final *Journal*, as in the earlier one, Sade paid special attention to his sexual thoughts and acts. For example, in the earlier one, on July 29, 1807, he noted that he had conducted a reading of a play for Coulmier's name day and that Mme Santeuil, another patient, had been present. "That night," he recorded, "the idea of ϕ" occurred to him.[144] This peculiar symbol, "ϕ," clearly has some sexual significance. It appears several times in the earlier *Journal*, as when two individuals visited him on January 15, 1808, and provoked the "idea of $\phi \phi$."[145] His entry for July 4, 1808, recorded "at night the idea of ϕ," and added that this was "the 82nd" occurrence of the idea.[146] The symbol also appears on October 23, 1814, in his final *Journal*.[147] Sade's sexual body and thoughts became the objects of his scientific curiosity. They became objectified, quantified, turned into data, and remained a fascinating puzzle to him all his life. It was as if he expected to find in the data some explanation for the way he was.

What occupied the vast majority of Sade's *Journal* entries during the last four months of his life was not mere fantasizing, but a sexual affair with a young woman, Magdeleine Leclerc, who was a part-time worker at Charenton. Her mother was a regular worker there. Magdeleine Leclerc was born on December 19, 1796, the very year when Sade, laid up with gout and desperate for money, had been obliged to sell his château at La Coste. When she made her first appearance in Sade's final *Journal* on July 21, 1814, she was seventeen and a half years old, and he was seventy-four. He kept a running account of her visits and of their sexual relations (a lesser number). For example, on July 21, he recorded that "Mgl made her 57th [sexual relation] and her 81st [visit] in all."[148] Clearly, their relations had begun long before the date of this journal entry. If the other journals had survived, it might be known exactly how and when their relationship began. Since Sade made a record of each of her visits, it is possible to count backward and to estimate the onset of their affair. However, the frequency of their meetings may have changed, and even in the extant *Journal*, Sade sometimes miscounted, as when he noted that she paid her eighty-ninth visit on both September 9 and September 17.[149] Whenever and however it began, the affair met with the approval of Magdeleine's mother. Sade gave Magdeleine a few francs from time to time. On November 6, when Sade told her he had only 1 franc, "she was content with that and said some kind things on this subject." Moreover, as a present, Sade noted, "she brought me a pair of stockings."[150]

During the last months of his life, Sade was even hoping to obtain his release and to live with Magdeleine Leclerc. She told him on August 12 that she was willing, but "that, if her mother did not approve, she could not do it, not yet being old enough to follow her own will."[151] Sade was thrown into an almost adolescent anxiety about what Mme Leclerc would say to his scheme. He began to doubt Magdeleine's affection for him. On August 12, he wondered whether Magdeleine was putting on an act when her manner seemed to say, *"Oh, dear God, don't go to any expense on my account, Monsieur, because you never have to with me."* His paranoia came to the fore once more. He reminded himself "that she visits you only as *télégraphe*"—that is, to send him some sort of signal, just as his enemies had always done. Sade warned himself, "You will have absolute proof that you are nothing but a dupe in this whole affair." He even imagined that his enemies put her up to spying on him: "They have turned this girl into one of those spies who are placed next to the condemned in order to learn their secrets." He believed he could see "definite proof" of her betrayal in "her coldness, her lack of interest in pleasure and in conversation." It had been different before (further proof that their relationship had developed some time ago), "for in her childhood," he noted, "she had much more honesty and candor."[152]

Sade need not have worried so much. In a few days, on August 17, Mme Leclerc finally appeared for the dreaded interview and agreed to whatever Sade wished—that is, "to let me have her daughter without any conditions other than those I had made myself." From the same passage, it appears that Sade also promised Mme Leclerc some employment once he got out and set up house with her daughter.[153] Mme Leclerc and Sade discussed the same matter two months later with equally agreeable results: "With regard to M[agdeleine], she asked me if I had spoken to her daughter about it. I told her yes. She asked me what she had replied. 'In the affirmative,' I answered. 'Very well,' she said, 'how could I refuse after that?' She displayed the greatest eagerness to see her daughter happy."[154] Mme Leclerc was not only eager to countenance this May–December relationship, she was positively conspiratorial, even to the point of commiserating with Sade on August 17 over the fact that Magdeleine was not a partisan of soap and water: "She said that her daughter never bathed." And when Sade had "scolded" Magdeleine over the "bad company" she was keeping, Mme Leclerc explained that "she was not able to prevent her daughter from working [at Charenton] with those sorts of girls," but assured him that "she saw them no more."[155] The oddity of this arrangement seemed not to bother anyone, including Mme Quesnet, who continued to run Sade's errands in Paris. Only once did Sade record in his *Journal* that Mme Quesnet lost her temper. Sade regularly had his trysts with Magdeleine on Sundays from October to December of 1814. On Sunday, November 13, 1814, when Magdeleine was expected but did not show up, Mme Quesnet paid a "surprise" visit, "to create a scene, believing that she was there." A few days later, on November 17, Sade had a "discussion" with Mme Quesnet and admitted "that it was I who was wrong."[156]

Sade's *Journal* accounts of his affair with Magdeleine Leclerc during the last months of his life are by turns funny, poignant, and sad. It would seem that there was some affection and attachment on both sides. Some excerpts might give the flavor of their relationship.

July

21, Mgl: made her 57th and her 81st in all. I warned her in advance that Annette would come in to bring the newspaper, first knocking on the door. She arrived, and Mgl. was completely disconcerted. She nearly did not recover, and in general was cold throughout the entire ϕ, which was begun without a conclusion.

Magdeleine was embarrassed by the appearance of Annette, but Sade had warned her about it, perhaps had even arranged this intrusion to satisfy his curiosity. Then he took Magdeleine to task about the friends she saw, in particular about a certain Lefebvre, over whom Sade was visibly jealous. Long ago, in 1781, when Sade was in Vincennes, he had become violently jealous over a presumed affair between Renée and her servant—Lefèvre. Now, about this new Lefebvre, Magdeleine assured Sade that she "knew him by sight but she never spoke to him at all, and she assured me that she would not speak with him."[157] Here is Sade's entry for August 12:

> Mgl. came as she promised. I was quite ill. She noticed it and seemed troubled, said that she was also ill. . . . She calmed me [over his jealousy], told me not to worry myself, said that she would not go to the ball with her friends.[158]

September

2, Mgl. made her 88th in all and her 64th. It was easy to see that she had been ill. She looked it. She had snipped off her c[unt] h[airs]. Someone knocked on the door and disturbed us.

17, Mgl. made her 89th in all. . . . Very agreeable, and never was I more pleased by her. She borrowed *Le Portier des C[hartreux]* [an eighteenth-century pornographic novel] and was very obligingly ardent, etc. . . .[159]

Sade was teaching her how to read, and also how to write, as would appear from his record of her ninety-first visit, on October 9: "I gave her a short lesson in writing and reading. She promised me to occupy herself with that during the long evenings."[160]

October

23, . . . she came at a quarter past noon and stayed until 2 o'clock, cold throughout, and when I expressed some reproaches to her about it, she said that it was the Institution that was the cause of it all, and that she would be entirely different on the outside. She earnestly promised me to remain faithful and attached to me and that I could count on her. She was having her period. . . . There occurred nevertheless a sudden thought of ϕ and she promised it for next Sunday.[161]

30, Mgl. came, as she had promised, and made her 93rd. She stayed two hours. She arrived at 8 [in the morning] and did not leave until after 10. She was very pleasant, promised to devote herself entirely to me when we are together. She drank, wrote, and sang.[162]

As the following excerpt indicates, Sade did not force any of his unusual sexual tastes on Magdeleine, nor could he have done so: young as she was, she understood herself and her power over her aged lover.

November

6, Mg. made her 94th; she entered at 9 o'clock and was very nice, displayed a good deal of consideration, but gave me to understand, despite the submission that she had vowed to me, that there were two things that she would not perform, and I realized that, as a rule, she would do only what she wished. She continued to be passive and without feeling and even cold throughout the session.

20, Mg., who had promised to come at the hour of mass [this was a Sunday], dallied over breakfast and instead of coming at 9 o'clock as she had promised, did not come until a quarter past 10. She was having her period, was very lively in conversation but without feeling in the pleasures, spoke of wanting to be a governess, said that she did not like to eat in the kitchen or with the cook. She had not been working at all on her writing, which made me angry, but she did not read badly.[163]

The reader may note that Sade divided his sessions with Magdeleine Leclerc into conversation, sex acts ("the pleasures"), and instruction. This is the formula of all of his erotic novels, in which a girl (Magdeleine was young enough to be his granddaughter), willing or not, is indoctrinated into the libertine mind and body. In this final romance with Magdeleine Leclerc, Sade relived in a sometimes tender, sometimes poignant form the essential dream of his long and tortured life.

On November 11, a new intern, L.-J. Ramon, nineteen years old, arrived at Charenton to take up his medical duties. He arrived in time to witness the last few weeks of Sade's life. Fifty-three years later, in 1867, he wrote down his recollections of Sade in "Notes sur M. de Sade": "I frequently encountered him, walking alone with a heavy, shuffling step, dressed quite carelessly, in the corridor adjoining his apartment; I never found him chatting with anyone. Coming up to him, I would greet him, and he would answer my greeting with that cold politeness that puts at a distance any idea of entering into conversation." Sade appeared to Dr. Ramon as a lonely, remote, proud old man, whose sufferings were almost over. In a way, his life had been over long before, doomed by his own improvidence, by his bad luck, by the need families and societies sometimes have for scapegoats. Even for young Dr. Ramon, Sade was a walking fossil, a barely living legend of the excesses of the ancien régime: "M. de Sade was for me one of those curious personages of the last half of the eighteenth century, curious because of what I had heard about him, since I had never read his works, although I knew of them, very imperfectly it is true, by tradition." Nothing has changed. Today, time has made the myth of Sade into an even more brazen, fleering mask. But of Sade the man as he appeared in 1814, Dr. Ramon said, "Nothing could have made me suspect in him the author of *Justine* and of *Juliette;* he only seemed an old gentleman, haughty and lonely."[164]

Sade observed the beginning of his final illness on November 20, 1814. He mentioned it to Magdeleine Leclerc: "I told her, since it was true, that for the past two weeks my health had not been good. She appeared moved by that."[165] A day later, on November 21, Mme de Talaru—his "cousin," as he called her—paid Sade a visit (her eighth, he noted). She saw at once that he was not well. "In a very tender manner," she asked if she could send him some of the aged wine that he liked so much: it might soothe his stomach trouble. She also "spoke several times of *liberty.*" But it was too late for such talk. By November 26, Sade recorded in his *Journal* that "my pains were still very sharp." Dr. Ramon was called, and he applied "a suspensory bandage"—a support for his testicles, which, Sade wrote in his *Journal,* had been paining him for a week, "especially when they were touched."[166]

Almost nine years earlier, on January 30, 1806, Sade had drawn up his will at Charenton. He appeared to have had some fear of being autopsied or buried while still alive—as if he were a character in one of his own novels. "I absolutely forbid that my body be opened, under whatever pretext there could be," he insisted in his will. Moreover, he continued, "I ask with the greatest solicitude that it be kept forty-eight hours in the room where I die, placed in a wooden coffin that will not be nailed shut until the conclusion of the above-mentioned forty-eight hours." Then he stipulated that a cart would transport his body to Malmaison, his farm—which, however, by 1814 had long ago been sold. He wished to be buried there "without any kind of ceremony":

> Once the pit is filled, it will be sown over with acorns, so that in the future, the ground of the said pit will again be overgrown, and the copse will once again be wooded as it had been before, all signs of my grave erased from the surface of the earth, as I hope that my memory will be effaced from the minds of men, except, of course, from the minds of those few who were pleased to love me until my last breath, and whose dear memory I carry to my grave.[167]

Magdeleine Leclerc, as she had promised, arrived on Sunday, November 27, for what would turn out to be her last visit, "her 97th," Sade, meticulous to the end, recorded in his *Journal:*

> She seemed deeply affected by my suffering, which I described to her; she had not gone to any ball and promised not to go to any, spoke of the future, said that she will be 18 years old the 19th of next month, lent herself as usual to our little amusements, promised to return next Sunday or Monday, thanked me for what I did for her, and made it clear that she has not deceived me nor did she have any wish to deceive.

Sade's final note on this Sunday's conversation and pleasures reads, "Mgl: stayed for 2 hours, and I was very pleased by it."[168] He would die almost as he had written that the man had died in his *Dialogue entre un prêtre et un moribond,* surrounded by female companions and arguing his libertine philosophy even in the face of the attending priest.

On December 1, 1814, according to Dr. Ramon's account,[169] Sade's condition radically worsened, and he was moved to an apartment where he could be better observed. During the afternoon of December 2, Claude-Armand arrived at the asylum and asked Dr. Ramon to watch over his father during the night. As evening approached and Dr. Ramon arrived at Sade's rooms, he ran into a priest on the way out. It was the Abbé Geoffroy, the chaplain of the institution, who seemed to Dr. Ramon, "if not inspired, then at least satisfied with his visit," for he told the doctor that Sade had agreed to another meeting the following morning. Dr. Ramon entered the room and studied his patient. Sade's "breathing, which had been noisy and labored, became more and more difficult." Dr. Ramon administered a few swallows of an infusion, as well as a potion prescribed to relieve the congestion in Sade's lungs. Then Dr. Ramon seated himself beside the bed of the dying man and waited. At around ten o'clock, Dr. Ramon became aware that the room had grown suddenly quiet.

Following Sade's death on December 2, Dr. Ramon admitted that he was eagerly looking forward to the customary autopsy, and especially to "the examination of Sade's skull and of the brain." However, Claude-Armand, who ignored most of Sade's stipulations in his will, was assiduous in petitioning the director of Charenton to forgo the autopsy—"perhaps the only one" Dr. Ramon says he did not perform from the end of 1814 to 1817. Following a mass in the chapel of Charenton, Sade's body was buried, not at Malmaison, of course, but in the cemetery of the Charenton asylum. A stone was lowered to close the grave. It bore no name. Sade might have liked that, but not the cross that was erected above it.

Some years later, Dr. Ramon could not say exactly how many, he finally got a chance to examine Sade's skull when his grave, among others, required exhumation for a reason that Dr. Ramon did not elaborate on. Dr. Ramon, a student of phrenology, then very much in fashion, reached the following conclusions: the cranial vault indicated "theosophy" and "benevolence"; the absence of protrusions in the temporal region indicated a "complete lack of ferocity"; and the moderate distance between one mastoid apophysis to the other suggested "nothing excessive in the area of physical love." In short, he concluded, Sade's skull "was in every respect exactly like that of a Father of the Church." Even as Dr. Ramon was solemnly extracting these ridiculous conclusions, even as he sat in his office with Sade's skull in the palm of his hand—poor Yorick!—who should come through his door but the great Dr. Spurzheim, the "celebrated phrenologist," who made off with the skull, promising to send it back to Dr. Ramon as well as some plaster copies of it. But Spurzheim died soon after, and Dr. Ramon never saw the skull again. However, one of the plaster copies made for Spurzheim was eventually found sitting peacefully in the Musée de l'Homme in Paris.

But Sade's skull itself, where is it now? And where, indeed, was the rest of his body reinterred at Charenton? Nobody knows. It is emblematic of Sade's misunderstood life and career that all that is left of him is a plaster simulacrum of his skull. And it is equally emblematic that the man who tried to argue the indivisibility of the body and the mind should end up with his skull in one place and his bones someplace else, and all lost.

Sade would have liked the irony. He saw himself as a victim of family, of government, of history, of fate. Read the epitaph that he wrote in his *Notes littéraires*, dating from 1803–1804:

> *Epitaph of D.-A.-F. Sade,*
> *prisoner under all the regimes.*
>
> Traveler,
> Stay and bend your knee to pray
> Near the most ill-fated of men.
> He was born in the last century
> And died in the current one.
>
> Despotism, with frightful mien,
> Against him waged unending strife;

Under Monarchs, this hateful fiend
Stole away the rest of his life.

Under the Terror, it lived once more,
Set Sade on the abyss's rim.
Under the Consulate it was reborn
And still Sade is its victim.[170]

Sade portrayed himself as a martyr to three governments, a rare distinction
and an ironical joke of fortune. It was as if he could sense the tragicomic destiny that fate had designed for him and would continue to fashion for him
even after his death. For today, he is a martyr to a quirk in history that
attached his name to a species of violent disease that represents only a very
small fraction of his own character. His wit, the playfulness of his ideas, his
extremist and ironical mentality, his essential ineluctability—all these are now
ignored. But the painful life he had fashioned for himself, the writings
pitched to extremes that define what it means to be human at the farthest
limits of the imagination, deserve to be better known. The leaves that he
wanted to obscure his unmarked grave ought to be swept away. The leaves of
his books ought to be read with care. For he, more than anyone, can teach us
what it means to be human in the extreme.

NOTES

NOTE: When in one of my paragraphs I quote from several pages in one of Sade's published letters, I have chosen to give inclusive page numbers at the end of the quotations. This procedure will minimize endnotes and should not inconvenience readers who wish to examine the original text in French.

I have used the following abbreviated references for works frequently cited in the text:

Bourdin   *Correspondance inédite du marquis de Sade.* Edited by Paul Bourdin. Paris, 1929.

Debauve   *Lettres inédites et documents retrouvés.* Edited by Jean-Louis Debauve. Paris, 1990.

Laborde   *Correspondances du marquis de Sade et de ses proches enrichies de documents, notes et commentaires.* Edited by Alice M. Laborde. 19 vols. (1–11, 20–27) to date. Genève, 1991–.

Lettres   *Lettres et mélanges littéraires.* Edited by Georges Daumas and Gilbert Lely. 3 vols. in 1. Paris, 1980.

Lely   Gilbert Lely. *Vie du marquis de Sade.* 2 vols. Paris, 1952–57.

OC   *Oeuvres complètes du marquis de Sade.* Edited by Annie Le Brun and Jean-Jacques Pauvert. 15 vols. Paris, 1986–91.

Oeuvres   *Oeuvres complètes.* Edited by Gilbert Lely. 16 vols. Paris, 1966–67.

1: Son and Heir

1. *Oeuvres,* 12:181. In modern numbering, this is Petrarch's sonnet 81, beginning *"Io son sì stanco sotto 'l fascio antico"* ("I am so weary under the burden of my sins") (*Petrarch's Lyric Poems,* 185).

2. *OC,* 1:78.

3. Jean-Jacques Pauvert dates the separation "probably in 1747 or 1748" (*Sade,* 1:25), and Maurice Lever states that Sade's parents were living separately by 1758 (*Donatien,* 87).

4. Lely, 1:290.

5. Laborde, *Le Mariage,* 35.

6. Ibid., 37.

7. *OC,* 4:40.

8. Laborde, *Le Mariage,* 74.

9. Laborde, 4:103.

10. Lely, 1:43.

11. Laborde, *Le Mariage,* 76.

12. *Lettres,* 1:341.

13. Lely, 1:138. Lely dates this letter June 1, 1766 (1:137); see p. 520, n. 21, for the reasons in favor of the earlier date.

14. Sade's grandmother may have had help from her five daughters, Sade's aunts: Henriette-Victoire, married to the Marquis de Villeneuve-Martignan; Gabrielle-Laure, Abbesse of Saint-Laurent d'Avignon; Gabrielle-Éléonore, Abbesse of Saint-Benoît de Cavaillon; Anne-Marie-Lucrèce, nun in Avignon; and Marguerite-Félicité, nun in Cavaillon.

15. Lely, 1:35–36.

16. Benabou, *Prostitution*, 128.

17. Lely implies that the Abbé's "amorous nature" (1:35) had some effect. Lever offers broader, almost snickering allusions to the Abbé's "libertinage" (*Donatien*, 66–67). Laborde disagrees entirely (*Le Mariage*, 80).

18. *Oeuvres*, 12:24.

19. The Abbé de Sade wrote to his brother on January 26 announcing the arrival of the tutor Amblet. Lever conjectures that the year was 1745 (*Donatien*, 672 n. 11).

20. Lever, *Donatien*, 62.

21. *Lettres*, 2:311.

22. *Oeuvres*, 12:201.

23. Laborde, *Le Mariage*, 99.

24. Laborde, 3:361–62, 364.

25. *Lettres*, 3:177.

26. Ibid., 2:349.

27. Lely, 1:224.

28. *Oeuvres*, 12:282–83.

29. Rochemonteix, *Un Collège*, 2:28.

30. Bluche, *La Vie*, 49.

31. Lely, 1:49.

32. Rochemonteix, *Un Collège*, 2:41.

33. Lely, 1:48.

34. Rochemonteix, *Un Collège*, 2:89.

35. Lever has offered these speculations, and further suggested that Jesuit schools like Louis-le-Grand were "veritable centers of pederasty" (*Donatien*, 72–73).

36. Rousseau, *Confessions*, 25–28.

37. Ibid., 27.

38. Laborde, *Le Mariage*, 24ff.; Lever, *Donatien*, 69.

39. Laborde, *Le Mariage*, 29.

40. Ibid., 31.

41. Lever, *Donatien*, 77–79.

42. Lely, 1:53.

43. Bluche, *La Vie*, 121.

44. Ibid., 122.

45. Ibid., 148.

46. Lever, *Donatien*, 82–83.

47. *OC*, 4:41.

48. Laborde, 3:363.

49. Ibid., 361.

50. Lever, *Donatien*, 86.

51. Bluche, *La Vie*, 143.

52. Ibid., 151.

53. Pauvert, *Sade*, 1:58.

54. Or Castéja, as Lever suggests (*Donatien*, 95).

55. Lely found this name illegible (1:58), but it is identified by Pauvert as that of Sade's valet (1:58).

56. *Oeuvres*, 12:8–9.

57. Ibid., 9.

58. The conclusion of this sentence and the beginning of the next one are based on an improvement of Lely's reading of the manuscript by Laborde (3:65).

59. *Oeuvres*, 12:7–8.

60. Ibid., 8.

61. Lely speculates it may date from 1758 (1:55); Lever, with more assurance, dates it April 22, 1759 (*Donatien*, 92); Pauvert assigns it a range, from 1758 to 1760 (*Sade*, 1:54).

62. *OC*, 16:34.

63. *Oeuvres*, 12:11–13.

2: Love and Marriage

1. Laborde, *Le Mariage*, 135.

2. Ibid., 136.

3. Lever, *Donatien*, 98ff.

4. Ibid., 101.

5. Laborde, *Le Mariage*, 123; Lever, *Donatien*, 98.

6. Laborde, *Le Mariage*, 208–9.

7. Laborde, 3:81–82.

8. *Lettres*, 1:69.

9. Laborde, *Le Mariage*, 133.

10. *OC*, 11:104.

11. Laborde, *Le Mariage*, 136.

12. Letter of July 1, 1762, quoted in Lever, *Donatien*, 106.

13. Laborde, *Le Mariage*, 139.

14. Ibid., 145.

15. Ibid., 139.

16. Ibid., 141–42.

17. Letter from the Comte to the Abbé, March 17, 1763, in ibid., 143–44.

18. The details in this paragraph come from the letter Sade wrote to Laure in the first days of April from Avignon (Laborde, 3:121–24).

19. Laborde, *Le Mariage*, 165.

20. Debauve, 67–68.
21. Laborde, *Le Mariage,* 150.
22. *Oeuvres,* 12:13–16.
23. Laborde, *Le Mariage,* 163–64.
24. Ibid., 166.
25. Laborde, 3:161.
26. Laborde, *Le Mariage,* 166.
27. *Lettres,* 1:342.
28. Laborde, *Le Mariage,* 169.
29. Lely, 1:86–87.
30. Laborde, *Le Mariage,* 166.
31. Details in this paragraph are drawn from the *contrat de mariage* and the *brevet de retenue* as printed at length by Laborde (*Le Mariage,* 201–16). Summaries of the contract are offered by Lely (1:86–87) and by Lever (*Donatien,* 116).
32. Laborde, 3:143.
33. Laborde, *Le Mariage,* 175.
34. Ibid., 208.
35. Ibid., 174–75.
36. Ibid., 180.
37. Ibid., 173.
38. Laborde, 3:161.
39. Laborde, *Le Mariage,* 175.
40. Ibid., 177.
41. Ibid., 174.
42. Benabou, *Prostitution,* 181–82.
43. Delpech, *La Passion,* 26.
44. Lever, *Donatien,* 125.
45. Laborde, 3:181.
46. *OC,* 12:39.
47. Ibid., 2:87–88.
48. Laborde, *Le Mariage,* 177.
49. Letter of June 1, 1765, in Lely, 1:138.
50. Laborde, 3:246–47.
51. *OC,* 1:60.
52. Letter of May 21, 1781, in *Oeuvres,* 12:324.
53. Letter of November 23–24, 1783, in ibid., 412.
54. Lely, 1:102; Lever, *Donatien,* 125.
55. Laborde, *Le Mariage,* 172.
56. Ibid., 177. In July 1763, Sade's investigation of the missing money revealed that it had been paid to a M. de Chevin, to whom Sade wrote a very clear, stern, lawyerly letter, possibly assisted (or provoked) by M. de Montreuil, who was a judge (ibid., 180).
57. Ibid., 182.
58. Ibid., 184–85.
59. Ibid., 187.
60. Ibid., 189.
61. Ibid., 190.
62. Ibid., 178–79.
63. Ibid., 182.
64. Ibid., 174.
65. Ibid., 182.
66. Ibid., 189.
67. Ibid., 191, 173.

3: Scandalous Debauch

1. Laborde, *Le Mariage,* 191.
2. Letter of September 14, 1763, in ibid., 183.
3. Letter of October 20, 1763, in ibid., 191.
4. The former standards of *pied* and *pouce* must be adjusted to modern feet and inches. Testard's estimate of around five *pieds* three *pouces* translates to around five feet seven inches. Sade's height, as recorded later on various administrative documents, was measured as five feet six inches or a bit more (see Lely, 1:91–93).
5. *Oeuvres,* 12:644–47. This document was discovered in 1963 by M. Jean Pomarède (ibid., xi, 644).
6. Laborde, 3:194.
7. Bluche, *La Vie,* 73.
8. Casanova, *Memoirs,* 2:140.
9. Benabou, *Prostitution,* 247.
10. *OC,* 1:225.
11. Ibid., 117.
12. Benabou, *Prostitution,* 394.
13. Ibid., 396.
14. Ibid., 394.
15. Rousseau, *Confessions,* 27–28.
16. Ibid., 25.
17. Lely, 1:108.
18. Ibid., 109.
19. Quoted in Lever, *Donatien,* 129.
20. Laborde, 3:190.
21. Ibid., 191–92.

22. Lely, 1:112.
23. Ibid., 144.
24. Laborde, 3:228.
25. Lely, 1:115.
26. Laborde, 3:228–29.
27. Letter of November 7, 1765, in ibid., 243.
28. Ibid., 202.

29. Ibid., 203.
30. Lely, 1:115.
31. Ibid., 116.
32. Ibid., 115.
33. Ibid., 116.
34. *Oeuvres*, 16:31.
35. *OC*, 1:458.

4: In the Flames of Passion

1. Lely, 1:116.
2. Ibid., 118.
3. Letter to Renée, May 21, 1781, in *Oeuvres*, 12:324.
4. Ibid., 19.
5. Ibid., 20–21.
6. Lely, 1:119–20.
7. Ibid., 151–52.
8. Letter to Renée, summer or fall of 1781, in *Oeuvres*, 12:330.
9. Lely, 1:152.
10. Letter of August 8, 1765, in Laborde, 3:234.
11. Letter of August 26, 1765, in ibid., 237.
12. *Oeuvres*, 12:22.
13. It is possible that Mlle C—— was Mlle de Cambis of Avignon, a young woman considered by the Comte as a potential bride for his son in a letter to the Abbé in March 1763 (Laborde, *Le Mariage*, 146–47). Sade himself did not mention her at that time and appears to have been unaware of his father's speculations.
14. *Oeuvres*, 16:36–37.
15. Ibid., 37.
16. Lever, *Donatien*, 139.
17. Lely, 1:121.
18. Ibid., 122.
19. Letter of March 29, 1765, in Laborde, 3:220.
20. Ibid., 221.
21. Lely dates this letter June 1, 1766. But the Abbé suggests that this was Sade's first trip to La Coste, which was true of his visit during the summer of 1765. Lely merely observes this incongruity in his dating of this letter a year later, and lets it go at that (1:138 n. 1). There are other clues for the earlier date. In this letter, the Abbé said that he waited for

his nephew at Avignon. This was true of Sade's 1765 visit, but not of his trip during the summer of 1766, when he made plans to meet the Abbé at Ébreuil, as he wrote in a letter dating from early in 1766 (see Laborde, 3:260).
22. Lely, 1:138–39.
23. Fauville, *La Coste*, 51.
24. Laborde, 3:230–31.
25. Letter of July 17, 1765, in ibid., 228–29.
26. Ibid., 233–35.
27. Ibid., 246; I have preserved Sade's punctuation in this passage.
28. Ibid., 237.
29. Lely, 1:131.
30. Bourdin, xvii.
31. Pauvert, *Sade*, 1:164.
32. Lely, 1:131.
33. Laborde, 3:239.
34. Letter of November 7, 1765, in ibid., 243.
35. Ibid.
36. Lely, 1:134.
37. Ibid., 135.
38. Pauvert, *Sade*, 1:168.
39. *Oeuvres*, 12:24–25.
40. Lely, 1:135.
41. *Oeuvres*, 12:26.
42. Bourdin, xvii.
43. This incident was discovered in eighteenth-century legal archives by Arlette Farge and reported in *Le Goût de l'archive* (Paris, 1989), 84–85. My account is based on details quoted in Debauve, 86–87, and Lever, *Donatien*, 686 n. 42.
44. Debauve, 79–80.
45. However, Lely (1:137) and Lever (*Donatien*, 151 and 686 n. 20) attribute a tryst at Melun to the summer of 1766, because they date Sade's June 1 letter to the Abbé to the

year 1766. For reasons already given, I agree
with Laborde in dating this letter as June 1,
1765 (see p. 520 n. 21).

46. Fauville, *La Coste*, 58.

47. Lely, 1:139.

48. Bourdin, xvii.

49. Lever, *Donatien*, 156.

50. Laborde, *Le Marquis et la marquise*, 16.

51. Laborde, 3:264.

52. Letter of January 30, 1767, in ibid., 265.

53. Ibid., 265–66.

54. Lely, 1:140.

55. Unaccountably, Lever places the conception in October 1765 at Échauffour (*Donatien*, 149). It actually occurred in Paris in
November 1766. Sade's first child, Louis-
Marie, was born on August 27, 1767.

56. Lely, 1:141–42.

57. Laborde, 4:20–21.

58. Fauville, *La Coste*, 72.

59. Laborde, *Le Marquis et la marquise*, 16.

5: The Arcueil Affair

1. Lely, 1:144.

2. Bourdin, xvii.

3. Lely, 1:201.

4. Laborde, 4:74.

5. Ibid., 65.

6. Ibid., 74.

7. Details of the events of April 3 and following, unless otherwise noted, are drawn from
official depositions and court records repro-
duced by Lely (1:197ff.), Laborde (4:26ff.),
and originally by Maurice Heine (*Le Marquis
de Sade*, 159ff.). Rose Keller gave two depositions: one on the night of April 3, and the
other on April 21 for the criminal division of
the High Court, known as La Tournelle. Her
testimony was essentially the same on both
occasions; the few differences will be noted as
necessary.

8. However, this detail about the church was
neither in Keller's first deposition nor in the
depositions of any other witness to whom
she told her story.

9. As reported in the deposition of Marguerite Sixdeniers (Laborde, 4:73).

10. The woman was Marie-Louis Jouette,
wife of Charles Lambert, the registrar to the
court for the town of Arcueil. Her deposition
was taken for the court on April 21.

11. Lely, 1:230–31.

12. Pauvert, *Sade*, 1:188 n. 3.

13. Walpole, *Correspondence*, 58.

14. Fauville, *La Coste*, 76.

15. Lely, 1:225.

16. Ibid., 224.

17. The above details are from Sohier's deposition for the court made on April 22, published by Heine (*Le Marquis de Sade*, 183–84)
and Laborde (4:75–76); and from Amblet's
deposition on April 26, published by Heine
(*Le Marquis de Sade*, 190–92) and Laborde
(4:94–96).

18. *Oeuvres*, 12:269.

19. *OC*, 2:126.

20. Ibid., 5:160 n.

21. *Oeuvres*, 12:393.

22. Ibid., 269.

23. Ibid., 273.

24. Lely, 1:197.

25. Ibid., 225.

26. Ibid., 204–6.

27. *Oeuvres*, 12:28–29.

28. Lely, 1:224–25.

29. Ibid., 231.

30. Lever, *Donatien*, 802–3.

31. To be sure, we know that Sade's mother
had written a complaint about her son's treatment at Pierre-Encize to the minister of the
King's household, M. de Saint-Florentin; on
May 3, he replied that, if he brought her
complaint before the King, the King might
decide to turn Sade over to the court, and
then things would only be worse for her son
(Lely, 1:231).

32. Laborde, 4:102–3.

33. Ibid., 113.

34. Lely, 1:229.

35. Ibid., 235.

36. Mme de Montreuil mentioned this sale,

"although she carefully hid it from me," in her letter to the Abbé of March 2, 1769 (Laborde, 4:129).

37. Lely, 1:235.

38. See Lely, 1:236–37; Laborde, 4:122.

39 Laborde, 4:126.

40. Ibid., 125.

41. Letter of May 29, 1772, in Lely, 1:254.

42. Debauve, 87.

43. Lely, 1:124 n. 3.

44. Laborde, 4:134.

45. One researcher into Sade's finances, Alice Laborde, observes that, when Sade's father died in 1767, he left his son with his own debts, amounting to as much as 86,000 livres. Laborde notes that on the day Sade married he "was already faced with a very complicated financial situation which he will *never* resolve." Laborde's belief is that Mme de Montreuil exaggerated her son-in-law's image as a spendthrift in order to provide herself with "an excellent excuse to meddle in his affairs." ("The Marquis de Sade's Biography Revisited," 14–15.)

46. Laborde, 4:127–34.

47. Ibid., 130.

48. Ibid., 133.

49. Laborde dates this letter March 4, 1770 (4:170).

50. Ibid., 170–72.

51. Ibid., 135.

52. Ibid., 137.

53. Ibid.

54. Laborde 4:142.

55. Ibid., 144.

56. Quotations from Sade's journal-letters of this trip are in ibid., 153, 156, 154, 165.

57. Ibid., 132.

58. Lely, 1:245.

59. Laborde, 4:174.

60. Lely found no trace of Sade from the fall of 1770 until March 13, 1771, when Sade petitioned the King for a promotion (1:247). Lely speculates that Sade may have made a trip to London during the fall or winter of 1770, based upon a note in his novel *Isabelle de Bavière* in which Sade claimed he did research for this novel in London in 1770 (*OC*, 12:264 n. 59). However, there is no other indication of Sade's familiarity with London. The evidence that Sade remained in France consists of letters concerning business matters, dating during this period or conjectured to do so. For details, see Lever, *Donatien*, 689 n. 14; Laborde, 4:176–81.

61. Laborde, 4:183.

62. Ibid., 186.

63. Ibid., 185.

64. Ibid., 194.

65. Ibid., 193.

66. Ibid., 191.

67. *Lettres*, 1:332.

68. *Oeuvres*, 12:209.

69. Laborde, 4:201.

70. Ibid., 202–3.

71. Letter of July 10, 1792, in Bourdin, 318.

72. Letter of May 5, 1793, in ibid., 341.

73. Letter of July 12, 1797, in Debauve, 392.

74. Letter of May 18, 1799, in ibid., 443.

75. Letter of January 26, 1800, in Bourdin, 442.

76. Laborde, 4:204.

77. Ibid., 201–2.

78. *Lettres*, 1:83–85.

79. Laborde, 4:202.

80. Ibid., 203.

6: Fatal Passion

1. Lely, 1:252–53.

2. Lely had estimated that Anne-Prospère had been born between 1743 and 1745 (1:271). Lever, however, has recently discovered Anne-Prospère's birthdate in family records to be December 27, 1751 (*Donatien*, 192). Renée was born in December 1741.

3. A letter from the Abbé de Sade to Anne-Prospère indicated his belief that her convent was in the Auvergne (Lely, 1:290–91). Lever, however, has discovered that she was a resident of the Priory of Alix, near Lyons (*Donatien*, 192), although he acknowledges that she may have resided in two convents at different times (690 n. 24).

4. Bourdin, xix.

5. Lely, 1:273.
6. Laborde, 5:215.
7. Fauville, *La Coste,* 88.
8. Laborde, 5:280–81.
9. *OC,* 13:23.
10. Ibid., 27–29.
11. Ibid., 28.
12. Ibid., 40.
13. Ibid., 41–42.
14. Ibid., 45.
15. Fauville, *La Coste,* 86.
16. *Théâtre de Sade,* 1:82–83.
17. Laborde, 5:266.
18. Lely, 1:287–88.
19. Ibid., 289–91.
20. Bourdin, 9–10.

21. Lely, 1:251.
22. Laborde, 4:172.
23. *Sade,* 1:242.
24. *OC,* 1:389.
25. Ibid., 440.
26. Ibid., 556.
27. Ibid., 558.
28. *Totem and Taboo,* 69.
29. *Théâtre de Sade,* 2:128.
30. Ibid., 137.
31. Debauve, 109. To be sure, Sade soon wrote Ripert to change these plans, saying that he would arrive a day earlier and would "be alone with one of his friends," emphasizing, "There will be no lady at all" (ibid., 110).

7: Marseilles

1. Laborde, 5:281.
2. Ibid., 292.
3. Ibid., 294.
4. Fauville, *La Coste,* 97 n. 10.
5. *Travels in France,* 229.
6. *OC,* 11:349–50.
7. The details of Sade's activities at Marseilles come from court depositions and documents published first by Heine (*Le Marquis de Sade,* 127–50), later by Lely (1:304–26), and most recently by Laborde (6:19–42).
8. As will be seen, Marguerite Coste's recantation on the capital crime of sodomy came as the result of a sum of money paid by Renée.
9. *Psychopathia Sexualis,* 141.
10. *Lettres,* 1:283–94.
11. *Oeuvres,* 12:449–51.
12. Ibid., 340.
13. Ibid., 125.
14. Ibid., 130.
15. *OC,* 1:316.
16. Ibid., 161.
17. Ibid., 163.
18. *Oeuvres,* 12:320.
19. Ibid., 327.
20. Ibid., 371.
21. See, for example, letters written from Vincennes on October 26, 1781, "They are giving me drugs that upset my stomach" (*Oeuvres,* 12:340); on October 10, 1782, "having put drugs in my food" and "having tried to poison my food" (*Lettres,* 3:116–17); October 21, 1782, "For the past six weeks that rascal endeavored to give me drugs that impaired my health" (*Oeuvres,* 12:365).
22. *Lettres,* 1:81.
23. *OC,* 11:149.
24. Quoted in Lely, 1:348.
25. Laborde, 6:52.
26. *Oeuvres,* 12:284.
27. Laborde, 6:66.
28. Bourdin, 10.
29. Lely, 1:339.
30. Laborde, 6:58.
31. Ibid., 59. Laborde asserts that the postscript is in Sade's handwriting, proving that Sade had not yet left La Coste (6:59 n.).
32. Lever, *Donatien,* 213.
33. Laborde, 6:69.
34. *Oeuvres,* 12:351–52.
35. There is considerable debate among Sade's biographers about the timing of his flight to Italy and about whether or not he was accompanied by his sister-in-law. According to Lely, Sade immediately fled to Italy with Anne-Prospère, around July 3 (1:278). The argument against Lely's view depends primarily upon Renée's *requête,* in

which she acknowledged that she had become aware of the "fatal passion" between her husband and her sister, and that she and Anne-Prospère nevertheless went to Marseilles to see what could be done (Bourdin, 10). If Anne-Prospère was at Marseilles in July, she could not have run off to Italy with her brother-in-law around July 3. Lely lamely argued that the statement in the *requête* in which Renée said that her sister accompanied her to Marseilles was a mistake on the part of the lawyer who took down Renée's account of the events (1:278 n. *a*). It is not likely there was a mistake in such an important legal document prepared by the Sades' otherwise meticulous lawyer Gaufridy. But the two sisters could have made the trip together to

Marseilles, and Sade could have fled with Anne-Prospère later than around July 3, the date Lely guessed the elopement had taken place. Laborde, however, uses Renée's *requête* and circumstantial arguments to discredit Lely's view ("The Marquis de Sade," 16–18). Pauvert also doubts that Anne-Prospère ever went to Italy with Sade (1:280). And Lever offers new but ambiguous evidence that the trip had occurred (*Donatien*, 218 and 696 n. 34).

36. Bourdin, 10.
37. Laborde, 6:91.
38. Ibid., 175.
39. Ibid., 238.
40. Ibid., 112.
41. Letter of April 10, 1780, in *Lettres*, 3:37.

8: In Prison at Miolans

1. Laborde, 6:132.
2. Ibid., 92.
3. Ibid., 96.
4. Ibid., 101.
5. Ibid., 102–3.
6. Ibid., 109.
7. Ibid., 121.
8. Ibid., 116–17.
9. Ibid., 129.
10. Ibid., 124–25.
11. The fort comprised the donjon, the Tower of Saint-Pierre, and the Bas-Fort. The latter contained quarters for the garrison, the canteen, the church, and storerooms.
12. Laborde, 6:125.
13. Ibid., 124.
14. Ibid., 125.
15. Ibid., 130.
16. Ibid., 135–36.
17. Augustin Ansard was the merchant who rented Sade the furnishings for his cell and supplied other provisions.
18. Major de la Balme was second in command at the fort.
19. Laborde, 6:136–37.
20. Letter of January 21, 1773, in ibid., 140.
21. For example, in February 1773, the Chevalier de Mouroux showed Renée's letter

to the King of Sardinia (ibid., 149), and as a consequence, on March 1, the Sardinian ambassador to France reported on a discussion about the letter that he had conducted in Paris with the French minister of foreign affairs, the Duc d'Aiguillon (ibid., 162–63).
22. Ibid., 140.
23. Ibid., 146–47.
24. Letter of February 19, 1773, in ibid., 156.
25. Ibid., 133.
26. Ibid., 139.
27. Ibid., 142.
28. Letter of January 24, 1773, in ibid., 140.
29. Ibid., 141–43, 189–92.
30. Letter of February 14, 1773, in ibid., 150–51.
31. Ibid., 153–54.
32. Sade made this admission in a letter to Renée on May 21, 1781 (*Oeuvres*, 12:318).
33. Laborde, 6:154.
34. Ibid., 155.
35. Ibid., 157.
36. Letter of March 1, 1773, in ibid., 162–63.
37. For example, in a letter to Renée in January 1784, Sade wrote that Albaret "was a rogue driven from my house for *slander* and *for theft*" (*Lettres*, 3:176). In other letters to Renée, Sade called Albaret a "scoundrel," a

"c[a]t[a]mite," and Mme de Montreuil's "gigolo" (*Oeuvres*, 12:165, 175, 261).

38. Letter of March 10, 1773, in Laborde, 6:168.

39. Ibid., 166.

40. Ibid., 164.

41. Albaret made three visits to the Comte: (1) on Monday, March 8, when he brought Renée's "Barraux" letter; (2) on Tuesday, March 9 ("yesterday" in the Comte's March 10 letter to the Chevalier de Mouroux), when Albaret asked for horses for their departure on Friday, March 12; and (3) "again the day before yesterday," when Albaret "postponed" the request for a team of horses to Sunday, March 14. This postponement must have occurred before March 12, the intended date of departure, and after March 9, the date of Albaret's second interview with the Comte. Thus, Albaret's third interview occurred on either March 10 or 11, and the Comte's letter was therefore written two days later, on March 12 or 13. My reading of the Comte's two letters clarifies errors by Lely (1:517) and Lever (*Donatien*, 233), who conflate Albaret's second and third visits into one, and by Georges Daumas, who mistakenly puts Albaret's first demand for horses during his first visit on Monday, March 8 (Lely, 1:420 n. 2).

42. Daumas was convinced that Renée's tactics were somehow designed to support her husband's escape from Miolans; Lely considered this theory interesting but unsupported (1:429 n. 2).

43. Ibid., 395 n. 2.

44. Ibid.

45. Laborde, 6:179.

46. This is Lely's view (1:444 n. 2).

47. Laborde, 6:170.

48. Letter of March 19, 1773, in ibid., 179.

49. Ibid.

50. Ibid., 159–61.

51. Letter of March 12, 1773, in ibid., 172.

52. Letter of March 17, 1773, in ibid., 175.

53. Ibid., 186–87.

54. Ibid., 198.

55. The dating and the size of this letter have caused some confusion in the versions published by Lely (1:445–48), by Desbordes (*Le Vrai Visage,* 122–23), by Debauve (115–18), and by Laborde (6:181–83). Lely prints this letter directly following one by Commandant de Launay of March 19, in which the commandant says he is attaching one by Sade. But the letter in question cannot be the one the commandant means, because in it Sade makes reference to the new King of Sardinia's General Amnesty for prisoners, and Lely himself prints Daumas's comment that this edict could not have been published before March 20 (1:447 n. 1). However, Commandant de Launay's letter to the Comte of March 26 also promises an attached letter from Sade (Lely 1:459), but Lely offers no letter by Sade at all in this place. Debauve's version of the letter in question has no month, but does have the date, "26." Debauve conjecturally gives the month as March. Since Sade's letter expresses exactly the same conciliatory tone that the commandant reports in his letter of March 26, and since the commandant describes the enclosed letter by Sade as dealing with the topic of speedier postal delivery (which is the topic of the opening paragraph of the letter in question), it is clear that Sade's letter is of the same date and was meant to accompany it, and not the commandant's letter of March 19. Unaccountably, Laborde gives Sade's letter to the Comte de la Tour of April 1 as the one the commandant enclosed in his dispatch of March 26 (6:199); these dates make no sense. It is also to be noted that Laborde's version contains a beginning as well as three concluding paragraphs that Lely says are missing (1:445 n. 1).

56. Laborde, 6:182–83.

57. Ibid., 199.

58. Ibid., 205.

59. Letter of April 16, 1773, in ibid., 206.

60. Letter of April 30, 1773, in ibid., 209.

61. Unless otherwise indicated, the succeeding references to details of the escape in this and the next two paragraphs are to this letter (Laborde, 6:218–21).

62. Laborde, 6:244. This citation and those below to "Laborde, 6:244–45," refer to the King of Sardinia's letter to the Comte de la Tour sentencing Violon to permanent banishment from the realm.

63. Measures given in this passage are modern, adjusted from the eighteenth-century Savoy measures of *pied* and *pouce* (Lely, 1:478 n. 1).

64. Laborde, 6:245.

65. Ibid., 223.

66. Ibid., 216.

67. Ibid., 210–11.

68. Ibid., 222.

69. Ibid., 213–15.

70. *Oeuvres*, 12:378.

9: Wolf-Man

1. Lely, 1:484–85.

2. Laborde, 6:239.

3. Lely, 1:599.

4. Laborde, 6:226.

5. Bourdin, 11.

6. Laborde, 7:84. Laborde attributes this letter, marked only "November 22," to the year 1773, because it refers to Sade's imprisonment at Miolans, which ended with his escape in 1773. However, 1774 is the correct year, since Mme de Montreuil refers to the *requête* that Renée was to sign "on her arrival in Provence" from Paris (ibid., 85). Renée did in fact return to La Coste in November 1774.

7. Lever, *Donatien*, 247.

8. Lely, 1:534.

9. Farge and Foucault, *Le Désordre des familles*, 9–10.

10. Ibid., 93.

11. Ibid., 95.

12. Ibid., 29.

13. Ibid., 28.

14. Lever, *Donatien*, 248.

15. Goupil eventually fell afoul of the law himself and was imprisoned in Vincennes, where he died on April 28, 1780. In 1791, Pierre Manuel in *La Police de Paris dévoilée* called Goupil "one of those knaves who always deserved to be hanged, were it only to test the rope" (1:262–63).

16. Discovered and first published in 1939 by Desbordes in *Le Vrai Visage* (136–37).

17. Laborde, 7:98–101.

18. Lely, 1:544.

19. Bourdin, 46–47.

20. Laborde, 7:100.

21. This detail was noted by Renée in her account of the raid for her *requête* (Bourdin, 12).

22. Reported in Fage's letter to Mme de Montreuil, dated by Lever as January 7–8, 1774 (*Donatien*, 250).

23. Laborde, 7:114.

24. Ibid., 6:243.

25. Ibid., 7:114.

26. Bourdin, 14.

27. Ibid., 11.

28. Ibid., 11–12.

29. Laborde, 7:111.

30. Bourdin, 9.

31. Laborde, 7:112–13.

32. Ibid., 136–37.

33. Ibid., 120.

34. Lely, following Bourdin (6), very tentatively suggests (though offering no evidence) that Sade spent some time first at Bordeaux, then at Grenoble, before returning to La Coste in June (1:541–44). Lever (*Donatien*, 253) and Pauvert (*Sade*, 1:340) assert that Sade went to Italy, although they offer no evidence of this particular destination.

35. Bourdin, 15.

36. Lely, again citing Bourdin, said that in September Sade was in Savoy, where he suffered a fall from his horse (1:546). Bourdin had been able to examine all of Gaufridy's correspondence held intact by Gaufridy's descendants, only a fraction of which he published in 1939; after this, all of the letters were dispersed into private collections. Bourdin's familiarity with all of the information contained in the letters gives his albeit uncorroborated statements particular value.

37. Bourdin, 9.

38. Ibid., 14.

39. Ibid.

40. Ibid., 15–16.

41. Ibid., 15.

42. Sade's "Grande Lettre," written to Renée from prison on February 20, 1781, is a comprehensive defense against almost every charge of misconduct then outstanding against him.
43. *Oeuvres*, 12:267–68.
44. *OC*, 15:73–74.
45. Bourdin, 13.
46. Laborde, 7:85.
47. Lely, 1:544.
48. This information was reported by an Aix lawyer in a letter to Gaufridy on January 11, 1776 (Bourdin, 53).
49. Sade discussed these two "Nanon"s in his "Grande Lettre" (*Oeuvres*, 12:268, 271).
50. *Oeuvres*, 12:269.
51. Benabou, *Prostitution*, 220.
52. *Oeuvres*, 12:268.
53. Ibid., 269.
54. Laborde, 7:76.
55. Bourdin, 84.
56. Ibid., 16.
57. *Oeuvres*, 12:270–71.
58. Laborde, 7:83–85.
59. Ibid., 189.
60. Debauve, 586.
61. Bourdin, 16.
62. Bourdin, 19; Lever, *Donatien*, 264.
63. Bourdin, 18–19.
64. Lely, 1:530.
65. *Lettres*, 2:12.
66. Lever, *Donatien*, 265.
67. Laborde, *Le Marquis et la marquise*, 21.
68. Quoted in Darnton, "Artist as Lover," 133.
69. Biographies of Mme de Sade have been only adequate at best. See Ginisty's *La Marquise;* Delpech, *La Passion;* Crosland, *Sade's Wife.*
70. A partial cause of this oversight was the peculiar editorial decision of Lely and Daumas to compile Sade's letters to Renée and hers to him in separate volumes of their edition of *Lettres et mélanges littéraires,* thus obscuring their relationship.
71. *Oeuvres*, 12:114.
72. *Lettres*, 2:114.
73. *Oeuvres*, 12:259.
74. *Lettres*, 2:285.

75. *Oeuvres*, 12:419.
76. Ibid., 277.
77. Ibid., 276.
78. One girl was identified by Bourdin as Marie Tussin of the hamlet of Villeneuve-de-Marc. After the scandal, she was sent to a convent at Caderousse (Bourdin, 18). In addition, Mme de Montreuil's letter to Gaufridy on April 8, 1775, mentioned a man named Berh, a woman named Abbadie, and a woman named Lagrange (Bourdin, 31) or Desgranges, according to Sade in a letter to Gaufridy (Bourdin, 27).
79. Lely, although citing Bourdin, mistakenly dates this letter January 21 (1:551).
80. Bourdin, 25.
81. *Oeuvres*, 12:269.
82. Bourdin, 26.
83. Lely, 1:552–53.
84. This information derives from a letter no longer available but seen by Heine (*Le Marquis de Sade*, 239).
85. Lely, 1:552–53.
86. Ibid., 553.
87. Bourdin, 26–27.
88. Lely, 1:554.
89. Bourdin, 32.
90. Ibid., 28.
91. Ibid., 29.
92. Lely, 1:560.
93. Bourdin, 30.
94. Ibid.
95. *Oeuvres*, 12:269–70.
96. Bourdin, 55.
97. *Oeuvres*, 12:269.
98. Lely, 1:565.
99. Bourdin, 58.
100. Ibid.
101. Laborde, 7:320.
102. *Oeuvres*, 12:270.
103. Ibid., 271. The postmaster is Louis Charvin, whom Sade took with him on his tour of Italy (see below page 195).
104. *Oeuvres*, 12:269.
105. Bourdin, 127.
106. *Oeuvres*, 12:271–72.
107. Bourdin, 38.
108. Heine, *Le Marquis de Sade*, 239.
109. Bourdin, 38.

110. Ibid., 53.

111. Ibid., 35–36.

112. Ibid., 37.

113. Ibid., 38–39.

114. Ibid., 38.

115. Ibid., 43–44.

116. Ibid., 55.

117. Ibid., 56.

118. Ibid., 88.

119. Ibid., 92.

120. Ibid., 95.

121. Ibid., 34.

122. Ibid., 30–32.

123. Ibid., 31–32.

124. Ibid., 39.

125. Ibid., 46.

126. Ibid., 39.

127. Ibid., 35.

128. Sade recalled this humiliation fifteen years later in a letter to Gaufridy on August 18, 1790 (Lely, 1:563 n. 2).

129. Bourdin, 39.

10: Italy

1. Lever has found Charvin's name among the daily expense accounts in the Sade family archives (*Donatien*, 704 n. 24). Sade also mentioned Charvin by name in a letter to Gaufridy dating probably from September 1775, in which Sade complained about Charvin's "gluttony" and his "disgraceful" consumption of "most of the chocolate" that Sade had intended to send to Gaufridy (Bourdin, 42).

2. Unless otherwise identified, parenthetical page numbers in this chapter refer to the text of the *Voyage d'Italie*, as published for the first time by Gilbert Lely in *Oeuvres*, vol. 16.

3. *OC*, 4:311 n.

4. Lely, 1:499–500.

5. Letter of September 29, 1775, in Bourdin, 43.

6. Ibid., 45.

7. Ibid., 44–45.

8. Bourdin indicates that the crate weighed "more than six quintaux" (50). One quintal equals a hundred kilograms, and six hundred kilograms equal 1,323 pounds (*Collins Robert French-English English-French Dictionary*, 2nd ed., s.v. "quintal").

9. Bourdin, 49.

10. Ibid., 50.

11. *Lettres*, 1:85.

12. Based upon Dr. Mesny's letters to Sade in Rome and Naples, Lever concluded that Sade had become her lover in Florence (*Donatien*, 279). However, Mesny's letters that Lever includes in his appendix VII (813–36), though they frequently mention Sarah Goudar's name, often in response to Sade's questions about her, do not conclusively prove an amorous relationship.

13. Lever was the first to discover this relationship (*Donatien*, 276–77). In his appendix VIII (837–47), he published Mme Moldetti's amorous, then confused, and finally plaintive letters (written in Italian) to Sade after he left Florence for Rome and Naples.

14. Lever, *Donatien*, 838.

15. Ibid., 847.

16. Lely, 1:570–71.

17. *OC*, 9:129.

18. Bourdin, 55.

19. Renée recounts the story in a letter to Gaufridy on February 9, 1776, in ibid., 53.

20. Ibid., 54–55.

21. Ibid., 51.

11: The Shot

1. Bourdin, 51.

2. Ibid.

3. Ibid., 87.

4. Ibid., 83.

5. Ibid., 59–60.

6. The details of the scandal now under dis-

cussion derive from the deposition filed at
Aix by the father of the cook Sade hired,
Catherine Trillet (Lely, 1:588–90). Sade's
response to this deposition, including his
point-by-point rebuttal of M. Trillet's statements, is to be found in an undated letter
Sade wrote to Gaufridy (Bourdin, 64–65).

7. *Oeuvres*, 12:271.

8. Lely, 1:589.

9. Ibid., 588.

10. Bourdin, 64.

11. Ibid., 68.

12. Sade said only one of the Besson girls
appeared (Bourdin, 64).

13. Lely, 1:589.

14. Ibid.

15. Bourdin, 65.

16. Lely, 1:589.

17. Bourdin, 65.

18. In addition to M. Trillet's deposition filed
at Aix (Lely, 1:588–90) and Sade's letter to
Gaufridy (Bourdin, 64–65), further details of
M. Trillet's activities at La Coste can be found
in another undated letter from Sade to
Gaufridy (Bourdin, 60–3) and in the record
of the preliminary inquiry conducted at La
Coste by Jean-Baptiste Viguier, lieutenant to
the judge of La Coste, on January 18 (Lely,
1:584–86).

19. Lely, 1:590.

20. Bourdin, 65.

21. Lely, 1:590.

22. Ibid., 590 n. 1.

23. Bourdin, 64–65.

24. Ibid., 67.

25. Ibid., 60.

26. Lely, 1:585.

27. Bourdin, 60–61.

28. Lely, 1:585.

29. Bourdin, 61.

30. Ibid.

31. Lely, 1:585.

32. Bourdin, 62.

33. Ibid.

34. Ibid., 67–68.

35. Ibid., 62–63.

36. Ibid.

37. Ibid., 65.

38. Ibid., 66.

39. Ibid., 78.

40. Ibid., 67.

41. Ibid., 68–69.

42. Ibid., 69.

43. Ibid., 77.

44. Ibid., 67.

45. Ibid., 79.

46. A few months later, on April 29, 1777,
Mme de Montreuil would inform Gaufridy
of Catherine Trillet's departure for Montpellier (ibid., 84).

47. Ibid., 79.

48. Ibid., 72.

12: Vincennes—House of Silence

1. Bourdin, 79.

2. Ibid., 80.

3. Ibid., 71.

4. Ibid., 80.

5. Lely, 1:594–95.

6. Debauve, 151. The copy of this letter is
without a date or the name of its recipient. It
has been ascribed to the end of 1777 by
Debauve (151), and to March or April 1777 by
Pauvert (*Sade*, 2:43).

7. Debauve, 151.

8. Lely blames Renée for having revealed

Sade's presence in Paris to her mother (1:595),
but Renée had never acted independently of
her husband.

9. *Oeuvres*, 12:121.

10. Bourdin, 84.

11. *Oeuvres*, 12:121.

12. Debauve, 151.

13. *Oeuvres*, 12:112.

14. Ibid., 120–21.

15. Lemarchand, *Château royal de Vincennes*,
141–42.

16. Lely, 2:17 n. 3.

17. Rousseau, *Confessions,* 326.
18. Quoted in Maquet, *Donjon de Vincennes,* 2:102.
19. Mirabeau, *Lettres de cachet,* 338–39.
20. *Oeuvres,* 12:122.
21. Mirabeau, *Lettres de cachet,* 339–40.
22. Bourdin, 80.
23. Letter of February 25, 1777, in ibid.
24. Ibid., 84.
25. Ibid., 86; see also 87–88.
26. Ibid., 86.
27. Ibid., 91.
28. Ibid., 126.
29. *Lettres,* 2:101, 137 n. 6.
30. Ibid., 102.
31. Bourdin, 86.
32. Desbordes, *Le Vrai Visage,* 173.
33. *Oeuvres,* 12:111–13.
34. Bourdin, 81.
35. Ibid., 82.
36. Letter of April 6, 1777, in ibid, 83.
37. Letter to Gaufridy, April 6, 1777, in ibid., 82.
38. Letter of May 9, 1777, in ibid., 85.
39. Letter to Gaufridy, December 20, 1777, in ibid., 93.
40. Ibid., 102.
41. Ibid., 103.
42. During this same month, on April 18, 1777, Sade himself called M. de Montreuil mentally "thick" (*Oeuvres,* 12:123).
43. Letter of April 29, 1777, in Bourdin, 84.
44. *Lettres,* 2:102.
45. *Oeuvres,* 12:124.
46. Ibid., 161.
47. Letter of April 18, 1777, in ibid., 123–24.
48. Ibid., 113.
49. My version of this letter, based upon a reading of the manuscript, restores to completion a letter that Daumas unaccountably divided between two letters that he dated June and October 1777 (*Lettres,* 1:58–59, 61–62).

13: A Surprise at Aix

1. Letter to Gaufridy, June 18, 1777, in Bourdin, 87.
2. Ibid., 88.
3. Renée alluded to this plan in writing to Sade in invisible ink on October 13, 1777: "The Chanoine [Vidal] has neither forgotten nor given up our travel plans" (*Lettres,* 2:111).
4. Bourdin, 86–87.
5. *Lettres,* 1:56–57.
6. Ibid., 2:107.
7. Ibid., 112–13.
8. Bourdin, 94–95.
9. Quoted in Lever, *Donatien,* 303.
10. Debauve, 155–61.
11. Letter from Mme de Montreuil to Gaufridy, February 28, 1778, in Bourdin, 102.
12. Letter of April 29, 1777, in ibid., 84–85.
13. Ibid., 91.
14. Ibid., 102.
15. Ibid., 103.
16. Lely, 1:612.
17. Lever, *Donatien,* 850.
18. Letter of April 14, 1778, in Bourdin, 103.
19. Letter to Gaufridy, June 8, 1778, in ibid., 104.
20. Ibid., 101–2.
21. *Lettres,* 1:407–8.
22. Lely, 1:616.
23. Letter to Gaufridy, July 14, 1778, in Bourdin, 109.
24. Unless otherwise indicated, details of Sade's stay at Aix derive from his "Histoire de ma détention" (Lely, 1:648–50), in which he noted the day and the date of his arrival as Saturday, June 20 (648).
25. Letter of June 27, 1778, in Bourdin, 107.
26. Lely, 1:620.
27. Ibid., 623.
28. Bourdin, 97.
29. Ibid., 115.
30. Ibid., 173.
31. Ibid., 183. Mme de Baudoin's "gratitude" may refer to a small gift of money Sade gave her in prison. Shortly after the event, on August 8, 1778, Sade wrote to Gaufridy to repay Reinaud "the 7 livres 10 sols that I

bestowed on the poor [female] prisoner" (ibid., 118). This unnamed prisoner may well be Mme de Baudoin. Seven and a half livres was not a sum likely to buy anyone's affection (Sade paid Jeanne Testard 48 livres for a night of pleasure). Nevertheless, Mme de Baudoin's affection appears strong, eager, and sincere, even after the passage of time.

32. Ibid., 105.

33. Ibid., 106.

34. Ibid., 108.

35. Unless otherwise noted, my account derives from Marais's letter of July 1, 1788 (Lely, 1:622–23).

36. Bourdin, 97.

37. Letter of January 19–20, 1778, in Debauve, 159.

38. Bourdin, 109.

39. Lely, 1:626.

40. Ibid., 644.

14: The Golden Dawn of a Beautiful Day

1. Marais's "Deposition" of July 17, 1778 (Lely, 1:644–47)—hereafter cited as "Deposition." Other details of the events of the next few days derive from Sade's recollection made several years later, entitled "Histoire de ma détention" (Lely, 1:648–50)—hereafter cited as "Histoire"; and Sade's letter to Gaufridy dated July 18, 1778, but actually written a few days later and antedated (Bourdin, 109–12)—hereafter cited as "July 18 letter."

2. Deposition.

3. "Histoire."

4. July 18 letter.

5. Letter to Renée, March 1781, in *Lettres*, 3:79.

6. Deposition.

7. Ibid.

8. Bourdin, 121.

9. "Histoire."

10. Ibid.

11. Bourdin, 109.

12. Ibid., 115.

13. Debauve, 163–64.

14. Ibid., 165; the first half of this letter was also published by Bourdin (118).

15. Debauve, 165.

16. Bourdin, 127.

17. Ibid., 126–27. Bourdin believes that chief among the "cabal" was Chanoine Vidal (99).

18. Ibid., 109.

19. A few months later, on October 4, 1778, Sade wrote bitterly to Renée, complaining that it took him two hours to figure out what she meant by this letter, which, moreover, contained no money and no real prospect of

any from that "rascal of a lawyer" Gaufridy (*Oeuvres*, 12:166).

20. Bourdin, 112.

21. Ibid., 114.

22. Ibid., 118.

23. Ibid., 116.

24. Ibid., 117.

25. Ibid., 121.

26. Ibid., 120–21.

27. Ibid., 118.

28. Ibid., 120.

29. Ibid., 121.

30. Ibid., 115.

31. Ibid., 124.

32. *Oeuvres*, 12:155–56.

33. Ibid., 217–18.

34. Bourdin, 136.

35. Letter of March 22, 1779, in *Oeuvres*, 12:184.

36. Letter of May 6, 1779, in *Lettres*, 2:195; and throughout Renée's correspondence.

37. Letter of October 4, 1779, in *Oeuvres*, 12:219, 221.

38. Letter of April 1779, in *Lettres*, 1:63.

39. Letter of April 26, 1783, in *Oeuvres*, 12:386.

40. Letter of April 30, 1779, in *Lettres*, 1:339.

41. Letter of May 7, 1779, in ibid., 346.

42. Letter of April 26, 1783, in *Oeuvres*, 12:386. For further discussion of the significance of *Clarissa* to Sade and Mlle de Rousset, see p. 271 below.

43. Ibid., 188.

44. *Lettres*, 1:321.

45. Ibid., 63–64.

46. Lely does not ask the question when he discusses the time Mlle de Rousset spent at La Coste during the summer of 1778 (see 2:631ff.); Bourdin, without elaboration, says she was "only a friend" (98); Fauville (*La Coste*, 131) and Pauvert (*Sade*, 2:98) are not sure; and Lever prevaricates (*Donatien*, 322).

47. *Oeuvres*, 12:389.

48. *Lettres*, 1:367–68.

49. Bourdin, 187.

50. Ibid., 139–40.

51. Ibid., 149.

52. Ibid., 157.

53. *Lettres*, 1:368.

54. Bourdin, 126.

55. *Oeuvres*, 12:154.

56. Bourdin, 126.

57. *Oeuvres*, 12:157.

58. Ibid., 158.

59. *Lettres*, 1:285.

60. Ibid., 283.

61. However, on September 1, Sade would write to Gaufridy that the sale of his title was of no moment: "As for the title and the honor: I care little for both; they have made me too many enemies. When one has the misfortune to have as many of them as I do, it is necessary to have a small fortune, which incites no envy, and to renounce all pomp and show" (Bourdin, 123). This pose was bravado. He would write to his wife in September about "all the grief I suffered from the loss of my office" (*Oeuvres*, 12:160). Actually, Sade was not sure how he felt. He could feel and express quite opposite ideas on the same topic, depending upon his correspondent.

62. *Oeuvres*, 12:155.

63. Ibid., 158.

64. Bourdin, 126–27.

65. Ibid., 127.

66. Ibid., 128.

67. Letter from Renée to her husband, October 23, 1778, in *Lettres*, 2:152.

68. Ibid., 3:72.

69. Benabou, *Prostitution*, 103.

70. *Oeuvres*, 12:152.

71. Ibid., 159.

72. Bourdin, 122.

73. Ibid., 122–23.

15: Vincennes, Again

1. Sade's letter to Renée of February 17, 1779, in *Oeuvres*, 12:180.

2. Bourdin, 122.

3. Ibid., 124.

4. Ibid., 125.

5. Ibid., 125–26.

6. "Histoire de ma détention," in Lely, 1:649.

7. *Oeuvres*, 12:159.

8. Letter of October 26, 1778, in *Lettres*, 2:155.

9. Letter of May 16, 1779, in *Oeuvres*, 12:205.

10. Letter of July 27, 1780, in ibid., 252.

11. Letter of December 14, 1780, in ibid., 257.

12. Letter of January 1783, in *Lettres*, 3:126.

13. Letter of July 27, 1780, in *Oeuvres*, 12:251.

14. Letter of October 4, 1778, in ibid., 167.

15. Letter of March 22, 1779, in ibid., 189.

16. Letter of October 4, 1778, in ibid., 167.

17. Ibid., 226.

18. *Lettres*, 3:22.

19. *Oeuvres*, 12:226.

20. Sterne, *Tristram Shandy*, 1:88.

21. Letter of September 1783, in *Oeuvres*, 12:404.

22. Letter of November 1, 1779, in *Lettres*, 3:30.

23. Letter of January 18, 1779, in ibid., 1:331.

24. Laborde, *Le Marquis et la marquise*, 2.

25. Letter of November 1, 1779, in *Lettres*, 3:29.

26. Letter of August 17, 1780, in ibid., 50.

27. Letter of October 21, 1782, in *Oeuvres*, 12:365.

28. Letter of March 4, 1783, in *Lettres*, 3:130.

29. Letter of July 27, 1780, in *Oeuvres*, 12:251.

30. Letter of 1781, in ibid., 344.

31. Letter of April 10, 1780, in *Lettres*, 3:37.

32. *Oeuvres*, 12:231.

33. Letter of August 22, 1779, in *Lettres*, 3:27.
34. Bourdin, 126.
35. Ibid., 147.
36. Ibid., 128.
37. Ibid., 127.
38. Ibid., 128.
39. *Lettres*, 1:315–16.
40. Bourdin, 129.
41. Ibid., 129–30.
42. Lever, *Donatien*, 352.
43. Letter of December 27, 1778, in *Lettres*, 1:321.
44. Letter of March 6, 1779, in ibid., 2:183.
45. Lely, 2:298.
46. *Lettres*, 2:408–9.
47. Ibid., 409–10.
48. Ibid., 3:15.
49. Letter of January 18, 1779, in Bourdin, 138.
50. *Lettres*, 2:155.
51. Ibid., 159.
52. Ibid., 172.
53. Letter of December 27, 1778, in ibid., 173–74.
54. Bourdin, 129.
55. *Lettres*, 2:177.
56. Bourdin, 139.
57. *Oeuvres*, 12:191.
58. Ibid., 197.
59. Bourdin, 140.
60. Ibid., 143–44.
61. Ibid., 144–45.
62. Ibid., 143.
63. *Lettres*, 1:328–30.
64. Ibid., 349.
65. Letter of May 12, 1779, in ibid., 68.
66. Ibid., 414–15.
67. Ibid., 417.
68. Letter of April 3, 1779. in ibid., 2:185.
69. Shakespeare, *As You Like It*, 5.2.41–42, in *Complete Works*.
70. *Lettres*, 2:190.

71. Letter of October 1783, in ibid., 3:164.
72. *Oeuvres*, 12:218–19.
73. Bourdin, 148.
74. Letter to Gaufridy, November 9, 1779, in ibid., 146.
75. Ibid.
76. Letter of November 11, 1779, in ibid., 150. Lely, who came into possession of this letter, revised Bourdin's dating, observing that the date is clearly visible as December 11, 1779 (2:61 n. 2).
77. Bourdin, 157.
78. Ibid., 158.
79. *Oeuvres*, 12:237–38.
80. *Lettres*, 3:40–41.
81. Maquet, *Le Donjon de Vincennes*, 2:100.
82. Letter of August 1785, in *Lettres*, 3:207.
83. Mirabeau, *Lettres de cachet*, 333.
84. *Oeuvres*, 12:324–25.
85. Ibid., 316.
86. Letter of April 12, 1781, in ibid., 294.
87. Letter to Mlle de Rousset, April 20–25, 1781, in ibid., 312.
88. Letter to Renée, May 21, 1781, in ibid., 321.
89. Letter of 1781, in ibid., 346.
90. Letter of February 1785, in *Lettres*, 3:203.
91. Letter of February 17, 1779, in *Oeuvres*, 12:179–80.
92. Ibid., 345–47.
93. *Lettres*, 3:43–44.
94. Lely, 2:71–72.
95. Ibid., 73–74.
96. Ibid., 72.
97. Bourdin, 158–59. Unaccountably, this letter, following one for July 24, is dated by Bourdin as July 7. This would appear to be a typographical error for July 27.
98. *Oeuvres*, 12:248–50.
99. *Lettres*, 2:248.
100. Bourdin, 159.
101. Ibid., 160.

16: Signals

1. In a letter of April 18, 1777, in *Oeuvres*, 12:122. In a letter to Mlle de Rousset on March 22, 1779, Sade wrote that in order to survive at Vincennes "you have to be between ten and fifteen years old." As for himself, he added, "I am only eleven, so I get along very well here" (ibid., 189).
2. Ibid., 122.

3. *Oeuvres,* 12:122.

4. Ibid.

5. Letter of June 4, 1777, in Bourdin, 86.

6. Letter of April 11, 1781, in *Oeuvres,* 12:290.

7. Letter of October 4, 1778, in ibid., 165.

8. Ibid., 120.

9. *Lettres,* 1:61–62. Daumas unaccountably dates this letter as October 1777, though there are good reasons to believe it belongs to June.

10. Ibid., 2:167.

11. Letter of December 27, 1778, in ibid., 173.

12. Ibid., 3:18–20.

13. *Oeuvres,* 12:235–36.

14. *Lettres,* 2:331.

15. Ibid., 362 n. 11.

16. Ibid., 332.

17. Ibid., 362 n. 12.

18. Ibid., 264.

19. *Oeuvres,* 12:405–6.

20. *Oeuvres,* 12:393–95.

21. *OC,* 1:194; see also 208.

17: Sex in Prison

1. *Lettres,* 1:279. Lely's footnote unaccountably dates this letter in error as January 1, 1780 (*Lettres,* 1:218 n. 16).

2. *Donatien,* 358.

3. *Lettres,* 1:291.

4. Ibid., 284.

5. Ibid., 283–94.

6. Ibid.

7. Ibid., 289.

8. *Lettres,* 3:92. Again, accounting for differences between ancient and modern measurements, these come to approximately six and a third inches in circumference by eight and a half or nine and a half inches in height.

9. Ibid., 2:282.

10. Ibid., 285.

11. Ibid., 292.

12. Ibid., 3:135.

13. Letter of November 23, 1783, in ibid., 2:344.

14. Letter of November 23–24, 1783, in *Oeuvres,* 12:414.

15. *Lettres,* 2:344.

16. *Oeuvres,* 12:417–18. In modern measures, eight and a half and nine *pouces* are nine and nine and a half inches respectively.

17. *Lettres,* 3:135.

18. Ibid., 2:259.

19. Ibid., 261.

20. *Oeuvres,* 12:412–17.

21. *OC,* 2:37.

22. *Oeuvres,* 12:413–14.

23. Ibid., 383–84.

24. This undated letter has been variously placed by Lely in May 1783 (*Oeuvres,* 12:387) and in May 1782 (2:119).

25. Sade later added the following note to his letter: "These couplets must be sung to the tune of the carillon, or throw them into the fire, because they are not made to be read" (ibid., 12:387 n. 2).

26. Ibid., 387–89.

27. Ibid., 382.

28. *Lettres,* 1:88–89.

29. Ibid., 3:156.

30. *Oeuvres,* 12:372.

31. Ibid., 397.

18: The Visit

1. Bourdin, 158.

2. Ibid., 159.

3. Letter of November 15, 1780, in ibid., 160.

4. Letter of January 12, 1781, in ibid., 168.

5. *Lettres,* 3:74–75.

6. Letter of March 18, 1781, in ibid., 75.

7. Bourdin, 146.

8. Letter of March 10, 1781, in ibid., 169.

9. Letter of March 31, 1781, in ibid., 170.

10. *Oeuvres,* 12:285–86.

11. *Lettres,* 3:80.

12. Ibid., 87.

13. Bourdin, 145. Bourdin inadvertently placed this letter from 1781 among those for 1779.

14. *Lettres,* 3:91.

15. Ibid., 2:371.

16. *Oeuvres*, 12:290–94.

17. *Lettres*, 3:83–84.

18. *Oeuvres* 12:303.

19. *Lettres*, 3:91.

20. Ibid., 2:277

21. Ibid., 358 n. 23.

22. *Oeuvres*, 12:327–28.

23. Mlle de Rousset referred to Renée's "moving costs" in a letter to Gaufridy on October 21, 1780 (Bourdin, 159).

24. Letter of July 27, 1781, in ibid., 172.

25. *Lettres*, 2:168–69.

26. Ibid., 193.

27. Ibid., 297.

28. Ibid., 3:94.

29. Ibid., 2:296.

30. Letter of July 21, 1781, in ibid., 289–90.

31. *Oeuvres*, 12:329.

32. *Lettres*, 3:71.

33. Ibid., 2:239, 353 n. 11.

34. Lely, 2:97–98.

35. *Oeuvres*, 12:331.

36. Bourdin, 172.

37. Ibid., 173.

38. *Lettres*, 2:298, 358 n. 35.

39. Bourdin, 174.

40. *Lettres*, 2:299.

41. Ibid., 298.

42. *Oeuvres*, 12:332.

43. Ibid., 337.

44. *Lettres*, 2:301, 359 n. 46.

45. *Oeuvres*, 12:342.

46. Ibid., 341.

47. *Lettres*, 2:306.

48. Ibid., 307.

49. Lely, 2:117.

50. *Lettres*, 2:308–9.

19: Writer

1. Bourdin, 181.

2. Ibid., 182–83.

3. *Lettres*, 1:359–60.

4. Letter to Gaufridy, January 1, 1782, in Bourdin, 180.

5. Ibid., 187.

6. Ibid., 188.

7. Ibid., 189.

8. *Oeuvres*, 12:369.

9. Renée acknowledged receipt of it in her letter to Sade on May 24, 1782 (*Lettres*, 2:319).

10. Ibid., 2:322.

11. *Oeuvres*, 12:369.

12. *Lettres*, 3:115.

13. Lely, 2:121.

14. Ibid., 122.

15. In a note at the end of the manuscript, Sade wrote: "This work was begun on December 24, 1780; the first draft was finished on January 8, 1781, and the work completed on the night of the 24th of the same month." (*OC*, 13:305).

16. Letter of March 26, 1781, in *Lettres*, 3:77.

17. *OC*, 13:314.

18. Ibid., 310.

19. Ibid., 320.

20. Ibid., 312.

21. *Lettres*, 1:71.

22. Letter of March 25, 1781, in ibid., 2:271.

23. *OC*, 13:268.

24. *Lettres*, 3:77–78.

25. *OC*, 13:431.

26. Ibid., 451.

27. *OC*, 14:446.

28. Letter to Amblet, January 1782, in *Oeuvres*, 12:347.

29. *OC*, 1:502.

30. Ibid., 504.

31. Ibid., 509.

32. Ibid., 510–11.

33. Ibid., 512.

34. *Lettres*, 1:453–56.

35. Ibid., 3:125.

36. *Oeuvres*, 12:374.

37. Bourdin, 196.

38. *Lettres*, 3:129.

39. Ibid., 223 n. 65.

40. Ibid., 135–36.

41. *OC*, 1:476.

42. See ibid., 4:346–47.

43. Ibid., 1:477.

44. *Oeuvres*, 12:409–10.

45. See for example, Sade's letters to Renée requesting answers to his questions about Spain and Portugal on November 9, 1786 (*Lettres*, 1:101), on November 25, 1786 (*Oeuvres*, 12:455), on December 2, 1786, (*Lettres*, 1:103), on December 14, 1786 (*Lettres*, 1:104), and on December 24, 1786 (*Lettres*, 1:105). For further discussion, see below page 370.

46. *Lettres*, 2:268.

47. Ibid., 1:359.

48. *Oeuvres*, 12:407–08.

49. *Lettres*, 3:151–52.

50. This play bore various titles, including *La Folle épreuve (The Foolish Test)* and *Le Mari crédule (The Gullible Husband)*. The play is found in *OC*, vol. 13.

51. *Oeuvres*, 12:381.

52. Ibid., 384.

53. *Lettres*, 2:338.

54. *Oeuvres*, 12:390.

55. This novel was written in the Bastille during 1787 and 1788, and underwent later enlargements as *Justine, ou les malheurs de la vertu* and as *La Nouvelle Justine, ou les mal-heurs de la vertu*.

56. *OC*, 2:383.

57. *Oeuvres*, 12:420–21.

58. Ibid., 422.

59. Ibid., 424.

60. Ibid., 429.

61. Ibid., 423–24.

62. Bourdin, 203.

63. *Oeuvres*, 12:353.

64. Rousseau, *Confessions*, 166–67.

65. *Lettres*, 1:71.

66. Lely, 2:231.

67. *Lettres*, 2:349.

68. Ibid., 3:179.

69. Ibid., 226 n. 15.

70. Funck-Brentano, *Bastille et Faubourg Saint-Antoine*, 39.

71. Carlyle, *French Revolution*, 1:54.

72. Letter of March 8, 1784, in *Oeuvres*, 12:433.

73. Fossa, *Le Château de Vincennes*, 2:52.

74. Bloit and Payen-Appenzeller, *Mystères de Paris*, 111.

75. *Lettres*, 3:179.

20: The Bastille

1. Quétel, *Bastille*, 53.

2. Ibid., 304.

3. The news that Breteuil had replaced Amelot in this post in 1783 had prompted Renée to write optimistically to Gaufridy on January 13, 1784: "I have a good deal of hope for the new minister" (Bourdin, 202).

4. Quoted in Quétel, *Bastille*, 184.

5. *Oeuvres*, 12:434–36.

6. *Lettres*, 1:77.

7. Ibid., 78.

8. Quétel, *Bastille*, 314–16.

9. Renée's first visit to her husband in the Bastille occurred during this same month, on March 16. Prison records show that she brought Sade six pounds of candles (Lely, 2:163).

10. *Lettres*, 1:79.

11. Ibid., 78.

12. Ibid., 3:228 n. 40.

13. Quétel, *Bastille*, 268.

14. *Lettres*, 3:188.

15. Ibid., 189.

16. *Oeuvres*, 12:447–48.

17. *Lettres*, 1:491–92.

18. Letter of June 8, 1784, in ibid., 3:190.

19. Bourdin, 228.

20. Taine, *French Revolution*, 1:25.

21. Bourdin, 244.

22. Ibid., 226.

23. *Lettres*, 2:374.

24. Ibid., 1:114.

25. Bourdin, 206.

26. Ibid., 210–11.

27. Ibid., 205.

28. *Lettres*, 2:281.

29. Ibid., 318.

30. Ibid., 342–43.

31. Bourdin, 211–12. La Jeunesse's debauchery in the capital (or elsewhere) may have led

to his death from syphilis, as Lely (2:173 n. 2) and Fauville (*La Coste,* 155) suspect.

32. Bourdin, 227.

33. Lever reprints the document from the Sade family archives (*Donatien,* 732 n. 172).

34. Bourdin, 227.

35. Ibid.

36. Ibid., 238.

37. Ibid., 234.

38. Ibid., 219.

39. Lely, 2:185.

40. Manuel, *La Police de Paris,* 2:41.

41. *Lettres* 1:442.

42. Ibid., 126.

43. Ibid., 80–81.

44. Ibid., 3:204–5.

45. Ibid., 206–7.

46. Ibid., 1:108.

47. Lely, 2:204.

48. *Lettres,* 1:100.

49. Ibid., 2:372.

50. Ibid., 374.

51. Ibid., 369.

52. Ibid., 375.

21: Sodom

1. *OC,* 1:51. Hereafter in this chapter, references to *OC* 1 will be cited by page number in parentheses or brackets.

2. The following (from Lely, 1:49) is the schedule for scholars at Sade's Collège Louis-le-Grand:

Morning:		Afternoon and Evening:	
5:30	Rise	1:15	Study and classes
6:00	Prayers		
6:15	Bible study	4:30	Snack and recreation
7:45	Breakfast and recreation		
		5:00	Study and classes
8:15	Study and classes		
		7:15	Supper and recreation
10:30	Mass		
11:00	Study	8:45	Prayers
Noon	Dinner and recreation	9:00	Bedtime

3. Johnson, *Rasselas,* 118–19.

4. Freud, *A Case of Hysteria,* 150.

5. Ibid., 151–52.

6. Yeats, "Crazy Jane Talks with the Bishop," in *Collected Poems,* 255.

7. Freud, *Jensen's "Gradiva,"* 212.

8. Melanie Klein has written that "the first object" of a child's "instinct for knowledge is the interior of the mother's body" (*Psychoanalysis,* 174).

9. Bataille, *Literature and Evil,* 121–22.

10. Paglia, *Sexual Personae,* 235.

11. Krafft-Ebing, *Psychopathia Sexualis,* 262.

12. Ibid., 243.

13. Ibid., 105.

14. Ibid., 499.

15. Freud, *A Case of Hysteria,* 50.

16. Chasseguet-Smirgel, *Creativity and Perversion,* 56. Freud earlier expressed this idea as follows: "We were driven to the conclusion that a disposition to perversions is an original and universal disposition of the human sexual instinct" (*A Case of Hysteria,* 231).

17. Freud, *A Case of Hysteria,* 149.

18. Ibid., 50.

19. Ibid., 151.

20. Ibid., 151–52.

21. Ibid., 50.

22. Ibid., 148–49.

23. Sade's numbering problems derive from the fact that December has thirty-one days, so, in order to have 150 examples told, Sade has to give only four examples on five days, instead of the customary five examples. He does manage to do so. See the 12th of December (373), the 20th (377), the 26th (380–81), the 29th (383), and the 30th (383–84). However, when he ends up with only four examples on December 31, making up 151 altogether, he does not realize that he skipped number 69 and also that he gave six rather than five examples on the 21st (379), so there really were 150 after all. Sade has similar problems for the thirty-one days of January, when he properly reduces five days'

narrations to four examples, but unaccountably gives six examples for another day, and so ends up with 151 and again leaves a note for himself, "Ascertain why there is one too many" (406). The twenty-eight days of February pose a different problem, for now Sade must increase on ten days the number of examples from five to six. This he manages to do for only eight days, and so ends up on February 28 with 148, and leaves another note for himself: "Ascertain why there are two missing, they were all in the outline" (443).

24. Barthes, *Sade, Fourier, Loyola*, 27.

25. I regard the text of *Les Cent Vingt Journées de Sodome* as essentially complete and as Sade intended it to be. As he noted at the end of the manuscript scroll, he completed it in the Bastille on October 22, 1785 (*OC*, 1:451). If he had wanted to make any significant changes, he had almost three years and nine months to do them before he was removed from the Bastille on July 4, 1789.

26. Any reader wishing to pursue these themes ought to consult the works of Melanie Klein and Janine Chasseguet-Smirgel listed in the bibliography.

27. *Lettres*, 3:68.

22: The Revolution

1. *Lettres*, 1:89.
2. Quétel, *La Bastille*, 116.
3. Bourdin, 214.
4. *Lettres*, 1:441
5. Ibid., 2:369.
6. Young, *Travels in France*, 85.
7. Ibid., 87.
8. Ibid., 81.
9. *Lettres*, 1:119. Unlike at Vincennes, where the original letters were sent after being censored by means of ink blots, at the Bastille, letters were vetted and were then completely transcribed by the censor, thereby producing the oddly impersonal style found in this and other letters.
10. Bourdin, 235.
11. Ibid., 236.
12. Ibid., 238.
13. *Lettres*, 2:374.
14. Bourdin, 239.
15. *Lettres*, 1:101.
16. Ibid., 103–4.
17. Ibid., 104–5.
18. Ibid., 105.
19. Bourdin, 213.
20. *Lettres*, 2:371–72.
21. *Oeuvres*, 12:459.
22. *OC*, 2:412.
23. Ibid., 427.
24. Ibid., 393.

25. *Lettres*, 2:387.
26. Ibid., 388.
27. Ibid., 389.
28. Ibid., 390.
29. *OC*, 5:227.
30. *Lettres*, 2:389.
31. *OC*, 4:121.
32. Ibid., 122.
33. *Lettres*, 2:389.
34. Ibid., 390.
35. Ibid., 389–90.
36. Ibid., 390.
37. Ibid., 397.
38. Ibid., 398.
39. Ibid., 395.
40. Ibid., 394.
41. Ibid., 375.
42. Bourdin, 247.
43. Ibid., 248.
44. *Lettres*, 2:394.
45. Ibid., 376.
46. Taine, *French Revolution*, 1:2.
47. *Lettres*, 2:376–77.
48. Ibid., 1:133.
49. Bourdin, 244.
50. Ibid., 245.
51. Ibid., 247.
52. Quétel, *La Bastille*, 351.
53. Bloit and Payen-Appenzeller, *Mystères de Paris*, 47–51.

54. Ibid., 57–60.

55. According to Bourdin, Gaufridy mistakenly marked this letter "Received April 11, 1789" (the Réveillon riot began on April 27). Suggesting that Gaufridy made a slip of one month, Bourdin revised the date of reception to May 11 (245). If it had been received in Provence by May 11, then it would appear that Renée wrote a few days before the "procession" of May 4 that she mentioned at the end of the letter. Lely, however, accepts without comment Bourdin's date of May 11 (2:189).

56. Bourdin, 245–46.

57. Bloit and Payen-Appenzeller, *Mystères de Paris*, 55.

58. *Lettres*, 1:134.

59. Bourdin, 248.

60. *Lettres*, 2:397.

61. Bourdin, 247–48.

62. Sade's judgment of de Launay's character was confirmed by events and by Louis Deflue, the commander of a small brigade of Swiss guards detached to the Bastille on July 7. Deflue later commented on Governor de Launay's "continual anxiety and his irresolution": de Launay, he said, "was a man without great military understanding, without experience, and of little courage" (Quétel, *La Bastille*, 353).

63. *Lettres*, 1:134.

64. Ibid., 2:377.

65. Young, *Travels in France*, 132–35.

66. *Lettres*, 2:378.

67. Ibid., 379.

68. Bourdin, 248.

69. Young, *Travels in France*, 154.

70. Ibid., 157.

71. Ibid., 158.

72. Laborde, 21:91.

73. Lely, 2:191.

74. Bourdin, 269.

75. Laborde, 21:91.

76. Debauve, 209.

77. Bourdin, 269.

78. Ibid.

79. Lely, 2:263–72.

80. Bourdin, 270.

81. Lely, 2:251–52; Lever, *Donatien*, 408–9.

82. Bourdin, 270.

83. Ibid., 264–65.

84. Ibid., 248.

85. Taine, *French Revolution*, 1:40.

86. Quétel, *La Bastille*, 356.

87. Laborde, 21:94.

88. Bourdin, 270.

89. Lever, *Donatien*, 384.

90. Bloit and Payen-Appenzeller, *Mystères de Paris*, 102.

91. Quétel, *La Bastille*, 375.

92. Bourdin, 249.

93. Young, *Travels in France*, 188.

94. Ibid., 223.

95. Bourdin, 250.

96. Ibid.

97. Ibid., 252.

98. Ibid., 253.

99. Ibid., 254.

100. Young, *Travels in France*, 251.

101. Ibid., 246–47.

102. Letter of February 13, 1790, in Bourdin, 260.

103. Ibid., 261.

23: "Amidst Madmen and Epileptics"

1. Bourdin, 269.

2. Letter of May 19, 1790, in ibid., 266.

3. Tenon, *Mémoires sur les hôpitaux*, 1.

4. Ibid., 179.

5. Ibid., 184.

6. Ibid., 209.

7. Ibid., 211–12.

8. Quoted in Pinon, *L'Hospice de Charen-ton*, 70.

9. Pinel, *Treatise on Insanity*, 67.

10. Ibid., 116.

11. Ibid., 5.

12. Ibid., 186.

13. Ibid., 109.

14. Ibid., 103.

15. Ibid., 250.

16. Pinon, *L'Hospice de Charenton,* 79.

17. Ibid., 108.

18. Ibid., 251.

19. Sade's letter was a response to a letter published in the journal *Révolutions de Paris dédiés à la nation* on October 3, 1789, in which a Paris lawyer asked for information about an individual named Drouillère, who had been arrested (possibly wrongly) and who may have been hidden away in the Charenton asylum (Lever, *Donatien,* 862–64).

20. All of the above quotes come from Sade's letter first published by Lever (*Donatien,* 864–68).

21. Castel, *Regulation of Madness,* 25.

22. Lely, 2:280–81.

23. Quoted in Pinon, *L'Hospice de Charenton,* 70.

24. Bourdin, 261–62.

25. Lely, 2:282.

26. Letter of May 19, 1790, in Bourdin, 266.

24: "Free at Last"

1. Bourdin, 263.

2. Ibid., 264.

3. Ibid., 263.

4. Ibid., 262–63.

5. Ibid., 261.

6. Renée misdated this letter as April 2, but since she referred to her husband's release "yesterday," the letter must have been written on April 3.

7. Bourdin, 262.

8. Ibid., 269.

9. Letter written shortly after April 14, 1790, in ibid., 265.

10. Lever, *Donatien,* 735 n. 6.

11. Bourdin, 263.

12. Ibid., 272.

13. Ibid., 264–65.

14. Ibid., 270.

15. Ibid., 272.

16. Lely, 2:296.

17. Bourdin, 270.

18. Ibid., 265–66.

19. Debauve, 211.

20. Ibid., 270–71.

21. Bourdin noted that Sade must have continued this letter beyond May 22, because Sade mentioned the decree of that date limiting the King's power to make war and peace (267 n. 1).

22. Ibid., 266–67.

23. Ibid., 268–69.

24. Ibid., 271.

25. Ibid., 271–72.

26. Ibid., 272.

25: Citizen Sade

1. Letter of November 26, 1793, in Debauve, 274.

2. Letter of August 3, 1793, in Bourdin, 342.

3. Letter of August 15, 1793, in ibid., 346.

4. Hemmings, *Culture and Society in France,* 53.

5. Bourdin, 272.

6. Debauve, 214. Note that this detail is in Debauve's complete version of Sade's letter, and it is not in Bourdin's abridgment.

7. Carlyle, *French Revolution,* 1:370.

8. Sade, *Théâtre,* 2:117–18.

9. Lely, 2:297 n. 5.

10. Debauve, 218–19.

11. Sade, *Théâtre,* 2:88.

12. Ibid., 211–21.

13. Ibid., 119–20.

14. Sade gave the day he first met Mme Quesnet as August 25, 1790, in his will, which he wrote on January 30, 1806 (Laborde, 24:256). Lever establishes the ages of Mme Quesnet and her son from Mme Quesnet's death records (*Donatien,* 741 n. 1, 742 n. 9).

15. Bourdin, 317.

16. Ibid., 311–12.
17. Letter of December 18, 1790, in ibid., 276.
18. Ibid., 286.
19. Ibid., 310.
20. Ibid., 274.
21. Letter of May 5, 1793, in ibid., 341.
22. Ibid., 274–75.
23. Letter of November 26, 1790, in ibid., 274.
24. Ibid., 276.
25. Ibid., 289.
26. Cabanis, *Journal de la maladie,* 40–41.
27. Ibid., 65.
28. Bourdin, 286.
29. Ibid., 280.
30. Ibid., 287–88.
31. Letter of June 12, 1791, in ibid., 289.
32. Ibid.
33. *OC,* 3:32.
34. Ibid., 86.
35. Ibid., 112.
36. Ibid., 167.
37. Ibid., 17–18.
38. Ibid., 13.
39. Letter of May 22, 1791, in Bourdin, 287.
40. Ibid., 288.
41. *OC,* 3:323.
42. Ibid., 324.
43. Ibid., 322.
44. Ibid., 326.
45. Bourdin, 301–2.
46. Debauve, 286.
47. Lely, 2:311–12.
48. Bourdin, 295.
49. Ibid., 297.
50. Ibid., 299–300.
51. Ibid., 309.
52. Ibid., 310.
53. Letter to Gaufridy, April 1792, in Debauve, 238.
54. Letter to Gaufridy, December 5, 1791, in ibid., 301.
55. Sade, *Théâtre,* 2:11.
56. *OC,* 15:89.
57. Ibid., 90.
58. Bourdin, 298.
59. Sade, *Théâtre,* 2:17–18.
60. Lely, 2:322.
61. Bourdin, 313.
62. Lely, 2:328.
63. Bourdin, 313.
64. Letter of April 19, 1792, in ibid., 314.
65. Ibid., 315.
66. Ibid., 316.
67. Ibid., 317.
68. Debauve, 239.
69. Letter of July 10, 1792, in Bourdin, 318.
70. Ibid.
71. Ibid., 319.
72. Debauve, 286.
73. *OC,* 11:20.
74. Bourdin, 322.
75. Ibid., 319.
76. Ibid., 320.
77. Ibid., 322. A few years later, Sade was still troubled by Soton's daughter, who had remained in Paris. On February 22, 1795, Sade informed Gaufridy that she "continues to act impertinently toward me here." Sade's solution was bizarre: "I would very much like someone [presumably Gaufridy] to warn her, in a charitable way, that if she persists she will soon find herself in the hospital" (Debauve, 330).
78. Bourdin, 323.
79. Lely, 2:341 n. 1.
80. Bourdin, 323–24.
81. Ibid., 332.
82. My account of the riot depends on Paulet's letter (Bourdin, 335–36) and on the reports drafted by the municipal officials of La Coste (Laborde, 22:210–21).
83. Lever, *Donatien,* 489; Fauville, *La Coste,* 177.
84. Bourdin, 329.
85. Ibid., 330.
86. Letter of October 30, 1792, in ibid., 333–34.
87. Ibid., 334.
88. *OC,* 3:331.
89. Ibid., 332.
90. Ibid., 333.
91. Ibid., 338.
92. Ibid., 339.
93. Bourdin, 334.
94. Letter of December 10, 1792, in ibid., 337.

95. Debauve, 287.
96. Lely, 2:361.
97. Bourdin, 338.
98. Ibid., 339.
99. Debauve, 226 n. 2.
100. Ibid., 287.
101. Sade, *Théâtre*, 2:92.
102 Ibid., 93.
103. Ibid., 94.
104. Ibid., 94–95.
105. Debauve, 251.
106. Bourdin, 339–40.
107. Ibid., 340.
108. Ibid., 339.
109. Ibid.
110. Letter of April 13, 1793, in ibid., 340.
111. Debauve, 256.
112. Sade would later refer to this event and take credit for the correctness of his views: "I had the honor of personally presenting" this petition "at the head of the forty-eight sections of Paris, in which I expressed the dangers of the revolutionary army; one can today see if I was correct then" (letter to the Comité de Sûreté Générale, May 7, 1794, in Debauve, 287).
113. *OC*, 3:341–2.
114. Laborde, 23:92.
115. Bourdin, 341.
116. Laborde, 23:97.

117. Bourdin, 342.
118. Ibid., 318.
119. Pauvert, *Sade*, 3:73.
120. Bourdin, 342.
121. *OC*, 3:360.
122. Lever, *Donatien*, 505.
123. *OC*, 3:358.
124. Schama, *Citizens*, 740.
125. Ibid., 738.
126. *OC*, 3:359.
127. Lely suggests that Sade's fulsome praise of Marat, "the hideous vampire of the Revolution," can be considered as "a parody" of irresponsible and deceptive political rhetoric (2:379). Similarly, Lever considers the speech Sade's private joke, made all the more enjoyable because of the applause it evoked from the crowd of Jacobins (*Donatien*, 506). Pauvert, however, argues that Sade was far from being a political moderate and that some part of him fully entered into the logic and the rhetoric of Jacobin extremism (*Sade*, 3:75).
128. Debauve, 287.
129. *OC*, 11:19.
130. Schama, *Citizens*, 791–92.
131. Ibid., 789.
132. Carlyle, *French Revolution*, 2:351.
133. *OC*, 3:369–73.
134. Ibid., 363.
135. Ibid., 364.

26: The Guillotine Beneath Our Windows

1. This and subsequent quotes are from the full text of the arrest report, in Laborde, 23:135–38.
2. In May 1795, Sade would tell Gaufridy that at the time of his arrest he believed it was due to his son's emigration (Bourdin, 372).
3. Pauvert, *Sade*, 3:123.
4. Laborde, 23:138.
5. Ibid., 134–35.
6. Schama, *Citizens*, 793.
7. Letter of November 19, 1794, in Bourdin, 360.
8. I.e., December 8. "Frimaire" ("the cold month") was part of the new revolutionary

calendar adopted by the National Convention in October 1793 to replace the old Gregorian calendar. All of the old months were given descriptive or agricultural names: "Pluviose" ("the rainy month"), "Thermidor" ("the hot month"), etc. The idea was to purge the Republic of all old associations.
9. Laborde, 23:141–43.
10. Bourdin, 366.
11. Ibid., 360.
12. Lely, 2:401 n. 2.
13. Ibid., 401.
14. Ibid., 402.
15. Ibid., 401.
16. Laborde, 23:167–71.

17. Letter of December 6, 1794, in Bourdin, 362.

18. Laborde, 23:175–76.

19. Ibid., 178.

20. Ibid., 177.

21. To this letter of May 7, Sade added a list of items in his possession that the committee might wish to see, including his speech on Marat, receipts for revolutionary taxes, and his copy of the letter from the governor of the Bastille to Minister Villedeuil (Laborde, 23:194–96).

22. Ibid., 192–93.

23. Lely, 2:409.

24. Letter of November 19, 1794, in Bourdin, 360.

25. Pauvert, *Sade,* 3:143.

26. Laborde, 25:256–57. Lely deprecated Quesnet's role, arguing that Sade's crediting her with saving his life was done "in order to increase" her role and "thereby to justify, in the eyes of his natural heirs, the bequest" that he gave her (2:417 n. 2).

27. Letter to Gaufridy, November 19, 1794, in Bourdin, 361.

28. See, for example, Sade's letter to Gaufridy on December 6, 1794, when he said that, "by the greatest good fortune," Goupilleau "happens to be a member" of the Committee for General Security (Bourdin, 362); again, on December 12, he announced the good news that Gaufridy's son could come out of hiding, adding that the success of the petition was due solely to Mme Quesnet, who "would be pleased with a little letter of gratitude from you" (ibid., 363).

29. Letters to Gaufridy, on November 30, 1794, in Bourdin, 362; and November 19, 1794, in Debauve, 317.

30. Debauve, 317. These details are not in Bourdin's version of this letter of November 19, 1794 (360–61). Typically, Bourdin used

ellipsis marks to indicate his abridgments. Debauve's version is complete (314–20).

31. Blanc, *La Dernière Lettre,* 221.

32. Bourdin, 361.

33. Letter of January 6, 1795, in ibid., 364.

34. Letter of January 21, 1795, in ibid., 365.

35. Laborde, 23:203.

36. Ibid., 204.

37. Olivier Blanc identified this individual as Courlet de Boulot, who claimed he had been the Comte de Vernantois (*La Dernière Lettre,* 57–59). Slight differences in spelling were common in the eighteenth century. In any case, the Vermantois on Sade's list was guillotined on the same day as the Vernantois cited above.

38. Even though Sade had never been in Cossé-Brissac's guard, this trumped-up charge stuck.

39. Laborde, 23:205.

40. Lely, 2:402.

41. Blanc, *La Dernière Lettre,* 64.

42. Carlyle, *French Revolution,* 2:412. Carlyle also gave the following example of a mix-up at Saint-Lazare, in which a father was able to sacrifice himself to save his son: "Lieutenant-General Loiserolles, a nobleman by birth and by nature, . . . hurrying to the Grate to hear the Death-list read, . . . caught the name of his son. The son was asleep at the moment. 'I am Loiserolles,' cried the old man: at Tinville's bar, an error in the Christian name is little" (*French Revolution,* 2:412).

43. Lely, 2:417.

44. Lever, *Donatien,* 534.

45. Letter to Gaufridy, November 19, 1794, in Bourdin, 361.

46. Ibid.

47. Laborde, 23:212.

48. Ibid., 215.

49. Ibid., 220.

50. Bourdin, 361.

27: *On My Knees, Dying of Hunger*

1. Bourdin, 359.

2. Debauve, 311.

3. Letter of November 12, 1794, in Bourdin,

359–60.

4. Ibid., 361.

5. The above details of Sade's letter to

Gaufridy of November 19, 1794, are from Debauve's version (316–19) rather than Bourdin's (360–61). Bourdin abridged a great many of the letters in his edition.

6. Bourdin, 364–65.

7. Letter to Gaufridy, January 18, 1795, in Debauve, 327.

8. Bourdin, 363; letter of January 6, 1795.

9. Debauve, 325. Once again, this passage is not in Bourdin's version of the letter.

10. Laborde, 23:240.

11. Letter of January 31, 1795, in Bourdin, 365.

12. Letter of February 10, 1795, in ibid., 365.

13. Ibid., 367.

14. Letter of February 22, 1795, in ibid., 369.

15. Letter of March 13, 1796, in ibid., 387.

16. Letter to Gaufridy, August 5, 1795, in ibid., 375.

17. Ibid., 376.

18. Debauve, 334. Again, these details are not in Bourdin's version of the letter.

19. Bourdin, 377.

20. Laborde, 24:62. Sade was assiduous in promoting *Aline et Valcour*. On March 2, 1796, when he discovered that the bookseller Deterville had failed to include this novel in his catalogue, Sade wrote to protest: "*Aline et Valcour, ou le roman philosophique*, the most extraordinary work, the most powerful, the most interesting, the best written that has appeared in thirty years, certainly deserved to be included in your catalogue" (Debauve, 352).

21. This and the following parenthetical page references to *La Philosophie dans le boudoir* are for *OC*, vol. 13.

22. Debauve, 339.

23. Bourdin, 383.

24. Ibid., 388.

25. Ibid., 391.

26. Ibid., 392.

27. Ibid., 392–93.

28. Ibid., 396.

29. Letter of October 15, 1796, in ibid., 401.

30. Letter of September 11, 1796, in Laborde, 24:153.

31. Ibid., 170–71.

32. Ibid., 175–76.

33. Letter of January 2, 1797, in Bourdin, 401–2.

34. Ibid., 402.

35. Ibid., 397–98.

36. Lever, *Donatien*, 554.

37. Bourdin, 404.

38. Ibid., 404–5.

39. Ibid., 406.

40. Debauve, 391.

41. Bourdin, 406–7.

42. Ibid., 408.

43. Debauve, 392–93.

44. Ibid., 393.

45. Ibid., 394.

46. Bourdin, 400.

47. Debauve, 401–2.

48. Ibid., 409.

49. Letter of December 7, 1797, in Bourdin, 417–18.

50. Letter of May 3, 1798, in ibid., 421.

51. Debauve, 428.

52. Ibid., 429.

53. Letter of January 24, 1799, in Bourdin, 428.

54. Lely, 2:453.

55. Ibid., 457.

56. Pauvert calls it *"quite simply the greatest publishing venture in the history of pornography"* (*OC*, 8:18). Pauvert raises reasonable questions about the date, 1797, and the order of publication of *La Nouvelle Justine* and the *Histoire de Juliette*. He argues that there was an early version of *Juliette* in 1796, followed by *La Nouvelle Justine* in August 1800, and a new, larger version of *Juliette* in March 1801 (*OC*, 8:14ff.).

57. Paglia, *Sexual Personae*, 236.

58. Ibid., 238.

59. Bourdin, 428.

60. Letter of January 24, 1799, in ibid., 429.

61. Debauve, 435–36.

62. Letter of January 24, 1799, in Bourdin, 429.

63. Laborde, 25:179.

64. *OC*, 15:114.

65. Bourdin, 440.

66. Ibid., 434.

67. Ibid., 443.

68. Ibid., 442.

69. Ibid., 444.

70. Ibid.

71. Ibid., 445.

72. Ibid., 439.

73. In 1832, Sade's son Claude-Armand acquired this manuscript and destroyed it (Lely, 2:535 n. 2).

74. In his *Notes littéraires*, Sade described *Le Boccace français* as a two-volume collection, containing twelve stories he probably had written in the Bastille but had not included in his *Crimes de l'amour*. Sade listed the titles, a few of which include "Il y a place pour deux" ("There's Room for Two"), "La Cruauté fraternelle" ("Brotherly Cruelty"), and "Les Inconvénients de la pitié" ("The Disadvantages of Pity") (*OC*, 11:41–42). Sade intended to recast one story he had written in the Bastille, "La Marquise de Thélème, ou les effets du libertinage," situating it during the revolutionary Terror, when a deputy to the Convention, Joseph Le Bon, first satisfies his lust for Mme de Thélème and her daughter, and then has them guillotined. The "sole moral" of this story, Sade noted, is "to raise detestation for the crimes of those times" (*OC*, 11:38).

75. Pauvert, *Sade,* 3:278–79.

76. *OC*, 10:29.

77. Ibid., 39.

78. Ibid., 34.

79. Ibid., 35–36.

80. Ibid., 37.

81. Ibid., 38.

82. Restif de la Bretonne, *Oeuvres érotiques,* 287.

83. Lely, 2:472.

84. *OC*, 10:80.

85. Lely, 2:521.

86. *OC*, 10:570.

87. Ibid., 567.

88. Ibid., 566.

28: Charenton

1. The following details of Sade's account of his arrest are to be found in *Notes littéraires*, a kind of commonplace book he kept during 1803–4 (*OC*, 11:26–27).

2. The following details of Dubois's version come from a report he drew up on September 8, 1804 (Lely, 2:544–46).

3. Lely, 2:536.

4. *OC*, 11:29–30.

5. Ibid., 34–35.

6. Laborde, 25:287.

7. Debauve, 487.

8. Lely, 2:541–42.

9. Lever, *Donatien,* 591–93.

10. Lever was the first to reprint these verses in appendix XIII of his biography (*Donatien,* 870).

11. Lely, 2:546.

12. Ibid., 543.

13. Ibid., 543 n. 2.

14. Ibid., 546.

15. Pinel, *Treatise on Insanity,* 284.

16. Quoted in Pinon, *L'Hospice de Charenton,* 71–72.

17. Ibid., 8.

18. Sade, *Cahiers personnels,* 118.

19. *OC*, 15:501.

20. Ibid., 497.

21. Debauve, 488–89.

22. *OC*, 15:505–6.

23. Ibid., 499.

24. Debauve, 489.

25. Laborde, 25:397.

26. Ibid., 398–401.

27. Ibid., 408–9.

28. Ibid., 401.

29. Lely, 2:548.

30. Debauve, 491–92.

31. Lely conjectured that Mme Quesnet moved to Charenton in 1806 (2:548 n. 1). However, Pauvert (*Sade,* 3:337) and Lever (*Donatien,* 601) provide conclusive evidence that she entered the asylum as a "self-admitted pensioner" in August 1804.

32. *OC*, 15:512.

33. Ibid., 511.

34. Ibid., 494–95.

35. Ibid., 512–13.

36. Pierre Pinon was the first to point out Esquirol's plagiarism from Colins (*L'Hospice de Charenton,* 79). For example, the following phrases are to be found, word for word, in Colins's earlier memorandum: "objects of the curiosity . . . of a frivolous, thoughtless, and sometimes wicked public"; "the derisive laughter and the insulting pity" of the audience (*OC,* 15:514–15).

37. *OC,* 15:513–14.

38. Ibid., 514.

39. Ibid., 512.

40. Laborde, 25:303–4.

41. *OC,* 15:502.

42. Laborde, 25:302.

43. *OC,* 15:102. The journals written at Charenton were first edited and published by Georges Daumas in *Journal inédit* (1970). I am using the reprint in *OC,* vol. 11.

44. Ibid., 15:105.

45. Ibid., 107.

46. Sade's counting mania had returned, and also his belief that cryptographic messages were being sent to him in the form of numerical "signals."

47. *OC,* 11:110.

48. Ibid., 111.

49. Ibid., 112.

50. Ibid., 127.

51. Mlle Flore was at least a few years off in her estimate of Sade's age.

52. *OC,* 15:499–500.

53. Ibid., 501.

54. Ibid.

55. Ibid., 501–2.

56. Ibid., 516.

57. Ibid., 515.

58. Ibid., 291.

59. Lely, 2:550.

60. Ibid., 552.

61. *OC,* 11:77. There is a typographical error in this epigram in Pauvert's edition of Sade's "Notes," where *"la vie"* appears instead of *"la vice."*

62. *OC,* 11:59.

63. Lely, 2:553–54; Lever, *Donatien,* 602.

64. *OC,* 11:99–100.

65. Sade's "Notes" for *Les Journées de Florbelle* were fortunately preserved in a photo-

copy made by Maurice Heine before the originals disappeared during World War II.

66. *OC,* 11:70, 73, 79. For a complete discussion of what might be the earlier versions of *Les Journées de Florbelle,* see Pauvert's argument in his introduction to the "Notes" (*OC,* 11:60–63). Lely also mentions an earlier version, entitled *Conversations du château de Charmelle,* seized when Sade was arrested at his editor's house in 1801 (2:535 n. 1, 601, 604 n. 1).

67. *OC,* 11:108.

68. Ibid., 112–13.

69. Ibid., 115.

70. Ibid., 111.

71. Ibid., 109.

72. Ibid., 106.

73. January 2 and 29, and May 7, 1808 (ibid., 107–8, 109–10, and 115–6, respectively).

74. Sade ignored his earlier stays at Vincennes, Saumur, Pierre-Encize, Fort-l'Évêque, and Miolans. He also ignored his nearly three years in various prisons during the Terror.

75. *OC,* 11:116.

76. Ibid., 117.

77. Ibid., 116.

78. Ibid., 108.

79. Ibid., 103.

80. Ibid., 117.

81. Ibid., 113.

82. Ibid., 109.

83. Ibid., 105.

84. Ibid., 106.

85. Ibid., 107.

86. Ibid., 106.

87. Lever, *Donatien,* 624–25.

88. *OC,* 11:119.

89. The journal for that period was lost or destroyed.

90. *OC,* 11:122.

91. Ibid., 123. Louis-Marie was assiduous in his campaign: during his visits on July 5, July 14, and July 20, "he continued to express the same ideas concerning his brother that he had previously given," and he also continued to hold out hope of the return of Sade's manuscripts (ibid., 125–26).

92. Laborde, 25:276–77.

93. Additional details about the confrontations over this marriage can be found in Lever (*Donatien,* 622–27), Lely (2:554–57), and Pauvert (*Sade,* 3:392–96).

94. *OC,* 11:127.

95. Debauve, 530.

96. *OC,* 15:505–6.

97. Ibid., 11:102.

98. Laborde, 25:281.

99. Ibid., 283.

100. Lely, 2:564–65.

101. Lever, *Donatien,* 631–32.

102. Lely, 2:567. Note that when Sade said that he was seventy, he was making himself almost a whole year older.

103. Debauve, 503.

104. Ibid., 505.

105. Ibid., 506.

106. Ibid., 508.

107. Bourdin, 448–49.

108. Ibid., 450.

109. Debauve, 519.

110. Ibid., 530.

111. Laborde, 25:329–30.

112. Ibid., 331–32. Coulmier also noted that Sade was penniless, "without any resources," because "his children" took "advantage of his detention to steal his last sou." Moreover, Coulmier said, the institution was owed 9,000 francs, and he asked Montalivet's help in getting Claude-Armand to pay up (ibid., 332).

113. Ibid., 375–76. The above excerpts are taken from a long memorandum on Sade's detention at Charenton drawn up by its new director, Roulhac du Maupas, on September 7, 1814 (ibid., 374–83).

114. Ibid., 369.

115. Debauve, 555.

116. Ibid., 553.

117. Laborde, 25:371.

118. *OC,* 15:513.

119. Ibid., 11:268.

120. Ibid., 12:11

121. Ibid., 314.

122. Even such a stalwart admirer as Lely is obliged to admit that *Adélaïde de Brunswick* "scarcely rises above the mediocre" (2:609). Pauvert bluntly states that this novel is "bio-graphical proof" of Sade's mental "decline" (*Sade,* 3:441).

123. Pauvert, remarking on the strength of the style of this novel, which was not in accord with his view of Sade's creative decline during this period, and also noticing that Sade mentioned that his work during the summer of 1813 consisted of a "final draft," speculated that this novel was originally composed some years earlier (*OC,* 12:12).

124. Ibid., 259.

125. Ibid., 152.

126. Ibid., 187.

127. Ibid., 85.

128. Ibid., 147.

129. Ibid., 204.

130. Ibid., 60.

131. Ibid., 71.

132. Lely, 2:216–17.

133. Ibid., 218–19.

134. *OC,* 11:189.

135. Ibid., 129.

136. Ibid., 129, 136.

137. Ibid., 141.

138. Lely, 2:584.

139. *OC,* 11:131.

140. Ibid., 139.

141. Ibid., 135.

142. Laborde, 25:378.

143. Ibid., 374.

144. *OC,* 11:103.

145. Ibid., 109.

146. Ibid., 125.

147. Ibid., 139.

148. Ibid., 130.

149. Ibid., 136. Georges Daumas estimates that their first sexual encounter occurred on May 15, 1813, when she was sixteen and a half years old. Daumas also believes that Sade may have caught his first glimpse of her on January 9, 1808, in Mme Quesnet's room (Sade, *Journal inédit,* 34). Pauvert dates the beginning of sexual relations around the end of 1812 (*Sade,* 3:451), and Lever believes the date was before March 1811, when Sade wrote a defense against the charge of corrupting a girl in the asylum (*Donatien,* 650). If Lever is right, Magdeleine Leclerc had recently turned fourteen.

150. *OC,* 11:141.
151. Ibid., 132.
152. Ibid., 132–33.
153. Ibid., 133.
154. Ibid., 140.
155. Ibid., 133.
156. Ibid., 141.
157. Ibid., 130.
158. Ibid., 132.
159. Ibid., 136.
160. Ibid., 138.
161. Ibid., 139.

162. Ibid., 140.
163. Ibid., 141.
164. Sade, *Cahiers personnels,* 109–10.
165. *OC,* 11:141.
166. Ibid., 142.
167. Laborde, 25:258.
168. *OC,* 11:142.
169. The details in this and the next two paragraphs are taken from Dr. Ramon's "Notes sur M. de Sade" (Sade, *Cahiers personnels,* 110–14).
170. *OC,* 11:24–25.

BIBLIOGRAPHY

Barthes, Roland. *Sade, Fourier, Loyola.* Translated by Richard Miller. New York, 1976.

Bataille, Georges. *Literature and Evil.* Translated by Alastair Hamilton. London, 1985.

Beauvoir, Simone de. *Faut-il brûler Sade?* Paris, 1955.

Benabou, Erica-Marie. *La Prostitution et la police des moeurs au XVIIIe siècle.* Paris, 1987.

Blanc, Olivier. *La Dernière Lettre: Prisons et condamnés de la Révolution, 1793–1794.* Paris, 1984.

Bloit, Michel, and Pascal Payen-Appenzeller. *Les Mystères de Paris en l'an 1789.* Paris, 1989.

Bluche, François. *La Vie quotidienne de la noblesse Française au XVIIIe siècle.* Paris, 1973.

Brinton, Crane. *A Decade of Revolution: 1789–1799.* New York, 1934. Reissued, New York, 1963.

Cabanis, P. J. G. *Journal de la maladie et de la mort de . . . Mirabeau.* Paris, 1791.

Carlyle, Thomas. *The French Revolution: A History.* Edited by K. J. Fielding and David Sorensen. 2 vols in 1. Oxford, 1989.

Carter, Angela. *The Sadeian Woman and the Ideology of Pornography.* New York, 1979.

Casanova, Jacques. *The Memoirs of Jacques Casanova de Seingalt.* 6 vols. Translated by Arthur Machen. New York, n.d.

Castel, Robert. *The Regulation of Madness: The Origins of Incarceration in France.* Translated by W. D. Halls. Berkeley, Calif., 1988.

Chasseguet-Smirgel, Janine. *Creativity and Perversion.* New York, 1984.

————. *The Ego Ideal: A Psychoanalytic Essay on the Malady of the Ideal.* Translated by Paul Barrows. London, 1985.

Crosland, Margaret. *Sade's Wife: The Woman behind the Marquis.* London, 1995.

Darnton, Nina. "Artist as Lover: Bergman." *Elle.* May 1993. Pp. 130–33.

Delpech, Jeanine. *La Passion de la marquise de Sade.* Paris, 1970.

Desbordes, Jean. *Le Vrai Visage du marquis de Sade.* Paris, 1939.

Farge, Arlette, and Michel Foucault. *Le Désordre des familles: Lettres de cachet des Archives de la Bastille.* Paris, 1982.

Fauville, Henri. *La Coste: Sade en Provence.* Aix-en-Provence, 1984.

Fossa, F. de. *Le Château de Vincennes.* 2 vols. Paris, 1908.

Foucault, Michel. *Discipline and Punish: The Birth of the Prison.* Translated by Alan Sheridan. New York, 1979.

————. *Madness and Civilization: A History of Insanity in the Age of Reason.* Translated by Richard Howard. New York, 1965. Reprint, New York, 1973.

Freud, Sigmund. *A Case of Hysteria, Three Essays on Sexuality, and Other Works.* Vol. 7 of *The Standard Edition of the Complete Psychological Works.* Edited and translated by James Strachey. London, 1953.

————. *Jensen's "Gradiva" and Other Works.* Vol. 9 of *The Standard Edition.* London, 1959.

————. *Totem and Taboo and Other Works.* Vol. 13 of *The Standard Edition.* London, 1955.

Funck-Brentano, Frantz. *Bastille et Faubourg Saint-Antoine.* Paris, 1925.

Ginisty, Paul. *La Marquise de Sade.* Paris, 1901.

Giraud, "Citoyen." *Observations sommaires sur toutes les prisons du département de Paris.* Paris, 1793.

Giraudy, Charles François S., and Dominique Raymond. *Traité des maladies qu'il est dangereux de guérir.* Paris, 1808.

Goldstein, Jan. *Console and Classify: The French Psychiatric Profession in the Nineteenth Century.* New York, 1987.

Gorer, Geoffrey. *The Marquis de Sade: A Short Account of His Life and Work.* New York, 1934.

Gray, Francine du Plessix. *At Home with the Marquis de Sade: A Life.* New York, 1998.

Hayman, Ronald. *De Sade: A Critical Biography.* London, 1978.

Heine, Maurice. *Le Marquis de Sade.* Edited by Gilbert Lely. Paris, 1950.

Hemmings, F. W. J. *Culture and Society in France: 1789–1848.* N.p., 1987.

Jean, Raymond. *Un Portrait de Sade.* Arles, 1989.

Johnson, Samuel. *Rasselas and Other Tales.* Edited by Gwin J. Kolb. Vol. 16 of *The Yale Edition of the Works of Samuel Johnson.* New Haven, Conn., 1990.

Kearney, Patrick J. *A History of Erotic Literature.* London, 1982.

Klein, Melanie. *The Psycho-analysis of Children.* Translated by Alix Strachey. London, 1932. Revised by H. A. Thorner, London, 1975. Reprint, London, 1989.

Klossowski, Pierre. *Sade mon prochain.* Paris, 1947. Reprint, Paris, 1967.

Krafft-Ebing, R. von. *Psychopathia Sexualis.* Translated by F. J. Rebman. Brooklyn, 1931.

Laborde, Alice M. *Les Infortunes du marquis de Sade.* Paris, 1990.

———. *Le Mariage du marquis de Sade.* Paris, 1988.

———. "The Marquis de Sade's Biography Revisited." In *Sade: His Ethics and Rhetoric*, edited by Colette V. Michael. New York, 1989.

———. *Le Marquis et la marquise de Sade.* New York, 1990.

———. *Sade romancier.* Neuchâtel, 1974.

Le Brun, Annie. *Soudain un bloc d'abîme, Sade.* Paris, 1986.

Lely, Gilbert. *Vie du marquis de Sade.* 2 vols. Paris, 1952–57.

Lemarchand, Ernest. *Le Château royal de Vincennes.* Paris, 1907.

Lever, Maurice. *Donatien Alphonse François, marquis de Sade.* Paris, 1991.

Manuel, Pierre. *La Police de Paris dévoilée.* 2 vols. Paris, "second year of The Liberty" [1791].

Maquet, Alboize and Auguste. *Le Donjon de Vincennes.* 2 vols. Paris, 1844.

Mirabeau, Honoré-Gabriel-Riquetti, comte de. *Des Lettres de cachet et des prisons d'état.* Vol. 7 of *Oeuvres de Mirabeau.* Paris, 1835.

Moore, Thomas. *Dark Eros: The Imagination of Sadism.* Dallas, 1990.

Paglia, Camille. *Sexual Personae: Art and Decadence from Nefertiti to Emily Dickinson.* New Haven, Conn., 1990.

Pauvert, Jean-Jacques. *Sade vivant.* 3 vols. Paris, 1986–90.

Petrarch's Lyric Poems. Edited by Robert M. Durling. Cambridge, Mass., 1976.

Pinel, Philippe. *A Treatise on Insanity.* Translated by D. D. Davis. New York, 1962.

Pinon, Pierre. *L'Hospice de Charenton.* Translated by Murray Wyllie. Liège, Belgium, 1989.

Piton, Camille. *Paris sous Louis XV: Rapports des inspecteurs de police au roi.* 5 vols. Paris, 1914.

Praz, Mario. "Chapter III: The Shadow of the Divine Marquis." In *The Romantic Agony.* Translated by Angus Davidson. 2nd ed. Oxford, 1951. Reissued, Oxford, 1970.

Quétel, Claude. *La Bastille: Histoire vraie d'une prison légendaire.* Paris, 1989.

Restif de la Bretonne. *Oeuvres Érotiques.* Paris, 1985.

Richardson, Samuel. *Clarissa, or The History of a Young Lady.* 4 vols. London, 1932. Reprinted with an introduction by John Butt, London, 1962.

————. *Pamela, or Virtue Rewarded.* 2 vols. London, 1914. Reprinted with an introduction by M. Kinkead-Weeks, London, 1962.

Rochemonteix, Père Camille de. *Un Collège de Jésuites aux XVIIe & XVIIIe Siècles: Le Collège Henri IV de la Flèche.* 4 Vols. Le Mans, 1889.

Rousseau, Jean-Jacques. *The Confessions.* Translated by J. M. Cohen. 1953. Reprint, New York, 1988.

Sade, Donatien Alphonse François, marquis de. *Cahiers personnels, 1803–1804.* Edited by Gilbert Lely. Paris, 1953.

————. *Correspondance inédite du marquis de Sade, de ses proches et de ses familiers.* Edited by Paul Bourdin. Paris, 1929.

————. *Correspondances du marquis de Sade et de ses proches enrichies de documents, notes et commentaires.* Edited by Alice M. Laborde. 19 vols. (1–11, 20–27) to date. Genève, 1991–.

————. *Journal inédit.* Edited by Georges Daumas. Paris, 1970.

————. *Lettres et mélanges littéraires.* Edited by Georges Daumas and Gilbert Lely. 3 vols. in 1. Paris, 1980.

————. *Lettres inédites et documents retrouvés.* Edited by Jean-Louis Debauve. Paris, 1990.

————. *Oeuvres complètes.* Edited by Gibert Lely. 16 vols. Paris, 1966–67.

————. *Oeuvres complètes du marquis de Sade.* Edited by Annie Le Brun and Jean-Jacques Pauvert. 15 vols. Paris, 1986–91.

————. *Le Théâtre de Sade.* Edited by Jean-Jacques Brochier. 4 vols. Paris, 1970.

Schama, Simon. *Citizens: A Chronicle of the French Revolution.* New York, 1989.

Shakespeare, William. *The Complete Works.* Edited by Stanley Wells and Gary Taylor. Oxford, 1986.

Sterne, Laurence. *The Life and Opinions of Tristram Shandy, Gentleman.* Edited by Melvyn New and Joan New. 2 vols. 1978.

Stoller, Robert J. *Presentations of Gender.* New Haven, Conn., 1985.

————. *Sex and Gender: On the Development of Masculinity and Femininity.* New York, 1968.

Taine, Hippolyte Adolphe. *The French Revolution.* Translated by John Durand. 3 vols. Gloucester, Mass., 1962.

Tenon, [Jacques]. *Mémoires sur les hôpitaux de Paris.* Paris, 1788.

Thomas, Donald. *The Marquis de Sade.* London, 1976. Reissued, London, 1992.

Walpole, Horace. *Horace Walpole's Correspondence with Madame du Deffand.* Edited by W. S. Lewis and Warren Hunting Smith. Vol. 4 of *The Yale Edition of Horace Walpole's Correspondence.* New Haven, Conn., 1939.

Williams, Alan. *The Police of Paris: 1718–1789.* Baton Rouge, La., 1979.

Yeats, W. B. *The Collected Poems of W. B. Yeats.* New York, 1952.

Young, Arthur. *Travels in France During the Years 1787, 1788 & 1789.* Edited by Constantia Maxwell. Cambridge, Eng., 1950.

INDEX

A NOTE ABOUT THE AUTHOR

NEIL SCHAEFFER is Professor of English Literature at Brooklyn
College. He lives in New York and Vermont.

A NOTE ON THE TYPE

THIS BOOK was set in Adobe Garamond. Designed for the Adobe Corporation by Robert Slimbach, the fonts are based on types first cut by Claude Garamond (c. 1480–1561). Garamond was a pupil of Geoffroy Tory and is believed to have followed the Venetian models, although he introduced a number of important differences, and it is to him that we owe the letter we now know as "old style." He gave to his letters a certain elegance and feeling of movement that won their creator an immediate reputation and the patronage of Francis I of France.

Composed by Creative Graphics,
Allentown, Pennsylvania
Printed and bound by R.R. Donnelley & Sons,
Harrisonburg, Virginia
Designed by Virginia Tan